DISCOVERING THE WESTERN PAST

A LOOK AT THE EVIDENCE

VOLUME II: SINCE 1500

FIFTH EDITION

Merry E. Wiesner
University of Wisconsin—Milwaukee

Julius R. Ruff
Marquette University

William Bruce Wheeler
University of Tennessee

HOUGHTON MIFFLIN COMPANY   Boston   New York

Sponsoring Editor: Nancy Blaine
Development Editor: Julie Dunn
Associate Project Editor: Reba Libby
Editorial Assistant: Kendra Johnson
Production/Design Coordinator: Lisa Jelly Smith
Manufacturing Manager: Florence Cadran
Senior Marketing Manager: Sandra McGuire

Cover Image: Derain, Andre (1880–1954), London Bridge. 1906. Oil on canvas, 26″ × 39″. Digital image © the Museum of Modern Art. Gift of Mr. and Mrs. Charles Zadok. (195. 1952)/Licensed by SCALA/Art Resource, NY/© ARS, NY.

Printed in the U.S.A.

Library of Congress Catalog Card Number: 2002109689

ISBN: 0-618-31293-5

56789-QF-09 08 07 06 05

CONTENTS

Rousseau regarding the poem. David Hume's "The Essay on Miracles," 1748. *The System of Nature,* by Paul-Henry Thiry, Baron d'Holbach, 1770.

CHAPTER FOUR
A Statistical View of European Rural Life, 1600–1800 95

Tables and graphs depicting data on agricultural yields, nutrition, weather and food prices, salaries, epidemics, crises, birth and death rates, infant and child mortality, life expectancy, marriages, and seasonal incidence of conception. Pictures illustrating agricultural techniques and living conditions.

CHAPTER FIVE
A Day in the French Revolution: July 14, 1789 116

Paintings of the Palais Royal and Camille Desmoulins speaking at the Palais Royal. Photograph of the rue de Fer-à-Moulin, 1870. Floor plan of a typical residential building in Faubourg Saint-Antoine. Graphs depicting wheat prices in Paris and France in the eighteenth century. Table of bread and wage earner's budget. Map of Paris by economic circumstances of residents, 1790. Table of the trades of the Bastille insurgents, 1789. Marguerite Painaigre's petition to the French National Assembly. Travel account, Arthur Young, 1789. Duke of Dorset's report on Paris to the Foreign Office in London. Report by bookseller Siméon-Prosper Hardy on the background of the Bastille attack.

CHAPTER SIX
Labor Old and New: The Impact of the Industrial Revolution 143

CHAPTER SEVEN
Two Programs for Social and Political Change: Liberalism and Socialism   178

CHAPTER EIGHT
Vienna and Paris, 1850–1930: The Development of the Modern City   210

THE EVIDENCE   307

World War I verses by Rupert Brooke, Charles Péguy, and Ernst Lissauer. Photographs of German infantry and British infantry attacks. *Under Fire*, by Henri Barbusse, 1916. Excerpt from Erich Maria Remarque's *All Quiet on the Western Front*, 1928. Verses by Wilfred Owen and Siegfried Sassoon. Letter from a former German student serving in France, 1914. Vera Brittain's account of a London air raid, 1917. German wartime civilian rations, 1918. Report on French public opinion in the Department of the Isère. Tables depicting the employment of women in wartime British industry and estimated military casualties by nation.

QUESTIONS TO CONSIDER   331
EPILOGUE   332

CHAPTER TWELVE
Selling a Totalitarian System   335

THE PROBLEM   335
SOURCES AND METHOD   340
THE EVIDENCE   344

Excerpts from Hitler's *Mein Kampf*. Joseph Goebbels's directives for the presidential campaign of 1932. Adolf Hitler's S.A. Order 111, 1926. Photographs of Regensburg S.A. banners, 1923, and S.A. propaganda rally in Spandau, 1932. Report of a Nazi meeting held in a heavily communist quarter of Berlin, 1927. Political posters from 1924 and 1932. Photograph of a National Socialist rally in the Berlin Sports Palace, 1930. Verses from "The Horst Wessel Song." Otto Dietrich's description of Hitler's campaign by airplane, 1932. Text from a Nazi pamphlet, ca 1932. Graph depicting types and amounts of political violence in Northeim, Germany, 1930–1932. *My Part in Germany's Fight*, by Joseph Goebbels, 1934. Report on the problem of stemming the spread of Nazi ideas in the Protestant Youth Movement, 1931. William L. Shirer's reactions to the Nazi party rally at Nuremberg, 1934.

QUESTIONS TO CONSIDER   361
EPILOGUE   363

CHAPTER THIRTEEN
Berlin: The Crux of the Cold War, 1945–1990   365

THE PROBLEM   365
SOURCES AND METHOD   373
THE EVIDENCE   378

Protocol of the Proceedings of the Berlin Conference. Map of Europe after World War II. The Novikov telegram. Reports and summaries from the

PREFACE

The first four editions of *Discovering the Western Past: A Look at the Evidence* elicited a very positive response from instructors and students alike, and that response encouraged us to proceed with this Fifth Edition. As authors, we were particularly gratified by the widespread acceptance of the central goal of *Discovering the Western Past*, that of making students active analysts of the past and not merely passive recipients of its factual record.

The title of this book begins with a verb, a choice that reflects our basic philosophy about history. History is not simply something one learns about; it is something one does. One discovers the past, and what makes this pursuit exciting is not only the past that is discovered but also the process of discovery itself. This process can be simultaneously exhilarating and frustrating, enlightening and confusing, but it is always challenging enough to convince those of us who are professional historians to spend our lives at it. And our own students, as well as many other students, have caught this infectious excitement.

The recognition that history involves discovery as much as physics or astronomy does is often not shared by students, whose classroom experience of history frequently does not extend beyond listening to lectures and reading textbooks. The primary goal of *Discovering the Western Past: A Look at the Evidence* is to allow students enrolled in the Western Civilization course to *do* history in the same way we as historians do—to examine a group of original sources in order to answer questions about the past. We feel that contact with original sources is an excellent means of communicating the excitement of doing history, but incorporating complete works or a collection of documents into a Western Civilization course can be problematic for many instructors.

The evidence in this book thus differs from that in most source collections in its variety. We have included visual evidence such as coins, paintings, aerial photographs, cartoons, buildings, architectural plans, maps, and political posters. In choosing written evidence we again have tried to offer a broad sample—songs, plays, poems, novels, court records, notarial contracts, statistical data, and work regulations all supplement letters, newspapers, speeches, autobiographies, and other more traditional sources.

For students to learn history the way we as historians do, they must not only be confronted with the evidence; they must also learn how to use that evidence to arrive at a conclusion. In other words, they must learn historical methodology. Too often methodology (or even the notion that historians *have* a methodology) is reserved for upper-level majors or graduate students; beginning students are simply presented with historical facts and interpretations without being shown how these were unearthed or formulated. Students may learn that historians hold different interpretations of the significance of an event or individual or different ideas about causation, but they are not informed of how historians come to such conclusions.

Thus, along with evidence, we have provided explicit suggestions about how one might analyze that evidence, guiding students as they reach their own conclusions. As they work through the various chapters, students will discover not only that the sources of historical information are wide-ranging but also that the methodologies appropriate to understanding and using them are equally diverse. By doing history themselves, students will learn how intellectual historians handle philosophical treatises, economic historians quantitative data, social historians court records, and political and diplomatic historians theoretical treatises and memoirs. They will also be asked to consider the limitations of their evidence, to explore what historical questions it cannot answer as well as those it can. Instead of passive observers, students become active participants.

Following an approach that we have found successful in many different classroom situations, we have divided each chapter into five parts: The Problem, Sources and Method, The Evidence, Questions to Consider, and Epilogue. The section called "The Problem" presents the general historical background and context for the evidence offered and concludes with the central question or questions explored in the chapter. The section titled "Sources and Method" provides specific information about the sources and suggests ways in which students might best study and analyze this primary evidence. It also discusses how previous historians have evaluated such sources and mentions any major disputes about methodology or interpretation. "The Evidence" forms the core of each chapter, presenting a variety of original sources for students to use in completing the central task. In "Questions to Consider," suggestions are offered about connections among the sources, and students are guided to draw deductions from the evidence. The final section, "Epilogue," traces both the immediate effects of the issue under discussion and its impact on later developments.

Within this framework, we have tried to present a series of historical issues and events of significance to the instructor as well as of interest to the student. We have also aimed to provide a balance among political, social, diplomatic, intellectual, and cultural history. In other words, we have attempted to create a kind of historical sampler that we believe will help students learn the methods and skills used by historians. These skills—analyzing arguments, developing hypotheses, comparing evidence, testing conclusions, and reevaluating material—will not only enable students to master historical content; they will also provide the necessary foundation for critical thinking in other college courses and after college as well.

Discovering the Western Past is designed to accommodate any format of the Western Civilization course, from the small lecture/discussion class of a liberal arts or community college to the large lecture with discussions led by teaching assistants at a sizable university. The chapters may be used for individual assignments, team projects, class discussions, papers, and exams. Each is self-contained, so that any combination may be assigned. The book is not intended to replace a standard textbook, and it was written to accompany any Western Civilization text the instructor chooses. The *Instructor's Resource Manual*, written by the authors of the text, offers suggestions for class discussions, suggestions for ways in which students' learning may be evaluated, and annotated lists of suggestions for further reading.

New to the Fifth Edition

The Fifth Edition of *Discovering the Western Past* incorporates the responses to the book that we have received from our own students, as well as from student and faculty users of the book around the country. Many of the chapters in the two volumes have received some reworking, and new chapters are included in each volume.

Volume I includes new chapters on polytheism and monotheism in the fertile crescent, medieval infidels and heretics, and the impact of the Reformations. Volume II offers readers new chapters that examine the debates for and against extending women's citizenship and suffrage, the origins of the Cold War and the crises in Berlin, and the development of the European Union.

Acknowledgments

In the completion of this book, the authors received assistance from a number of people. Our colleagues and students at the University of Wisconsin—Milwaukee, Marquette University, and the University of Tennessee, Knoxville, have been generous with their ideas and time. Merry E. Wiesner (-Hanks) wishes especially to thank Judith Bennett, Judith Beall, Martha Carlin, Abbas Hamdani, and Marci Sortor for their critiques and suggestions, and Neil Wiesner-Hanks and Kai and Tyr Wiesner-Hanks for their help in maintaining the author's perspective. Julius Ruff acknowledges the assistance of two valued colleagues who aided in preparing all five editions of this work: the Reverend John Patrick Donnelly, S.J., of Marquette University and Michael D. Sibalis of Wilfrid Laurier University. He also wishes to thank Laura, Julia, and Charles Ruff for their continued support. William Bruce Wheeler wishes to thank Owen Bradley and John Bohstedt for their valuable assistance.

We wish to acknowledge particularly the following historians who read and commented on the manuscript of this Fifth Edition as it developed:

David Berry, *Rich Mountain Community College*

Daniel F. Callahan, *University of Delaware*

James R. Farr, *Purdue University*

Sally S. Fisher, *College of Charleston*

Paul B. Hatley, *Rogers State University*

Ann R. Higginbotham, *Eastern Connecticut State University*

Alison Williams Lewin, *St. Joseph's University*

Erick J. Mann, *Oakton Community College*

Molly McClain, *University of San Diego*

Sherri Olson, *University of Connecticut*

Carole A. Putko, *San Diego State University*

John Ramsbottom, *University of Illinois, Urbana-Champaign*

Alison A. Smith, *Wagner College*

Joseph P. Ward, *University of Mississippi*

Finally, the authors extend their thanks to the staff of Houghton Mifflin Company for their enthusiastic support.

M.E.W.

J.R.R.

W.B.W.

CHAPTER ONE

PEASANT VIOLENCE: REBELLION AND RIOT IN

EARLY MODERN EUROPE, 1525–1789

THE PROBLEM

Most of us, being all too familiar with the problems of twenty-first-century urban America, probably tend to have an idealized view of traditional rural societies as somehow more peaceful than our own. Yet historians are finding that the opposite was the case: Many traditional rural societies experienced quite high levels of violence.

In early modern Europe, violence was a commonplace of rural life. Historians of criminal justice have found that levels of individual acts of violence, in the form of assaults and murders, were quite high and that even social elites, such as the nobility, engaged in such behavior. Common, too, were collective acts of violence by European peasants. These were the people who tilled the soil and who owed a part of their produce, and sometimes their labor, to noble landowners, often called *seigniors*, in a society that was still widely feudalized.

Peasant collective violence assumed two chief forms, rebellions and riots. Rebellions were widespread expressions of collective violence that extended beyond the confines of individual villages and that endured for more than a few days. Rebels aimed at changing their government, its policies, or the society in which they lived. The occasions on which peasants took up arms were numerous. Indeed, one of the twentieth century's most insightful historians, noting the possibilities for conflict in a landholding system in which peasants owed rents and other dues to their seigniors, wrote:

> To the historian, whose task is merely to observe and explain, agrarian revolt is as natural to the seigniorial regime as strikes, let us say, are to large scale capitalism.[1]

---

1. Marc Bloch, *French Rural History: An Essay on its Basic Characteristics,* translated by Janet Sondheimer (Berkeley: University of California Press, 1966), p. 170.

Chapter 1

Peasant Violence:

Rebellion and

Riot in Early

Modern Europe,

1525–1789

Riots probably were more common than outright rebellions and differed from them in several ways. They were generally localized outbursts of group violence that were rather spontaneous and thus lacked planning and organization. Riots also generally were of short duration, rarely lasting more than one or two days, and they commonly represented an expression of local anger at some very tangible problem, rather than an attempt to effect sweeping change.

The origins and nature of these acts of peasant collective violence must be sought first in the outlook of the peasants. Early modern peasants had a distinct view of government. Their society retained memories of the individual's right to petition the monarch directly for solutions to problems. Many peasants saw their taking up of arms to protest government policy as a simple extension of their right to petition. In doing this, they believed that they were in no way being disloyal to the king; rather, they believed that their good king had been misled by evil or corrupt advisers into bad policies. "If the king only knew!" was a sentiment that was widely expressed by peasant rebels in this period to justify their uprisings to seek changes of officials or policies.

Popular religion also sometimes justified rebellion in the minds of peasants. Problems of late medieval and early modern Europe, including the bubonic plague, schisms in the Church, and the advance of the Turks, convinced some that the end of the world was approaching, and that a coming day of judgment would be followed by a new millennium, or period of peace and perfection. In preparation for the latter event, the world had to be purged of its evil, and some peasant revolts had this millenarian aspect to them.

Cultural historians also find a unique concept of time among early modern European peasants. While for us time is essentially a linear concept, marked, in human development, by progress, for peasants five centuries ago time could be circular. That is, human development could include the return of past conditions; in particular, the peasant mentality retained an idealized vision of an earlier "golden age" when conditions had been much better. The desire to recover those better times is often found as a goal of peasant violence.

The primitive agricultural methods of the age also were at the root of some peasant violence. Working the land with simple wooden plows that rarely broke the soil deeply enough and farming without modern techniques of fertilization and crop rotation, peasant cultivators lived a subsistence existence in which they barely met their families' needs, their obligations to Church and state, and their dues to their seigniors in years of good harvest. As a result, they were prone to panics and riots in the face of threats to their food supplies. Indeed, mere rumors of such threats would prompt local rioting.

Peasant revolts and riots erupted within the institution that was the essential focus of peasant existence: the village or parish community. Peasant social and economic life took place within this community, and it was within the village that peasants rallied to counter any real or perceived threat to their existence.

Two chief threats to that traditional existence arose during the period from 1525 to 1789 and were the main causes of rural violence in this period. The first of these threats was economic in nature. The economy of the West was beginning its slow evolution from a subsistence agricultural economy to an economy driven by exchange on international markets and nascent industrial capitalism. Our sources will reveal the effects of such changes on early modern peasants. They could be wrenching at times, manifesting themselves in such varied forms as increased seigniorial dues, innovative and disruptive ways of administering agricultural land, and higher food prices driven by market forces that were beyond the control or even the understanding of peasants. Such developments provoked considerable resistance to changes in traditional peasant ways.

The second cause of peasant unrest was the growing power of the state. This was felt in a variety of ways, including military conscription of peasant boys, but chiefly in the rising tax burden that governments imposed on their subjects. The sixteenth, seventeenth, and eighteenth centuries were periods of extensive warfare, and every state sought to increase its tax revenues to sustain the costs of war. To raise war taxes, expensive, centralized bureaucracies also had to be created, further increasing revenue demands on the peasants who formed the mass of the state's subjects and often intruding deeply into their rural worlds. The new government officials often tried to supplant traditional rural administrative practices in order to raise revenues more efficiently, and these governmental and fiscal innovations also encountered peasant resistance.

Peasants responded to these developments with violence that may appear rather bizarre to twenty-first-century students of history, who are accustomed to defining revolutions as movements aimed at creating new governmental or social orders. Many historians have noted that early modern peasant rebellions and riots aimed not at creating a new order, but, instead, at protecting the status quo or restoring an older social or governmental order.

In this chapter we will assess the origins and nature of European peasant rebellions and riots over three centuries. In the sources that constitute the core of this chapter, you should seek answers to several fundamental questions, understanding, of course, that the sources are describing just a few of thousands of such acts of violence. What were the causes of these acts of collective violence by European peasants? Were these actions revolutionary in that they sought a new social, political, or economic order? What do these events tell you about traditional rural society in Europe? Who participated in such violence, and who led it?

Chapter 1
Peasant Violence:
Rebellion and
Riot in Early
Modern Europe,
1525–1789

SOURCES AND METHOD

We have assembled a number of different kinds of sources to assist you in answering the basic questions posed in this chapter. Nonetheless, you quickly will perceive that this evidence has two basic origins. One part of the evidence is the work of nonpeasants, usually various people in authority who were concerned with the reestablishment of order after collective violence. Some of the authors of such sources, as you will see, had little concern with the peasants' point of view and assumed that rebellions and riots were the work of the very lowest, and materially the most dispossessed, elements of society. Persons in authority also tended to believe that outsiders often stirred up peasant revolts and riots, and that peasants themselves were incapable of mobilizing and directing a movement. Since for centuries historians chiefly consulted the works of such authority figures, their writings long reflected the opinions evident in these sources.

The second origin of our evidence is sources written by the peasants themselves, or their representatives. Until recently, these sources frequently were more difficult for historians to consult because they generally were buried in police and administrative archives. In such sources, we can come closer to ascertaining the causes of peasant unrest, but we often find that their authors lack a complete understanding of the problems that led them to revolt.

The sources are drawn from a number of different rebellions and riots from 1525 to 1789. The events recounted in these sources occurred all over Europe (in England, France, Germany, the Habsburg monarchy, Piedmont-Sardinia, and Russia) and were selected to illustrate several different manifestations of collective violence. Sources 1 and 2 originated in German peasant revolts in the late fifteenth and early sixteenth centuries. Germany was the scene of widespread, powerful peasant rebellions in this period; indeed, some observers estimate that as many as 300,000 peasants took up arms in the German Peasants' Revolt of 1525. A number of problems produced these disturbances, including the continuing effects of a late medieval economic crisis that was in part the result of the devastation of Europe's population by the bubonic plague.

By the second half of the fifteenth century, Germany's population, recovering from the plague's effects, was growing, and that growth dramatically affected the status of peasants. The increased labor supply drove wages downward, while the sheer growth in population increased demand for food, and therefore its price. Seigniors, seeking to profit from this situation, caused growing discontent among their peasants as they pursued several different strategies to maximize the income from their estates. The lords increasingly appropriated for their own use common lands that traditionally had been open to all for the grazing of livestock and other purposes. They also shortened the peasants' leases on lands in order to raise rents at each renewal to keep up with inflation and to collect the fees that peasants paid their lord at renewal. And seigniors increased labor services and other dues collected from their peasants, so that the latter sensed a real worsening of their conditions. Clerical institutions, to which the peasants owed the tithe, which was usually paid in agricultural goods, also sought to maximize their incomes, and peasant resentment of an increasingly rigorous collection of the tithe also rose.

Policies pursued by German rulers also dismayed peasants. Germany in this period was a collection of more than 300 independent principalities, loosely governed by the Holy Roman Emperor. The rulers of many of these German states in this period sought to strengthen and modernize their realms, at a rising cost to the peasant. New bureaucracies, increasingly costly in terms of taxes, eroded traditional regional or communal political autonomy and imposed, in place of old customary laws, new law codes based on Roman law principles.

Other factors affected peasant response to these developments. Early modern agriculture was extremely vulnerable to weather conditions, blights, and pests, and German peasants in this period endured a great deal of suffering from failed harvests; as an example, in one part of the Holy Roman Empire, Alsace, harvests failed fifteen times in the period from 1475 to 1525. Such failures, amid their other problems, led many

peasants to a belief that divine intervention might dramatically improve their lot. Indeed, astrological prediction, particularly attractive to the less educated, foretold dramatic events for the year 1525 and encouraged peasant action at that time.

One final element that also contributed to peasant unrest, at least after 1517, was the Protestant Reformation, whose main German leader was Martin Luther. Certainly Luther condemned peasant rebellion when it broke out, but his message defying the authority of Rome must have caused already restive peasants to question the established authority of their seigniors, and of at least local officials of Church and state.

The convergence of these developments produced widespread peasant rebellion in German lands, beginning with the Bundschuh Rebellion in Alsace as early as the 1439–1444 period. The name of this rebellion was derived from the symbol that the peasants displayed on their banners, the peasants' heavy work shoe (*schuh* is "shoe" in German), which was bound by a thong (*bund* in German; the word has a double meaning, "thong" or "tie" but also "association"). The shoe on rebel peasant banners often supported symbols of the papacy and the Holy Roman Emperor, representing the peasants' rejection of all authority save that of the pope and the emperor. German peasants also raised such banners in 1493, 1502, 1513, 1517, and 1525.

Source 1 is a wood block engraving of peasants with a *bundschuh* banner. The work of a sixteenth-century

[5]

Chapter 1

Peasant Violence:

Rebellion and

Riot in Early

Modern Europe,

1525–1789

engraver, the picture portrays the revolt of German peasants in 1525. What symbol rests on the shoe on the banner? What is the response to the banner of the peasants at the right of the picture? What do you conclude from this about peasant loyalties? Why does this picture suggest peasant millenarianism to you? In the background of the picture, among portrayals of peasant labor, you will notice a picture of the Old Testament prophet Abraham sacrificing his son Isaac. Why do you think the artist included this scene?

Source 2 also comes from the German Peasants' Revolt of 1525, the last and greatest of the early modern rebellions in Germany. It began in southwest Germany in the summer of 1524 and engulfed most of the southern and central parts of the country in 1525. The rebellion started as a strike rather than a rebellion, with peasant communities refusing to work until they negotiated better conditions from their lords. But soon peasants selected leaders, marched around their regions to rally support, and turned to violence. German peasant rebels chose the same targets in 1525 as they had in earlier uprisings: the authority represented by castles and monasteries. These places were plundered and sometimes their occupants were killed as the peasants forged themselves into military forces to oppose the armies of the German princes.

German peasants frequently asked literate members of their communities, such as priests or craftsmen, to draft lists of their demands for change. Since many peasant communities drafted such lists of the local problems that prompted them to revolt, historians have a good record of the rebellion's causes. Probably the most concise of these is the Twelve Articles of the Upper Swabian Peasants (Upper Swabia was a region in southwestern Germany), which represents a distillation of over 300 peasant grievances drafted by a Protestant pastor, Christoph Schappeler, and a Protestant layman, Sebastien Lutzer. Because the authors drew on actual peasant grievances in writing their document, the Twelve Articles, presented in Source 2, offer an authentic expression of peasant desires. This document also became a call to action for other peasants because the new printing presses of the early sixteenth century allowed the Twelve Articles to be reproduced in quantity and circulated widely. Moreover, there is evidence that they were read aloud to rally illiterate audiences to the cause of revolt, and even though the peasant rebels proved unable to unify their forces and, thus, were defeated and brutally punished by the armies of German rulers, the Twelve Articles had an enduring significance. Peasants in about one-third of the rebel areas, despite their defeat, succeeded in reaching agreements with their lords that met at least some of the desires stated in the articles.

What role in their revolt did the authors of the Twelve Articles ascribe to the new religious teaching of the Reformation? What are the peasants' demands in the area of religion? What view do the authors express on serfdom? What were peasant complaints with regard to noble rights to land use and feudal dues? How did the peasants justify their position? What effect do you think the Twelve Articles would have had on peasant audiences hearing them for the first time?

English peasants experienced some of the same problems as their German contemporaries. The growth of England's postplague population in the fifteenth and sixteenth centuries held down wages and drove up prices for necessities, while currency debasement to finance an ambitious foreign policy only added to inflation. Exacerbating the rural economic difficulties engendered by inflation was a substantial change in English agriculture. Landowners sought to benefit from rising prices for agricultural goods by increasing their production. This could be done in several ways. One way was to clear forest land and to bring wastelands under the plow, but the amount of such land was limited. Another way for landowners to increase output was through enclosure.

This practice, which had been occurring in England from as early as the thirteenth century, proceeded in two ways. Some nobles and gentry encroached on the common lands of their estates, chiefly pastures traditionally set aside for their tenants' livestock, enclosing these areas with fences or hedges for their own use. Other estate owners simply evicted tenants who could not prove their rights to small farms on large estates and consolidated these lands, again enclosing them with fences or hedges.

Landowners particularly engaged in enclosure to undertake large-scale sheep raising. The general population growth of the West in the fifteenth and sixteenth centuries led to demand for increasing quantities of wool cloth for clothing, and England long had been the source for much of Europe's raw wool. Thus, much of the newly enclosed land was used to pasture sheep. But this process of enclosure was not without cost for those who were not substantial landowners. Loss of common rights reduced the incomes of many peasants, while enclosure entirely displaced others from the land. Indeed, sixteenth-century officials charged with maintaining public order had to deal with large numbers of wandering poor, the victims of this structural change in agriculture. Such officials also faced rising peasant opposition to enclosure.

Anti-enclosure riots, in which crowds knocked down fences and leveled hedges, were the most common form of rural protest in the early sixteenth century. But in the late 1540s the number of such riots against agricultural innovation increased, and, as we will see in one case, some of them grew into outright rebellion. Several political developments seem to have contributed to this growing peasant militancy. King Henry VIII died on January 28, 1547, and the crown passed to his son, Edward VI, a boy of nine years of age, who lacked the authority of his father. Administrative authority in the late 1540s was in the hands of the monarch's uncle, Edward Seymour, Duke of Somerset and Lord Protector. Somerset had

Chapter 1

Peasant Violence:

Rebellion and

Riot in Early

Modern Europe,

1525–1789

considerable sympathy for the peasantry affected by enclosure. He issued two proclamations ordering the cessation of the practice and, over the opposition of landowners, sent out royal commissions to investigate enclosure abuses. The apparent support of the Protector encouraged many in their opposition to enclosure and hastened open rebellion in the county of Norfolk, an area of extensive wool and cloth production.

Events in that county moved toward violence in the summer of 1549, culminating at Wymondham on the feast of the Translation of St. Thomas Becket, a traditional gathering for peasants in the area. Much more than religious ceremony marked the observance of this day on Sunday, July 7, 1549. Peasants also seem to have heatedly discussed their grievances over enclosure, for the next day, crowds returning from Wymondham began to demolish fences and hedges in the area. Soon these violent crowds coalesced into a major force of perhaps 16,000 men under the leadership of Robert Kett (1492–1549), a local landowner. Kett led his followers to capture the county seat, Norwich, then England's second largest city. There Kett presided over a very conservative resistance to enclosure. He and his followers did not question royal authority and the law; rather, they set up law courts to try landowners for their abuses.

As much as he might have sympathized with the demands of Kett and his followers, Somerset could not ignore the threat to public order posed by such events. Thus, he dispatched an army that recaptured Norwich,

crushed the rebellion, and captured its leaders. The authorities executed Kett in December 1549.

Kett and his followers, like the German peasants of 1525, left a statement of their objectives, the Twenty-Nine Demands addressed to the king, which are excerpted in Source 3. This document reveals the causes of Kett's rebellion, but shows signs of having been hastily drafted: The demands represent a diverse list of grievances, presented in no systematic order. Indeed, although the rebels accepted the religious reforms of Henry VIII that had taken England out of the Roman Catholic Church, they also offered a number of demands for clerical reform (which are not included in Source 3). As you read these demands, you also will note that local concerns often intruded into the rebels' list. Thus, in the first demand that "no man shall enclose any more," drafters sought an exemption from this requirement for the large number of Norfolk residents who raised saffron for use as a textile dye.

Against what practices and which social group are these demands directed? In what tone do the drafters of these demands address the monarch? Why would you consider this an essentially conservative document rather than a revolutionary one? Given the great concern about property rights in the demands, what do you think was the social and economic status of their authors?

Numerous peasant rebellions erupted in France in the sixteenth and seventeenth centuries, particularly in the southwestern quarter of the kingdom. The cause of these rebellions was the rising royal tax burden imposed on the peasants and the way in which it was collected. Taxes were increasing during the sixteenth and seventeenth centuries because France frequently was at war and royal revenues had to rise to meet military costs. But often taxes went up far more than the government's expenses. This was because the monarchy, lacking a sufficient bureaucratic structure to collect all its taxes, "farmed out" most of its indirect taxes. Under this system, syndicates of investors bid for the right to collect a royal tax; in order to make a profit, they had to collect the amount the crown expected from the tax plus additional sums to defer the cost of collection and to provide a profit margin.

Peasant taxpayers were well aware of this system and scorned the collectors, whom they called *gabelleurs* after the *gabelle,* a tax-farmed fee on salt sales. Peasants also detested the new royal tax officials, the *élus,* charged with assessing the main royal tax, the *taille.* The taille, paid only by commoners, was levied on a parish, and then taxes were assessed on parish residents, in principle in proportion to their worth. But because this tax was a parish obligation and not an individual obligation, a taxpayer might have to pay more than his proportionate share if his neighbors were delinquent in paying or if wealthy and influential parishioners secured tax exemptions for themselves.

In 1636, amid a period of military emergency in which France was invaded by her enemies in the Thirty Years' War, taxes increased dramatically. So, too, did the local costs for garrisoning royal troops. The result was the revolt of the Croquants[2] of the Angoumois and Saintonge regions of southwestern France when officials tried to collect taxes in April 1636. Armed peasants assembled at the sound of their local parish alarm bells, selected leaders, and killed or drove off tax collectors, burned their homes, and besieged towns where they sought refuge. They were led by the wealthier peasants, parish priests, or local nobles forced by the crowd to take leadership roles because of their military experience.

With much of its military strength committed in the Thirty Years' War, the royal government at first met the Croquants' rebellion with a mixture of force and temporary concessions on tax issues, and the rebellion spread to the neighboring province of Périgord in 1637. Even though by the end of 1637 royal forces had defeated the peasants and captured and executed their leaders, extensive violence against tax officials continued until 1643.

The Angoumois rebels, in particular, left an excellent record of their objectives, as peasant leaders had assembled in June 1636 to draft lists of these goals. Seldom did peasants protest the power of local noblemen or the basic principle of royal taxation.

2. **Croquants:** the origin of this name, used as a term of derision for peasant rebels in several regions of southwestern France in the early modern period, is uncertain. Perhaps it is from the town of Crocq, or perhaps from *croc,* which is the name of the cudgel many peasants carried.

Chapter 1

Peasant Violence:

Rebellion and

Riot in Early

Modern Europe,

1525–1789

Rather, they argued against new royal taxes in the belief that these taxes were the work of corrupt royal officials and that the king would grant peasants tax relief if he only knew of his subordinates' dishonesty. In advancing their protest, peasants looked back nostalgically to an earlier age of lower taxes and demanded the return of those times.

While Angoumois Croquants stated their demands particularly well, their manifestos repeat themes that were common in the numerous French peasant rebellions from 1548 to 1675. Thus Source 4, a manifesto drafted by the peasants of Angoumois in 1636, typifies the demands of many early modern French peasant rebellions. What evidence do you find here of peasant concern for local problems and an effort on the part of peasants to exercise powers of government? What enemies in their own midst did the peasants single out? What abuses in taxation did the peasants protest? What response to their protest do you think they expected from the king? What role did peasants demand of the local nobility?

Seventeenth-century peasant revolts also challenged the authority of the tsar of Russia. As in France, we may find the roots of the greatest of these, that of Stepan Razin (1630?–1671), in the development of the early modern state. As we have seen in France, warfare placed extraordinary demands on the resources of the seventeenth-century monarchy, and the wars of Tsar Michael (r. 1613–1645) and Tsar Alexis (r. 1645–1676) with Sweden, Poland, Turkey, and the warlike Tartar tribes along Russia's southern borders required great increases in taxation.

To collect new taxes, the government had to create an efficient bureaucratic apparatus, and the seventeenth century witnessed a growing centralization of the Russian state. New officials from the capital, Moscow, assumed most of the authority formerly exercised by local officials, including those at the village level, who traditionally had been elected. Thus, many Russians perceived the new officials as usurpers. In addition, because Tsar Michael and Tsar Alexis both took the throne as adolescents and were weak rulers who often let avaricious groups of advisers run the state apparatus for them, these officials were also seen by many as rapaciously dishonest.

New taxes, however, would produce no revenue if there were no taxpayers, and many Russian peasants fled to the frontiers of the country, to the steppes and the fertile Volga River Valley in the south or to Siberia in the east, to escape taxes and military service. Indeed, on Russia's frontier in the southern valleys of the Don and Volga Rivers, a virtually independent society, that of the Cossacks, flourished and attracted many refugees fleeing from state authority.

Cossacks were descended from fugitives from the tsar's rule who recognized no authority but their own. They had their own general assembly, a *Krug;* elected their own chief, or *ataman;* and refused to pay taxes. They also forbade extensive agriculture in their lands, fearing the encroachment of Russian serfdom, and lived as hunters, fishermen, herders, and occasionally bandits and pirates. In return for their freedom and occasional payments from the treasury in Moscow, Cossacks performed services for the tsar, such as patrolling the frontier and providing defense against warlike tribes including the Crimean Tartars.

In response to the erosion of its tax base by the flight of taxpayers, the tsar's government produced the Sobornoye Ulozhenie, or Law Code of 1649, which sought to lock Russia's people into their existing condition in order to tax them efficiently. It required townsmen never to change their hometowns and to follow their fathers' occupations. Serfs lost any possibility of ever escaping their bondage to their lords.

In the years after 1649, the country experienced conditions that produced a great deal of unrest. Peasants continued to flee to the frontiers, and the numbers doing so grew greatly when Russia resumed its wars with Poland and Sweden after 1654. In response, the government for the first time sent agents to areas of the Volga Valley to recapture these fugitives. The financial demands of war also prompted the government to attempt to replace silver currency with copper, and the resulting inflation led to a revolt in Moscow in 1662. All the while, the country's losses mounted in the war with Poland, which lasted until 1667. And disease swept the country in the 1660s, killing perhaps 700,000 to 800,000 persons.

Out of these problems grew the Razin revolt. Razin was a Cossack leader who first achieved prominence in 1667 by leading a Cossack plundering expedition in the Volga Valley and the Caspian Sea. By 1670, his band of pirates had become a rebel army, and he announced his intention to march on Moscow to free the country from the tsar's evil advisers. His followers spread leaflets throughout the countryside as they advanced, proclaiming his loyalty to the tsar and his intent to "establish the Cossack way . . . so that all men will be equal."[3]

Razin amassed a great following, who often called him "Father." Escaped serfs, fearing recapture, joined his Cossack force, as did members of the lower clergy drawn from the peasantry, and even whole army units that also were of peasant origin. Everywhere Razin appeared, peasants burned local manor houses and the records of their obligations to their seigniors, and sometimes killed their lords. While Razin's force ultimately numbered perhaps 20,000 men, it was a poorly disciplined and ill-equipped force that was defeated in October 1670 when it encountered tsarist forces that were well equipped and well led.

Razin, wounded, retreated but was captured by Cossack leaders, who feared that his rebellion would lead to an increase in the tsar's authority in their region. They turned him over to the government, and he was executed in June 1671. The rebellion he had started dragged on for a while longer, but the army brutally crushed the revolt in the end; some

3. Quoted by Paul Avrich, *Russian Rebels, 1600–1800* (New York: Schocken Books, 1972), p. 89.

Chapter 1

Peasant Violence:

Rebellion and

Riot in Early

Modern Europe,

1525–1789

seventeenth-century observers estimated rebel losses in battle and in the ensuing repression at 100,000.

Source 5 recounts an incident in Razin's rebellion. It is part of a rather large literature written by foreign visitors to seventeenth-century Russia, a country then only poorly known in western Europe. Such accounts are not always reliable as sources because their value depends on their authors' knowledge of the country. The author of Source 5, Ludwig Fabritius, however, knew Russia well. A Dutch soldier employed with his stepfather, Paul Rudolph Breem, to serve as an expert on western European military methods in the Russian army, Fabritius lived in Russia from 1660 to 1677. He then served in the Swedish diplomatic corps, and died in Stockholm in 1729. While we must understand when we read Fabritius's account that his loyalties were with the tsar, he does provide a reliable account of events. Against whom does he say Razin directed his revolt? Who joined Razin's cause? Why might you think that Razin had not completely given up his earlier, plundering ways? What military effect do you think the decision, recounted here, to postpone the advance on Moscow in favor of an attack on Astrakhan had on Razin's campaign?

In the polyglot central European monarchy of the Habsburgs, such large-scale peasant rebellions also were a real concern to authorities, especially in the Bohemian lands that today form a large part of the Czech Republic. These lands had been the center of the religious reform movement of John Hus (1369–1415), which

had separated many residents of this area from the Roman Catholic Church. The Habsburgs, however, reimposed Catholicism in the wake of the Bohemian revolt that opened the Thirty Years' War, and the Habsburg defeat of Bohemian Protestants at the Battle of White Mountain (1620) permitted the monarchy to dispossess defeated Protestant noblemen of their lands and replace them with non-Bohemian lords who were loyal to the dynasty and its faith. These new, foreign seigniors imposed a harsh regime on peasants who, in the past, had achieved considerable freedom by converting their seigniorial obligations into cash payments; even the *robot* (*robota* is Slavonic for "work"), a requirement for peasant labor on the lord's behalf, had been convertible. The post-1620 settlement, however, confirmed the principle of *nexus subditelae,* which held that peasants on noble manors were subjects not of the monarch but of their seigniors, who thus had the power to administer justice on their lands, collect the peasants' taxes to the crown, and exact payments and labor from the peasants as their landlords. The new lords rigorously exacted their due, including the *robot,* which commonly came to represent a peasant obligation to the seignior of three days' labor per week. From the peasants' standpoint, this obligation was made worse by the fact that it took precedence over all their other responsibilities; thus, at harvest time, the peasants' own crops might remain uncut and susceptible to weather damage while they harvested the fields of the seignior. Peasants did not passively accept such changes, and a large peasant rebellion erupted in Bohemia in 1680.

By the mid-eighteenth century, however, change in these conditions seemed imminent. The government of Maria Theresa (Archduchess of Austria and Queen of Bohemia and Hungary, 1740–1780) recognized that a modern state required tax revenues, which could be raised only from free and prosperous farmers. The monarch therefore ordered government inquiries into peasant conditions as a basis for their reform. Source 6 is an excerpt from a report resulting from such an inquiry in 1769. This is part of a large body of investigatory material produced by most eighteenth-century governments, representing the pioneering efforts of early modern states to generate hard data on which to base policy decisions. Such reports provide twenty-first-century historians with essential information for understanding the society and economy of an earlier age. Source 6 is the work of an observant official of the Habsburg monarchy, who argues strongly for reform of the conditions of Bohemian peasants. Even with such evidence at hand, however, Maria Theresa was unable to achieve timely change in Bohemia as a result of the local nobility's opposition to reform. The monarch recognized that delay might prove costly. Indeed, in a letter in early 1775, she predicted that failure to achieve change in Bohemia might lead to revolt because desperate men could be dangerous. Her fears proved well founded. In January 1775, a revolt bred of discontent with

both the peasants' obligations to their seigniors and the reimposition of Catholicism broke out in eastern and northern Bohemia. Peasant leaders formed a government that declared its loyalty to Maria Theresa and proclaimed, mistakenly, that she actually had abolished the *robot* but that the nobility had suppressed her orders. Moreover, they led a large force against the capital, Prague, that required more than 40,000 troops to defeat. The monarchy's actions in the wake of its victory were conciliatory: Its officials executed only seven peasant leaders, and, more importantly, they renewed their efforts at reform in Bohemia.

Consider the conditions described in Source 6. What powers did Bohemian seigniors have over their peasants? What effect on the peasants did the report's author ascribe to the *robot*? How do you think peasants felt about such a significant decline in their condition over the previous several generations?

Rebellion in France is the subject of Source 7. In 1789, King Louis XVI (r. 1774–1792) called a meeting of the Estates General, a legislative body that had not met in 175 years, in an attempt to secure sufficient taxes to prevent his government's impending bankruptcy. Economic difficulties were the lot of the king's subjects, too; the harvest of 1788 had been a meager one because of late summer storms, and in 1789 food prices were extremely high and the wandering poor filled the roads in search of jobs and food.

Election of the Estates General had raised peasants' hopes for some

Chapter 1

Peasant Violence:

Rebellion and

Riot in Early

Modern Europe,

1525–1789

improvement in their lot, especially when the representatives of the Third Estate of the Estates General declared that they would write a constitution for the country in defiance of the king's wishes. Indeed, when the king began to move troops to Versailles, where the Estates met, to disband the body, Parisians rose in rebellion and seized control of the capital on July 14, 1789; in provincial cities, similar municipal revolutions occurred. Although the king abandoned his military coup, news of these events reached the countryside. There the numerous wandering poor seem to have been the root of wild rumors that bands of brigands or foreign troops were coming to punish the peasants for their support of reform by burning their ripening crops. Through much of rural France, parish alarm bells rang in late July and early August, calling peasants to arm themselves for defense.

Of course the "brigands" never appeared, but armed peasants vented their anger against the property of their local seigniors in the rebellion known as the Great Fear. The particular targets of peasant violence were the archives of local manor houses containing records of their obligations, and many of these were burned. Source 7 is an account of the peasant attack on the Château of Cuirieu, in the province of Dauphiné, drafted in October 1789 by an investigatory commission established by the provincial legislature. Written soon after the Great Fear, the account probably presents events accurately. What sorts of fears excited the peasants of Dauphiné? With what

did the peasants arm themselves? How many peasant bands stormed the Château of Cuirieu? What was their objective? What role did rumor and tales of plots play in this uprising? Why might you conclude that what is important for us to understand is what the peasants *thought* was happening rather than what we as historians know actually was happening?

Riots also disturbed the peace of early modern Europe, and many of them originated in the same problems that produced rural rebellion, often aristocratic attempts to modify the terms of peasant land tenure. But since early modern governments maintained none of the criminal justice data-gathering apparatus of the modern state, historians must carefully peruse sources like court records, the rather mundane administrative paperwork of government, and private correspondence for evidence of armed resistance. Indeed, Sources 8 and 9 come from the mass of petitions routinely received by every early modern ruler and from the voluminous private correspondence often carried on by educated early modern Europeans.

Source 8 includes two petitions originating in a series of large riots on the manor controlled by the Rottenbuch Abbey in Bavaria during the economic hard times of the Thirty Years' War. Beginning in the second decade of the seventeenth century, the abbey's prior sought to expel a number of peasant families from the manor in a dispute over land tenure. Peasants resisted these efforts over the period from 1619 to 1628 in a series of riots that required the ruler of Bavaria, Duke Maximilian I, to dispatch troops to the area to keep order and to arrest peasant leaders. One of these seemed to have been George Vend, whose personal property and home the authorities confiscated when they ordered Vend to leave his farm in Rottenbuch. Vend, however, defied this order, returning to his farm at least four times. Each defiance resulted in his arrest and expulsion from Rottenbuch.

In fact, Vend seems not to have left the area, for he participated in a mass two-day march of Rottenbuch peasants to Bavaria's capital, Munich, in August 1628 to petition the duke for redress of their grievances against the abbey and its prior. Vend was again arrested, and the authorities punished him by cutting off his ear and banishing him from Bavaria for life, a penalty that rendered him dead for purposes of civil law, as we will see in Source 8. Nevertheless, Vend ignored his banishment and returned to Rottenbuch with his family to plow his land. Again the authorities arrested him and expelled him from Bavaria, and the prior ordered that any local peasant feeding or sheltering Vend's wife, Christina, and his children would be fined. Christina then petitioned the duke to undo all of these penalties. The low rate of literacy among early modern peasant women suggests that Christina Vend must have used the services of a notary or attorney to draft the petitions reproduced in Source 8. She presented two petitions to the duke, the first one in February 1629 and the second the following month. The

duke rejected the first and granted the requests in the second.

What role do you think George Vend played in the events at Rottenbuch? What difference in tone may have accounted for the failure of the first petition and the success of the second? What does this suggest to you that Bavaria's ruler sought in the country's peasantry? What elements of the settlement proposed in the second petition might suggest to you that the whole dispute might have originated in the prior's attempt to increase the abbey's revenues at Rottenbuch?

Peasant riots also occurred in Savoy, a province in an emerging state whose eighteenth-century territories are now part of southern France and northern Italy. The territories of the dukes of Savoy experienced several problems in the early eighteenth century that contributed to peasant unrest. The duke chose to fight neighboring France in the War of the Spanish Succession (1701–1714), and enemy forces occupied part of his territories, at considerable cost to their inhabitants. The ducal foreign policy was costly to them, too, as it required tax increases. Taxes remained high after the war, when the duke, Victor Amadeus II (r. 1675–1730), added the island of Sardinia to his territories in Savoy and Piedmont (northern Italy) and acquired a royal title, king of Piedmont-Sardinia.

While war and taxes reduced peasant resources, the duke sought to enhance his own revenues by selling titles of nobility, often to middle-class persons who could ill afford the investment. These new nobles often

Chapter 1

Peasant Violence:

Rebellion and

Riot in Early

Modern Europe,

1525–1789

attempted to recoup their invest-ments quickly by redrafting surveys of their estate lands in their own favor and generally increasing peas-ants' seigniorial dues. This process of innovation encountered widespread resistance, as a nobleman named Vuy found in 1717.

Vuy had acquired the administra-tion of a domain in Gets, Savoy, that was the possession of the chapter of Barnabite monks at Thonon, Savoy. On Sunday, March 14, 1717, Vuy, with an armload of papers supporting his right to the revenues of Gets, assem-bled the local peasants after Mass in a customary meeting place, the village cemetery, to advise them of his newly acquired authority. The crowd of sev-eral hundred was armed with sticks and clubs, and their reaction to their new seignior was recounted by Vuy himself in the letter that is excerpted in Source 9. It is an eyewitness ac-count of events, although, since Vuy survived, we should probably as-sume that he embellished his account of the ferocity of the crowd.

What action did the crowd take against Vuy? Why do you think the crowd was so angry? Why would you not be surprised to learn that a careful study of Savoyard police and judicial records produced evidence of many other such violent incidents during this period?

Another frequent cause of early modern riots was the scarcity of food or its high price. The development of modern capitalism was fundamen-tally reshaping the provision of food-stuffs in the early modern period. Governments abandoned traditional controls on the trade and price of

bread and other staples, and food supplies flowed not so much to where they were needed as to the markets, often in large and wealthy cities, that offered the highest prices to sellers. The result in many cases was higher prices for basic foods or a sudden shortage in supply. People re-sponded violently to such develop-ments. Indeed, food riots posed such an important threat to peace in this period that most governments care-fully observed oscillations in food prices that might cause trouble, and some rulers attempted to restore reg-ulations on the distribution of flour and the price of bread to keep that staple affordable.

Food riots could take several forms. Market riots generally occurred in urban areas when city residents, sus-pecting that speculators were driving food prices higher by hoarding flour or bread, stormed granaries and bak-eries in search of those goods. An-other form of crowd action, generally known by its French name, *entrave,* was driven by fear of hunger. In this action, peasant mobs stopped grain shipments to markets outside of their regions. A third form of collective ac-tion, a variety of food riot that the French call *taxation populaire,* ex-pressed what one historian has called the "moral economy" of the crowd. In this form of riot, crowd members seized control of bread or grain in a period of shortage and high price and sold the foodstuffs at what they deemed a "just price." The "just price" always was far below market prices in times of shortage, but its uniformity throughout whole re-gions suggests widespread consensus among people as to the price that the poor could afford. Interestingly, the crowd turned the proceeds of such sales over to the merchants or bakers from whom it had seized the food.

A period of widespread food rioting, called the Flour War, erupted in the countryside around Paris in April 1775, as a result of the convergence of two developments. First, the grain harvest of 1774 was a poor one, and in 1775 bread prices rose as a consequence. Second, at almost the same time, the royal government announced complete freedom of the grain trade as a step toward implementing the economic thought of eighteenth-century Enlightenment thinkers, which called for free trade. From the peasants' perspective, rising food prices and the movement of grain to new markets outside their regions portended disaster and starvation, and they responded forcefully. Peasants stopped barges and wagons loaded with grain and brought *taxation populaire* to many a village, in some cases doubtlessly encouraged by unfounded rumors of royal orders to sell grain at a certain price. Violence abated only when the government moved two armies into the region in May 1775.

Source 10 presents a record of one riot in the Flour War. It is a record of an interrogation of a rioter by the Maréchaussée, or rural police, of eighteenth-century France. Such records can be very useful to the historian because they often provide researchers with almost verbatim accounts of the conflicts and actions of persons who normally leave historians no written records of their activities. The accused rioter, Louis Marais, did not deny being in the thick of the crowd action of May 3, 1775, but he did deny leading the riot. What evidence do you find that the peasants had an idea of a "just price" for wheat? Reflecting on the causes of the Flour War, why might you find the peasants' actions a political statement? How were these peasants simply responding to changes in government policy? How were the peasants attempting to restore earlier conditions?

Using this background on peasant violence, turn now to the evidence. As you read it, seek to formulate answers to the central questions of this chapter. What were the causes of these acts of collective violence by European peasants? Were these actions revolutionary in that they sought a new social, political, or economic order? What do these events tell you about traditional rural society in Europe? Who participated in such violence, and who led it?

Chapter 1

Peasant Violence:

Rebellion and

Riot in Early

Modern Europe,

1525–1789

THE EVIDENCE

Source 1 from Otto Brandt, Der deutsche Bauernkrieg *(1929), p. 25. German peasant revolt.* Reprinted in Roland H. Bainton, Here I Stand: A Life of Martin Luther *(New York: New American Library, 1963), p. 210.*

1. The German Peasants' Revolt of 1525: The *Bundschuh* Banner

Source 2 from James Harvey Robinson and Merrick Whitcomb, editors, Translations and Reprints from the Original Sources, vol. II, no. 6: The Period of the Early Reformation in Germany *(Philadelphia: University of Pennsylvania Press, 1902).*

2. The German Peasants' Revolt of 1525: The Twelve Articles of the Peasants

Peace to the Christian reader, and the Grace of God through Christ.

There are many evil writings put forth of late which take occasion on account of the assembling of the peasants, to cast scorn upon the Gospel, saying: Is this the fruit of the new teaching, that no one should obey but all should everywhere rise in revolt, and rush together to reform, or perhaps destroy entirely, the authorities, both ecclesiastical and lay? The articles below shall answer these godless and criminal fault-finders, and serve in the first place to remove the reproach from the word of God and, in the second place, to give a Christian excuse for the disobedience or even the revolt of the entire Peasantry. In the first place the Gospel is not the cause of revolt and disorder, since it is the message of Christ, the promised Messiah, the Word of Life, teaching only love, peace, patience and concord. Thus, all who believe in Christ should learn to be loving, peaceful, long-suffering and harmonious. This is the foundation of all the articles of the peasants (as will be seen) who accept the gospel and live according to it. . . . In the second place, it is clear that the peasants demand that this Gospel be taught them as a guide in life, and they ought not to be called disobedient or disorderly. . . . Therefore, Christian reader, read the following articles with care and then judge. Here follow the articles:

The First Article: First, it is our humble petition and desire, as also our will and resolution, that in the future we should have power and authority so that each community should choose and appoint a pastor, and that we should have the right to depose him should he conduct himself improperly. The pastor thus chosen should teach us the Gospel pure and simple, without any addition, doctrine or ordinance of man. For to teach us continually the true faith will lead us to pray God that through his grace this faith may increase within us and become a part of us. For if his grace work not within us we remain flesh and blood, which availeth nothing; since the Scripture clearly teaches that only through true faith can we come to God. . . .

The Second Article: According as the just tithe is established by the Old Testament and fulfilled in the New, we are ready and willing to pay the fair tithe of grain. The word of God plainly provides that in giving according to right to God and distributing to his people the services of a pastor are required. We will that for the future our church provost, whomsoever the community may appoint, shall gather and receive this tithe. From this he shall give to the pastor, elected by the whole community, a decent and sufficient maintenance for

[19]

Chapter 1

Peasant Violence:

Rebellion and

Riot in Early

Modern Europe,

1525–1789

him and his . . . , as shall seem right to the whole community (or, with the knowledge of the community). What remains over shall be given to the poor of the place, as the circumstances and the general opinion demand. Should anything farther remain, let it be kept, lest anyone should have to leave the country from poverty. Provision should also be made from this surplus to avoid laying any land tax on the poor. . . .

. . . The small tithes,[4] whether ecclesiastical or lay, we will not pay at all, for the Lord God created cattle for the free use of man. We will not, therefore, pay farther an unseemly tithe which is of man's invention.

The Third Article: It has been the custom hitherto for men to hold us as their own property, which is pitiable enough, considering that Christ has delivered and redeemed us all, without exception by the shedding of his precious blood, the lowly as well as the great. Accordingly, it is consistent with Scripture that we should be free and wish to be so. Not that we would wish to be absolutely free and under no authority. God does not teach us that we should lead a disorderly life in the lusts of the flesh, but that we should love the Lord our God and our neighbor. We would gladly observe all this as God has commanded us in the celebration of the communion. He has not commanded us not to obey the authorities, but rather that we should be humble, not only towards those in authority, but towards everyone. We are thus ready to yield obedience according to God's law to our elected and regular authorities in all proper things becoming to a Christian. We, therefore, take it for granted that you will release us from serfdom, as true Christians, unless it should be shown us from the Gospel that we are serfs.

The Fourth Article: In the fourth place it has been the custom heretofore, that no poor man should be allowed to touch venison or wild fowl, or fish in flowing water, which seems to us quite unseemly and unbrotherly, as well as selfish and not agreeable to the word of God. In some places the authorities preserve the game to our great annoyance and loss, recklessly permitting the unreasoning animals to destroy to no purpose our crops, which God suffers to grow for the use of man, and yet we must remain quiet. This is neither godly nor neighborly. For when God created man he gave him dominion over all the animals, over the birds of the air and over the fish in the water. Accordingly it is our desire if a man holds possession of waters that he should prove from satisfactory documents that his right has been unwittingly acquired by purchase. We do not wish to take it from him by force, but his rights should be exercised in a Christian and brotherly fashion. But whosoever cannot produce such evidence should surrender his claim with good grace.

---

4. **small tithe:** peasants owed tithes to support the Church, although the right to collect these could be owned by laymen. The small tithe was payable on the value of livestock in much of Germany and also as a percentage of the crop of fruits or vegetables. The great tithe was payable on grains.

The Fifth Article: In the fifth place we are aggrieved in the matter of wood-cutting, for the noble folk have appropriated all the woods to themselves alone. If a poor man requires wood he must pay double for it. . . . It is our opinion in regard to a wood, which has fallen into the hands of a lord, whether spiritual or temporal, that unless it was duly purchased it should revert again to the community. . . .

The Sixth Article: Our sixth complaint is in regard to the excessive services demanded of us, which are increased from day to day. We ask that this matter be properly looked into so that we shall not continue to be oppressed in this way, and that some gracious consideration be given us, since our forefathers were required only to serve according to the word of God.

The Seventh Article: Seventh, we will not hereafter allow ourselves to be farther oppressed by our lords, but will let them demand only what is just and proper according to the word of the agreement between the lord and the peasant. . . .

The Eighth Article: In the eighth place, we are greatly burdened by holdings which cannot support the rent exacted from them. The peasants suffer loss in this way and are ruined; and we ask that the lords may appoint persons of honor to inspect these holdings, and fix a rent in accordance with justice, so that the peasant shall not work for nothing, since the laborer is worthy of his hire.

The Ninth Article: In the ninth place, we are burdened with a great evil in the constant making of new laws. We are not judged according to the offence, but sometimes with great ill will, and sometimes much too leniently. In our opinion we should be judged according to the old written law, so that the case shall be decided according to its merits, and not with partiality.

The Tenth Article: In the tenth place, we are aggrieved by the appropriation by individuals of meadows and fields which at one time belonged to a community. These we will take again into our own hands. . . .

The Eleventh Article: In the eleventh place we will entirely abolish the due called *Todfall*[5] . . . , and will no longer endure it, nor allow widows and orphans to be thus shamefully robbed against God's will, and in violation of justice and right, as has been done in many places, and by those who should shield and protect them. . . .

Conclusion: In the twelfth place it is our conclusion and final resolution, that if one or more of the articles here set forth should not be in agreement with the word of God, as we think they are, such article we will willingly recede from, when it is proved really to be against the word of God by a clear

---

5. **todfall:** death tax. This was a sort of transfer fee, payable to the peasants' seignior, when the peasant proprietor died and his property passed to his heir. Its traditional form in Germany required a male heir to give up his best horse and best garment and a female heir to render her best cow and best garment.

Chapter 1

Peasant Violence:

Rebellion and

Riot in Early

Modern Europe,

1525–1789

explanation of the Scripture. . . . Likewise, if more complaints should be discovered which are based upon truth and the Scriptures, and relate to offences against God and our neighbor, we have determined to reserve the right to present these also, and to exercise ourselves in all Christian teaching. For this we shall pray God, since he can grant this, and he alone. The peace of Christ abide with us all.

Source 3 from Stephen K. Land, Kett's Rebellion: The Norfolk Rising of 1549 *(Ipswich: The Boydell Press; Totowa, N.J.: Rowman and Littlefield, 1977), pp. 63–66. Reprinted by permission of Boydell & Brewer Ltd.*

3. The Twenty-Nine Demands of Kett's Rebellion, 1549

1. We pray your grace that where it is enacted for inclosing that it be not hurtfull to such as have enclosed saffron grounds for they be greatly chargeable to them, and that from henceforth no man shall enclose any more.

2. We certifie your grace that whereas the lords of the manors have been charged with certain free rent, the same lords have sought means to charge the freeholders to pay the same rent, contrary to right.

3. We pray your grace that no lord of no manor shall common[6] upon the commons.

4. We pray that priests from henceforth shall purchase no lands neither free nor bond, and the lands that they have in possession may be letten to temporal men,[7] as they were in the first year of the reign of King Henry VII.[8]

5. We pray that reedground and meadowground[9] may be at such price as they were in the first year of King Henry VII.

6. We pray that all the marshes that are held of the King's majesty by free rent or of any other, may be again at the price that they were in the first year of King Henry VII. . . .

9. We pray that the payments of castleward rent,[10] and blanch farm,[11] and office lands,[12] which hath been accustomed to be gathered of the tenaments, whereas we suppose the lords ought to pay the same to their bailiffs for their rents gathering, and not the tenants.

6. **common:** to pasture one's herds.

7. **letten to temporal men:** leased to nonclergy.

8. King Henry VII, the first monarch of the governing Tudor family, ruled from 1485 to 1509.

9. **reedground and meadowground:** marshy areas and pasture land.

10. **castleward rent:** a levy on buildings in the proximity of a royal castle to pay for its upkeep.

11. **blanch farm:** sometimes also called "white rents," these were the fixed rents of tenants on manors and were so named because they were paid in silver, or "white" money.

12. **office lands:** crown lands. This article protests lords shifting their obligations to the crown to their tenants.

10. We pray that no man under the degree of a knight of esquire keep a dove house,[13] except it hath been of an old ancient custom.

11. We pray that all freeholders and copyholders may take the profits of all commons, and there to common, and the lords not to common nor take profits of the same. . . .

13. We pray your grace to take all liberty of leet[14] into your own hands whereby all men may quietly enjoy their commons with all profits.

14. We pray that copyhold[15] land that is unreasonable rented may go as it did in the first year of King Henry VII and that at the death of a tenant or of a sale the same lands to be charged with an easy fine as a capon[16] or a reasonable sum of money for a remembrance. . . .

16. We pray that all bond men[17] may be made free for God made all free with his precious blood shedding.

17. We pray that rivers may be free and common to all men for fishing and passage. . . .

21. We pray that it be not lawful to the lords of any manor to purchase lands freely and to let them out again by copy of court roll to their great advantage and to the undoing of your poor subjects. . . .

27. We pray your grace to give license and authority by your gracious commission under your great seal to such commissioners as your poor commons hath chosen, or to as many of them as your majesty and your council shall appoint and think meet, for to redress and reform all such good laws, statutes, proclamations, and all other your proceedings, which hath been bidden by your Justices of your peace, Sheriffs, Escheators,[18] and others your officers, from your poor commons, since the first year of the reign of your noble grandfather King Henry the seventh.[19] . . .

29. We pray that no lord, knight, esquire, nor gentleman do graze nor feed any bullocks or sheep if he may spend forty pounds a year by his lands but only for the provision of his house.[20]

---

13. **dove house:** a structure used as a nesting place for pigeons. English and European noblemen often maintained such structures for the pigeons that they hunted for sport. The pigeons often fed on the crops of neighboring peasants.

14. **leet:** a court meeting annually or semiannually in which certain manor lords judged local disputes.

15. **copyhold:** landholding rights proven by record in the rolls of a manorial court.

16. **capon:** a rooster castrated to improve its flesh when cooked.

17. **bond men:** literally, feudal serfs. Such persons were extremely rare in sixteenth-century England.

18. **Escheator:** a royal official appointed for each county to oversee escheats, that is, the property that reverted to the crown when its deceased owners had no legal heirs.

19. This demand calls for the election of delegates, or commissioners, from Norfolk to reform laws made since 1485.

20. **provision of his house:** those animals necessary to feed the households. This demand intends to limit the grazing of livestock by gentry to such a number, thus limiting their pursuit of large-scale stock raising.

Chapter 1

Peasant Violence:

Rebellion and

Riot in Early

Modern Europe,

1525–1789

Source 4 from Archives Nationales de France, U793, f°s 88–89 v°; reprinted in Yves-Marie Bercé, Histoire des Croquants: Étude des soulèvements populaires au XVIIe siècle dans le Sud-Ouest de la France *(Geneva: Librairie Droz, 1974), vol. II, p. 738. Translated by Julius R. Ruff.*

4. Manifesto of the Peasants of the Angoumois, 1636

The assembly of the common people, having deliberated, ordered the following in a few words.

All inhabitants of each parish are directed to gather all payments due the priest of each parish and place them in the safekeeping of the two richest parishioners who will give the inhabitants an exact count of them. The priest will receive 300 *livres*[21] of this free and clear in estimated value of goods or in money. The remainder will be used to repair the church and to care for the parish poor.

We also direct all inhabitants of each parish to arm themselves according to their means and to be well supplied with lead and powder under the threat of a 20 *livres* fine for lacking powder and lead and being rebels.

We also direct each parish in the future, when they have received their assessments, to tax only three-quarters of the principal of the *taille,* because His Majesty will have lowered it for us, and also to tax only one-half of the increase in garrison costs because this has gone up by one-half in six years.

We direct each parish, when it wishes to apportion the *taille* among its citizens, to call upon the parish priest to undertake the process conscientiously and to assess the tax obligations among those with sufficient property to pay them. This is to be done without regard for personal connections and without fear of the power of the rich in order to relieve the poor of God.

We direct each parish to make the nobility provide arms and march in our cause under threat of having their manor houses burned and being denied payment of rents and *agriers*[22] due them.

We direct each parish to pass on a copy of this decree under penalty of being destroyed by our movement.

Sirs, we warn you that the real *gabelleurs* are the *élus* . . . , the richest of each parish who pay practically nothing. It has been confirmed in Paris that the *élus* of Saintes and Fontenay gather impositions of 60,000 *livres* over and above the sums authorized by His Majesty. All things considered, we have or-

---

21. *livres:* the main unit of Old Regime French currency, containing 20 *sous. Livres* means "pounds," but it is not translated as such because the French *livre* and British pound sterling were not equal in value.

22. *agriers:* a payment in kind, about 12 percent of the crop, which peasants owed their lords.

dered without appeal that the *élus* will be arrested by the commune in order to render justice . . . and make them restore with interest the notorious sums that they have stolen.

And as for the rich of each parish who completed the people's ruin, they must be excluded from the apportioning of the *taille* in the future and assessed their correct portion.

Source 5 from Ludwig Fabritius, Account of the Razin Rebellion, Oxford Slavonic Papers, *vol. 10 (1955), reprinted in Anthony Cross, editor,* Russia Under Western Eyes, 1517–1825 *(London: Elek Books, 1971), pp. 120–123.*

5. Ludwig Fabritius's Account of the Stepan Razin Revolt, 1670

Then Stenka[23] with his company started off upstream, rowing as far as Tsaritsyn, whence it took him only one day's journey to Panshin, a small town situated on the Don. Here he began straightaway quietly gathering the common people around him, giving them money, and promises of great riches if they would be loyal to him and help to exterminate the treacherous boyars.[24]

This lasted the whole winter, until by about spring he had assembled 4,000 to 5,000 men. With these he came to Tsaritsyn and demanded the immediate surrender of the fortress; the rabble soon achieved their purpose, and although the governor tried to take refuge in a tower, he soon had to give himself up as he was deserted by one and all. Stenka immediately had the wretched governor hanged; and all the goods they found belonging to the Tsar and his officers as well as to the merchants were confiscated and distributed among the rabble.

Stenka now began once more to make preparations. Since the plains are not cultivated, the people have to bring their [grain] from Nizhniy-Novgorod and Kazan down the Volga in big boats known as *nasady,* and everything destined for Astrakhan has first to pass Tsaritsyn. Stenka Razin duly noted this, and occupied the whole of the Volga, so that nothing could get through to Astrakhan. Here he captured a few hundred merchants with their valuable goods, taking possession of all kinds of fine linen, silks, striped silk material, sables, soft leather, ducats, talers, and many thousands of rubles in Russian money, and merchandise of every description—these men used to do much trade with the Persians, the Bokharans, the Uzbeks, and the Tartars.

23. **Stenka:** the diminutive of "Stepan," that is, "little Stepan."
24. **boyars:** noblemen.

Chapter 1

Peasant Violence:
Rebellion and
Riot in Early
Modern Europe,
1525–1789

In the meantime four regiments of *streltsy*[25] were dispatched from Moscow to subdue these brigands. They arrived with their big boats and as they were not used to the water, were easily beaten. Here Stenka Razin gained possession of a large amount of ammunition and artillery-pieces and everything else he required. While the above-mentioned *streltsy* were sent from Moscow, about 5,000 men were ordered up from Astrakhan by water and by land to capture Stenka Razin. As soon as he had finished with the former, he took up a good position, and, being in possession of reliable information regarding our forces, he left Tsaritsyn and came to meet us half way at Chernyy Yar, confronting us before we had suspected his presence or received any information about him. . . .

. . . We got out of our boats and took up battle positions. General Knyaz Semen Ivanovich Lvov went through the ranks and reminded all the men to do their duty and to remember the oath they had taken to His Majesty the Tsar, to fight like honest soldiers against these irresponsible rebels, whereupon they all unanimously shouted: 'Yes, we will give our lives for His Majesty the Tsar, and will fight to the last drop of our blood.'

In the meantime, Stenka prepared for battle and deployed on a wide front; to all those who had no rifle he gave a long pole, burnt a little at one end, and with a rag or small hook attached. They presented a strange sight on the plain from afar, and the common soldiers imagined that, since there were so many flags and standards, there must be a host of people. They [the common soldiers] held a consultation and at once decided that this was the chance for which they had been waiting so long, and with all their flags and drums they ran over to the enemy. They began kissing and embracing one another and swore with life and limb to stand together and to exterminate the treacherous boyars, to throw off the yoke of slavery, and to become free men.

The general looked at the officers and the officers at the general, and no one knew what to do; one said this, and another that, until finally it was decided that they and the general should get into the boats and withdraw to Astrakhan. But the rascally *streltsy* of Chernyy Yar stood on the walls and towers, turning their weapons on us and opened fire; some of them ran out of the fortress and cut us off from the boats, so that we had no means of escape. In the meantime those curs of ours who had gone over to the Cossacks came up from behind. We numbered about eighty men, officers, noblemen, and clerks. Murder at once began. Then, however, Stenka Razin ordered that no more officers were to be killed, saying that there must be a few good men among them who should be pardoned, whilst those others who had not lived in

---

25. *streltsy:* literally "sharpshooters." These military units, organized by Ivan the Terrible in 1550, were the first Russian troops to carry firearms. Recruited from all classes of commoners, these soldiers lived in their own settlements until Peter the Great disbanded their units in 1698 after a series of mutinies.

amity with their men should be condemned to well-deserving punishment by the Ataman and his *Krug*. A *Krug* is a meeting convened by the order of the Ataman, at which the Cossacks stand in a circle with the standard in the centre; the Ataman then takes his place beside his best officers, to whom he divulges his wishes, ordering them to make these known to the common brothers and to hear their opinion on the matter; if the proposals of the Ataman please the commoners, they all shout together, 'Lyubo, lyubo'.

A *Krug* was accordingly called and Stenka asked through his chiefs how the general and his officers had treated the soldiers under their command. Thereupon the unscrupulous curs, *streltsy* as well as soldiers, unanimously called out that there was not one of them who deserved to remain alive, and they all asked that their father Stepan Timofeyevich Razin should order them to be cut down. . . .

. . . When all the bloodthirsty curs had lined up, each was eager to deal his former superior the first blow, one with the sword, another with the lance, another with the scimitar, and others again with martels, so that as soon as an officer was pushed into the ring, the curs immediately killed him with their many wounds; indeed, some were cut to pieces and straightaway thrown into the Volga. My stepfather, Paul Rudolf Beem, and Lt. Col. Wundrum and many other officers, senior and junior, were cut down before my eyes.

My own time had not yet come: this I could tell by the wonderful way in which God rescued me, for as I—half-dead—now awaited the final blow, my [former] orderly, a young soldier, came and took me by my bound arms and tried to take me down the hill. As I was already half-dead, I did not move and did not know what to do, but he came back and took me by the arms and led me, bound as I was, through the throng of curs, down the hill into the boat and immediately cut my arms free, saying that I should rest in peace here and that he would be responsible for me and do his best to save my life. . . . Then my guardian angel told me not to leave the boat, and left me. He returned in the evening and brought me a piece of bread which I enjoyed since I had had nothing to eat for two days.

The following day all our possessions were looted and gathered together under the main flag, so that both our bloodthirsty curs and the Cossacks got their share.

Chapter 1

Peasant Violence:

Rebellion and

Riot in Early

Modern Europe,

1525–1789

Source 6 from C. A. Macartney, editor, The Habsburg and Hohenzollern Dynasties in the Seventeenth and Eighteenth Centuries *(New York: Harper and Row, Publishers, 1970), pp. 173–174. Copyright © 1970 by C. A. Macartney. Reprinted by permission of HarperCollins Publisher, Inc.*

6. Report of the Commission of Enquiry into the Conditions of the Peasants of Bohemia, presented to the Council of State in Vienna, June 1769

The *robot* gives rise to continual vexations. Even those nobles who have the best intentions are unable to protect their peasants, because their agents are rough, evil, violent and grasping. These burdens are terrifyingly heavy, and it is not surprising that the peasants try to evade them by every means. In consequence of the arbitrary allocation of the *robot,* the peasants live in a condition of real slavery; they become savage and brutalized, and cultivate the lands in their charge badly. They are rachitic,[26] thin and ragged; they are forced to do *robot* from their infancy. In their ruinous huts, the parents sleep on straw, the children naked on the wide shelves of earthenware stoves; they never wash, which promotes the spread of epidemics; there are no doctors to look after them. . . . Even their personal effects are not safe from the greed of the great lords. If they own a good horse, the lord forces them to sell it him, or if their good horse succumbs to the severity of the *robot,* they are compensated with a blind, old screw. In many places the serfs are forced to buy sick sheep from their lord at an arbitrarily fixed price. Implements of torture are set up in every village market square, or in front of the castle; recalcitrant peasants are thrown into irons, they are forced to sit astride a sharp wooden horse, which cuts deeply into their flesh; stones are hung on their legs; for the most trifling offense they are given fifty strokes of the rod; the serf who arrives late for his *robot,* be it only half an hour, is beaten half-dead. Many flee into Prussia to escape this reign of terror; there are hundreds of huts which their occupants have abandoned because they threatened to collapse and they had not the means to repair them. In other places the thatches have been taken off to feed the horses for lack of fodder, because these wretched creatures are forbidden to gather leaves in the forest for fear of their disturbing the game. Even when the harvest has been good they are obliged to ask for seed from their lord, and he sells it them at an extortionate price. The big landlords drive away the Jews, who make loans on better terms. . . . The Kingdom of Bohemia is like a statue which is collapsing because its pedestal has been taken away, because

---

26. **rachitic:** afflicted by rickets, a bone disorder resulting from vitamin D deficiency that generally afflicts children.

all the charges of the Kingdom are born by the peasants, who are the sole tax-payers.

Source 7 from Xavier Roux, Mémoire détaillé et par ordre de la marche des brigandages qui se sont commis en Dauphiné en 1789 *(Grenoble, 1891); reprinted in Yves-Marie Bercé,* Croquants et Nu-Pieds les soulèvements paysans en France du XVIe au XIXe siècle *(Paris: Gallimard/Julliard, 1974), pp. 125–128. Translated by Julius R. Ruff.*

7. Note on What Occurred Before and During the Devastation of the Château of Cuirieu During the Great Fear of July–August 1789

On Monday, July 27, 1789, about four in the afternoon, the tocsin in the market town of La Tour-du-Pin was heard to ring; a little later it was heard ringing in all the neighboring parishes.

On every side were heard only laments and cries of alarm, repeated on everyone's lips, that ten to twenty thousand men . . . were coming from the direction of Savoy[27] who were indiscriminately burning and killing. No sooner had they been said to have entered Dauphiné than it was said that they had entered La Tour-du-Pin. . . .

Upon hearing this alarm, a peasant host from different places, armed with guns, pitchforks, scythes, etc. came to La Tour-du-Pin, claiming to bring it assistance.

Couriers were dispatched in the direction that it was said the brigands were coming from . . . and they brought word that everything was calm and that this false alarm was caused by merchants hoarding food who were [seeking to profit from the false emergency by] offering wheat at 10 *sous* per measure above the current price in the Pont-de-Beauvoisin market; others subsequently arrived who gave other causes for this alarm. Thus one cannot rely on any version.

The next day, Tuesday, a band of about 150 persons, armed as above and claiming to be from Biol, Torchefelon, Châteauvilain Saint-Victor, and neighboring places, arrived at four in the morning at the Château of Cuirieu. They presented themselves at the gate . . . demanding entry for shelter from the rain, and, without waiting for the estate agent to return with the key to open the door for them . . . , they pushed on the door so hard that they forced it open. . . . They renewed an earlier assurance to the agent that they would not

27. **Savoy:** in the eighteenth century, Savoy was part of the territory of the Kingdom of Piedmont-Sardinia in northern Italy. Thus, what the peasants feared was probably a foreign attack.

[29]

Chapter 1

Peasant Violence:

Rebellion and

Riot in Early

Modern Europe,

1525–1789

harm him and said that they only wanted to warm themselves and drink a draught since they all were soaked. They also said that they had come from the Château du Pin where they had smashed in the doors of the wine cellar; several of them had bottles full of wine and appeared drunk. . . .

The next day, Wednesday, they learned at the Château of Cuirieu that a second band was at Vallin and that it was coming from there to Cuirieu. At five in the evening this crowd arrived with the objective of burning the *terriers*.[28] . . . The agent recognized a young man armed with a drawn sword at the head of a crowd of about one-hundred and fifty persons armed with guns, scythes, and other weapons; they were led by a drummer and marched in two columns. A few steps in front of them was the unarmed Sieur Domenjon, and the agent approached him. Upon entering the poultry yard at Cuirieu, the band shouted: "Long live the King!" and "Long live the Third Estate!" Sieur Domenjon said to the agent: "These people want your *terriers*; they have come from Vallin where they burned all the papers; if you have any old scrap paper, give it to them to satisfy them. . . ."

As soon as the band entered, it demanded to drink and eat; at the same time it began to make a racket. Sieur Domenjon reprimanded them and said to them: "No more noise. You know that you forced me to come and that you promised me that you would only do what I told you; thus, if you make a din, I will go no further with you." With the whole band shouting "We want papers!", Sieur Domenjon, assisted by four others drawn from the crowd, went up to the archives. The agent asked the priest of Saint-Blondine to please go up with him as he sought to satisfy the crowd. When he got there he turned over several bundles of papers and one or two very old manuscript books. On the books were maps upon which was written: "Inspected on such and such a year, month and day; useless or reported useless. . . ." These were thrown from the window to the band awaiting them in the courtyard. The band seized them, heaped them up, and set fire to them, saying that these were not the best records but that they would return.

Thursday, July 30, about five in the morning, a third band of about thirty men arrived led by a notary who they called "the Commandant." The notary told the estate agent that these men wanted all the *terriers* of Cessieu to make a fire of joy with them. . . .

A fourth band arrived on August 7 at six in the morning composed at first of thirty to forty persons but which grew all the time. . . . In the space of three hours, the château was laid waste and pillaged, all the furniture smashed or stolen, the linens stolen, the doors of the apartments pulverized so to speak, all the locks carried off, and the windows and stained glass windows

28. **terriers:** surveys that showed the ownership of land and, thereby, indicated to whom seigniorial dues were owed. By the eighteenth century, specialists in seigniorial rights drafted these documents to achieve maximum profits for the lord. Almost every château library had its collections of local *terriers*.

smashed. In the end, only that which the people of the château and the domestic servant aided by farmers and neighbors were able to secure was saved.

It was rumored that there was a man armed with a double-barreled gun, in a gray suit with a stylish waistcoat, who walked in the courtyard during the disaster without eating or drinking anything but who had the air of laughing at what was going on. He shortly left.

Source 8 from Bavarian State Archives, Munich, K1 641 ad 18, fol. 418–420 (first petition) and fol. 425–426 (second petition). Transcripts courtesy of Renate Blickle. Translated by Merry E. Wiesner.

8. The Petitions of Christina Vend to Duke Maximilian I, Elector of Bavaria, in February and March 1629

First Petition, February 1629

Most illustrious Elector[29] and gracious Lord:

I, a poor afflicted woman, in need so pressing that I would not otherwise bother your Electoral Grace with this insignificant letter, through the will of God, his beloved Virgin Mary, the Mother of God, and the Last Judgment, do call upon the mercy of your Electoral Grace to graciously listen to and look at my misery and pain.

On our manor and in our law court there has been a long dispute between the authorities of the abbey Rottenbuch and all of its subjects, but now—God be praised—it has come to a peaceful resolution. My husband has been treated in these events as if he were one of the instigators or leaders, but events show that even though I was forbidden from going home, [we] must conclude, he could not have been one of the instigators.

Gracious Prince and Lord, he was imprisoned not only in Munich and also in Landsberg, but no grounds for suspicion were discovered or accusations made, nor could they ever be made. Despite this he was banished from the

---

29. **elector:** one of the seven German rulers who, under the decree known as the Golden Bull of 1356, voted to select Germany's monarch, the Holy Roman Emperor of the German Nation. These rulers were the archbishops of Mainz, Trier, and Cologne; the king of Bohemia; the duke of Saxony; the margrave of Brandenburg; and the count palatine of the Rhine. In 1623, Emperor Ferdinand II deprived the count palatine of the electoral dignity because of his defiance of imperial authority in leading a revolt in Bohemia that began the Thirty Years' War, awarding it to the duke of Bavaria. In 1648, the Treaty of Westphalia created an eighth elector by restoring the vote of the count palatine. A ninth elector was added in 1692 when the rulers of Hanover received the electoral dignity.

Chapter 1

Peasant Violence:

Rebellion and

Riot in Early

Modern Europe,

1525–1789

country [Bavaria], his ear was cut off, and he was driven out with sticks. All this he bore patiently.

What is even more, the judge in Rottenbuch not only banished me and my poor innocent children from the manor, but on the Sunday just past he announced in front of the church, and forbade the whole community, that whoever helped or housed me or my children or let us stay overnight would be punished with a 10 Thaler fine for the first instance and 20 Thaler for the second. This must be lamented to God the Almighty in Heaven, that we come into this situation and into poverty innocently, and my husband bore everything that happened to him obediently and with patience.

So, gracious Elector and Lord, if it is necessary, I will get a letter and petition from the whole community and manor of Rottenbuch, that he was not an instigator or agitator, no matter what else is said. . . . If he had been an instigator or agitator, he said himself that he would not only have withstood his punishment obediently, but would have even given his life. . . . So [he] and I as his afflicted wife and his innocent children do not have to suffer and be driven from our homeland, [we] shall not leave off calling to Your Electoral Illustriousness in our deepest need in God's name . . . to let us maintain our property and to open the country again to my husband and let him come home. . . .

Your Electoral Illustriousness's poor distressed abandoned wife with two innocent children, Your obedient,

Christina Vend, the wife of George Vend, who has been exiled from the country.

Second Petition, March 1629

Illustrious Duke, Gracious Elector and Lord. I have had read to me the answer of my Lord Prior of Rottenbuch to my humble supplication, about whether I must continue to stay away from my piece of property at Rottenbuch. With the most sorrowful heart I understood that my request was heard, but that the situation was still to remain the same. Through this I gathered and understood that I and my two young orphans,[30] because of our husband's and father's insubordination, must unfortunately leave and go to him in bitter misery, and must be dispossessed.

Now I must certainly acknowledge, that my aforementioned husband definitely did wrong and earned his punishment, because he so strongly resisted the many warnings given him in a fatherly way. However, I have learned, that

---

30. **orphans:** in law, the banishment of George Vend represented "civil death," that is, the termination of his civil and property rights. Thus, his children were legally fatherless in Bavaria, even if Vend lived on in banishment elsewhere. Children without a living father were considered orphans, even if their mother survived.

others who were just as active as my husband or even more so in stirring up the Rottenbuchers to rebellion have, by calling on the grace of the Lord Prior or on that of Your Electoral Illustriousness, been allowed to return to their lands. Therefore I ask Your Electoral Illustriousness most humbly, and make the same request of the graciousness of the Lord Prior in Rottenbuch, that you don't let it continue that my young innocent orphans have to stay in misery, paying and making good on the debt that their father created through his insubordination. I ask this even more as my aforementioned husband, accepting your electoral penance, says that if he were allowed back in the country and again in your good graces, he would swear, that just as previously he was a bad example to his neighbors through his obstinacy, he would become from then on an example of the most indebted obedience. The Lord Prior will not be sorry that he let me and my young children back into his grace, and in return for the purchase of a privilege, and the payment of all other changes, tolerated us again on the property. I beg for Your Electoral grace, and together with my small children beg Your Electoral Illustriousness daily for your intercession, for which I will serve you every day and night of my life in the lowliest obedience.

Your Electoral Illustriousness's most humble Christina Vend

Source 9 from Jean Nicolas, La Savoie au 18e siècle: Noblesse et bourgeoisie, *Tome I:* Situations au temps de Victor-Amédée II *(Paris: Maloine s.a., Editeur, 1978), p. 528. Translated by Julius R. Ruff.*

9. Riot in Savoy: Le Sieur[31]
Vuy at Gets, March 14, 1717

All the people, from the first to the last, threw themselves furiously onto me, except for five or six who sympathized with me without daring to assist me out of fear of being beaten to death by those who assaulted me. The crowd set upon me with calumnies, pushed and struck me with punch blows to the chin and blows of arms and legs from the rear, threatened me, and spat on me, shouting loudly that they must slaughter the Barnabites and all those acting on their behalf.

---

31. **le sieur:** a French legal term meaning, literally, "Mister."

Chapter 1

Peasant Violence:

Rebellion and

Riot in Early

Modern Europe,

1525–1789

Source 10 from Vladimir S. Ljublinski, La Guerre des farines: Contribution à l'histoire de la lutte des classes en France à la veille de la Révolution, *translated into French by Françoise Adiba and Jacques Radiguet (Grenoble: Presses universitaires de Grenoble, 1979), pp. 367–369. Translated into English by Julius R. Ruff.*

10. Interrogation of Louis Marais, May 6, 1775

Extract from the minutes of the scribe of the Generality of Paris[32] Maréchaussée quartered at Senlis drafted on May 6, 1775 in the Criminal Court of Senlis. Presiding were we, Charles Gabriel de la Balme, gentleman captain of cavalry and lieutenant of the Generality of Paris Maréchaussée quartered at Senlis, assisted by Jacques-Augustin De Bray, assistant Maréchaussée judge, and by our customary scribe.

We had an individual brought from his prison cell who had been arrested by the Louvres brigade on the third of the present month on charges of having led a riot. He had been transferred to the prisons of this town on the fourth, and was confined under the name Louis Marais. He is 5 *pieds* 3 *pouces*[33] tall, black haired and balding, with a high forehead, dark eyes, a big nose, and dressed in a short blue jacket, a blue and red printed cotton waistcoat, common pants, and black stockings. We made known to him our rank and that we would hear his case prevotally[34] and without appeal and then, having had him swear to tell the truth, we interrogated him as follows.

Interrogated about his name, surname, age, status, residence, and place of birth he said that his name was Louis de Marais, aged 42 years, a quarryman, living at Luzarches, native of Luzarches.

Interrogated if on the third of the present month he had not been at the head of a crowd of peasants and had not traveled to different farms in the village of Louvres for the purpose of forcing the farmers to sell wheat at 12 *livres* per *setier*[35] to this rabble, most notably at the farms of Brandin of the above-named place and Regnard. He answered that it is true that he went from Luzarches to Louvres that day with a number of peasants, without being at their head, for the purpose of getting wheat. It was said that wheat costing only 12 *livres* was available there. He went with a crowd first to the farm of

32. **Generality of Paris:** prior to the Revolution of 1789, France was divided into administrative units known as generalities, administered by officials called intendants.

33. **5 *pieds* 3 *pouces*:** measures of length used in eighteenth-century France. There were 12 *pouces* to a *pied,* and a *pied* was about 13 inches. Thus, the prisoner was about 5 feet 9 inches tall.

34. **prevotally:** the Maréchaussée Courts were called *prévôts.* Thus, the prisoner was to be judged by a police court that dealt out summary justice to criminals who threatened the public order. These courts judged without appeal and had a very high conviction rate.

35. ***setier:*** a measure used for grains and other goods in eighteenth-century France. There were four *minots* in a *setier,* and the *setier* of the Paris region equaled 4.43 bushels.

Brandin where, for his part, he took 3 *minots* of wheat for which he paid 3 *livres*, that is to say at a price of 12 *livres* per *setier*. Next he was at the farm of Renard in the hope of getting another 3 *minots* there. Seeing the majority of the women coming out carrying wheat for which they had not paid, he stationed himself at the door with Renard's sister to make the departing peasants pay 12 *livres* per *setier.*

Interrogated if he had not claimed to bear an order requiring the sale of wheat at 12 *livres* per *setier,* he replied that he had never said that he was carrying any order. But when the peasants demanded to know under what order he distributed wheat at a price of 12 *livres,* he replied that he had no more need of an order than those who had pillaged the lands of My Lord the Prince of Conti[36] and that, in addition, necessity dictates many things.

Interrogated about whether he had ever been a prisoner or whether he was a repeat offender, he replied no, and we found nothing to prove it [past offense].[37]

After the present interrogation was read, he replied that his statements contained the truth, and he repeated this and declared that he did not know how to sign this interrogation. . . .

Signed: De la Balme

De Bray

---

36. **Prince of Conti:** the head of a branch of the French royal family; the prince was a major landowner.

37. The judges apparently examined the defendant for the mark of the branding iron that was normally applied to the shoulders of those convicted of many crimes in eighteenth-century France to serve as a record of conviction.

QUESTIONS TO CONSIDER

The sources that you read allow you to examine closely six peasant rebellions and three examples of rioting drawn from the histories of six countries (England, France, Germany, the Habsburg monarchy, Piedmont-Sardinia, and Russia) over a period of three centuries. Your task in analyzing these events is to draw together their common features and thereby evolve explanations for and descriptions of rural collective violence. Use the chapter's central questions to guide you in this endeavor.

First, what were the causes of these acts of collective violence by European peasants? Remember that we have already noted that peasants rebelled against either the demands of their seigniors or the taxes imposed by their monarchs. To assess adequately the roots of rebellions, analyze the societies that produced them and how these basic issues prompted people to take up arms. Consider each society's landholding system and the condition of its peasantry.

Chapter 1

Peasant Violence:
Rebellion and
Riot in Early
Modern Europe,
1525–1789

Were peasants facing new exactions from their seigniors? Was the fiscal or governmental authority of the state encroaching on the lives of peasants in new ways? In the case of riots, what material ills affected peasants? What sort of rumors may have triggered their actions?

Second, were the collective actions of peasants revolutionary in that they sought a new social, political, or economic order? In each case, ask yourself what the goals of the peasant rebels or rioters were. How do you find many of them searching for the restoration of an earlier social, economic, or political order? How do peasants justify their revolts? Do they use modern revolutionary terms, or do they refer to traditions and scripture in their justifications? Even in riots by mobs, what sort of traditional moral justification for violence do you find?

Third, what do these events tell you about traditional rural society in Europe? Consider this question on several levels. First, what are the basic features of traditional peasant existence? How do peasant rebellions and riots illustrate the society and world-view of these peasants, people whose failure to produce many written records led historians, until recently, largely to ignore them? How

might peasant demands for release from seigniorial restrictions and dues perhaps unintentionally have paved the way for a very different society? Why might you conclude that during the three centuries looked at in this chapter, society was in transition? Next, consider the role of the state in the unrest you have examined. Why might you again conclude that, governmentally, Europe was in a period of transition? What aspects of the modern state can you discern in the issues raised by peasants?

Finally, who participated in such violence, and who led it? Why might you conclude that peasant rebellions had the support of a broad segment of rural society, not just of its poorest elements? To whom did peasants turn for leadership in addition to local community leaders? What evidence do you find of clerical, noble, or artisan leadership?

Your consideration of all these issues should permit you to answer this chapter's central questions. What were the causes of these acts of collective violence? Were these actions revolutionary in that they sought a new social, political, or economic order? What do these events tell you about traditional, rural society in Europe? Who participated in such violence, and who led it?

EPILOGUE

By the late eighteenth century, the conditions that had produced the rebellions and riots that we have examined began to disappear.

An agricultural revolution, gathering force in the eighteenth century, created a much more productive agriculture that freed western Europe from most of the material problems that had produced violence in an earlier age. Those riots and rebellions had been made possible, in part, by the military weakness of early modern monarchs. Beginning in the second half of the seventeenth century, however, the dramatic expansion of state military resources made localized, collective violence much less possible. In this, France led the way. Under Louis XIV (r. 1643–1715), the royal army mustered some 500,000 men, and the number of rebellions dropped dramatically. Indeed, from 1675 to 1789, the only widespread French peasant violence was the millenarian revolt of the Protestant Camisards of the south in the first decade of the eighteenth century and the riots we have seen in the Flour War and the Great Fear. Since other monarchs aspired to the military might of the French king, rebellions disappeared elsewhere, too, as armies grew.

Seigniorial dominance of the peasantry also collapsed in the course of the eighteenth century. In France, the Great Fear prompted the revolutionary government after 1789 to legislatively end the rural old order. Elsewhere, the growing power of kings worked against the seigniorial powers that had earlier generated so much peasant unrest. Eighteenth-century monarchs needed taxpayers who were free of competing demands on their resources in order to meet the growing revenue needs of the state. Thus, monarchs took the lead in emancipating peasants from their obligations to seigniors; between 1771 and 1864, state action in thirty-eight European countries freed peasants of obligations to their lords.

These developments made rural nineteenth- to twenty-first-century Europe, on the whole, a much more secure place than it had been a few centuries earlier.

CHAPTER TWO

STAGING ABSOLUTISM

The "Age of Absolutism" is the label historians often apply to the history of Europe in the seventeenth and eighteenth centuries. In many ways it is an appropriate description because, with the exception of England, where the Civil War (1642–1648) and the Glorious Revolution (1688) severely limited royal power and created parliamentary government, most European states in this era had monarchs who aspired to absolute authority in their realms.

The royal absolutism that evolved in seventeenth-century Europe represents an important step in governmental development. In constructing absolutist states, monarchs and their ministers both created new organs of administration and built on existing institutions of government to supplant the regional authorities of the medieval state with more centralized state power. In principle, this centralized authority was subject to the absolute authority of the monarch; in practice, royal authority was nowhere as encompassing as that of a modern dictator. Poor communication systems, the persistence of traditional privileges that exempted whole regions or social groups from full royal authority, and other factors all set limits on royal power. Nevertheless, monarchs of the era strove for the ideal of absolute royal power, and France was the model in their work of state building.

French monarchs of the seventeenth and early eighteenth centuries more fully developed the system of absolute monarchy. In these rulers' efforts to overcome impediments to royal authority, we can learn much about the creation of absolutism in Europe. Rulers in Prussia, Austria, Russia, and many smaller states sought not only the real power of the French kings, but also the elaborate court ceremony and dazzling palaces that symbolized that power.

Absolutism in France was the work of Henry IV (r. 1589–1610), Louis XIII (r. 1610–1643) and his minister Cardinal Richelieu, and Louis XIV (r. 1643–1715). These rulers established a system of centralized royal political authority that destroyed many remnants of the feudal monarchy. The reward for their endeavors was great: With Europe's largest population and immense wealth, France was potentially the mightiest country on the continent in 1600 and its natural leader, if only these national strengths could be unified and directed by a strong government. Creation of such a government around an absolute monarch was the aim of French rulers, but they confronted formidable problems, common to many early modern states in achieving their goal. Nobles everywhere still held considerable power, in part a legacy of the system of feudal monarchy. In France they possessed military power, which they used in the religious civil wars of the sixteenth century and in their Fronde revolt against growing royal power in the mid-seventeenth century. Nobles also exercised considerable political power through such representative bodies as the Estates General and provincial assemblies, which gave form to their claims for a voice in government. Moreover, nobles served as the judges of the great law courts, the *parlements*, which had to register all royal edicts before they could take effect.

A second obstacle to national unity and royal authority in many states, in an age that equated national unity with religious uniformity, was the presence of a large and influential religious minority. In France the Protestant minority was known as the Huguenots. Not only did they forswear the Catholic religion of the king and the majority of his subjects, but they possessed military power through their rights, under the Edict of Nantes,[1] to fortify their cities.

A third and major impediment to unifying a country under absolute royal authority was regional differences. The medieval monarchy of France had been built province by province over several centuries, and the kingdom was not well integrated. Some provinces, like Brittany in the north, retained local estates or assemblies with which the monarch actually had to bargain for taxes. Many provinces had their own cultural heritage that separated them from the king's government centered in Paris. These differences might be as simple as matters of local custom, but they might also be as complex as unique systems of civil law. A particular problem was the persistence of local dialects, which made the French of royal officials a foreign and incomprehensible tongue in large portions of the kingdom.

The only unifying principle that could overcome all these centrifugal forces was royal authority. The task in the seventeenth century was to build a theoretical basis for a truly powerful monarch, to endow the king with tangible power that gave substance to theory, and to place the sovereign in a setting that would never permit the country to forget his new power.

To establish an abstract basis for absolutism, royal authority had to be strengthened and reinforced by a veritable cult of kingship. Seventeenth-

1. **Edict of Nantes:** In this 1598 decree, King Henry IV sought to end the civil warfare between French Catholics and Huguenots. He granted the Protestants basic protection, in the event of renewed fighting, by allowing them to fortify some 200 of their cities. The edict also accorded the Protestants freedom of belief with some restrictions, and civil rights equal to those of Catholic Frenchmen.

century French statesmen built on medieval foundations in this task. Medieval kings had possessed limited tangible authority but substantial religious prestige; their vassals had rendered them religious oaths of loyalty. French monarchs since Pepin the Short had been anointed in a biblically inspired coronation ceremony in which they received not only the communion bread that the Catholic church administered to all believers, but also the wine, which was normally reserved for clerics; once crowned, they claimed to possess mystical religious powers to heal with the royal touch. All these trappings served to endow the monarch with almost divine powers, separating him from and raising him above his subjects. Many seventeenth-century thinkers emphasized this traditional divine dimension of royal power. Others, as you will see, found more practical grounds for great royal power.

To achieve greater royal power, Henry IV reestablished peace after the religious civil warfare of the late sixteenth century, and Cardinal Richelieu curbed the military power of the nobility. With the creation of loyal provincial administrators, the *intendants,* and a system of political patronage that he directed, the cardinal also established firmer central control in the name of Louis XIII. Richelieu, moreover, ended Huguenot political power by crushing their revolt in 1628, and he intervened in the Thirty Years' War to establish France as a chief European power.

The reign of Louis XIV completed the process of consolidating royal authority in France. Louis XIV created much of the administrative appara-

tus necessary to centralize the state. The king brought the nobility under even greater control, building in Europe's largest army a force that could defeat any aristocratic revolt and creating in Versailles a court life that drew nobles away from provincial plotting and near to the king, where their actions could be observed. The king also sought to extend royal authority by expanding France's borders through a series of wars and to eliminate the Huguenot minority completely by revoking the religious freedoms embodied in the Edict of Nantes.

The king supplemented his military and political work of state building with other projects to integrate France more completely as one nation. With royal patronage, authors and scholars flourished and, by the example of their often excellent works, extended the French dialect in the country at the expense of provincial tongues. In the king's name, his finance minister, Jean-Baptiste Colbert (1619–1683), sought to realize a vision of a unified French economy. He designed mercantilist policies to favor French trade and build French industry, and he improved transportation to bind the country together as one unit. The result of Louis's policies, therefore, was not only a stronger king and a more powerful France but a more unified country as well.

Far more than previous French monarchs, Louis XIV addressed the third task in establishing absolutism. In modern terms, it consisted of effective public relations, which required visible evidence of the new royal authority. The stage setting for the royal display of the symbols of absolute authority was Versailles, the site of a new royal palace. Built between 1661 and 1682, the palace itself was massive, with a façade one-quarter mile long pierced by 2,143 windows. It was set in a park of 37,000 acres, of which 6,000 acres were embellished with formal gardens. These gardens contained 1,400 fountains that required massive hydraulic works to supply them with water, an artificial lake one mile long for royal boating parties, and 200 statues. The palace grounds contained various smaller palaces as well, including Marly, where the king could entertain small, select groups away from the main palace, which was the center of a court life embracing almost 20,000 persons (9,000 soldiers billeted in the town; and 5,000 royal servants, 1,000 nobles and their 4,000 servants, plus the royal family, all housed in the main palace). Because the royal ministers and their secretaries also were in residence, Versailles was much more than a palace: It was the capital of France.

Royal architects deliberately designed the palace to impart a message to all who entered. As a guidebook of 1681 by Laurent Morellet noted regarding the palace's art:

The subjects of painting which complete the decorations of the ceilings are of heroes and illustrious men, taken from history and fable, who have deserved the titles of Magnanimous, of Great, of Fathers of the People, of Liberal, of Just, of August and Victorious, and who have possessed all the Virtues which we have seen appear in the Person of our Great Monarch during the fortunate course of his reign; so that everything remarkable which one sees in the Château and in the garden always has some relationship with the great actions of His Majesty.[2]

The court ritual and etiquette enacted in this setting departed markedly from the simpler court life of Louis XIII and were designed to complement the physical presence of the palace itself in teaching the lesson of a new royal power.

In this chapter we will analyze royal absolutism in France. What was the theoretical basis for absolute royal authority? What was traditional and what was new in the justification of royal power as expressed in late sixteenth- and seventeenth-century France? How did such early modern kings as Louis XIV communicate their absolute power in the various ceremonies and symbols of royal authority presented in the evidence that follows?

2. Laurent Morellet, *Explication historique de ce qu'il y a de plus remarquable dans la maison royale de Versailles et en celle de Monsieur à Saint-Cloud* (Paris, 1681), quoted in Robert W. Hartle, "Louis XIV and the Mirror of Antiquity" in Steven G. Reinhardt and Vaughn L. Glasgow, eds., *The Sun King: Louis XIV and the New World* (New Orleans: Louisiana State Museum Foundation, 1984), p. 111.

SOURCES AND METHOD

This chapter assembles several kinds of sources, each demanding a different kind of historical analysis. Two works of political theory that were influential in the formation of absolutism open the evidence. To analyze these works effectively, you will need some brief background information on their authors and on the problems these thinkers discussed.

Jean Bodin (1530–1596) was a law professor, an attorney, and a legal official. His interests transcended his legal education, however. He brought a wide reading in Hebrew, Greek, Italian, and German to the central problem addressed in his major work, *The Six Books of the Republic* (1576), that of establishing the well-ordered state. Writing during the religious wars of the sixteenth century, when government in France all but broke down, Bodin offered answers to this crisis. Especially novel for the sixteenth century was his call for religious toleration. Although he was at least formally a Catholic[3] and recognized unity in religion as a strong unifying factor for a country, Bodin was unwilling to advocate the use of force in eliminating Protestantism from France. He believed that acceptance was by far the better policy.

Bodin's political thought was also significant, and his *Republic* immediately was recognized as an important work. Published in several editions and translated into Latin, Italian, Spanish, and German, the *Republic* influenced a circle of men, the *Politiques*, who advised Henry IV. Through the process of seeking to explain how to establish the well-ordered state, Bodin contributed much to Western political theory. Perhaps his most important idea was that there was nothing divine about governing power. Men created governments solely to ensure their physical and material security; to meet those needs, the ruling power had to exercise a sovereignty on which Bodin placed few limits.[4] Indeed, Bodin's concept of the ruler's power is his most important contribution to political thought. In the brief selection from Jean Bodin's complex work, examine his conception of the sovereign power required to establish a well-ordered state in France, and contrast this conception with the feudal state that still partially existed in his time.

The second work of political theory was written by Jacques Bénigne Bossuet (1627–1704), Bishop of Meaux. A great orator who preached at the court of Louis XIV, Bossuet was entrusted with the education of the king's son and heir, the Dauphin. He wrote three works for that prince's instruction, including the one excerpted in this chapter, *Politics Drawn from the Very Words of the Holy Scriptures* (1678).

As tutor to the Dauphin and royal preacher, Bossuet expressed what has been called the *divine right* theory of kingship: that is, the king was God's deputy on earth, and to oppose him was to oppose divine law. Here, of course, the bishop was drawing on those medieval beliefs and practices

3. Bodin's religious thought evolved in the course of his life. Although he was brought up a Catholic and was briefly a Carmelite friar, his knowledge of Hebrew and early regard for the Old Testament led some to suspect that he was a Jew. The writings of his middle years indicate some Calvinist leanings. Later in life, his thought seems to have moved beyond traditional Catholic and Protestant Christianity. He was nevertheless deeply religious.

4. Bodin saw the sovereign power as limited by natural law and the need to respect property (which meant that the ruler could not tax without his subjects' consent) and the family.

imputing certain divine powers to the king. Because Bossuet was an influential member of the court of Louis XIV, his ideas on royal authority carried considerable weight. Trained as a theologian, he buttressed his political theories with scriptural authority. In this selection, determine the extent of the royal link to God. Why might such a theory be particularly useful to Louis XIV?

Source 3 is a selection from the *Memoirs* of Louis de Rouvroy, Duke of Saint-Simon (1675–1755). Saint-Simon's memoirs of court life are extensive, comprising forty-one volumes in the main French edition. They constitute both a remarkable record of life at Versailles and, because of their style, an important example of French literature. As useful and important as the *Memoirs* are, however, they must be read with care. All of us, consciously or unconsciously, have biases and opinions, and memoirists are no exception. In fact, memoir literature illustrates problems of which students of history should be aware in everything they read. The way in which authors present events, even what they choose to include or omit from their accounts, reflects their opinions. Because memoir writers often recount events in which they participated, they may have especially strong views about what they relate. Thus, to use Saint-Simon's work profitably, it is essential to understand his point of view. We must also ask if the memoir writer was in a position to know firsthand what he or she was relating or was simply recounting less reliable rumors.

Saint-Simon came from an old noble family that had recently risen to prominence when his father became a royal favorite. Ironically, no one was more deeply opposed to the policies of Louis XIV, which aimed to destroy the traditional feudal power of the nobility in the name of royal authority, than this man whose position rested on that very authority. Saint-Simon was, quite simply, a defender of the older style of kingship, in which sovereignty was limited by the monarch's need to consult with his vassals. His memoirs reflect this view and are often critical of the king. But even with his critical view of the king and his court, Saint-Simon was an important figure there, an individual privy to state business and court gossip, who gives us a remarkable picture of life at Versailles. Analyze the court etiquette and ritual that Saint-Simon describes as a nonverbal message from the king to his most powerful subjects. For example, what message did the royal waking and dressing ceremony convey to the most powerful and privileged persons in France, who crowded the royal bedroom and vied for the privilege of helping the king dress? What message did their very presence convey in turn to Louis XIV? Recall Bossuet's ideas of kingship. Why might public religious ritual such as that attending the royal rising be part of the agenda of a king who was not particularly noted for his piety during the first half of his life?

Studied closely, the three different kinds of written evidence presented—the work of a sixteenth-century political theorist, the writings of a contemporary supporter, and the memoirs of one of the king's opponents—reveal much about the growing power of the French monarchy. What common

[43]

themes do you find in these works? What were the sources of the king's political authority?

From these written sources, we move on to pictorial evidence of the symbols of royal authority. Symbols are concrete objects possessing a meaning beyond what is immediately apparent. We are all aware of the power of symbols, particularly in our age of electronic media, and we all, perhaps unconsciously, analyze them to some extent. Take a simple example drawn from modern advertising: The lion appears frequently as an image in advertisements for banks and other financial institutions. The lion's presence is intended to convey to us the strength of the financial institution, to inspire our faith in the latter's ability to protect our funds. Using this kind of analysis, you can determine the total meaning of the symbols associated with Louis XIV.

Consider the painting presented as the fourth piece of evidence, *Louis XIV Taking Up Personal Government* in 1661. Louis XIV had been king in name since the age of five after his father's death in 1643, but only in 1661, as an adult, did he assume full power. Remember that such art was generally commissioned by the king and often had an instructional purpose. What do the following elements symbolize: the portrayal of Louis XIV as a Roman emperor; the positioning of a figure representing France on his right; the crowning of the king with a wreath of flowers; the figure of Time (note the hourglass and scythe) holding a tapestry over the royal head; and the presence of herald angels hovering above?

Now go on to the other pictures and perform the same kind of analysis, always trying to identify the symbolic message that the painter or architect wished to convey. For Source 5, study the royal pose and such seemingly superficial elements in the picture as the king's dress and the background details. Ask yourself what ideas these were intended to convey. Source 6 presents the insignia Louis XIV chose as his personal symbol, which decorated much of Versailles. Reflect on Louis's reasons for this choice in reading his explanation:

The symbol that I have adopted and that you see all around you represents the duties of a Prince and inspires me always to fulfill them. I chose for an emblem the Sun which, according to the rules of this art [heraldry], is the noblest of all, and which, by the brightness that surrounds it, by the light it lends to the other stars that constitute, after a fashion, its court, by the universal good it does, endlessly promoting life, joy, and growth, by its perpetual and regular movement, by its constant and invariable course, is assuredly the most dazzling and most beautiful image of the monarch.[5]

Finally, Source 7 portrays Louis XIV costumed for one of the many pageants enjoyed by the king in his younger years. He wears the garb of a Roman emperor, an official who ruled much of the ancient world. What does the king's choice of costume suggest about his vision of his own role in the world?

5. Quoted in Reinhardt and Glasgow, *The Sun King*, p. 181.

With Sources 8 through 13, we turn to analysis of architecture, which of course also served to symbolize royal power. You must ask yourself how great that concept of royal power was as you look at the pictures of Versailles. The palace, after all, was not only the royal residence but also the setting for the conduct of government, including the king's reception of foreign ambassadors. At the most basic level, notice the scale of the palace. What impression might its size have been intended to convey? At a second level, examine decorative details of the palace. Why might the balustrade at the palace entry have been decorated with statuary symbolizing Magnificence, Justice, Wisdom, Prudence, Diligence, Peace, Europe, Asia, Renown, Abundance, Force, Generosity, Wealth, Authority, Fame, America, Africa, and Victory?

Observe the views of the palace's interior, considering the functions of the rooms and their details. Source 10 offers a view of the royal chapel at Versailles. Richly decorated in marble and complemented with ceiling paintings such as that depicting the Trinity, the chapel was the site of daily masses as well as of royal marriages and celebrations of victories. Note that the king attended mass in the royal gallery, joining the rest of the court on the main floor only when the mass celebrant was a bishop. Why might such a magnificent setting be part of the palace? More important, what significance do you place on the position the king chose for himself in this grand setting?

Sources 11 and 12 present the sites of the royal rising ceremony described by Saint-Simon. The royal bedroom, Source 11, was richly decorated in gilt, red, and white, and was complemented by paintings of biblical scenes. Notice the rich decoration of the Bull's Eye Window Antechamber (Source 12), just outside the bedroom, where the courtiers daily awaited the king's arising. Why were the rooms decorated in such a fashion?

Source 13 offers an artist's view of Marly. Again, notice the scale of this palace, reflecting that it was, according to Saint-Simon, a weekend getaway spot for Louis XIV and selected favorites. How might the king have used invitations to this château, with the closeness to the royal person they entailed? Examine details of the palace. The central château had twelve apartments, four of which were reserved for the royal family, the others for its guests. The twelve pavilions around the lake in the center of the château's grounds each housed two guest apartments and represented the twelve signs of the zodiac. What symbolic importance might you attach to this?

Finally, return to Source 7, which recreates the pageant known as the Carousel of 1662, one of many such entertainments at court. The scale of such festivals could be huge. In 1662, 12,197 costumed people took part in a celebration that included a parade through the streets of Paris and games. Costumed as ancient Romans, Persians, and others, the participants must have made quite an impression on their audience. What kind of impression do you think it was?

What common message runs through the art and architecture you have analyzed? As you unravel the message woven into this visual evidence, combine it with the evidence you derived from Saint-Simon's portrayal of court life and the political theory of absolutism. Remember, too, the unstated message: that the monarchy of Louis XIV possessed in Europe's largest army the ultimate means for persuading its subjects to accept the divine powers of the king. You should be able to determine from all this material what was new in this conception of royal authority and the ways in which the new authority was expressed.

THE EVIDENCE

Source 1 from Francis William Coker, editor, Readings in Political Philosophy *(New York: Macmillan, 1926), pp. 235–236.*

1. From Jean Bodin, *The Six Books of the Republic*, Book I, 1576

The first and principal function of sovereignty is to give laws to the citizens generally and individually, and, it must be added, not necessarily with the consent of superiors, equals, or inferiors. If the consent of superiors is required, then the prince is clearly a subject; if he must have the consent of equals, then others share his authority; if the consent of inferiors—the people or the senate—is necessary, then he lacks supreme authority. . . .

It may be objected that custom does not get its power from the judgment or command of the prince, and yet has almost the force of law, so that it would seem that the prince is master of law, the people of custom. Custom, insensibly, yet with the full compliance of all, passes gradually into the character of men, and acquires force with the lapse of time. Law, on the other hand, comes forth in one moment at the order of him who has the power to command, and often in opposition to the desire and approval of those whom it governs. Wherefore, Chrysostom[6] likens law to a tyrant and custom to a king. Moreover, the power of law is far greater than that of custom, for customs may be superseded by laws, but laws are not supplanted by customs; it is within the power and function of magistrates to restore the operation of laws which by custom are obsolescent. Custom proposes neither rewards nor penalties; laws carry one or the other, unless it be a permissive law which nullifies the penalty of some other law. In short, a custom has compelling force only as long as the prince, by adding his endorsement and sanction to the custom, makes it a law.

6. **Chrysostom:** Saint John Chrysostom (ca 347–407), an early Father of the Greek church and a brilliant preacher whose religion led him to condemn the vices of the court of the Eastern Roman emperor.

It is thus clear that laws and customs depend for their force upon the will of those who hold supreme power in the state. This first and chief mark of sovereignty is, therefore, of such sort that it cannot be transferred to subjects, though the prince or people sometimes confer upon one of the citizens the power to frame laws (*legum condendarum*), which then have the same force as if they had been framed by the prince himself. The Lacedæmonians bestowed such power upon Lycurgus, the Athenians upon Solon;[7] each stood as deputy for his state, and the fulfillment of his function depended upon the pleasure not of himself but of the people; his legislation had no force save as the people confirmed it by their assent. The former composed and wrote the laws, the people enacted and commanded them.

Under this supreme power of ordaining and abrogating laws, it is clear that all other functions of sovereignty are included; that it may be truly said that supreme authority in the state is comprised in this one thing—namely, to give laws to all and each of the citizens, and to receive none from them. For to declare war or make peace, though seeming to involve what is alien to the term law, is yet accomplished by law, that is by decree of the supreme power. It is also the prerogative of sovereignty to receive appeals from the highest magistrates, to confer authority upon the greater magistrates and to withdraw it from them, to allow exemption from taxes, to bestow other immunities, to grant dispensations from the laws, to exercise power of life and death, to fix the value, name and form of money, to compel all citizens to observe their oaths: all of these attributes are derived from the supreme power of commanding and forbidding—that is, from the authority to give law to the citizens collectively and individually, and to receive law from no one save immortal God. A duke, therefore, who gives laws to all his subjects, but receives law from the emperor, Pope, or king, or has a co-partner in authority, lacks sovereignty.

Source 2 from Richard H. Powers, editor and translator, Readings in European Civilization Since 1500 *(Boston: Houghton Mifflin, 1961), pp. 129–130.*

2. From Jacques Bénigne Bossuet, *Politics Drawn from the Very Words of the Holy Scriptures,* 1678

TO MONSEIGNEUR LE DAUPHIN

God is the King of kings. It is for Him to instruct and direct kings as His ministers. Heed then, Monseigneur, the lessons which He gives them in His

---

7. **Lacedæmonians:** the Spartans of ancient Greece. **Lycurgus:** traditional author of the Spartan constitution. **Solon:** sixth-century B.C. Athenian lawgiver.

Scriptures, and learn . . . the rules and examples on which they ought to base their conduct. . . .

BOOK II: OR AUTHORITY...

CONCLUSION: Accordingly we have established by means of Scriptures that monarchical government comes from God. . . . That when government was established among men He chose hereditary monarchy as the most natural and most durable form. That excluding the sex born to obey[8] from the sovereign power was only natural. . . .

BOOK III: THE NATURE OF ROYAL AUTHORITY...

FIRST ARTICLE: Its essential characteristics. . . . First, royal authority is sacred; Second, it is paternal; Third, it is absolute; Fourth, it is subject to reason. . . .

SECOND ARTICLE: Royal authority is sacred.

FIRST PROPOSITION: God establishes kings as his ministers and reigns over people through them.—We have already seen that all power comes from God. . . .

Therefore princes act as ministers of God and as His lieutenants on earth. It is through them that he exercises His empire. . . .

Thus we have seen that the royal throne is not the throne of a man, but the throne of God himself. So in Scriptures we find "God has chosen my son Solomon to sit upon the throne of the kingdom of Jehovah over Israel." And further, "Solomon sat on the throne of Jehovah as king."

And in order that we should not think that to have kings established by God is peculiar to the Israelites, here is what Ecclesiastes says: "God gives each people its governor; and Israel is manifestly reserved to Him.". . .

SECOND PROPOSITION: The person of the king is sacred.—It follows from all the above that the person of kings is sacred. . . . God has had them anointed by His prophets with a sacred ointment, as He has had His pontiffs and His altars anointed.

But even before actually being anointed, they are sacred by virtue of their charge, as representatives of His divine majesty, delegated by His providence to execute His design. . . .

The title of *christ* is given to kings, one sees them called *christs* or the Lord's *anointed* everywhere.

Bearing this venerable name, even the prophets revered them, and looked upon them as associated with the sovereign empire of God, whose authority they exercise on earth. . . .

THIRD PROPOSITION: Religion and conscience demand that we obey the prince.—After having said that the prince is the minister of God Saint Paul concluded: "Accordingly it is necessary that you subject yourself to him out of fear of his anger, but also because of the obligation of your conscience. . . ."

8. **sex born to obey:** women. The Salic Law, mistakenly attributed to the medieval Salian Franks, precluded women from inheriting the crown of France.

And furthermore: "Servants, obey your temporal masters in all things. . . ." Saint Peter said: "Therefore submit yourselves to the order established among men for the love of God; be subjected to the king as to God . . . be subjected to those to whom He gives His authority and who are sent by Him to reward good deeds and to punish evil ones."

Even if kings fail in this duty, their charge and their ministry must be respected. For Scriptures tell us: "Obey your masters, not only those who are mild and good, but also those who are peevish and unjust."

Thus there is something religious in the respect which one renders the prince. Service to God and respect for kings are one thing. . . .

Thus it is in the spirit of Christianity for kings to be paid a kind of religious respect. . . .

BOOK IV: CONTINUATION OF THE CHARACTERISTICS OF ROYALTY

FIRST ARTICLE: Royal authority is absolute.

FIRST PROPOSITION: The prince need render account to no one for what he orders. . . .

SECOND PROPOSITION: When the prince has judged there is no other judgment. . . . Princes are gods.

Source 3 from Bayle St. John, translator, The Memoirs of the Duke of Saint-Simon on the Reign of Louis XIV and the Regency, *8th ed. (London: George Allen, 1913), vol. 2, pp. 363–365; vol. 3, pp. 221–227.*

3. The Duke of Saint-Simon on the Reign of Louis XIV

[*On the creation of Versailles and the nature of its court life*]

He [Louis XIV] early showed a disinclination for Paris. The troubles that had taken place there during the minority made him regard the place as dangerous;[9] he wished, too, to render himself venerable by hiding himself from the eyes of the multitude; all these considerations fixed him at St. Germains[10] soon after the death of the Queen, his mother. It was to that place he began to attract the world by fêtes and gallantries, and by making it felt that he wished to be often seen.

9. During the Fronde revolt of 1648–1653, the royal government lost control of Paris to the crowds and the royal family was forced to flee the city. Because Louis XIV was a minor (only ten years of age) when the revolt erupted, the government was administered by his mother, Anne of Austria, and her chief minister, Cardinal Mazarin.

10. **St. Germain-en-Laye:** site of a royal château, overlooking the Seine and dating from the twelfth century, where Louis XIV was born. The court fled there in 1649 during the Fronde.

His love for Madame de la Vallière,[11] which was at first kept secret, occasioned frequent excursions to Versailles, then a little card castle, which had been built by Louis XIII—annoyed, and his suite still more so, at being frequently obliged to sleep in a wretched inn there, after he had been out hunting in the forest of Saint Leger. That monarch rarely slept at Versailles more than one night, and then from necessity; the King, his son, slept there, so that he might be more in private with his mistress; pleasures unknown to the hero and just man, worthy son of Saint Louis, who built the little château.[12]

These excursions of Louis XIV by degrees gave birth to those immense buildings he erected at Versailles; and their convenience for a numerous court, so different from the apartments at St. Germains, led him to take up his abode there entirely shortly after the death of the Queen.[13] He built an infinite number of apartments, which were asked for by those who wished to pay their court to him; whereas at St. Germains nearly everybody was obliged to lodge in the town, and the few who found accommodation at the château were strangely inconvenienced.

The frequent fêtes, the private promenades at Versailles, the journeys, were means on which the King seized in order to distinguish or mortify the courtiers, and thus render them more assiduous in pleasing him. He felt that of real favours he had not enough to bestow; in order to keep up the spirit of devotion, he therefore unceasingly invented all sorts of ideal ones, little preferences and petty distinctions, which answered his purpose as well.

He was exceedingly jealous of the attention paid him. Not only did he notice the presence of the most distinguished courtiers, but those of inferior degree also. He looked to the right and to the left, not only upon rising but upon going to bed, at his meals, in passing through his apartments, or his gardens of Versailles, where alone the courtiers were allowed to follow him; he saw and noticed everybody; not one escaped him, not even those who hoped to remain unnoticed. He marked well all absentees from the court, found out the reason of their absence, and never lost an opportunity of acting towards them as the occasion might seem to justify. With some of the courtiers (the most distinguished), it was a demerit not to make the court their ordinary abode; with others 'twas a fault to come but rarely; for those who never or scarcely ever came it was certain disgrace. When their names were in any way mentioned, "I do not know them," the King would reply haughtily. Those who presented themselves but seldom were thus characterized: "They are people I never see;" these decrees were irrevocable. . . .

11. **Madame de la Vallière:** Louise de la Baume le Blanc, Duchesse de la Vallière (1644–1710), the king's first mistress.

12. Saint-Simon greatly admired Louis XIII, whom he had never met, and for over half a century attended annual memorial services for the king at the royal tombs in the basilica of St. Denis.

13. Anne of Austria (1601–1666), the mother of Louis XIV.

Louis XIV took great pains to be well informed of all that passed every-where; in the public places, in the private houses, in society and familiar inter-course. His spies and tell-tales were infinite. He had them of all species; many who were ignorant that their information reached him; others who knew it; others who wrote to him direct, sending their letters through channels he in-dicated; and all these letters were seen by him alone, and always before every-thing else; others who sometimes spoke to him secretly in his cabinet, enter-ing by the back stairs. These unknown means ruined an infinite number of people of all classes, who never could discover the cause; often ruined them very unjustly; for the King, once prejudiced, never altered his opinion or so rarely, that nothing was more rare.

[*On the royal day and court etiquette*]

[*The royal day begins*]

At eight o'clock the chief valet de chambre on duty, who alone had slept in the royal chamber, and who had dressed himself, awoke the King. The chief physician, the chief surgeon, and the nurse (as long as she lived), entered at the same time. The latter kissed the King; the others rubbed and often changed his shirt, because he was in the habit of sweating a great deal. At the quarter, the grand chamberlain was called (or, in his absence, the first gentle-man of the chamber), and those who had, what was called the *grandes entrées.* The chamberlain (or chief gentleman) drew back the curtains which had been closed again, and presented the holy water from the vase, at the head of the bed. These gentlemen stayed but a moment, and that was the time to speak to the King, if any one had anything to ask of him; in which case the rest stood aside. When, contrary to custom, nobody had aught to say, they were there but for a few moments. He who had opened the curtains and presented the holy water, presented also a prayer-book. Then all passed into the cabinet of the council. A very short religious service being over, the King called, they re-entered. The same officer gave him his dressing-gown; immediately after, other privileged courtiers entered, and then everybody, in time to find the King putting on his shoes and stockings, for he did almost everything himself and with address and grace. Every other day we saw him shave himself; and he had a little short wig in which he always appeared, even in bed, and on medicine days. He often spoke of the chase, and sometimes said a word to somebody. No toilette table was near him; he had simply a mirror held before him.

As soon as he was dressed, he prayed to God, at the side of his bed, where all the clergy present knelt, the cardinals without cushions, all the laity re-maining standing; and the captain of the guards came to the balustrade dur-ing the prayer, after which the King passed into his cabinet.

He found there, or was followed by all who had the entrée, a very numer-ous company, for it included everybody in any office. He gave orders to each

[51]

for the day; thus within a half a quarter of an hour it was known what he meant to do; and then all this crowd left directly. The bastards, a few favourites, and the valets alone were left. It was then a good opportunity for talking with the King; for example, about plans of gardens and buildings; and conversation lasted more or less according to the person engaged in it.

All the Court meantime waited for the King in the gallery, the captain of the guard being alone in the chamber seated at the door of the cabinet.

[*The business of government*]

On Sunday, and often on Monday, there was a council of state; on Tuesday a finance council; on Wednesday council of state; on Saturday finance council. Rarely were two held in one day or any on Thursday or Friday. Once or twice a month there was a council of despatches[14] on Monday morning; but the order that the Secretaries of State took every morning between the King's rising and his mass, much abridged this kind of business. All the ministers were seated according to rank, except at the council of despatches, where all stood except the sons of France, the Chancellor, and the Duc de Beauvilliers.[15]

[*The royal luncheon*]

The dinner was always *au petit couvert*,[16] that is, the King ate by himself in his chamber upon a square table in front of the middle window. It was more or less abundant, for he ordered in the morning whether it was to be "a little," or "very little" service. But even at this last, there were always many dishes, and three courses without counting the fruit. The dinner being ready, the principal courtiers entered; then all who were known; and the first gentlemen of the chamber on duty, informed the King.

I have seen, but very rarely, Monseigneur[17] and his sons standing at their dinners, the King not offering them a seat. I have continually seen there the Princes of the blood and the cardinals. I have often seen there also Monsieur,[18] either on arriving from St. Cloud to see the King, or arriving from the council of despatches (the only one he entered), give the King his napkin and remain

---

14. **Council of Despatches:** the royal council in which ministers discussed the letters from the provincial administrators of France, the *intendants*.

15. **Sons of France:** The royal family was distinguished from the rest of the nobility as "children of France." The "sons of France" in the last decade of the seventeenth century thus were the king's son, his grandsons, and his brother. **Duc de Beauvilliers:** Paul de Beauvilliers, Duc de St. Aignan (1648–1714), was a friend of Saint-Simon and tutor of Louis XIV's grandsons, the dukes of Burgundy, Anjou, and Berry.

16. *au petit couvert:* a simple table setting with a light meal.

17. **Monseigneur:** Louis, Dauphin de France (1661–1711), son of Louis XIV and heir to the throne.

18. **Monsieur:** Philippe, Duc d'Orléans (1640–1701), Louis XIV's only sibling. His permanent residence was at the Château of St. Cloud near Paris.

standing. A little while afterwards, the King, seeing that he did not go away, asked him if he would not sit down; he bowed, and the King ordered a seat to be brought for him. A stool was put behind him. Some moments after the King said, "Nay then, sit down, my brother." Monsieur bowed and seated himself until the end of the dinner, when he presented the napkin.

[*The day ends*]

At ten o'clock his supper was served. The captain of the guard announced this to him. A quarter of an hour after the King came to supper, and from the ante-chamber of Madame de Maintenon[19] to the table again, any one spoke to him who wished. This supper was always on a grand scale, the royal household (that is, the sons and daughters of France), at table, and a large number of courtiers and ladies present, sitting or standing, and on the evening before the journey to Marly all those ladies who wished to take part in it. That was called presenting yourself for Marly. Men asked in the morning, simply saying to the King, "Sire, Marly." In later years the King grew tired of this, and a valet wrote up in the gallery the names of those who asked. The ladies continued to present themselves.

After supper the King stood some moments, his back to the balustrade of the foot of his bed, encircled by all his Court; then, with bows to the ladies, passed into his cabinet, where on arriving, he gave his orders. He passed a little less than an hour there, seated in an arm-chair, with his legitimate children and bastards, his grandchildren, legitimate and otherwise, and their husbands or wives. Monsieur in another arm-chair; the princesses upon stools, Monseigneur and all the other princes standing.

The King, wishing to retire, went and fed his dogs; then said good night, passed into his chamber to the *ruelle*[20] of his bed, where he said his prayers, as in the morning, then undressed. He said good night with an inclination of the head, and whilst everybody was leaving the room stood at the corner of the mantelpiece, where he gave the order to the colonel of the guards alone. Then commenced what was called the *petit coucher,* at which only the specially privileged remained. That was short. They did not leave until he got into bed. It was a moment to speak to him. Then all left if they saw any one buckle to the King. For ten or twelve years before he died the *petit coucher* ceased, in consequence of a long attack of gout he had had; so that the Court was finished at the rising from supper.

---

19. **Madame de Maintenon:** Françoise d'Aubigné, Marquise de Maintenon (1635–1719), married Louis XIV after the death of his first wife, Marie Thérèse of Spain.

20. *ruelle:* the area in the bedchamber in which the bed was located and in which the king received persons of high rank.

Source 4 from Giraudon/Art Resource, NY.

4. **Charles Le Brun,** *Louis XIV Taking Up Personal Government,* **ca 1680, from the Ceiling of the Hall of Mirrors at Versailles**

Source 5 from Réunion des Musées Nationaux/Art Resource, NY.

5. Hyacinthe-François-Honoré-Pierre-André Rigaud, *Louis XIV,*
King of France and Navarre, **1701**

[55]

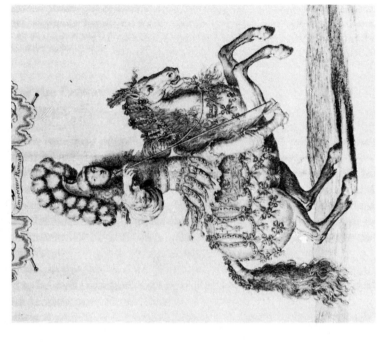

Source 7 from Charles Perrault, Festiva ad captia, 1670. British Library, London.

7. Rousselet, Louis XIV as "Roman Emperor" in an Engraving from the Carousel of 1662

Source 6 from Musée de la Marine, Photographic Service.

6. Mask of Apollo, God of Light, 17th Century

[56]

8. Garden Façade of Versailles

9. Aerial View of Versailles

Sources 10 through 12 from Réunion des Musées Nationaux/Art Resource, NY.

10. The Royal Chapel at Versailles

11. Reconstruction of the King's Chamber at Versailles, After 1701

12. Antechamber of the Bull's Eye Window at Versailles

13. Pierre Denis Martin, *Château of Marly*, 1724

QUESTIONS TO CONSIDER

Louis XIV is reputed to have said, "I am the state." Whether the king actually uttered those words is immaterial for our purpose; they neatly summarize the unifying theme in all this chapter's evidence, which demonstrates how royal power was defined as absolute and how that authority was expressed in deeds, art, and architecture.

Consider first the theories of royal authority, comparing the political ideas of Bodin and Bossuet. What are the origins of sovereignty for Bodin and Bossuet? How do they differ? Why can Bodin be said to have justified absolutism on the basis of expediency, that is, that absolute royal power was the only way to ensure order? Do the two thinkers ultimately arrive at the same conclusions? What is the difference between Bodin's conclusion that the royal power permitted the king to hand down laws to his subjects and receive them from no one and Bossuet's definition of the king as virtually a god on earth?

Royal ceremony and etiquette enforced this view of the king. Consider Saint-Simon's *Memoirs* again. The selection describes only limited aspects of court etiquette, but it conveys to us a vivid image of court life. Who was the center of this court made up of the country's most prominent nobles? Analyze individual elements of court ceremony. How does each contribute to a consistent message? Consider the royal dining ritual. To reinforce the lesson of royal power, who was kept standing during the king's luncheon? Who had the task, for most commoners performed by an ordinary waiter, of handing the king his napkin? A message of royal power is being expressed here in a way that is almost theatrical.

Indeed, the image of theater can be useful in further structuring your analysis. The stage setting for this royal display, the palace of Versailles, shows the work of a skilled director in creating a remarkably uniform message in landscape and architecture alike. Who do you suppose that director was? Examine his statement at Versailles. Look first at the exterior views of both Versailles (Sources 8 and 9) and Marly (Source 13). How do the grounds add to the expression of royal power? What view of nature might they suggest to a visitor? How did the stage set enhance the play described by Saint-Simon? How did it encourage the French to accept the authority of Louis XIV?

Look next at the interior of the palace. It was, of course, a royal residence. But do you find much evidence of its function as a place to live in? Examine the royal bedroom and its outer room (Sources 11 and 12). Modern bedrooms are generally intimate in size and decoration; how does the king's differ? Why? Notice, too, the art and use of symbols in the palace. Why might the king's artists and architects have decorated the palace so richly with biblical and classical heroes and themes (Sources 8, 9, 10, 11, 12)?

Finally, consider the principal actor, Louis XIV. Notice how his self-presentation is consistent with the trappings of the stage set. We find him consciously acting a role in Source 7, portraying an emperor in the Carousel of 1662. That engraving embodies a great deal of indirect information. What details reinforce the aura of royal power? Why should the king be mounted and in Roman costume? What strikes you about the king's attitude atop the prancing horse? Compare this picture with the Le Brun (Source 4) and Rigaud (Source 5) paintings. What elements do you find these pictures to have in common? How does the royal emblem of the sun (Source 6) contribute to the common message?

With these considerations in mind, return now to the central questions of this chapter. What was the theoretical basis for absolute royal authority? What was traditional and what was new in the justification of royal power expressed in late sixteenth- and seventeenth-century France? How did such early modern kings as Louis XIV communicate their absolute power in the various ceremonies, displays, and symbols of royal authority presented in the evidence?

EPILOGUE

We all know that any successful act produces imitators. In the seventeenth century, the monarchy of Louis XIV looked for a long time like the most successful regime in Europe. Royal absolutism had seemingly unified France. Out of that unity came a military power that threatened to overwhelm Europe; an economic strength, based on mercantilism, that increased French wealth; and an intellectual life that gave the culture of seventeenth- and eighteenth-century Europe a distinctly French accent. Imitators of Louis XIV's work were therefore numerous. At the very least, kings sought physically to express the unifying and centralizing monarchical principle of government in palaces recreating Versailles.[21]

But the work of such monarchs as Louis XIV involved far more than the construction of elaborate palaces in which to stage the theater of their court lives. The act of focusing the state on the figure of the monarch began the transition to the centralized modern style of government and marked the beginning of the end of the decentralized medieval state that bound subjects in an almost contractual relationship to their ruler. The king now emerged as theoretically all-powerful and also as a symbol of national unity.

The monarchs of the age did their work of state building so effectively that the unity and centralization they created often survived the monarchy itself. The French monarchy, for example, succumbed to a revolution in 1789 that in large part stemmed from the bankruptcy of the royal govern-

21. Palaces consciously modeled on Versailles multiplied in the late seventeenth and early eighteenth centuries. They included the Schönbrunn Palace in Vienna (1694), the Royal Palace in Berlin (begun in 1698), Ludwigsburg Palace in Württemberg, Germany (1704–1733), the Würzburg Residenz in Franconia, Germany (1719–1744), and the Stupinigi Palace (1729–1733) near Turin, Italy.

ment after too many years of overspending on wars and court life in the name of royal glory. But the unified state endured, strong enough to retain its sense of unity despite challenges in war and changes of government that introduced a new politics of mass participation.

The methods employed by Louis XIV and other monarchs also transcended their age. Modern governments understand the importance of ritual, symbolism, and display in creating the sense of national unity that was part of the absolute monarch's goal. Ritual may now be centered on important national observances. The parades on such days as July 4 in the United States, July 14 in France (commemorating one of the earliest victories of the Revolution of 1789), and the anniversary of the October 1917 Revolution as it was celebrated until 1990 in the former Soviet Union all differ in form from the rituals of Louis XIV. They are designed for a new political age, one of mass participation in politics, in which the loyalty of the whole people, not just that of an elite group, must be won. But their purpose remains the same: to win loyalty to the existing political order.

Modern states also use symbolism to build political loyalty. Artwork on public buildings in Washington, D.C., and the capital cities of other republics, for example, often employs classical themes. The purpose of such artwork is to suggest to citizens that their government perpetuates the republican rectitude of Athens and Rome. Display also is part of the political agenda of modern governments, even governments of new arrivals in the community of nations. This is why newly independent, developing nations of the twentieth and twenty-first century expend large portions of their meager resources on such things as grand new capital cities, the most sophisticated military weaponry, and the latest aircraft for the national airline. These are symbols of their governments' successes and thus the basis for these regimes' claims on their peoples' loyalty. These modern rituals, symbols, and displays perform the same function for modern rulers as Versailles did for the Sun King.

CHAPTER THREE

THE MIND OF AN AGE:

SCIENCE AND RELIGION

CONFRONT EIGHTEENTH-CENTURY

NATURAL DISASTER

THE PROBLEM

Because of the tremendous loss of life and damage to property that great natural disasters, such as earthquakes and floods, inflict on their victims, survivors of such events require some explanation of them. What was the reason for the disaster? Why did it occur where it did? In the answers that the thinkers of an age propose for such questions, we may find indications of the general thought patterns that characterize that particular era in history.

In the late twentieth century, for example, most of us would understand earthquakes scientifically, as the result of pressures along geological faults that occasionally produce cataclysmic movements of the earth's surface. Earlier ages often understood earthquakes in terms of supernatural action. The eighteenth century, the focus of this chapter, is an

age whose intellectual life we may investigate with particularly rewarding results. We will find that the intellectual life of this century illustrates the persistence of traditional thought patterns, increasingly challenged by a new, scientific vision of the physical world.

By the middle of the eighteenth century, Europe was approaching the culmination of an intellectual revolution that had been under way since the sixteenth century. Scientific discoveries of the sixteenth and seventeenth centuries, which your textbook describes as the Scientific Revolution, had produced a wholly new outlook on the physical world that was gaining increasing acceptance among educated Europeans. The result of the sixteenth- and seventeenth-century work of Nicholas Copernicus, Johannes Kepler, Galileo Galilei, René Descartes, Sir Isaac Newton, and others was a growing certainty that the physical world

Chapter 3

The Mind of an

Age: Science

and Religion

Confront

Eighteenth-

Century

Natural Disaster

could be understood through the ability of human reason to discern immutable mathematical laws that governed it. No longer did intellectuals explain the world in terms of supernatural action. The physical world increasingly appeared to be a great machine, and many eighteenth-century thinkers, called Deists in their religious outlook, posited a novel relationship between God and the physical world. The movements of the world-machine might have been created by God, but Deists believed that they could not be interrupted by him. Some thinkers also had faith that a divine plan governed the world, affirming that all would be well. But all agreed that nothing happened in such a world without sufficient cause or reason. This was a true revolution in thought, espoused by intellectuals called *philosophes*, who sought to apply their faith in the existence of reasonable and comprehensible natural laws to all aspects of the human experience. Their efforts in this regard constitute the intellectual milieu that historians call the Enlightenment of the eighteenth century.

The Enlightenment's concept of a machine-like universe contradicted much in the traditional Judeo-Christian concept of God. Most important, perhaps, Enlightenment thought precluded any belief in divine intervention in the physical world. Miracles or divinely ordained disasters, for example, simply were impossible for the *philosophes* because they violated natural laws of cause and effect. Traditional religious beliefs, however, were not without their defenders. Often these defenders were clergymen who, using the same tools of

reason employed by the Enlightenment's exponents, strongly disagreed with the *philosophes*. In Catholic Europe, members of the Society of Jesus, or Jesuits, were important defenders of traditional beliefs; in France they even published an influential monthly journal for their cause, the *Journal de Trevoux*. Clergymen in Protestant countries also espoused traditional beliefs concerning a divine presence in the world.

Debate between the proponents of these differing visions of the world's relationship to God had been under way for years before a major earthquake in Lisbon, Portugal, in 1755 forced Western thinkers to focus closely on the problem of explaining the causes of natural disasters. The Lisbon earthquake particularly captured the attention of Western thinkers because it struck a major political capital and international trading center close to Europe's heart.[1] Moreover, it was quite destructive.[2] The earthquake struck the Portuguese capital on November 1, 1755, All Saints' Day. At 9:30 A.M. on that holy day, on which Roman Catholics like the inhabitants of Lisbon are obligated to attend mass in commemoration of all of the church's saints, a

1. Other earthquakes of the period struck either on the fringes of the West, as in Jamaica in 1692 and Peru in 1746, or in isolated parts of Europe, as in Sicily in 1693. The few that had occurred in major cities—like London's quakes of 1750—had been slight in comparison to Lisbon's.

2. A number of twentieth-century earthquakes, for which we have accurate casualty counts, have clearly been more devastating. For example, the quake that struck Yokohama, Japan, on September 1, 1923, took about 200,000 lives; another in Tangshan, China, on July 28, 1976, killed about 242,000 persons.

loud rumbling disturbed a peaceful morning marked by religious observance or preparation for church attendance. Then three great seismic shocks rocked the city and ended its citizens' religious devotions. Churches and homes alike tumbled during this earthquake, whose shocks were felt as far away as Switzerland and northern France, and many persons perished. Other disasters resulting from the earthquake soon increased the loss of life. Fires spread from the hearths of the damaged city and burned for almost a week before they could be extinguished. The trembling of the earth created ocean waves fifteen to twenty feet high that swept up the Tagus River, on which Lisbon is situated, and broke over the city's waterfront. The combined destruction of earthquake, fires, and tidal waves left about 10,000 to 15,000 dead on that holy day of November 1.[3]

3. Estimates on the earthquake toll vary greatly, ranging as high as 60,000 persons. T. D. Kendrick, the author of a modern study, *The Lisbon Earthquake* (Philadelphia: J. B. Lippincott, 1957), accepts 10,000–15,000 as the probable number of dead, and, indeed, as the city's population was only about 275,000, the figure of 60,000 dead is difficult to accept.

Natural disasters like that at Lisbon elicited explanations from theologians who sought the work of God's hand in the Portuguese capital. The *philosophes,* however, differed markedly among themselves on the earthquake's significance. By reading selections on the exchange of ideas quickened by the Lisbon earthquake, the background on how some of these ideas developed, and the later implications of these thoughts, you will gain a deeper understanding of eighteenth-century thought about God and his relationship to the world. This was a key issue for the age, and one that was widely debated. Examining it allows us to learn a great deal about the Enlightenment by posing basic questions to the sources presented in this chapter: Why did the Lisbon earthquake present such an intellectual crisis for eighteenth-century thinkers? How did theologians explain the disaster within the framework of their beliefs? How did Enlightenment thinkers explain it? In what direction was their thought on the physical world and its relationship to divine forces leading them?

SOURCES AND METHOD

The problem at hand presents you with questions in the history of ideas, or what historians call "intellectual history." For generations, intellectual historians wrote about the ideas of the past without asking a question that seems central to historians

today: "Who, in a certain period, held a particular set of ideas?" or, more precisely, "How representative were these ideas of the society as a whole?" In other words, "How broad was the impact of these ideas in their own time?"

As your text probably notes, literacy was not widespread in eighteenth-century Europe, and so the

Chapter 3

The Mind of an

Age: Science

and Religion

Confront

Eighteenth-

Century

Natural Disaster

majority of the continent's population never had access to the ideas of the Scientific Revolution or the Enlightenment. Indeed, historians in recent years have come to recognize the persistence of a culture of the people, a popular culture, sometimes pre-Christian in its roots, that coexisted with the ideas of the *philosophes.* The intellectual world of the unlettered was one inhabited by witches and warlocks, in which people readily accepted supernatural explanations for physical phenomena. Such people might be frightened almost to death by an earthquake, but they took little part in the discussion of its philosophical ramifications presented here.

If the majority of the population of eighteenth-century Europe had little or no access to the ideas we will examine, are those ideas still relevant to our study of the past? The answer is certainly yes, although we must take care not to attribute the ideas to all persons. We are discussing ideas that were current among the small, educated elite of the eighteenth century. We must recognize, however, that this privileged group had tremendous influence in a societal and governmental system that accorded little role to anyone born outside that class. Moreover, such persons were the opinion makers of their age. Their ideas would have had considerable influence among those of the middle classes with some education. Thus the thought of this minority of Europe's total population had an impact well outside the boundaries of the social group from which it arose and so is quite worthy of study.

The evidence that follows has been chosen to present you with a broad sample of the thought of Europe's eighteenth-century intellectual elite and the background of its development. The Lisbon earthquake raised the immediate problem of explaining the disaster. This question involved large issues, chief among them the relationship of the physical world to God. Did God intervene in the world's daily operation, as theologians argued? Was he, as Deists said, like a watchmaker, creating a world-machine and then standing back and letting it operate on its own? Or was no divine hand at work in the world at all? In reading these selections, you should gain an understanding of why the Lisbon disaster preoccupied so many eighteenth-century thinkers.

Sources 1 and 2 represent a tendency perhaps as old as humankind, that is, the attempt to explain natural phenomena in terms of supernatural or divine forces. Source 1, "An Opinion on the True Cause of the Earthquake," was a pamphlet written by a Roman Catholic priest, the Jesuit Gabriel Malagrida (1689–1761). Born in Italy, Malagrida spent much of his life in missionary work in Portugal's Brazilian colony and lived in Lisbon after 1754. It is not insignificant that he was a Jesuit; the Society of Jesus was one of the most influential orders in the early modern Roman Catholic church. The absolute loyalty of the Jesuits to the papacy, combined with their energy and preaching ability, had done much to stem the spread of sixteenth-century European Protestantism. In subsequent centuries, the order's excellent schools had strengthened Catholicism, as had the influence its members wielded as spiritual advisers to monarchs. Malagrida in every way typified his order. He was an excellent preacher and well connected at court, and consequently his attempt to justify the earthquake in theological terms had an impact in Catholic Portugal. How did he account for the earthquake?

Source 2 is a sermon by John Wesley (1703–1791), one of the most influential English Protestant leaders of the eighteenth century. Ordained a priest of the Church of England, Wesley experienced a religious conversion in 1738 that led him to found a new Protestant faith, Methodism. In the eighteenth century, Methodism represented a dynamic new faith, espousing an emotional and personal kind of religion that contrasted with the practices of both Catholics and traditional Protestant groups.

Wesley preached widely in the cause of his faith; he is estimated to have journeyed 250,000 miles in the course of delivering 40,000 sermons, often to large audiences. Because many of his sermons were published in pamphlet form, he reached an even larger public than only those able to attend his sermons. According to this influential Protestant clergyman, what was the cause of the Lisbon earthquake? How might future earthquakes be avoided?

With Source 3 we encounter the thought of the Enlightenment. Voltaire was the pen name of François-Marie Arouet (1694–1778), one of the greatest of the *philosophes* and the author of Source 3. Born the son of a Parisian notary, Voltaire received a traditional education from French Jesuits but early developed an independence of thought and an irreverence toward established creeds and institutions that plunged him into difficulties. In 1717 the royal government imprisoned him for eleven months for alleged insults to the regent of France. In 1726 his writings provoked the authorities once again, and he avoided a second, lengthy imprisonment by agreeing to leave France for an extended stay in England. Voltaire remained in England for more than two years.

The lack of official tolerance for Voltaire's early writings defined the theme that became a constant in his writings: the cause of toleration. In England, he believed he had found a much freer and more tolerant society than that in France, and his *Letters Concerning the English Nation* (published 1733) contrasted France very unfavorably with England. The book also reflected the deep impact of the ideas of the English thinkers Newton and Locke on Voltaire. He would go on to write an extensive popular version of Newtonian physics, *Elements of the Philosophy of Newton* (1736), but in the earlier work on England, excerpted in Source 3, we find a brief summary of Newton's thought. What sort of world did Newton describe? What was the relationship of God to this world? In what ways does Voltaire express a Deistic interpretation of God's relationship to the physical world?

Source 4 is a passage from the poem "An Essay on Man" by Alexander Pope (1688–1744), an English poet whose acquaintance Voltaire made

Chapter 3

The Mind of an

Age: Science

and Religion

Confront

Eighteenth-

Century

Natural Disaster

during his English sojourn. As a member of England's Roman Catholic minority, Pope was excluded from educational opportunities open to Protestants, and he was largely self-taught. "An Essay on Man," published in 1734, is therefore remarkable as a summary of the philosophical speculation of the day on God's relationship to the world described by Newton. What is that relationship, according to Pope? Why does Pope tell his readers to accept the world as they find it?

Source 5 is an excerpt from the *Encyclopedia: The Rational Dictionary of the Sciences, the Arts, and the Crafts*, edited by Denis Diderot. Conceived as an attempt to summarize the knowledge of the eighteenth century and especially the results of the Scientific Revolution, the *Encyclopedia* also served to recapitulate Enlightenment thought. Many of the chief *philosophes*, including Voltaire, wrote its articles and brought to the work their criticism of the institutions of their age. Controversy was the immediate result. Church authorities sought to stop publication of the *Encyclopedia*, but slowly, over the years 1751 to 1772, the work appeared in seventeen volumes of text and eleven volumes of illustrations. The entry reproduced here as Source 5 is on the subject "Observation." What methods of research did its anonymous author urge scientific researchers to adopt? How does this article reflect the Scientific Revolution? Is there any role for the intervention of God in this method of amassing knowledge?

In Source 6 we have evidence of the effort to apply these methods of research. This selection is the work of Georges Louis Leclerc, Comte de Buffon (1707–1788), a nobleman and scientist who served as director of the French royal botanical gardens in Paris. In addition, he devoted himself for forty years to writing a forty-four-volume *Natural History*, his attempt to summarize and popularize the results of the Scientific Revolution. Although Buffon may not have been a particularly original thinker and his observation of earthquakes clearly was confined to their above-ground effects, his work was a great success, becoming something of a best seller that greatly influenced his age. Certainly we cannot scientifically accept Buffon's explanation of earthquakes today. But what approach to the physical world does his work represent? Would he in any way be able to accept the ideas of Malagrida or Wesley? Does Buffon see any evidence of divine design? How does his concept of the world grow out of Newton's science?

In Source 7 we encounter a rather different Voltaire from the man who discussed Newton. In his "Poem on the Lisbon Disaster, or An Examination of That Axiom 'All Is Well,'" published twenty years after *Letters*, we have the work of an older Voltaire, whose words reflect a growing doubt about the ideas of the early Enlightenment on the relationship of the physical world to God. What is Voltaire's view of God's role in the physical world in this poem he wrote on receiving the news of the Lisbon disaster? Why can Voltaire accept neither a theological explanation of the event nor the faith of some Deists that a divine plan dictated that all would work out for the best? What possible implications for the later Enlightenment's views on God do you find in this work of the influential Voltaire?

Voltaire's Lisbon poem elicited a forceful response in the form of a letter from Jean-Jacques Rousseau (1712–1778), given here as Source 8. Rousseau was born in Geneva, Switzerland, and his mother died shortly after his birth; his subsequent haphazard upbringing was followed by a wandering life that permitted few lasting relationships. His works, including *The Social Contract*, a work of political theory, and *Emile*, a work of educational philosophy, rank Rousseau among the eighteenth century's greatest thinkers. But he was not part of the company of the *philosophes* and ultimately disassociated himself from them. Rousseau's works glorify the simplicity to be found in nature, and in many ways he was a precursor of the Romantic movement in early-nineteenth-century literature, which consciously sought to negate the Enlightenment.

It was only natural, therefore, for Rousseau to have intellectual differences with Voltaire. When he wrote his letter in 1755, however, Rousseau's great work was still in the future and he was as yet relatively unknown. His letter to Voltaire, who was already an internationally known thinker, was thus rather audacious. What does Rousseau find wrong in Voltaire's view of the Lisbon earthquake? What relationship between God and humans does Rousseau express?

The author of Source 9, "The Essay on Miracles," was David Hume (1711–1776), a Scottish philosopher who lived for a time in France and who briefly befriended Rousseau. (Hume offered Rousseau a home when the latter was expelled from Bern, Switzerland, for his ideas. Rousseau soon quarreled with Hume, however, as he did with many persons.) Hume's thought reflects the Enlightenment search for hard, observable facts to justify conclusions, whether historical, philosophical, or theological. Could Hume find evidence of the God of Malagrida and Wesley on the one hand or of the God of Newton and the early Voltaire on the other? According to Hume, is any divine scheme at work in the world?

If Hume represents the skepticism of the Enlightenment, the work of Baron d'Holbach, a German-born nobleman who passed much of his life in France, perhaps reflects a logical culmination of Enlightenment thought about the physical world. Source 10 presents an expression of Holbach's views in a selection from his most important work, *The System of Nature*. What room is there for a divinity in Holbach's view, which sees the world as an "uninterrupted succession of causes and effects" in which "matter always existed"? Why do you think Holbach's contemporaries, including Voltaire, criticized his position as atheistic?

As you read these selections, you should be able to answer the central

Chapter 3

The Mind of an

Age: Science

and Religion

Confront

Eighteenth-

Century

Natural Disaster

questions of this chapter: Why did the Lisbon earthquake pose an intellectual crisis for eighteenth-century thinkers? How did theologians explain the disaster? How did Enlightenment thinkers explain it? In what direction was their thought on the physical world and its relationship to divine forces leading them?

THE EVIDENCE

Source 1 from T. D. Kendrick, The Lisbon Earthquake *(Philadelphia: Lippincott, 1957), pp. 137–138. Translated by T. D. Kendrick.*

1. Gabriel Malagrida, "An Opinion on the True Cause of the Earthquake," 1756

Learn, O Lisbon, that the destroyers of our houses, palaces, churches, and convents, the cause of the death of so many people and of the flames that devoured such vast treasures, are your abominable sins, and not comets, stars, vapours and exhalations, and similar natural phenomena. Tragic Lisbon is now a mound of ruins. Would that it were less difficult to think of some method of restoring the place; but it has been abandoned, and the refugees from the city live in despair. As for the dead, what a great harvest of sinful souls such disasters send to Hell! It is scandalous to pretend the earthquake was just a natural event, for if that be true, there is no need to repent and to try to avert the wrath of God, and not even the Devil himself could invent a false idea more likely to lead us all to irreparable ruin. Holy people had prophesied the earthquake was coming, yet the city continued in its sinful ways without a care for the future. Now, indeed, the case of Lisbon is desperate. It is necessary to devote all our strength and purpose to the task of repentance. Would to God we could see as much determination and fervour for this necessary exercise as are devoted to the erection of huts and new buildings! Does being billeted in the country outside the city areas put us outside the jurisdiction of God?[4] God undoubtedly desires to exercise His love and mercy, but be sure that wherever we are, He is watching us, scourge in hand.

4. Many of Lisbon's citizens fled the danger of the city for the countryside and remained there in shacks and tents until the earthquake danger passed.

Source 2 from The Works of John Wesley, *vol. 11 (Grand Rapids, Mich.: Zondervan, 1958),* pp. 1–2, 6–7, 8, 11.

2. John Wesley, "Some Serious Thoughts Occasioned by the Late Earthquake at Lisbon," 1755

Tua res agitur, paries quum proximus ardet.[5]

Thinking men generally allow that the greater part of modern Christians are not more virtuous than the ancient Heathens; perhaps less so; since public spirit, love of our country, generous honesty, and simple truth, are scarce anywhere to be found. On the contrary, covetousness, ambition, various injustice, luxury, and falsehood in every kind, have infected every rank and denomination of people, the Clergy themselves not excepted. Now, they who believe there is a God are apt to believe he is not well pleased with this. Nay, they think, he has intimated it very plainly, in many parts of the Christian world. How many hundred thousand men have been swept away by war, in Europe only, within half a century![6] How many thousands, within little more than this, hath the earth opened her mouth and swallowed up! Numbers sunk at Port-Royal, and rose no more! Many thousands went quick into the pit at Lima! The whole city of Catanea, in Sicily, and every inhabitant of it, perished together.[7] Nothing but heaps of ashes and cinders show where it stood. Not so much as one Lot escaped out of Sodom![8]

And what shall we say of the late accounts from Portugal? That some thousand houses, and many thousand persons, are no more! that a fair city is now

5. From the Roman poet Horace: "'Tis your own interest that calls, when flames invade your neighbor's walls."

6. Intense warfare did mark the half-century preceding the earthquake. The great Northern War (1700–1716) pitted Sweden against Russia. In the War of the Spanish Succession (1702–1714), France and Spain fought against England, Holland, the armies of the Holy Roman Emperor, and most of the German states. In the War of the Polish Succession (1733–1735), Spain and France confronted Russia and the forces of the Holy Roman Emperor. Almost all of Europe was involved in the War of the Austrian Succession (1740–1748), in which France, Spain, Prussia, and a number of the German states fought England and Austria. At the time Wesley wrote, fighting between English and French forces had already broken out in North America and would lead to the Seven Years War of 1756–1763. And these were only the major wars! Minor conflicts also raged. One historian reckoned that all of Europe was at peace for only two years in the century spanning 1700–1800.

7. Wesley refers here to the earthquakes of 1692, 1693, and 1746 mentioned in note 1.

8. In the Bible's book of Genesis, chapters 11–14 and 19, God destroyed Sodom and Gomorrah with fire because of their wickedness. Abraham's nephew, Lot, a resident of Sodom, was warned of the destruction and escaped.

Chapter 3

The Mind of an

Age: Science

and Religion

Confront

Eighteenth-

Century

Natural Disaster

in ruinous heaps! Is there indeed a God that judges the world? And is he now making inquisition for blood? If so, it is not surprising, he should begin there, where so much blood has been poured on the ground like water! where so many brave men have been murdered, in the most base and cowardly as well as barbarous manner, almost every day, as well as every night, while none regarded or laid it to heart.[9] "Let them hunt and destroy the precious life, so we may secure our stores of gold and precious stones."[10] How long has their blood been crying from the earth! Yea, how long has that bloody *House of Mercy*,[11] the scandal not only of all religion, but even of human nature, stood to insult both heaven and earth! "And shall I not visit for these things, saith the Lord? Shall not my soul be avenged on such a city as this?". . .

But alas! why should we not be convinced sooner, while that conviction may avail, that it is not chance which governs the world? Why should we not now, before London is as Lisbon, Lima, or Catanea, acknowledge the hand of the Almighty, arising to maintain his own cause? Why, we have a general answer always ready, to screen us from any such conviction: "All these things are purely natural and accidental; the result of natural causes." But there are two objections to this answer: First, it is untrue: Secondly, it is uncomfortable.

First. If by affirming, "All this is purely natural," you mean, it is not providential, or that God has nothing to do with it, this is not true, that is, supposing the Bible to be true. For supposing this, you may descant ever so long on the natural causes of murrain, winds, thunder, lightning, and yet you are altogether wide of the mark, you prove nothing at all, unless you can prove that God never works in or by natural causes. But this you cannot prove; nay, none can doubt of his so working, who allows the Scripture to be of God. For this asserts, in the clearest and strongest terms, that "all things" (in nature) "serve him;" that (by or without a train of natural causes) He "sendeth his rain on the earth;" that He "bringeth the winds out of his treasures," and "maketh a way for the lightning and the thunder;" in general, that "fire and hail, snow and

9. In this sentence, Wesley is referring to the executions resulting from trials by the Portuguese Inquisition. The Inquisition was a system of Roman Catholic courts created to identify and judge heretics. Like all continental European courts of the day, these courts could torture the defendant to gather evidence against him or her. Civil, not church, authorities, however, executed sentences.

10. **precious stones:** "Merchants who have lived in Portugal inform us that the King has a large building filled with diamonds; and more gold stored up, coined and uncoined, than all the other monarchs of Europe." [Wesley's note] This may or may not have been true, but Lisbon certainly received gold from New World mines and diamonds from mines discovered in the Portuguese colony of Brazil in the 1730s.

11. **House of Mercy:** "The title which the Inquisition of Portugal (if not in other countries also) takes to itself." [Wesley's note]

vapour, wind and storm, fulfil his word." Therefore, allowing there are natural causes of all these, they are still under the direction of the Lord of nature: Nay, what is nature itself, but the art of God, or God's method of acting in the material world? . . .

A Second objection to your answer is, It is extremely uncomfortable. For if things really be as you affirm; if all these afflictive incidents entirely depend on the fortuitous concourse and agency of blind, material causes; what hope, what help, what resource is left for the poor sufferers by them? . . .

What defence do you find from thousands of gold and silver? You cannot fly; for you cannot quit the earth, unless you will leave your dear body behind you. And while you are on the earth, you know not where to flee to, neither where to flee from. You may buy intelligence, where the shock was yesterday, but not where it will be to-morrow,—to-day. It comes! The roof trembles! The beams crack! The ground rocks to and fro! Hoarse thunder resounds from the bowels of the earth! And all these are but the beginning of sorrows. Now, what help? What wisdom can prevent, what strength resist, the blow? What money can purchase, I will not say deliverance, but an hour's reprieve? Poor honourable fool, where are now thy titles? Wealthy fool, where is now thy golden god? If any thing can help, it must be prayer. But what wilt thou pray to? Not to the God of heaven; you suppose him to have nothing to do with earthquakes. . . .

But how shall we secure the favour of this great God? How, but by worshipping him in spirit and in truth; by uniformly imitating Him we worship, in all his imitable perfections? without which the most accurate systems of opinions, all external modes of religion, are idle cobwebs of the brain, dull farce and empty show. Now, God is love: Love God then, and you are a true worshipper. Love mankind, and God is your God, your Father, and your Friend. But see that you deceive not your own soul; for this is not a point of small importance. And by this you may know: If you love God, then you are happy in God; if you love God, riches, honours, and the pleasures of sense are no more to you than bubbles on the water: You look on dress and equipage, as the tassels of a fool's cap; diversions, as the bells on a fool's coat. If you love God, God is in all your thoughts, and your whole life is a sacrifice to him. And if you love mankind, it is your own design, desire, and endeavour, to spread virtue and happiness all around you; to lessen the present sorrows, and increase the joys, of every child of man; and, if it be possible, to bring them with you to the rivers of pleasure that are at God's right hand for evermore.

Chapter 3

The Mind of an

Age: Science

and Religion

Confront

Eighteenth-

Century

Natural Disaster

Source 3 from Voltaire, Letters Concerning the English Nation *(New York: Burt Franklin Reprints, 1974), pp. 65–66, 96–97, 100, 103, 105–106.*

3. Voltaire on Newtonian Physics, 1733

Not long since, the trite and frivolous Question following was debated in a very polite and learned Company, *viz.* (namely) who was the greatest Man, *Cæsar, Alexander, Tamerlane, Cromwell,* & *c.*[12]

Some Body answer'd, that Sir *Isaac Newton* excell'd them all. The Gentleman's Assertion was very just; for if true Greatness consists in having receiv'd from Heaven a mighty Genius, and in having employ'd it to enlighten our own Minds and that of others; a Man like Sir *Isaac Newton,* whose equal is hardly found in a thousand Years, is the truly great Man. And those Politicians and Conquerors, (and all ages produce some) were generally so many illustrious wicked Men. That Man claims our Respect, who commands over the Minds of the rest of the World by the Force of Truth, not those who enslave their Fellow Creatures; He who is acquainted with the Universe, not They who deface it. . . .

The Discoveries which gain'd Sir *Isaac Newton* so universal a Reputation, relate to the System of the World, to Light, to Geometrical Infinites; and lastly to Chronology, with which he us'd to amuse himself after the Fatigue of his severer Studies.

I will now acquaint you (without Prolixity if possible) with the few Things I have been able to comprehend of all these sublime Ideas. With Regard to the System of our World, Disputes were a long Time maintain'd, on the Cause that turns the Planets, and keeps them in their Orbits; and on those Causes which make all Bodies here below descend towards the Surface of the Earth.

Having . . . destroy'd the *Cartesian* Vortices,[13] he despair'd of ever being able to discover, whether there is a secret Principle in Nature which, at the same Time, is the Cause of the Motion of all celestial Bodies, and that of Gravity on the Earth. But being retir'd in 1666, upon Account of the Plague, to a Solitude near *Cambridge;* as he was walking one Day in his Garden, and saw some Fruits fall from a Tree, he fell into a profound Meditation on that Grav-

---

12. **Julius Caesar** (102–44 B.C.) dominated Rome during the last years of the republic. **Alexander the Great** (356–323 B.C.) was the king of Macedonia who led the Greeks on wars of conquest to create an empire that included modern Greece, Turkey, Egypt, and much of the Middle East to the borders of India. **Tamerlane** (ca 1336–1405) was a Turkish chieftain who created an empire embracing parts of southern Russia, Turkey, the Middle East, Afghanistan, Pakistan, and northern India. **Oliver Cromwell** (1599–1658) led Parliament's armies against the king in the English Civil War. After the king's defeat and execution, he ruled England as virtual dictator.

13. **Cartesian vortices:** René Descartes (1546–1650), a French philosopher and mathematician, accounted for planetary motion in terms of vortices, that is, a rapid movement of cosmic bodies in a fluid or ether around an axis. Newtonian physics, with its law of gravity, dispensed with such theories.

ity, the Cause of which had so long been sought, but in vain, by all the Philosophers, whilst the Vulgar think there is nothing mysterious in it. He said to himself, that from what height soever, in our Hemisphere, those Bodies might descend, their Fall wou'd certainly be in the Progression discover'd by *Galileo*;[14] and the Spaces they run thro' would be as the Square of the Times. Why may not this Power which causes heavy Bodies to descend, and is the same without any sensible Diminution at the remotest Distance from the Center of the Earth, or on the Summits of the highest Mountains; Why, said Sir *Isaac,* may not this Power extend as high as the Moon? And in Case, its Influence reaches so far, is it not very probable that this Power retains it in its Orbit, and determines its Motion? But in case the Moon obeys this Principle (whatever it be) may we not conclude very naturally, that the rest of the Planets are equally subject to it? In case this Power exists (which besides is prov'd) it must increase in an inverse *Ratio* of the Squares of the Distances. All therefore that remains is, to examine how far a heavy Body, which should fall upon the Earth from a moderate height, would go; and how far in the same time, a Body which should fall from the Orbit of the Moon, would descend. To find this, nothing is wanted but the Measure of the Earth, and the Distance of the Moon from it.

This is Attraction, the great Spring by which all Nature is mov'd. Sir *Isaac Newton* after having demonstrated the Existence of this Principle, plainly foresaw that its very Name wou'd offend; and therefore this Philosopher in more Places than one of his Books, gives the Reader some Caution about it. He bids him beware of confounding this Name with what the Ancients call'd occult Qualities; but to be satisfied with knowing that there is in all Bodies a central Force which acts to the utmost Limits of the Universe, according to the invariable Laws of Mechanicks.

Give me Leave once more to introduce Sir *Isaac* speaking: . . . "The Spring that I discover'd was more hidden and more universal, and for that very Reason Mankind ought to thank me the more. I have discover'd a new Property of Matter, one of the Secrets of the Creator; and have calculated and discover'd the Effects of it. After this shall People quarrel with me about the Name I give it."

Vortices may be call'd an occult Quality because their Existence was never prov'd; Attraction on the contrary is a real Thing, because its Effects are demonstrated, and the Proportions of it are calculated. The Cause of this Cause is among the *Arcana*[15] of the Almighty.

Procedes huc, & non amplius.
Hither thou shalt go, and no farther.

---

14. **Galileo Galilei:** Italian astronomer, mathematician, and physicist (1564–1642) whose work was an important contribution to the Scientific Revolution. He developed the mathematical explanation of the rates at which bodies fall to earth in his law of falling bodies.
15. **Arcana:** secrets or mysteries.

Chapter 3

The Mind of an

Age: Science

and Religion

Confront

Eighteenth-

Century

Natural Disaster

Source 4 from A. W. Ward, editor, The Poetical Works of Alexander Pope *(London: Macmillan, 1879), pp. 199–200.*

4. From Alexander Pope, "An Essay on Man," 1734

All are but parts of one stupendous whole,
Whose body Nature is, and God the soul;
That, chang'd thro' all, and yet in all the same;
Great in the earth, as in th' ethereal[16] frame;
Warms in the sun, refreshes in the breeze,
Glows in the stars, and blossoms in the trees,
Lives thro' all life, extends thro' all extent,
Spreads undivided, operates unspent;
Breathes in our soul, informs our mortal part,
As full, as perfect, in a hair as heart:
As full, as perfect, in vile Man that mourns,
As the rapt Seraph[17] that adores and burns:
To him no high, no low, no great, no small;
He fills, he bounds, connects, and equals all.

Cease then, nor Order Imperfection name:
Our proper bliss depends on what we blame.
Know thy own point: This kind, this due degree
Of blindness, weakness, Heav'n bestows on thee;
Submit.—In this, or any other sphere,
Secure to be as blest as thou canst bear:
Safe in the hand of one disposing Pow'r,
Or in the natal, or the mortal hour.
All Nature is but Art, unknown to thee;
All Chance, Direction, which thou canst not see;
All Discord, Harmony not understood;
All partial Evil, universal Good:
And, spite of Pride, in erring Reason's spite,
One truth is clear, WHATEVER IS, IS RIGHT.

16. **ethereal:** heavenly.

17. **Seraph:** one of the heavenly creatures hovering around the throne of God described in Isaiah 6.

Source 5 from Denis Diderot, The Encyclopedia: Selections, *edited and translated by Stephen J. Gendzier (New York: Harper & Row, 1967), pp. 175–177. Used by permission of Stephen J. Gendzier.*

5. From the *Encyclopedia,* Anonymous Entry on "Observation," ca 1765

OBSERVATION (*Gram. Physic. Med.*) is the attention of the soul focused on objects offered by nature. An experiment is the result of this same attention directed toward phenomena produced by the labors of man. We must, therefore, include within the meaning of the generic noun *observation* the examination of all natural effects, not only of those that present themselves at once and without intermediary to our sight but also those we would not be able to discover without the hand of a worker, provided that this hand has not changed, altered, or disfigured them. The work necessary to reach a mine does not prevent the examination that is made of the metal's distribution, position, quantity, and color from being a simple *observation.* It is also by *observation* that we know the interior geography, that we estimate the number, position, and nature of the layers of earth, although we are obliged to resort to instruments for the excavation that allows us to see the mine. We must not consider as an *experiment* the opening of cadavers, the dissection of plants or animals, and certain analyses or mechanical sorting of mineral matter that scientists are obliged to do in order to be able to *observe* the parts that enter into their composition. The telescope of astronomers, the magnifying glass of the naturalist, and the microscope of the physicist do not prevent the knowledge acquired by these means from being the exact product of *observation.* All these preparations, these instruments only serve to render the different objects of *observation* more concrete, to remove the obstacles that prevent us from perceiving them, or to pierce the veil that hides them. But no change results from this, and there is not the slightest alteration in the nature of the *observed* object. It appears, nevertheless, such as it is; and this is the main difference between an *observation* and an *experiment* which decomposes, combines, and thereby gives use to rather different phenomena from those which nature presents. . . .

Observation is the primary foundation of all the sciences, the most reliable way to arrive at one's goal, the principal means of extending the periphery of scientific knowledge and of illuminating all its points. The facts, whatever they are, constitute the true wealth of the philosopher and the subject of *observation:* the historian collects them, the theoretical physicist combines them, and the experimenter verifies the results of their synthesis. Several facts taken separately appear dry, sterile, and unfruitful. The moment we compare them, they acquire a certain power, assume a vitality that everywhere results from the mutual harmony, from the reciprocal support, and from a chain that binds them together. The connection of these facts and the general cause that links

Chapter 3

The Mind of an

Age: Science

and Religion

Confront

Eighteenth-

Century

Natural Disaster

them together are some of the objects of reasoning, theories, and systems, while the facts are the materials. The moment a certain number of them have been gathered, some people hasten to construct; and the building is the more solid as the materials are more numerous and each one of them finds a more appropriate place.

Source 6 from Georges Louis Leclerc, Comte de Buffon, Histoire naturelle, générale et particulière, avec description du cabinet du roi, *vol. 1 (Paris: De l'Imprimerie Royale, 1749), pp. 526–529. Translated by Julius R. Ruff.*

6. From Georges Louis Leclerc, Comte de Buffon, *Natural History, General and Specific,* ca 1750

There are two kinds of earthquakes. One type is caused by the action of subterranean fires and by the explosion of volcanoes and is only felt over small distances when volcanoes are active or when they erupt. When the materials which make up subterranean fires begin to ferment, to heat up, and to ignite, the fire expands on all sides and, if it does not naturally find outlets, it heaves up the ground and makes a passage by throwing out the earth in its way. This produces a volcano, the effects of which repeat themselves and endure in proportion to the inflammable materials.

But there is another kind of earthquake, very different as regards its effects and perhaps as regards its causes. These are the earthquakes which are felt over long distances and which shake a large area of terrain without the appearance of a new volcano or an eruption. We have examples of earthquakes which are felt at the same time in England, France, Germany, and as far away as Hungary. These earthquakes always extend over an area much longer than it is wide. They shake a band or zone of the earth with varying force in different locations. They are almost always accompanied by a muffled sound, similar to that of a large, quickly rolling coach.

To understand more fully the causes of this kind of earthquake, it is necessary to remember that all inflammable and explosive materials produce . . . a great deal of air in igniting.[18] This air produced by the fire is in a very highly rarefied state and, because of its state of compression in the depths of the earth, it must produce very violent effects. Let us therefore suppose that at a very great depth, say 600 to 1200 feet, there are found pyrites and other sulphurous materials and that by the fermentation produced by the filtration

---

18. Buffon advanced this description of combustion a quarter of a century before the great French chemist Antoine Laurent Lavoisier (1743–1794) accurately described combustion and the role of oxygen in this process.

of water or by other causes, these materials ignite. Let us see what must happen. These materials are not regularly arranged in horizontal strata . . . they are, on the contrary, in perpendicular clefts in the caverns . . . where water can penetrate and have an effect. These materials ignite, producing a large quantity of air, the force of which, compressed in a small space like a cavern, not only will shake the terrain above but will look for routes of escape. . . . The routes which are available are caverns and cuts by water and subterranean streams. The rarefied air will rush violently through all of these passages which are open to it. It will form a raging wind in its subterranean paths, the noise of which will be heard on the earth's surface, and it will be accompanied by shock and concussions. This subterranean wind produced by the fire will extend as far as the subterranean cavities and cuts, and will cause a tremor the violence of which will depend on the distance from the source and the narrowness of the passages through which the wind passes. . . . This air will produce no eruption or volcano because it will have found enough space in which to expand or indeed because it will have found escapes and will have left the earth in the form of wind or vapor.[19]

Source 7 from Oeuvres complètes de Voltaire, *nouvelle edition, vol. 9 (Paris: Garnier frères, 1877), p. 470. Translated by Julius R. Ruff.*

7. From Voltaire, "Poem on the Lisbon Disaster, or An Examination of That Axiom 'All Is Well,'" 1755

Oh, miserable mortals! Oh wretched earth!
Oh, dreadful assembly of all mankind!
Eternal sermon of useless sufferings!
Deluded philosophers who cry, "All is well,"
Hasten, contemplate these frightful ruins,
This wreck, these shreds, these wretched ashes of the dead;
These women and children heaped on one another,
These scattered members under broken marble;
One-hundred thousand unfortunates devoured by the earth,[20]

19. The article on "Earthquakes" in the *Encyclopedia* edited by Diderot also explains this phenomenon with a theory of subterranean fire. Modern geologists have shown earthquakes to be the result of stresses in the earth's crust. Interestingly, however, modern research also has shown that the eighteenth-century theories of subterranean fire were not entirely incorrect: The earth does have a liquid core of practically molten rock.

20. Voltaire wrote this poem on hearing the first news of the disaster. Those first reports grossly exaggerated the number of deaths, as does the poem.

Chapter 3

The Mind of an

Age: Science

and Religion

Confront

Eighteenth-

Century

Natural Disaster

Who, bleeding, lacerated, and still alive,
Buried under their roofs without aid in their anguish,
End their sad days!
In answer to the half-formed cries of their dying voices,
At the frightful sight of their smoking ashes,
Will you say: "This is the result of eternal laws
Directing the acts of a free and good God!"
Will you say, in seeing this mass of victims:
"God is revenged, their death is the price for their crimes?"
What crime, what error did these children,
Crushed and bloody on their mothers' breasts, commit?
Did Lisbon, which is no more, have more vices
Than London and Paris immersed in their pleasures?
Lisbon is destroyed, and they dance in Paris!

Source 8 from Theodore Bestermann, editor, Voltaire's Correspondence, *vol. 30 (Geneva: Institut et Musée Voltaire, 1958), pp. 102–115. Translated by Julius R. Ruff.*

8. From Jean-Jacques Rousseau's Letter to Voltaire Regarding the Poem on the Lisbon Earthquake, August 18, 1756

All my complaints are . . . against your poem on the Lisbon disaster, because I expected from it evidence more worthy of the humanity which apparently inspired you to write it. You reproach Pope[21] and Leibnitz[22] with belittling our misfortunes by affirming that all is well, but you so burden the list of our miseries that you further disparage our condition. Instead of the consolations that I expected, you only vex me. It might be said that you fear that I don't feel my unhappiness enough, and that you are trying to soothe me by proving that all is bad.

Do not be mistaken, Monsieur, it happens that everything is contrary to what you propose. This optimism which you find so cruel consoles me still in

---

21. Alexander Pope, whose "An Essay on Man" is Source 4 in this chapter.

22. **Gottfried Wilhelm von Leibnitz:** a German mathematician and philosopher (1646–1716), the author of *Essays on Theodicy,* in which he examined the origins of evil in the world. Leibnitz saw the universe operating according to a divine plan, and therefore this was the best of all possible worlds. He was not a total optimist, however, because he recognized the existence of evil. Incompletely understanding the thought of Leibnitz, Voltaire satirized him as a blind optimist in his novel *Candide* (1759).

the same woes that you force on me as unbearable. Pope's poem[23] alleviates my difficulties and inclines me to patience; yours makes my afflictions worse, prompts me to grumble, and, leading me beyond a shattered hope, reduces me to despair. . . .

"Have patience, man," Pope and Leibnitz tell me, "your woes are a necessary effect of your nature and of the constitution of the universe. The eternal and beneficent Being who governs the universe wished to protect you. Of all the possible plans, he chose that combining the minimum evil and the maximum good. If it is necessary to say the same thing more bluntly, God has done no better for mankind because (He) can do no better."

Now what does your poem tell me? "Suffer forever unfortunate one. If a God created you, He is doubtlessly all powerful and could have prevented all your woes. Don't ever hope that your woes will end, because you would never know why you exist, if it is not to suffer and die. . . ."

I do not see how one can search for the source of moral evil anywhere but in man. . . . Moreover . . . the majority of our physical misfortunes are also our work. Without leaving your Lisbon subject, concede, for example, that it was hardly nature that there brought together twenty-thousand houses of six or seven stories. If the residents of this large city had been more evenly dispersed and less densely housed, the losses would have been fewer or perhaps none at all. Everyone would have fled at the first shock. But many obstinately remained . . . to expose themselves to additional earth tremors because what they would have had to leave behind was worth more than what they could carry away. How many unfortunates perished in this disaster through the desire to fetch their clothing, papers, or money? . . .

There are often events that afflict us . . . that lose a lot of their horror when we examine them closely. I learned in *Zadig*,[24] and nature daily confirms my lesson, that a rapid death is not always a true misfortune, and that it can sometimes be considered a relative blessing. Of the many persons crushed under Lisbon's ruins, some without doubt escaped greater misfortunes, and . . . it is not certain that a single one of these unfortunates suffered more than if, in the normal course of events, he had awaited [a more normal] death to overtake him after long agonies. Was death [in the ruins] a sadder end than that of a dying person overburdened with useless treatments, whose notary[25] and heirs do not allow him a respite, whom the doctors kill in his own bed at

---

23. **Pope's poem:** "An Essay on Man."

24. **Zadig:** a story published by Voltaire in 1747 that still reflected some faith on his part that a divine order for the world assured that all would work out for the best. In the story, Zadig, the main character, endures a lengthy series of misfortunes.

25. **notary:** in France and other Continental countries, a professional person specializing in drafting wills and inventorying the property involved in them as well as drawing up other property arrangements.

[83]

Chapter 3

The Mind of an

Age: Science

and Religion

Confront

Eighteenth-

Century

Natural Disaster

their leisure, and whom the barbarous priests artfully try to make relish death? For me, I see everywhere that the misfortunes nature imposes upon us are less cruel than those which we add to them. . . .

I cannot prevent myself, Monsieur, from noting . . . a strange contrast between you and me as regards the subject of this letter. Satiated with glory . . . you live free in the midst of affluence.[26] Certain of your immortality, you peacefully philosophize on the nature of the soul, and, if your body or heart suffer, you have Tronchin[27] as doctor and friend. You however find only evil on earth. And I, an obscure and poor man tormented with an incurable illness, meditate with pleasure in my seclusion and find that all is well. What is the source of this apparent contradiction? You explained it yourself: you revel but I hope, and hope beautifies everything.

. . . I have suffered too much in this life not to look forward to another. No metaphysical subtleties cause me to doubt a time of immortality for the soul and a beneficent providence. I sense it, I believe it, I wish it, I hope for it, I will uphold it until my last gasp. . . .

I am, with respect, Monsieur,

Jean-Jacques Rousseau

Source 9 from David Hume, Essays: Moral, Political and Literary *(Oxford: Oxford University Press, 1963), pp. 519–521, 524–526, 540–541.*

9. David Hume, "The Essay on Miracles," 1748

There is, in Dr. Tillotson's[28] writings, an argument against the *real presence*,[29] which is as concise, and elegant, and strong, as any argument can possibly be supposed against a doctrine so little worthy of a serious refutation. It is acknowledged on all hands, says that learned prelate, that the authority, either of the Scripture or of tradition, is founded merely on the testimony; of the Apostles, who were eye-witnesses to those miracles of our Saviour, by which he proved his divine mission. Our evidence, then, for the truth of the *Christian* religion, is less than the evidence for the truth of our senses; because, even in

---

26. Voltaire had prospered from his publishings and also had invested well. He owned property in Geneva, Switzerland, and a large estate at Ferney, France, on the Swiss border.

27. **Theodore Tronchin:** a physician (1709–1781) of Geneva, Switzerland. A pioneer in smallpox inoculation in Switzerland, he was a member of Voltaire's circle.

28. **Dr. John Tillotson:** Archbishop of Canterbury (1630–1694), that is, spiritual leader of the Church of England.

29. **real presence:** the presence of Jesus Christ in the sacramental bread and wine of Christian Communion.

the first authors of our religion, it was no greater; and it is evident it must diminish in passing from them to their disciples; nor can any one rest such confidence in their testimony as in the immediate object of his senses. But a weaker evidence can never destroy a stronger; and therefore, were the doctrine of the real presence ever so clearly revealed in Scripture, it were directly contrary to the rules of just reasoning to give our assent to it. It contradicts sense, though both the Scripture and tradition, on which it is supposed to be built, carry not such evidence with them as sense, when they are considered merely as external evidences, and are not brought home to every one's breast by the immediate operation of the Holy Spirit.

Nothing is so convenient as a decisive argument of this kind, which must at least *silence* the most arrogant bigotry and superstition, and free us from their impertinent solicitations. I flatter myself that I have discovered an argument of a like nature, which, if just, will, with the wise and learned, be an everlasting check to all kinds of superstitious delusion, and consequently will be useful as long as the world endures; for so long, I presume, will the accounts of miracles and prodigies be found in all history, sacred and profane.

Though experience be our only guide in reasoning concerning matters of fact, it must be acknowledged, that this guide is not altogether infallible, but in some cases is apt to lead us into errors. One who in our climate should expect better weather in any week of June than in one of December, would reason justly and conformably to experience; but it is certain that he may happen, in the event, to find himself mistaken. However, we may observe that, in such a case, he would have no cause to complain of experience, because it commonly informs us beforehand of the uncertainty, by that contrariety of events which we may learn from a diligent observation. All effects follow not with like certainty from their supposed causes. Some events are found, in all countries and all ages, to have been constantly conjoined together: others are found to have been more variable, and sometimes to disappoint our expectations; so that in our reasonings concerning matter of fact, there are all imaginable degrees of assurance, from the highest certainty to the lowest species of moral evidence.

A wise man, therefore, proportions his belief to the evidence. In such conclusions as are founded on an infallible experience, he expects the event with the last degree of assurance, and regards his past experience as a full *proof* of the future existence of that event. In other cases he proceeds with more caution: he weighs the opposite experiments: he considers which side is supported by the greater number of experiments: to that side he inclines with doubt and hesitation; and when at last he fixes his judgment, the evidence exceeds not what we properly call *probability*. All probability, then, supposes an opposition of experiments and observations, where the one side is found to overbalance the other, and to produce a degree of evidence proportioned to the superiority. A hundred instances or experiments on one side, and fifty on another, afford a doubtful expectation of any event; though a hundred uni-

Chapter 3

The Mind of an

Age: Science

and Religion

Confront

Eighteenth-

Century

Natural Disaster

form experiments, with only one that is contradictory, reasonably beget a pretty strong degree of assurance. In all cases, we must balance the opposite experiments, where they are opposite, and deduct the smaller number from the greater, in order to know the exact force of the superior evidence. . . .

A miracle is a violation of the laws of nature; and as a firm and unalterable experience has established these laws, the proof against a miracle, from the very nature of the fact, is as entire as any argument from experience can possibly be imagined. Why is it more than probable that all men must die; that lead cannot, of itself, remain suspended in the air; that fire consumes wood, and is extinguished by water; unless it be that these events are found agreeable to the laws of nature, and there is required a violation of these laws, or, in other words, a miracle to prevent them? Nothing is esteemed a miracle, if it ever happen in the common course of nature. It is no miracle that a man, seemingly in good health, should die on a sudden; because such a kind of death, though more unusual than any other, has yet been frequently observed to happen. But it is a miracle that a dead man should come to life; because that has never been observed in any age or country. There must, therefore, be an uniform experience against every miraculous event, otherwise the event would not merit that appellation. And as an uniform experience amounts to a proof, there is here a direct and full *proof*, from the nature of the fact, against the existence of any miracle. . . .

The plain consequence is (and it is a general maxim worthy of our attention), "That no testimony is sufficient to establish a miracle, unless the testimony be of such a kind, that its falsehood would be more miraculous than the fact which it endeavours to establish: and even in that case there is a mutual destruction of arguments, and the superior only gives us an assurance suitable to that degree of force which remains after deducting the inferior." When any one tells me that he saw a dead man restored to life, I immediately consider with myself whether it be more probable that this person should either deceive or be deceived, or that the fact which he relates should really have happened. I weigh the one miracle against the other; and according to the superiority which I discover, I pronounce my decision, and always reject the greater miracle. If the falsehood of his testimony would be more miraculous than the event which he relates, then, and not till then, can he pretend to command my belief or opinion.

Upon the whole, then, it appears, that no testimony for any kind of miracle has ever amounted to a probability, much less to a proof; and that, even supposing it amounted to a proof, it would be opposed by another proof, derived from the very nature of the fact which it would endeavour to establish. It is experience only which gives authority to human testimony; and it is the same experience which assures us of the laws of nature. When, therefore, these two kinds of experience are contrary, we have nothing to do but to subtract the one from the other, and embrace an opinion either on one side or the other, with that assurance which arises from the remainder. But according to the principle here explained, this subtraction with regard to all popular religions amounts to an entire annihilation; and therefore we may establish it as a maxim, that no human testimony can have such force as to prove a miracle, and make it a just foundation for any such system of religion. . . .

What we have said of miracles, may be applied without any variation to prophecies; and, indeed, all prophecies are real miracles, and as such, only can be admitted as proofs of any revelation. If it did not exceed the capacity of human nature to foretell future events, it would be absurd to employ any prophecy as an argument for a divine mission or authority from heaven. So that, upon the whole, we may conclude, that the *Christian Religion* not only was at first attended with miracles, but even at this day cannot be believed by any reasonable person without one. Mere reason is insufficient to convince us of its veracity: and whoever is moved by *Faith* to assent to it, is conscious of a continued miracle in his own person, which subverts all the principles of his understanding, and gives him a determination to believe what is most contrary to custom and experience.

Source 10 from Paul-Henry Thiry, Baron d'Holbach, The System of Nature, *translated by H. D. Robinson (Boston: J. P. Mendum, 1853), pp. viii–ix, 12–13, 15, 19–23.*

10. From Paul-Henry Thiry, Baron d'Holbach, *The System of Nature,* 1770

Preface

The source of man's unhappiness is his ignorance of Nature. The pertinacity with which he clings to blind opinions imbibed in his infancy, which interweave themselves with his existence, the consequent prejudice that warps his mind, that prevents its expansion, that renders him the slave of fiction, appears to doom him to continual errour. He resembles a child destitute of experience, full of idle notions: a dangerous leaven mixes itself with all his knowledge: it is of necessity obscure, it is vacillating and false:—He takes the tone of his ideas on the authority of others, who are themselves in errour, or else have an interest in deceiving him. To remove this Cimmerian darkness,[30] these barriers to the improvement of his condition; to disentangle him from the clouds of errour that envelop him, that obscure the path he ought to tread; to guide him out of the Cretan labyrinth,[31] requires the clue of Ari-

---

30. **Cimmerian darkness:** in Greek mythology, the Cimmerians were a people inhabiting a land of perpetual darkness.

31. **Cretan labyrinth:** according to Greek mythology, there existed on the island of Crete a structure of winding passages leading to a monster with the body of a man and the head of a bull, the Minotaur. This monster was annually fed seven young men and seven young women from Athens as that city's tribute to the rulers of Crete.

Chapter 3

The Mind of an

Age: Science

and Religion

Confront

Eighteenth-

Century

Natural Disaster

adne,[32] with all the love she could bestow on Theseus. It exacts more than common exertion; it needs a most determined, a most undaunted courage—it is never effected but by a persevering resolution to act, to think for himself; to examine with rigour and impartiality the opinions he has adopted. . . .

Man seeks to range out of his sphere: notwithstanding the reiterated checks his ambitious folly experiences, he still attempts the impossible; strives to carry his researches beyond the visible world; and hunts out misery in imaginary regions. He would be a metaphysician before he has become a practical philosopher. He quits the contemplation of realities to meditate on chimeras. He neglects experience to feed on conjecture, to indulge in hypothesis. He dares not cultivate his reason, because from his earliest days he has been taught to consider it criminal. He pretends to know his fate in the indistinct abodes of another life, before he has considered of the means by which he is to render himself happy in the world he inhabits: in short, man disdains the study of Nature, except it be partially. . . .

The most important of our duties, then, is to seek means by which we may destroy delusions that can never do more than mislead us. The remedies for these evils must be sought for in Nature herself; it is only in the abundance of her resources, that we can rationally expect to find antidotes to the mischiefs brought upon us by an ill-directed, by an over-powering enthusiasm. It is time these remedies were sought; it is time to look the evil boldly in the face, to examine its foundations, to scrutinize its super-structure: reason, with its faithful guide experience, must attack in their entrenchments those prejudices to which the human race has but too long been the victim. For this purpose reason must be restored to its proper rank,—it must be rescued from the evil company with which it is associated. . . .

Truth speaks not to these perverse beings [the enemies of the human race]:—her voice can only be heard by generous minds accustomed to reflection, whose sensibilities make them lament the numberless calamities showered on the earth by political and religious tyranny—whose enlightened minds contemplate with horrour the immensity, the ponderosity of that series of misfortunes with which errour has in all ages overwhelmed mankind. . . .

Of Nature

. . . The *civilized man*, is he whom experience and social life have enabled to draw from nature the means of his own happiness; because he has learned to oppose resistance to those impulses he receives from exterior beings, when experience has taught him they would be injurious to his welfare.

The *enlightened man*, is man in his maturity, in his perfection; who is capable of pursuing his own happiness; because he has learned to examine, to

32. **Ariadne:** a daughter of the King of Crete who fell in love with Theseus, an Athenian hero and one of the youths sent by Athens to be offered to the Minotaur. Ariadne gave Theseus a ball of thread, which he unwound as he penetrated the labyrinth and there killed the Minotaur. He then followed the thread back out of the labyrinth.

think for himself, and not to take that for truth upon the authority of others, which experience has taught him examination will frequently prove erroneous. . . .

It necessarily results, that man in his researches ought always to fall back on experience, and natural philosophy: These are what he should consult in his religion—in his morals—in his legislation—in his political government—in the arts—in the sciences—in his pleasures—in his misfortunes. Experience teaches that Nature acts by simple, uniform, and invariable laws. It is by his senses man is bound to this universal Nature; it is by his senses he must penetrate her secrets; it is from his senses he must draw experience of her laws. Whenever, therefore, he either fails to acquire experience or quits its path, he stumbles into an abyss, his imagination leads him astray. . . .

Man did not understand that Nature, equal in her distributions, entirely destitute of goodness or malice, follows only necessary and immutable laws, when she either produces beings or destroys them, when she causes those to suffer, whose organization creates sensibility; when she scatters among them good and evil; when she subjects them to incessant change—he did not perceive it was in the bosom of Nature herself, that it was in her abundance he ought to seek to satisfy his wants; for remedies against his pains; for the means of rendering himself happy: he expected to derive these benefits from imaginary beings, whom he erroneously imagined to be the authors of his pleasures, the cause of his misfortunes. From hence it is clear that to his ignorance of Nature, man owes the creation of those illusive powers under which he has so long trembled with fear; that superstitious worship, which has been the source of all his misery. . . .

The universe, that vast assemblage of every thing that exists, presents only matter and motion: the whole offers to our contemplation nothing but an immense, an uninterrupted succession of causes and effects; some of these causes are known to us, because they strike immediately on our senses; others are unknown to us, because they act upon us by effects, frequently very remote from their original cause. . . .

Of Motion and Its Origin

. . . Observation and reflection ought to convince us, that every thing in Nature is in continual motion. . . . Thus, the idea of Nature necessarily includes that of motion. But, it will be asked, from whence did she receive her motion? Our reply is, from herself, since she is the great whole, out of which, consequently, nothing can exist. . . .

If they [natural philosophers] had viewed Nature uninfluenced by prejudice, they must have been long since convinced, that matter acts by its own peculiar energy, and needs not any exterior impulse to set it in motion. They would have perceived, that whenever mixed bodies were placed in a capacity to act on each other, motion was instantly engendered, and that these mixtures acted with a force capable of producing the most surprising effects. If

[89]

Chapter 3
The Mind of an
Age: Science
and Religion
Confront
Eighteenth-
Century
Natural Disaster

filings of iron, sulphur and water be mixed together, these bodies thus capacitated to act on each other, are heated by degrees, and ultimately produce a violent combustion. If flour be wetted with water, and the mixture closed up, it will be found, after some little lapse of time, by the aid of a microscope, to have produced organized beings that enjoy life, of which the water and the flour were believed incapable: it is thus that inanimate matter can pass into life, or animate matter, which is in itself only an assemblage of motion. Reasoning from analogy, the production of a man, independent of the ordinary means, would not be more marvellous than that of an insect with flour and water. . . .

Those who admit a cause exterior to matter, are obliged to suppose, that this cause produced all the motion by which matter is agitated in giving it existence. This supposition rests on another, namely, that matter could begin to exist; a hypothesis that, until this moment, has never been demonstrated by any thing like solid proof. To produce from nothing, or the *Creation*, is a term that cannot give us the most slender idea of the formation of the universe; it presents no sense, upon which the mind can fasten itself.

Motion becomes still more obscure, when creation, or the formation of matter, is attributed to a *spiritual* being, that is to say, to a being which has no analogy, no point of contact, with it; to a being which has neither extent, nor parts, and cannot, therefore, be susceptible of motion, as we understand the term; this being only the change of one body relatively to another body, in which the body moved, presents successively different parts to different points of space. Moreover, as all the world are nearly agreed that matter can never be totally annihilated, or cease to exist, how can we understand, that that which cannot cease to be, could ever have had a beginning?

If, therefore, it be asked, whence came matter? it is a very reasonable reply to say, it has always existed. . . .

Let us, therefore, content ourselves with saying *that* which is supported by our experience, and by all the evidence we are capable of understanding; against the truth of which, not a shadow of proof such as our reason can admit, has ever been adduced; which has been maintained by philosophers in every age; which theologians themselves have not denied, but which many of them have upheld; namely, that *matter always existed; that it moves by virtue of its essence; that all the phenomena of Nature is ascribable to the diversified motion of the variety of matter she contains; and which, like the phenix,*[33] *is continually regenerating out of her own ashes.*

33. **phenix:** the common modern spelling is "phoenix." In Egyptian mythology, the phoenix was a large bird with a life span of 500 to 600 years, living in the Arabian desert. At the end of its life the phoenix was consumed in fire, and from its ashes a new phoenix arose.

QUESTIONS TO CONSIDER

The selections that you have read allow you to trace one of the major issues raised by the *philosophes* as they sought to use the discoveries of the Scientific Revolution to comprehend the physical world more completely. Your consideration of this issue—the relationship of God to the physical world—should give you some clear understanding of the thought of the *philosophes* and its implications.

Consider first the traditional views expressed by Catholic and Protestant theologians. What caused the Lisbon earthquake, according to Malagrida? Did he foresee further disaster overtaking the city? Can you find in his pamphlet possible remedies for the city's misery from which Lisbon residents might have derived comfort? Contrast Malagrida's view of the plight of Lisbon with that of John Wesley, bearing in mind, of course, the latter's Protestantism. To what cause did Wesley ascribe the earthquake? Did he see any way to avoid such disasters? Despite their obvious differences, do you find any similarity in outlook in Malagrida and Wesley?

Now move on to Enlightenment sources, which are arranged to permit you to trace the development of the *philosophes'* responses to the disaster and the implications of their thought. Voltaire's distillation of Newton's physics in Source 3 is fundamental to understanding the Enlightenment because Newton's work provided the basis for the *philosophes'* understanding of the world in which

they lived. Through what method did Newton propose to understand the physical world? What relationships did he find governing the physical world? In what way did Newton's ideas provide a governing theory to explain much of that physical world? Why might you expect those influenced by Newton to describe the physical world as a machine?

Source 4, Alexander Pope's "An Essay on Man," represents an early-eighteenth-century attempt to balance a belief in God with the new scientific discoveries of Newton and others. How does Pope reflect traditional religion? What elements of sixteenth- and seventeenth-century scientific thought do you find in Pope? Most important, what role does God play in the world, according to Pope? What effect does that divine role have on humankind?

Reconsider the entry on "Observation" from the *Encyclopedia.* What view of reason does the article offer to its readers? How does Buffon attempt to apply this vision in his discussion of earthquakes? What sort of causal pattern does he find for earthquakes? Despite his explanation of earthquakes, which is recognized today as incorrect, is there any room for a divine role in Buffon's explanation of these disasters? Whose view do you identify with more closely, Buffon's or Malagrida's?

Voltaire's "Poem on the Lisbon Disaster" is the reaction of the Enlightenment's most celebrated thinker to the earthquake. Contrast it with the account he had written earlier of Newton's science. How had Voltaire's

Chapter 3

The Mind of an

Age: Science

and Religion

Confront

Eighteenth-

Century

Natural Disaster

point of view changed during this interval? How does Voltaire respond to the views of his friend Alexander Pope? What response does he have to the theological explanation of the quake? Do you detect a growing skepticism in the thought of the older Voltaire? If so, in what ways? What response to Voltaire does Jean-Jacques Rousseau make in his letter? What similarities in thinking with earlier selections do you find in Rousseau?

Next examine Source 9, the selection by David Hume. Compare Voltaire's skepticism about a divine role in the world with the position Hume takes in "The Essay on Miracles." Also contrast Hume with Rousseau; how might intellectual differences have helped to cause their break? Where had Enlightenment skepticism, evident in Voltaire's later thought, led Hume? What religious implications of the Enlightenment's search to apply human reason to all issues do

you find in Hume's work? Is any room left here for a divine role in the natural order? Trace this tendency in the thought of Baron d'Holbach, whose ideas shocked even some *philosophes*. Where have the principles of the Enlightenment led in Holbach's *System of Nature*? As we noted earlier, some of Holbach's contemporaries called him an atheist. How else might you describe his thought?

Your answers as you carefully consider these questions should provide you with the basis for responding to the main questions in this chapter: Why did the Lisbon earthquake pose such an intellectual crisis for eighteenth-century thinkers? How did theologians explain the disaster? How did Enlightenment thinkers explain it? In what direction was their thought on the physical world and its relationship to divine forces leading them?

EPILOGUE

The difference in outlook between Malagrida and Wesley on the one hand and the older and skeptical Voltaire and Baron d'Holbach on the other is immense, and it represents a long intellectual journey for eighteenth-century thinkers. The culmination of this journey represented the success of the Scientific Revolution in modeling for the Western mind a method of searching for reasonable, scientific explanations of natural phenomena as well as imparting its faith in human ability to find these answers.

The Enlightenment, however, meant much more than even this. The implications of a movement that ultimately was unprepared, as we have seen, to accept traditional religion were tremendous beyond the fields of theology and natural science. Enlightenment skepticism in matters religious is controversial even to the present day. Its search for reasonable and comprehensible natural laws to govern all aspects of the human experience helped to change the Western world. Though a new and grander Lisbon arose out of the old city's ruins, much else did not long survive the intellectual crisis of mid-century that earthquake embodied. The *philosophes'* search failed to uncover rational, natural laws to justify many human institutions of the eighteenth century. As a result, they called for sweeping changes of such existing institutions as divine right monarchy (see Chapter 2). In his *Social Contract*, for example, Rousseau argued for a new governing principle in which the general will of the people should govern. In the criminal justice practiced by governments of the day, the *philosophes* found a brutal system in which courts might employ torture to force defendants to testify against themselves and in which capital punishment was common. Many *philosophes* argued against the barbarism of such a system. In the work of the Italian thinker Cesare Bonesana, Marchese di Beccaria (1738–1794), the Enlightenment produced a strong statement against the death penalty and in favor of punishments based on prison terms graduated to fit the offense.

In religious matters, *philosophes* everywhere found an intolerance that to them seemed irrational, and Voltaire led their call for toleration and freedom of thought. Not even economic affairs escaped the attention of the *philosophes*. Eighteenth-century economic life was still dominated by guilds that set prices and government mercantilist policies that regulated trade. Adam Smith (1723–1790), a Scottish economist, led many Enlightenment thinkers in calling for a free economy. Let the natural laws of the economy work unimpeded and unregulated and the needs of all would be met, they argued. Everywhere the *philosophes* looked, they saw the need

for reform. The existence today in the modern West of much of what they called for testifies to the wide-ranging influence of their thought.

A further casualty of the earthquake in Portugal was the Society of Jesus, one of the great opponents of much of Enlightenment thought. The Society fell victim to the Marquis of Pombal, chief minister of Portugal's weak-willed monarch, Joseph I, and the man who led the relief and rebuilding efforts in the devastated city. The Portuguese version of that eighteenth-century phenomenon described in your text as the "enlightened despot," Pombal wielded more and more royal power even though he never wore the crown.

Like a number of enlightened despots, including Frederick the Great of Prussia and Joseph II of Austria, Pombal had a vision of a government that was first of all absolute in power and only secondarily reforming in its policies. He found the great power of the Catholic church in Portugal a formidable obstacle to his hopes of building the secular strength of the state. Armed with greater prestige after the earthquake, Pombal attacked the greatest bastion of clerical power, the Society of Jesus, and expelled almost all of Portugal's Jesuits on September 1, 1759. In 1761 he ordered the execution of Gabriel Malagrida, the Society's most visible Portuguese spokesman. Malagrida's ideas stood in the way of reconstruction because he preached a need for spiritual regeneration and focused people's attentions on the next life. Pombal, in contrast, required all of Portugal's energies for rebuilding in the here and now. Other Catholic

Chapter 3

The Mind of an

Age: Science

and Religion

Confront

Eighteenth-

Century

Natural Disaster

countries duplicated the Portuguese expulsion of the Jesuits. Local political or theological issues were often at the root of such expulsions, but they resulted in the worldwide abolition of the Society of Jesus from 1773 to 1814.[34]

The postearthquake Western world, thanks to the natural forces of the Lisbon disaster and the intellectual forces of the Enlightenment, would be considerably transformed on a number of levels. The fruits of Enlightenment thought are still with us in many forms.

34. On the French experience, see Dale Van Kley, *The Jansenists and the Expulsion of the Jesuits from France* (New Haven: Yale University Press, 1974).

CHAPTER FOUR

A STATISTICAL VIEW

OF EUROPEAN RURAL LIFE,

1600–1800

Chapter 3 gave us a glimpse into the intellectual currents circulating among the educated upper classes of eighteenth-century Europe. Such groups have left historians ample evidence of their intellectual milieu in the works of figures like Voltaire, as well as copious records of their lives and activities in correspondence, autobiographies, and other written sources. As a consequence, historians have been able to describe in great detail both the thought and the daily routine of Europe's opinion molders and governing classes. No matter how much influence these groups wielded, however, ultimately they represented only a small minority of the total population of their countries.

Most Europeans in the seventeenth and eighteenth centuries were illiterate or barely literate, and they left none of the conventional written records that have long provided historians their raw material for reconstructing the world of the privileged classes. Moreover, the majority of the population was rural, earning its living from the land, far from London, Paris, Venice, Vienna, and the other great urban centers that traditionally have attracted the research efforts of historians. Consequently we know a great deal about Voltaire as a member of the European elite, for example, but very little about the many peasants who worked his estate at Ferney—or about any other peasants, for that matter.

Only relatively recently have historians developed the methodological skills to penetrate the world of the majority of early modern Europe, the nonelites who left no written records of their own. Twentieth-century French scholars led the way in research in this area, and consequently the largest body of materials now available is devoted to France. Here two groups of French scholars have advanced our knowledge. One school, associated with the historical journal *Annales: Economies, sociétés, civilisations,*

Chapter 4

A Statistical

View of

European

Rural Life,

1600–1800

attempts to write "total history." Their search to understand the entirety of human existence, not just the actions of generals and kings and the thought of the great philosophers, has led them into many interesting lines of research, including studies of climatic changes and of literacy.[1] Because the ability to read and write largely defines the relationships an individual or a group forms with the wider world, the presence or absence of literacy is a fundamental issue in studying historic populations. Based on the frequency with which persons were able to sign their names to such documents as marital registers and court records, these historians have reconstructed the literacy pattern of western Europe during the seventeenth and eighteenth centuries. A more literate north and a less literate south characterized western Europe at this time, a regional difference that can be attributed partially to religious factors: northern European countries like England and Sweden were Protestant and emphasized individual reading of the Bible as an integral part of religious practice. Throughout Europe, a direct relationship existed between the ability to read and write on the one hand and personal wealth and social class on the other.

A second school of French researchers has focused attention on historical demography, that is, the historical study of population.[2] Because the existence of regular census data on populations is largely a nineteenth-century development, these historians have reconstructed the past by means of other data, as you will see.

English and other historians followed the French lead, with the result that our knowledge of Europe's unlettered majority has grown immensely over the past five decades. Whatever their nationalities, however, historians examining Europe's ill-educated majority have adopted a common approach in reconstructing the past. Because there is little information about any given seventeenth- or eighteenth-century individual, historians have employed the technique of *collective biography*: They attempt to reconstruct the life of a community or social group and often express the results of their studies statistically.

The picture that emerges from these statistical studies is one of deep poverty for Europe's farming majority, a poverty that left them utterly at the mercy of nature. This is how the French demographic historian, Pierre Goubert, draws on his many years of study to describe the lifestyle of poorer French peasants in the late seventeenth century:

> The humble day-labourer, with a garden, a plot of land, a couple of sheep, working seasonally for other people, spinning or woodworking at home, would live in the classic cottage, the *chaumine enfumée* (smoky cottage) spec-

---

1. The journal *Annales* espoused this approach to history from its founding in 1929 by the French historians Marc Bloch and Lucien Febvre. The influence of this approach to historical study grew immensely after World War II.

2. Historical demography is also a relatively new field of study. The major early works of the French pioneers in the field date only from the 1950s.

ified by La Fontaine,[3] and these would certainly have been the commonest dwellings in France at that time. Made of stone or daub, depending on the region, but always with a solid chimney, stone surrounds for door and windows, it would be built around a simple frame of local wood, and roofed with reeds, rye straw, heather, or fern, topped with some large stones to protect the thatch from the wind. Inside there would be a single room, square or elongated (sometimes with a stable at one end). Beneath its occupants' bare feet (they put clogs on to go out) would be a floor of trodden earth, sometimes strewn with reeds or branches, all pretty well soaked with rain, damp from the walls, and chicken urine and droppings. The "hearth," the heart of the house, usually had a hook and a pot; there they warmed themselves, when the door was not open to make the chimney draw. Wind, rain, small animals, and every sort of parasite—creeping, scratching, jumping—came in all the time. Apart from cold (which they could protect themselves from by means of old cloaks, flea-ridden blan-

kets, and *poches* [sacks]), their chief enemy was *arsin*, fire.[4]

The methodology that allows historians to portray the details of a vanished way of life in this manner consists of two basic operations: first compiling the statistical data and then analyzing them, that is, asking the right questions of the figures. The goal is to understand the life of the rural farming poor, to learn if any change in that life occurred over time, and to attempt to explain changes through other sets of data. Your objective in this chapter is to ask and respond to the kinds of questions of statistical data that historians pose to understand better the lifestyle of Europe's majority from 1600 to 1800. What were the natural forces that affected these people? How can we measure the effects of these forces on Europe's farming population? Can we discern any changes that might have allowed Europe's illiterate, rural majority to escape the grip of these natural forces?

3. **Jean de La Fontaine** (1621–1695): a French poet and author of fables often describing rural life.

4. Pierre Goubert, *The French Peasantry in the Seventeenth Century,* trans. Ian Patterson (New York: Cambridge University Press, 1986), p. 37.

SOURCES AND METHOD

The evidence in this chapter assembles pictorial sources and a wide variety of the types of tables and graphs in which historians advance the statistical results of their research. Analyzing these materials jointly will allow you to understand more fully the lives led by seventeenth- and eighteenth-century Europeans.

Source 1 is a primary record of early modern agricultural methods. It is an illustration for a fifteenth-century book of hours, the Très Riches Heures du Duc de Berry. Illustrated by the Limbourg brothers, Flemish artists known for their attention to detail, the picture in Source 1 portrays agricultural activities for the month of March. Note, in particular, the cumbersome wheeled plow, used in much of northern Europe, whose

Chapter 4

A Statistical

View of

European

Rural Life,

1600–1800

design did not change for centuries. Typically constructed of wood, some early modern plows would have had an iron plowshare, but few plowed deeply. Deep plowing is essential for productive agriculture, both to cut off and bury surface vegetation like weeds and to loosen the soil in preparation of seeding. What sort of furrow does this peasant plowman seem to be making? What sort of expenditure of human and animal labor was required even to achieve these results? The plowman would have been followed by a sower, sowing seeds broadcast style, a highly inefficient and wasteful way to plant by our standards today. Indeed, many early modern farmers had little understanding of the basic principles of modern scientific farming; even by the eighteenth century, only educated and affluent landowners employed such techniques as crop rotation, fertilization of the soil, and selective livestock breeding. How productive do you think the peasant illustrated in Source 1 was?

Source 2 presents data on European agricultural productivity for the grains wheat, rye, and barley, the mainstays of the European diet during the period 1600–1800. The data are arranged by regions and expressed in terms of yield ratios. *Yield ratios* are a basic statistical tool employed by historians of agriculture; they give the number of bushels harvested from one bushel of seed. Thus, from 1600 to 1649 in Zone I, 1 bushel of grain seed produced 6.7 bushels at harvest. To put these data in perspective, you need to understand that modern farming methods on amply watered wheat fields in the U.S. Midwest produce yield ratios of at least

40:1 and often much higher. What do you conclude about the productivity of agriculture in the period that is the subject of this chapter? Which areas of Europe were most and least productive? Which areas showed the greatest advance toward a more productive farming? Given such an agriculture, why would you not be surprised to find the majority of the population occupied with farming?

Sources 3 and 4 present the dietary consequences of this primitive agriculture and also illustrate how the historian uses old sources and new scientific methods to reconstruct the past. Source 3 illustrates a meal in a Dutch peasant household in 1653. The poverty of the household, largely due to the unproductive agriculture of the age, is evident; there is not even a table on which to place the evening meal. The meal is quite characteristic of the diet of most early modern Europeans: It was largely based on cereals, and in this case the Dutch family is preparing to consume a gruel made by boiling oats or some other cereal with water or milk. Elsewhere, people of similar economic status consumed large quantities of bread, oatmeal, polenta (a cornmeal mush prepared in Italy), or *Kasha* (ground and roasted rye cooked like rice in Poland and Russia). Proteins from meat and other nutrients were deficient in such diets, as we will see in Source 4.

Source 4 is a "Nutritional Balance Sheet" drawn from the records of a notary in the Gévaudan region of southern France in the eighteenth century. Notaries were legal specialists, found even in the most isolated villages of France, who dealt with property matters. They drafted wills, inventories of the property of deceased persons, and marital agreements that specified property arrangements. Most important for the historian, notaries kept their documents for many years, preserving them until they came to be housed in modern archives funded by the French government, which opened them as important sources for historians. From notarial records, historians can determine marital patterns and individual and collective wealth within a community.

The table in Source 4 is drawn from a particular kind of notarial concern. Often the notary recorded arrangements for the care of aged parents or a disabled sibling when, for example, an aging father transferred ownership of the family farm to his son. In order to avoid later conflict within the family, notarial documents often spelled out quite precisely what food the aging parent or sibling was to be provided with by the person taking control of the family property. The result is a kind of record, rarely found, that tells us what people ate. Each of the eleven entries on the table represents one family's arrangements for the feeding of one of its members.

In order to adequately interpret Source 4, you need to know something of human dietary needs, because the historian who assembled these data has interpreted food allotments in terms of their nutritional content. Most of the recipients of these food allotments were expected to work, and a daily food intake of about 2,400 calories is necessary to sustain moderate labor

(1,500 calories per day is necessary simply to sustain life). But modern nutritionists know that diet must also be analyzed to determine if it is sufficiently rich in certain energy-producing substances, and the historian who assembled the data in Source 4 has expressed the amount of those substances in each family's allotment in grams. Proteins supply the body with essential nitrogens and amino acids, and about one gram of protein per kilogram of body weight is necessary daily. Assume an average male weight of 65 kilograms (143 lbs.). Are there sufficient proteins in these diets? Ideally, too, 40 percent of daily proteins should be of animal origin. What is the source of most of the proteins in Source 4? What role does meat assume in these diets?

Lipids, or fats, are essential in maintaining body temperature, and about 40 grams daily are necessary. What do you find these diets provide in lipids? Combine this with your findings on proteins. What impact do you think such diets would have on an individual's ability to sustain physical labor in sometimes rigorous weather?

Glucides, or sugars, provide muscle energy, and an adult requires a minimum of 40 grams of these per day. What do the diets in Source 4 provide in sugars? Why do you find this the only source of energy provided in sufficient amount?

Various minerals also are essential to good nutrition. Minerals like calcium and phosphorus are necessary for skeletal development and sound teeth, and they must be present in the diet in certain proportions. Ideally, an

[99]

Chapter 4

A Statistical

View of

European

Rural Life,

1600–1800

adult's calcium consumption should be between 60 and 80 percent of his or her phosphorus consumption. Pregnant women and children require even more calcium. Consult Source 4 to determine whether the Gévaudan residents were getting sufficient calcium by simply dividing calcium consumption by phosphorus consumption. Why would you not be surprised to find calcium deficiency–related problems like poor teeth, bow legs, and scoliosis (abnormal curvature of the spine) in this population?

Now consider the diets as a group. What foods do you find missing? What food type, based on the calories it represents in daily consumption, seems to dominate the diet of the peasant farmers who consumed these rations? What do you think the health consequences of such a diet, more or less generalized in this population, would have been?

We must understand, too, that the diet presented in Source 4 represents the ideal, not the norm. Weather factors often affected European farming, resulting in diminished agricultural yields. Insufficient or excessive rainfall, abnormally low temperatures, and other climatological phenomena all influenced the harvest. The graphs in Source 5 represent some of the most interesting research of modern historians—the study of weather and its consequences. The work of such historians is showing the climatic differences that have affected the West over the last millennium. The diagrams in Source 5 illustrate the impact of weather changes over the period 1699–1789. These diagrams are de-

signed to be read together. Diagram 1 presents temperature data for England in the eighteenth century as evidence of general European temperature trends. Note that the scale of temperatures on this diagram has been inverted so that the temperature graph goes up for colder temperatures and down for higher ones. This has been done to allow you to correlate increases in food prices with abnormally low temperatures more readily. In what years do the data in Diagram 1 show abnormally cool spring and summer temperatures? What effect would such temperatures have had on agricultural products such as grapes and wheat? Diagram 2 presents the effects of temperature trends by showing simultaneously the dates of grape harvests and the advance of glaciers in the Alps. An especially extended period of glacial advance indicates a period of cool weather, as does an unusually late grape harvest. Diagram 3 draws on the data that the French government (like other early modern European governments) kept on the price of food, the ultimate consequence of weather trends. How do seasonal temperatures correlate with wheat prices? In what years did weather adversely affect agriculture and drive up prices?

The data presented in Source 6 may seem abstract to twenty-first-century readers, who, after all, live in a society in which social welfare agencies prevent actual starvation among the poor despite price increases for dietary essentials. We must remember that such agencies are relatively recent additions to Western life; two centuries ago they did not exist. The graph in Source 6 presents the consequences of periodic food price increases for a French wagoner. You should understand that the graph assigns a value of 100 to wages and prices in the period 1726–1735, establishing that period as the base "index" for the graph. An index of 155 for the price of wheat in Arles in the late 1740s thus represents a 55 percent increase over wheat prices in the base period. What do you observe in long-term salary trends? What do you note about the long-term trends in the price of wheat, which was essential in making bread, the dietary staple of the poor? What sorts of conditions did the wagoners of Basse-Provence experience in the 1730s, the late 1740s, and especially from the 1760s into the late 1780s?

Poverty and dietary insufficiencies breed a multitude of maladies. The living conditions of the majority of Europeans especially endangered their health. Source 7 is a photograph of a museum's reconstruction of a peasant residence in the South Tyrol region of Austria. It is typical of many early modern peasant dwellings in several ways. Most notably, many humans shared their residences with livestock, including animals of some size, like cows and sheep. While such large animals added their body warmth to the residence in winter, the excreta of such beasts, and the insects that infested them, certainly posed health risks for humans. In the kitchen area illustrated in Source 7, notice the earthen floor and the chicken coop on the left, the top of which serves as a counter. Note, too, that this kitchen lacks even a fireplace

with a chimney to draw out the smoke of the cooking fire that has blackened the wall in the room's right corner. The smoke, instead, slowly exited through an opening in the roof. What do you think were the health implications of such living conditions? If you combine such conditions with the poor diet of the age, what sort of health was probably the lot of many early modern Europeans?

Many epidemic diseases struck even well-fed populations. None of these was more feared in medieval and early modern Europe than the bubonic plague. Physicians knew no cure for this fatal disease, which had ravaged Europe since its first appearance there in the fourteenth century. By the eighteenth century, Europeans at least understood somewhat the importance of quarantining districts afflicted by the plague as a means of stemming its spread. The table in Source 8 represents plague mortalities in southern France in 1720–1721 as the disease spread. Plague broke out first in the large port of Marseilles and spread to much of the surrounding region, grievously afflicting some towns and not others. Quarantines restricted the disease to the southern part of France, and the Marseilles epidemic was the last great outbreak of the plague in the modern West to date. In what towns did the greatest portion of the population die? What impact would such losses have had on the towns?

Disease was common in early modern Europe, as were famine conditions. When disease coincided with agricultural failure, the result could be what historians call a *demographic*

[101]

Chapter 4

A Statistical

View of

European

Rural Life,

1600–1800

or *population crisis,* a period in which deaths exceed births and the population declines. Information on such crises in the population history of Europe has been amassed laboriously by historians, using records left by the literate members of early modern society about the largely illiterate majority. Priests, for example, kept parish registers of baptisms, marriages, and burials, which, in the hands of skilled historical demographers, permit the scholarly reconstitution of the history of past populations. Sources 9 through 14 are assembled to reflect the combined effects of the agricultural cycle and disease on population.

Inadequate means of transportation often affected the condition of the population in early modern Europe. An area experiencing poor harvests might confront outright starvation simply because of the impossibility of moving food supplies to it from prosperous neighboring areas. Source 9 presents demographic data from Bresles-en-Beauvaisis, a town in northern France, for the seventeenth and early eighteenth centuries. Compare the graphs of food prices and of births and burials. In what years were food prices high? In what years did burials exceed births? What do you think caused the excessive burials? How often, over the period 1655–1745, did burials exceed births? Do you think this population grew much in this period?

Our data thus far suggest that a very high death rate affected early modern Europeans. But death did not claim all equally. Examine Source 10, which presents data on infant and child mortality in several parts of

France. Approximately what percentage of eighteenth-century French children might hope to live to age ten?

Source 11 employs the statistical tool of average life expectancy to show living conditions in Colyton, England. Average life expectancy is a statistical construct in which the life spans of all persons born at a given point in time are averaged together. In deriving such averages, historians of population and public health specialists average the life spans of the infant dying within minutes or hours of birth and the old person who reaches the age of eighty or ninety. The resulting figure offers a perspective on how well a given society provides for the health and welfare of its members. For purposes of comparison, the average life expectancy in modern England in the 1980s was 70.2 years for males and 76.2 years for females, whereas in some impoverished Third World countries today life expectancy is roughly 43 years for both men and women.

The Colyton figures show average life expectancy for years of high, low, and average death rates. How do such life expectancies compare with those of modern England and the modern Third World? What role do you think infant mortality had in keeping average life expectancy low?

The lives of early modern Europeans clearly were affected by the fortunes of agriculture. But even in noncrisis years, the regular rhythm of the agricultural year ruled early modern rural Europeans' lives. The rural French experience was probably typical of Europe as a whole: The year opened with January and February, cold months when agricultural labor was light because of weather conditions. Food reserves, however, were beginning to shrink at this time, and farmers often slaughtered pigs and other livestock because fodder for the animals was running low. By March, April, and May, the fruits of the previous autumn's harvests were dwindling for humans, too, as agricultural labor resumed with plowing and planting. Late May and June, after the crops were planted, might bring a slight respite from work. But late summer and early autumn brought the more taxing labor of the harvest. In these months, epidemics of disease and health problems resulting from the drinking of impure water and the eating of partially ripened fruits and vegetables, made necessary by summer shortages, affected the health of the rural population. Once the harvest was in, of course, winter's rigors resumed.

Source 12 presents the seasonal incidence of death in Morannes, France. How does the death rate reflect the impact of the agricultural year and climatic conditions on French people? Note that this graph distinguishes the deaths of the young from those of the old. When did children die? Why? In Sources 13 and 14, you find data on marriages and conceptions in rural France. To analyze the marriage data, you must remember that France is largely a Catholic country, and you should understand that the Church forbade marriages during Advent (the period in late November and December beginning on the fourth Sunday before Christmas on Decem-

ber 25) and Lent (the period, usually in March and early April, of the forty weekdays before Easter. Lent begins on Ash Wednesday). Bearing in mind these religious strictures and the agricultural cycle, determine when rural Frenchmen married and why they chose the months they did. Why would these months in the agricultural cycle be propitious times for wedding feasts? When did French rural couples conceive their children? How might the agricultural cycle affect reproduction?

Your task in this chapter is to reconstruct the lifestyle of Europe's majority using the statistical sets provided. Use the mode of analysis suggested in this section, taking care to do the following: (1) Study each data set, observing changes over time— for instance, increased agricultural productivity in some areas. (2) Once you have identified a change, seek an explanation in the other data sets. For example, what weather trends affected areas with improved agricultural output? How might they help to account for increased productivity? What role might diet have played? (3) Pose basic questions of your data. What trends were affecting the population?

Making use of this methodology, you should be able to answer the central questions of this chapter: What were the natural forces that affected these people? How can we measure the effects of these forces on Europe's farming population? Can we discern any changes that might have allowed Europe's illiterate, rural majority to escape the grip of these natural forces?

Chapter 4

A Statistical

View of

European

Rural Life,

1600–1800

THE EVIDENCE

Source 1 published in Georges Duby and Armand Wallon, eds., Historire de la France rurale, *vol. 2,* L'âge classique, 1340–1789 *by Hugues Neveux, Jean Jacquart, and Emmanuel Le Roy Ladurie (Paris: Éditions du Seuil, 1975), p. 184. Original picture source: Réunion des Musées Nationaux/Art Resource, NY.*

1. Spring Agricultural Labor, from a Fifteenth–Century French Book of Hours[5] of Jean, Duc de Berry[6]

Source 2 from E. E. Rich and C. H. Wilson, editors, The Cambridge Economic History of Europe, *vol. 5,* The Economic Organization of Early Modern Europe *(New York: Cambridge University Press, 1977), p. 81. Used by permission of Cambridge University Press.*

2. Combined Yield Ratios of Wheat, Rye, and Barley, 1600–1820

Period	Zone I[a]	Zone II[b]	Zone III[c]	Zone IV[d]
1600–1649	6.7:1	—	4.5:1	4.0:1
1650–1699	9.3	6.2:1	4.1	3.8
1700–1749	—	6.3	4.1	3.5
1750–1799	10.1	7.0	5.1	4.7
1800–1820	11.1	6.2	5.4	—

a. Zone I: England, Low Countries.
b. Zone II: France, Spain, Italy.
c. Zone III: Germany, Switzerland, Scandinavia.
d. Zone IV: Russia, Poland, Czechoslovakia, Hungary.

5. Books of hours were devotional works containing religious texts for each liturgical hour of the day, as well as other devotional matter, calendars, and sometimes illustrations.

6. Jean, Duc de Berry (d. 1416), the brother of King Charles V, was one of France's most prominent noblemen.

Source 3 published in Fernand Braudel, Civilization and Capitalism, 15th–18th Century, *vol. 1,* The Structures of Everyday Life, *translated by Siân Reynolds (New York: Harper and Row, 1979), p.138. Original picture source: engraving by A. Van Ostade in the Bibliothèque Nationale, Paris. Photograph: Bibliothèque Nationale.*

3. A Meal of Gruel in a Dutch Peasant Family, 1653

Chapter 4

A Statistical

View of

European

Rural Life,

1600–1800

Source 4 adapted from R.-J. Bernard, "Peasant Diet in Eighteenth-Century Gévaudan" in Robert and Elborg Forster, eds., European Diet from Pre-Industrial to Modern Times (New York: Harper and Row, 1975), p. 38. © École des Hautes Études en Sciences Sociales. Reprinted by permission.

4. A Nutritional Balance Sheet

	Protein (in grams)			Lipids (in grams)					Glucides (in grams)			Trace Elements (milligrams)			Calories	
	Bread	Cheese	Total	Bread	Butter	Cheese	Salt Lard	Total	Bread	Cheese	Total	Phosphorus	Calcium	Iron	Total	% from Bread
1.	45.93	1.64	47.57	5.74	4.99	1.76	10.14	22.63	287.01	0.02	287.03	1,070.62	386.26	17.26	1,576.07	89.80
2.	48.00	5.01	53.01	6.00	10.14	5.37	15.21	36.72	300.00	0.71	300.71	1,171.28	486.49	18.10	1,665.51	83.20
3.	67.19	4.17	71.36	8.40	12.49	4.47	30.43	55.79	420.00	0.59	420.59	1,521.65	609.79	26.15	2,359.04	82.10
4.	36.55	1.97	38.52	4.55	5.99	2.11	8.11	20.76	227.83	0.02	227.85	860.10	324.65	14.20	1,195.20	88.10
5.	36.77	1.97	38.74	4.59	5.99	2.11	5.99	18.68	279.87	0.02	279.89	863.85	325.90	14.34	1,386.00	80.25
6.	54.30	2.05	56.35	6.78	7.60	2.21	20.28	36.87	339.43	0.03	339.46	1,230.45	418.22	20.45	1,861.28	84.10
7.	61.44	1.97	63.41	7.68	5.99	2.11	12.17	27.95	384.00	0.02	384.02	1,418.70	510.85	23.09	1,955.60	90.81
8.	68.08	6.82	74.90	8.51	20.28	7.30	20.28	56.37	425.50	0.97	426.47	1,607.18	683.35	26.12	2,487.01	83.04
9.	63.36	1.97	65.33	6.33	10.14	2.11	20.28	38.86	396.04	0.02	396.06	1,052.79	389.12	17.86	2,163.69	86.92
10.	84.75	3.94	88.69	10.59	10.14	4.22	15.21	40.76	529.71	0.04	529.75	1,979.25	735.54	32.68	2,816.25	90.60
11.	61.43	2.50	63.93	7.67	7.60	2.68	15.21	33.16	383.96	0.04	384.00	1,438.39	527.66	23.71	1,998.75	93.70

Sources 5 and 6 adapted from Ernest Labrousse et al., Histoire économique et sociale de la France, vol. II, Des derniers temps de l'âge seigneurial aux préludes de l'âge industriel (1660–1789) (Paris: Presses Universitaires de la France, 1970), pp. 392, 537. Reprinted by permission.

5. Wheat Prices and Weather, France, 1699–1789

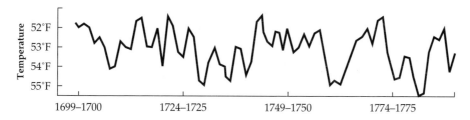

1. Spring and summer temperatures for England (two-year moving averages; temperature scale in Fahrenheit; graph of temperatures inverted for better comparison with the graph of grape harvests).

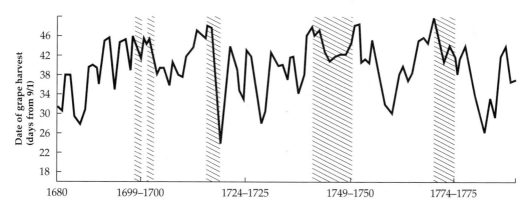

2. Dates of grape harvests (counted in days from September 1, in moving two-year averages); glacial maximums in the Alps shown in shading.

3. Price of wheat per *setier* of Paris in *livres tournois* (French currency of eighteenth century).

Chapter 4

A Statistical

View of

European

Rural Life,

1600–1800

6. Contrast Between Fixed Salary of a Typical Agricultural Worker and Price of Wheat in Basse-Provence, France, 1726–1789

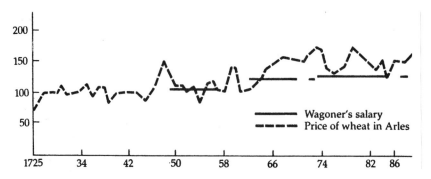

Source 7 published in Raffaella Sarti, Europe at Home: Family and Material Culture, 1500–1800 *(New Haven: Yale University Press, 2002). Original picture source: Sudtiroler Volkskunde Museum, Dietenheim/Teodone (Bolzano/Bozen).*

7. Peasant Kitchen with Open Fire in the South Tyrol

Source 8 from Jean-Noël Biraben, "Certain Demographic Characteristics of the Plague Epidemic in France, 1720–1722," Daedalus, *Spring 1968, pp. 541–542. Reprinted by permission.*

8. Epidemics: The Plague in Southern France, 1720–1721

Place	Approximate Preplague Population	Date of First Appearance of Plague	Number of Plague Deaths	Percentage of Population Killed
Marseilles and environs	90,000	20 June 1720	39,334	43.7
Vitrolles	770	2 August	210	27.3
Gignac	470	15 August	42	8.9
Septèmes	940	26 August	200	21.3
Gaubert	500	4 September	29	5.8
Nans	500	27 September	125	25.0
Auriol	3,200	3 October	1,319	41.2
Villars Brancas	300	9 October	12	4.0
Martigues	6,000	1 November	2,200	36.7
Arles	22,000	26 November	9,400	42.7
Orgon	1,700	29 December	105	6.2
La Valette	1,600	20 February 1721	1,068	64.3
Trinquetaille-les-Arles	1,157	11 June	80	6.9
St. Nazaire (Sanary)	1,200	1 July	51	4.2
La Roquebrussane	997	14 August	201	20.1

Chapter 4

A Statistical

View of

European

Rural Life,

1600–1800

Source 9 adapted from Pierre Goubert and Daniel Roche, Les français et l'Ancien Régime, *vol. I (Paris: Armand Colin, 1984), p. 45. Reprinted by permission.*

9. Local Crises at Bresles-en-Beauvaisis, France, Late 17th and Early 18th Centuries

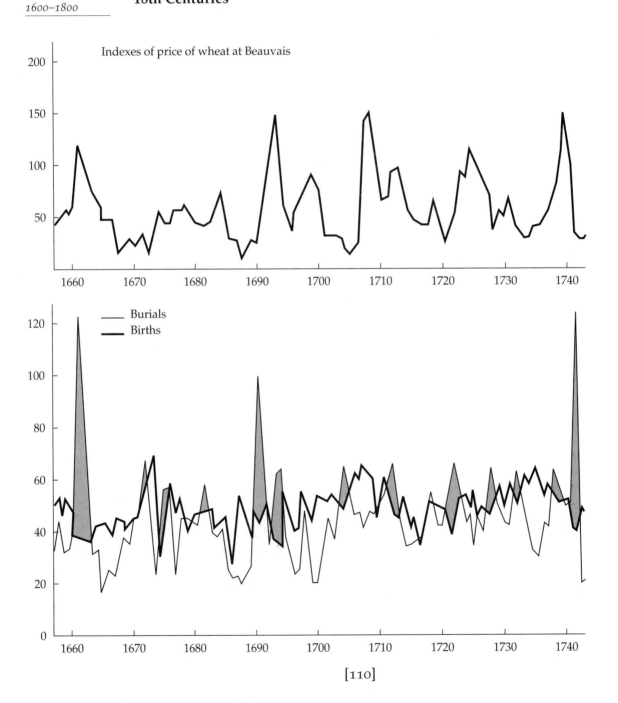

Indexes of price of wheat at Beauvais

Burials
Births

Source 10 from Pierre Goubert, "Legitimate Fecundity and Infant Mortality in France During the Eighteenth Century: A Comparison," Daedalus, *Spring 1968, pp. 599–600. Reprinted by permission.*

10. Infant and Child Mortality in France: Children Living to the Age of 10 Years

Brittany:

Saint-Aubin (1748–1789)	580 of 1,000
La Guerche (1720–1790)	510 of 1,000
Saint-Méen (1720–1792)	463 of 1,000

Elsewhere (Southwest and Normandy):

Thézels (1747–1782)	645 of 1,000
Azereix (18th century)	639 of 1,000
Crulai (1674–1742)	672 of 1,000

Source 11 from E. A. Wrigley, "Mortality in Pre-Industrial England: The Example of Colyton, Devon, Over Three Centuries," Daedalus, *Spring 1968, p. 574. Reprinted by permission.*

11. Life Expectancy in Colyton, England, in Years

Period	High Mortality	Low Mortality	Midpoint
1538–1624	40.6	45.8	43.2
1625–1699	34.9	38.9	36.9
1700–1774	38.4	45.1	41.8

Source 12 from François Lebrun, Les hommes et la morte en Anjou aux 17e et 18e siècles. Essai de démographie et de psychologie historiques *(Paris and The Hague: Mouton, 1971), p. 190. Copyright © École des Hautes Études en Science Sociales. Reprinted by permission of Éditions de l'École des Hautes Études et Sciences Sociales, Paris.*

12. Seasonal Incidence of Mortality in Morannes, France, 17th and 18th Centuries

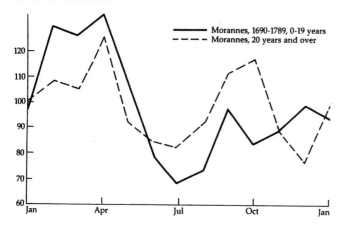

Chapter 4

A Statistical

View of

European

Rural Life,

1600–1800

Sources 13 and 14 from Pierre Guillaume and Jean-Pierre Poussou, Demographie historique *(Paris: Armand Colin, 1970), p. 184; p. 172. Used by permission of Armand Colin Editeur, Paris.*

13. Seasonal Incidence of Marriage in France, Showing the Three Most Common Months (1–3) and the Three Least Common Months (10–12), by Location

Parishes	Period of Observation	1	2	3	10	11	12
Thézels-Saint-Sernin (Lot)	1700–1792	Feb.	Nov.	June	Sept.	Aug.	Dec.
Castelnau-de-Montratier (Lot)	1716–1789	Feb.	Nov.	Jan.	Aug.	March	Dec.
La Rochelle, Saint-Barthélemy parish	1677–1685	Feb.	Jan.	July	April	March	Dec.
Chef-Boutonne (Deux-Sèvres)	1722–1792	Feb.	Jan.	Nov.	Aug.	March	Dec.
Avits (Tarn)	1692–1717	Feb.	June	Jan.	Aug.	March	Dec.
Lyon	1750–1774	Feb.	Jan.	Nov.	April	March	Dec.
Saint-Romain-d'Urfé (Loire)	1740–1749	Nov.	Feb.	Jan.	April	March	Dec.
Bonneuil-sur-Marne (Seine)	1680–1790	Nov.	Jan.	Feb.	Aug.	March	Dec.
Bagneux (Seine)	1691–1789	Feb.	Nov.	Jan.	April	Dec.	March
Paris	{ 1728–1737	Feb.	Nov.	Jan.	April	March	Dec.
	1778–1787	Feb.	Nov.	Jan.	Aug.	March	Dec.
Crulai (Orne)	1675–1798	Nov.	Feb.	Jan.	April	March	Dec.

14. Seasonal Incidence of Conceptions in France, Showing the Three Most Common Months (1–3) and the Three Least Common Months (10–12), by Location

Parishes	Period of Observation	1	2	3	10	11	12
Thézels-Saint-Sernin (Lot)	1700–1792	June	May	July	Oct.	March	Sept.
Castelnau-de-Montratier (Lot)	1716–1789	June	May	April	Aug.	Sept.	March
Divillac (Lot)	1671–1692	June	May	April	Aug.	March	Nov.
Ile de Ré, 8 parishes	1764–1773	June	Jan.	April	Aug.	Sept.	Oct.
La Rochelle, Saint-Barthélemy parish	1677–1685	Feb.	June	May	Oct.	Dec.	Sept.
Chef-Boutonne (Deux-Sèvres)	1722–1792	June	May	April	Aug.	Oct.	Sept.
Avits (Tarn)	1692–1717	June	Jan.	Nov.	Feb.	Sept.	Oct.
Saint-Romain-d'Urfé (Loire)	1740–1749	June	May	July	Oct.	Sept.	Nov.
Crulai (Orne)	1700–1799	June	May	April	Sept.	Nov.	Oct.

QUESTIONS TO CONSIDER

Each of the sources of evidence you considered in this chapter represents a piece of a puzzle that, when assembled, presents a picture of the life of the rural majority of seventeenth- and eighteenth-century Europe. Let us now begin to fit those pieces together.

Consider first what the various sources tell you about the health of seventeenth- and eighteenth-century Europeans in "average" times. How did the productivity of farming compare to that today? What sort of diet did it provide Europeans of those centuries? Why would you not be surprised to learn that modern scientists have found evidence that nutritionally based ailments like rickets abounded among these people and that historians have discovered that they were of much shorter stature than twentieth-century Europeans? What would you conclude about this population's resistance to disease?

Next you should determine the frequency with which a physically vulnerable population faced the physical stress of nonaverage times. Note in Source 8 how disastrous an epidemic could be in early modern times. Then recall the sanitary conditions described by Pierre Goubert earlier in this chapter. How common do you think diseases other than the plague must have been, given such sanitary conditions and the physical condition of the population? To arrive at a partial answer to this question, count the demographic crises at Bresles-en-Beauvaisis (Source 9) in the 1655–1745 period. How many times did burials exceed births in this period? How often, on the average, did crises combining disease and food shortage recur? To generalize from the French case, reflect how much more productive agriculture in the French zone of Europe was than that in some other parts of the Continent. What groups in society, based on the evidence in Sources 10 through 12, were most vulnerable to disease and poor nutrition?

You should also consider the effect that climate and agricultural life had on those who survived the threats to life in seventeenth- and eighteenth-century Europe. How did the cycle of agriculture affect such basic events of human life as marriage and reproduction?

You also ought to consider the cultural ramifications of the material life we have examined in this chapter. How do you think an illiterate population, cut off by poor transportation from outside assistance in time of famine and also isolated from more sophisticated ideas originating in cities, explained the disasters that overtook it periodically? Why would you not be surprised to find in other historical sources a high level of superstition among Europe's peasant population and a persistence of beliefs in the existence of witches, who were thought to bring evil upon their neighbors? What chance did scientific farming methods have to influence the agricultural methods of a widely illiterate European population? If farm productivity could have been improved, what sort of effects do you think western Europe would have experienced?

Chapter 4

A Statistical

View of

European

Rural Life,

1600–1800

As you formulate answers to these questions that transcend the lessons of the individual pieces of evidence and lead you to general conclusions, you should be on the way to putting together the puzzle. As you do so, you should be able to answer the main questions of this chapter. What were the natural forces that affected the majority of seventeenth- and eighteenth-century Europeans? How can we measure the effects of these forces on Europe's farming population? Can we discern any changes that might have allowed Europe's illiterate, rural majority to escape the grip of these natural forces?

EPILOGUE

The world we have sketched here was, until the late eighteenth century, one of limited literacy, poverty, and precarious existence, characterized by a stagnant or slowly growing population. Educational levels improved slowly in the late eighteenth century and more rapidly along with the spread of public education in the nineteenth century. But the biggest change was the transformation of the demographic system of western Europe.

After a century and a half of little growth, Europe's population rapidly expanded after about 1750. The population in England and Wales increased more than fivefold between 1750 and 1900, and that of France almost doubled in the same period. Other countries experienced similar dramatic population increases.

This population explosion was primarily the result of a reduced mortality rate. In particular, losses of life to famine and disease decreased. Famines declined in frequency and severity for several reasons. Some western European farmers applied more scientific techniques to improve their output, first in England and Holland but later elsewhere. New crops of American origin, like corn and the potato, were introduced to European agriculture. Yielding more food per acre than wheat and often cultivable on marginal lands unsuited for that grain, these crops also increased the food supply. All these developments were part of a phenomenon that many textbooks call the Agricultural Revolution, a process that greatly reduced the numbers of deaths from starvation or the effects of malnutrition.

Deaths from diseases also diminished in the eighteenth century, when physicians began inoculation for smallpox and more effective quarantining of infectious diseases. As a result of the more bountiful and reliable food supply and reduced mortality from disease, the population swelled.

A second transformation of society, the Industrial Revolution, also dramatically altered the lifestyle we examined in this chapter. Beginning in the late eighteenth century in England and later elsewhere in Europe, the Industrial Revolution drew increasing numbers of people away from agriculture to employment in factories and residence in the cities that grew up around the new plants (see Chapters 6 and 8). The Agricultural Revolution aided this process by creating harvests so productive that a farming minority of the population could feed an urbanized majority employed in manufacturing and service industries. The result was an increasingly urbanized Europe.

The Industrial Revolution also helped to destroy the demographic system we explored in this chapter. Improved transportation, like the railroads made possible by the modern steel industry, permitted food products to be moved rapidly to areas in need of them, eliminating local famines. Some historians argue that at least in England, the Industrial Revolution may also have helped to increase the birth rate. Because marriage has always depended on the existence of the financial means to establish a new household, industrialization may have created the wealth necessary to allow more women than ever before to marry and to have children.

A variety of factors thus combined in the nineteenth and early twentieth centuries to alter beyond recognition the rural world we have explored. Its isolation bred of illiteracy, its poverty rooted in an unproductive agriculture, and its high mortality now represent a lifestyle foreign to modern Europe, a Western society preserved only in museums and history books.

CHAPTER FIVE

A DAY IN

THE FRENCH REVOLUTION:

JULY 14, 1789

Tuesday, July 14, 1789, dawned cool and cloudy in Paris. Leaden skies threatening heavy rainfall cast little light into the narrow, crowded streets of the capital. But the rain held off until evening, thereby providing the opportunity for events to occur in the city's streets and squares that set off a fundamental change in the political history of France and the West as a whole. When rain finally fell, sending Parisians scurrying home, the forces of King Louis XVI had lost control of the capital, and, in hindsight, the principle of royal absolutism was clearly in decline.

On that Tuesday, the people of Paris seized the great fortress and prison on the city's eastern edge known as the Bastille. Construction of the Bastille had begun in 1370 as part of the eastern defenses of Paris. The fortress had eight towers, set in walls about 80 feet high and 10 feet thick. Its only entrance was by two drawbridges across a moat that was dry in 1789; by

that date the Bastille had been obsolete as a fort for several centuries. Developments in modern artillery had rendered its walls vulnerable, and the growth of Paris meant that the Bastille was no longer on the city's periphery, but instead was surrounded by the streets of the suburb known as the Faubourg Saint-Antoine.

As early as the fifteenth century, the monarchy had confined prisoners in the Bastille, but the systematic use of the old fort as a prison began during the ministry of Cardinal Richelieu in the early seventeenth century. The Bastille confined persons whose offenses were not punishable under the regular criminal laws of France, and received political prisoners held without trial under royal orders known as *lettres de cachet*. Religious dissenters joined the prison's inmates during the reign of Louis XV (1715–1774). The nature of this prison made it a symbol of despotism in the eighteenth century, but such notoriety was little warranted by 1789. Although the Bastille had a capacity for forty-two prisoners in cells, with room for additional inmates in a dungeon that had been unused for twenty years, it held only seven prisoners on July 14, 1789. These seven—four forgers, two noblemen locked away at the behest of their families for immoral behavior, and one murder suspect—hardly seemed victims of royal injustice. Indeed, the monarchy was considering plans to demolish this outdated structure when the Paris crowd captured it.

The origins of the crowd's storming of the Bastille, the first—but not the last—mass action of its kind in Paris during the Revolution, may be found in a political and economic crisis that had kept France in turmoil during the preceding thirty months. As a consequence of the costly wars of the eighteenth century and a system of taxation that largely exempted the clergy and nobility from fiscal obligations, the French monarchy faced bankruptcy by 1787.[1] Several finance ministers struggled with the crown's fiscal problems, but all eventually arrived at the same solution: fundamental financial reform that would tax the Church and the nobility, not simply the commoners. In proposing such changes, however, the royal ministers encountered constitutional problems. The proposed reforms violated traditional rights of the clergy and nobility, and the king was forced to call for the meeting of a French representative body—the Estates General, which had not met since 1614—to consider reform.[2]

The election campaign for the Estates General stirred up the country, creating expectations of change. Election regulations enfranchised almost all male taxpayers, and these voters did not select a legislature prepared simply to approve tax reform and go home. Some representatives of the clergy and nobility resisted any change. More seriously, the monarchy confronted the defiant members of the Third Estate, representing the commoners, who demanded tax reform and greater political equality.[3] They declared themselves a National Assembly, the rightful representatives of the French people, and then, on June 20, 1789, in their Tennis Court oath, called for a constitution to limit royal power. This defiance of royal authority really had been the first act of revolution.

The king vacillated at first in the face of such defiance but then resolved on two steps. On June 22, 1789, he signed orders for the movement of troops into the region of Paris and Versailles to regain control of events. Those assigned were largely foreign soldiers (Swiss and German regiments especially) in French service, who presumably

1. France's successful intervention in the American War of Independence played no small part in this situation. The American war cost France 2 billion livres, a figure about four times the government's tax receipts in 1788. By that year, interest payments on the government's debts consumed 51 percent of its receipts.

2. Royal failure to call the Estates General was deliberate; the body was an obstacle to royal absolutism.

3. Representatives of the clergy constituted the First Estate of the Estates General; representatives of the nobility made up the Second Estate of what had been traditionally a three-house legislature. In 1789 the king required this traditional style of meeting, which gave great voice to the small minority of the population who were clerics and nobles.

would be more willing to use force on civilians than would French soldiers. Such troop movements, however, could not be kept secret. There was growing fear in Versailles and Paris of a royal coup in early July directed against the defiant National Assembly and its supporters in the capital.

The king's second step was the dismissal of Jacques Necker as royal finance minister on July 11, 1789. Popular opinion regarded Necker as a liberal financial genius whose skills kept the government solvent, stabilized financial markets, and kept Paris supplied with food. But he and the ministers associated with him were replaced with officials more fully committed to Louis's impending use of force to reestablish royal authority.

Political events of the preceding months and a rapid rise in bread prices caused by recent bad harvests had heightened tension in Paris even before the king reached this decision. The concurrence of political and economic unrest already had led to large-scale rioting on April 27–28, 1789, when rumors spread that a wallpaper manufacturer, Reveillon, had advocated reduction of workers' wages.[4] Troops had been needed to restore order in the capital in April. News of Necker's firing reached Paris about 9:00 A.M. on July 12, a Sunday, when the population's release from normal weekday duties favored the spread of rumor and political agitation. One of the agitators, the demagogic Camille Desmoulins, effectively directed the thoughts of many Parisians to action when he said to his listeners at the popular gathering place, the Palais Royal:

> Citizens, you know that the Nation had asked for Necker to be retained, and he has been driven out! Could you be more insolently flouted? After such an act they will dare anything, and they may perhaps be planning and preparing a Saint-Bartholomew massacre of patriots for this very night! . . . To arms! To arms![5]

Demonstrations broke out in Paris by the middle of the day on July 12, bolstered by the adherence of the French Guards, a unit charged with keeping order in the city, to the cause of the crowds. By evening, fighting was taking place between demonstrators and units of the foreign troops ordered to Paris by the king, and their commanders withdrew royal forces from the city. Unrest continued through the night without opposition. At about 1:00 A.M. on July 13, crowds began to burn the tax stations along the wall surrounding Paris, since the majority of the commoners blamed the tax on goods en-

---

4. Reveillon was one of Paris's largest manufacturers; his wallpaper works employed about 300 persons. He had not, however, precisely advocated a reduction of wages in a speech he gave at his local assembly to elect representatives to the Estates General. On April 23, Reveillon had said that if the price of bread could be reduced, workers' wages would follow, resulting in a lower cost for the goods they produced. Sources vary widely on the human cost of the rioting. Jacques Godechot, *The Taking of the Bastille: July 14, 1789* (trans. Jean Stewart; New York: Scribner's, 1970, p. 147), accepts a figure of 300 dead.

5. Quoted by Godechot, pp. 187–188. **Saint-Bartholomew Massacre:** on August 24, 1572, Catholic forces killed several thousand Protestants all over France during the French wars of religion.

tering the capital for higher food prices. At 6:00 A.M., crowds attacked a monastery where they believed food was stored.

As disorder grew in the capital, on the morning of July 13, the men who had served as electors of the Parisian deputies to the Estates General assembled at the Paris city hall and implemented two important decisions.[6] First, they constituted a committee from their ranks to administer the city, in effect creating a revolutionary municipal government; second, they called for the founding of a "civic militia." The militia's stated purpose was to keep order in the capital, but the formation of such an armed force, obeying the orders of the electors rather than the king, was another revolutionary act.

The creation of the militia, soon to be called the *National Guard*, required arms, and the search for guns and ammunition became the next object of crowd action. On the morning of July 14, a crowd estimated at 80,000 persons forced its way into the In-

valides, an old soldiers' home/barracks, and seized all of the 32,000 muskets stored there. Muskets were of little value without gunpowder and musket balls, however, and the crowd found few of these commodities at the Invalides. They surged on that morning to the Bastille, to which royal officers earlier had transferred 250 barrels of powder for safekeeping as Paris grew restive. Defending the fortress against a growing crowd were eighty-two *invalides* (older or partially disabled soldiers fit only for garrison duty) and thirty-two soldiers of the Swiss regiments in French service. After two deputations from the crowd failed to secure the commander's surrender, the attack began around 1:30 P.M. By 5:00 P.M. the Bastille and its supplies had fallen to the crowd.

You now have a summary of what the crowd did on July 14, 1789. Such mass actions were common in early modern Europe, as we have seen in Chapter 1. Your task in this chapter is to analyze the evidence presented here to answer basic questions about the crowd. Why were the people of Paris angry in mid-July 1789? How were Parisians mobilized for action? Who made up the crowd that stormed the Bastille?

6. Rules for Estates General elections in Paris required that voters in each of the city's sixty electoral districts select electors, who in turn would vote for representatives to the Estates General.

SOURCES AND METHOD

This chapter presents a variety of evidence to assist you in answering the basic questions about the atmosphere in Paris in July 1789 that produced the attack on the Bastille. The first

pieces of evidence you encounter in the chapter are visual. You already have analyzed such sources in Chapter 2, and you should examine the pictures presented in this chapter to reconstruct the physical setting for the events of 1789. In analyzing the evidence, your objective should be to derive answers to this question: What features of the physical layout of Paris were conducive to the spread of rumors and agitation?

Sources 1 and 2 offer views of the Palais Royal, the property of the Duke of Orléans, a member of the royal family. On the grounds of this palace, the duke developed a commercial and entertainment area lined with shops and cafés. The palace and its grounds were outside of police jurisdiction because they belonged to the duke and so attracted political agitators, prostitutes, and criminals such as pickpockets. Much of the politically active population of Paris would have been familiar with the grounds of the Palais Royal. What role might such a site have played on July 14, 1789? Why might the significance of the Palais Royal for the political climate of 1789 have been so great that a few historians have seen it as evidence of a plot by its owner to foment a revolution that might benefit his own political ambitions?

Source 3 shows the rue du Fer-à-Moulin, a street typical of many of those of eighteenth-century Paris at the time of the Revolution. In 1789 much of the Parisian population of about 600,000 still lived in such streets, crowded inside the boundaries set by the city's former medieval fortifications. To accommodate this dense population, residential buildings were six or seven stories high and crowded, with an average of almost thirty residents in each one. Try to imagine life in these buildings and streets. Do you think people would have spent a great deal of time in the streets? Why? What sorts of exchanges of information might have occurred in streets like these?

Source 4 introduces a new form of evidence, architectural drawings of residential buildings, to enhance your understanding of the physical aspect of Paris in 1789. The floor plan for 18, rue Contrescarpe is of a house very near the Bastille. Such multi-storied structures typically had a ground floor that was rented out to a merchant or craftsman who maintained a shop that opened on the street. A craftsman might also have rented a workshop behind the shop on the ground floor. Access to the residential upper floors was through the gate opening onto the street at the end of the passage leading to the interior courtyard. Each building's numerous residents would cross the courtyard daily going in and out or fetching water from the well. All would have needed to mount the staircase to rooms whose prices decreased as the number of steps separating them from the ground increased. As a consequence of this pricing procedure, a master craftsman might occupy a large apartment on the first floor up these stairs; his employees, the tiny rooms in the attic. Reflect on this living situation. How might news and rumor have spread in such a setting? How might a crowd be mobilized there? Why might the economic power of an employer and his residential proximity to his workers in such buildings permit an employer who was committed to a political cause to draw his workers along with him?

This chapter also presents quantitative data similar to those that you analyzed in Chapter 4, in the form of graphs, tables, and a map. The information presented here is essential to understanding which social groups participated in the events of July 14, 1789, and why. As we found in Chapter 4, the largely illiterate majority of pre-nineteenth-century Europe left few conventional written records, like letters and diaries, that might allow historians to interpret their thought. Historians' ingenuity, however, has allowed them to understand these people through other sources. In constructing the data sets on food prices in this chapter, historians drew on a rich source for understanding seventeenth- and eighteenth-century life. Because early modern governments recognized a correlation between high food prices during periods of dearth on one hand and riots and other acts of public disorder on the other, they kept close watch on such prices. Their effort generated excellent records of food prices, especially of the cost of wheat, the essential ingredient for the bread that was the staple of early modern diets. Look at the graphs numbered 5 and 6 among the evidence for this chapter. Although the two researchers used slightly different measures of wheat in assembling their data, you are presented with significant price trends: Long-term trends in wheat prices for France as a whole are in Source 5 and short-term trends for Paris alone are in Source 6. Analyze the price trends presented here. Between the 1730s and mid-1780s, the highest prices were the result of failed harvests in

the early 1770s. During that period, the rural poor in some regions of the country resorted at times to eating boiled grass or acorns when bread became too scarce and costly. The high food prices resulting from harvest failures also generated popular fear that the elevated cost of food was the result not of dearth, but of speculators unscrupulously hoarding large quantities of grain to artificially drive up prices and increase their own profits. Such fears, indeed, earlier had caused widespread rioting in the Paris region in the 1770s. How did prices in 1789 in Paris and France compare with those of the 1770s? Imagine yourself a Frenchman aged forty in 1789. What would your memory of food prices be? How would those of 1789 strike you? Consult Source 7, a table. How would price trends in 1788–1789 have affected your family's income? Reflect, too, on the fact that women did their families' marketing in the eighteenth century. Why would you not be surprised to find women protesting food prices and other issues? Why might you have been concerned about the preservation of order in Paris in July 1789 if you had been a police official?

Historians drew on a second kind of source—tax data—in formulating the map presenting the composition of the various Paris sections by income (Source 8). These data are your basis for understanding the economic structure of Paris's population and, most important for our purposes, the economic background of the crowd members who stormed the Bastille. For centuries, historians and government officials held that the lowest and most criminal elements comprised these crowds. Indeed, eighteenth-century French police records use a phrase that may be translated as "the scum of the people" in describing the composition of crowds. What do we find about the Bastille crowd, however? Notice that the map in Source 8 provides data on the taxes paid by residents of the forty-eight sections into which early revolutionary Paris was divided. From those data we may judge each section's relative wealth because, of course, wealthier citizens paid more taxes. To completely analyze the data you need to know that "active" citizens under the 1791 constitution were those who could vote by virtue of paying taxes worth three days' labor (nationally, 41 percent of citizens did not meet this minimum standard). "Eligible" citizens were "active" citizens qualified for administrative office by paying taxes worth at least ten days' labor. Using this information, ascertain from the table in Source 8 the sections of Paris that housed those who made up the Bastille crowd. Why do you think that the police would have erred had they characterized that crowd in their usual manner?

Other data might also allow historians further to identify the members of the crowd, if not by name, at least by social group. Police records of those arrested in unsuccessful rebellions that provide personal data on participants have been systematically exploited only recently by historians. But the Bastille attack began a successful revolution, and the crowd members became heroes and heroines who received the title *Vainqueurs de la Bastille* ("Conquerors of the Bastille") and state pensions if they had been disabled in the attack. The list of these persons is one among many functions of the administrative and fiscal record keeping of a modern state, but it provides you, in the table that is Source 9, with an occupational listing of the Bastille's conquerors. From a distance of two hundred years, it is probably impossible to reconstruct the precise income of each conqueror. Moreover, each trade, like the cabinetmaking common in the Faubourg Saint-Antoine, would have shown a variety of incomes within the ranks of its practitioners—another frustration. We do know, however, that in skilled trades the self-employed tended to be masters of their trades and therefore probably more affluent than journeymen wage earners or apprentices employed by others. Examine the table. What were the most common trades of the Bastille's attackers? Who predominated, wage earners or the self-employed? What conclusion do you draw from the fact that most of the conquerors had definite trades and were not unskilled or poor?

Written sources can supplement quantitative evidence and supply historians with information on public opinion in Paris during the month of July 1789. This chapter presents several types of such evidence, which you have not previously analyzed. Source 10 is another part of the massive bureaucratic record generated by modern states, in this case a petition addressed to the French national legislature by a woman seeking compensation for herself and her husband as conquerors of the Bastille. In reading her petition, ask yourself how her account further contributes to your knowledge of the crowd's composition. Remember that the division of household labor in the eighteenth century gave housewives the major marketing responsibility. Why might women be involved in crowd actions in 1789 or at other points in the Revolution?

Next you will read a travel account, a literary form very common in the early modern period. Europe's curiosity about the outside world grew with the Age of Exploration during the sixteenth century, and a large reading audience developed for accounts by European travelers. The usefulness of such works in reconstructing a society varies, however, according to the intelligence and observational skills of their authors. In the case of Arthur Young, whose Paris report is excerpted as Source 11, we have the work of a master of the travel genre.

Arthur Young (1741–1820) was a wealthy and educated Englishman who sought out and publicized the latest agricultural techniques. Before visiting France to examine French farming, a journey that produced the selection here, Young, who was well known as an agricultural expert and as an economist, published descriptions of his travels through England, Wales, and Ireland. The record of his travels in France is valuable, therefore, for several reasons. Young's fame and his knowledge of the French language gained him access to many prominent Frenchmen. The

observational skills he had honed on earlier trips allowed him quickly to appreciate the economic problems of France and to assess public reaction to them. Finally, as luck would have it, his journey took him through France in the years 1787, 1788, and 1789, so that he was present in the country during the early days of the Revolution. His account, consequently, is extremely useful in understanding the events of the year 1789. Young tells us a great deal about modern politics and the spread of revolution. Thanks to parish schools that offered inexpensive elementary education, the population of Paris was much more literate than the rural population of France. How did Young find this literacy affecting politics in the capital? How did political news spread to provincial cities like Metz? Do you find in any of this description a political life that in some ways presages that of our modern age? Recall, too, the fears many Frenchmen had about having adequate food supplies in the eighteenth century. Why did Young believe that troop movements would renew such fears?

The third kind of written evidence presented in this chapter is diplomatic correspondence. The letters of ambassadors to their home governments long have been useful sources for historians. Their utility derives from the very functions of ambassadors. Since the posting of the first permanent ambassadors by Italian Renaissance states, these officials performed several roles. First, they represented their countries' interests to foreign courts, and thus we can identify the policies of their states in ambassadors' correspondence with their superiors. Additionally, from their earliest days ambassadors kept their governments informed of conditions in their host countries that might affect international relations; they functioned almost like spies, gathering all available information for use by their governments. In this regard, the British ambassador's reports to his superiors in the Foreign Office are extremely important. In 1789 France was a major power that had long been in conflict with England and one most influential in achieving American victory over the English in the War of Independence. As a result, information on political events in France was crucial to English policymakers, and their ambassador supplied detailed reports on France. As with all sources, however, the historian must approach such correspondence with a critical eye. Was the ambassador writing from firsthand knowledge of events? Is his information verified by other sources? How would you assess the reliability of the Duke of Dorset, the English ambassador to France, whose letters are presented as Source 12?

What do they tell you about events in Paris?

The fourth written source in this chapter is an excerpt from the journal and diary literature written by many educated persons in the centuries before our own. The historical utility of such sources again depends on their authors' activities and abilities to record accurately events of their times. In the journal of the Parisian bookseller Siméon-Prosper Hardy we have the work of a reasonably well-educated man who was something of a busybody, alert for all news. However, Hardy was also a cautious man who took no part in the dangerous events of July 14 and whose residence was far from the Bastille. He can therefore be relied on only for noting general trends in Paris, not for details on the Bastille attack. What picture of general events does the selection in Source 13 from his journal present?

All these sources should fit together in your mind like the pieces of a puzzle, allowing you to reconstruct the state of public opinion in Paris in July 1789, to determine how crowds were mobilized, and to understand who stormed the Bastille on July 14.

Source 1 from Musée Carnavalet, Paris. © Photothèque des Musées de la Ville de Paris.

1. Henri Monnier, *The Palais Royal*

Source 2 from Bibliothèque Nationale, Paris; Vinck Collection.

2. Camille Desmoulins Speaking to the Crowds at the Palais Royal, July 12, 1789

Source 4 adapted from David Garrioch, Neighborhood and Community in Paris, 1740–1790 (New York: Cambridge University Press, 1986), p. 222. Reprinted by permission.

4. Plan of a Typical Parisian Residential Building, 18, Rue Contrescarpe, Faubourg St.-Antoine

Small courtyard

Well

Workshop

Shop

Passage

Source 3 from Musée Carnavalet, Paris. © Photothèque des Musées de la Ville de Paris.

3. Rue du Fer-à-Moulin, 1870

Source 5 adapted from Ernest Labrousse, Ruggiero Romano, and F.-G. Dreyfus, Le prix du froment en France au temps de la monnaie stable (1726–1913) *(Paris: Ecole des Hautes Études en Sciences Sociales, 1970), p. xiv.*

5. Average Price of a Hectoliter (100 liters) of Wheat in France, 1726–1790

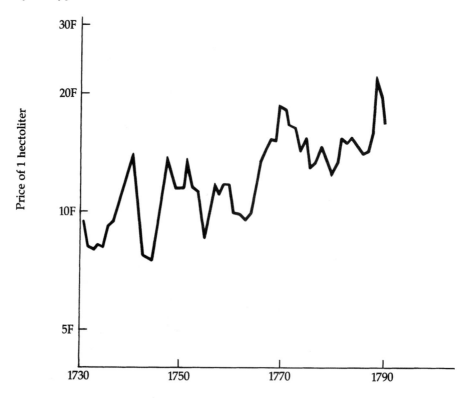

Source 6 from Jacques Godechot, The Taking of the Bastille, July 14, 1789 *(New York: Scribner's, 1970), p. 13. Used by permission.*

6. Price of 100 Kilograms of Wheat in Paris, 1770–1790

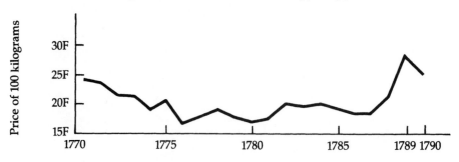

[128]

Source 7 from George Rudé, "Prices, Wages and Popular Movements in Paris During the French Revolution," Economic History Review, 2nd ser., vol. 6 (1953), p. 248. Used by permission of Basil Blackwell Ltd.

7. Bread and the Wage Earner's Budget[a]

Occupation	Effective Daily Wage in Sous (s)[b]	Expenditure on Bread as Percentage of Income with Bread at	
		9s (Aug 1788)	14½s (Feb–July 1789)
Laborer in Reveillon wallpaper works	15	60	97
Builder's laborer	18	50	80
Journeyman mason	24	37	60
Journeyman, locksmith, carpenter, etc.	30	30	48
Sculptor, goldsmith	60	15	24

[a]The price of the 4-pound loaf consumed daily by a workingman and his family as the main element in their diet.
[b]"Effective" wage represents the daily wage adjusted for 111 days of nonwork per calendar year for religious observation, etc.

Source 8 map from Marcel Reinhard, Nouvelle histoire de Paris: La Révolution *(Paris: Distributed by Hachette for the Association pour la publication d'une Histoire de Paris, 1971), pp. 66–67. Key and table from George Rudé,* The Crowd in the French Revolution *(New York: Oxford University Press, 1959), pp. 244–245. Copyright © 1959. Used by permission of Oxford University Press.*

8. Map of Paris by Economic Circumstances of Residents, 1790

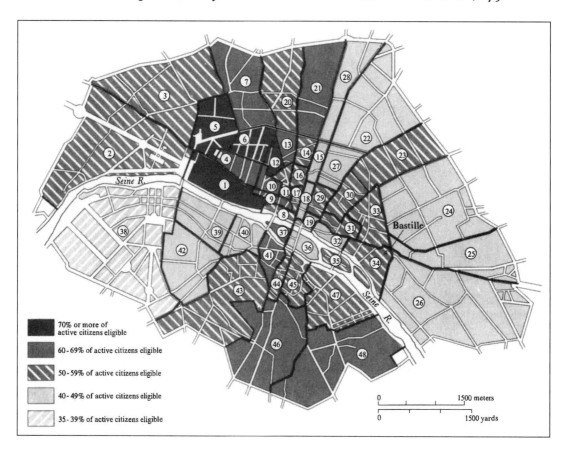

Section[a]	Bastille July[b]	Section	Bastille July	Section	Bastille July
1. Tuileries	2	17. Marché des Innocents	6	34. Arsenal	23
2. Champs Élysées	—	18. Lombards	5	35. Île Saint-Louis	—
3. Roule	2	19. Arcis	3	36. Notre Dame	1
4. Palais Royal	1	20. Faubourg Montmartre	—	37. Henri IV	2
5. Vendôme	1	21. Poissonière	1	38. Invalides	5
6. Bibliothèque	2	22. Bondy	4	39. Fontaine de Grenelle	2
7. Grange Batelière	2	23. Temple	9	40. Quatre Nations	6
8. Louvre	1	24. Popincour	87	41. Théâtre Français	6
9. Oratoire	2	25. Montreuil	139	42. Croix Rouge	2
10. Halle au Blé	6	26. Quinze Vingts	193	43. Luxembourg	7
11. Postes	4	27. Gravilliers	3	44. Thermes de Julien	3
12. Louis XIV	—	28. Faubourg St. Denis	1	45. Sainte-Geneviève	10
13. Fontaine Montmorency	—	29. Beaubourg	5	46. Observatoire	3
		30. Enfants Rouges	2	47. Jardin des Plantes	3
14. Bonne Nouvelle	—	31. Roi de Sicile	3	48. Gobelins Outside Paris	3
15. Ponceau	3	32. Hôtel de Ville	18		
16. Mauconseil	4	33. Place Royale	17	*Total*	602

[a]Names of sections are as in 1790–1791.
[b]Numbers arrested, killed, wounded, or participated in the attack on the Bastille.

Source 9 from George Rudé, The Crowd in the French Revolution (New York: Oxford University Press, 1959), pp. 246–248. Copyright © 1959. Used by permission of Oxford University Press.

9. Trades of the Bastille Insurgents, 1789

Trade	Participants (no.)	Trade	Participants (no.)	Trade	Participants (no.)
1. Food, Drink		Cabinet makers	48 (9)	*9. Leather*	
Bakers	5	Chandlers	—	Curriers	—
Brewers	2 (1)a	Fancy ware	9 (1)	Leather, skin dressers	2
Butchers	5 (3)	Joiners	49 (8)	*10. Print and Paper*	
Cafés, restaurants	4	Upholsterers	4 (1)	Bookbinders	—
Chocolate	—	*5. Transport*		Booksellers	—
Cooks	2 (2)	Bargemen	3 (3)	Papermakers	1
Fruit vendors	—	Blacksmiths	—	Printers	8 (4)
Grocers	—	Carters	5 (5)	*11. Glass, Pottery*	
Innkeepers	2	Coachmen	2 (1)	Earthenware	1
Pastry chefs	4	Farriers	4 (1)	Potters	7
Tobacco	—	Harness, saddlers	5	Royal Glass factory	1 (1)
Wine merchants	11	Porters	16 (16)	*12. Miscellaneous*	
2. Building, Roads		Riverside workers	5 (5)	Actors, artists, musicians, etc.	—
Carpenters	3	Shipyard workers	5 (5)	Beggars	—
Glaziers	—	Wheelwrights	—	Bourgeois	—
Locksmiths	41 (8)	*6. Metal*		Businessmen	4
Monumental masons	9 (1)	Braziers	7 (1)	Charcoal burners	3
Navvies	2 (2)	Buttonmakers	3	Civil servants	—
Painters	4	Cutlers	—	Clerks	5
Paviors	—	Edge-tool makers	2	Domestic servants, cleaners	—
Plasterers	—	Engravers, gilders	13	Deputies	—
Quarrymen	—	Founders	9 (2)	Fishermen	2 (1)
Sawyers	4 (1)	Goldsmiths	6 (1)	Housewives	—
Sculptors	20 (1)	Instrument makers	—	Journalists, publishers	—
Stonecutters	4 (4)	Jewelers	5	Laborers	2 (2)
Stonemasons	7 (5)	Mechanics	—	Launderers	3 (1)
Surveyors	—	Nailsmiths	9 (1)	Newsagents, vendors	—
Tilers	—	Pewterers	2	Peasants	—
3. Dress		Stovemakers	5 (3)	Priests	—
Beltmakers	—	Tinsmiths	5 (2)	Professional (lawyers, doctors)	—
Boot and shoe	28 (5)	Watchmakers	3	Shopkeepers, assistants	22 (1)
Dressmakers	—	*7. Wood*		"Smugglers"	—
Dyers, cleaners	3	Coopers	3 (1)	Teachers	1
Florists, gardeners	6 (3)	Turners	10	Trades	56 (1)
Furriers	2 (1)	*8. Textiles*		Army, police, National Guard:	
Hairdressers	10	Cotton	—	a. Officers	—
Hatters	9 (4)	Gauze	22 (22)	b. Others	77
Ribbon weavers	3 (3)	Silk	1 (1)		
Stocking weavers	4 (4)	Weavers	1	*Total*	662 (149)
Tailors	7 (1)				
4. Furnishing					
Basketmakers	2				
Boxmakers	1				

aFigures in parentheses represent insurgents who probably were wage-earners (i.e., not self-employed).

Source 10 from selected documents translated with notes and commentary by Darline Gay Levy, Harriet Branson Applewhite, and Mary Durham Johnson, from Women in Revolutionary Paris, 1789–1795 *(Urbana: University of Illinois Press, 1979), pp. 29–30. Copyright © 1979 by the Board of Trustees of the editors of the University of Illinois. Used with permission of the editors of the University of Illinois Press.*

10. Petition Addressed by Marguerite Pinaigre to the French National Assembly

Legislators:

The person named here, Margueritte Piningre [*sic*], wife of Sieur Bernard Vener, one of the Vainqueurs de la Bastille, has the honor of appearing today before your august assembly to reclaim the execution of the decree issued by the Constituent Assembly in his [her husband's] favor in 1789. This intrepid citizen, who has the misfortune of being crippled for the rest of his days without ever being able to work again in his life because of wounds received on all parts of his body, yes, Legislators, not only has this dear citizen fought in the conquest of the Bastille with the greatest courage, but furthermore, his *citoyenne*[7] wife, who is present here, worked equally hard with all her might, both of them having resolved to triumph or to die. It is she who ran to several wineshops to fill her apron with bottles, both broken and unbroken, which she gave to the authorities to be used as shot in the cannon used to break the chain on the drawbridge of the Bastille. Therefore, by virtue of these legitimate claims the petitioner believes herself justified in coming before the National Assembly today to advise it concerning the nonexecution of laws relative to conquerors who were severely maimed, as was the petitioner's husband. This law awards a pension to those who are really crippled and without the means for earning their living. Such is the situation of the latter, who is offering to provide evidence in the form of authentic statements. Nevertheless, he still has not been awarded this pension which he so richly deserves, he as well as his wife, as a consequence of the dangers they faced. The only gratification which this citizen has received is a small sum of four hundred *livres*, which since 1789 has barely sufficed to care for him and to help him get over the severe wounds he suffered.

Under these circumstances, and in the light of such a compelling account, the petitioner dares hope, Messieurs, for your justice and your usual generosity. May you be willing to take under urgent consideration the object of a request which is becoming as pressing as it is urgent—assuming that surely you would not allow one of the most zealous and intrepid Vainqueurs de la Bastille to languish any longer bent under the weight of the indigence to

---

7. *citoyenne:* citizeness. As an expression of revolutionary equality, during the Revolution, the terms of address "citizen" and "citizeness" replaced the traditional "Monsieur" and "Madame," based as they were on "My Lord" and "My Lady."

[133]

which he is presently reduced, along with his wife and his children, who expect his every minute to be his last—because from this period [July 14, 1789] on he has always been ill and continues to suffer cruelly every day. The petitioner expects the favor of the representatives of the French nation, to whom she will never cease to offer her most heart-felt gratitude.

[signed] Marguerite Pinaigre

Source 11 from Arthur Young, Travels in France During the Years 1787, 1788 and 1789, *edited by Jeffry Kaplow (Gloucester, Mass.: Peter Smith, 1976), pp. 104–105, 130, 145–146.*

11. Arthur Young's Report from France

[June 1789 (in Paris)]

THE 9TH.—The business going forward at present in the pamphlet shops of Paris is incredible. I went to the Palais Royal to see what new things were published, and to procure a catalogue of all. Every hour produces something new. Thirteen came out to-day, sixteen yesterday, and ninety-two last week. We think sometimes that Debrett's or Stockdale's shops at London are crouded, but they are mere deserts, compared to Desenne's, and some others here, in which one can scarcely squeeze from the door to the counter. The price of printing two years ago was from 27 liv. to 30 liv.[8] per sheet, but now it is from 60 liv. to 80 liv. This spirit of reading political tracts, they say, spreads into the provinces, so that all the presses of France are equally employed. Nineteen-twentieths of these productions are in favour of liberty, and commonly violent against the clergy and nobility; I have to-day bespoken[9] many of this description, that have reputation; but enquiring for such as had appeared on the other side of the question, to my astonishment I find there are but two or three that have merit enough to be known. Is it not wonderful,[10] that while the press teems with the most levelling and even seditious principles, which put in execution would overturn the monarchy, nothing in reply appears, and not the least step is taken by the court to restrain this extreme licentiousness of publication? It is easy to conceive the spirit that must thus be raised among the people. But the coffee-houses in the Palais Royal present yet more singular and astonishing spectacles; they are not only crouded within, but other expectant crouds are at the doors and windows, listening *à gorge déployée*[11] to certain

8. **livre:** the main unit of Old Regime currency, made up of 20 sous (s). Each sou contained 12 deniers (d); 6 livres equaled 1 écu.
9. **bespoken:** Young employs an archaic usage of this word, whose meaning here may most clearly be rendered as "encountered."
10. **wonderful:** another older usage. Young does not state approval here but indicates that the contents of the press were surprising.
11. *à gorge déployée:* enthusiastically.

[134]

orators, who from chairs or tables harangue each his little audience: the eager-ness with which they are heard, and the thunder of applause they receive for every sentiment of more than common hardiness or violence against the pres-ent government, cannot easily be imagined. I am all amazement at the min-istry permitting such nests and hot-beds of sedition and revolt, which dissem-inate amongst the people, every hour, principles that by and by must be opposed with vigour, and therefore it seems little short of madness to allow the propagation at present.

THE 10TH.—Every thing conspires to render the present period in France criti-cal: the want of bread is terrible: accounts arrive every moment from the provinces of riots and disturbances, and calling in the military, to preserve the peace of the markets. The prices reported are the same as I found at Abbeville and Amiens 5s. (2½d.) a pound for white bread, and 3½s. to 4s. for the common sort, eaten by the poor: these rates are beyond their faculties, and occasion great misery.

THE 26TH.—Every hour that passes seems to give the people fresh spirit: the meetings at the Palais Royal are more numerous, more violent, and more as-sured; and in the assembly of electors, at Paris, for sending a deputation to the National Assembly, the language that was talked, by all ranks of people, was nothing less than a revolution in the government, and the establishment of a free constitution: what they mean by a free constitution, is easily under-stood—*a republic*; for the doctrine of the times runs every day more and more to that point; yet they profess, that the kingdom ought to be a monarchy too; or, at least, that there ought to be a king. In the streets one is stunned by the hawkers of seditious pamphlets, and descriptions of pretended events, that all tend to keep the people equally ignorant and alarmed. The supineness, and even stupidity of the court, is without example: the moment demands the greatest decision—and yesterday, while it was actually a question, whether he should be a Doge of Venice,[12] or a King of France, the King went a hunting! The spectacle of the Palais Royal presented this night, till eleven o'clock, and, as we afterwards heard, almost till morning, is curious. The croud was prodi-gious, and fireworks of all sorts were played off, and all the building was illu-minated: these were said to be rejoicings on account of the Duc d'Orléans[13]

---

12. **Doge of Venice:** in principle the head of Venetian government, the Doge in reality was a fig-urehead.

13. **Duc d'Orléans:** Louis Philippe Joseph, Duke of Orléans (1747–1793), was a member of the royal family who played an equivocal role in the Revolution's early years. As a member of the Assembly of Notables, he opposed new royal taxing authority. On June 25, 1789, the duke answered the call of the Third Estate of the Estates General for noblemen to join it, in defiance of royal order, as the National Assembly. This is the event celebrated in Young's account. The duke's ownership of the Palais Royal has led generations of historians to ac-cuse him of inciting the revolutionary agitation that took place there. Before his death in the Reign of Terror, he served as a member of the legislature and in 1792 cast his vote for the death of Louis XVI.

and the nobility joining the commons; but united with the excessive freedom, and even licentiousness of the orators, who harangue the people; with the general movement which before was threatening, all this bustle and noise, which will not leave them a moment tranquil, has a prodigious effect in preparing them for whatever purposes the leaders of the commons shall have in view; consequently they are grossly and diametrically opposite to the interests of the court;—but all these are blind and infatuated.

> [July 1789 (on the road at Metz, a city
> about 150 miles east of Paris)]

THE 14TH.—They have a *cabinet littéraire*[14] at Metz, something like that I described at Nantes, but not on so great a plan; and they admit any person to read or go in and out for a day, on paying 4s. To this I eagerly resorted, and the news from Paris, both in the public prints, and by the information of a gentleman, I found to be interesting. Versailles and Paris are surrounded by troops: 35,000 men are assembled, and 20,000 more on the road, large trains of artillery collected, and all the preparations of war. The assembling of such a number of troops has added to the scarcity of bread; and the magazines[15] that have been made for their support are not easily by the people distinguished from those they suspect of being collected by monopolists. This has aggravated their evils almost to madness; so that the confusion and tumult of the capital are extreme.

Source 12 from Keith Michael Baker, editor, Readings in Western Civilizations, *vol. 7,* The Old Regime and the Revolution *(Chicago: University of Chicago Press, 1987), pp. 193–196.*

12. Report of the British Ambassador, the Duke of Dorset, to the Foreign Office in London

(*25th June, 1789.*) The reports concerning the scarcity of corn[16] in the neighbourhood of Paris have but too much foundation: the deficiency of this material article extends to the distance of 15 leagues[17] round the City and is so severely felt that Administration has been obliged to supply the different great Markets, by sending corn from the Magazines of the *Ecole Militaire*[18] originally

14. *cabinet littéraire:* reading room.
15. **magazines:** storage depots.
16. **corn:** in British usage, this word refers to grain, not American corn or maize.
17. **league:** a unit of distance equal to 2.764 miles in English-speaking countries.
18. **Ecole Militaire:** the Military School in Paris.

intended for the consumption of the Capital: in regard to the other Provinces of the Kingdom there is no further apprehension, as they are sufficiently supplied 'till the ensuing harvest which has every appearance of being very plentifull. . . .

The French Guards have, in some few instances within these few days, shewn a great reluctance to act and some of the men have declared that if they should be called upon to quell any disturbance they will, if compelled to fire, take care not to do any mischief. The Archbishop of Paris was very ill-treated last night by the mob at Versailles: his coach was broke to pieces and his horses much bruised: if the Guards had not protected him he must himself have been inevitably destroyed.

The people now are disposed to any desperate act of violence in support of the *Assemblée Nationale*.[19] I shall not fail to send Your Grace immediate intelligence of any momentous occurrence during this critical state of affairs. . . .

(*16th July, 1789.*) I wrote to Your Grace on the 12th Inst. by a messenger extraordinary to inform you of the removal of M. Necker from His Majesty's Councils: I have now to lay before Your Grace an account of the general revolt, with the extraordinary circumstances attending it, that has been the immediate consequence of that step. On Sunday evening a slight skirmish happened in the Place de Louis XV, in which two Dragoons[20] were killed, and two wounded of the Duc de Choiseuil's Regiment: after which all the troops left the Capital, and the populace remained unmolested masters of everything: much to their credit however, uncontrouled as they now were, no material mischief was done; their whole attention being confined to the burning of some of the Barriers. Very early on Monday morning the Convent of St. Lazare was forced, in which, besides a considerable quantity of corn, were found arms and ammunition supposed to have been conveyed thither as a place of security, at different periods from the Arsenal: and now a general consternation was seen throughout the Town: all shops were shut; all public and private works at a stand still and scarcely a person to be seen in the Streets excepting the armed *Bourgeoisie,* a temporary police for the protection of private property, to replace the established one which no longer had any influence.

In the morning of Tuesday the Hospital of Invalids was summonsed to surrender and was taken possession of after a very slight resistance: all the cannon, small arms and ammunition were immediately seized upon, and every one who chose to arm himself was supplied with what was necessary . . . in the evening a large detachment with two pieces of cannon went to the Bastille

19. **Assemblée Nationale:** the National Assembly.

20. **Dragoon:** cavalryman equipped with both a sabre and a short musket and therefore capable of fighting either mounted or on foot.

to demand the ammunition that was there, the *Gardes Bourgeoises*[21] not being then sufficiently provided: a flag of truce was sent on before and was answered from within, notwithstanding which the governor (the Marquis de Launay) contrary to all precedent fired upon the people and killed several: this proceeding so enraged the populace that they rushed to the very gates with a determination to force their way through if possible: upon this the Governor agreed to let in a certain number of them on condition that they should not commit any violence: these terms being acceded to, a detachment of about 40 in number advanced and were admitted, but the drawbridge was immediately drawn up again and the whole party instantly massacred: this breach of honor aggravated by so glaring an act of inhumanity excited a spirit of revenge and tumult such as might naturally be expected: the two pieces of cannon were immediately placed against the Gate and very soon made a breach which, with the disaffection that as is supposed prevailed within, produced a sudden surrender of that Fortress: M. de Launay, the principal gunner, the tailer, and two old invalids who had been noticed as being more active than the rest were seized and carried to the *Hôtel de Ville*[22] where, after a very summary trial before the tribunal there, the inferior objects were put to death and M. de Launay had also his head cut off at the Place de Grève, but with circumstances of barbarity too shocking to relate. . . . In the course of the same evening the whole of the *Gardes Françoises*[23] joined the Bourgeoisie with all their cannon, arms and ammunition: the Regiments that were encamped in the *Champ de Mars*,[24] by an Order from Government left the ground at 2 o'Clock yesterday morning and fell back to Sêve, leaving all their camp equipage behind them; the magazines of powder and corn at the *Ecole Militaire* were immediately taken possession of and a *Garde Bourgeoise* appointed to protect them. Nothing could exceed the regularity and good order with which all this extraordinary business has been conducted: of this I have myself been a witness upon several occasions during the last three days as I have passed through the streets, nor had I at any moment reason to be alarmed for my personal safety.

21. **Gardes Bourgeoises:** the civic militia formed by the Parisian electors on July 13.

22. **Hôtel de Ville:** the Paris city hall.

23. **Gardes Françoises:** the French Guards, the unit normally charged with Parisian security, whose loyalty to the king had begun to erode as early as June 18, 1789.

24. **Champ de Mars:** the large parade ground in Paris in front of the Military School (Ecole Militaire).

Source 13 from Marcel Le Clère, editor, Paris de la préhistoire à nos jour *(Paris: Editions Bordessoules, 1985), p. 411. Translated by Julius R. Ruff.*

13. The Bookseller Hardy on the Background of the Bastille Attack

On Sunday, July 12, between five and six in the evening the news arrived from Versailles that Monsieur Necker, Minister of State and Director General of Finances, at the king's order had given up his office and had left incognito for Switzerland the previous night at one hour past midnight. If one believed the rumors, his departure came after he had told His Majesty that he deplored the disasters with which France was going to be overwhelmed, and warned him that before long there would, perhaps, not be a single *écu* left in the treasury. The resulting public outcry that worthy ministers had been dismissed and had been replaced by others who had no merit at all in public opinion led to the cancellation of all theatrical performances and the refunding of ticket prices to their audiences. This unexpected event causes a great clamor and spreads dread to all minds. In the Palais Royal, the Tuileries,[25] and in the Champs Elysées occurs an astonishing meeting of citizens of all social stations which results in the movements of large numbers of troops and guards charged with the city's security. People reported that various tragic events, of which I was unable to get precise details, had occurred in the Place Louis XV and on the Tuileries terrace. All the residents of the capital and its suburbs spend most of the night in the greatest anxiety.

QUESTIONS TO CONSIDER

Crowd violence was not uncommon in early modern Europe, and historians have recently shown that such violence, rather than reflecting blind rage, often represented the expression of very definite ideas. Recall the political crisis of June and July 1789. The National Assembly was defying the king, and many Parisians supported this stand. Both the legislators at Versailles and the people of Paris knew that royal troops were moving in the latter's direction. They correctly connected these military steps with Necker's dismissal and believed that the king was beginning a coup to suppress demands for change in France. How might political problems coinciding with other difficulties have helped to produce the Bastille attack? Your problem in this chapter is to reconstruct the nature and spread of certain ideas in Paris on July 14, 1789, by bringing together the various pieces of evidence presented here.

25. **Tuileries:** the gardens of the Tuileries Palace, open to the public. To their west was the Place Louis XV (now the Place de la Concorde) and an area still undeveloped in the eighteenth century, the Champs Elysées.

Consider first the physical setting of this historical drama. Examine the picture of the Palais Royal. How many people could congregate here in fair weather like that experienced on July 12–14? What effect did Camille Desmoulins appear to have on the crowd? If political agitation and rumors spread beyond the Palais Royal, what physical features of Paris, visible in the city's streets and residences, would have been conducive to their dispersion throughout the city? What conditions did Parisians encounter in the streets? How would these conditions affect the spread of news? What features of the floor plans of typical Parisian houses might have permitted the mobilization of all residents in a political cause? Combine all these facts and you should have an idea of the nature of political activity in the city in 1789.

Next, consider the prices for wheat in Paris. You need to know what these prices represented to Parisians in terms of daily survival. How might food prices have inspired the agitation made possible by the city's physical layout? Examine both national and Parisian trends in wheat prices. What impact did rising bread prices have on the budgets of even skilled workers like journeymen masons and locksmiths? What do you suppose their response to such prices might have been? Remember that Jacques Necker, who was widely regarded as an important factor in keeping Paris supplied with food, was dismissed on July 11.

Examine next the social background of the Bastille's attackers. Refer to the map and the table showing the trades and residences of Bastille insurgents to determine which groups felt the problems of 1789 most acutely. What social groups were represented in the crowd? What was their economic standing? What parts of the city did they come from? Why do you suppose such groups, rather than other residents of the city, were moved to action? What factors conducive to the mobilization of the insurgents would you expect to find among them? Why would you expect them to be accustomed to organization in trades still governed by guilds? Why would you expect them to have been involved in the business activities of Parisian streets and markets?

As you complete this analysis, you should have an understanding of the composition of the Bastille crowd, how it was mobilized, and why the population might be agitated by food problems in 1789. Remember that the food price crisis coincided with a political crisis. Consult the written sources to understand the conjunction of these problems. How does Arthur Young show the response of Parisian public opinion to all of this? Were the effects of the crisis felt beyond Paris? Look at the works of the British ambassador and the bookseller Hardy. What do they tell us about developments in Paris? Considering that the Bastille fell to a group of armed rebels, how do you account for the ambassador's assurances that he felt safe? Refer to your findings on the crowd's composition in answering this question and remember the creation of a civil guard made up of middle-class citizens.

What social group controlled Paris by the time rain fell on July 14?

By combining these sources, both the traditional written accounts long used by historians and the sociological material that establishes the composition of the crowd, you should be able now to answer the central questions of this chapter. What stirred Parisians to mass action? Who was in that crowd on July 14, 1789?

EPILOGUE

The fall of the Bastille to a popular attack whose genesis you have analyzed in this chapter was an event charged with both practical and symbolic significance. On the practical level, capturing the Bastille provided the crowd with the gunpowder it sought and made regaining control of Paris virtually impossible for the royal army. In consequence, the king's resolve to oppose the National Assembly evaporated along with his hopes of controlling Paris. Louis XVI announced to the National Assembly on July 15 that troops would be removed from the region of the capital; on July 16 he recalled Necker as finance minister. On the following day, July 17, the king went to Paris, where his actions publicly confirmed royal recognition and acceptance of the events of the preceding days. First he received the keys to the city from its new mayor, Jean-Sylvan Bailly, representative of the electors of Paris who now controlled the capital. At the city hall he affixed to his hat the blue, white, and red cockade,[26] composed of the blue and red of the Paris coat of arms and the white of the monarchy. That cockade would become the symbol of the Revolution, and its colors would come to form a new national flag.

With these actions, Louis XVI effectively surrendered control of events to the citizen rebels of Paris. Although we now know that his private sentiments remained steadfastly opposed to the widening Revolution, his public acquiescence was plain to Frenchmen of all political persuasions. The king's brother, the Count of Artois, left the country on the evening of July 16, the first of thousands who would flee the growing Revolution out of fear or hatred for what it represented. At the same time, towns and cities all over France imitated Paris by forming revolutionary governments and National Guards to consolidate the overthrow of the old regime in municipal administration. Disorder spread among peasants in the countryside, prompting the National Assembly on August 4, 1789, to end the distinct privileges of the nobility and clergy; henceforth, all citizens would be equal before the law, pay taxes, and enjoy equal rights and opportunities. The Revolution had won its first great victory, a fact that even the king later recognized. Planning an escape in 1792, Louis said that, in hindsight, he should

26. **cockade:** a rosette of ribbons often worn on the hat as a kind of badge in the eighteenth century.

have fled Paris on July 14, 1789, to rally his forces and undo the Revolution. He stated, "I know I missed my opportunity: that was on July 14th. I ought to have gone away then. . . . I missed my opportunity, and I've never found it again."[27]

The symbolic importance of the Bastille's fall also was great. Despite its small prisoner census by 1789, the old fortress-prison symbolized royal power to eighteenth-century Frenchmen. The Paris government conferred the job of physically smashing this symbol of the Old Regime on a patriotic contractor, Pierre-François Palloy (1755–1834). In his hands, the transformation of the Bastille into another sort of symbol began. Palloy demolished the prison and transformed its remains into physical symbols of liberty's victory. In 1790 he had stones of the prison carved into eighty-three small replicas of the Bastille and sent one to each of France's new administrative units, the *départements*. In 1793 he sent

stones from the Bastille to the 544 districts of France and a number of political clubs and prominent citizens. He also had the prison's irons struck into commemorative medals and sponsored festivals celebrating the prison's fall. Others followed his lead. Masonry taken from the prison was used in a Parisian bridge so that citizens could tread on the "stone of tyranny." Lafayette sent a key to the Bastille to George Washington as a symbol of the victory of liberty. This key hangs today at Mount Vernon. And on July 14, 1790, the city of Paris honored 954 citizens who had taken part in the prison's capture as conquerors of the Bastille.

Eighteenth-century Frenchmen recognized the great symbolic importance of July 14, 1789, and France commemorated the anniversary of the Bastille's fall throughout its Revolution. Future generations recognized the event's importance, too. In 1880 the Third Republic made July 14 the great national holiday, observed in France with as much patriotic fervor as Americans observe July 4.

27. Quoted in Godechot, p. 257.

CHAPTER SIX

LABOR OLD AND NEW:

THE IMPACT OF

THE INDUSTRIAL REVOLUTION

The main difficulty did not ... lie so much in the invention of a proper self-acting mechanism for drawing and twisting cotton as in the distribution of the different members of the apparatus into one cooperative body, in impelling each organ with its appropriate delicacy and speed, and above all, in training human beings to renounce their desultory habits of work, to identify themselves with the unvarying regularity of work of the complex automation. It requires in fact a man of Napoleonic nerve and ambition to subdue refractory tempers of work people accustomed to irregular spasms of diligence, and to urge on his multifarious and intricate constructions in the face of prejudice, passion, and envy.

This is how Andrew Ure, an early and enthusiastic analyst of the Industrial Revolution, characterized the problems of industrial management in his book *The Philosophy of Manufacturers* (1835). In these few sentences,

Ure identified the essence of the Industrial Revolution. As most Western Civilization courses correctly emphasize, the period of history this label describes did indeed represent an economic and technological revolution of the greatest magnitude. The manner in which the West produced its goods changed more in the century from 1750 to 1850 than in all the previous centuries of human history, making necessary, as Ure says, the solution of tremendous problems of technology and integration of industrial processes.

But the Industrial Revolution had another impact, one that Ure did not neglect, though he approached it from the managerial point of view in emphasizing the manager's need to train his employees. That Ure thought the disciplining of the work force was perhaps the manager's chief problem suggests the broad social impact of industrialization. The first generations of factory laborers encountered a world of work dramatically transformed from that of

Chapter 6

Labor Old

and New:

The Impact of

the Industrial

Revolution

their fathers and mothers, a laboring situation with which most were totally unfamiliar.

The work life of the preindustrial laborer certainly was not easy. Workdays were long, typically dawn to dusk, six days per week, and it was common for wives and children to labor alongside their husbands and fathers as part of a household economy. Indeed, for agricultural workers and craftsmen alike, labor took up so much of their time that little remained for other daily activities. The material rewards of labor often were meager, too; we saw the mass poverty of preindustrial Europe in Chapter 4. But preindustrial work, however long, hard, and unrewarding, had characteristics that distinguished it from early industrial labor.

Preindustrial work usually was conducted in and around the worker's residence. Such labor afforded the worker occasional variety and, in some instances, a measure of control over the pace of work. We may see this effect if we examine the various types of preindustrial workers. Agricultural workers certainly experienced periods of intensive labor, especially at spring plowing and at harvest time, but periods of less intensive labor, especially in the winter months, punctuated their work year and brought them a bit of respite from their duties.

Many of the skilled craftsmen who produced the consumer goods of preindustrial Europe were organized by trade into local, professional groups known as guilds. Guilds performed many functions for their members. By controlling the size of their member-

ship, guilds could limit the number of practitioners of a trade in their cities because practice of a trade often required guild membership. Such limitation of membership aimed at protecting the livelihoods of guild members by ensuring that there would be sufficient work, and thus income, for each one. Guilds set prices for their products as well, always at a level that would ensure an adequate income to guild members and prevent ruinous price competition. Guilds gave the consumer a measure of protection, too. Guilds regulated the quality of their members' output and, through a system of training known as *apprenticeship*, guaranteed consumers that producers had sufficient skills in their trades to produce a fine product. Apprenticeship gave a craftsman the essential skills of his trade, and most men followed apprenticeship with employment as *journeymen*, that is, as workers who were sufficiently skilled to command a daily wage in the shop of a guild master. Full guild membership, and the right to open one's own production unit in his trade, was reserved for those journeymen who completed a *masterpiece*, a fine example of their skills in their chosen profession, which won for them the title of guild master.

The production unit of a guild master afforded him some measure of freedom in plying his trade within guild regulations. The master supervised a production unit that often included members of his family, apprentices, and sometimes journeymen. The master set the pace for himself and his workers, who, particularly in Catholic countries, might look forward to a number of religious holidays, civic festivals, and fairs to interrupt their year's labor.

In the later centuries of the preindustrial age, another kind of labor began to emerge. Called the *putting-out system,* this form of employment became common in textile production. A merchant would purchase raw material, often wool, and deliver it to various rural workers, who would spin, weave, dye, and finish the cloth, using traditional methods. Often workers were farm families who took in textile work to supplement their incomes. Merchants sought such rural workers because they worked cheaply and because they were beyond the jurisdiction of urban authorities, who limited textile production to guild members. The putting-out system allowed merchants to gather large numbers of workers under their control and thus organize production more efficiently. Even workers in this more disciplined mode of production enjoyed some freedom in organizing their work, however, despite the low wages that often kept them in poverty. For example, consider a weaver employed as part of the putting-out system. The weaver might enjoy "holy Monday," that is, a prolongation of the Sabbath, by taking the first day of the week off. The weaver might also take a few hours off on Tuesday and Wednesday as well, completing the week's required production only by working all night Thursday and Friday. No matter how he or she scheduled his or her work time, however, the choice was the weaver's. The worker had some control over the labor.

Indeed, all these factors that somewhat lessened the intensity of preindustrial labor have led some historians to idealize preindustrial work. It is important that we do not follow their example. By perhaps the most important measure of a laborer's work life—the standard of living it supports—it is by no means certain that early industrial employment represented an overall worsening of workers' living conditions. Historians continue to debate the issue of standard of living, examining diverse data on wages, diet, and housing; the problem clearly is a complex one. Whereas the preindustrial skilled craftsman was generally well rewarded for his work, the agricultural laborer and putting-out worker usually were not, and peasant families on the Continent sometimes lived a subsistence existence. For some rural workers, early industrial labor may actually have improved their standard of living.

Industrial labor, however, definitely brought all those employed in the new mills, factories, and mines a new style of work. Hours in the new establishments remained long, and the work year was interrupted by fewer holidays because factory owners could maximize returns on their massive investments in plants and machines only by using them to their fullest. Labor by whole families often continued, too, but the factory system separated them from their homes, and the tasks and workplaces of family members were very

[145]

Chapter 6

Labor Old

and New:

The Impact of

the Industrial

Revolution

different. Husbands endured the heaviest labor in textile mills or mines. Their wives, research has shown, most often remained at home, keeping house, caring for young children, and often laboring many hours in low-paying tasks that could be done at home—"slop work," that is, needle trades, bookbinding, millinery, or other such occupations. Only a minority of married women worked in early mills and mines. Children and unmarried women, however, went out to work in mills, where their hands were better suited to intricate machinery than men's, or in mines, where their small statures allowed them to move through low mine tunnels more easily than men. Their wages always were very low.

Most significantly, perhaps, the worker lost control over the pace of his or her work. Modern factory production dictated that workers serve these new machines that had taken over the productive role. Barring breakdowns, the machine's pace never varied; the new work was monotonous. Workers found themselves endlessly repeating the same tasks in the production process with little autonomy. In addition, industrial work imposed a new punctuality on workers. For the factory system to function smoothly, all had to be at their work stations on time and remain there except during scheduled breaks. "Holy Monday" and unscheduled leisure time threatened the smooth operation of an industrial establishment. Early mines and factories posed significant safety problems, too, as we will see.

How did the first generations of industrial workers respond to such

fundamental changes? Some adapted. Others proved incapable of adjusting to the new working conditions, and absenteeism (especially on Mondays), chronic tardiness, and workers' inability to keep pace with machines plagued many early mills. Many other workers experienced a growing inner alienation, identified by such observers of industrialism as Karl Marx, that manifested itself in various forms of asocial behavior. When economic conditions were good and jobs were plentiful, early mills had problems with frequent employee resignations. Some mills experienced as much as 100 percent annual employee turnover.

Other new social problems also accompanied industrialization. Urban expansion accompanied the factory system (see Chapter 8), reflecting the movement of many rural families to growing cities in search of factory employment. Such moves separated the new arrivals from friends and from the social controls of village life. In the city they often found not only the poverty of early industrial work but also the anonymity of urban life and the wealth of modern society displayed by the privileged classes. The result was a rapid rise of crimes against property accompanying urban growth. Older social problems persisted, too. Preindustrial workers frequently consumed alcohol in excess as an escape from their tedious work lives. Indeed, "holy Monday" often reflected the effects of a worker's weekend of alcohol abuse. The early industrial age was little different. One English clergyman described to a committee of Parliament the sight of twelve-year-old coal miners staggering with drink.

The human response to this fundamental change in work thus assumed many forms; however, these did not include organized resistance to the machine age by industrial workers. Those employed in early mills and mines often were illiterate and consequently difficult to mobilize for collective actions such as strikes. Moreover, laws like the English Combination Acts (1799, 1800) and the French Le Chapelier Law (1791) actually forbade worker organizations; the few early unions were illegal and secretive. The only overt resistance to industrialization, therefore, came not from industrial workers but from one group of preindustrial laborers, namely, the artisans. Members of this class had a high rate of literacy and thus were aware that the new machines ultimately threatened both their livelihoods and their work autonomy. They lashed out with acts of machine smashing. English machine smashers were called *Luddites* after one Ned Ludd, who supposedly originated their movement.

Machine smashing, of course, could not stop industrialization, and workers in early mines and mills became the objects of an increasingly stringent discipline aimed at forcing their acceptance of the new labor. Overseers beat child laborers. Managers fined or dismissed adults and sometimes blacklisted particularly difficult workers to deny them any employment.

In this chapter you will be asked to contrast the working conditions of the preindustrial and industrial ages. How did industrial labor differ from preindustrial work? How did such labor evolve? What effects did the new labor have on the first generations of men, women, and children in Europe's mills and mines?

SOURCES AND METHOD

The central questions of this chapter require your analysis of both preindustrial and industrial labor. As an aid to this analysis, the evidence for this chapter is accordingly divided into two groups, one relating to the preindustrial age (the "old labor") and the other to the industrial era (the "new labor").

Let us begin our consideration of the old labor with its most traditional form, agricultural labor. Source 1 is the work of Sébastien Le Prestre de Vauban (1633–1707). Vauban was a brilliant military engineer whose skill in designing fortifications and conducting sieges for the army of Louis XIV of France propelled him to the highest rank in the army, Marshal of France. But Vauban's interests were not narrowly military in scope. This highly intelligent and observant man wrote extensively on a variety of problems; he was the author of treatises on agriculture, construction, and the need for religious toleration in an age of widespread persecution of religious minorities. The selection from Vauban's writings presented in Source

Chapter 6

Labor Old

and New:

The Impact of

the Industrial

Revolution

1 is drawn from one of his last works, a proposal for reforming the tax system of early-eighteenth-century France with the goals of both greater equity in assessing the tax burden and increased revenues to balance the royal budget. To adequately present his ideas, Vauban undertook a description of the economic situations of his fellow Frenchmen in this work, which gives the student of the eighteenth century a number of insights into the lot of common people who left little other record of their activities. In reading this source, pay particular attention to the agricultural workers Vauban describes. This group owned little property, but instead worked the lands of others. Lacking land of their own, this group of workers possessed a certain mobility, which would lead many of their number to factory employment a century after Vauban's analysis of their situation. How long was the agricultural work year of this group? Why were the earnings of such people from agriculture insufficient? What sort of nonagricultural employment did members of the family unit undertake?

In Source 2, you encounter further evidence on agricultural labor, this time on working conditions of farm workers in England almost a century and a half after Vauban wrote. Source 2 offers you for the first time a type of evidence you will analyze several times in this chapter, the record of hearings on early industrial working conditions conducted by legislative committees. From such records, committee members drew up recommendations, which often resulted in legislation to improve working conditions in early mills, factories, and mines.

These records have a great advantage for the historian because they also offer a glimpse into the world of the illiterate laboring poor of an earlier age. Secretaries to the investigating committees often took down the testimony of witnesses verbatim, providing an enduring record of all the difficulties of labor in the early industrial era. Mrs. Britton labored in the old style as an agricultural worker, but she brought a unique perspective to her testimony to a committee of the British Parliament because she once had worked in a factory also. What were the work conditions and the standard of living of agricultural workers like Mrs. Britton and her husband? How did agricultural labor compare with factory labor for Mrs. Britton?

With Source 3 we turn to the labor of the preindustrial craftsman. The evidence on craftsmen's labor opens with a summary of holidays in a textile-producing city, Lille, France, in the seventeenth century. How would you characterize the pace of labor in Lille, a city whose work calendar was not unusual in Catholic Europe?

Source 4 presents excerpts from guild regulations in the Prussian woolen industry. The Industrial Revolution began in England in the mid-eighteenth century but affected the Continent much later, only in the first decades of the nineteenth century. Thus, these guild regulations dating from 1797 describe the traditional labor of many Europeans. In reading them, ask yourself what sort of labor conditions these regulations sustained. A worker's demonstration of his mastery of all the processes of producing wool cloth won him the "freedom of the guild" and its privileges. The latter involved the right to establish his own production unit and market his goods, as well as guild assistance when old age or illness prevented work. What sort of limits on the activities of guild members accompanied these freedoms? What do you think were the reasons for these restrictions? What efforts to protect both the consumer and the guild members' market can you discern in these restrictions? Why was the putting-out system explicitly forbidden to guild members? What specifically in all these restrictions seems intended to create a protected monopoly for producers?

Source 5 describes another facet of the old style of labor in textile production, namely, the putting-out system. It is the work of François-Alexandre Frédéric, Duke of La Rochefoucauld-Liancourt (1747–1827), an astute observer of the social and economic problems of his day who applied his energy and wealth to various reform schemes, including experimental farms and an early cotton mill. La Rochefoucauld wrote persuasively on the need for improved poor relief and better education for all Frenchmen. Here, to support his call for social change, La Rochefoucauld provides a good description of the putting-out system in his travel account of 1781 to 1783, based on his visit to Rouen, the capital of the northern French province of Normandy. Who was employed in textiles in Rouen? What does the duke tell you about the quantity of production in Rouen, despite the continued use of hand looms? How did the organization of this work, the quantity

of production, and the destinations of its products foreshadow certain features of the industrial age?

Source 6, "The Clothier's Delight," is a popular song, a type of source you have not yet studied in Volume II. Historians examine songs as evidence of popular culture to understand the attitudes and lives of men and women who were often illiterate. We must understand that such songs may exaggerate their message a bit to achieve their desired effect among unsophisticated audiences. Nevertheless, we do have in this song some evidence of broad trends in the putting-out system and the concerns of those employed in it by English clothiers. Who controlled the material in this production process? Were the weavers and other textile workers the independent producers described in the guild regulations? Why did the workers view the clothiers as adversaries? How did the clothiers control the workers?

Next, consider the evidence on the new labor, that is, the work of the industrial age. Sources 7 and 8 in this section are regulations governing the conditions of work in early industrial enterprises. In using this material, the historian must remember that such regulations describe the behavior prescribed by persons in authority; they may not describe the actual comportment of those whose behavior the statutes aimed to control. Indeed, we can assume that there was frequent conflict between the prescribed rules and the actual behavior of working people as workers adapted to the new conditions of industrial work.

Examine the work code for the foundry and engineering works in

Chapter 6

Labor Old

and New:

The Impact of

the Industrial

Revolution

Moabit, an industrial suburb of Berlin, Germany, in 1844 (Source 7). What sort of habits did these regulations seek to inculcate in the foundry workers? Notice also the pay practices described in paragraph 18. Why would management have adopted these? What disadvantages did they represent for the worker?

The apprenticeship agreement for girls as silk workers in rural Tarare, France (Source 8), retains the terminology of the old labor in designating new workers as apprentices, but it lays down industrial-age work rules for the young women. Examine the agreement carefully, noting its disciplinary features. How long was the apprenticeship? When were wages paid? What happened if a girl left before the completion of her apprenticeship? What were the work hours? In what ways did management seek to increase production? Such mills as this were established in rural areas, away from cities like Lyons, where male preindustrial silk weavers had a centuries-long history of guild organization (and of unrest). Given that information, can you discern why the mill's location was chosen and why a female work force was sought? What attractions did the mill, with its long workday, offer unmarried rural women who otherwise would have been reluctant to seek industrial employment away from home?

The testimony of William Cooper to the Sadler Committee of the British Parliament (Source 9) provides dramatic evidence about the conditions of industrial labor in early textile mills. What effect did mill labor have on Cooper? What were the hours of work? How did overseers enforce punctuality and a faster work pace by young workers? Were conditions within the mills conducive to good health? Compare Cooper's height to that of his father. What could have accounted for Cooper's shorter stature? When he had health problems and was unable to work, what recourse did Cooper have?

Source 10 also describes the condition of labor in the textile industry, but it records the lot of women fifty or more years after William Cooper's experiences in the mills. Had working conditions improved very much since Cooper's day? How long was the workday? Did the work demand exceptional energy or skill from the workers? How did management impose discipline in such matters as punctuality?

With the selections brought together as Source 11, you will once more analyze the records of English parliamentary inquiries, but this time the committees examined coal mine labor in the 1840s. Read first the testimony of Joseph Staley. Note his position in the mine. How might this have affected his conclusion about his miners' health? How many boys did he employ, and what ages were they? What sort of labor did the boys do? What were their hours? Analyze the testimony of William Jagger. What age was he? How long had he worked in the mine? What were his hours? What do his testimony and the comment by the investigator following that testimony tell you about work conditions and mine safety?

With the testimony of Patience Kershaw we have a record of women's labor in the mines. What sort of labor did Kershaw do? What weight of coal did she move daily? What health effects did such labor have on women like Kershaw and her sisters? What impression did she make on the parliamentary investigator, as indicated in his comment following her testimony?

Industrialization transformed the Western world in many ways, and we will examine aspects of its consequences in other chapters of this book as well (see especially Chapters 8 and 14). Your analysis of the evidence presented here should aid you in understanding one aspect of that transformation: the emergence of a new world of industrial labor and how it affected men and women of the eighteenth and nineteenth centuries.

THE EVIDENCE

THE OLD LABOR

Source 1 from Sébastien Le Prestre de Vauban, Project d'une Dixme royale, *ed. by E. Coornaert (Paris: Alcan, 1933) reprinted in Pierre Goubert,* The Ancien Régime: French Society, *1600–1750, trans. by Steve Cox (New York: Harper and Row, 1974), pp. 116–118. Copyright © 1973 by George Weidenfeld & Nicholson Ltd. Reprinted with the permission of Steve Cox.*

1. Agricultural Labor Described by Vauban, About 1700

. . . It only remains to take stock of two million men[1] all of whom I suppose to be day-laborers or simple artisans scattered throughout the towns, *bourgs*[2] and villages of the realm.

What I have to say about all these workers . . . deserves serious attention, for although this sector may consist of what are unfairly called the dregs of the people, they are nonetheless worthy of high consideration in view of the services which they render to the State. For it is they who undertake all the great tasks in town and country without which neither themselves nor others could live. It is they who provide all the soldiers and sailors and all the serving women; in a word, without them the State could not survive. It is for this reason that they ought to be spared in the matter of taxes, in order not to burden them beyond their strength. . . .

1. Vauban wrote in an age that had no modern census data for accurately assessing the size of a population. His figures here, at best, are an estimate. Indeed, modern demographic historians generally find Vauban's population data highly inaccurate.

2. *bourgs:* market towns.

Chapter 6

Labor Old

and New:

The Impact of

the Industrial

Revolution

Among the smaller fry, particularly in the countryside, there are any number of people who, while they lay no claim to any special craft, are continually plying several which are most necessary and indispensable. Of such a kind are those we call *manoeuvriers,* who, owning for the most part nothing but their strong arms or very little more, do day- or piece-work for whoever wants to employ them. It is they who do all the major jobs such as mowing, harvesting, threshing, woodcutting, working the soil and the vineyards, clearing land, ditching, carrying soil to vineyards or elsewhere, labouring for builders and several other tasks which are all hard and laborious. These men may well find this kind of employment for part of the year, and it is true that they can usually earn a fair day's wage at haymaking, harvesting and grapepicking time, but the rest of the year is a different story. . . .

It will not be inappropriate [to give] some particulars about what the country day-laborer can earn.

I shall assume that of the three-hundred and sixty-five days in the year, he may be gainfully employed for one hundred and eighty, and earn nine *sols*[3] a day. This is a high figure, and it is certain that except at harvest and grapepicking time most earn not more than eight *sols* a day on average, but supposing we allow the nine *sols,* that would amount to eighty-five *livres* and ten *sols,* call it ninety *livres,* from which we have to deduct his liabilities (taxes plus salt[4] for a family of four, say 14l. 16s.) . . . leaving seventy-five *livres* four *sols.*

Since I am assuming that his family . . . consists of four people, it requires not less than ten *septiers*[5] of grain, Paris measure, to feed them. This grain, half wheat, half rye . . . commonly selling at six *livres* per *septier* . . . will come to sixty *livres,* which leaves fifteen *livres* 4 *sols* out of seventy-five *livres* four *sols,* out of which the labourer has to find the price of rent and upkeep for his house, a few chattels, if only some earthenware bowls, clothing and linen, and the needs of his entire family for one year.

But these fifteen *livres* four *sols* will not take him very far unless his industry[6] or some particular business supervenes and his wife contributes to their income by means of her distaff,[7] sewing, knitting hose or making small quan-

---

3. *sol:* sou.

4. Salt was subject to a form of tax in France before 1789. Tax farmers purchased the exclusive right to sell this dietary necessity to the public. The public was required by law to buy a certain amount of salt per year from these monopolists; in paying the price of the salt, buyers also paid a salt tax, the *gabelle,* to the tax farmers, who turned the proceeds of this over to the government. This form of taxation kept salt prices artificially high in much of France and was deeply resented by many taxpayers.

5. *septier:* a unit of measure in use in France prior to the Revolution of 1789. Its precise size varied from one district to another; hence here Vauban must specify that he is using the Parisian *septier.* Ten Parisian *septiers* would have equaled about 15.5 hectoliters or 43 bushels.

6. Many rural workers would have been employed in some phase of textile production, such as weaving.

7. **distaff:** a staff that holds unspun flax or wool during the process of spinning such material into thread. The word can also refer to women's work or interests, because spinning was women's work.

tities of lace . . . also by keeping a small garden or rearing poultry and perhaps a calf, a pig or a goat for the better-off . . . ; by which means he might buy a piece of larding bacon and a little butter or oil for making soup. And if he does not additionally cultivate some small allotment, he will be hard pressed to subsist, or at least he will be reduced, together with his family, to the most wretched fare. And if instead of two children he has four, that will be worse still until they are old enough to earn their own living. Thus however we come at the matter, it is certain that he will always have the greatest difficulty in seeing the year out. . . .

Source 2 from British Parliamentary Papers: Reports of Special Assistant Poor Law Commissioner on the Employment of Women and Children in Agriculture *(London: William Clowes and Sons for Her Majesty's Stationery Office, 1843), pp. 66–67.*

2. Testimony of an Agricultural Worker's Wife and Former Factory Worker, 1842[8]

Mrs. *Britton,* Wife of _____ *Britton, of Calne, Wiltshire,* Farm-labourer, examined.

I am 41 years old; I have lived at Calne all my life. I went to school till I was eight years old, when I went out to look after children. At ten years old I went to work at a factory in Calne, where I was till I was 26. I have been married 15 years. My husband is an agricultural labourer. I have seven children, all boys. The oldest is fourteen, the youngest three-quarters of a year old. My husband is a good workman, and does most of his work by the lump, and earns from 9s. to 10s. a-week pretty constantly, but finds his own tools,—his wheelbarrow, which cost 1l., pickaxe, which cost 3s., and scoop, which cost 3s.[9]

I have worked in the fields, and when I went out I left the children in the care of the eldest boy, and frequently carried the baby with me, as I could not

8. This testimony was delivered before a parliamentary committee studying the employment of women and children in British agriculture.
9. **by the lump:** Mr. Britton was paid by the job rather than by the hour or day. English coinage mentioned in this and following selections (with the abbreviations for each denomination where appropriate) includes:
   £ or l.: pound sterling.
   s.: shilling; 20 shillings to 1 pound sterling.
   d.: pence (from Latin *denari*); 12 pence to 1 shilling.
   crown: a coin worth 5 shillings.
   groat: a coin worth 4 pence.

Chapter 6

Labor Old

and New:

The Impact of

the Industrial

Revolution

go home to nurse it. I have worked at hay-making and at harvest, and at other times in weeding and keeping the ground clean. I generally work from half-past seven till five, or half-past. When at work in the spring I have received 10*d.* a-day, but that is higher than the wages of women in general; 8*d.* or 9*d.* is more common. My master always paid 10*d.* When working I never had any beer, and I never felt the want of it. I never felt that my health was hurt by the work. Hay-making is hard work, very fatiguing, but it never hurt me. Working in the fields is not such hard work as working in the factory. I am always better when I can get out to work in the fields. I intend to do so next year if I can. Last year I could not go out, owing to the birth of the baby. My eldest boy gets a little to do; he don't earn more than 9*d.* a-week; he has not enough to do. My husband has 40 lugs[10] of land, for which he pays 10*s.* a-year. We grow potatoes and a few cabbages, but not enough for our family; for that we should like to have forty lugs more. We have to buy potatoes. One of the children is a cripple, and the guardians[11] allow us two gallons of bread a-week for him.[12] We buy two gallons more, according as the money is. Nine people can't do with less than four gallons of bread a-week. We could eat much more bread if we could get it; sometimes we can afford only one gallon a-week. We very rarely buy butcher's fresh meat, certainly not oftener than once a-week, and not more than sixpenny worth. I like my husband to have a bit of meat, now he has left off drinking. I buy $\frac{1}{2}$ lb. butter a-week, 1 oz. tea, $\frac{1}{2}$ lb. sugar. The rest of our food is potatoes, with a little fat. The rent of our cottage is 1*s.* 6*d.* a-week; there are two rooms in it. We all sleep in one room, under the tiles. Sometimes we receive private assistance, especially in clothing. Formerly my husband was in the habit of drinking, and everything went bad. He used to beat me. I have often gone to bed, I and my children, without supper, and I have had no breakfast the next morning, and frequently no firing.[13] My husband attended a lecture on teetotalism one evening about two years ago, and I have reason to bless that evening. My husband has never touched a drop of drink since. He has been better in health, getting stouter, and has behaved like a good husband to me ever since. I have been much more comfortable, and the children happier. He works better than he did. He can mow better, and

10. **lug:** an old English measure of area equal to 49 square yards. The Brittons' 40 lugs would, therefore, have equaled 1,960 square yards, less than half of a full acre, which is 4,840 square yards.

11. **guardian:** Poor Law official.

12. **two gallons of bread:** the gallon as a gauge of wheat and other dry material is an archaic English measure, the weight of which was far from standard in the British Isles. Sources refer to gallons of wheat weighing anywhere from 8 to almost 10 pounds. If we assume a gallon to have been 9 pounds in the case of the Brittons, we find that the family claims to have required a minimum of 36 pounds of bread per week. For this time, in which bread was the basic dietary element of the poor, demographic historians assume an adult to have consumed 2 pounds per day. Even if the family comprised only two adults and the rest children, these were extremely short rations.

13. **firing:** that is, no morning hearth fire for want of the cost of fuel.

that is hard work, and he does not mind being laughed at by the other men for not drinking. I send my eldest boy to Sunday school; them that are younger go to the day school. My eldest boy never complains of work hurting him. My husband now goes regularly to church: formerly he could hardly be got there.

Source 3 from Alain Lottin, Chavatte, ouvrier lillois. Un contemporain de Louis XIV *(Paris: Flammarion, 1979), pp. 323–324. Reprinted with permission.*

3. The Work Year in 17th-Century Lille, France

Holidays in Seventeenth-Century Lille

January	Monday following Epiphany (January 6)
22 January	Feast of St. Vincent
25 January	Feast of St. Paul's Conversion
February	Ash Wednesday
22 February	Feast of the Chair of St. Peter
March or April	Tuesday of Holy Week until the Thursday after Easter (eight working days)
3 May	Feast of the Finding of the True Cross
9 May	Feast of St. Nicholas
May or June	Feast of Pentecost (seventh Sunday after Easter): Pentecost eve through the following Thursday (five days)
5 June	Corpus Christi
9 June or second Sunday in June	Municipal procession accompanied by banquets
11 June	Feast of St. Barnabas
June	Thursday after municipal procession is a holiday
2 July	Feast of the visitation of the Virgin
1 August	Feast of St. Peter in Chains
3 August	Feast of St. Stephen
29 August	Feast of the Beheading of St. John the Baptist, followed by five days off
1 October	Feast of St. Remy
18 October	Feast of St. Luke
1 November	All Saints Day
24–31 December	Christmas (eight days)

This represents a total of forty-four days off, in addition to Sundays.

Chapter 6

Labor Old

and New:

The Impact of

the Industrial

Revolution

Sources 4 and 5 from Sidney Pollard and Colin Holmes, editors, Documents in European Economic History, *vol. 1,* The Process of Industrialization, 1750–1870 *(New York: St. Martin's, 1968), pp. 45–48, pp. 91–92. Copyright © 1968 by St. Martin's Press. Reprinted with permission of St. Martin's Press, Inc., and Sidney Pollard.*

4. Guild Regulations in the Prussian Woolen Industry, 1797

§ 760

Although it is laid down in the General Privilege (8 Nov. 1734) that it shall not be necessary to produce a masterpiece in order to gain the master's freedom; yet it was ruled afterwards: that anyone aspiring to the freedom of the gild, shall (22 November 1772) apart from being examined by the Inspector of Manufactures and the Gild Master whether he be properly experienced in sorting and fulling, wool shearing and preparing and threading the looms, also weave a piece of cloth of mixed colour from wool dyed by himself.

§ 765–§ 771

The woollen weavers may sell by retail and cutting-up home produced cloths and baizes[14] on condition that they and their fellow gild members may not only sell in their own town the goods made locally, but may also offer them for sale at fairs and annual markets. The latter, however, is limited to this extent (1772 and 1791): that a gild member may not take part in any market or fair unless he has at least 12 pieces of cloth for sale, though it is permissible (18 December 1791) for two of them to enter a fair and to offer cloth for sale if they have at least 12 pieces of cloth between them; at the same time, this privilege is extended also to weavers (1772) who are no longer practising their trade themselves.

The woollen weavers of Salzwedel, however, may not sell the cloths produced by themselves, by retail and cutting-up, even in their own town, because the local cloth cutters' and tailors' gild enjoys, according to its old privilege (1233, 1323 and last confirmed on 26 January 1715) the sole right of cutting up woollen and similar cloth for sale, so that neither the local merchants, nor the mercers, nor the woollen weavers of the town, whose rights were recently confirmed, have the right to cut up woollen cloth for sale.

Woollen weavers may not trade in woollen cloths made outside their own town, unless they have been specially granted this right, because this would infringe the privileges granted to the merchants. . . .

---

14. **baize:** a soft woolen fabric.

Neither finishers nor croppers,[15] dyers or other craftsmen (1772) are permitted to trade in woollen cloths or undertake putting-out agencies on pain of losing their craft privileges.

In the countryside (28 August 1723, 14 November 1793) neither linen (?) weavers, nor vergers[16] or schoolmasters, nor husbandmen themselves, are permitted to manufacture woollen or worsted cloth not even for their own use. Neither are town linen weavers permitted to make goods wholly of wool.

Woollen weavers are permitted to dye their own cloths, but neither they nor the merchants are permitted to have the cloths made in the Electoral Mark finished or dyed in foreign towns, on pain of confiscation of the goods. While the export of unfinished and undyed cloths is permissible (1772), merchants and woollen weavers should be persuaded (26 October and 10 November 1791) to export only dyed and finished cloths.

Woollen weavers may not (1772) keep their own tenting frame and stretch their own cloths, but must leave this finishing process to the cloth finishers. They have however the concession (28 October and 11 November 1773) that they may keep 10–12 frames, but on these they may only stretch $\frac{3}{4}$ widths, and twill flannels. . . .

§ 798

On pain of requisition and, for repeated offences, on pain of loss of the freedom of the gild, better yarn may not be used for the ends of pieces of cloth than is used for the middle. No weaver is permitted to keep frames of his own, on pain of loss of his gild freedom, and he is obliged to take his cloths to the master shearmen; tanned wool and wool-fells may not be woven into pieces, but must be made only into rough goods and horse blankets. Finally it is laid down in detail how each type of woollen and worsted cloth shall be manufactured; and weavers have been advised several times to observe closely the detailed rules and regulations of the woollen and worsted order (20 September 1784, 9 September and 8 October 1787). . . .

§ 800

It is further laid down as a general rule, that all cloths shall be viewed by sworn aulnagers,[17] of whom eight shall be elected in large companies, six in medium sized ones, and two to four among small ones, and they shall be viewed three times, and sealed accordingly after each time. The first viewing shall determine that the piece is woven with sufficient and satisfactory yarn, woven sufficiently closely and without flaws, and of the correct length and

15. **cropper:** a craftsman who sheared the nap from woolen cloth.
16. **verger:** a parish official generally charged with care of the interior of a church.
17. **aulnager:** an official charged with measuring and inspecting woolen cloth.

Chapter 6

Labor Old

and New:

The Impact of

the Industrial

Revolution

width. The second, held on the frame, shall determine whether the cloth is overstretched, and has wholly pure wool, is fulled cleanly and free of errors in fulling, and the third, held on the frame after dyeing, whether it has suffered by the dyeing.

5. La Rochefoucauld Describes the Putting-Out System in Rouen, France, 1781–1783

I then saw the material called cotton check (*cotonnades*). There are all sorts of cotton manufacture made up at Rouen and in the area 15 leagues[18] around it. The peasant who returns to the plough to work his fields, sits at his cotton frame and makes either *siamoises*[19] or ticking or even white, very fine, cotton cloth. One must admire the activity of the Normans. This activity does not interfere at all with their daily work. Land is very dear and consequently very well cultivated. The farmer works on the land during the day and it is in the evening by the light of the lamp that he starts his other task. His workers and his family have to help. When they have worked all week they come into the town with horses or carts piled up with material. Goods are sold in the Hall, which is all that remains of the palace of the former Dukes of Normandy, on Thursdays. It is a truly wonderful sight. It takes place at a surprising speed. Almost 800,000 francs worth of business is transacted between 6.00 and 9.00 in the morning. Among those who do the buying there are many agents who buy for merchants and then the goods pass to America, Italy and Spain. The majority goes to America. I have seen many pieces destined to become shirts for negroes; but their skin will be seen through the material, since the cloth is thin and almost sufficiently coarse to make ticking. It costs 17, 20 and even 25 francs per aune[20] in the Hall.

18. **league:** a league equals 2.764 miles.

19. *siamoises:* common cotton goods.

20. **aune:** an old French measurement unit for textiles; equal to 45 inches.

Source 6 from James Burnley, The History of Wool and Wool Combing *(London: Sampson Low, Marston, Searle and Rivington, Ltd., 1889), pp. 160–163.*

6. "The Clothier's Delight; or, the Rich Men's Joy, and the Poor Men's Sorrow, Wherein Is Exprest the Craftiness and Subtility of Many Clothiers in England by Beatting Down Their Workmen's Wages," Song, 18th Century

Of all sorts of callings that in England be,
There is none that liveth so gallant as we;
Our trading maintains us as brave as a knight,
We live at our pleasure, and take our delight;
We heapeth up riches and treasure great store,
Which we get by griping and grinding the poor.
    And this is a way for to fill up our purse,
    Although we do get it with many a curse.

Throughout the whole kingdom, in country and town,
There is no danger of our trade going down,
So long as the Comber[21] can work with his comb,
And also the Weaver weave with his lomb;[22]
The Tucker[23] and Spinner[24] that spins all the year,
We will make them to earn their wages full dear.
    And this is the way, &c.

In former ages we us'd to give,
So that our work-folks like farmers did live;
But the times are altered, we will make them know
All we can for to bring them all under our bow;

21. **comber:** the person who performed one of the processes in finishing raw wool, the combing out of the wool.
22. **lomb:** archaic spelling of *loom.*
23. **tucker:** in the processing of wool, the person who performed the task of *fulling* the wool, that is, cleaning, shrinking, and thickening the fabric with moisture, heat, and pressure.
24. **spinner:** the person who spun the raw wool into thread on a spinning wheel or other device.

Chapter 6

Labor Old

and New:

The Impact of

the Industrial

Revolution

We will make to work hard for sixpence a day,[25]
Though a shilling they deserve if they had their just pay.
    And this is the way, &c. . . .

We'll make the poor Weavers work at a low rate;
We'll find fault where there's no fault, and so we will bate;[26]
If trading grows dead, we will presently show it;
But if it grows good, they shall never know it;
We'll tell them that cloth beyond sea will not go,
We care not whether we keep clothing or no.
    And this is the way, &c.

Then next for the Spinners we shall ensue,
We'll make them spin three pound instead of two;
When they bring home their work unto us, they complain,
And say that their wages will not them maintain;
But if that an ounce of weight they do lack,
Then for to bate threepence we will not be slack.
    And this is the way, &c.

But if it holds weight, then their wages they crave,
We have got no money, and what's that you'd have?
We have bread and bacon and butter that's good,
With oatmeal and salt that is wholesome for food;
We have soap and candles whereby to give light,[27]
That you may work by them so long as you have light.
    And this is the way, &c. . . .

Then hey for the Clothing Trade, it goes on brave;
We scorn for to toyl and moyl,[28] nor yet to slave.
Our workmen do work hard, but we live at ease;
We go when we will, and come when we please;
We hoard up our bags of silver and gold;
But conscience and charity with us are cold.
    By poor people's labour, &c.

25. There were 12 pence to a shilling; hence sixpence represented a 50 percent pay cut. In the next verse, the value of 8 groats was 32 pence, and half a crown was worth 30 pence. Thus the song portrays the clothiers as seeking to reduce wages a small and perhaps unnoticed amount, 2 pence.

26. **bate:** to beat back or reduce a worker's wages.

27. This whole verse refers to a practice, theoretically illegal in England after 1701, of paying putting-out workers in textiles with goods, not cash. This practice kept workers dependent on their employers because they lacked hard currency when they were paid in such commodities as bread, bacon, butter, oatmeal, salt, soap, and candles. That the practice endured despite the law is indicated by additional laws directed against it as late as 1779.

28. **toyl and moyl:** archaic spellings of *toil* and *moil*—that is, work and drudgery.

THE NEW LABOR

Source 7 from Sidney Pollard and Colin Holmes, editors, Documents in European Economic History, *vol. 1,* The Process of Industrialization, 1750–1870 *(New York: St. Martin's Press, 1968), pp. 534–536. Copyright © 1968 by St. Martin's Press. Reprinted with permission of St. Martin's Press, Inc., and Sidney Pollard.*

7. Rules for Workers in the Foundry and Engineering Works of the Royal Overseas Trading Company, Berlin, 1844

In every large works, and in the co-ordination of any large number of workmen, good order and harmony must be looked upon as the fundamentals of success, and therefore the following rules shall be strictly observed.

Every man employed in the concern named below shall receive a copy of these rules, so that no one can plead ignorance. Its acceptance shall be deemed to mean consent to submit to its regulations.

(1) The normal working day begins at all seasons at 6 a.m. precisely and ends, after the usual break of half an hour for breakfast, an hour for dinner and half an hour for tea, at 7 p.m., and it shall be strictly observed.

Five minutes before the beginning of the stated hours of work until their actual commencement, a bell shall ring and indicate that every worker employed in the concern has to proceed to his place of work, in order to start as soon as the bell stops.

The doorkeeper shall lock the door punctually at 6 a.m., 8.30 a.m., 1 p.m. and 4.30 p.m.

Workers arriving 2 minutes late shall lose half an hour's wages; whoever is more than 2 minutes late may not start work until after the next break, or at least shall lose his wages until then. Any disputes about the correct time shall be settled by the clock mounted above the gatekeeper's lodge.

These rules are valid both for time- and for piece-workers, and in cases of breaches of these rules, workmen shall be fined in proportion to their earnings. The deductions from the wage shall be entered in the wage-book of the gatekeeper whose duty they are: they shall be unconditionally accepted as it will not be possible to enter into any discussions about them.

(2) When the bell is rung to denote the end of the working day, every workman, both on piece- and on day-wage, shall leave his workshop and the yard, but is not allowed to make preparations for his departure before the bell rings. Every breach of this rule shall lead to a fine of five silver groschen to the sick fund. Only those who have obtained special permission by the overseer may stay on in the workshop in order to work.—If a workman has worked beyond

Chapter 6

Labor Old

and New:

The Impact of

the Industrial

Revolution

the closing bell, he must give his name to the gatekeeper on leaving, on pain of losing his payment for the overtime.

(3) No workman, whether employed by time or piece, may leave before the end of the working day, without having first received permission from the overseer and having given his name to the gatekeeper. Omission of these two actions shall lead to a fine of ten silver groschen payable to the sick fund.

(4) Repeated irregular arrival at work shall lead to dismissal. This shall also apply to those who are found idling by an official or overseer, and refuse to obey their order to resume work.

(5) Entry to the firm's property by any but the designated gateway, and exit by any prohibited route, e.g., by climbing fences or walls, or by crossing the Spree, shall be punished by a fine of fifteen silver groschen to the sick fund for the first offences, and dismissal for the second.

(6) No worker may leave his place of work otherwise than for reasons connected with his work.

(7) All conversation with fellow-workers is prohibited; if any worker requires information about his work, he must turn to the overseer, or to the particular fellow-worker designated for the purpose.

(8) Smoking in the workshops or in the yard is prohibited during working hours; anyone caught smoking shall be fined five silver groschen for the sick fund for every such offence.

(9) Every worker is responsible for cleaning up his space in the workshop, and if in doubt, he is to turn to his overseer.—All tools must always be kept in good condition, and must be cleaned after use. This applies particularly to the turner, regarding his lathe.

(10) Natural functions must be performed at the appropriate places, and whoever is found soiling walls, fences, squares, etc., and similarly, whoever is found washing his face and hands in the workshop and not in the places assigned for the purpose, shall be fined five silver groschen for the sick fund.

(11) On completion of his piece of work, every workman must hand it over at once to his foreman or superior, in order to receive a fresh piece of work. Pattern makers must on no account hand over their patterns to the foundry without express order of their supervisors. No workman may take over work from his fellow-workman without instruction to that effect by the foreman.

(12) It goes without saying that all overseers and officials of the firm shall be obeyed without question, and shall be treated with due deference. Disobedience will be punished by dismissal.

(13) Immediate dismissal shall also be the fate of anyone found drunk in any of the workshops.

(14) Untrue allegations against superiors or officials of the concern shall lead to stern reprimand, and may lead to dismissal. The same punishment shall be meted out to those who knowingly allow errors to slip through when supervising or stocktaking.

(15) Every workman is obliged to report to his superiors any acts of dishonesty or embezzlement on the part of his fellow workmen. If he omits to do so, and it is shown after subsequent discovery of a misdemeanour that he knew about it at the time, he shall be liable to be taken to court as an accessory after the fact and the wage due to him shall be retained as punishment. Conversely, anyone denouncing a theft in such a way as to allow conviction of the thief shall receive a reward of two Thaler, and, if necessary, his name shall be kept confidential.—Further, the gatekeeper and the watchman, as well as every official, are entitled to search the baskets, parcels, aprons etc. of the women and children who are taking the dinners into the works, on their departure, as well as search any worker suspected of stealing any article whatever. . . .

(19) A free copy of these rules is handed to every workman, but whoever loses it and requires a new one, or cannot produce it on leaving, shall be fined $2\frac{1}{2}$ silver groschen, payable to the sick fund.

Moabit, August, 1844.

Source 8 from Erna Olafson Hellerstein, L. P. Hume, and K. M. Offen, editors, Victorian Women: A Documentary Account of Women's Lives in Nineteenth-Century England, France, and the United States *(Stanford, Calif.: Stanford University Press, 1981), pp. 394–396. Used by permission of Stanford University Press.*

8. Apprenticeship Contract for Young Women Employed in the Silk Mills of Tarare, France, 1850s

MILLING, REELING, AND WARP-PREPARATION OF SILKS

Conditions of Apprenticeship

Art. 1. To be admitted, young women must be between the ages of thirteen and fifteen, of good character and in good health, intelligent and industrious, and must have been vaccinated. They must present their birth certificate, a certificate of vaccination, and a trousseau.

Art. 2. Girls who are accepted by the establishment will be placed in milling, reeling, or warp[29] preparation by the director, according to the needs of the establishment and their intelligence.

Art. 3. During the apprenticeship period, the pupil will be paid wages, fed, lodged, given heat and light, and laundry *for her body linen only*; she will also be furnished with aprons.

---

29. **warp:** in the weaving process, threads placed lengthwise in the loom. They were woven with threads called the *weft* or *woof* placed perpendicularly to them.

Chapter 6

Labor Old

and New:

The Impact of

the Industrial

Revolution

Art. 4. The pupil promises to be obedient and submissive to the mistresses charged with her conduct and instruction, as well as to conform to the rules of the establishment.

Art. 5. In case of illness the director will notify the father or guardian of the sick apprentice, and if her state necessitates a leave, it will be granted until her recovery.

Art. 6. If the sick pupil remains in the establishment, every care necessitated by her condition will be given to her.

Art. 7. In case of illness or any other serious cause that warrants her leaving, the apprentice who must absent herself from the establishment will be obligated to prolong her apprenticeship during a time equal to that of her absence.

Art. 8. The director alone has the right to authorize or refuse leaves. They will be granted only on the request of the father or guardian of the pupil.

Art. 9. Apprenticeship is for three consecutive years, *not including an obligatory trial month.* In order to encourage the pupil, she will be paid:

1st year:	a wage of 40 to 50 francs
2nd year:	″ ″ ″ 60 to 75 ″
3rd year:	″ ″ ″ 80 to 100 ″

After the apprenticeship the wage will be established according to merit.

At the end of the apprenticeship, a gratuity of 20 francs will be given to the apprentice to reward her for her exactitude in fulfilling her engagements.

Art. 10. The effective work time is twelve hours. Summer and winter, the day begins at 5 o'clock and ends at 7:15.

Breakfast is from 7:30 to 8:15; lunch is from 12:00 to 1:00; snack is from 5:00 to 5:30; supper is at 7:15.

After the second year, pupils will receive lessons in reading, writing, and arithmetic. They will be taught to sew and do a little cooking.

Art. 11. As a measure of encouragement and with no obligation, it is established that at the end of each month the young people will be graded as follows:

1st class, gift for the month 1 fr. 50 c.	
2nd class	1 ″ —
3rd class	50 c.
4th class	——30

Each month a new classification will take place, and the young person will rise or fall according to her merit. This classification will be based on an overall evaluation of conduct, quantity and quality of work, docility and diligence, etc.

---

30. Abbreviations for French currency.
 fr.: franc.
 c.: centime; 100 centimes to 1 franc.

Art. 12. Wages are not due until the end of the year. They will be paid during the month following their due date. Gifts, incentive pay, and compensation for extra work will be paid each month.

Art. 13. Any apprentice who leaves the establishment before the end of her term, or who has been dismissed for bad conduct, conspiracy, rebellion, laziness, or a serious breach of the rules loses her rights to wages for the current year; beyond this, in such a case, the father or guardian of the pupil agrees to pay the director of the establishment the sum of one hundred francs to indemnify him for the non-fulfillment of the present agreement: half of this sum will be given to the *bureau de bienfaisance*[31] in the pupil's parish.

Art. 14. If, during the first year, apprentice is recognized as unfit, despite the agreement and in the interest of both parties the director reserves the right to send her away without indemnity.

Art. 15. The apprentice who leaves the establishment at the end of the first month under the pretext that she cannot get used to the place, will pay 50 centimes per day toward the costs she has occasioned, as well as her travel expenses.

Art. 16. On her arrival, the apprentice will submit to inspection by the house doctor. Any girl who has a skin disease or who is found to be sickly will not be accepted and will be sent away immediately at her own expense. . . .

Source 9 from British Parliamentary Papers: Reports from Committees, *vol. 15,* Labour of Children in Factories *(London: House of Commons, 1832), pp. 6–13.*

9. Report of the Sadler Committee, 1832[32]

William Cooper, called in; and Examined.

What is your business?—I follow the cloth-dressing at present.

2. What is your age?—I was eight-and-twenty last February.

3. When did you first begin to work in mills or factories?—When I was about 10 years of age.

4. With whom did you first work?—At Mr. Benyon's flax[33] mills, in Meadowland, Leeds.

5. What were your usual hours of working?—We began at five, and gave over at nine; at five o'clock in the morning.

6. And you gave over at nine o'clock?—At nine at night.

---

31. *bureau de bienfaisance:* Catholic social welfare organization.

32. **Sadler Committee:** the Committee on the Bill to Regulate the Labour of Children in the Mills and Factories of the United Kingdom.

33. **flax:** a plant whose fiber is manufactured into linen for thread or weaving into fabrics.

Chapter 6

Labor Old

and New:

The Impact of

the Industrial

Revolution

7. At what distance might you have lived from the mill?—About a mile and a half.

8. At what time had you to get up in the morning to attend to your labour?—I had to be up soon after four o'clock.

9. Every morning?—Every morning.

10. What intermissions had you for meals?—When we began at five in the morning, we went on until noon, and then we had 40 minutes for dinner.

11. Had you no time for breakfast?—No, we got it as we could, while we were working.

12. Had you any time for an afternoon refreshment, or what is called in Yorkshire your "drinking?"—No; when we began at noon, we went on till night; there was only one stoppage, the 40 minutes for dinner.

13. Then as you had to get your breakfast, and what is called "drinking" in that manner, you had to put it on one side?—Yes, we had to put it on one side; and when we got our frames doffed, we ate two or three mouthfuls, and then put it by again.[34]

14. Is there not considerable dust in a flax mill?—A flax mill is very dusty indeed.

15. Was not your food therefore frequently spoiled?—Yes, at times with the dust; sometimes we could not eat it, when it had got a lot of dust on.

16. What were you when you were ten years old?—What is called a bobbin-doffer; when the frames are quite full, we have to doff them.

17. Then as you lived so far from home, you took your dinner to the mill?—We took all our meals with us, living so far off.

18. During the 40 minutes which you were allowed for dinner, had you ever to employ that time in your turn in cleaning the machinery?—At times we had to stop to clean the machinery, and then we got our dinner as well as we could; they paid us for that.

19. At these times you had no resting at all?—No.

20. How much had you for cleaning the machinery?—I cannot exactly say what they gave us, as I never took any notice of it.

34. Vocabulary of the textile mill:
> **frame:** the water frame, an early spinning machine.
> **doff:** the task, in the industrial spinning process, of removing spindles filled with yarn from the spinning machine.
> **bobbin:** a reel, cylinder, or spoollike apparatus on which thread is wound.
> **card:** a tool used to comb out textile fibers (wool, flax, etc.) in preparation for spinning them into thread.
> **gigger:** a person who worked in the gigging process, a step in dressing wool cloth in which loose fibers are drawn off the fabric and in which the fabric's nap is raised. The process used **teasles,** thistlelike plants that hooked the fabric and raised it.
> **boiler:** part of the processing of wool involved boiling and scrubbing to remove oils.
> **primmer, brusher:** workers involved in the final preparation of woolen cloth.

21. Did you ever work even later than the time you have mentioned?—I cannot say that I worked later there: I had a sister who worked up stairs, and she worked till 11 at night, in what they call the card-room.

22. At what time in the morning did she begin to work?—At the same time as myself.

23. And they kept her there till 11 at night?—Till 11 at night.

24. You say that your sister was in the card-room?—Yes.

25. Is not that a very dusty department?—Yes, very dusty indeed.

26. She had to be at the mill at five, and was kept at work till eleven at night?—Yes.

27. During the whole time she was there?—During the whole time; there was only 40 minutes allowed at dinner out of that.

28. To keep you at your work for such a length of time, and especially towards the termination of such a day's labour as that, what means were taken to keep you awake and attentive?—They strapped us at times, when we were not quite ready to be doffing the frame when it was full.

29. Were you frequently strapped?—At times we were frequently strapped.

30. What sort of strap was it?—About this length [*describing it*].

31. What was it made of?—Of leather.

32. Were you occasionally very considerably hurt with the strap?—Sometimes it hurt us very much, and sometimes they did not lay on so hard as they did at others.

33. Were the girls strapped in that sort of way?—They did not strap what they called the grown-up women.

34. Were any of the female children strapped?—Yes; they were strapped in the same way as the lesser boys. . . .

44. Were your punishments the same in that mill as in the other?—Yes, they used the strap the same there.

45. How long did you work in that mill?—Five years.

46. And how did it agree with your health?—I was sometimes well, and sometimes not very well.

47. Did it affect your breathing at all?—Yes; sometimes we were stuffed.

48. When your hours were so long, you had not any time to attend to a day-school?—We had no time to go to a day-school, only to a Sunday-school,[35] and then with working such long hours we wanted to have a bit of rest, so that I slept till the afternoon, sometimes till dinner, and sometimes after.

49. Did you attend a place of worship?—I should have gone to a place of worship many times, but I was in the habit of falling asleep, and that kept me away; I did not like to go for fear of being asleep.

50. Do you mean that you could not prevent yourself from falling asleep, in consequence of the fatigue of the preceding week?—Yes. . . .

35. **Sunday-school:** churches often ran schools for mill children on their day off (Sunday) to teach the rudiments of reading and writing along with religious instruction.

Chapter 6

Labor Old

and New:

The Impact of

the Industrial

Revolution

85. After working at a mill to this excess, how did you find your health at last?—I found it very bad indeed; I found illness coming on me a long time before I fell down.

86. Did you at length become so ill as to be unable to pursue your work?—I was obliged to give it up entirely.

87. How long were you ill?—For six months.

88. Who attended?—Mr. Metcalf and Mr. Freeman.

89. What were you told by your medical attendants was the reason of your illness?—Nothing but hard labour, and working long hours; and they gave me up, and said no good could be done for me, that I must go into the country.

90. Did this excessive labour not only weaken you, but destroy your appetite?—It destroyed the appetite, and I became so feeble, that I could not cross the floor unless I had a stick to go with; I was in great pain, and could find ease in no posture.

91. You could drink in the meantime, if you could not eat?—Yes, I could drink.

92. But you found that did not improve your health?—No.

93. Has it been remarked that your excessive labour from early life has greatly diminished your growth?—A number of persons have said that such was the case, and that I was the same as if I had been made of iron or stone.

94. What height are you?—About five feet. It is that that has hindered me of my growth.

95. When you were somewhat recovered, did you apply for labour?—I applied for my work again, but the overlooker said I was not fit to work; he was sure of that, and he would not let me have it. I was then obliged to throw myself on the parish.[36]

96. Have you subsisted on the parish ever since?—Yes.

97. Have you been always willing and anxious to work?—I was always willing and anxious to work from my infancy.

98. Have you been on the parish since your severe illness?—Yes.

99. How long is that ago?—Six months. When I was ill I got something from the Society; they relieved me then, but when I became better I received no benefit from it.

100. Yours is not what is called a Friendly Society?—No, it is what we call Odd Fellows.[37]

101. And they do not extend relief after a certain period?—Not after you get better. . . .

---

36. **on the parish:** under existing English laws, poor relief was the responsibility of the local parish.

37. **Friendly Society, Odd Fellows Society:** organizations founded to benefit workers through "self-help." They took up small weekly sums from their members and used the funds thus collected to aid sick or injured members who were unable to work, or to assist the widows and orphans of members.

124. You say that you had no time to go to school during the week, but that you went on Sunday?—I went on Sunday; I had no time to go to a day-school.

125. Can you read or write?—I can read, but I cannot write. . . .

150. Do you work anywhere now?—I have not worked anywhere for rather more than a year. I have been constantly out to seek for employment since I have been better.

151. How are you supported?—By the town.

152. Do you mean by the parish?—Yes.

153. Of what place?—Leeds. . . .

184. How did you contrive to be awake so early in the morning?—My father used to call me up.

185. Did he get up so early as that for his own business?—He got up on purpose to call me.

186. How many hours did he work in a day at his own business?—Sometimes from five in the morning till eight at night.

187. You say he was a shoemaker?—Yes.

188. Then, according to this, he worked more hours than you did?—I think not so long.

189. Did your father take his regular intervals for his meals?—I should think so.

190. And walked about to market for his family; had he not many pauses in his labour?—He worked at home, and therefore could do as he pleased. . . .

198. Has your health improved since you left off working long hours?—I am a deal better than I was; but I believe that if I could have got work, and have had something to support me, I should have recruited my health better. I have been very poorly kept for these last six months, having been out of work. I have only half a crown a week allowed from the parish for my wife and myself. . . .

206. When you were working these very long hours in a mill as a gigger and boiler, had you the liberty, if you wished to be away for a day or part of a day, to send another person to do your work?—Yes; if we were poorly, we had liberty to send another person in our place.

207. If you wished to rest for half a day, you could send another man in your place?—I was once poorly, and I sent another workman, and they let me have the job again; now that I have been ill six months, they will not let me have the job again. . . .

217. Do you think you would be able to stand your work?—I should like to try; I cannot bear to go wandering about the streets. . . .

220. Is being a gigger harder than the others?—Yes, gigging is very hard work; the fleeces are so heavy and full of water, and you have to stand in this position [*describing it*] to support them and turn the fleece over; if you are not over strong it makes you rather deformed in your legs.

221. At what age do people generally begin gigging?—Some begin about 15, 16 or 17, and some lads begin when about 14.

Chapter 6

Labor Old

and New:

The Impact of

the Industrial

Revolution

222. At what age did your father die?—He was 60 when he died.

223. Have you seen the man lately who is doing your work at Mr. Brown's?—Yes.

224. Is he in good health?—I do not know; I must not say a thing that I do not know; it is a good while since I saw him.

225. Was your father a tall or a short man?—He stood about five feet seven.

226. And you are five feet?—Yes.

227. Have you any brothers or sisters?—Two brothers and a sister.

228. Do they work in the same trade?—I have a brother working now at the same trade; he was seventeen the 14th of last February.

229. Has he good health?—He had not over good health when I came from Leeds.

Source 10 from Sidney Pollard and Colin Holmes, editors, Documents in European Economic History, *vol. 2,* Industrial Power and National Rivalry *(New York: St. Martin's, 1972), pp. 322–323. Copyright © 1972 by St. Martin's Press. Reprinted with permission of St. Martin's Press, Inc., and Sidney Pollard.*

10. Working Conditions of a Female Textile Worker in Germany, 1880s and 1890s

In the weaving sheds the girls work in an atmosphere which, on the third day of my work there, gave me bad lung catarrh; tiny flakes of the twisted wool fill the air, settle on dress and hair, and float into nose and mouth; the machines have to be swept clean every two hours; the dust is breathed in by the girls, since they are not allowed to open the windows. To this has to be added the terrible nerve-racking noise of the rattling machines so that no one can hear himself speak. No communication with one's neighbour is possible except by shouting on the top of one's voice. In consequence, all the girls have screeching, irritating voices: even when the shop has gone quiet, at the end of the working day, on the street, at home, they never converse quietly like other people, their conversation is a constant yelling, which produces the impression among outsiders that they are quarrelling.

It is truly a miracle that so many girls still look fresh and blooming, and that they still feel like singing at work, usually sentimental folk songs. . . .

Many girls work happily, particularly those weaving small carpets or curtains woven as one piece who can observe the building up of the pattern. They love their machines like loving a faithful dog; they polish them, and tie coloured ribbons, little pictures of saints and all sorts of gaudy tinsel given to them by their sweethearts at the summer fairs, to the crossbars.

The girls work hard, very hard, and quite a few told me how they collapsed with the exertion of the first four weeks of work, and how most of them suffer for months with irritations of the lung and throat until they get used to the dust. To this has to be added the poor, miserable food, the short periods of rest in rooms which don't deserve the name of "dwelling"—and yet the girls remain cheerful, healthy, lively and enterprising.

I have always watched this with admiration; I could not have stood this for long. I could not take anything in the morning beside coffee; only in the evening I hurried, totally exhausted, to my hotel, to swallow some nourishing food with great difficulty. . . .

No one would dream of stopping work and taking a rest even when suffering from violent headache or toothache, not even a quarter of an hour of being late was tolerated without a substantial fine at the end of the week. . . .

The work of the carpet weavers should not be underrated, it is anything but monotonous or repetitive. When working the complex Turkish patterns, the weaver has to catch the exact moment for changing the different coloured reels. She has to think and coordinate, calculate and pay attention and concentrate all her thoughts. This work requires far more mental activity and sense of responsibility than the crochet work and needlework done by hundreds of girls of society, year after year, in expectation of the shining knight who would one day come and rescue them.

Most factories start work at half past six, pause for breakfast from 8 to 8.30, dinner 12–1; at 4 there are 20–30 minutes for tea, and work goes on until 7. On Saturdays work ends at 5.30, in order to give time to the workers to clean the machines thoroughly and to oil them by 6; Mondays, work starts half an hour later probably because all the girls have a hangover from Sunday.

Source 11 from British Parliamentary Papers: Reports from Commissioners: Children's Employment (Mines), *vol. 17*, Appendix to the First Report of the Commissioners (Mines) *(London: William Clowes for Her Majesty's Stationery Office, 1842), pp. 39, 103, 107–108.*

11. Report on the Employment of Children in British Mines, 1841–1842

May 14, 1841:

No. 49. Mr. *Joseph Staley,* Managing Partner in Coal-works at Yate Common, in the parish of Yate (Two Pits), carried on under the firm of *Staley* and *Parkers.*

Employ from 30 to 35 hands; not more than five or six boys under 13; the two youngest are from eight to nine years old, who work with their father; perhaps three boys not more than 10 years of age; they assist in cutting and carting out the coal from a one-foot seam; no doorboys employed, because there is sufficient ventilation without being particular about closing them; the

Chapter 6

Labor Old

and New:

The Impact of

the Industrial

Revolution

carters generally manage the doors as they pass; the boys earn from 6s. to 9s. per week when they get handy at cutting; have not more than three or four under 18; all over 15 are earning nearly men's wages—say 15s. per week; the men earn from 18s. to 20s.; considers two tons a fair day's work; wages paid in money every Saturday; the older boys receive their own; the boys, in carting out the coals from the *googs* [narrow inclined planes up which the coal is pulled by a chain and windlass], when short distances, draw by the *girdle* or *lugger, i.e.* a rope round the waist, with an iron hook depending in front, to which a chain, passing between the legs, is attached; if for longer distances, they use wheeled-carriages on a railway; no horses are employed under ground at present; the smaller boys do not tug more than 1 cwt.[38] at a time; the carts generally hold about 2 cwt. each; the thickest vein is two feet six inches, and is worked by the young men; the boys cart through a two feet six inches passageway; the young men have four feet, there being a bed of soft stuff above the coal, to cut away before they come to the roof; the shaft is 45 fathoms,[39] worked by a steam-engine, and strong-plaited rope; thinks rope decidedly safer than chain, as it gives more timely notice of any defect, by a strand or two giving way, whereas a link of iron is sometimes near breaking, a good while before it is discovered, and then separates on a sudden. Has had many years' experience in Staffordshire and Derbyshire, having been brought up a collier; say for 40 years; has been engaged 23 years in this coal-field; the workings are quiet dry; a pumping-engine of 60-horse power, is constantly at work when there is water; three or four days a-week is sufficient in summer; hours of work average eight to nine hours a-day; no night-work at present; always employ two sets when it occurs.

Some of the boys and young persons attend the Church Sunday-school, and others the Dissenting Sunday-school; most of them can read a little; look clean and tidy on Sundays; thinks there are no healthier boys in the country.

MESSRS. WILLSON, HOLMES, AND STOCKS, QUARRY-HOUSE PIT.

No. 6. *William Jagger,* aged 11.   May 6:

I am a hurrier[40] for my father, Benjamin Jagger; have been in here four years and upwards; I come to work at seven o'clock, and go home at four, five, and six; I get breakfast afore I come down; I get my dinner down here, I get it about one o'clock; I don't know how long I am taking it; I get it as I can; I go to

---

38. **cwt.:** hundredweight, i.e., 100 pounds.

39. **fathom:** a fathom equals 6 feet; the shaft of 45 fathoms thus extended 270 feet below the earth's surface.

40. Mining vocabulary:
    hurrier: a person who drew a wagon loaded with coal through mine tunnels to the shaft up which the load would be raised to the earth's surface.
    corve: small wagon for carrying coal or ore in a mine.

work directly after; I get currant-cake and buttered cake sometimes, never any meat; I get a bit of meat for supper when I go up. I went to day-school often; I comed to work about half a year; I go to Sunday-school now at church; I cannot read or write. I have got to hurry a corve 400 yards; I don't know what weight it is [$2\frac{1}{2}$ cwt.]; it runs upon rails; I push the corves; some of the boys push when there is no rail. I do not oft hurt my feet; I never met with an accident. The men serve me out sometimes—they wallop me; I don't know what for, except 'tis when I don't hurry fast enough; I like my work very well; I would rather hurry than set cards.

The mainway of this pit is 3 feet 6 inches high and 400 yards in length; seams 17 inches thick; gear in good order; shaft not walled up. At the moment of stepping out of the corve at the pit's bottom, a stone weighing from five to seven pounds fell in the water close by my feet from the unlined shaft near the top, or from the bank, a circumstance at once illustrative of the importance of protecting persons in their descent, by walling up the sides of the shaft, and thereby preventing loose measures from falling.

MR. JOSEPH STOCKS, BOOTH TOWN PIT, HALIFAX.

No. 26. *Patience Kershaw*, aged 17.   May 15:

My father has been dead about a year; my mother is living and has ten children, five lads and five lasses; the oldest is about thirty, the youngest is four; three lasses go to mill; all the lads are colliers, two getters and three hurriers; one lives at home and does nothing; mother does nought but look after home.

All my sisters have been hurriers, but three went to the mill, Alice went because her legs swelled from hurrying in cold water when she was hot. I never went to day-school; I go to Sunday-school, but I cannot read or write; I go to pit at five o'clock in the morning and come out at five in the evening; I get my breakfast of porridge and milk first; I take my dinner with me, a cake, and eat it as I go; I do not stop or rest any time for the purpose; I get nothing else until I get home, and then have potatoes and meat, not every day meat. I hurry in the clothes I have now got on, trousers and ragged jacket; the bald place upon my head is made by thrusting the corves; my legs have never swelled, but sisters' did when they went to mill; I hurry the corves a mile and more under ground and back; they weigh 3 cwt.; I hurry 11 a-day; I wear a belt and chain at the workings to get the corves out; the getters that I work for are *naked* except their caps; they pull off all their clothes; I see them at work when I go up; sometimes they beat me, if I am not quick enough, with their hands; they

---

getter: a person who cut the coal from the seam. Young male hurriers, who often suffered stunted growth because of their excessive labor in moving coal as children, often graduated to the occupation of getter. Short stature was an asset in the restricted spaces of mine tunnels. The mining commission report from which this testimony is drawn notes that getters described themselves as "mashed up."

Chapter 6

Labor Old

and New:

The Impact of

the Industrial

Revolution

strike me upon my back; the boys take liberties with me sometimes, they pull me about; I am the only girl in the pit; there are about 20 boys and 15 men; all the men are naked; I would rather work in mill than in coal-pit.

This girl is an ignorant, filthy, ragged, and deplorable-looking object, and such a one as the uncivilized natives of the prairies would be shocked to look upon.[41]

QUESTIONS TO CONSIDER

Let us bring together your findings on the old and new labor of European working men and women. Your goal is to understand the changes affecting them in the late eighteenth and nineteenth centuries and how these changes came about. You may want to review the questions in Sources and Method before continuing your study of the evidence.

First, consider the length of time workers devoted to labor. Was the preindustrial workday much different in length from the early-industrial-age workday? Note especially the findings of the Sadler Committee on the workdays of William Cooper, employed in industrial labor, and his father, a craftsman of the old school. Next, consider the number of workdays per year. Both old and new labor generally required a six-day workweek. But reexamine the holidays at Lille, remembering to punctuate the work year with a liberal number of "holy Mondays." On how many days per year did Vauban estimate his workers were employed in agriculture? Compare this quantity of work with that demanded of William Cooper.

Like many nineteenth-century miners, this textile worker could probably have looked forward to holidays only on Christmas, Easter Monday, and the Monday after Pentecost. What other time off from work could he have expected? What effect did the Industrial Revolution have on the annual quantity of work for many laborers?

Those employed in both old and new styles of labor certainly worked hard. But the quality, pace, and discipline of their respective work situations certainly varied. Let us first consider the quality or nature of the old labor. What sort of variety characterized the work of agricultural workers like those described by Vauban and Mrs. Britton? Where was much of their work carried on? Where did most industrial-age labor take place? Why do you think Mrs. Britton testified that she preferred physically taxing agricultural work to factory labor? Why do you think William Cooper would have preferred the craftsman's work of his father to industrial labor? How do you think the necessity of working with machinery would have shaped Cooper's opinion? What basic qualitative differences distinguished the old from the new labor?

41. This comment by the mine commissioners is amplified elsewhere in their report, where they note that Kershaw worked in a mine whose tunnels contained 3 or 4 inches of water at all times and that she moved her corve 1,800 to 2,000 yards on each trip.

Consider the pace of work. Who set the pace for guild members? Who set the pace in the putting-out system, the factory, and the mine? Notice the discipline of the industrial-era workplace, too. What sort of punishments and incentives prodded employees to work quickly? Considering the conditions of preindustrial labor, why do you think the specific regulations in Source 8 were necessary? Recall the statement by Andrew Ure that opened this chapter. What were management's goals in imposing this kind of discipline?

Other changes in labor also accompanied the Industrial Revolution. What do the testimonies from the coal miners and the records of French and German textile workers tell us about the labor of women in the industrial age? Reexamine Mrs. Britton's testimony. In what setting did she labor after her marriage? What effect might female and child industrial labor have had on the family? What educational opportunities existed for boys and girls in industrial labor?

Finally, let us consider the health and safety of workers under both the old and the new systems. Which style of labor do you think Mrs. Britton and William Cooper would have considered more healthful? What hazards awaited textile workers like Cooper and miners like William Jagger and Patience Kershaw?

In other ways, old and new labor were not quite so different. Ideally, any job should provide some security of continuing employment. How did the Prussian guild regulations seek to protect the markets and incomes of

the textile workers? Did any other workers, old or new, benefit from such efforts to protect job security? Consider the problems of Mr. Britton and Vauban's workers, the effect of cycles of economic prosperity and depression on William Cooper and his fellow textile workers, and the experiences of putting-out workers described in the song. Did any of them have hopes of continuing employment opportunity?

Consider, too, the problems all these workers confronted when illness, injury, or economic conditions denied them employment. What recourse did Mrs. Britton and her family have in the face of poverty? Did William Cooper have any additional resources to draw on when illness struck? Were they sufficient for his needs?

Your comparative analysis of this chapter's sources provides one more insight into the industrialization of western Europe. Economic historians speak of *proto-industrialization,* a process that paved the way for industrialization by organizing production into larger units employing traditional technologies. Industrial capitalists later combined experience in such organization with new machines to produce the Industrial Revolution. To understand this process, consider what the factory system meant: large units of production, controlled by capitalists who were prepared to organize labor and resources for a profit, and competition among producers who sought worldwide markets. What evidence of modern industrial organization do you find in the putting-out system? In what ways did it occupy a transitional role? Were its methods of pro-

[175]

Chapter 6

Labor Old

and New:

The Impact of

the Industrial

Revolution

duction old or new? Was its organization of production old or new? How were its labor-management relations similar to those of the industrial age? Compare the discipline Andrew Ure advocated for industrial managers with the alleged goal of the clothiers in the popular song. What significance do you attach to the putting-out workers' complaint that they could no longer buy land? Would you say that they were slipping into a work status similar to that of later industrial workers?

Now you are ready to provide detailed answers to the main questions of this chapter: What was the nature of the new labor? How did it evolve? How did it differ from the old labor? Be sure to base your responses on the evidence you have assessed.

EPILOGUE

A combination of developments served to improve conditions for later generations of workers. Early industrial workers won such improvements in their lot only slowly and with considerable struggle, however. The right to take part in government by voting was one common demand of nineteenth-century workers in a Europe that accorded a political voice only to the wealthy and privileged, if it accorded one to anyone at all. Workers in England began to win the vote only in 1867 after considerable agitation; a revolution in France in 1848 established the right of universal suffrage for men. Elsewhere the vote came more slowly, and Russian workers lacked voting rights until 1906.

In the more democratic western European nations, a widened right to vote in the nineteenth century made political institutions more responsive to workers' needs. During that century, several European parliaments passed legislation that sought to regulate working conditions for women and children, to establish minimum safety standards, and to begin to provide the accident, health, and old age insurance plans that protect modern workers. Real improvements, however, often lagged behind such legislation. Early wage, hour, and safety regulations ran counter to an important political philosophy of the nineteenth century, liberalism (see Chapter 7), which viewed such legislation as interference in freedom of management. Thus, when early regulations were passed, there frequently were not enough officials to enforce them by comprehensive factory inspections. If you refer to William Cooper's testimony, you will find him completely unaware of a parliamentary act to regulate work hours, eloquent proof of this early lack of enforcement. Governments were slow to create the machinery necessary to enforce these rules.

The nineteenth century also witnessed an often bitter struggle by workers to form their own organizations promoting their common welfare. Because unions and strikes, as we have seen, were illegal in many countries, the first worker organizations of the early nineteenth century often were self-help groups such as the one that aided William Cooper. Only after much struggle did governments in countries like England and France legalize labor unions and the right to strike.

The legalization of unions, however, allowed industrial workers to take collective action in strikes to win better wages and conditions. Early strikes often produced bloody conflict between labor on one side and management, sometimes backed by police or the army in the name of keeping order, on the other. The first major victory for a noncraft union, however, occurred in the London dockworkers' strike of 1889. Twentieth-century developments have improved the lot of workers in other ways, especially through increased leisure time, realized in the forty-hour workweek and paid vacations.

Improvements in wages and working conditions, however, did not change the basic nature of modern factory labor. In the industrial workplace, the pace of work continued to be set by machines, granting little independence to the individual worker, who remained a human cog in the greater modern industrial machine. Though most workers adjusted to this kind of labor, manifestations of their discontent have not disappeared entirely. In 1968, as you will see in Chapter 14, millions of French workers went on strike and occupied their factories. One of their chief demands was for a concept they called *autogestion,* that is, some voice in the workplace decisions that governed their lives on the job.

Such demands by employees have not gone entirely unheeded by management. There have been efforts to reintroduce some worker input into the production process through such practices as quality circles, in which workers engaged in the same phases of production meet periodically to discuss their jobs and to make suggestions for improving the production process. Other experiments in such industries as automobile assembly have sought to involve individual workers in several phases of the production process as a way of mitigating the monotony of assembly-line work. Nevertheless, for the majority of Western workers today, the basic nature of industrial employment, as symbolized by the production line, remains unchanged.

CHAPTER SEVEN

TWO PROGRAMS FOR

SOCIAL AND POLITICAL

CHANGE: LIBERALISM

AND SOCIALISM

THE PROBLEM

"Workingmen of all countries unite!" proclaimed Karl Marx and Friedrich Engels in *The Communist Manifesto* of 1848, urging working people to overthrow the capitalist system and end the working conditions of the early Industrial Revolution, which we explored in Chapter 6. Marx and Engels were partisans in a nineteenth-century ideological clash in which they and other proponents of socialism opposed liberalism, the dominant doctrine among the rising class of factory owners and managers. Nineteenth-century liberals and socialists differed greatly in their views on such issues as the definition of freedom and democracy, the role of government, and their visions of the future.

We must be careful in this chapter to understand liberalism in its nineteenth- and not its twenty-first-century sense. For most twenty-first-century Americans, *liberalism* describes an ideology that calls for an activist role for government in ensuring the basic needs of its citizens in a variety of areas, including civil rights, material wants, and health and safety protection. In the nineteenth century, liberals sought to maximize the freedom of the individual from government control. Drawing on traditions restricting royal authority that dated back to medieval times, liberals saw in the French Revolution the essential victory they sought to win all over Europe. In destroying the Old Regime, with its absolute monarchy and privilege for the aristocratic few, the Revolution had created a new political order based on individual freedom. Everywhere, liberals sought to draft constitutions that would limit royal authority and ensure basic individual rights. The citizen was to be safe from arbitrary arrest and was to enjoy freedom of speech, assembly, religion, and the press.

For the early or classical liberals, however, individual freedom did not mean political democracy, a voice for all in government. The constitutional arrangements created by liberals usually included some sort of property qualification for voting. Most liberals were members of the middle classes and believed that to exercise the right to vote, a citizen had to have some stake in the existing social and economic order in the form of property. The majority lacked sufficient wealth to vote in all early-nineteenth-century countries under liberal rule. But one liberal French minister, François Guizot, noted that the poor possessed full freedom to increase their wealth so that they could acquire property and participate in political life! Extreme as this view may seem to us, it does express the liberal faith that peaceful political change was possible. The key to the success of such a system of government was the establishment of a society of laws protecting individual freedoms.

Liberal economic thought was also a doctrine of absolute freedom. Liberals opposed the guild and aristocratic privileges that had limited career opportunities in Old Regime Europe. Thus, individual economic opportunity, embodied in the opening of all careers to citizens on the basis of their talents, not their titles, became the central liberal economic tenet. But liberals' faith in economic freedom had far greater implications.

Liberals believed that immutable natural laws, like supply and demand, regulated economic life. Government interference in economic life, they believed, violated not only these laws but individual freedom as well. Based in large part on the writings of such classical liberal economists as the Englishmen Adam Smith (1723–1790), Thomas Malthus (1766–1834), and David Ricardo (1772–1823), liberal economic thought defended the right of early industrial employers to be free of government regulation. Their doctrine was summed up in the French phrase *laissez-faire* (literally, "leave it alone").

Socialists differed from liberals in that they saw the French Revolution of 1789 as simply the first step in revamping Europe's old order. The Revolution had established individual freedom but not political democracy. More important for socialists, the Revolution had not brought social democracy. To achieve this goal, they advocated a more equitable distribution of society's wealth. Their message, as you might imagine, had considerable appeal to those workers employed in the mills, factories, and mines of the early Industrial Revolution whose lot we explored in Chapter 6.

Some early socialist thinkers expressed the view that economic equality could be realized by peaceful evolutionary change. Karl Marx applied the label "utopian" to those thinkers because of the impracticality, in his view, of their schemes. Charles Fourier (1771–1837) advocated a restructuring of society around essentially agricultural communities that represented an attempt to turn the clock back to a preindustrial economy. Louis Blanc (1811–1882) advocated state assistance in the creation of worker-owned units of production, which was difficult to imagine in a Europe dominated by

Chapter 7

Two Programs

for Social

and Political

Change:

Liberalism

and Socialism

the liberal ideology of government noninterference in economic life. But some utopian socialists, notably Robert Owen (1771–1858), who created a model industrial town around his textile mills in New Lanark, Scotland, achieved real improvements for working people.

Utopian socialism did not transform society. Some of its ideas, however, did influence other socialist thinkers, including Karl Marx, who advocated a revolutionary transformation of society. Indeed, revolutionary socialism gained large numbers of working-class followers and by the middle and late nineteenth century threatened western Europe's liberal political

leaders with the possibility of a complete overhaul of society in the name of political and social democracy.

Nineteenth-century liberalism and socialism both produced important thinkers who analyzed the ills of their society and advanced not only plans for change but critiques of the opposing ideology. What visions of the future did liberals and socialists propose? How did they hope to realize their ideals? How did their ideologies differ? Your task in this chapter is to answer these questions by examining the ideas of two nineteenth-century political and social theorists.

<hr>

SOURCES AND METHOD

Liberalism and socialism each had large numbers of eloquent proponents in the nineteenth century. This chapter presents you with samples of liberal and socialist thought in the nineteenth century drawn from the writings of but one advocate of each cause. Your sources in this chapter are the works of the liberal Alexis de Tocqueville and the revolutionary socialist Karl Marx. These two thinkers have been selected because they expressed strikingly different views on similar subjects: the historical development of the West, the nature of democracy, and the role of revolution. Tocqueville and Marx also analyzed the French Revolution of 1848, a topic you may wish to review in your textbook. Their contrasting views on the same issues will provide the

basis for your answers to the general questions on liberalism and socialism.

In analyzing the works of Tocqueville and Marx, you must understand that these works were polemic in character—that is, they were all written to advocate the causes espoused by their authors. All such works may be expected to emphasize their authors' viewpoints and summarily dismiss opposing points of view that may have considerable validity. Because each theorist was an eloquent advocate of his cause, some examination of their separate backgrounds and viewpoints is necessary to permit you to analyze their ideas fruitfully.

Alexis Charles Henri Clérel de Tocqueville was born in 1805, the son of an aristocratic father who hoped for the restoration of the French monarchy destroyed by the Revolution of 1789. When Napoleon's fall from power finally brought a restored monarchy, the Tocquevilles rose to positions of importance in government. Alexis de Tocqueville's talents gained early recognition with his appointment as a judge at the youthful age of twenty-one. It was not as a jurist that Tocqueville gained fame, however, but rather as a liberal political theorist and as an early student of what we would call today sociology and political science.

In 1831 Tocqueville and his longtime friend Gustave de Beaumont undertook a fact-finding tour in the United States to study that country's pioneering penitentiary system. For nine months Tocqueville and Beaumont traveled through the United States, observing prisons and much more. The fruit of their trip was a study of prisons based largely on Beaumont and Tocqueville's observations on American society and government, published as *Democracy in America* (1835–1840). Tocqueville's keen analysis of American society in this work gained him immediate international recognition, and he received an honor unusual for a person of his age: election to the French Academy in 1841.[1]

In 1839 Tocqueville had already won election to the French Chamber of Deputies, which permitted him an active role in French politics. He joined the opposition to the government of King Louis Philippe and rejected especially the monarchy's restriction of the right to vote to wealthy Frenchmen. As a deputy, Tocqueville wrote a report on slavery that contributed to its abolition in France's colonies. Further, in a speech to the Chamber of Deputies in January 1848 during a period of apparent political calm, his analysis of social conditions led him to predict the imminence of revolution. Indeed, revolution broke out less than four weeks later.

Despite his opposition to Louis Philippe, Tocqueville long had criticized revolution, perceiving a danger that individual liberty could be lost in revolutionary enthusiasm. Nevertheless, he was elected to the legislature of the new Second Republic created by the Revolution of 1848 and took part in the drafting of its constitution, arguing unsuccessfully against a directly elected president. He correctly foresaw the possibility that an ambitious demagogue could sway the people to gain election and threaten democracy. In December 1848, the victor in the presidential elections was Louis-Napoleon Bonaparte. This nephew of Emperor Napoleon I destroyed the republic in favor of an authoritarian empire, naming himself Emperor Napoleon III.[2] Tocqueville

1. **French Academy:** an association of scholars, writers, and intellectual leaders founded in 1635 to maintain the purity of the French language and establish standards of correct usage. The Academy has only forty members, called the "immortals," who vote to fill vacancies in their ranks caused by deaths of members. The dignity of such election is usually confined to persons of advanced years and long-proven merit.

2. **Emperor Napoleon III:** Bonapartists recognize the son of Emperor Napoleon I (ruled 1804–1814, 1815) as Napoleon II. But Napoleon II never actually ruled France. Aged three years when his father abdicated, he was taken to Vienna by his maternal grandfather, the emperor of Austria, and spent his brief life there until his death in 1832.

Chapter 7

Two Programs

for Social

and Political

Change:

Liberalism

and Socialism

retired permanently from public life after Bonaparte's seizure of power, unable to support the new, undemocratic regime.

Returning to writing, Tocqueville produced two more important works before his death from tuberculosis in 1859. The first was his *Recollections* of the Revolution of 1848 and the Second Republic, based on his experiences in Paris in 1848 and 1849; the second was a study of the French Revolution of 1789, *The Old Regime and the Revolution*. Both works demonstrate again Tocqueville's liberal ideology and political astuteness.

In reading the selections by Tocqueville, you should ascertain the nature of his liberal thought. In Source 1, what does Tocqueville identify as the main trend in historical development? What implications did this trend, which he found strong in America, have for Europe's existing class structure? What problems does Tocqueville, in Source 2, find accompanying American democracy? What threatened the individual? What danger did centralized authority pose? In Source 3, Tocqueville treats revolution. Why does he see the danger of revolution diminishing with the advance of political democracy? Does he find revolution justified at times?

Sources 3 and 4 provide you with summations of Tocqueville's political thought and his view of the future. Under what sort of government had he spent his youth? What did it contribute to his political thought?

Born in Germany in 1818, thirteen years after Tocqueville, Karl Marx was the advocate of a very different

political order, one of socialist revolution. The son of a successful attorney, Marx enjoyed an excellent education. He studied law first and then philosophy, a field in which he completed the doctoral degree that normally would have led to an academic career. Young Marx, however, was an advocate of political and economic democracy whose growing radicalism and atheism precluded such a career. When he turned instead to journalism, his ideas quickly offended the Prussian censors, who suppressed his newspaper.

Marx left Germany in 1843 for Paris, a city in which there was considerable discussion of utopian socialist ideas. Perhaps the greatest single event in Marx's two-year stay in Paris was his meeting with a young businessman, Friedrich Engels, with whom he was to enjoy a lifelong friendship. Engels shared Marx's socialist ideas, gave him intellectual support, and provided financial aid that allowed Marx to devote his life to writing.

French authorities expelled Marx for his radical political ideas in 1845. He moved to Brussels, Belgium, where he and Engels wrote *The Communist Manifesto*, an abstract declaration of war between the working class and its capitalist exploiters. Belgian authorities ultimately also expelled Marx. Back in Paris by March 1848, Marx, like Tocqueville, based his writings on some firsthand experience of the French Revolution of 1848. He also returned to Germany during 1848 before settling in England in 1849, where he spent the rest of his life.

Marx's poor command of spoken English and his illegible handwriting precluded his employment in white-collar jobs, and he and his family often lived in poverty when there were delays in Engels's generosity. In England, Marx drew on his own excellent education, his knowledge of French socialist thought from his Paris days, and his daily research in the British Museum Library to refine his views on socialist revolution. He wrote studies of contemporary events, including *Class Struggles in France* and *The Eighteenth Brumaire of Louis Bonaparte,* which dealt with the French Revolution of 1848 and its aftermath. The final product of his labors was the first volume of *Capital* (1867), a work Engels completed after Marx's death in 1883.

Marx was not to witness the implementation of his ideals during his life. His chief attempt at revolutionary organization, the International Workingmen's Association or First International, founded in 1864, broke up as a result of ideological disputes in 1876. In those disputes, the always irascible Marx found his viewpoints challenged by another revolutionary activist, Mikhail Bakunin (1814–1876). Marx, who prided himself on what he believed was the scientific certainty of his ideas, found Bakunin insufficiently "scientific" and ruptured socialist unity in securing the latter's expulsion from the association. Bakunin went on to become one of the founders of modern anarchism, a movement advocating the destruction of all institutions of modern society. Marx spent the few years remain-

ing before his death in 1883 drained and embittered by his struggle in the International and by family problems. He died believing that his ideas would have little impact. Nevertheless, his writings became the basis for the international socialist movement.

As you read the selections by Marx, you should answer a number of questions to aid you in formulating your responses to the central problems of this chapter. Marx, like Tocqueville, had a definite view of history. Examine Source 5, a selection from *The Communist Manifesto.* What basic event, according to Marx, has characterized and shaped all historical development? Why does Marx find the latest phase of history, modern middle-class ("bourgeois") capitalism, particularly oppressive? What is Marx's view of the free economy advocated by nineteenth-century liberals?

In Source 6, Marx deals with the French Revolution of 1848. That revolution, of course, failed to bring the working classes to power. Whom did it bring to power in France? In Source 7 we have Marx's statement of his ideals in government. Marx proclaims that he advocates democracy. How does that democracy differ from the kind of democracy acceptable to liberals like Tocqueville?

Now you are ready to read the selections with an eye to answering the main questions of this chapter: What were Tocqueville's and Marx's separate political visions? How did they hope to see their visions realized? How did these two thinkers and their liberal and socialist ideologies differ?

Chapter 7

Two Programs

for Social

and Political

Change:

Liberalism

and Socialism

THE EVIDENCE

ALEXIS DE TOCQUEVILLE

Sources 1 and 2 from Alexis de Tocqueville, Democracy in America, *edited by J. P. Mayer and Max Lerner, translated by George Lawrence (New York: Harper & Row, 1965), pp. 3–5, 610–611, 613, 618; pp. 231–233, 665, 667–669. English translation copyright © 1965 by Harper & Row Publishers, Inc. Copyright renewed. Reprinted by permission of HarperCollins Publishers, Inc.*

1. Tocqueville's View of History

No novelty in the United States struck me more vividly during my stay there than the equality of conditions. It was easy to see the immense influence of this basic fact on the whole course of society. It gives a particular turn to public opinion and a particular twist to the laws, new maxims to those who govern and particular habits to the governed.

I soon realized that the influence of this fact extends far beyond political mores and laws, exercising dominion over civil society as much as over the government; it creates opinions, gives birth to feelings, suggests customs, and modifies whatever it does not create.

So the more I studied American society, the more clearly I saw equality of conditions as the creative element from which each particular fact derived, and all my observations constantly returned to this nodal point.

Later, when I came to consider our own side of the Atlantic, I thought I could detect something analogous to what I had noticed in the New World. I saw an equality of conditions which, though it had not reached the extreme limits found in the United States, was daily drawing closer thereto; and that same democracy which prevailed over the societies of America seemed to me to be advancing rapidly toward power in Europe. . . .

A great democratic revolution is taking place in our midst; everybody sees it, but by no means everybody judges it in the same way. Some think it a new thing and, supposing it an accident, hope that they can still check it; others think it irresistible, because it seems to them the most continuous, ancient, and permanent tendency known to history. . . .

Running through the pages of our history, there is hardly an important event in the last seven hundred years which has not turned out to be advantageous for equality.

The Crusades and the English wars decimated the nobles and divided up their lands. Municipal institutions introduced democratic liberty into the heart of the feudal monarchy; the invention of firearms made villein and noble equal on the field of battle; printing offered equal resources to their minds; the post brought enlightenment to hovel and palace alike; Protestantism maintained that all men are equally able to find the path to heaven. America, once discovered, opened a thousand new roads to fortune and gave any obscure adventurer the chance of wealth and power.

If, beginning at the eleventh century, one takes stock of what was happening in France at fifty-year intervals, one finds each time that a double revolution has taken place in the state of society. The noble has gone down in the social scale, and the commoner gone up; as the one falls, the other rises. Each half century brings them closer, and soon they will touch.

And that is not something peculiar to France. Wherever one looks one finds the same revolution taking place throughout the Christian world.

WHY GREAT REVOLUTIONS
WILL BECOME RARE

When a people has lived for centuries under a system of castes and classes, it can only reach a democratic state of society through a long series of more or less painful transformations. These must involve violent efforts and many vicissitudes, in the course of which property, opinions, and power are all subject to swift changes.

Even when this great revolution has come to an end, the revolutionary habits created thereby and by the profound disturbances thereon ensuing will long endure.

As all this takes place just at the time when social conditions are being leveled, the conclusion has been drawn that there must be a hidden connection and secret link between equality itself and revolutions, so that neither can occur without the other.

On this point reason and experience seem agreed.

Among a people where ranks are more or less equal, there is no apparent connection between men to hold them firmly in place. None of them has any permanent right or power to give commands, and none is bound by his social condition to obey. Each man, having some education and some resources, can choose his own road and go along separately from all the rest.

The same causes which make the citizens independent of each other daily prompt new and restless longings and constantly goad them on.

It therefore seems natural to suppose that in a democratic society ideas, things, and men must eternally be changing shape and position and that ages of democracy must be times of swift and constant transformation.

But is this in fact so? Does equality of social conditions habitually and permanently drive men toward revolutions? Does it contain some disturbing principle which prevents society from settling down and inclines the citizens constantly to change their laws, principles, and mores? I do not think so. The subject is important, and I ask the reader to follow my argument closely.

Almost every revolution which has changed the shape of nations has been made to consolidate or destroy inequality. Disregarding the secondary causes which have had some effect on the great convulsions in the world, you will

[185]

Chapter 7

Two Programs

for Social

and Political

Change:

Liberalism

and Socialism

almost always find that equality was at the heart of the matter. Either the poor were bent on snatching the property of the rich, or the rich were trying to hold the poor down. So, then, if you could establish a state of society in which each man had something to keep and little to snatch, you would have done much for the peace of the world. . . .

Such men are the natural enemies of violent commotion; their immobility keeps all above and below them quiet, and assures the stability of the body social.

I am not suggesting that they are themselves satisfied with their actual position or that they would feel any natural abhorrence toward a revolution if they could share the plunder without suffering the calamities; on the contrary, their eagerness to get rich is unparalleled, but their trouble is to know whom to despoil. The same social condition which prompts their longings restrains them within necessary limits. It gives men both greater freedom to change and less interest in doing so.

Not only do men in democracies feel no natural inclination for revolutions, but they are afraid of them.

Any revolution is more or less a threat to property. Most inhabitants of a democracy have property. And not only have they got property, but they live in the conditions in which men attach most value to property. . . .

Therefore the more widely personal property is distributed and increased and the greater the number of those enjoying it, the less is a nation inclined to revolution.

Moreover, whatever a man's calling and whatever type of property he owns, one characteristic is common to all.

No one is fully satisfied with his present fortune, and all are constantly trying a thousand various ways to improve it. Consider any individual at any period of his life, and you will always find him preoccupied with fresh plans to increase his comfort. Do not talk to him about the interests and rights of the human race; that little private business of his for the moment absorbs all his thoughts, and he hopes that public disturbances can be put off to some other time.

This not only prevents them from causing revolutions but also deters them from wanting them. Violent political passions have little hold on men whose whole thoughts are bent on the pursuit of well-being. Their excitement about small matters makes them calm about great ones. . . .

There are also other, and even stronger, reasons which prevent any great change in the doctrines of a democratic people coming about easily. I have already indicated them at the beginning of this book.

Whereas, in such a nation, the influence of individuals is weak and almost nonexistent, the power of the mass over each individual mind is very great. . . .

Whenever conditions are equal, public opinion brings immense weight to bear on every individual. It surrounds, directs, and oppresses him. The basic constitution of society has more to do with this than any political laws. The more alike men are, the weaker each feels in the face of all. Finding nothing that raises him above their level and distinguishes him, he loses his self-confidence when he comes into collision with them. Not only does he mistrust his own strength, but even comes to doubt his own judgment, and he is brought very near to recognizing that he must be wrong when the majority hold the opposite view. There is no need for the majority to compel him; it convinces him.

Therefore, however powers within a democracy are organized and weighted, it will always be very difficult for a man to believe what the mass rejects and to profess what it condemns.

This circumstance is wonderfully favorable to the stability of beliefs.

2. Tocqueville on the Problems of Democracy

TYRANNY OF THE MAJORITY

I regard it as an impious and detestable maxim that in matters of government the majority of a people has the right to do everything, and nevertheless I place the origin of all powers in the will of the majority. Am I in contradiction with myself?

There is one law which has been made, or at least adopted, not by the majority of this or that people, but by the majority of all men. That law is justice.

Justice therefore forms the boundary to each people's right.

A nation is like a jury entrusted to represent universal society and to apply the justice which is its law. Should the jury representing society have greater power than that very society whose laws it applies?

Consequently, when I refuse to obey an unjust law, I by no means deny the majority's right to give orders; I only appeal from the sovereignty of the people to the sovereignty of the human race. . . .

Omnipotence in itself seems a bad and dangerous thing. I think that its exercise is beyond man's strength, whoever he be, and that only God can be omnipotent without danger because His wisdom and justice are always equal to His power. So there is no power on earth in itself so worthy of respect or vested with such a sacred right that I would wish to let it act without control and dominate without obstacles. So when I see the right and capacity to do all given to any authority whatsoever, whether it be called people or king, democracy or aristocracy, and whether the scene of action is a monarchy or a republic, I say: the germ of tyranny is there, and I will go look for other laws under which to live.

My greatest complaint against democratic government as organized in the United States is not, as many Europeans make out, its weakness, but rather its irresistible strength. What I find most repulsive in America is not the extreme freedom reigning there but the shortage of guarantees against tyranny.

[187]

Chapter 7

Two Programs

for Social

and Political

Change:

Liberalism

and Socialism

When a man or a party suffers an injustice in the United States, to whom can he turn? To public opinion? That is what forms the majority. To the legislative body? It represents the majority and obeys it blindly. To the executive power? It is appointed by the majority and serves as its passive instrument. To the police? They are nothing but the majority under arms. A jury? The jury is the majority vested with the right to pronounce judgment; even the judges in certain states are elected by the majority. So, however iniquitous or unreasonable the measure which hurts you, you must submit.[3]

But suppose you were to have a legislative body so composed that it represented the majority without being necessarily the slave of its passions, an executive power having a strength of its own, and a judicial power independent of the other two authorities; then you would still have a democratic government, but there would be hardly any remaining risk of tyranny.

WHAT SORT OF DESPOTISM DEMOCRATIC NATIONS HAVE TO FEAR

I noticed during my stay in the United States that a democratic state of society similar to that found there could lay itself peculiarly open to the establishment of a despotism. And on my return to Europe I saw how far most of our princes had made use of the ideas, feelings, and needs engendered by such a state of society to enlarge the sphere of their power. . . .

---

3. [Tocqueville's note:] At Baltimore during the War of 1812 there was a striking example of the excesses to which despotism of the majority may lead. At that time the war was very popular at Baltimore. A newspaper which came out in strong opposition to it aroused the indignation of the inhabitants. The people assembled, broke the presses, and attacked the house of the editors. An attempt was made to summon the militia, but it did not answer the appeal. Finally, to save the lives of these wretched men threatened by the fury of the public, they were taken to prison like criminals. This precaution was useless. During the night the people assembled again; the magistrates having failed to bring up the militia, the prison was broken open; one of the journalists was killed on the spot and the others left for dead; the guilty were brought before a jury and acquitted.

I once said to a Pennsylvanian: "Please explain to me why in a state founded by Quakers and renowned for its tolerance, freed Negroes are not allowed to use their rights as citizens? They pay taxes; is it not right that they should vote?"

"Do not insult us," he replied, "by supposing that our legislators would commit an act of such gross injustice and intolerance."

"So, with you, Negroes do have the right to vote?"

"Certainly."

"Then how was it that at the electoral college this morning I did not see a single one of them in the meeting?"

"That is not the fault of the law," said the American. "It is true that Negroes have the right to be present at elections, but they voluntarily abstain from appearing."

"That is extraordinarily modest of them."

"Oh! It is not that they are reluctant to go there, but they are afraid they may be maltreated. With us it sometimes happens that the law lacks force when the majority does not support it. Now, the majority is filled with the strongest prejudices against Negroes, and the magistrates do not feel strong enough to guarantee the rights granted to them by the lawmakers."

"What! The majority, privileged to make the law, wishes also to have the privilege of disobeying the law?"

Our contemporaries are ever a prey to two conflicting passions: they feel the need of guidance, and they long to stay free. Unable to wipe out these two contradictory instincts, they try to satisfy them both together. Their imagination conceives a government which is unitary, protective, and all-powerful, but elected by the people. Centralization is combined with the sovereignty of the people. That gives them a chance to relax. They console themselves for being under schoolmasters by thinking that they have chosen them themselves. Each individual lets them put the collar on, for he sees that it is not a person, or a class of persons, but society itself which holds the end of the chain.

Under this system the citizens quit their state of dependence just long enough to choose their masters and then fall back into it.

A great many people nowadays very easily fall in with this brand of compromise between administrative despotism and the sovereignty of the people. They think they have done enough to guarantee personal freedom when it is to the government of the state that they have handed it over. That is not good enough for me. I am much less interested in the question who my master is than in the fact of obedience. . . .

Subjection in petty affairs is manifest daily and touches all citizens indiscriminately. It never drives men to despair, but continually thwarts them and leads them to give up using their free will. It slowly stifles their spirits and enervates their souls, whereas obedience demanded only occasionally in matters of great moment brings servitude into play only from time to time, and its weight falls only on certain people. It does little good to summon those very citizens who have been made so dependent on the central power to choose the representatives of that power from time to time. However important, this brief and occasional exercise of free will will not prevent them from gradually losing the faculty of thinking, feeling, and acting for themselves, so that they will slowly fall below the level of humanity.

I must add that they will soon become incapable of using the one great privilege left to them. Those democratic peoples which have introduced freedom into the sphere of politics, while allowing despotism to grow in the administrative sphere, have been led into the strangest paradoxes. For the conduct of small affairs, where plain common sense is enough, they hold that the citizens are not up to the job. But they give these citizens immense prerogatives where the government of the whole state is concerned. They are turned alternatively into the playthings of the sovereign and into his masters, being either greater than kings or less than men. When they have tried all the different systems of election without finding one to suit them, they look surprised and go on seeking for another, as if the ills they see did not belong much more to the constitution of the country itself than to that of the electoral body.

It really is difficult to imagine how people who have entirely given up managing their own affairs could make a wise choice of those who are to do that for them. One should never expect a liberal, energetic, and wise government to originate in the votes of a people of servants.

[189]

Chapter 7

Two Programs

for Social

and Political

Change:

Liberalism

and Socialism

3. Tocqueville on Revolution

[*The general danger of revolution*]

There are some habits, some ideas, and some vices which are peculiar to a state of revolution and which any prolonged revolution cannot fail to engender and spread, whatever may be in other respects its character, object, and field of action.

When in a brief space of time any nation has repeatedly changed its leaders, opinions, and laws, the men of that nation will in the end acquire a taste for change and grow accustomed to see all changes quickly brought about by the use of force. Then they will naturally conceive a scorn for those formalities of whose impotence they have been daily witnesses, and they will be impatient to tolerate the sway of rules which they have so often seen infringed.

As ordinary ideas of equity and morality are no longer enough to explain and justify all the innovations daily introduced by revolution, men fall back on the principle of social utility, political necessity is turned into a dogma, and men lose all scruples about freely sacrificing particular interests and trampling private rights beneath their feet in order more quickly to attain the public aim envisaged.

Such habits and ideas, which I call revolutionary since all revolutions give rise to them, are seen as much in aristocracies as among democratic peoples. But in the former case they are often less powerful and always less permanent, because there they come up against habits, ideas, faults, and eccentricities which are opposed to them. They therefore vanish of their own accord when the revolution is at an end and the nation recovers its former political ways. However, that is not always the case in democratic countries, for in them there is always a danger that revolutionary instincts will mellow and assume more regular shape without entirely disappearing, but will gradually be transformed into mores of government and administrative habits.

Hence, I know of no country in which revolutions are more dangerous than in a democracy, because apart from the accidental and ephemeral ills which they are ever bound to entail, there is always a danger of their becoming permanent, and one may almost say, eternal.

I think that resistance is sometimes justified and that rebellion can be legitimate. I cannot therefore lay it down as an absolute rule that men living in times of democracy should never make a revolution. But I think that they, more than others, have reason to hesitate before they embark on such an enterprise and that it is far better to put up with many inconveniences in their present state than to turn to so dangerous a remedy.

[*Tocqueville on the Revolution of 1848
in France*]

*My Explanation of the 24th of February and My Thoughts as to Its
Effects upon the Future*[4]

And so the Monarchy of July[5] was fallen, fallen without a struggle, and before rather than beneath the blows of the victors, who were as astonished at their triumph as were the vanquished at their defeat. . . .

I had spent the best days of my youth amid a society which seemed to increase in greatness and prosperity as it increased in liberty; I had conceived the idea of a balanced, regulated liberty, held in check by religion, custom and law; the attractions of this liberty had touched me; it had become the passion of my life; I felt that I could never be consoled for its loss, and that I must renounce all hope of its recovery.

I had gained too much experience of men to be able to content myself with empty words; I knew that, if one great revolution is able to establish liberty in a country, a number of succeeding revolutions make all regular liberty impossible for very many years.

I could not yet know what would issue from this last revolution, but I was already convinced that it could give birth to nothing that would satisfy me; and I foresaw that, whatever might be the lot reserved for our posterity, our own fate was to drag on our lives miserably amid alternate reactions of licence and oppression. . . .

I spent the rest of the day with Ampère, who was my colleague at the Institute,[6] and one of my best friends. He came to discover what had become of me in the affray, and to ask himself to dinner. I wished at first to relieve myself by making him share my vexation. . . .

I saw that he not only did not enter into my view, but that he was disposed to take quite an opposite one. Seeing this, I was suddenly impelled to turn against Ampère all the feelings of indignation, grief and anger that had been accumulating in my heart since the morning; and I spoke to him with a violence of language which I have often since recalled with a certain shame, and which none but a friendship so sincere as his could have excused. I remember saying to him, *inter alia*.[7]

"You understand nothing of what is happening; you are judging like a poet or a Paris cockney.[8] You call this the triumph of liberty, when it is its final de-

---

4. On Thursday, February 24, 1848, King Louis Philippe abdicated the throne in the face of the Paris revolution and fled the capital for England.

5. **Monarchy of July:** the term often used for the regime of King Louis Philippe because that government came to power in July 1830.

6. **Institute:** Institut de France, the cultural institution including the French Academy, of which Tocqueville was a member. **Jean-Jacques Ampère** (1800–1864): a philologist and professor of French literature.

7. **inter alia:** Latin, "among other things."

8. **Cockney:** generally a person of the lower classes born in London's East End. In this context, it refers to someone from that same class in Paris.

Chapter 7

Two Programs

for Social

and Political

Change:

Liberalism

and Socialism

feat. I tell you that the people which you so artlessly admire has just succeeded in proving that it is unfit and unworthy to live a life of freedom. Show me what experience has taught it! Where are the new virtues it has gained, the old vices it has laid aside? No, I tell you, it is always the same, as impatient, as thoughtless, as contemptuous of law and order, as easily led and as cowardly in the presence of danger as its fathers were before it. Time has altered it in no way, and has left it as frivolous in serious matters as it used to be in trifles."

After much vociferation we both ended by appealing to the future, that enlightened and upright judge who always, alas! arrives too late.

Source 4 from Roger Boesche, editor, James Toupin and Roger Boesche, translators, Alexis de Tocqueville: Selected Letters on Politics and Society *(Berkeley: University of California Press, 1985), pp. 112–113. Copyright © 1985 The Regents of the University of California. Reprinted with permission.*

4. Tocqueville's Ideals of Government (Letter to Eugène Stoffels)[9]

I do not think that in France there is a man who is less revolutionary than I, nor one who has a more profound hatred for what is called the revolutionary spirit (a spirit which, parenthetically, is very easily combined with the love of an absolute government). What am I then? And what do I want? Let us distinguish, in order to understand each other better, between the end and the means. What is the end? What I want is not a republic, but a hereditary monarchy. I would even prefer it to be legitimate rather than elected like the one we have, because it would be stronger, especially externally. What I want is a central government energetic in its own sphere of action. Energy from the central government is even more necessary among a democratic people in whom the social force is more diffused than in an aristocracy. Besides our situation in Europe lays down as imperative law for us in what should be a thing of choice. But I wish that this central power had a clearly delineated sphere, that it were involved with what is a necessary part of its functions and not with everything in general, and that it were forever subordinated, in its tendency, to public opinion and to the legislative power that represents this public opinion. I believe that the central power can be invested with very great prerogatives, can be energetic and powerful in its sphere, and that at the same time provincial liberties can be well developed. I think that a government of this kind can exist, and that at the same time the majority of the nation itself

---

9. **Eugène Stoffels** (1805–1852): an official in Metz, France, and a friend of Tocqueville from their days together in secondary school.

can be involved with its own affairs, that political life can be spread almost everywhere, the direct or indirect exercise of political rights can be quite extensive. I wish that the general principles of government were liberal, that the largest possible part were left to the action of individuals, to personal initiative. I believe that all these things are compatible; even more, I am profoundly convinced that there will never be order and tranquility except when they are successfully combined.

As for the means: with all those who admit that we must make our way gradually toward this goal, I am very much in accord. I am the first to admit that it is necessary to proceed slowly, with precaution, with legality. My conviction is that our current institutions are sufficient for reaching the result I have in view. Far, then, from wanting people to violate the laws, I profess an almost superstitious respect for the laws. But I wish that the laws would tend little and gradually toward the goal I have just indicated, instead of making powerless and dangerous efforts to turn back. I wish that the government would itself prepare mores and practices so that people would do without it in many cases in which its intervention is still necessary or invoked without necessity. I wish that citizens were introduced into public life to the extent that they are believed capable of being useful in it, instead of seeking to keep them away from it at all costs. I wish finally that people knew where they wanted to go, and that they advanced toward it prudently instead of proceeding aimlessly as they have been doing almost constantly for twenty years.

KARL MARX

Source 5 from Karl Marx and Friedrich Engels, The Communist Manifesto, *translated by Samuel Moore (New York: Penguin, 1977), pp. 79–83, 85–92, 95–96.*

5. Marx's View of History

1

BOURGEOIS AND PROLETARIANS[10]

The history of all hitherto existing society is the history of class struggles.

Freeman and slave, patrician and plebeian, lord and serf, guild-master[11] and journeyman, in a word, oppressor and oppressed, stood in constant opposition to one another, carried on an uninterrupted, now hidden, now open fight, a fight that each time ended, either in a revolutionary reconstitution of society at large, or in the common ruin of the contending classes.

10. **bourgeois, proletarian:** "By bourgeoisie is meant the class of modern Capitalist, owners of the means of social production and employers of wage labour. By proletariat, the class of modern wage-labourers who, having no means of production of their own, are reduced to selling their labour power in order to live" (note by Engels to the English edition, 1888).

11. **guild-master:** "that is, a full member of a guild, a master within, not a head of a guild" (note by Engels to the English edition, 1888).

Chapter 7

Two Programs

for Social

and Political

Change:

Liberalism

and Socialism

In the earlier epochs of history, we find almost everywhere a complicated arrangement of society into various orders, a manifold gradation of social rank. In ancient Rome we have patricians, knights, plebeians, slaves; in the Middle Ages, feudal lords, vassals, guild-masters, journeymen, apprentices, serfs; in almost all of these classes, again, subordinate gradations.

The modern bourgeois society that has sprouted from the ruins of feudal society has not done away with class antagonisms. It has but established new classes, new conditions of oppression, new forms of struggle in place of the old ones.

Our epoch, the epoch of the bourgeoisie, possesses, however, this distinctive feature: it has simplified the class antagonisms. Society as a whole is more and more splitting up into two great hostile camps, into two great classes directly facing each other: Bourgeoisie and Proletariat.

From the serfs of the Middle Ages sprang the chartered burghers of the earliest towns. From these burgesses the first elements of the bourgeoisie were developed.

The discovery of America, the rounding of the Cape, opened up fresh ground for the rising bourgeoisie. The East-Indian and Chinese markets, the colonization of America, trade with the colonies, the increase in the means of exchange and in commodities generally, gave to commerce, to navigation, to industry, an impulse never before known, and thereby, to the revolutionary element in the tottering feudal society, a rapid development.

The feudal system of industry, under which industrial production was monopolized by closed guilds, now no longer sufficed for the growing wants of the new markets. The manufacturing system took its place. The guild-masters were pushed on one side by the manufacturing middle class; division of labour between the different corporate guilds vanished in the face of division of labour in each single workshop.

Meantime the markets kept ever growing, the demand ever rising. Even manufacture no longer sufficed. Thereupon, steam and machinery revolutionized industrial production. The place of manufacture was taken by the giant, Modern Industry, the place of the industrial middle class, by industrial millionaires, the leaders of whole industrial armies, the modern bourgeois.

Modern industry has established the world market, for which the discovery of America paved the way. This market has given an immense development to commerce, to navigation, to communication by land. This development has, in its turn, reacted on the extension of industry; and in proportion as industry, commerce, navigation, railways extended, in the same proportion the bourgeoisie developed, increased its capital, and pushed into the background every class handed down from the Middle Ages.

We see, therefore, how the modern bourgeoisie is itself the product of a long course of development, of a series of revolutions in the modes of production and of exchange.

Each step in the development of the bourgeoisie was accompanied by a corresponding political advance of that class. An oppressed class under the sway of the feudal nobility, an armed and self-governing association in the medieval commune;[12] here independent urban republic (as in Italy and Germany), there taxable "third estate" of the monarchy (as in France), afterwards, in the period of manufacture proper, serving either the semi-feudal or the absolute monarchy as a counterpoise against the nobility, and, in fact, cornerstone of the great monarchies in general, the bourgeoisie has at last, since the establishment of Modern Industry and of the world market, conquered for itself, in the modern representative State, exclusive political sway. The executive of the modern State is but a committee for managing the common affairs of the whole bourgeoisie.

The bourgeoisie, historically, has played a most revolutionary part.

The bourgeoisie, wherever it has got the upper hand, has put an end to all feudal, patriarchal, idyllic relations. It has pitilessly torn asunder the motley feudal ties that bound man to his "natural superiors," and has left remaining no other nexus between man and man than naked self-interest, than callous "cash payment." It has drowned the most heavenly ecstasies of religious fervour, of chivalrous enthusiasm, of philistine sentimentalism, in the icy water of egotistical calculation. It has resolved personal worth into exchange value, and in place of the numberless indefeasible chartered freedoms, has set up that single, unconscionable freedom—Free Trade. In one word, for exploitation, veiled by religious and political illusions, it has substituted naked, shameless, direct, brutal exploitation.

The bourgeoisie has stripped of its halo every occupation hitherto honoured and looked up to with reverent awe. It has converted the physician, the lawyer, the priest, the poet, the man of science, into its paid wage-labourers.

The bourgeoisie has torn away from the family its sentimental veil, and has reduced the family relation to a mere money relation. . . .

The bourgeoisie cannot exist without constantly revolutionizing the instruments of production, and thereby the relations of production, and with them the whole relations of society. Conservation of the old modes of production in unaltered form, was, on the contrary, the first condition of existence for all earlier industrial classes. Constant revolutionizing of production, uninterrupted disturbance of all social conditions, everlasting uncertainty and agitation distinguish the bourgeois epoch from all earlier ones. All fixed, fast-frozen relations, with their train of ancient and venerable prejudices and

12. **commune:** "the name taken, in France, by the nascent towns even before they had conquered from their feudal lords and masters local self-government and political rights as the 'Third Estate.' Generally speaking, for the economical development of the bourgeoisie, England is here taken as the typical country; for its political development, France" (note by Engels to the English edition, 1888). "This was the name given their urban communities by the townsmen of Italy and France, after they had purchased or wrested their initial rights of self-government from their feudal lords" (note by Engels to the German edition, 1890).

Chapter 7

Two Programs

for Social

and Political

Change:

Liberalism

and Socialism

opinions are swept away, all new-formed ones become antiquated before they can ossify. All that is solid melts into air, all that is holy is profaned, and man is at last compelled to face with sober senses, his real conditions of life, and his relations with his kind.

The need of a constantly expanding market for its products chases the bourgeoisie over the whole surface of the globe. It must nestle everywhere, settle everywhere, establish connexions everywhere. . . .

Modern bourgeois society with its relations of production, of exchange and of property, a society that has conjured up such gigantic means of production and of exchange, is like the sorcerer, who is no longer able to control the powers of the nether world whom he has called up by his spells. For many a decade past the history of industry and commerce is but the history of the revolt of modern productive forces against modern conditions of production, against the property relations that are the conditions for the existence of the bourgeoisie and of its rule. It is enough to mention the commercial crises that by their periodical return put on its trial, each time more threateningly, the existence of the entire bourgeois society. In these crises a great part not only of the existing products, but also of the previously created productive forces, are periodically destroyed. In these crises there breaks out an epidemic that, in all earlier epochs, would have seemed an absurdity—the epidemic of overproduction. . . .

And how does the bourgeoisie get over these crises? On the one hand by enforced destruction of a mass of productive forces; on the other, by the conquest of new markets, and by the more thorough exploitation of the old ones. That is to say, by paving the way for more extensive and more destructive crises, and by diminishing the means whereby crises are prevented.

The weapons with which the bourgeoisie felled feudalism to the ground are now turned against the bourgeoisie itself.

But not only has the bourgeoisie forged the weapons that bring death to itself; it has also called into existence the men who are to wield those weapons—the modern working class—the proletarians.

In proportion as the bourgeoisie, i.e., capital, is developed, in the same proportion is the proletariat, the modern working class, developed—a class of labourers, who live only so long as they find work, and who find work only so long as their labour increases capital. These labourers, who must sell themselves piecemeal, are a commodity, like every other article of commerce, and are consequently exposed to all the vicissitudes of competition, to all the fluctuations of the market.

Owing to the extensive use of machinery and to division of labour, the work of the proletarians has lost all individual character, and, consequently, all charm for the workman. He becomes an appendage of the machine, and it is only the most simple, most monotonous, and most easily acquired knack, that is required of him. Hence, the cost of production of a workman is restricted, almost entirely, to the means of subsistence that he requires for his maintenance, and for the propagation of his race. . . .

Modern industry has converted the little workshop of the patriarchal master into the great factory of the industrial capitalist. Masses of labourers, crowded into the factory, are organized like soldiers. As privates of the industrial army they are placed under the command of a perfect hierarchy of officers and sergeants. Not only are they slaves of the bourgeois class, and of the bourgeois State; they are daily and hourly enslaved by the machine, by the overlooker, and, above all, by the individual bourgeois manufacturer himself. The more openly this despotism proclaims gain be its end and aim, the more petty, the more hateful and the more embittering it is. . . .

The proletariat goes through various stages of development. With its birth begins its struggle with the bourgeoisie. At first the contest is carried on by individual labourers, then by the work-people of a factory, then by the operatives of one trade, in one locality, against the individual bourgeois who directly exploits them. They direct their attacks not against the bourgeois conditions of production, but against the instruments of production themselves; they destroy imported wares that compete with their labour, they smash to pieces machinery, they set factories ablaze, they seek to restore by force the vanished status of the workman of the Middle Ages.

At this stage the labourers still form an incoherent mass scattered over the whole country, and broken up by their mutual competition. If anywhere they unite to form more compact bodies, this is not yet the consequence of their own active union, but of the union of the bourgeoisie, which class, in order to attain its own political ends, is compelled to set the whole proletariat in motion, and is moreover yet, for a time, able to do so. At this stage, therefore, the proletarians do not fight their enemies, but the enemies of their enemies, the remnants of absolute monarchy, the landowners, the non-industrial bourgeois, the petty bourgeoisie. Thus the whole historical movement is concentrated in the hands of the bourgeoisie; every victory so obtained is a victory for the bourgeoisie.

But with the development of industry the proletariat not only increases in number; it becomes concentrated in greater masses, its strength grows, and it feels that strength more. The various interests and conditions of life within the ranks of the proletariat are more and more equalized, in proportion as machinery obliterates all distinctions of labour, and nearly everywhere reduces wages to the same low level. The growing competition among the bourgeois, and the resulting commercial crises, make the wages of the workers ever more fluctuating. The unceasing improvement of machinery, ever more rapidly developing, makes their livelihood more and more precarious; the collisions between individual workmen and individual bourgeois take more and more the character of collisions between two classes. Thereupon the workers begin to form combinations (Trades Unions) against the bourgeois; they club together

[197]

Chapter 7
Two Programs
for Social
and Political
Change:
Liberalism
and Socialism

in order to keep up the rate of wages; they found permanent associations in order to make provision beforehand for these occasional revolts. Here and there the contest breaks out into riots.

Now and then the workers are victorious, but only for a time. The real fruit of their battles lies, not in the immediate result, but in the ever-expanding union of the workers. This union is helped on by the improved means of communication that are created by modern industry and that place the workers of different localities in contact with one another. It was just this contact that was needed to centralize the numerous local struggles, all of the same character, into one national struggle between classes. But every class struggle is a political struggle. And that union, to attain which the burghers of the Middle Ages, with their miserable highways, required centuries, the modern proletarians, thanks to railways, achieve in a few years. . . .

Of all the classes that stand face to face with the bourgeoisie today, the proletariat alone is a really revolutionary class. The other classes decay and finally disappear in the face of modern industry; the proletariat is its special and essential product.

The lower middle class, the small manufacturer, the shopkeeper, the artisan, the peasant, all these fight against the bourgeoisie, to save from extinction their existence as fractions of the middle class. They are therefore not revolutionary, but conservative. Nay more, they are reactionary, for they try to roll back the wheel of history. . . .

In the conditions of the proletariat, those of old society at large are already virtually swamped. The proletarian is without property; his relation to his wife and children has no longer anything in common with the bourgeois family relations; modern industrial labour, modern subjection to capital, the same in England as in France, in America as in Germany, has stripped him of every trace of national character. Law, morality, religion, are to him so many bourgeois prejudices, behind which lurk in ambush just as many bourgeois interests.

All the preceding classes that got the upper hand sought to fortify their already acquired status by subjecting society at large to their conditions of appropriation. The proletarians cannot become masters of the productive forces of society, except by abolishing their own previous mode of appropriation, and thereby also every other previous mode of appropriation. They have nothing of their own to secure and to fortify; their mission is to destroy all previous securities for, and insurances of, individual property.

All previous historical movements were movements of minorities, or in the interest of minorities. The proletarian movement is the self-conscious, independent movement of the immense majority, in the interest of the immense majority. The proletariat, the lowest stratum of our present society, cannot stir, cannot raise itself up, without the whole superincumbent strata of official society being sprung into the air.

2
PROLETARIANS AND COMMUNISTS

In what relation do the Communists stand to the proletarians as a whole?

The Communists do not form a separate party opposed to other working-class parties.

They have no interests separate and apart from those of the proletariat as a whole.

They do not set up any sectarian principles of their own, by which to shape and mould the proletarian movement.

The Communists are distinguished from the other working-class parties by this only: 1. In the national struggles of the proletarians of the different countries, they point out and bring to the front the common interests of the entire proletariat, independently of all nationality. 2. In the various stages of development which the struggle of the working class against the bourgeoisie has to pass through, they always and everywhere represent the interests of the movement as a whole.

The Communists, therefore, are on the one hand, practically, the most advanced and resolute section of the working-class parties of every country, that section which pushes forward all others; on the other hand, theoretically, they have over the great mass of the proletariat the advantage of clearly understanding the line of march, the conditions, and the ultimate general results of the proletarian movement.

The immediate aim of the Communists is the same as that of all the other proletarian parties: formation of the proletariat into a class, overthrow of the bourgeois supremacy, conquest of political power by the proletariat.

The theoretical conclusions of the Communists are in no way based on ideas or principles that have been invented, or discovered, by this or that would-be universal reformer.

They merely express, in general terms, actual relations springing from an existing class struggle, from a historical movement going on under our very eyes. The abolition of existing property relations is not at all a distinctive feature of Communism.

All property relations in the past have continually been subject to historical change consequent upon the change in historical conditions.

The French Revolution, for example, abolished feudal property in favour of bourgeois property.

The distinguishing feature of Communism is not the abolition of property generally, but the abolition of bourgeois property. But modern bourgeois private property is the final and most complete expression of the system of producing and appropriating products, that is based on class antagonisms, on the exploitation of the many by the few.

In this sense, the theory of the Communists may be summed up in the single sentence: Abolition of private property.

Chapter 7

Two Programs

for Social

and Political

Change:

Liberalism

and Socialism

Source 6 from Karl Marx, The Class Struggles in France (1848–1850), *edited by C. P. Dutt (New York: International Publishers, 1964), pp. 33–34, 39–40, 50–52, 55, 56, 58–59. Used by permission of International Publishers.*

6. Marx on the Revolution of 1848 in Paris

1
FROM FEBRUARY TO JUNE 1848

With the exception of a few short chapters, every important part of the annals of the revolution from 1848 to 1849 carries the heading: Defeat of the revolution!

But what succumbed in these defeats was not the revolution. It was the pre-revolutionary traditional appendages, results of social relationships, which had not yet come to the point of sharp class antagonisms—persons, illusions, conceptions, projects, from which the revolutionary party before the February Revolution was not free, from which it could be freed, not by the victory of February, but only by a series of defeats.

In a word: revolutionary advance made headway not by its immediate tragi-comic achievements, but on the contrary by the creation of a powerful, united counter-revolution, by the creation of an opponent, by fighting whom the party of revolt first ripened into a real revolutionary party.

To prove this is the task of the following pages.

I. THE DEFEAT OF JUNE 1848

After the July Revolution, when the Liberal banker, Laffitte, led his godfather, the Duke of Orleans, in triumph to the Hôtel de Ville,[13] he let fall the words: "From now on the bankers will rule." Laffitte had betrayed the secret of the revolution. . . .

It was not the French bourgeoisie that ruled under Louis Philippe, but a fraction of it, bankers, Stock Exchange kings, railway kings, owners of coal and iron works and forests, a section of landed proprietors that rallied around them—the so-called finance aristocracy. It sat on the throne, it dictated laws in the Chambers, it conferred political posts from cabinet portfolios to the tobacco bureau.

The real industrial bourgeoisie formed part of the official opposition, *i.e.,* it was represented only as a minority in the Chambers. . . .

The petty bourgeoisie of all degrees, and the peasantry also, were completely excluded from political power. Finally, in the official opposition or

---

13. **Hôtel de Ville:** City Hall. The Duke of Orleans emerged from the July Revolution as King Louis Philippe.

entirely outside the *pays légal*,[14] there were the ideological representatives and spokesmen of the above classes, their savants, lawyers, doctors, etc., in a word: their so-called talents. . . .

The Provisional Government which emerged from the February barricades, necessarily mirrored in its composition the different parties which shared in the victory.[15] It could not be anything but a compromise between the different classes which together had overturned the July throne, but whose interests were mutually antagonistic. A large majority of its members consisted of representatives of the bourgeoisie. . . . The working class had only two representatives, Louis Blanc and Albert. . . .

Up to noon on February 25, the republic had not yet been proclaimed; on the other hand, the whole of the Ministries had already been divided among the bourgeois elements of the Provisional Government and among the generals, bankers and lawyers of the *National*. But the workers were this time determined not to put up with any swindling like that of July 1830. They were ready to take up the fight anew and to enforce the republic by force of arms. With this message, Raspail betook himself to the Hôtel de Ville. In the name of the Parisian proletariat he commanded the Provisional Government to proclaim the republic; if this order of the people were not fulfilled within two hours, he would return at the head of 200,000 men. The bodies of the fallen were scarcely cold, the barricades were not yet cleared away, the workers not yet disarmed, and the only force which could be opposed to them was the National Guard. Under these circumstances the prudent state doubts and juristic scruples of conscience of the Provisional Government suddenly vanished. The interval of two hours had not expired before all the walls of Paris were resplendent with the tremendous historical words:

République française! Liberté, Egalité, Fraternité![16]. . .

The proletariat, by dictating the republic to the Provisional Government and through the Provisional Government to the whole of France, stepped into the foreground forthwith as an independent party, but at the same time challenged the whole of bourgeois France to enter the lists against it. What it won

14. *pays légal:* literally, "legal country." Here Marx refers to the fact that the monarchy established by the July Revolution created a very limited right to vote. One had to possess a substantial amount of property to qualify for the right to vote, with the result that only 170,000 men, out of a population of about 30,000,000, qualified to vote for the Chamber of Deputies in the 1830s.

15. In his work *The Eighteenth of Brumaire of Louis Bonaparte* (New York: International Publishers, 1935), p. 101, Marx referred to the participation of a broad spectrum of social groups in the February Revolution as the "Universal brotherhood swindle." This means that, in his view, the lower classes were seduced into revolutionary action by bourgeois promises of democracy that were unfilled in the postrevolutionary government.

16. *République française: Liberté, Egalité, Fraternité:* "The French Republic: Liberty, Equality, Fraternity," the motto of the Revolution of 1789.

Chapter 7

Two Programs

for Social

and Political

Change:

Liberalism

and Socialism

was the terrain for the fight for its revolutionary emancipation, but in no way this emancipation itself! . . .

A hundred thousand workers thrown on the streets through the crisis and the revolution were enrolled by the Minister Marie in so-called National *Ateliers*![17] Under this grand name was hidden nothing but the employment of the workers on tedious, monotonous, unproductive earthworks at a wage of 23 sous.[18] English *workhouses* in the open—that is what these National *Ateliers* were. . . .

All the discontent, all the ill humour of the petty bourgeois was simultaneously directed against these National *Ateliers,* the common target. With real fury they reckoned up the sums that the proletarian loafers swallowed, while their own situation became daily more unbearable. A state pension for sham labour, that is socialism! they growled to themselves. They sought the basis of their misery in the National *Ateliers,* the declarations of the Luxembourg,[19] the marches of the workers through Paris. And no one was more fantastic about the alleged machinations of the Communists than the petty bourgeoisie who hovered hopelessly on the brink of bankruptcy.[20] . . .

In the National Assembly all France sat in judgment on the Paris proletariat. It broke immediately with the social illusions of the February Revolution; it roundly proclaimed the bourgeois republic, nothing but the bourgeois republic. It at once excluded the representatives of the proletariat, Louis Blanc and Albert, from the Executive Commission appointed by it; it threw out the proposal of a special Labour Ministry,[21] and received with stormy applause

17. *atelier:* workshop. The National Ateliers were government-funded projects to provide work to the unemployed.

18. **23 sous:** The sou was a French coin worth 5 centimes (100 centimes to 1 franc). Thus Marx cites a wage of a little over 1 **franc** per day for the labor. Initially, wages in the workshops were 2 francs per day for laborers and 1 franc per day for those unemployed for whom labor could not be found. Even 2 francs per day was less than the usual wage for skilled artisans like tailors and shoemakers.

19. **The Luxembourg:** the revolutionary government established a commission to study labor problems; chaired by the socialist Louis Blanc and composed of representatives of various trades, it was headquartered in the Luxembourg Palace. The commission secured the government's enactment of a ten-hour workday in Paris and a twelve-hour workday in the provinces. This reform would have reduced most workers' hours of labor had it been enforced by government supervision.

20. One of the causes of the Revolution of 1848 was a general European economic crisis in 1846–1848 that had its origins in agricultural problems. Potato harvests were disastrously deficient in Ireland and other countries in 1845–1848 because of a blight. Weather factors conspired to reduce wheat harvests in these same years, creating rising food prices and general distress in the economies of most European countries.

21. The National Assembly, elected by universal manhood suffrage in April 1848, had a moderate to conservative majority: Of the 900 members, about 500 were moderate republicans and 300 were monarchists. In such a chamber, proposals for a Ministry of Labor and for a guaranteed right to work, proposed by Louis Blanc, gained little support.

the statement of the Minister Trélat: "The question is merely one of bringing labour back to its old conditions."

But all this was not enough. The February republic was won by the workers with the passive support of the bourgeoisie. The proletarians regarded themselves, and rightly, as the victors of February, and they made the proud claims of victors. They had to be vanquished on the streets, they had to be shown that they were worsted as soon as they fought, not with the bourgeoisie, but against the bourgeoisie. Just as the February republic, with its socialist concessions, required a battle of the proletariat, united with the bourgeoisie, against monarchy, so a second battle was necessary in order to sever the republic from the socialist concessions, in order to officially work out the bourgeois republic as dominant. The bourgeoisie had to refute the demands of the proletariat with arms in its hands. And the real birthplace of the bourgeois republic is not the February victory; it is the June defeat. . . .

The Executive Commission began by making entry into the National *Ateliers* more difficult, by turning the day wage into a piece wage, by banishing workers not born in Paris to Sologne, ostensibly for the construction of earthworks. These earthworks were only a rhetorical formula with which to gloss over their expulsion, as the workers, returning disillusioned, announced to their comrades. Finally, on June 21, a decree appeared in the *Moniteur*,[22] which ordered the forcible expulsion of all unmarried workers from the National *Ateliers*, or their enrolment in the army.

The workers were left no choice: they had to starve or start to fight. They answered on June 22 with the tremendous insurrection in which the first great battle was joined between the two classes that split modern society. It was a fight for the preservation or annihilation of the bourgeois order. The veil that shrouded the republic was torn to pieces.

It is well known how the workers, with unexampled bravery and talent, without chiefs, without a common plan, without means and, for the most part, lacking weapons, held in check for five days the army, the Mobile Guard, the Parisian National Guard, and the National Guard that streamed in from the provinces. It is well known how the bourgeoisie compensated itself for the mortal anguish it underwent by unheard of brutality, and massacred over 3,000 prisoners.[23] . . .

By making its burial place the birth place of the bourgeois republic, the proletariat compelled the latter to come out forthwith in its pure form as the state whose admitted object is to perpetuate the rule of capital, the slavery of labour. With constant regard to the scarred, irreconcilable, unconquerable

22. *Moniteur:* a journal that published parliamentary debate and government decrees.

23. Marx does not wildly exaggerate the losses here. Casualties in the actual fighting and in the retribution following it were high.

Chapter 7

Two Programs

for Social

and Political

Change:

Liberalism

and Socialism

enemy—unconquerable because its existence is the condition of its own life—bourgeois rule, freed from all fetters, was bound to turn immediately into bourgeois terrorism. With the proletariat removed for the time being from the stage and bourgeois dictatorship recognised officially, the middle sections, in the mass, had more and more to side with the proletariat as their position became more unbearable and their antagonism to the bourgeoisie became more acute. Just as earlier in its upsurge, so now they had to find in its defeat the cause of their misery. . . .

Only through the defeat of June, therefore, were all conditions created under which France can seize the initiative of the European revolution. Only after baptism in the blood of the June insurgents did the tricolour[24] become the flag of the European revolution—the red flag.

And we cry: *The revolution is dead!—Long live the revolution!*

Source 7 from Karl Marx and Friedrich Engels, The Communist Manifesto, *translated by Samuel Moore (New York: Penguin, 1977), pp. 104–105.*

7. Marx's Ideals of Government and Economy

We have seen above, that the first step in the revolution by the working class, is to raise the proletariat to the position of ruling class, to win the battle of democracy.

The proletariat will use its political supremacy to wrest, by degrees, all capital from the bourgeoisie, to centralize all instruments of production in the hands of the State, i.e., of the proletariat organized as the ruling class; and to increase the total of productive forces as rapidly as possible.

Of course, in the beginning, this cannot be effected except by means of despotic inroads on the rights of property, and on the conditions of bourgeois production; by means of measures, therefore, which appear economically insufficient and untenable, but which, in the course of the movement, outstrip themselves, necessitate further inroads upon the old social order, and are unavoidable as a means of entirely revolutionizing the mode of production.

These measures will of course be different in different countries.

Nevertheless, in the most advanced countries, the following will be pretty generally applicable:

1. Abolition of property in land and application of all rents of land to public purposes.

2. A heavy progressive or graduated income tax.

24. **tricolor:** the three-colored flag, composed of vertical stripes of blue, white, and red, adopted in the 1789 Revolution and today the flag of France.

3. Abolition of all right of inheritance.

4. Confiscation of the property of all emigrants and rebels.

5. Centralization of credit in the hands of the State, by means of a national bank with State capital and an exclusive monopoly.

6. Centralization of the means of communication and transport in the hands of the State.

7. Extension of factories and instruments of production owned by the State; the bringing into cultivation of wastelands, and the improvement of the soil generally in accordance with a common plan.

8. Equal liability of all to labour. Establishment of industrial armies, especially for agriculture.

9. Combination of agriculture with manufacturing industries; gradual abolition of the distinction between town and country, by a more equable distribution of the population over the country.

10. Free education for all children in public schools. Abolition of children's factory labour in its present form. Combination of education with industrial production, &c., &c.

When, in the course of development, class distinctions have disappeared, and all production has been concentrated in the whole nation, the public power will lose its political character. Political power, properly so called, is merely the organized power of one class for oppressing another. If the proletariat during its contest with the bourgeoisie is compelled, by the force of circumstances, to organize itself as a class, if, by means of a revolution, it makes itself the ruling class, and, as such, sweeps away by force the old conditions of production, then it will, along with these conditions, have swept away the conditions for the existence of class antagonisms and of classes generally, and will thereby have abolished its own supremacy as a class.

In place of the old bourgeois society, with its classes and class antagonisms, we shall have an association, in which the free development of each is the condition for the free development of all.

QUESTIONS TO CONSIDER

Tocqueville and Marx pose different responses to many of the same issues in the selections presented in this chapter. Your basic task in answering the main questions of this chapter is to compare their ideas.

Central to the thought of both men is a certain vision of historical evolution. Indeed, Marx called himself a "scientific socialist" because, in his view, he had discovered the immutable course of historical development. What was this historical process for Marx? What patterns of history did Tocqueville identify? As you continue your study of modern Western history in this course, consider which of these thinkers' ideas seem most adequately to have predicted the political and economic development of the West.

Chapter 7

Two Programs

for Social

and Political

Change:

Liberalism

and Socialism

Both Marx and Tocqueville address the problem of revolution in the selections that you have read. First consider Tocqueville. What threats to democracy did he see emerging in the West? Why did he believe that revolution was not likely to be a threat to democracy? What dangers, according to Tocqueville, did revolution pose when it did erupt? Did Tocqueville's liberal principles admit any circumstances under which society should resort to revolution as a means of change? Recall Tocqueville's attitude toward the government of King Louis Philippe in Source 3. Why did Tocqueville oppose the Revolution of 1848 despite this view?

Now analyze Marx's ideas on revolution. Examine the historical role for revolution that Marx believed he had found. Why did Marx see the middle class, those who owned the factories and embraced liberal ideas, as revolutionary? In what ways, according to Marx, was capitalism sowing the seeds of its destruction? What class would challenge the factory owners in revolution? What vision of the future did that class have, according to Marx? Did they want the political democracy Tocqueville was prepared to accept or a broader reorganization of society? How did Marx and Tocqueville differ in their views of the desirability of revolution?

Both authors also wrote on the same revolution, the French uprising of 1848, providing us a further opportunity to contrast their views. As your study of the 1848 revolutions no doubt has demonstrated, it is impossible to consider the uprisings of that year a success. Whether revolution-aries' goals were nationalist or liberal, the revolutions ended in defeat everywhere. This was certainly the case in France, where the conflict of June 1848 between the government of the Second Republic and the Parisian unemployed created the political climate for the election of Louis-Napoleon Bonaparte.

How did each author view the revolution of 1848? What guiding emotion do you detect in Tocqueville's *Recollections* of February 24, 1848? What was its source? In formulating your answer, consult the selection in which Tocqueville discusses general aspects of revolution and expresses his ideals of government. What was Marx's view of the failure of the June 1848 revolt? Why was the victory that emerged in 1848 an essential step for Marx toward the final revolution?

Finally, let us compare the political and economic ideals advocated by the liberal Tocqueville and the socialist Marx. Your task here is made more challenging by the assertion of both these political thinkers that they advocated democracy. To understand the differences between them, review their writings to determine how each defined "democracy." Is Tocqueville's conception of democracy expressed primarily in terms of political participation? Is there any room in his thought for social democracy, that is, a more egalitarian distribution of society's wealth? How does Tocqueville characterize his political thought in Source 4? Recall France's history of recurring revolution. Why might he accept a monarch in Europe and an elected head of government in America?

Sources 5 through 7 express especially clearly Marx's democratic philosophy. Does Marx believe in political democracy? How is he concerned with social democracy? Who would control property, credit, and the means of production in his ideal society? What answers does Marx have to such abuses of industrialization as child labor? What impact would his system have on the lives of its citizens?

Finally, consider the two thinkers' views on the role of government. What role in the lives of its citizens does Tocqueville assign to the government? How does that view mark him as a nineteenth-century liberal? What sort of postrevolutionary government does Marx envision? How does it differ from Tocqueville's ideal? Are there areas where Marx and Tocqueville might agree?

With answers to these fairly specific questions in mind, you are now ready to answer the general questions presented earlier in this chapter: What visions of the future did liberals and socialists propose? How did they hope to realize their ideals? How did their ideologies differ?

EPILOGUE

The selections in this chapter present two contrasting nineteenth-century visions of Western society. Most of what you have read appeared around the middle of the nineteenth century, much of it in the midst of the West's last general outbreak of revolution in 1848. Because both authors wrote about that event and had a definite view of revolution, perhaps it is appropriate to examine briefly how their predictions fared after 1848.

The events of 1848 shook Tocqueville's faith in the growth of democracy founded on limited government and increasing equality of property as well as in political stability and evolutionary change based on respect for the rule of law. Indeed, in 1850 he wrote to his friend Eugène Stoffels of events in France with considerable despair:

What is clear to me is that for sixty years we have fooled ourselves by believing that we could see the end of revolution. The revolution was thought to have finished at 18 *brumaire*, the same was thought in 1814; I thought myself in 1830 that it could well be at an end . . . I was wrong. It is clear today . . . not only that we have not seen the end of the immense revolution which started before our time, but that today's child will probably not see it.[25]

25. Tocqueville to Eugène Stoffels, quoted in Jack Lively, *The Social and Political Thought of Alexis de Tocqueville* (Oxford: Clarendon Press, 1962), p. 211. The radical leaders of the French Revolution of 1789–1799 had sought to break with the traditional Western calendar and its Christian observances. Thus they created a new calendar devoid of Christian holidays and with renamed months. The date 18 *brumaire* was the day in 1799 that marked Napoleon's seizure of power in France; 1814 was the year of the restoration of the French monarchy after Napoleon's fall; 1830, of course, was the year King Louis Philippe came to power.

Chapter 7

Two Programs

for Social

and Political

Change:

Liberalism

and Socialism

Tocqueville died in 1859 questioning his vision of the future, and Marx lived on until 1883, also disillusioned, as we have noted, by his own apparent failure decisively to affect the socialist movement. Events after their deaths would have surprised both men. Political change in much of Europe proved to be far more evolutionary than revolutionary in the years after 1848, thanks to several developments predicted neither by Tocqueville nor by Marx.

The liberal ideology represented by Tocqueville became less and less a narrow doctrine of individual freedom. Later liberals, such as the Englishman John Stuart Mill (1806–1873), emphasized that economic liberty reached its limits when it allowed employers to abuse their employees with the low wages and poor working conditions we examined in Chapter 6. Consequently, they supported legislation to rectify many of the worst abuses of industrial employment. Such liberals also believed in political democracy and won extended franchises in countries like England and Italy.

Communist revolution occasionally did break out, as Marx had predicted. But he utterly misjudged the historical developments that produced such revolutions. Writing from the vantage point of the early Industrial Revolution, Marx assumed that working-class misery would intensify and produce communist revolution only in the most industrialized nations. Instead, Marx's revolution broke out in places where he never would have expected it. Peasant pop-

ulations in countries either on the threshold of industrialization, like Russia in 1917, or not yet industrialized, like China and Vietnam in the 1940s and 1950s, have been the chief adherents of communist revolution. Marx had believed peasants incapable of such ideological mobilization, counting them a politically inert "sack of potatoes." And, contrary to Marx's prediction that communism would constitute the final stage of human development, such regimes, like that in the former Soviet Union, were breaking down by the early 1990s.

In much of the industrialized West, the widened right to vote, in fact, engendered a new kind of evolutionary socialism quite distinct from Marx's revolutionary socialism. The German Eduard Bernstein (1850–1932) was among the first to recognize that working-class voting rights eliminated the need for Marx's class warfare and revolution. Armed with the vote, Bernstein emphasized, workers could elect parliaments favoring their needs and peacefully win a better life through legislation. The need for revolution was at an end.

In the twenty-first century, socialist parties committed to political democracy, sometimes allied with liberals, have been instrumental in bringing greater social equality for working people in much of Western Europe. In modern England, France, Italy, Germany, and other nations, legislation improving working conditions and wages as well as establishing the protection of health and unemployment insurance and old age pensions stands as monument to the widened vote created by liberals and the use of that vote by democratic socialists. The consequent improvement in working-class conditions ultimately resulted in the decline in the broad popular appeal of Marxian revolutionary socialists in much of the West.

CHAPTER EIGHT

VIENNA AND PARIS,

1850–1930:

THE DEVELOPMENT OF

THE MODERN CITY

The nineteenth century was a period of great change in Europe. Just as the Industrial Revolution transformed the Continent's mode of production and, as we have seen in Chapter 6, its patterns of work, it also greatly accelerated the urbanization of the West. Individual cities grew rapidly as large numbers of immigrants from rural areas came in search of industrial jobs, and society was transformed as urban rather than rural life became the lifestyle of the majority. By the second half of the nineteenth century, over half of the population of England and Wales, the original centers of the Industrial Revolution, dwelt in cities, and Germany and other countries reached that level of urban concentration of population within several decades.

Unfortunately for the residents of Europe's growing nineteenth-century cities, living conditions in these centers often were very difficult. This is how one French author described Paris in 1848:

If you contemplate from the summit of Montmartre or any other hill in the neighborhood, the congestion of houses piled up at every point of a vast horizon, what do you observe? Above, a sky that is always overcast, even on the finest day. Clouds of smoke, like a vast floating curtain, hide it from view. A forest of chimneys with black or yellowish chimneypots renders the sight singularly monotonous. . . . Looking at it, one is tempted to wonder whether this is Paris; and, seized with sudden fear, one is reluctant to venture into this vast maze, in which a million beings jostle each other, where the air, vitiated by unhealthy effluvia, rising in a poisonous cloud, almost obscures the sun. Most of the streets in this wonderful Paris are nothing but filthy alleys forever damp from a reeking flood. Hemmed in between two rows of tall houses, they never get the sun; it reaches only the tops of the chimneys dominating them. To catch a glimpse of the sky you have to look straight up above your head. A haggard and sickly crowd perpetually throngs these streets, their feet in the gutter, their noses in infection, their eyes outraged by the most repulsive garbage at every street corner. The best-paid workmen live in these streets. There are alleys, too, in which two cannot walk abreast, sewers of ordure and mud, in which the stunted dwellers daily inhale death. These are the streets of old Paris, still intact.[1]

Rapid population growth overwhelmed the capacity of early-nineteenth-century municipal governments to provide for the needs of their new citizens. The problems described in the quotation were almost universal. Many cities in Continental Europe remained hemmed in by medieval or early modern fortifications designed to protect much smaller populations from military attack. Even without this obstacle to expansion, however, urban spread was limited by the almost complete absence of cheap, public transportation. People had to live close to their jobs because they walked to them, and essentially medieval residential patterns persisted in which craftsmen and merchants dwelled behind or above their places of business and poorer persons occupied the upper floors of the same buildings.

1. H. Lecouturier, *Paris incompatible avec la République, plan d'un nouveau Paris où les révolutions seront impossibles* (Paris: 1848), quoted in Louis Chevalier, *Laboring Classes and Dangerous Classes in Paris during the First Half of the Nineteenth Century,* trans. by Frank Jellinek (Princeton, N.J.: Princeton University Press, 1981), p. 155. Montmartre is the highest point in Paris.

The growth in the urban population within the old walls led to an increasingly dense pattern of residence. Landlords added additional floors to existing buildings, cut up once spacious apartments into many smaller living units, erected inferior dwellings in courtyards and other open spaces, and rented basement and attic rooms. Sunlight and fresh air disappeared as building heights increased along narrow, medieval streets. Basements were particularly unhealthy dwellings; they often leaked and seldom received sunlight or ventilation. With little but musty, stale air available to them, it was a custom of basement residents to get an occasional "airing" out of doors.

Simple movement of people was a problem in the streets of such cities. Lacking sidewalks, pedestrians competed with horse-drawn vehicles for the opportunity to move through cramped streets wet with household waste water and soiled by horse droppings. A trip across a major city, which today would require a matter of minutes by subway, consumed considerably more time in the early nineteenth century. Many cities were almost strangled by such transportation difficulties within their old walls.

Rapid population growth in the limited spaces of many cities produced serious health and social problems. Extremely primitive methods for disposal of human wastes often led to pollution of water supplies, and in the first decades of the nineteenth century, sewers in Paris and other cities emptied into the very rivers that were the main sources of municipal water. Under such conditions, disease

Chapter 8

Vienna

and Paris,

1850–1930:

The Development

of the Modern

City

spread rapidly, and life could be short. Epidemics of cholera, a disease often transmitted by polluted drinking water, struck many cities in the nineteenth century; 20,000 persons died in one outbreak of the disease in Paris in 1832. Indeed, well into the nineteenth century, most cities retained an age-old urban demographic pattern in which death rates among their citizens exceeded birth rates. The limited urban population growth that occurred prior to about 1850 was almost entirely the result of immigration to the cities from rural areas.

A rapidly rising crime rate was probably the most vexing of the social consequences of urban growth. Urban life often plunged unskilled immigrants of rural origin into deep poverty. Though crime sometimes stemmed from poverty, certain features of urban life encouraged it. The social controls of rural village life largely were absent in the cities, where the anonymity of the individual in the urban mass facilitated lawbreaking. Police resources for controlling such behavior were limited or nonexistent during the first half of the nineteenth century, too. The pioneering effort at urban crime control, the London Metropolitan Police Force, was created only in 1829, and was imitated widely only after 1850.

In fact, only after about 1850 can we find Western society systematically attempting to solve the real problems of urban living. Collectively, these responses transformed city life and produced our modern pattern of urban living. Several nineteenth-century developments made possible this important transforma-

tion. We should note first that the power of central governments grew everywhere. The state's ability to command resources in the form of taxes financed many improvements. Its growing bureaucracy also provided the personnel to undertake the first modern urban planning. And its need to maintain order in growing cities led to improved police services and better street lighting to inhibit crime, wider streets to allow for troop movements in case of urban rebellion, and better sanitation to protect the health of its citizens and taxpayers.

The Industrial Revolution played a major role in the urban transformation, too. It created new technologies whose application to city life would improve conditions, and it produced wealth, increasingly shared by more and more persons, which could finance private projects of urban building and improvement. Industrialization also sustained a new consumer-oriented economy characterized by the mass distribution of the products of the new factories to large urban markets. Modern science played a part in urban improvements, too. The work of Louis Pasteur (1822–1895) and other scientists made possible purer water and food to protect public health.

The combination of these nineteenth-century developments would transform the Western city by 1930. Your problem in this chapter is to examine the physical expressions and social consequences of this transformation in two major cities: Paris, France, and Vienna, Austria. How were these cities physically reshaped in response to early-nineteenth-century problems? How did this physi-cal transformation affect the lifestyle of urban dwellers?

SOURCES AND METHOD

In order to analyze this chapter's sources, you will require some specific information on nineteenth-century Paris and Vienna. In the 1870s, Paris and Vienna, respectively, were Europe's second- and third-largest cities; only the population of Greater London was larger. As the political capitals of their nations and as major cultural, commercial, and industrial centers, they experienced rapid growth during much of the period from 1850 to 1930. The population of Paris grew from 547,000 persons in 1800 to 2,714,000 persons a century later, a growth rate of 496 percent. For the same period, Vienna's population grew even more rapidly: from 247,000 persons to 1,675,000 persons, for a growth rate of 678 percent.[2] With such rapid growth, Paris and Vienna experienced the full range of urban problems we examined earlier in this chapter. The two cities' responses to these problems are typical of those of most Continental European cities in our period. But to analyze our evidence on these changes, some background on Paris and Vienna is necessary.

Unlike English cities, which early abandoned their defensive walls be-cause of the protection from attack afforded all of England by its surrounding seas, most Continental European cities retained their walls into the nineteenth century because of the probability of military assault. Thus, Paris traditionally had been confined by fortifications against attackers and by barriers erected to enforce the collection of taxes on goods entering the city. Within those confines, the city described at the beginning of this chapter developed. Only in the 1850s did major improvements of the central city begin. But these improvements in Paris were centrally planned because the national government administered the French capital through its prefect of the Seine Department.[3] As a result, change in Paris could come about rapidly, since the financial resources of the national government could be brought to the process, and the prestige of that government aided private investment schemes for civic improvements like new housing.

From 1852 to 1870, Emperor Napoleon III governed France. He personally drafted detailed plans for the improvement of Paris and entrusted these to his energetic prefect of the

2. B. R. Mitchell, *European Historical Statistics 1750–1970*, abridged edition (New York: Columbia University Press, 1978), pp. 12–15. This is the source for all population statistics through 1970 in this chapter.

3. In 1791 the Legislative Assembly divided France into eighty-three departments for administrative purposes. Paris was the Department of the Seine until twentieth-century reforms subdivided the metropolitan area into a number of new departments in the interest of efficiency. Napoleon I instituted the office of the prefect as the central government's administrator in each department.

Chapter 8

Vienna

and Paris,

1850–1930:

The Development

of the Modern

City

Seine, Baron Georges Eugène Haussmann (1809–1891). Haussmann's projects combined government initiative and money with private capital, and his results were sweeping and rapid. He cut new boulevards through the warren of narrow, medieval streets in the city's center and began the construction of peripheral boulevards along the line of the tax wall of 1784 that once enclosed the city. The new boulevards were wide. Indeed, some of them were almost 400 feet in width. Such street-building efforts eased movement of goods and persons through the city and improved health standards by opening the center of Paris to more light and fresh air. At the same time, the city's physical appearance changed dramatically as private investors erected new apartment buildings along Haussmann's broad boulevards.

Matters of public health also occupied Haussmann. The government greatly expanded the Paris sewer system and built aqueducts to bring clean drinking water into the city. Haussmann's work also added to the cityscape of Paris parks where residents could enjoy recreational opportunities and unrestricted sunlight and fresh air. Former royal hunting preserves at the western and eastern borders of the city, the Bois de Boulogne (the Boulogne Wood) and the Bois de Vincennes (the Vincennes Wood), became great new public parks, and Haussmann added major new innercity parks: the Buttes-Chaumont, Monceau, and Montsouris parks.

Urban improvements continued in Paris after Haussmann. More major new thoroughfares opened, including the Avenue de l'Opéra in 1877, and

public transportation soon flowed on the new boulevards. Paris had had slow-moving and rather expensive horse-drawn buses called omnibuses since 1828. But the new boulevards permitted the city to lead Europe in the introduction of horse-drawn tramcars running much more quickly on steel tracks. By the end of the nineteenth century, electrification of trams provided increasingly efficient and inexpensive public transportation. And in 1900 the city opened a subway system, the Métropolitain, which many urban transportation specialists regard as the world's most comprehensive public transportation system.

The twentieth century also witnessed greater attention to solving the housing problems of working people in Paris. The apartment buildings constructed along Haussmann's boulevards, built at private expense, were intended to provide real estate investors a good return on their capital. These new buildings housed the middle- and upper-class Parisians, who, like their counterparts throughout Continental Europe, preferred the city to the suburbs, which were already drawing affluent English and Americans out of their cities. These new buildings and Haussmann's boulevards, however, destroyed much old working-class housing, and Paris's near suburbs, like those of many European cities, became zones of cheap worker housing as well as home to industries too large for the city itself.

Much of this housing for workers was of poor quality, however, because building expenses had to be kept low to keep rents affordable. Also to keep prices low, such housing was densely built; in Paris, working-class suburbs often had greater population densities than the central city. Worse still, there was an increasing shortage of low-cost housing in the early twentieth century in Paris. Rent controls, made necessary by World War I (1914–1918), continued until after World War II (1939–1945) and made private construction of low-cost housing unprofitable. As a result, French national and city governments cooperated to construct low-cost housing called HBM (Habitation de Bon Marché, that is, inexpensive housing). Built as multistoried apartment buildings, some of this new housing arose in the zone that had been occupied by Paris's most recent city wall, which was built in 1841–1845 and which the government razed after World War I.

Vienna, like Paris, sustained a rapid and planned transformation from a congested, walled city to a modern metropolis in the nineteenth century. As in Paris, the initiative came from the central government. In December 1857, Emperor Francis Joseph ordered the destruction of Vienna's fortifications and the implementation of a plan for his capital's expansion into the area of the old walls and the open spaces, called the *glacis*, surrounding them.[4] Just as Haussmann had promoted the construction of peripheral boulevards along the old tax wall of Paris, Viennese planners mapped out a broad system of boulevards, collectively called the *Ringstrasse*, along the old defense lines. As in Paris, this new boulevard system was grand: the Ringstrasse's builders made it 2.5 miles long and 185 feet wide. Along it rose new public buildings and privately financed apartment buildings.

Just as in Paris, such construction affected the human geography of Vienna. The old city within the walls had been densely populated before 1857, but it had never been squalid. The Imperial Court resided within the walls, and many of Austria's great nobles maintained residences nearby. Most of Vienna's suburbs, on the other hand, had long contained the residences of the economically disadvantaged: densely built tenements of two- and three-room apartments, structures that Viennese called "rent barracks" and "bedbug castles." The construction of the Ringstrasse reinforced this segregation, as its new apartment buildings became the residences of affluent families whose wealth was derived from new industries or service in the expanding governmental institutions of nineteenth-century Austria-Hungary. Even though the city of Vienna annexed numerous suburbs in 1867 and again in 1890, many neighborhoods just beyond the Ringstrasse retained their working-class character.

A new street system encouraged the development of public transportation in Vienna as it did in Paris. Horse-drawn trams began to run in 1868, and these were electrified at the turn of the century. Also at the century's end, in

4. Early modern fortifications customarily were surrounded by a *glacis,* an unbuilt area intended to provide free-fire zones for the fortifications' defenders. By the nineteenth century, as artillery ranges increased, these zones often had become quite broad indeed. In Vienna's case, the glacis was 1,485 feet wide. Destruction of constraining fortifications was a common feature of urban development in the nineteenth and early twentieth centuries. The following cities tore down their defensive walls in the years indicated: Brussels (1830s), Geneva (1851), Barcelona (1854), Basel (1860–1867), Madrid (1868), and Bologna (1902).

Chapter 8

Vienna

and Paris,

1850–1930:

The Development

of the Modern

City

1894, the city began construction of a peripheral railroad, the Stadtbahn (or S-Bahn), that ran in tunnels for about a quarter of its 16.5-mile route. A true subway system was planned, too, but World War I prevented its construction, and Vienna opened its subway system only in 1980.

Late-nineteenth-century Viennese planners effected many other improvements in their city. They initiated a system providing pure water to the city in 1860 and rechanneled the Danube in 1870–1875 to prevent dangerous flooding. Most importantly, they, like Haussmann, opened parks to provide healthful recreation opportunities for citizens. The Ringstrasse itself included a great deal of green space, but the most important park opened to citizens in the 1880s when Emperor Francis Joseph turned a former hunting preserve on the Danube River over to the city. This new park, the Prater, had some 3,200 acres and by the end of the nineteenth century offered something for almost everyone. It had paths for walking, riding, or bicycling; lakes for boating; soccer fields; an amusement park with a large Ferris wheel; and Europe's largest outdoor theater.

Such development made Vienna a much more attractive city by the outbreak of World War I in 1914. But that war drastically changed the city. Austria-Hungary broke up at the war's end, and Vienna found itself not the political and cultural center of a cosmopolitan empire of 54 million, but the capital of a republic of 6 million, with one-third of those living in Vienna. The capital of the small Republic of Austria faced great problems.

Population growth outstripped the construction of new, privately owned housing even before World War I, and wartime rent controls, as in Paris, ended most private construction during and after the war. Thus the city found itself with a major housing shortage at the war's end, when soldiers returned from the army to marry and establish families, and refugees from the former empire's territories crowded the city.

In Vienna, as in Paris and many other cities, the government sought to address this and other problems. The postwar constitution of Austria gave Vienna the status of a province, with authority to raise and spend substantial revenues. The government of this city was in the hands of the Socialist party until 1934, and that party used public funds for the construction of 63,924 low-cost housing units to meet the housing shortage and to provide better residences for those dwelling in Vienna's tenements. Other projects improved recreational opportunities; these included public swimming pools and a 60,000-seat stadium in the Prater.

Now let us use this background material on Paris and Vienna to consider the evidence. Your sources for answering the questions posed in this chapter are of two chief types. You first encounter pictorial evidence, a type of historical source that you have analyzed in earlier chapters. In the present chapter, you will wish to examine this evidence carefully, to discern the solutions to the urban problems that the pictures present. The pictures also present various architectural answers to the problems of living in the city.

You should consider carefully the solutions posed by architects and builders to society's needs, because architecture is an important source for the historian. Architects do not design for themselves, but at the commission of their customers. As a result, their designs generally reflect the needs and values of their employers.

This chapter presents a second kind of evidence, one which so far you have not analyzed extensively: maps and city plans. Maps are important records of human activity that often are underused by historians. Many historians simply employ maps to illustrate their narratives, as a military historian frequently does when he or she presents a map to describe a battle. Other social scientists, like sociologists and human geographers, make more extensive use of maps. Their study of maps as primary sources allows them to discover basic elements of human activity, such as residential patterns. It is in this fashion that you should view the maps.

Let us now apply these general guidelines to analysis of specific pieces of evidence. Sources 1 through 3 provide pictorial evidence on the pre-industrial city. Observe the pictures carefully, recalling our description of such cities in the Problem section of this chapter. Source 1 is a picture of Vienna in 1850, before the Ringstrasse development, showing the city walls and the glacis. What is your impression of the city within those walls? In which direction have buildings grown because of the city's confinement within these walls? What sort of opportunities did the glacis offer urban planners?

Sources 2 and 3 take us within early-nineteenth-century Paris. Consider Source 2, a photograph of the rue Bernard de Palissy. What kind of housing did such a street seem to offer? What do you think the population density in such a neighborhood would have been? Consider health conditions. How much sunlight probably reached the residences on this street? Given the city's lack of sewers in the early nineteenth century, what function do you think the central gutter performed? Why do you think such a street would offend your senses and prove unhealthful? Source 3 is a photograph of leather workshops along the Bièvre River. This district was in a densely populated area of the city on a river flowing into the Seine River, from which Parisians drew much of their drinking water in the early nineteenth century. Leather processing produces strong chemical odors and much toxic waste. Why do you think the workshops were built along the Bièvre? What sort of health impact do you suppose these workshops had?

Sources 4 and 5 present a map and photograph of Vienna's Ringstrasse. Study the map in Source 4. It shows central Vienna, with the Danube Canal curving across the lower right of the map near building Number 13. What evidence of deliberate planning efforts do you see in the development? Does the Ringstrasse, which intermingled new apartment buildings with both public and commercial buildings, seem to have certain functional zones? Why might you conclude that commerce occupied one zone? Moving along the Ringstrasse, what sort of functional change do you observe at

Chapter 8

Vienna

and Paris,

1850–1930:

The Development

of the Modern

City

the area's first building, the Votiv-kirche, a church built in the 1850s in thanksgiving for the emperor's escape from an assassination attempt? What sort of institutions surround the Hof-burg, or imperial palace?

Source 5 offers you a photograph of key Ringstrasse buildings. Do you find any harmony of architectural styles in the public buildings? Why do you think architects adopted clas-sical Greek architecture for the houses of Parliament? Why might they have adopted Gothic architecture for the city hall? Do you think such tactics heightened the sense of different func-tional zones within the Ringstrasse? Consider the scale of the boulevard. How might its great width have im-proved communications and public health?

In Sources 6 through 9, you must analyze evidence on Paris. The map in Source 6 is particularly rich in de-tail on the city improvements wrought by Baron Haussmann during the Sec-ond French Empire. How has Hauss-mann improved Paris streets? What other transportation improvements do you find on the map? Consider, too, the impact Haussmann's work had on the quality of life for Parisians. How many new parks were opened during Haussmann's tenure in of-fice? What problems dictated the aqueducts in the lower center of the map and in its upper right? What do you notice about the city's growth? What suburbs did it annex to provide for growth?

Sources 7 through 9 illustrate a major project in Paris's nineteenth-century improvements, the Avenue de l'Opéra. Source 7 is a map showing

the creation of the avenue. Hauss-mann began this broad avenue in the 1850s to provide better communica-tion in western Paris, but it was com-pleted only in 1878, after he left of-fice. The complexities of property acquisition for the new street played a major role in its delayed comple-tion. What was the street pattern in this area of the city before the av-enue's construction? What effects do you think the avenue had on its dis-trict? Refer to Source 8 as well now. How does this photograph affect your opinion of the complexity of this project? How would knowing that street builders had to level a large hill, the Butte Saint-Roch, to provide a level path for the avenue change your assessment of the proj-ect's difficulty? What sort of housing, judging by Source 8, was removed to make way for the avenue? Refer to Source 9 at this juncture, a photo-graph of the completed avenue look-ing toward the new opera house, which opened in 1875. How did the avenue improve communications in the city? What health benefits proba-bly resulted from its construction? What sort of housing seems to sur-round the avenue?

Sources 10 through 12 provide you with detailed examples of the housing built along the Ringstrasse and Hauss-mann's new streets. Examine Source 10, paying particular attention to the ornamentation around the windows and their size in this building con-structed in the late nineteenth century, before elevators came into widespread use. What about the building's façade suggests to you that the building's upper floors might contain less prestigious, cheaper, and smaller apartments than the lower floors? Why might you conclude that, in the absence of elevators, some former patterns of social segregation by floor persisted?

Source 11 is an engraving of a building typical of those that arose along Haussmann's new boulevards in Paris. Such structures usually had shops facing the street on the ground floor with apartments on upper floors. Access to the buildings' residential sections often was through a large double door (at lower left in the picture) leading past the lodging of a *concièrge,* who controlled access to the building and kept it clean, to an inner courtyard.

Source 12 illustrates an architect's plan for another such apartment building. Such plans, showing the building literally as it would look if you removed its roof and looked down into it, are easy to read, when you know a few rules. On this plan, doorways are shown as openings in the dark outline of the building, and windows are shown as white, narrower areas in the building's outline. The rest of the features of the building may be analyzed through the keys.

Remember that architects design buildings with a definite clientele in mind. Examine the apartment on the ground floor and the two apartments found on each of the first, second, and third floors (floors above the third contained smaller apartments and servants' quarters). How many rooms do these apartments contain? Consider, too, other features like service staircases, stables, and coach houses. What do these features of the building floor plan suggest to you

about the types of residents expected for these apartments? Compare your conclusions with those you derived from analyzing the exterior decoration of the Vienna apartment building in Source 10. Why might you conclude that the same class of resident lived in both the Vienna and Paris buildings?

Sources 13 and 14 present examples of the recreational areas added to nineteenth-century cities. Source 13 is a photograph of the Prater in the late nineteenth century. What sort of diversions did this part of the great park offer? What developments in nineteenth-century urban life would have made such a place more accessible to citizens of all classes? Source 14 illustrates Haussmann's Buttes-Chaumont Park, constructed in 1864–1867 near Belleville, one of the nineteenth-century worker suburbs annexed by Paris. On an area formerly occupied by quarries and dumps, Haussmann's engineers created a lake surrounded by a dramatically landscaped park with a view of the entire Paris area. Note that a multitrack railroad line traverses a corner of the park and that the smokestacks of industrial enterprises cluster around its periphery. What does the presence of these activities suggest to you about the suburbs of cities like Paris and Vienna?

Sources 15 through 17 focus on the near suburbs of both cities. Source 15 is a photograph of the working-class neighborhood of Belleville. What sort of concentration of people might you imagine inhabited a narrow street such as this one? Having examined the landscape around Buttes-Chau-

Chapter 8

Vienna

and Paris,

1850–1930:

The Development

of the Modern

City

mont Park in Source 14, examine Source 16, a picture of a suburban factory that opened in 1873 at Ivry. Why might you conclude that such suburbs would have been rather unhealthy places of residence? Turn to Source 17, which illustrates Viennese worker housing. Why do you find late-nineteenth-century conditions in Vienna little different from those in Paris?

Sources 18 and 19 illustrate the impact of the Industrial Revolution on urban life. Sources 18 and 19 in particular show new modes of transportation made possible by industrialization. The Stadtbahn, or S-Bahn, encircled Vienna, and buses and electric trolleys like those of Paris appeared on the streets of all European cities. The fares on such vehicles were low at all times and often were discounted for workers at rush hours. What impact might the availability of such transportation have had on worker living patterns? Since public transportation ran seven days per week, why do you think recreational opportunities for workers increased?

Our final sources illustrate post–World War I answers to the problems of city life, whose growing complexity dictated state rather than private action. Almost all major European cities built public, low-cost housing for workers after World War I. Source 20 illustrates the largest such Viennese housing project, the Karl Marx Hof, which provided homes for 5,000 persons in 1,382 apartments. Such projects really were small cities, equipped with common laundries, child-care facilities, and parklike courtyards.

Contrast this block of apartments with the tenements in Source 17. Why would you think that such large complexes would have been more healthful for workers than the old tenements?

Source 21 is a floor plan of a Parisian low-cost housing project with two apartments sharing a common stair. The Parisian solution to the housing shortage differed in detail, but not in substance, from the Viennese apartments of the Karl Marx Hof. Observe the floor plans carefully. What common late-twentieth-century amenities are missing? Floor plans always show placement of radiators. Do you find any? Indeed, do you find any heat source for multiroom apartments other than fireplaces? While each apartment has a toilet, does each have a shower? Notice the sizes of the rooms. How do they compare with those to which you are accustomed? For what class of residents do you think such apartments were designed?

Source 22 is a photo of Vienna's Kongressbad swimming pool. It was one of the largest pools in Europe, measuring 66′ × 330′. Built at public expense, such a pool represented the culmination of many trends. Why would such projects as this pool, which attracted 450,000 bathers in 1930, have been virtually impossible without developments in public transportation during our period? How do the pool and public housing developments reflect a government attitude toward the solution of urban problems different from that of the earlier nineteenth century?

As you examine the evidence that follows, you should be able to formulate answers to this chapter's central questions. How were these cities physically reshaped in response to the problems of the early nineteenth century? How did this physical transformation affect the lifestyles of urban dwellers?

Source 1 from Donald J. Olsen, The City as a Work of Art (New Haven, Conn.: Yale University Press, 1986), p. 61. Photograph: Historisches Museum der Stadt Wien.

1. **Vienna in 1850**

Source 2 from Donald J. Olsen, The City as a Work of Art *(New Haven, Conn.: Yale University Press, 1986), p. 222. Photograph: © Photothèque des Musées de la Ville de Paris/Cliché Lauros-Giraudon by SPADEM.*

2. A Paris Street in the 1850s: The Rue Bernard de Palissy

Source 3 from Mark Girouard, Cities and People: A Social and Architectural History (New Haven, Conn.: Yale University Press, 1985), p. 298. Photograph: © Photothèque des Musées de la Ville de Paris/Cliché Lauros-Giraudon by SPADEM.

3. Leather Workshops on the Bièvre River in Paris in the Mid-19th Century

Source 4 from Wolfgang Braunfels, translated by Kenneth J. Northcott, Urban Design in Western Europe: Regime and Architecture, 900–1900 *(Chicago: University of Chicago Press, 1988), p. 304.*

4. Schematic Drawing of the Viennese Ringstrasse and Its Major Buildings

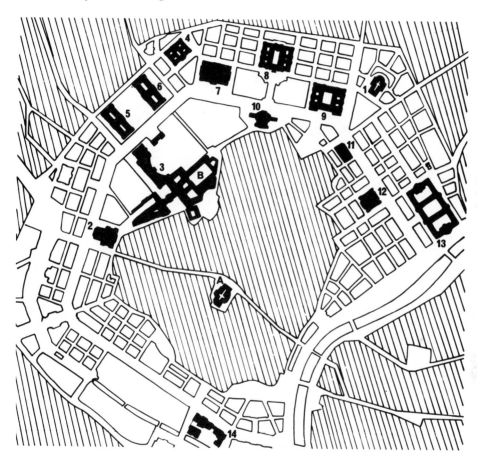

Key

Pre-1857 Buildings
A St. Stephen's Cathedral
B *Hofburg* (Imperial Palace)

Post-1857 Buildings
1 Votivkirche (the Votive Church or Church of the Divine Savior)
2 Opera House
3 New Hofburg
4 Courthouse
5 Art History Museum
6 Natural History Museum
7 Parliament
8 City Hall
9 University
10 Burgtheater
11 Banking Union
12 Stock Exchange
13 Army Barracks
14 School of Arts and Crafts

Chapter 8
Vienna
and Paris,
1850–1930:
The Development
of the Modern
City

Source 5 from William M. Johnston, Vienna, Vienna: The Golden Age, 1815–1914 *(New York: Clarkson N. Potter, 1981), p. 128. Photograph courtesy of Mondadori Press.*

5. Vienna Ringstrasse in the Late 19th Century

The Parliament building is in the foreground; city hall is the spired building in the upper left; the university is the domed building right of center; and the Burgtheater appears in the upper right.

Source 6 from Thomas F. X. Noble et al., Western Civilization: The Continuing Experiment, 2d ed. (Boston: Houghton Mifflin, 1998), p. 859.

6. Paris, 1850–1870

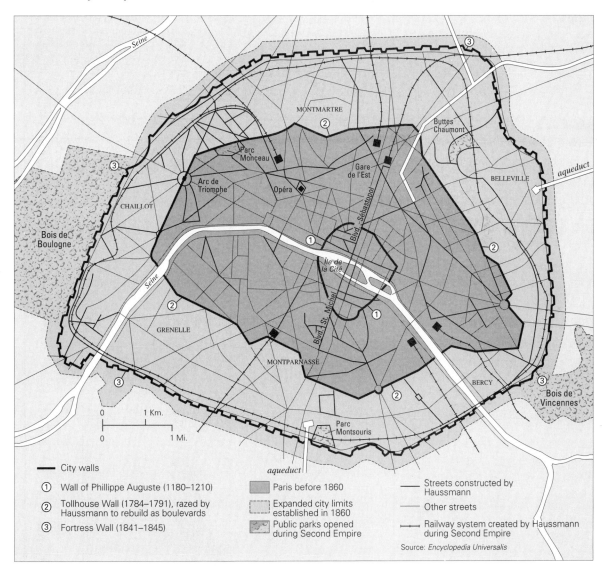

City walls

① Wall of Phillippe Auguste (1180–1210)

② Tollhouse Wall (1784–1791), razed by Haussmann to rebuild as boulevards

③ Fortress Wall (1841–1845)

Paris before 1860

Expanded city limits established in 1860

Public parks opened during Second Empire

Streets constructed by Haussmann

Other streets

Railway system created by Haussmann during Second Empire

Source: *Encyclopedia Universalis*

Chapter 8

Vienna

and Paris,

1850–1930:

The Development

of the Modern

City

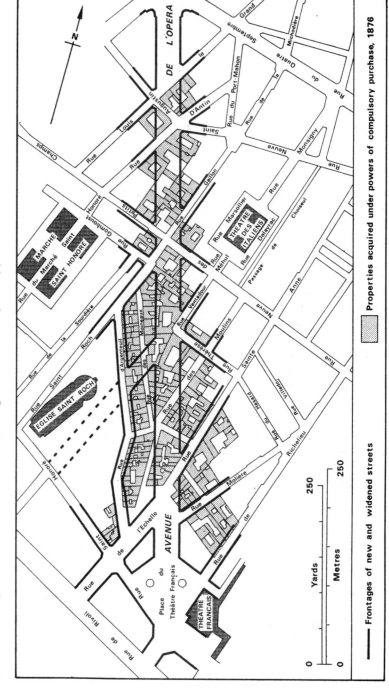

7. **The Completion of the Avenue de l'Opéra, Paris, 1876–1877**

Source 8 from Photothèque des Musées de la Ville de Paris/Cliché Dubuisson by SPADEM.

8. Clearing Old Neighborhoods for the Avenue de l'Opéra, Paris, 1876

Chapter 8

Vienna

and Paris,

1850–1930:

The Development

of the Modern

City

Source 9 from F. Roy Willis, Western Civilization, *vol. IV,* From the Seventeenth Century to the Contemporary Age *(Lexington, Mass.: D. C. Heath, 1985), 4th ed., p. 269. Photograph by H. Roger-Viollet.*

9. Avenue de l'Opéra, Paris, Late 19th Century

Source 10 from Donald J. Olsen, The City as a Work of Art *(New Haven, Conn.: Yale University Press, 1986), p. 156. Original source: Kunstgeschichte Institut Universität Wien. Photograph by Johanna Fiegl.*

10. Ringstrasse Apartment Building, Schottenring 25

Chapter 8
Vienna
and Paris,
1850–1930:
The Development
of the Modern
City

Source 11 from David H. Pinkney, Napoleon III and the Rebuilding of Paris *(Princeton, N.J.: Princeton University Press, 1958), Plate 16. Original Source:* The Builder *(London), XVI (March 6, 1858).*

11. A Paris Apartment Building, Late 19th Century

Source 12 from Donald J. Olsen, The City as a Work of Art *(New Haven, Conn.: Yale University Press, 1986), p. 118. Original source:* Revue générale d'architecture, *XVIII (1860), p. 41.*

12. Floor Plan of Apartment Building at 39, Rue Neuve des Mathurins, Paris

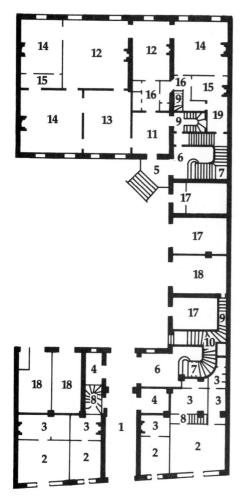 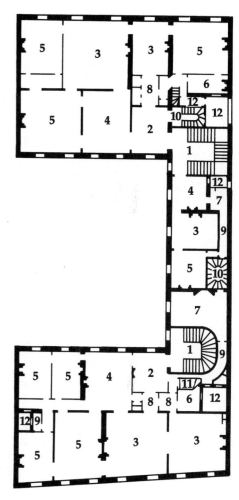

Ground floor

1 Passage from carriage entrance
  to courtyard
2 Shops
3 Shop backrooms
4 Concierge residence and kitchen
5 Entry steps
6 Grand staircase vestibule
7 Grand staircase

8,9,10 Service staircases
11 Antechamber
12 Parlors
13 Dining rooms
14 Bedrooms
15 Bathrooms
16 Cloakroom
17 Stables
18 Coach house
19 Light/air shafts

First, second, third floors

1 Grand staircase
2 Antechambers
3 Parlors
4 Dining rooms
5 Bedrooms
6 Bathrooms
7 Kitchens
8 Cloakrooms
9 Corridors
10,11 Service stairs
12 Light/air shafts

Chapter 8
Vienna
and Paris,
1850–1930:
The Development
of the Modern
City

Source 13 from William M. Johnston, Vienna, Vienna: The Golden Age, 1815–1914 *(New York: Clarkson N. Potter, 1981), p. 228. Photograph courtesy of Raccolta delle Stampe Bertarelli, Milan, Italy.*

13. The Prater, Vienna

Source 14 from Maurice Agulhon et al., Histoire de la France urbaine, *vol. IV,* La ville de l'âge industriel: Le cycle haussmannien *(Paris: Éditions du Seuil, 1983), p. 48. Photograph from Bibliothèque Historique de la Ville de Paris/Seuil.*

14. The Buttes-Chaumont Park, Paris

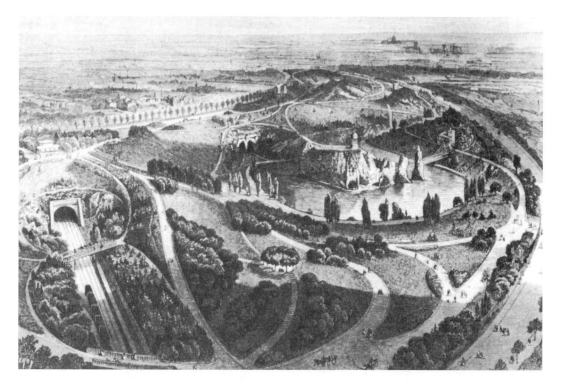

Chapter 8

Vienna

and Paris,

1850–1930:

The Development

of the Modern

City

Source 15 from Lapi-Viollet.

15. A 19th-Century Parisian Working-Class Suburb in Belleville

Source 16 from Maurice Agulhon et al., Histoire de la France urbaine, *vol. IV,* La ville de l'age industriel: Le cycle haussmannien *(Paris: Éditions du Seuil, 1983), p. 202. Photograph courtesy of Archives Seuil, Paris.

16. The Lemoine Forges at Ivry, 1881

Chapter 8

Vienna

and Paris,

1850–1930:

The Development

of the Modern

City

Source 17 from Helmut Gruber, Red Vienna: Experiment in Working-Class Culture, *1919–1934 (New York: Oxford University Press, 1991), p. 47. Original source: Verein für Geschichte der Arbeiterbewegung, Vienna.*

17. Vienna Workers' Tenement, Early 20th Century

Source 18 from William M. Johnston, Vienna, Vienna: The Golden Age, 1815–1914 *(New York: Clarkson N. Potter, 1981), p. 240. Photograph courtesy of Mondadori Press.*

18. The Vienna S-Bahn and Its Schönbrunn Station, Built Between 1894 and 1897

Source 19 from Maurice Agulhon et al., Histoire de la France urbaine, *vol. IV,* La ville de l'âge industriel: Le cycle haussmannien *(Paris: Éditions du Seuil, 1983), p. 350. Photograph by Harlingue/Viollet.*

19. The Gare de l'Est Bus and Tramway Stop in 1936

Source 20 from Paul Hoffmann, Viennese: Splendor, Twilight, and Exile *(New York: Doubleday, 1988). Photograph from Austrian Press and Information Service.*

20. The Karl Marx Hof, Erected 1927–1929

Chapter 8

Vienna

and Paris,

1850–1930:

The Development

of the Modern

City

Source 21 from Norma Evenson, Paris: A Century of Change, 1878–1978 *(New Haven, Conn.: Yale University Press, 1979), p. 219. Original source:* La vie urbaine *(Published by the Institut d'Urbanisme de Paris), No. 18, Nov. 15, 1933.*

21. Floor Plan of Parisian HBM (Low-Cost Housing) Apartments, 1933

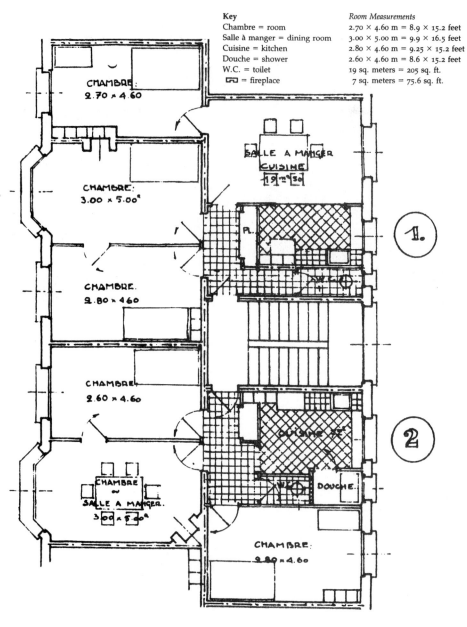

Key

Chambre = room
Salle à manger = dining room
Cuisine = kitchen
Douche = shower
W.C. = toilet
⌐⌐ = fireplace

Room Measurements

2.70 × 4.60 m = 8.9 × 15.2 feet
3.00 × 5.00 m = 9.9 × 16.5 feet
2.80 × 4.60 m = 9.25 × 15.2 feet
2.60 × 4.60 m = 8.6 × 15.2 feet
19 sq. meters = 205 sq. ft.
7 sq. meters = 75.6 sq. ft.

Source 22 from Helmut Gruber, Red Vienna: Experiment in Working-Class Culture, 1919–1934 *(New York: Oxford University Press, 1991), p. 122. Original source: Verein für Geschichte der Arbeiterbewegung, Vienna.*

22. Kongressbad, Vienna, One of Europe's Largest Pools, About 1930

Chapter 8

Vienna

and Paris,

1850–1930:

The Development

of the Modern

City

QUESTIONS TO CONSIDER

In the previous sections of this chapter, we considered each city individually. To answer the chapter's central questions, we now need to study the cities jointly, drawing general trends from their individual experiences in urban development.

Consider first the core of the cities. Notice the street patterns and recall the problems that faced early-nineteenth-century cities. What common approaches to street building do you find in Paris and Vienna? Notice how the ring boulevards of Vienna connect every area of the city with the riverfront. Notice how Haussmann's boulevards facilitate direct north-south and east-west movement in Paris. Why did city and national governments lay out such streets? What facilities for recreation do you find incorporated into many of the cities? Consult especially the maps of Paris and Vienna. Why do you think a Parisian or Viennese of 1800 would have had difficulty recognizing his or her city in 1900?

Improvements in the urban cores of cities benefited all to some extent. Let us look more deeply into these physical improvements, however, to discern whether one class, at least initially, benefited more than others from private and government initiatives for municipal improvements. Consult the sources to determine the kinds of buildings arising in the central cities in the late nineteenth century. Paris and Vienna continued to employ a large part of their central cores for residential use. What classes seem to

have occupied the new buildings constructed along Haussmann's boulevards and the Ringstrasse boulevards in Vienna? Where do the sources for Paris and Vienna suggest that persons of lower income were forced to live when the wealthy appropriated much of the central city for residential purposes? Why do you find an economically segregated housing pattern evolving? How might transportation developments have supported residential segregation?

Reflect also on the buildings erected at public expense in the second half of the nineteenth century, remembering all the while that universal, free public education became a reality only in the late nineteenth or early twentieth century in most countries. The opera in Paris, completed in 1875, typifies such buildings, as do the museums and theaters built in Vienna in the same period. What social groups do you think initially benefited most from such institutions? What does this tell you about the groups most influencing late-nineteenth-century politics? Why would you perhaps agree with those historians who call the nineteenth century the century of the middle class?

The right to vote became increasingly universal among European males in the late nineteenth and early twentieth centuries. Indeed, in many countries all women also gained the vote after World War I. At the same time, political parties addressing working-class needs arose in many countries. What evidence of such new political empowerment do you see in Parisian and Viennese urban development in the early twentieth century? Why do you think improved, low-cost public transport would have allowed lower income groups an improved lifestyle by the early twentieth century?

Finally, consider whether the developments reflected in your sources, including the construction projects, railroads, sewers, and water supply systems, would have been possible without the advances of industrialization. Why can you say with some justice that in the second half of the

nineteenth century, the Industrial Revolution helped to solve some of the problems it created in the first half?

After considering the sources as a unit, you should be ready to formulate answers to the chapter's main questions. How were the cities physically reshaped in response to the problems of the first decades of the early nineteenth century? How did this physical transformation affect the lifestyle of urban dwellers?

EPILOGUE

The development of Paris and Vienna after our period typifies one major trend in twentieth-century urban affairs: the end of urban growth in much of the West. Northern Europe led the way, as its rapid nineteenth-century population growth ended by the first decades of the twentieth century. The dramatic growth of urban populations characteristic of the nineteenth century ended as overall population growth rates diminished. Indeed, many cities had an actual decline in population in the twentieth century, and this was the case with Paris and Vienna.

The chief cause of Vienna's population decline was Austria-Hungary's defeat in World War I. The peace treaties ending that war left Vienna the capital of a truncated Austria, a city with the buildings for imperial glory, but without the old imperial territory and population. Vienna's population growth ended with the empire, and the city's population ac-

tually shrank. The 1910–1911 population was 2,031,000 people; the city's population in 1981 was 1,504,200.

Paris better illustrates trends in modern urban life because twentieth-century warfare less seriously affected that city. Paris continues to be a major cultural hub, and twentieth-century improvements have made it a bit more livable, although modern ecological problems like air pollution from large concentrations of motor vehicles are posing new problems for solution. Nevertheless, Paris reached its population peak in 1920–1921 at 2,907,000 persons and was inhabited by 2,152,423 in 1992.[5]

Urban growth in Paris and many other cities ceased in the twentieth century in large part because of a suburbanization that was much more extensive than that of the nineteenth century. In the nineteenth century, as we've seen, suburban growth fol-

5. Other major cities reached their population peaks as follows: Amsterdam, 1960–1961; Birmingham, 1950–1951; Glasgow, 1940–1941; London, 1940–1941; Manchester, 1930–1931; Rotterdam, 1960–1961; Stockholm, 1960–1961.

Chapter 8

Vienna

and Paris,

1850–1930:

The Development

of the Modern

City

lowed the roads, railroads, and later subways. In the twentieth and twenty-first centuries, limited-access highways also have abetted suburban sprawl. However, the social divisions of the nineteenth century persist. Paris continues to have a greater portion of its population ranked among economically and professionally higher status groups than the rest of France, but its suburbs still have a marked working-class complexion. Improved transportation has carried the working classes to communities more distant from the capital. The often drab working-class outer districts of Paris and its near suburban communities until recently have reflected their social composition at election time, voting so heavily for socialist or communist candidates committed to workers' causes that they have been nicknamed "the Red Belt."

In fact, suburbanization has become so extensive that modern planners in Western Europe are being forced to direct its course the way nineteenth-century planners tried to shape urban development. In the late twentieth century, French planners, for example, began to lay out large population centers on the distant periphery of Paris. Such centers, like Cergy-Pontoise, northeast of Paris, are suburban in their location and connected to the city by train and highway, but are almost urban in their population density. The modern city thus continues as the locus of Western civilization, but it is now a smaller city influencing a much broader area.

CHAPTER NINE

EXPANSION AND PUBLIC

OPINION: ADVOCATES OF

THE "NEW IMPERIALISM"

THE PROBLEM

From the 1870s until around 1905, Western nations engaged in a brief but extremely intense period of imperial expansion. In one sense, of course, this was not entirely a new phenomenon. From the sixteenth through the eighteenth centuries, the emerging nations of western Europe had struggled over possession of the New World. Between roughly 1815 and 1871, the West, beset with internal problems, had engaged in only limited attempts at colonialism, but some nations, principally England, nevertheless had sought to expand their economic spheres of influence. In some ways, then, the "new imperialism" of the late nineteenth century was not dramatically different from the old.

Yet to many living at the time (as well as to a number of later historians), the imperialism of the late nineteenth and early twentieth centuries seemed markedly different from earlier forms of territorial expansion. For one thing, the number of contestants for empire had increased with the addition of the newly formed nations of Germany and Italy. Indeed, even the United States, itself a nation composed of former European colonies, joined in the headlong scramble for new territories. The increased number of empire-seeking nations probably contributed to the speed with which unclaimed areas were brought under Western control.

Another factor that made the colonial expansion of the late nineteenth and early twentieth centuries appear "new" was that many people believed that this was their nation's last opportunity to build or enlarge an empire. Only Africa and parts of Asia remained vulnerable to imperialistic ventures. Awareness of this fact filled the nations of the West with a sense of urgency: If a nation did not acquire colonies quickly, other nations would do so. This feeling of urgency doubtless contributed to the speed of empire building as well as to the heightened sense of national competition for greatness. So powerful was this sentiment that by the turn of the

Chapter 9

Expansion

and Public

Opinion:

Advocates of

the "New

Imperialism"

century almost all of Africa and parts of Asia had fallen under Western control, and the West, accurately or not, could boast of itself as the master of much of the world.

A third factor that made the "new imperialism" seem different from the old was that advocates and opponents of colonial expansion felt the need to sway public opinion. Before the late eighteenth century, public opinion was not considered a crucial factor when monarchs or bodies representing a limited electorate decided what policies their respective governments should pursue. To be sure, certain powerful interest groups had to be consulted or appealed to, but the opinion of the general public was rarely heeded. The expansion of the electorate,[1] however, together with increased educational opportunities and literacy, the corresponding mass circulation of newspapers, and the evolution of modern political campaign techniques, served to make the general public more aware of the government's policies and even to give them a limited voice in the shaping of those policies. Hence, supporters or opponents of particular policies were obliged to appeal to—and, in some cases, manipulate—public opinion. Thus, the new imperialism also appeared different in that it was warmly debated not only in palaces and parliaments but also in the streets, the press, the workingmen's halls, and the public houses ("pubs") of the Western nations.

No historical trend such as the new imperialism takes place in a vacuum, unaffected by other trends and events that precede and parallel it and, in some cases, help to cause it. In the West, several important developments in the second half of the nineteenth century not only acted to create the new imperialism but also helped impart to that movement its particular shape and character.

One of the most important occurrences in the West preceding and paralleling the new imperialism was that of rapid population growth. Between 1850 and 1900, the population of Europe (including Russia) increased 54 percent, from approximately 274 million to 423 million. Germany's population jumped over 62 percent, Great Britain's 41 percent, Italy's around 41 percent, and Belgium's 48 percent. This population boom was primarily the result of falling death rates, in turn caused by the controlling of epidemic diseases, increased food production, and improvements in transportation that allowed food supplies to reach cities and regions of local famines. In the United States, where massive immigration from Europe supplemented the large natural increase, the population increased an astounding 227 percent.[2]

This dramatic jump in population, especially in the cities of Europe, created a serious need for jobs, particularly in the nonagricultural sector. The pressure for greater employment in turn increased Europe's demand for raw materials for industrial production and markets for those manufactured goods. Moreover, in some

---

1. The expansion of the electorate took place in the United Kingdom in 1867–1884, in Germany in 1871, in France in 1875, and in Italy in 1913.

2. Between 1846 and 1900, the number of emigrants from Europe to the United States and Latin America probably exceeded 30 million.

areas of Europe (notably Italy), the rise in rural population put a heavy strain on land and agricultural resources, which resulted in increased emigration. It is easy to imagine how these problems, caused by population pressures, might be linked to calls for expansionism.

A second important trend during this time was the spread and apparent peaking of the Industrial Revolution. By the latter part of the nineteenth century, much of the West had joined in the Industrial Revolution and thus (as noted earlier) needed raw materials and, equally important, markets for manufactured goods. A severe depression struck Europe and the United States in 1873 and lasted into the 1890s, making it impossible for the West to consume all the manufactured goods it could produce. Unless industries were to shut down, bringing on massive unemployment, new markets would have to be found. With most of the Western countries erecting protective tariff barriers to keep out each other's manufactured goods, these new markets would have to be found outside the West, in areas that could be exploited almost at will.

The Industrial Revolution not only provided an incentive for a new upsurge of imperialism, but also gave the West the means to accomplish this expansion. Technological improvements, especially in transportation and communications, allowed Western mercantile and financial houses gradually to draw much of the world into an integrated global market dominated by Western merchants and financiers. As English economist Stanley Jevons boasted in 1866:

The several quarters of the globe are our willing tributaries. The plains of North America and Russia are our cornfields; Chicago and Odessa our granaries; Canada and the Baltic our forests; Australia contains our sheep farms, and in South America are our herds of oxen . . . the Chinese grow tea for us; and coffee, sugar and spice arrive from East Indian plantations. Spain and France are our vineyards, and the Mediterranean our fruit garden.[3]

Advances in medicine and in weapons technology made it further possible for Westerners to subdue non-Western peoples and live for extended periods in non-Western climates. Great Britain, for example, acquired the Upper Nile River area in 1898, but only after slaughtering 20,000 tribesmen at Omdurman, thanks to the newly invented machine gun. As Hilaire Belloc's "Modern Traveler" would sing,

Whatever happens, we have got
The Maxim gun; and they have not.[4]

A third important trend that contributed to late-nineteenth-century imperialism was that of intensified competition among Western nations. It was obvious at the time to many people that Western nations did not have to seize non-Western territories in order to dominate them economically. Moreover, some of the

3. Quoted in R. R. Palmer and Joel Colton, *A History of the Modern World* (New York: Alfred A. Knopf, 1965), pp. 574–575.

4. Quoted in Roland Oliver and G. N. Sanderson, *The Cambridge History of Africa* (Cambridge: Cambridge University Press, 1985), vol. 6, p. 98. The Maxim gun was the brainchild of British engineer Sir Hiram Maxim, who in 1889 perfected the machine gun.

Chapter 9

Expansion

and Public

Opinion:

Advocates of

the "New

Imperialism"

territories that Western nations colonized could offer no immediate profits to their conquerors. Yet in this era of intensified rivalry, colonies were widely regarded as assets that could be exploited in the increased competition among Western nations and also as potential military bases to protect the extraction of raw materials and the maintenance of trade lanes. Safe harbors and coaling stations for a modern steam-powered navy were seen as critically important to each Western nation's power and survival. At the same time, no single country could be allowed to gain an advantage over others in the rush for colonies and the establishment of national "greatness." Thus U.S. president William McKinley justified taking the Philippine Islands partly to keep them out of the hands of any other national competitor seeking to exploit Asia and the Pacific. Truly, heightened national competition, along with other trends, helped renew the spirit of imperialism in the West. With the new nations of Germany and Italy and the newly imperialistic United States added to the race, the scramble for colonies at times seemed almost frantic.

Paralleling the rise in imperialistic sentiment were two important and, in some ways, contradictory intellectual trends. The first of these was Social Darwinism, a system of ideas that spread rapidly throughout the West in the second half of the nineteenth century. An application of the theories of biological evolution to human affairs, Social Darwinism taught that peoples, like species, were engaged in a life-or-death struggle to determine

the "survival of the fittest." Those classes or nations that emerged triumphant in this struggle were considered the most fit, and hence best suited to carry on the evolution of the human race. Therefore the subjugation of weak peoples by strong ones not only was in accordance with the laws of nature, but was bound to result in a more highly civilized world as well. Most celebrated among the Social Darwinists was the Englishman Herbert Spencer, a diminutive and eccentric writer who became a worldwide celebrity through his writings. (A letter was once addressed to him, "Herbert Spencer. England. And if the postman doesn't know the address, he ought to." It was delivered.)

Although Spencer himself disapproved of imperialism, it is easy to see how his writings could be used as a justification for empire building. At the conclusion of the Spanish-American War in 1898, whereby the United States acquired its empire from Spain, Senator Henry Cabot Lodge justified the transfer of colonies by asserting that "Spain . . . has proved herself unfit to govern, and for the unfit among nations there is no pity in the relentless world-forces which shape the destinies of mankind."[5]

At the same time that many in the West embraced this notion of a struggle for survival between the "fittest" and the "unfit" (a doctrine with strong racist overtones), they also adopted the concept of the "White Man's Burden." This concept held that it was the duty of the "fittest" not so much

5. Henry Cabot Lodge, *The War with Spain* (New York: Harper and Brothers, 1899), p. 2.

to destroy the "unfit" as to "civilize" them; white people, according to this view, had a responsibility to educate the rest of the world to the norms of Western society. As racist as Social Darwinism, the belief in the White Man's Burden downplayed the idea of a struggle for survival between peoples and emphasized the "humanitarian" notion of bringing the benefits of "civilization" to the "uncivilized." Using this argument, many in the West justified imperialism as an obligation, a sacrifice that God had charged the "fittest" to make. In his 1876 speech to the International Conference of Geographers, King Leopold II of Belgium declared:

> The matter which brings us together today is one most deserving the attention of the friends of humanity. For bringing civilization to the only part of the earth [Africa] which it has not yet reached and lightening the darkness in which whole peoples are plunged is, I venture to say, a crusade worthy of this century of progress. . . .[6]

6. From Henri Brunschwig, *French Colonialism 1871–1914: Myths and Realities* (New York: Praeger, 1966), p. 35.

Although the doctrine of the White Man's Burden differed in tone from that of Social Darwinism, one can see that its practical results might well be the same.

Thus, a number of important trends preceded and paralleled the rising imperialist tide in the West in the late nineteenth and early twentieth centuries. As we shall see, not only did these demographic, economic, technological, diplomatic, and intellectual trends profoundly alter the lives and attitudes of most Westerners, but they also gave power to the expansionist surges of the new imperialism.

Your task in this chapter is to analyze the writings of important advocates of imperialism from four of the most active expansionist nations: Germany, Great Britain, France, and Italy. What were the main arguments used by each spokesman in favor of colonial expansion? How did each attempt to appeal to public opinion? Finally, how can their speeches and writings help us identify the principal motives and justifications for the new imperialism?

SOURCES AND METHOD

One of the most significant currents in the West during the last half of the nineteenth century was the popular identification of the common people with the symbols and traditions of their respective nations. Although

roots of this modern sense of nationalism can be found in Napoleonic France, this tendency gained enormous strength and momentum in the latter part of the nineteenth century, fueled by national holidays and celebrations (Bastille Day in France, begun in 1880; Queen Victoria's jubilees in Great Britain in 1887 and 1897; the

Chapter 9

Expansion

and Public

Opinion:

Advocates of

the "New

Imperialism"

massive funerals of King Victor Emmanuel II of Italy in 1878 and of Tsar Alexander III of Russia in 1894), the erection of enormous monuments to the nation (the Eiffel Tower in France; the Washington Monument in the United States; the national monument to William I of Germany), the renovation of capital cities on magnificent scales (London, Paris, Berlin, Vienna, Rome, and Washington, D.C.), the commemoration of national heroes and historical events on postage stamps, and the creation or re-creation of international athletic competitions (the Davis Cup in tennis, begun in 1900; the Olympic Games, revived in 1896). This new sense of popular nationalism in which people of different classes, religions, and ethnic groups identified with the nation itself rather than with its monarch or government or with their own particular groups was a crucial step in the creation of the modern nation-state. Against the powerful force of modern nationalism, competing ideas such as Marxism had little initial effect.[7]

And yet, if the people were expected to identify with their nation, it seemed logical that their opinions about that nation and the policies of its government ought to be heard. And although few advocated actual rule by "the people," the prevailing sentiment was that their opinions should at least be heeded. Indeed, the few remaining autocrats, like the stubborn Nicholas II of Russia, would ignore

7. For an excellent discussion of this trend, see Eric Hobsbawm and Terence Ranger, eds., *The Invention of Tradition* (Cambridge: Cambridge University Press, 1983), especially pp. 263–307.

this impulse at their peril—and to their ultimate destruction. Therefore, when some political leaders in the West began to embrace imperialist ideas and ventures, they had to appeal to the populace for their support.

The evidence in this chapter, selections from five writings and one speech, is arranged in chronological order. Source 1 is from the extremely popular short book *Bedarf Deutschland der Kolonien?* (*Does Germany Need Colonies?*) by Friedrich Fabri (1824–1891), a longtime inspector of the Barmen Rhine Mission in German Southwest Africa. Originally published in 1879, the book was so popular that it ran through numerous editions in the late nineteenth and early twentieth centuries (the edition you will be reading was the original one, published in 1879).

Source 2 is from an 1883 letter written by John Gibson Paton (1824–1907) to James Service, governor-general of Australia. Paton was a Scotsman who in 1857 was ordained by the Reformed Presbyterian Church of Scotland and sent to be a missionary in the New Hebrides Islands (east of Australia). Missionaries such as Paton at first glance may not appear to be very important or influential. Yet their writings and occasional lectures during visits home had an enormous impact on churchgoers, and most of the men in the congregation were voters. For example, in 1889 fear of Scottish Presbyterian voters prompted Lord Salisbury to alter Great Britain's policy toward Nyasaland in southeast Africa. In 1889, Paton's autobiography (actually written by his brother from Paton's notes and letters) was published and was an extremely popular volume (a children's edition appeared in 1892).

Source 3 is a selection from an 1890 work by Jules Ferry (1832–1893). Born into a solidly bourgeois and well-to-do family (his father was a lawyer), Ferry had enough money to travel, study, take up painting, and write. He was a Republican who approved of the overthrow of Napoleon III (although he winced at the fact that the emperor's downfall had been brought on by Prussia) and served as the premier of France's Third Republic twice between 1880 and 1885. Although Ferry came late to his advocacy of imperialism, his popularity made him an important figure in appealing to the people of France to support the building of the second colonial empire. He was responsible for the French annexation of Tunisia.

Source 4 is from a speech made by Joseph Chamberlain (1836–1914), a wealthy manufacturer and member of the British Parliament since 1876, to a city relief association on January 22, 1894. Chamberlain, a former mayor of Birmingham (1873–1875) who was an advocate of social reforms to aid the working classes, was invited to speak at the meeting, which was called to discuss widespread unemployment and hard times in Birmingham.

The fifth piece of evidence is taken from a book that gained wide circulation in Italy, *Cose affricane (Concerning Africa)* (Milan, 1897), by Ferdinando Martini. Martini (1841–1928) was a well-known author, playwright, theater producer, and government offi-

cial (he was governor of the Italian colony Eritrea from 1897 to 1900). *Cose affricane* was written in the wake of the Italian defeat by Ethiopia when Italy attempted to seize that African nation. This was a major humiliation for Italy.

The final piece of evidence (Source 6) is a selection from the enormously popular book *With Kitchener to Khartum* (1898) by British journalist and war correspondent George Warrington Steevens (1869–1900). In 1884, General Charles Gordon was sent by the British government to suppress a rebellion in the Sudan that threatened the stability of Egypt. Surrounded at Khartoum, Gordon and his force were wiped out on January 25, 1885, before relief could reach them (the reaction in Great Britain was about the same as the shock Americans felt when they learned of the "last stand" of General George Armstrong Custer in 1876). When Major General Horatio Herbert Kitchener was ordered to smash the rebellion and avenge Gordon, Steevens went along as a war correspondent for the London *Daily Mail*. His vivid dispatches were read avidly throughout Great Britain and later collected into the book *With Kitchener to Khartum*. Steevens died of typhoid fever during the siege of Ladysmith (in Natal) during the Boer War.

All the pieces of evidence presented here were designed to influence or sway public opinion on imperialistic ventures. To help you answer the central questions in this chapter, you will want to examine each piece of evidence for the following points:

Chapter 9

Expansion

and Public

Opinion:

Advocates of

the "New

Imperialism"

(1) Does the author identify a problem or problems which he thinks imperialism can solve? What are they? If more than one, which is the most important? How will imperialism solve it? (2) How (if at all) does the author regard the "host populations" in the regions to be colonized? What adjectives, if any, are used to describe them? Does the author mention what effect Western imperialism will have on the "host populations"? (3) How does the author deal (if at all) with opponents of imperialism? How are they characterized? (4) How (if at all) does the author connect imperialism with one or more of the parallel trends and events? (5) In what other ways does the author attempt to influence public opinion?

Remember that each piece of evidence may include more than one reason to undertake imperialistic ventures. It would be helpful to take notes as you examine the evidence.

Keep the central questions in mind: What were the main arguments in favor of colonial expansion used by the six advocates of imperialism? How did each spokesman attempt to appeal to public opinion? How can these selections aid in identifying the principal motives and justifications for the new imperialism?

THE EVIDENCE

Source 1 from Friedrich Fabri, Bedarf Deutschland der Kolonien? *(Gotha: Friedrich Andreas Berthes, 1879), pp. 106–108. Translated by David E. Lee.*

1. Friedrich Fabri's *Bedarf Deutschland der Kolonien?*, 1879

But the German nation, which is fundamentally seaworthy and adept both commercially and industrially, which is more skillful at agricultural colonization than others, and is provided with a workforce more abundant and available than that of any other civilized people, should that nation not now successfully set off on this new path? We doubt this all the less the more we are convinced that today the colonial question has already become a vital question for the development of Germany. Dealing thoughtfully but also forcefully with this question will have profitable results for our economic situation and for our entire national development. Just the fact that we are dealing with a new question, whose multifaceted importance for the German people represents still untrodden virgin soil, can prove beneficial in many ways. In the new German Reich many things are already so embittered and soured and poisoned by sterile partisan squabbles that opening up a new, promising path of national development could have a liberating effect in many areas because it could be a powerful stimulant to the spirit of the people, propelling them in new directions. That too would be a joy and a plus. Of greater consequence is the consideration that a people guided to the height of its political power can maintain its historical position successfully only as long as it can both recognize itself as and prove itself to be *the bearer of a cultural mission.* At the same time this is the only course that guarantees the durability and growth of national prosperity, the necessary basis of a lasting development of power. The times in which Germany contributed to the challenges of our century only through intellectual and literary activity are past. We have become political and we have also become powerful. But political power, when it pushes itself into the foreground of our national ambitions as an end in itself, leads to harshness, even to barbarity, if it is not ready and willing to serve the spiritual and the moral as well as the economic cultural missions of its time. The French national economist Leroy Beaulieu ends his work on colonization with these words: "The greatest nation in the world is the one that colonizes the most; if it is not that today, it will be tomorrow." No one can deny that in this regard England is far superior to all other states. During the last decade, of course, we often heard people, especially in Germany, talking about "England's declining power." The person who knows how to calculate the relative power of a state only according to the number of troops prepared to fight a war—as has become almost customary in our iron age—may think that such a position can be easily justified. Whoever lets his eye wander round the globe, however, and takes in the constantly growing, powerful colonial possessions of Great Britain, whoever mulls over the power that it draws from these possessions, the skill with which it administers them, and indeed the dominant position that the anglo-saxon people assume in all overseas lands, for such a person that sort of talk will seem to be the reasoning of a philistine. England maintains its worldwide possessions, its suzerainty over all the oceans with a troop strength that hardly equals one quarter the army of a single one of our continental military states. This is not only a great economic boon but also at the same time the ultimate proof of the solid power, the cultural strength of England. Certainly England will stay as far away from the mass wars of the Continent as it can, or it will only enter the action together with allies; and none of this will bring any harm to the position of power occupied by the island empire. In any case it would be good if we Germans would begin to learn from the colonial skill of our anglo-saxon cousins. Centuries ago, when the German Reich stood at the head of the states of Europe, it was the leading commercial and maritime power. If the new German Reich wants to justify and maintain its power, then it will have to grasp it as a cultural mission and no longer hesitate to renew once again its colonial calling.

Chapter 9

Expansion
and Public
Opinion:

Advocates of
the "New
Imperialism"

Source 2 from John G. Paton (Senior Missionary, New Hebrides Mission) to the Hon. James Service (Governor-General of Australia), August 1883, quoted in Louis L. Snyder, editor, The Imperialism Reader *(Princeton, N.J.: D. Van Nostrand, 1962), pp. 295–297. Reprinted by permission.*

2. Letter from John G. Paton to James Service Urging British Possession of the New Hebrides, 1883

The Hon. James Service,
Premier

Sir:

For the following reasons we think the British government ought now to take possession of the New Hebrides group of the South Sea islands, of the Solomon group, and of all the intervening chain of islands from Fiji to New Guinea.

1. Because she has already taken possession of Fiji in the east, and we hope it will soon be known authoritatively that she has taken possession of New Guinea at the northwest, adjoining her Australian possessions, and the islands between complete this chain of islands lying along the Australian coast. Taking possession of the New Hebrides would not add much to her expenses, as her governments on Fiji and New Guinea with the visits of her men-of-war passing through the group of the New Hebrides and intervening islands on their way to New Guinea, would almost be sufficient for all her requirements on the islands between.

2. The sympathy of the New Hebrides natives are all with Great Britain, hence they long for British protection, while they fear and hate the French, who appear eager to annex the group, because they have seen the way the French have treated the native races in New Caledonia, the Loyalty Islands, and other South Sea islands.

3. Till within the past few months almost all the Europeans on the New Hebrides were British subjects, who long for British protection.

4. All the men and all the money (over £140,000) used in civilizing and Christianizing the New Hebrides have been British. Now fourteen missionaries and the Dayspring mission ship, and about 150 native evangelists and teachers are employed in the above work on this group, in which over £6000 yearly of British and British-colonial money is expended; and certainly it would be unwise to let any other power now take possession and reap the fruits of all this British outlay.

5. Because the New Hebrides are already a British dependency in this sense—all its imports are from Sydney and Melbourne and British colonies, and all its exports are also to British colonies.

6. The islands of this group are generally very rich in soil and in tropical products so that if a possession of Great Britain, and [if] the labour traffic stopped so as to retain what remains of the native populations on them, they would soon, and for ages to come, become rich sources of tropical wealth to these colonies, as sugar cane is extensively cultivated on them by every native of the group, even in his heathen state. For natives they are an industrious, hard-working race, living in villages and towns, and, like farmers, depending on the cultivation and products of the ground for their support by their plantations. The islands also grow maize, cotton, coffee, arrowroot, and spices, etc., and all tropical products could be largely produced on them.

7. Because if any other nation takes possession of them, their excellent and spacious harbors, as on Efate, so well-supplied with the best fresh water, and their near proximity to Great Britain's Australasian colonies, would in time of war make them dangerous to British interests and commerce in the South Seas and her colonies.

8. The thirteen islands of this group on which life and property are now comparatively safe, the 8,000 professed Christians on the group, and all the churches formed among them, are by God's blessing the fruits of the labours of British missionaries, who, at great toil, expense, and loss of life, have translated, got printed, and taught the natives to read the Bible in part or in whole in nine different languages of this group, while 70,000 at least are longing and ready for the gospel. On this group twenty-one members of the mission families died or were murdered by the savages in beginning God's work among them, not including good Bishop Peterson, of the Melanesian mission, and we fear all this good work would be lost if the New Hebrides fall into other than British hands.

9. Because we see no other way of suppressing the labour traffic in Polynesia, with all its many evils, as it rapidly depopulates the islands, being attended by much bloodshed, misery, and loss of life.[8] It is an unmitigated evil to the natives, and ruinous to all engaged in it, and to the work of civilizing and Christianizing the islanders, while all experience proves that all labour laws and regulations, with government agents and gunboats, cannot prevent such evils, which have always been the said accompaniments of all such traffic in men and women in every land, and because this traffic and its evils are a sad stain on our British glory and Australasian honor, seeing Britain has done so much to free the slave and suppress slavery in other lands.

For the above reasons, and others that might be given, we sincerely hope and pray that you will do all possible to get Victoria and the other colonial

---

8. For decades the South Sea Islands had been plagued by unscrupulous men known as "blackbirders" who abducted laborers and sold them as slaves to work in the cotton fields of Fiji and Queensland, the sugar fields of New Caledonia, and the sheep stations of Australia. See Cyril S. Belshaw, *Changing Melanesia: Social Economics and Cultural Contact* (London: Oxford University Press, 1954), pp. 17–19.

Chapter 9

Expansion
and Public
Opinion:
Advocates of
the "New
Imperialism"

governments to help and unite in urging Great Britain at once to take possession of the New Hebrides group. Whether looked at in the interests of humanity, or of Christianity, or commercially, or politically, surely it is most desirable
that they should be at once British possessions; hence we plead for your judi-
cious and able help, and remain, your humble servant,

JOHN G. PATON
Senior Missionary
New Hebrides Mission

Source 3 from Jules Ferry, Tonkin et la Mère-Patrie *(1890), translated by and quoted in Har-*
vey Goldberg, editor, French Colonialism *(New York: Rinehart & Co., 1959), pp. 3–4.*

3. Jules Ferry's Appeal to the French to Build the Second Colonial Empire, 1890

Colonial policy is the child of the industrial revolution. For wealthy countries
where capital abounds and accumulates fast, where industry is expanding
steadily, where even agriculture must become mechanized in order to survive, exports are essential for public prosperity. Both demand for labor and
scope for capital investment depend on the foreign market. Had it been possible to establish, among the leading industrial countries, some kind of rational
division of production, based on special aptitudes and natural resources, so
that certain of them engaged in, say, cotton and metallurgical manufacture,
while others concentrated on the alcohol and sugar-refining industries, Europe might not have had to seek markets for its products in other parts of the
world. . . . But today every country wants to do its own spinning and weaving, forging and distilling. So Europe produces, for example, a surplus of
sugar and must try to export it. With the arrival of the latest industrial giants,
the United States and Germany; of Italy, newly resurrected; of Spain, enriched
by the investment of French capital; of enterprising little Switzerland, not to
mention Russia waiting in the wings, Europe has embarked on a competitive
course from which she will be unable to turn back.

All over the world, beyond the Vosges and across the Atlantic, the raising of
high tariffs has resulted in an increasing volume of manufactured goods, the
disappearance of traditional markets, and the appearance of fierce competition. Countries react by raising their own tariff barriers, but that is not
enough. . . . The protectionist system, unless accompanied by a serious colonial policy, is like a steam engine without a safety valve. An excess of capital
invested in industry not only reduces profits on capital but also arrests the
rise of wages. This phenomenon cuts to the very core of society, engendering

passions and countermoves. Social stability in this industrial age clearly depends on outlets for industrial goods. The beginning of the economic crisis, with its prolonged, frequent strikes—a crisis which has weighed so heavily on Europe since 1877—coincided in France, Germany, and England with a marked and persistent drop in exports. Europe is like a commercial firm whose business turnover has been shrinking for a number of years. The European consumer-goods market is saturated; unless we declare modern society bankrupt and prepare, at the dawn of the twentieth century, for its liquidation by revolution (the consequences of which we can scarcely foresee), new consumer markets will have to be created in other parts of the world. . . . Colonial policy is an international manifestation of the eternal laws of competition.

Without either compromising the security of the country or sacrificing any of its past traditions and future aspirations, the Republicans have, in less than ten years, given France four kingdoms in Asia and Africa. Three of them are linked to us by tradition and treaty. The fourth represents our contribution to peaceful conquest, the bringing of civilization into the heart of equatorial Africa. Suppose the Republic had declared, with the doctrinaires of the Radical school, that the French nation ends at Marseilles. To whom would Tunisia, Indochina, Madagascar, and the Congo belong today?

Source 4 from Joseph Chamberlain, M. P., Foreign & Colonial Speeches *(London: George Routledge & Sons, 1897), pp. 131–139.*

4. Joseph Chamberlain, Speech to the West Birmingham Relief Association, January 22, 1894

We must look this matter in the face, and must recognise that in order that we may have more employment to give we must create more demand. (Hear, hear.) Give me the demand for more goods and then I will undertake to give plenty of employment in making the goods; and the only thing, in my opinion, that the Government can do in order to meet this great difficulty that we are considering, is so to arrange its policy that every inducement shall be given to the demand; that new markets shall be created, and that old markets shall be effectually developed. (Cheers.) You are aware that some of my opponents please themselves occasionally by finding names for me—(laughter)—and among other names lately they have been calling me a Jingo.[9] (Laughter.) I am no more a Jingo than you are. (Hear, hear.) But for the reasons and arguments I have put before you tonight I am convinced that it is a necessity as

9. **Jingo:** a belligerent patriot; a chauvinist.

Chapter 9

Expansion

and Public

Opinion:

Advocates of

the "New

Imperialism"

well as a duty for us to uphold the dominion and empire which we now possess. (Loud cheers.) For these reasons, among others, I would never lose the hold which we now have over our great Indian dependency—(hear, hear)—by far the greatest and most valuable of all the customers we have or ever shall have in this country. For the same reasons I approve of the continued occupation of Egypt; and for the same reasons I have urged upon this Government, and upon previous Governments, the necessity for using every legitimate opportunity to extend our influence and control in that great African continent which is now being opened up to civilisation and to commerce; and, lastly, it is for the same reasons that I hold that our navy should be strengthened—(loud cheers)—until its supremacy is so assured that we cannot be shaken in any of the possessions which we hold or may hold hereafter.

Believe me, if in any one of the places to which I have referred any change took place which deprived us of that control and influence of which I have been speaking, the first to suffer would be the working-men of this country. Then, indeed, we should see a distress which would not be temporary, but which would be chronic, and we should find that England was entirely unable to support the enormous population which is now maintained by the aid of her foreign trade. If the working-men of this country understand, as I believe they do—I am one of those who have had good reason through my life to rely upon their intelligence and shrewdness—if they understand their own interests, they will never lend any countenance to the doctrines of those politicians who never lose an opportunity of pouring contempt and abuse upon the brave Englishmen, who, even at this moment, in all parts of the world are carving out new dominions for Britain, and are opening up fresh markets for British commerce, and laying out fresh fields for British labour. (Applause.) If the Little Englanders[10] had their way, not only would they refrain from taking the legitimate opportunities which offer for extending the empire and for securing for us new markets, but I doubt whether they would even take the pains which are necessary to preserve the great heritage which has come down to us from our ancestors. (Applause.)

When you are told that the British pioneers of civilisation in Africa are filibusters,[11] and when you are asked to call them back, and to leave this great continent to the barbarism and superstition in which it has been steeped for centuries, or to hand over to foreign countries the duty which you are unwilling to undertake, I ask you to consider what would have happened if 100 or 150 years ago your ancestors had taken similar views of their responsibility? Where would be the empire on which now your livelihood depends? We should have been the United Kingdom of Great Britain and Ireland; but those vast dependencies, those hundreds of millions with whom we keep up a mu-

10. **Little Englanders:** Britain's anti-imperialists.

11. **filibuster:** a person engaged in a private military action against a foreign government.

tually beneficial relationship and commerce would have been the subjects of other nations, who would not have been slow to profit by our neglect of our opportunities and obligations. (Applause.)

Let me give you one practical illustration, in order to show what ought to be done, and may be done, in order to secure employment for our people. I will take the case of a country called Uganda, of which, perhaps, you have recently heard a good deal. A few years ago Uganda was only known to us by the reports of certain enterprising and most venturesome travellers, or by the accounts which were given by those self-denying missionaries who have gone through all these wild and savage lands, endeavouring to carry to the people inhabiting them the blessings of Christianity and civilisation. (Applause.) But within very recent times English authority has been established in Uganda, and an English sphere of influence has been declared. Uganda is a most fertile country. It contains every variety of climate; in a large portion of it European colonisation is perfectly feasible; the products are of the utmost richness; there is hardly anything which is of value or use to us in our commerce which cannot be grown there; but in spite of these natural advantages, during the past generation the country has been desolated by civil strife and by the barbarities of its rulers, barbarities so great that they would be almost incredible if they did not come to us on the authority of thoroughly trustworthy eye-witnesses.

All that is wanted to restore this country to a state of prosperity, to a commercial position which it has never attained before, is settled peace and order. (Hear, hear.) That peace and order which we have maintained for so long in India we could secure by a comparatively slight exertion in Uganda, and, when this is proposed to us, the politicians to whom I have referred would repudiate responsibility and throw back the country into the state of anarchy from which it has only just emerged; or they would allow it to become an appendage or dependency of some other European nation, which would at once step in if we were to leave the ground free to them. I am opposed to such a craven policy as this. (Applause.) I do not believe it is right. I do not believe it is worthy of Great Britain; and, on the contrary, I hold it to be our duty to the people for whom at all events we have for the time accepted responsibility, as well as to our own people, even at some cost of life, some cost of treasure, to maintain our rule and to establish settled order, which is the only foundation for permanent prosperity. When I talk of the cost of life, bear in mind that any cost of life which might result from undertaking this duty would be a mere drop in the ocean to the bloodshed which has gone on for generations in that country before we ever took any interest in it.

But I will go further than that. This rich country should be developed. It is at the present time 800 miles from the sea, and unless we can reach a country by the sea we cannot obtain its products in a form or at a cost which would be likely to be of any use to us, nor can we get our products to them. Therefore

Chapter 9

Expansion

and Public

Opinion:

Advocates of

the "New

Imperialism"

what is wanted for Uganda is what Birmingham has got—an improvement scheme. (Laughter.) What we want is to give to this country the means of communication by a railway from the coast which would bring to that population—which is more intelligent than the ordinary populations in the heart of Africa—our iron, and our cloths, and our cotton, and even our jewelry, because I believe that savages are not at all insensible to the delights of personal adornment. (Laughter.) It would bring to these people the goods which they want and which they cannot manufacture, and it would bring to us the raw materials, of which we should be able to make further use.

Now, it is said that this is the business of private individuals. Private individuals will not make that railway for fifty years to come, and for the good reason that private individuals who go into investments like railways want to see an immediate prospect of a return. They cannot afford to go for ten or twenty years without interest on their money, and accordingly you will find that in undeveloped countries no railway has ever been made by private exertion, but has always been made by the prudence and foresight and wisdom of a government. . . .

Source 5 from Ferdinando Martini, Cose affricane: da Saati ad Abba Carmina: discoursi e scritti *(Milan: Fratelli Treves, 1897), pp. 122, 136, 140. Translated by Gina Pashko.*

5. Ferdinando Martini, from
Cose affricane, 1897

Italy has 108 inhabitants per square kilometer; France has only 73. In proportion to its territory, only three countries in Europe surpass Italy in population density: Belgium, Holland, and Great Britain. If we continue at this rate, Italy will soon take the lead: in the decade of 1871–1881, the birth rate exceeded the death rate by seven percent, and in the following years, by eleven percent. Every year 100,000 farmers and agricultural laborers emigrate from Italy. In spite of this immense exodus, the country witnesses its place in the family of civilized people growing smaller and smaller as it looks on with fear for its political and economic future. In fact, during the last eighty years, the English-speaking population throughout the world has risen from 22 to 90 million; the Russian-speaking population from 50 to 70; and so forth, down to the Spanish-speaking population, who were 18 million and are now 39. On the other hand, the Italian-speaking population has only increased from 20 to 31 million, and most of this growth has taken place within Italy's own geographical borders. This is not very surprising. At first, our emigrants were spreading Italy's name, language, and prestige in foreign countries, but since all, or nearly all, of them went to highly developed areas, their sons and grandsons were surrounded and attracted to the life of the vigorous people of the nations giving them hospitality, and ended up by forgetting the language of their fathers and forefathers. Now they merely increase the population of other nations, like branches that are grafted on a plant of a different species. . . .

Realizing that our stubbornness and our mistakes have cost us so much in the past and continue to cost us today, I believe that, even leaving aside all other considerations and taking into account only expenditures and the chances of success, it is less secure and more expensive to endeavor to cultivate three million hectares of barren land in Italy than to insure the prosperity of a large agricultural colony in Eritrea. . . .

Source 6 from G. W. Steevens, With Kitchener to Khartum, *first published 1898 (London: Greenhill Books photocopy of 1898 original, 1990), pp. 317–322.*

6. G. W. Steevens on the Sudan, 1898

The curtain comes down; the tragedy of the Sudan is played out. Sixteen years of toilsome failure, of toilsome, slow success, and at the end we have fought our way triumphantly to the point where we began.

It has cost us much, and it has profited us—how little? It would be hard to count the money, impossible to measure the blood. Blood goes by quality as well as quantity; who can tell what future deeds we lost when we lost Gordon . . .? By shot and steel, by sunstroke and pestilence, by sheer wear of work, the Sudan has eaten up our best by hundreds. Of the men who escaped with their lives, hundreds more will bear the mark of its fangs till they die; hardly one of them but will die the sooner for the Sudan. And what have we to show in return?

At first you think we have nothing; then you think again, and see we have very much. We have gained precious national self-respect. We wished to keep our hands clear of the Sudan; we were drawn unwillingly to meddle with it; we blundered when we suffered Gordon to go out; we fiddled and failed when we tried to bring him back. We were humiliated and we were out of pocket; we had embarked in a foolish venture, and it had turned out even worse than anybody had foreseen. Now this was surely the very point where a nation of shopkeepers should have cut its losses and turned to better business elsewhere. If we were the sordid counter-jumpers that Frenchmen try to think us, we should have ruled a red line, and thought no more of a worthless land, bottomless for our gold, thirsty for our blood. We did nothing such. We tried to; but our dogged fighting dander would not let us. We could not sit down till the defeat was redeemed. We gave more money; we gave the lives of men we loved—and we conquered the Sudan again. Now we can permit ourselves to think of it in peace.

Chapter 9

*Expansion
and Public
Opinion:
Advocates of
the "New
Imperialism"*

The vindication of our self-respect was the great treasure we won at Khartum, and it was worth the price we paid for it. Most people will hardly persuade themselves there is not something else thrown in. The trade of the Sudan? For now and for many years you may leave that out of the account. The Sudan is a desert, and a depopulated desert. Northward of Khartum it is a wilderness; southward it is a devastation. It was always a poor country, and it always must be. Slaves and ivory were its wealth in the old time, but now ivory is all but exterminated, and slaves must be sold no more. Gum-arabic and ostrich feathers and Dongola dates will hardly buy cotton stuffs enough for Lancashire to feel the difference. . . .

It will recover—with time, no doubt, but it will recover. Only, meanwhile, it will want some tending. There is not likely to be much trouble in the way of fighting: in the present weariness of slaughter the people will be but too glad to sit down under any decent Government. There is no reason—unless it be complications with outside Powers, like France or Abyssinia—why the old Egyptian empire should not be reoccupied up to the Albert Nyanza and Western Darfur. But if this is done—and done it surely should be—two things must be remembered. First, it must be militarily administered for many years to come, and that by British men. Take the native Egyptian official even today. No words can express his ineptitude, his laziness, his helplessness, his dread of responsibility, his maddening red-tape formalism. His panacea in every unexpected case is the same. "It must be put in writing; I must ask for instructions." He is no longer corrupt—at least, no longer so corrupt as he was—but he would be if he dared. The native officer is better than the civilian official; but even with him it is the exception to find a man both capable and incorruptible. To put Egyptians, corrupt, lazy, timid, often rank cowards, to rule the Sudan, would be to invite another Mahdi as soon as the country had grown up enough to make him formidable.

The Sudan must be ruled by military law strong enough to be feared, administered by British officers just enough to be respected. For the second point, it must not be expected that it will pay until many years have passed. The cost of a military administration would not be very great, but it must be considered money out of pocket. . . .

Well, then, if Egypt is not to get good places for her people, and is to be out of pocket for administration—how much does Egypt profit by the fall of Abdullahi and the reconquest of the Sudan? Much. Inestimably. For as the master-gain of England is the vindication of her self-respect, so the master-gain of Egypt is the assurance of her security. As long as dervish raiders loomed on the horizon of her frontier, Egypt was only half a State. She lived on a perpetual war-footing. . . . Without us there would have been no Egypt to-day; what we made we shall keep.

That is our double gain—the vindication of our own honour and the vindication of our right to go on making Egypt a country fit to live in. Egypt's gain is her existence to-day. The world's gain is the downfall of the worst tyranny in the world, and the acquisition of a limited opportunity for open trade. The Sudan's gain is immunity from rape and torture and every extreme of misery.

The poor Sudan! The wretched, dry Sudan! Count up all the gains you will, yet what a hideous irony it remains, this fight of half a generation for such an emptiness. People talk of the Sudan as the East; it is not the East. The East has age and colour; the Sudan has no colour and no age—just a monotone of squalid barbarism. It is not a country; it has nothing that makes a country. Some brutish institutions it has, and some bloodthirsty chivalry. But it is not a country: it has neither nationality, nor history, nor arts, nor even natural features. Just the Nile—the niggard Nile refusing himself to the desert—and for the rest there is absolutely nothing to look at in the Sudan. Nothing grows green. . . .

QUESTIONS TO CONSIDER

Begin by examining each piece of evidence separately. Your task is to identify the principal arguments each speaker used to support imperialist ventures by his nation. To help you complete that task, recall the questions in Sources and Method: (1) What problem or problems does the speaker identify that he claims imperialism will solve? (2) How does the speaker regard the "host populations" of the regions to be colonized? (3) How does the speaker treat (if at all) the opponents of imperialism? How does he characterize them? (4) Does the speaker connect imperialism with other important and simultaneous trends and events? If so, how?

Friedrich Fabri offered many reasons for Germany's getting into the imperialist "scramble." And yet, in essence he put forth three principal reasons. What does he mean when he refers to the "unproductive political quarreling" that is going on within the new German state? How does he propose that colonialism can solve

that problem? Second, recall that Germany was a very new nation in 1879 (when Fabri's work first appeared). What material gains might this new nation realize through imperialism? What nonmaterial gains might be made? Finally, Fabri spends a good deal of time analyzing the British. What does he want his readers to conclude? Was his work likely to produce some sort of rivalry between Germany and Great Britain? In your view, what is Fabri's strongest argument?

In his letter to the governor-general of Australia, missionary John G. Paton listed nine reasons why the British government should "take possession of the New Hebrides group of the South Sea islands." In your opinion, which of Paton's nine reasons were intended to impress the governor-general? Of the nine reasons, which ones do you think Paton cared about the most? How does Paton characterize the "host population" in the New Hebrides? What does that characterization reveal about Paton's thinking?

Many Westerners would have agreed with Jules Ferry when he

[265]

Chapter 9

Expansion

and Public

Opinion:

Advocates of

the "New

Imperialism"

wrote that "Colonial policy is the child of the industrial revolution." And yet Ferry went on to explain precisely how, in his view, this "child" was born. In his opinion, what might the industrialized nations of the West have done in order to avoid colonization? What, therefore, made that colonization inevitable? What role was played by high tariffs? According to Ferry, what would have happened to Tunisia, Indochina (Vietnam), Madagascar, and the Congo had the French not enveloped them? Why would that have been undesirable?

Historian Henri Brunschwig claims that Britain's was the most commercially motivated imperialism of all European nations. Does Joseph Chamberlain's speech support Brunschwig's hypothesis? How does Chamberlain attempt to convince the British working classes that imperialism will help them? Is the argument convincing?

Chamberlain barely refers to the "host populations." When he does, however, how does he portray them? On another note, how does Chamberlain characterize British anti-imperialists?

Chamberlain strikes a responsive chord (as evidenced by the applause he receives) when he refers to "those self-denying missionaries who have gone through all these wild and savage lands." What is the nature of that appeal to the working people of Birmingham? Finally, what principal trends and events does Chamberlain link to imperialism? In what way does he make those connections?

In contrast, in what ways does Ferdinando Martini see Italy's situation as unique among European nations? How does he see the power and prestige of Italy changing? What accounts for that change? More important, how might building an empire help to solve Italy's problems?

War correspondent Steevens admits that Britain's conquest of the Sudan would reap no economic gains for many years. How, then, does he justify what he admits was the enormous expenditure of blood and treasure? How would Great Britain benefit? How can Steevens's view of Britain's benefits be contrasted with those of Chamberlain? How would Egypt benefit? How does Steevens view the "host population"? Do you think he believes it capable of being "civilized"?

After reading all the selections and answering these questions, look at the six pieces of evidence collectively. What were the most important arguments imperialists used in trying to influence public opinion? How did they view the "host populations"? The anti-imperialists? Did the arguments in favor of imperialism differ significantly from nation to nation? If so, can you explain these differences?

EPILOGUE

The brief imperialistic surge of the late nineteenth and early twentieth centuries profoundly altered the history of the world. Because of it, most of the earth's lands fell under Western political and economic influence. In 1880 only about 10 percent of

Africa was controlled by European nations; by 1900, however, only Ethiopia and Liberia had been able to resist the imperialist onslaught. In Asia, Western nations acquired some territory and effectively dominated the trade of most of the rest of the continent. And when Europe greedily eyed the vulnerable nations of Latin America, the United States—by 1900 itself a colonial power—announced that, in effect, that area fell within its national "sphere of influence." Indeed, by 1905 the nations of the West had come to believe that they were the center of the universe and that the rest of the earth existed to work for, produce profits for, and please the peoples of Europe and the United States. In their arrogance as the self-proclaimed "fittest" peoples in the world, most Westerners believed this dominance was only right and just.

This is not to say, however, that all Westerners approved of empire building. Though a minority, these critics of imperialism were extremely vocal and their criticisms could not be entirely ignored. In England, economist J. A. Hobson attacked colonialism as economically unprofitable to all but a few and morally bankrupting to the West. He characterized his foes, the advocates of imperialism, as "parasites upon patriotism." For his part, Vladimir Ilyich Lenin, soon to be leader of the Bolshevik Revolution, saw imperialism as the last stage of capitalism, which ultimately would lead to war and revolution. Building upon the work of Hobson, Lenin argued that investors were actually exporting investment capital from Europe to the developing colonies, to the

detriment of the workers in the West. Instead of helping workers, therefore, it was Lenin's contention that colonial expansion actually hurt them.

In France, the critics of imperialism were equally vocal. In 1904 French writer Anatole France warned that French imperialism was for the benefit of the military establishment, and that its ultimate result was a barbarism of both the military and civilian populations. For his part, socialist Jean Jaurès argued that the "host populations" would not remain a subjugated people for long, and that France was opening a Pandora's box that it would be unable to close.

In the United States, anti-imperialists counted among their number industrialist Andrew Carnegie, author Mark Twain, philosopher William James, reformer Jane Addams, and political leader William Jennings Bryan. Yet these and other voices, though loud and articulate, for the most part went unheeded amid the almost frantic scramble for colonial possessions.

Armed with hindsight, we can see that these critics of colonialism had much stronger arguments than their contemporaries either realized or appreciated. For one thing, few of these colonies could provide the markets for European manufactured goods that Ferry and Chamberlain claimed. For example, between 1909 and 1913, tropical Africa represented only about 2 percent of Great Britain's total non-European trade.

Moreover, acquiring and administering an empire was an enormously expensive process, draining off funds that might have been used for economic and social reforms. Snuffing

Chapter 9

Expansion

and Public

Opinion:

Advocates of

the "New

Imperialism"

out resistance to colonial rule required the maintenance of a strong military presence that often responded to anti-Western upsurges with extreme brutality. In China, resistance to imperialism was countered with naval bombardments of cities and wholesale executions of resisters. In the Philippines, the United States used approximately 74,000 troops to crush the movement for independence, resorting to torture, repression, and other atrocities in order to "civilize" the Filipinos. In the Congo Free State, agents of Leopold II resorted to forced labor and incredibly brutal treatment, including mutilations of protestors, in order to extract ivory and rubber.[12] In truth, colonialism could be both an exceedingly expensive and a morally reprehensible activity.

Finally, the scramble for empire heightened the rivalry and conflict among Western nations and was one factor leading to World War I in 1914. In 1898 England and France very nearly came to blows at Fashoda (on the upper Nile River) until the French backed down. In 1905 Germany's attempts to intrude into Morocco almost brought it to war with France until the Algeciras Conference of 1906 awarded control of Morocco to

12. The situation in the Congo Free State, Leopold's personal possession, became so scandalous that the king was forced to turn over control to the Belgian government in 1908.

the French. In 1904–1905, Russian imperialism in East Asia brought Russia into a war with Japan in which it suffered a humiliating defeat. As Western nations looked for power vacuums to exploit in Africa, China, and the Balkans, the threat of armed hostilities increased. Indeed, it was Russia's efforts to penetrate the Balkan tinderbox that led directly to war in 1914.

At the same time, the West's control of its newly acquired territories was never strong. Movements for national independence constantly had to be put down. Efforts to "westernize" Africans and Asians were never very successful, except among some of the elites of those regions. Though an increasing number of non-Westerners gradually came to embrace Western technology and political ideas in the twentieth century, they nevertheless insisted that the West should withdraw so that they could govern themselves. Thus, later movements for independence often tended to be "anti-Western" as well, to purge those societies of westernized elites, if not of Western technology. Within a half-century, all the empires built by the West in the late nineteenth century would be in shambles. For a time, the West lived in an imperialistic sunshine. Yet—to paraphrase Herman Melville—the brighter the sunshine, the greater the resulting shadows.

CHAPTER TEN

CITIZENSHIP AND SUFFRAGE

FOR WOMEN

The notion of citizenship—membership in an abstract body of individuals that carries with it both rights and duties—is a very old one in Europe. Though most European governments in the ancient and medieval periods were hereditary monarchies in which people were subjects rather than citizens, a few developed institutions of government based on citizenship. The first of these was the Greek city of Athens in the fifth and fourth centuries B.C., when various leaders transformed Athens from a government ruled by a few individuals into a limited democracy, one in which adult free males who held a certain amount of property and who had lived for several generations in the city made political decisions by voting directly. The easiest way to become a citizen was to be the son of one, with the handing on of citizenship from father to son symbolized by

a ceremony held on the tenth day after a boy was born. A citizen father laid his son on the floor of the house and gave him a name; this ceremony, rather than his actual physical birth, marked a boy's legal birth, and was not carried out for girls.

Women were not citizens in Athens and played no political role, other than in the comedies of the playwright Aristophanes, in which he portrays women with power as examples of democracy run amok, or the utopian writings of Plato, in which he proposes that the best form of government might be one in which talented men and women who lived independently from their families made all decisions. In both Athenian reality and Plato's *Republic*, having a political voice was linked with financial and legal independence; slaves and people who worked for a living were certainly not free enough, nor were women who were married or could marry, for marriage placed them in a dependent relationship.

[269]

The notion of citizenship continued in the Mediterranean after hereditary monarchies again came to power, though in both the Hellenistic monarchies and the Roman Empire, citizenship primarily gave one legal privileges rather than a political voice. Women as well as men were officially described as citizens in legal cases, and in the Roman Empire even the children of former slaves could eventually become citizens. This more legal and economic form of citizenship emerged again in European towns and cities in the Middle Ages. Being the citizen of a town gave one preferential legal treatment and certain privileges: One paid lower taxes than noncitizens, could live in the city and buy property there without seeking anyone's permission, and could claim certain services if one fell ill or became incapacitated and had to stay in a city hospital or receive public support. (In short, urban citizenship brought many of the same benefits we associate with national citizenship today, particularly the ability to live and work undisturbed in a particular location.) Citizenship also brought obligations, such as the duty to pay taxes and to defend the city if it were attacked. As in the Roman Empire, both women and men were citizens, obligated, if they were heads of household, to swear oaths of loyalty and provide soldiers and arms for the city's defense. Some towns and villages had an annual oath-swearing in which women did not participate, but the other obligations of citizenship were the same.

This rather offhand acceptance of women as citizens began to change in the sixteenth century. Towns often became worried about the number of citizens who might claim public support, and they increased fees for new citizens. (Worries about people moving in and becoming a burden on welfare rolls are not simply a modern phenomenon.) Greek philosophy and Roman law became more widely known and accepted, and both emphasized the mental weakness of women as a reason to exclude them from politics and limit their legal privileges. The middle-class men such as merchants or artisans who actually ran city governments increasingly regarded women who had independent power not as a necessary expedient because there wasn't a son around (as hereditary monarchs did), but as disruptive and disorderly; in their minds, women's authority was to be derivative only, coming from their status as wife or widow of the male household head. Men thus began to put more emphasis on the annual oath-swearing as a symbol of citizenship and to regard women's citizenship as secondary and "passive" whereas men's was "active."

Concepts of national citizenship that developed in the seventeenth and eighteenth centuries built on this more gendered tradition. Women petitioned Parliament in England during the period of the Civil War after the monarchy was overthrown, claiming "a proportional share in the Freedoms of this Commonwealth," but even the most radical groups in the English Civil War never suggested that ending the power of the monarch over his subjects should be matched by ending the power of husbands over their wives.

The former was unjust and against God's will, while the latter was "natural," as the words of the radical Parliamentarian Henry Parker make clear. "The wife is inferior in nature, and was created for the assistance of man, and servants are hired for their Lord's mere attendance; but it is otherwise in the State between man and man, for that civill difference ... is for ... the good of all, not that servility and drudgery may be imposed upon all for the pompe of one."[1] In English common law (as well as in the legal systems of Continental Europe and the English colonies), marriage continued to be one of "coverture," a permanent relationship in which the husband's authority was absolute and the wife was not a legal person and so had no rights to goods or property, including her own wages.

Eighteenth-century thinkers and political leaders began to add moral issues to women's inferior reason and wives' dependence in marriage as a grounds for denying women political rights. Thomas Jefferson noted: "Were our state a pure democracy . . . there would still be excluded from our deliberations . . . women, who, to prevent deprivation of morals and ambiguity of issue [children born out of wedlock], should not mix promiscuously in the public meetings of men."[2] Whether women ought to "partake in civil government dominions and sovereignty" was a topic of formal debate for the male students at Yale University in the 1770s, but there was little serious discussion of this question in the founding of the new republic after the American Revolution. In a few cases in the early United States, voting was based solely on property ownership and unmarried female property owners were allowed to vote, but these anomalies did not last long because they were not an intentional extension of voting rights to women, but simply accidental. By the nineteenth century such anomalies disappeared when voting rights in elections were specifically limited to males, leaving women along with children, criminals, and the mentally ill among the disenfranchised.

Most of the thinkers of the French Revolution agreed with Jefferson. There were a few exceptions; the Marquise de Condorcet, for example, commented in 1790: "Why should beings to whom pregnancy and passing indispositions are incident, not be able to exercise rights, of which nobody ever dreamt of depriving people who have gout every winter, or who easily catch cold?"[3] But for most of the revolutionaries, the possibility of getting pregnant created a type of distinction unlike any other. Whereas wealth, family background, social class, and status of birth were distinc-

1. [Henry Parker], *Observations upon Some of His Majesties Late Answers and Expresses* (London, 1642), p. 14.

2. Letter from Thomas Jefferson to Samuel Kercheval (September 5, 1816), in *The Writings of Thomas Jefferson*, edited by Andrew A. Lipscomb (Washington, D.C.: Thomas Jefferson Memorial Association, 1904), vol. 15, pp. 71–72.

3. Marquise de Condorcet "Condorcet's Pleas for the Citizenship of Women," translated by John Morley, *Fortnightly Review* 13 (June 1 1870): 718. Reprinted in Susan Groag Bell and Karen M. Often, eds., *Women, the Family, and Freedom: The Debate in Documents*, vol. I (Stanford: Stanford University Press, 1983). p. 99.

tions they increasingly took to be meaningless in terms of the limits of citizenship—the 1791 French Constitution limited voting rights to those men who had some property, but by 1792 all men over twenty-one could vote—sex remained, in their eyes, an unbridgeable chasm. Pierre-Gaspard Chaumette, a Parisian official, commented in 1792: "Since when is it permitted to give up one's sex? Since when is it decent to see women abandoning the pious cares of their households, the cribs of their children, to come to public places, to harangues in the galleries, at the bar of the Senate? Is it to men that nature has confided domestic cares? Has she given us breasts to feed our children?"[4] (Parisian revolutionaries were obsessed with women's breasts—not only did they constantly use images of nursing mothers in their speeches and paintings, but in 1793 at the festival of Unity and Indivisibility honoring the new republic, the deputies pledged their loyalty to the nation by drinking water spouting from the breasts of a large statue of an Egyptian goddess.)

Considerations—and rejections—of women's citizenship in 1792 did not simply arise out of abstract discussions of rights, but were in response to dramatic actions on the part of women, particularly in Paris, in the first years of the Revolution. Women

4. Pierre-Gaspard Chaumette, speech to the Commune of Paris, November 17, 1793. Translated and reprinted in *Women in Revolutionary Paris, 1789–1795*, edited by Darlene Levy, Harriet Applewhite, and Mary Durham Johnson (Urbana: University of Illinois Press, 1979), p. 215.

drafted official grievance lists for elected deputies to take to the king, marched from Paris to Versailles demanding that the king return to Paris, attended meetings and signed petitions concerning the future of the constitutional monarchy, and, as you saw in Chapter 5, participated in the fall of the Bastille. Throughout all of these activities, they identified themselves as citizens—*citoyennes* in the feminine in French—and as patriots. Women such as Olympe de Gouges wrote and spoke vigorously about the need for women to be part of political categories currently being discussed— "the nation," "the individual," and "the people." This politicization of women shocked both conservatives and revolutionaries, and none of the various constitutions drafted during the Revolution allowed women to vote, though they did allow women some civil rights, such as divorce and property ownership. These were taken away again in Napoleon's Civil Code of 1804, which left adult unmarried women relatively free to engage in business and legal affairs but made married women totally subservient to their husbands and decreed that a wife's nationality should follow her husband's. This code became the basis of many law codes in Europe after the Napoleonic conquests.

Subsequent political revolutions in France and other parts of Europe in 1830 and 1848, combined with more gradual reforms that extended voting rights and other political benefits of citizenship to wider groups of men, led to continued debates about women and citizenship. Women were inspired by both the liberal and socialist programs of change that you read about in Chapter 7 to call for more opportunities in education and employment, for their right to own property and control their own wages, and for access to an expanded public role. By the middle of the nineteenth century, groups specifically devoted to women's political rights began to be established in many countries of the world and to communicate with each other in what became an international feminist movement; international meetings included ones in Washington, D.C., in 1888 and in Buenos Aires in 1910.

Just as they had during the French Revolution, calls for women's citizenship and political rights in the nineteenth and early twentieth centuries were answered by individuals and groups who fervently opposed extending rights to women. Suffragists were ridiculed and attacked physically, and in many countries antisuffrage groups were formed whose tactics paralleled those of the suffrage groups; such groups included women

as well as men, for women have been the only group in history to mobilize both for and against their own enfranchisement. The debate took many forms: letters to the editor in newspapers, pamphlets, cartoons, specialized journals either supporting or opposing women's rights, and oral debates at meetings and in government bodies. As in most political debates, the arguments included references to both abstract principles and practical consequences, and they involved what we now term "negative advertising"—the portrayal of the other side in an unfavorable light—as well as advocacy of a position. Your task in this chapter will be to analyze material from both sides of this debate to answer the following questions: What arguments do both sides give for extending or not extending full citizenship to women? How do they use language and images, particularly in portrayals of themselves and their opponents, to make their points?

SOURCES AND METHOD

Analyzing political debates has been a part of history for a long time. The earliest works usually labeled "history" in Western civilization, the stories by Herodotus and Thucycides of various wars in which the ancient Greeks engaged, included descriptions of political debates along with portrayals of battles and heroes. Like the sources you are reading for this chapter, those debates referred to abstract principles

such as justice as well as to practical concerns such as military fitness; like the subject of this chapter, those ancient Greek debates often centered on how broad the group of decision-making citizens should be (though only Plato seriously considered including women in that group).

The authors and artists in this chapter were all intentionally engaged in the debate about women's rights and desired to make their points in ways that would be clear to their readers and viewers. This means that they are quite direct, even blunt, in their message, and it should not be difficult for you to follow their basic line of argument. As you read and look at the sources, it would be useful to keep notes about the abstract principles to which the authors refer and about the consequences they see if rights were extended to women. You should also keep notes about the words they use to describe themselves and their opponents. How does this language reinforce their positions?

The first five sources in this chapter come from those who argued against extending political rights to women. Source 1 comes from a long theoretical work, *De la Justice dans la Révolution et dans l'Église (On Justice in the Revolution and the Church)*, written in 1858 by Pierre-Joseph Proudhon (1809–1865), a French socialist writer and reformer. Proudhon includes two chapters on love and marriage, and in these he sets out his views of women and marriage very clearly. Read this carefully. To what does Proudhon attribute women's secondary status? Does he view this as something that can be changed? How does he relate women's inferiority to their exclusion from full citizenship? On what abstract principles does he base his argument?

Source 2 comes from a letter to the editor of a popular magazine, *The Nineteenth Century*, written by Mrs. Humphrey Ward (1851–1920), a well-known and respected English author. Mrs. Ward published this with the signed endorsement of a number of other upper-class women. What arguments does she give for not granting women the right to vote in national elections? In what ways does her argument agree with Proudhon's, and in what ways does it differ? What does she see as the consequences of extending voting rights? Source 3 comes from a small book, *The Unexpurgated Case Against Woman Suffrage*, published in 1913 by Sir Almroth Wright (1861–1947), a prominent physician and immunologist. What does he say would happen if voting rights were extended to women? Why does he expect men to be hostile to this idea? How does he portray the women who advocate education and votes for women?

The women's rights debate provided opportunities for artists on both sides. Source 4 is a German cartoon from 1847 showing four variations of "emancipated women": The top two depict "the female Don Juan" and "the female painter," and the bottom two "the female professor" and the "female protector." What do the physical attributes and postures of the four women suggest? How does the artist depict the men associated with these women? What does the artist portray as the consequences of women's emancipation? Source 5 is a cartoon by the popular French artist Honoré Daumier, from a 1849 series called "Socialist Women." Daumier had earlier published a series of cartoons much like Source 4 showing women who aspired to learning or political rights as ugly, fat, and unfaithful to their husbands, and in this he shows a domestic scene in which the woman says, "So you're my husband, you're the master. . . . But I've got the right to throw you out of the house. . . . Jeanne Deroin [see Source 6] proved it to me yesterday evening! Go have it out with her!" What does Daumier suggest will happen if women gain political rights? How does he depict the relations among the woman, her husband, and their child?

Sources 6 through 9 provide the other side of the argument. Source 6 includes several brief works by Jeanne Deroin (1805–1894), a self-educated working-class woman who sought to improve women's condition and in 1849 put herself forward to the Paris Democratic Socialist party as a candidate for the Legislative Assembly. Source 6A is a brief editorial printed in 1848 in a daily woman's newspaper, *La Voix des Femmes* (*The Voice of Women*), that had been founded just a week before; Source 6B gives Deroin's statements declaring her candidacy; Source 6C comes from a pamphlet Deroin published in 1850 answering Proudhon and the historian Jules Michelet on the issue of women's rights. Why does she think the time is right for women's full citizenship? What principles does she stress in her arguments? How does she portray those who oppose her?

In the same way that women's voices were heard arguing against women's rights, men's voices were heard in favor of them. Source 7 is from John Stuart Mill's *The Subjection of Women*, published in 1869. Mill was a philosopher and a liberal member of the British Parliament; in 1867 he introduced a bill that would have extended voting rights to women, which was defeated by a vote of 194 to 74. To what does Mill attribute women's subordination? What reasons does he give for extending political rights to them? What does he see as the consequences of having denied women access to citizenship and employment?

Source 8 is an extract from a pamphlet written in 1913 by the French Union for Women's Suffrage, a group founded by Jeanne Schmahl (1836–1915). Schmahl had been instrumental in achieving passage of the first married women's property act in France, which granted married women the right to their own wages. What reasons does this group give in favor of suffrage for women? Why does it feel the time is right for this change? What results does it anticipate if women are able to vote?

Source 9 is a pro-suffrage cartoon that appeared in the September 26, 1913, issue of the *Vote*, the newspaper of the Women's Freedom League, which was one of the main suffrage organizations in Britain. How does the cartoon portray those who opposed suffrage?

◼ THE EVIDENCE

Source 1 from Pierre-Joseph Proudhon, De la Justice dans la Révolution et dans l'Église (Paris, 1935). Excerpts from Susan Groag Bell and Karen M. Offen, eds., Women, the Family, and Freedom: The Debate in Documents, Vol. 1 (Stanford: Board of Trustees of the Leland Stanford Jr. University, 1983), pp. 325–330. Used with the permission of Stanford University Press, www.sup.org.

1. Pierre-Joseph Proudhon on Women's Equality, 1858

Are man and woman each other's equals or equivalents? Or are they merely complementary to one another, in such a manner that there can be neither equality nor equivalence between them? In any case, what is the social function of woman? Following from this, what is her dignity? What is her right? How should she be considered in the Republic? . . .

PHYSICAL INFERIORITY OF WOMEN

It is a fact of life, common to all mammals, that until puberty the make-up of the young man and the girl are scarcely different, but from the moment masculine development begins, man takes the lead in several respects: the squareness of his shoulders, the thickness of his neck, the hardness of his muscles, the girth of his biceps, the strength of his loins, the agility of his entire body, the power of his voice. It is a fact that the development can be arrested and retained, so to speak, in the neutral state by mutilating the young male; and that the adult male himself, undergoing castration, redescends insensibly and loses his virile qualities, as if by the generative faculties with which he is endowed the man, before engendering his kind, engenders himself and brings himself to a degree of strength such as woman never attains.

It is also a fact of life that the abuse of amorous encounters and seminal losses, like castration itself, deprives man of his strength and its accompanying qualities—agility, ardor, courage—and that the age at which he begins to grow old is that at which his organs produce less of this semen, of which the greatest part is used, it appears, for the production of strength.

Finally, it is a fact of life that between individual males the differences in strength and physical agility are not generally proportional to the height, mass, and weight, but to virile energy and to the relative efficiency with which this energy serves and maintains the system. . . .

According to these observations, therefore, the physical inferiority of woman is the product of her *non-masculinity*.

The complete human being, adequate to his destiny (I am speaking here of physique), is the male, who by means of his virility attains the highest degree of muscular and nervous tension that his nature and his destiny require, and thereby the maximum of activity in work and in combat.

The woman is a diminutive of man, and lacks an organ necessary to become anything other than a potential adult.

Why has nature given only to man this seminal virtue, whereas it has made woman a passive being, a receptacle for the seed that man alone produces, a place of incubation—like the earth for the grain of wheat—by itself an inert organ, lacking its own goal, which can be activated only by the fertilizing action of the father, but for another goal than that of the mother? This contrasts with the case of man, for whom the generative power has its positive utility independent of generation itself.

Such an arrangement can have no reason to exist other than in the couple and the family; it presupposes the subordination of the subject, outside which its self-sufficiency would be impossible, and it could rightly speak of itself as afflicted by nature and as the suffering victim of Providence. . . .

Whatever the inequality of vigor, suppleness, agility, constancy, that one can observe between men and women, it can be said without much risk of error that on the average the ratio of physical force of man to that of woman is 3 to 2.

Thus, from this perspective, the numerical ratio of 3 to 2 indicates the ratio of value between the sexes. . . .

What I have said so far is based on theory: in practice, the condition of woman encounters an even greater subordination through maternity. . . .

Without mentioning her periods, which take up eight days of the month, ninety-six days per year, one must count nine months for pregnancy; for recovery, forty days; for nursing, 12 to 15 months; for child care after weaning, five years: for a total of seven years for a single birth. In the case of four births at two-year intervals, maternity requires twelve years from a woman.

Here we must not engage in quibbling or haggling. No doubt the pregnant woman and the nursing mother, along with some one who cares for bigger children, is capable of some service. In my own estimate, during these twelve years the woman's time is absorbed almost entirely in bearing and raising children; whatever she can do beyond this without deteriorating is strictly fortuitous, and thus she and her children inevitably become dependent on man.

If, therefore, during the better part of her existence, woman is condemned by her nature to subsist only with the help of a man; if he—whether father, brother, husband, or lover—definitively becomes her sole protector and supplier, how (I reason always from pure logic and without regard to any other influence), how, I say, will he be able to submit to the control and the direction of a woman? How is it that she who does not work [for a living], who lives on the work of others, could—in her continual pregnancies and births—govern the worker? However you propose to regulate the relations of the sexes and the education of children—whether in a Platonic community or by an insurance system, as M. de Girardin proposes—or, if you prefer, by maintaining the monogamous couple and the family—whatever you do, you arrive at this same result—that woman, because of her organic weakness and the *interesting situation* she inevitably falls into (however little the man contributes to it), will be fatally and juridically excluded from all political, administrative, doctrinal, industrial governance, and from all military action.

INTELLECTUAL INFERIORITY OF WOMEN

. . . Like man, woman has five senses; she is constituted like man; like man she sees, she smells, she feeds herself, she walks, she loves. From the standpoint of physical force, she lacks only one thing in order to rival man, which is to produce seed.

Similarly, from the standpoint of intelligence, woman has perceptions, memory, imagination; she is capable of paying attention, of reflecting, of judging. What does she lack? To produce seeds, that is to say, ideas; what the Latins called *genius*, the generative faculty of the mind.

What is genius? . . .

Genius is . . . virility of spirit and its accompanying powers of abstraction, generalization, invention, conceptualization, which are lacking in equal measure in children, eunuchs, and women. And such is the solidarity of the two organs that, just as the athlete must separate himself from woman in order to conserve his vigor, the thinker must also separate himself in order to conserve his genius—as if the reabsorption of the semen were any less necessary to the brain of the latter than to the muscles of the former.

. . . To the generation of ideas as to the generation [of children] woman brings nothing of her own; she is a passive, enervating being, whose conversation exhausts you as much as her embraces. He who wishes to conserve in its entirety the strength of his body and his mind will flee her: she is a murderer. . . .

Since, in view of all that I have said, intelligence correlates with strength, we rediscover here the ratio established earlier, that is, that the intellectual power of man is 3, and that of woman, 2.

And insofar as in economic, political, and social action the strength of the body and that of the mind go in tandem and are multiplied by one another, the physical and intellectual value of man will be, with respect to the physical and intellectual value of woman, as 3×3 is to 2×2, that is as 9 is to 4.

No doubt woman contributes, insofar as she is able, to the social order and to the production of wealth, and it is just that her voice should be heard. But, whereas in general assembly the vote of the man will count as 9, that of woman will count as 4. Thus do arithmetic and Justice agree.

MORAL INFERIORITY OF WOMAN

. . . But is it true that in the moral order of things, from the standpoint of Justice, of liberty, courage, and modesty, woman might be the equal of man? Already we have seen that, in both, intelligence is proportional to strength; how can virtue not also be proportional? . . .

The question becomes one of asking whether woman possesses her own virtue, every bit of it, or whether by chance she does not derive her moral value, in part or in totality, from man, just as we know she derives her intellectual value thus. . . .

Woman is a receptacle. Just as she receives the embryo from man, so too she receives her intellect and her sense of duty from him.

By nature unproductive, inert, lacking industry or understanding, lacking a sense of Justice or modesty, she requires a father, a brother, a lover, a husband, a master, a man of some sort to give her, if I may put it this way, the wherewithal that will render her capable of the virile virtues, and of social and intellectual faculties.

From this one can appreciate her devotion to love; it is not merely the instinct for maturity that encourages her; it is the emptiness of her soul, the need for courage, Justice, and honor that propel her. For her it is insufficient to be chaste, *virgo*; she must also become a heroine, *virago*. Her heart and her brain require fertilization no less than her body. . . .

All these facts about the physical and moral comparableness of man and woman must be stated, not in a vain spirit of denigration and for the stupid pleasure of exalting one sex at the expense of the other, but because they reveal the truth, because truth alone is moral and cannot be mistaken by anyone for either praise or insult. If Nature wanted the two sexes to be unequal and thereby united according to the law of subordination rather than by that of equivalence, she had her reasons—deeper and more conclusive than the utopias of the philosophers, and more advantageous not only to man, but to woman, to the child, to the entire family. It has long been said that the further humanity has risen from its base origins, the more glorious its morality has become. What is true for the conjugal collectivity is equally true for each individual partner; leave to man the heroism, the genius, the jurisdictions that are his prerogative, and you will soon see woman succeed in overcoming the imperfections of her nature to arrive at an incomparable transparence, which by itself is worth the sum of our virtues.

Thus, follow our reasoning to its conclusion.

Inferior to man in conscience as much as in intellectual and muscular power, woman finds herself as member of domestic as well as of civil society definitively relegated to the second rank; from the moral point of view as well as from the physical and intellectual point of view, her comparative value is still 2 to 3.

And since society is constituted according to a combination of these three elements—work, science, and Justice—the total value of man and woman—their relationship and consequently their comparative share of influence will be $3 \times 3 \times 3$ to $2 \times 2 \times 2$, or 27 to 8.

Under these conditions, woman cannot pretend to balance man's virile power; her subordination is inevitable. According both to Nature and before Justice she weighs only a third of man; this means that the emancipation being sought in her name would be the legal consecration of her misery, if not of her servitude. The sole hope remaining to her is to find, without violating Justice, an arrangement that will redeem her: all my readers have identified this arrangement as marriage.

Source 2 from "An Appeal Against Female Suffrage," The Nineteenth Century 147 (June 1889): 781–785. Reprinted in Bonnie G. Smith, Changing Lives: Women in European History Since 1700 (Lexington, Mass.: D.C. Heath, 1989), pp. 358–359.

2. Mrs. Humphrey Ward, "An Appeal Against Female Suffrage," 1889

We, the undersigned, wish to appeal to the common sense and the educated thought of the men and women of England against the proposed extension of the Parliamentary suffrage to women.

While desiring the fullest possible development of the powers, energies, and education of women, we believe that their work for the State, and their responsibilities towards it, must always differ essentially from those of men, and that therefore their share in the working of the State machinery should be different from that assigned to men. Certain large departments of the national life are of necessity worked exclusively by men. To men belong the struggle of debate and legislation in Parliament; the working of the army and navy; all the heavy, laborious, fundamental industries of the State, such as those of mines, metals, and railways; the lead and supervision of English commerce, the service of that merchant fleet on which our food supply depends.

At the same time we are heartily in sympathy with all the recent efforts which have been made to give women a more important part in those affairs of the community where their interests and those of men are equally concerned; where it is possible for them not only to decide but to help in carrying out, and where, therefore, judgment is weighted by a true responsibility, and can be guided by experience and the practical information which comes from it. As voters for or members of School Boards, Boards of Guardians, and other important public bodies, women have now opportunities for public usefulness which must promote the growth of character, and at the same time strengthen among them the social sense and habit. But we believe that the emancipating process has now reached the limits fixed by the physical constitution of women, and by the fundamental difference which must always exist between their main occupations and those of men. The care of the sick and the insane; the treatment of the poor; the education of children: in all these matters, and others besides, they have made good their claim to larger and more extended powers. We rejoice in it. But when it comes to questions of foreign or colonial policy, or of grave constitutional change, then we maintain that the necessary and normal experience of women does not and can never provide them with such materials for sound judgment as are open to men.

In conclusion: nothing can be further from our minds than to seek to depreciate the position or the importance of women. It is because we are keenly alive to the enormous value of their special contribution to the community, that we oppose what seems to us likely to endanger that contribution. We are convinced that the pursuit of a mere outward equality with men is for women not only vain but demoralizing. It leads to a total misconception of women's true dignity and special mission. It tends to personal struggle and rivalry, where the only effort of both the great divisions of the human family should be to contribute the characteristic labour and the best gifts of each to the common stock.

Source 3 from Almroth E. Wright, The Unexpurgated Case Against Woman Suffrage *(London, 1913). Reprinted and excerpted in Marvin Perry,* Sources of the Western Tradition: from the Renaissance to the Present *(Boston: Houghton Mifflin, 1999), pp. 226–228.*

3. Almroth E. Wright, *The Unexpurgated Case Against Woman Suffrage,* 1913

The primordial argument against giving woman the vote is that that vote would not represent physical force.

Now it is by physical force alone and by prestige—which represents physical force in the background—that a nation protects itself against foreign interference, upholds its rule over subject populations, and enforces its own laws. And nothing could in the end more certainly lead to war and revolt than the decline of the military spirit and loss of prestige which would inevitably follow if man admitted woman into political co-partnership. . . .

[A] virile and imperial race will not brook any attempt at forcible control by women. Again, no military foreign nation or native race would ever believe in the stamina and firmness of purpose of any nation that submitted even to the semblance of such control. . . .

The woman voter would be pernicious to the State not only because she could not back her vote by physical force, but also by reason of her intellectual defects.

Woman's mind . . . arrives at conclusions on incomplete evidence; has a very imperfect sense of proportion; accepts the congenial as true, and rejects the uncongenial as false; takes the imaginary which is desired for reality, and treats the undesired reality which is out of sight as nonexistent—building up for itself in this way, when biased by predilections and aversions, a very unreal picture of the external world.

The explanation of this is to be found in all the physiological attachments of woman's mind: in the fact that mental images are in her overintimately linked up with emotional reflex responses; that yielding to such reflex responses gives gratification; that intellectual analysis and suspense of judgment involve an inhibition of reflex responses which is felt as neural distress; that precipitate judgment brings relief from this physiological strain; and that woman looks upon her mind not as an implement for the pursuit of truth, but as an instrument for providing her with creature comforts in the form of agreeable mental images. . . .

In further illustration of what has been said above, it may be pointed out that woman, even intelligent woman, nurses all sorts of misconceptions about herself. She, for instance, is constantly picturing to herself that she can as a worker lay claim to the same all-round efficiency as a man—forgetting that woman is notoriously unadapted to tasks in which severe physical hardships have to be confronted; and that hardly any one would, if other alternative offered, employ a woman in any work which imposed upon her a combined physical and mental strain, or in any work where emergencies might have to be faced. . . .

Yet a third point has to come into consideration in connexion with the woman voter. This is, that she would be pernicious to the State also by virtue of her defective moral equipment. . . .

It is only a very exceptional woman who would, when put to her election between the claims of a narrow and domestic and a wider or public morality, subordinate the former to the latter.

In ordinary life, at any rate, one finds her following in such a case the suggestions of domestic—I had almost called it animal—morality.

It would be difficult to find any one who would trust a woman to be just to the rights of others in the case where the material interests of her children, or of a devoted husband, were involved. And even to consider the question of being in such a case intellectually just to any one who came into competition with personal belongings like husband and child would, of course, lie quite beyond the moral horizon of ordinary woman. . . . In this matter one would not be very far from the truth if one alleged that there are no good women, but only women who have lived under the influence of good men. . . .

The proposal to bring man and woman together everywhere into extremely intimate relationships raises very grave questions. It brings up, first, the question of sexual complications; secondly, the question as to whether the tradition of modesty and reticence between the sexes is to be definitely sacrificed; and, most important of all, the question as to whether [bringing men and women together] would place obstacles in the way of intellectual work. . . .

What we have to ask is whether—even if we leave out of regard the whole system of attractions or, as the case may be, repulsions which comes into operation when the sexes are thrown together—purely intellectual intercourse between man and the typical unselected woman is not barred by the intellectual immoralities and limitations which appear to be secondary sexual characters of woman. . . .

Wherever we look we find aversion to compulsory intellectual co-operation with woman. We see it in the sullen attitude which the ordinary male student takes up towards the presence of women students in his classes. We see it in the fact that the older English universities, which have conceded everything else to women, have made a strong stand against making them actual members of the university; for this would impose them on men as intellectual associates. Again we see the aversion in the opposition to the admission of women to the bar.

But we need not look so far afield. Practically every man feels that there is in women—patent, or hidden away—an element of unreason which, when you come upon it, summarily puts an end to purely intellectual intercourse. . . .

From these general questions, which affect only the woman with intellectual aspirations, we pass to consider what would be the effect of feminism upon the rank and file of women if it made of these co-partners with man in work. They would suffer, not only because woman's physiological disabilities and the restrictions which arise out of her sex place her at a great disadvantage when she has to enter into competition with man, but also because under feminism man would be less and less disposed to take off woman's shoulders a part of her burden.

And there can be no dispute that the most valuable financial asset of the ordinary woman is the possibility that a man may be willing—and may, if only woman is disposed to fulfil her part of the bargain, be not only willing but anxious—to support her, and to secure for her, if he can, a measure of that freedom which comes from the possession of money.

In view of this every one who has a real fellow-feeling for woman, and who is concerned for her material welfare, as a father is concerned for his daughter's, will above everything else desire to nurture and encourage in man the sentiment of chivalry, and in woman that disposition of mind that makes chivalry possible.

And the woman workers who have to fight the battle of life for themselves would indirectly profit from this fostering of chivalry; for those women who are supported by men do not compete in the limited labour market which is open to the woman worker.

From every point of view, therefore, except perhaps that of the exceptional woman who would be able to hold her own against masculine competition—and men always issue informal letters of [admission] to such an exceptional woman—the woman suffrage which leads up to feminism would be a social disaster.

Source 4 from the Research Libraries, New York Public Library. 1847, German cartoon. Reprinted in Bonnie S. Anderson, Joyous Greetings: The First International Women's Movement, 1830–1860 *(New York: Oxford University Press, 2000), p. 98.*

4. German Cartoons of
"Emancipated Women," 1847

Source 5 from the Print Collection, New York Public Library. Honore Daumier, from Les Femmes Socialistes for Charivari, *May 23, 1849.*

5. Daumier Cartoon from the Series "Socialist Women," 1849

Source 6A from Jeanne Deroin, "Aux Citoyens Français," La Voix des Femmes, no. 7 (March 27, 1848). Translated and reprinted in Susan Groag Bell and Karen M. Offen, eds., Women, the Family, and Freedom: The Debate in Documents, *vol. 1 (Stanford: Stanford University Press, 1983), pp. 247–248.*

Source 6B from Deroin's election poster and "Réponse à Proudhon." Translated and reprinted in Susan Groag Bell and Karen M. Offen, eds., Women, the Family, and Freedom: The Debate in Documents, *vol. 1 (Stanford: Stanford University Press, 1983), pp. 280, 281.*

Source 6C from [Jeanne Deroin], "À M. Michelet. Droit politique des femmes." Translated and reprinted in Susan Groag Bell and Karen M. Offen, eds., Women, the Family, and Freedom: The Debate in Documents, *vol. 1 (Stanford: Stanford University Press, 1983), pp. 282–284.*

6. Jeanne Deroin on Women's Rights, 1848–1849

6A.

The reign of brute force has ended; that of morality and intelligence has just begun. The motives that led our fathers to exclude women from all participation in the governance of the State are no longer valid. When every question was decided by the sword, it was natural to believe that women—who could not take part in combat—should not be seated in the assembly of warriors. In those days it was a question of destroying and conquering by the sword; today it is a question of building and of organizing. Women should be called on to take part in the great task of social regeneration that is under way. Why should our country be deprived of the services of its daughters?

Liberty, equality, and fraternity have been proclaimed for all. Why should women be left only with obligations to fulfill, without being given the rights of citizens? Will they be excused from paying taxes and from obeying the laws of the State? Will they be obliged to obey the laws and to pay the taxes imposed upon them?

Are they to become the helots of your new Republic? No, citizens, you do not want this; the mothers of your sons cannot be slaves. We address this just demand not merely to the provisional government, which alone cannot decide a question that is of interest to the entire nation. We come to plead our cause—so holy, so legitimate—before the citizens' assembly: our cause is theirs. They will not want to be accused of injustice. When they abolish all privileges, they will not think of conserving the worst one of all and leaving one-half of the nation under the domination of the other half. They will at least give us a role in national representation; some women chosen among the most worthy, the most honorable, the most capable, will be nominated by the men themselves, to come forth in defense of the rights of their sex and the generous principles of our glorious Revolution. Liberty, equality, and fraternity will thus be realized.

6B.

[Deroin's election poster, addressed to the Electors of the Department of the Seine]

Citizens:

I present myself for your votes, out of devotion to the consecration of a great principle: the civil and political equality of the sexes.

It is in the name of justice that I appeal to the sovereign people against negating the great principles that are the foundation for the future of our society.

If, using your right, you call upon woman to take part in the work of the Legislative Assembly, you will consecrate our republican dogmas in all their integrity: Liberty, Equality, Fraternity for all women as well as for all men.

A Legislative Assembly composed entirely of men is as incompetent tc make the laws that rule a society of men and women, as an assembly composed entirely of privileged people to debate the interests of workers, or an assembly of capitalists to sustain the honor of the country.

Jeanne Deroin, Candidate

[Jeanne Deroin: "Reply to Proudhon"]

Citizen Editor!

I beg you to insert my reply to the peculiar protest on the subject of my candidacy that appeared in the journal *Le Peuple.*

By putting forth my candidacy to the Legislative Assembly I have accomplished a duty: I demanded, in the name of public morality and in the name of justice, that the dogma of equality should not be a lie.

It is precisely because woman is equal to man, and yet not identical to him, that she should take part in the work of social reform and incorporate in it those necessary elements that are lacking in man, so that the work can be complete.

Liberty for woman, as for man, is the right to utilize and to develop one's faculties freely.

6C.

That's better! The lines are drawn and clear! To the question so often asked of you: "What do you think of women's political rights?" you replied in your last lecture: "Women have the same rights as men, but the means of exercising these rights is not possible under present conditions—we therefore appeal to women themselves." . . .

Because you appealed to women's sentiments in this circumstance, Monsieur, I shall try to reply in their name. I ought to do so all the more, perhaps, because of a remarkable fact, which cannot have escaped attentive observers, that proves to me that in contradicting your conclusions on this subject I am in truth the faithful interpreter of woman's sentiments.

Men, to judge by your auditors, agree entirely with your views on votes for women. . . . But did the women agree with this point of view? Did they also applaud? No, Monsieur, not one did so; and yet usually on every other question, upon hearing your sympathetic voice the applause of both sexes is mingled and blended. Whence came this quite exceptional reserve of the women upon a point that touches them so closely? Did that reserve not carry the weight of a protest? As far as I am concerned, I did not understand it otherwise and, moreover, I have observed that woman's good sense, easily displayed on the spur of the moment, has later been proved correct by reason.

But let us return to your very words, in order to examine various statements.

When you say: "Women have the same rights as men," you offer in its completeness a principle that is increasingly accepted by free thinkers and independent spirits.

But is it the same when you add: "Women under present conditions cannot exercise their political rights without compromising the cause of progress:"?

On this point we utterly disagree. I believe, on the contrary, that our actual conditions are eminently favorable for the exercise of political rights by women.

Let us consider a case in which women present themselves at the ballot boxes. What would happen in such a case?

Are there large numbers of politically inclined women? That is the first question. This is immaterial; it is not the right question to ask. Are these women of the people or of the bourgeoisie? Are they those who are called Ladies? None of this is significant. Those women who would like to exercise their right to vote would present themselves in the name of the law; they would claim their privilege, they would base themselves on our republican institutions; that is all. What would happen then? The situation, it will no doubt be said, could become embarrassing, if not downright ridiculous. That is no response. Republicans, Democrats, Socialists all agree unanimously that allowing women to vote under present conditions would be the greatest disaster for the Republic and for the cause of progress and, consequently, women who present themselves must be told that they cannot be allowed to vote. Very well, but if these ladies persist, saying that to let them vote is not at all the same thing as to make them vote; if they protest against the illegality committed against their persons, concerning their RIGHTS as women? If, finally, they require that a formal attestation of denial of justice be drawn up, to document the injustice they claim to have suffered, how will you extricate yourself from that embarrassment, and which side will you take?

Have no doubt, sir; this is the manner in which the question will soon be posed and, indeed, the manner in which it has already been raised by a courageous woman, Madame Pauline Roland.[5] But that was an individual case, which occurred in the provinces and, thus, did not make a great noise.

5. N. Pauline Roland was a Frenchwomen who tried to register to vote in 1848.

Do not believe, however, that this example will be lost. On the contrary, you may be sure that it will be repeated and multiplied. Do you not sense this when you see the persistence with which women come back to that very question on every occasion? Is this not a sure indication of the importance they attach to this question?

One woman presented herself in the provinces but in Paris a hundred will present themselves.

That number is not at all impressive, you say? So much the better! You will be better able to choose sides before the number increases to infinity.

Do you wish to make a fiction of the law? Do you wish to repulse women in spite of the law and in the most flagrantly illegal manner? . . . That would be a disastrous course.

This protest of a few women, this example of civic courage and, above all else, your moral persecution will perhaps produce the spark that will leap all the way to the domestic hearth to kindle the fire of independence and liberty!

One should not play either with justice or with fire. Justice is the sacred fire of the conscience; cursed be they who do not tend it! . . .

To return to the question that concerns us—and to preserve the future from the evils we fear just as much as you do—I have but one thing to say, and I address it to all who cherish the realization of orderly progress.

Do you wish to be *just* as well as prudent? Do you wish to remain within the bounds of legality? Then let women vote freely, and take care only that nothing is changed for them in the present conditions of the vote. These conditions are the very guarantees of progress; every honest opinion submits to them easily.

Source 7 from John Stuart Mill, The Subjection of Women *(London, 1869). Reprinted and excerpted in Marvin Perry,* Sources of the Western Tradition: From the Renaissance to the Present *(Boston: Houghton Mifflin, 1999), pp. 219–221.*

7. From John Stuart Mill, *The Subjection of Women*, 1869

The object of this Essay is to explain, as clearly as I am able, the grounds of an opinion which I have held from the very earliest period when I had formed any opinions at all on social or political matters, and which, instead of being weakened or modified, has been constantly growing stronger by the progress of reflection and the experience of life: That the principle which regulates the existing social relations between the two sexes—the legal subordination of one sex to the other—is wrong in itself, and now one of the chief hindrances to human improvement; and that it ought to be replaced by a principle of perfect equality, admitting no power or privilege on the one side, nor disability on the other. . . .

. . . The adoption of this system of inequality never was the result of deliberation, or forethought, or any social ideas, or any notion whatever of what conduced to the benefit of humanity or the good order of society. It arose simply from the fact that from the very earliest twilight of human society, every woman (owing to the value attached to her by men, combined with her inferiority in muscular strength) was found in a state of bondage to some man. . . .

But, it will be said, the rule of men over women differs from all these others in not being a rule of force: it is accepted voluntarily; women make no complaint, and are consenting parties to it. In the first place, a great number of women do not accept it. Ever since there have been women able to make their sentiments known by their writings (the only mode of publicity which society permits to them), an increasing number of them have recorded protests against their present social condition: and recently many thousands of them, headed by the most eminent women known to the public, have petitioned Parliament for their admission to the parliamentary suffrage. The claim of women to be educated as solidly, and in the same branches of knowledge, as men, is urged with growing intensity, and with a great prospect of success; while the demand for their admission into professions and occupations hitherto closed against them becomes every year more urgent. Though there are not in this country, as there are in the United States, periodical Conventions and an organized party to agitate for the Rights of Women, there is a numerous and active Society organized and managed by women, for the more limited object of obtaining the political franchise. Nor is it only in our own country and in America that women are beginning to protest, more or less collectively, against the disabilities under which they labour. France, and Italy, and Switzerland, and Russia now afford examples of the same thing. How many more women there are who silently cherish similar aspirations, no one can possibly know; but there are abundant tokens how many *would* cherish them, were they not so strenuously taught to repress them as contrary to the proprieties of their sex. . . .

Men do not want solely the obedience of women, they want their sentiments. All men, except the most brutish, desire to have, in the woman most nearly connected with them, not a forced slave but a willing one; not a slave merely, but a favourite. They have therefore put everything in practice to enslave their minds. The masters of all other slaves rely, for maintaining obedience, on fear; either fear of themselves, or religious fears. The masters of women wanted more than simple obedience, and they turned the whole force of education to effect their purpose. All women are brought up from the very earliest years in the belief that their ideal of character is the very opposite to that of men; not self-will, and government by self-control, but submission, and yielding to the control of others. All the moralities tell them that it is the duty of women, and all the current sentimentalities that it is their nature, to live for others; to make complete abnegation of themselves, and to have no life but in their affections. And by their affections are meant the only ones they are allowed to have—those to the men with whom they are connected, or to the children who constitute an additional and indefeasible tie between them and a man. When we put together three things—first, the natural attraction between opposite sexes; secondly, the wife's entire dependence on the husband, every privilege or pleasure she has being either his gift, or depending entirely on his will; and lastly, that the principal object of human pursuit, consideration, and all objects of social ambition, can in general be sought or obtained by her only through him—it would be a miracle if the object of being attractive to men had not become the polar star of feminine education and formation of character. And, this great means of influence over the minds of women having been acquired, an instinct of selfishness made men avail themselves of it to the utmost as a means of holding women in subjection, by representing to them meekness, submissiveness, and resignation of all individual will into the hands of a man, as an essential part of sexual attractiveness. Can it be doubted that any of the other yokes which mankind have succeeded in breaking would have subsisted till now if the same means had existed, and had been as sedulously [diligently] used to bow down their minds to it?

On the other point which is involved in the just equality of women, their admissibility to all the functions and occupations hitherto retained as the monopoly of the stronger sex. . . . I believe that their disabilities [in occupation and civil life] elsewhere are only clung to in order to maintain their subordination in domestic life; because the generality of the male sex cannot yet tolerate the idea of living with an equal. Were it not for that, I think that almost every one, in the existing state of opinion in politics and political economy, would admit the injustice of excluding half the human race from the greater number of lucrative occupations, and from almost all high social functions; ordaining from their birth either that they are not, and cannot by any possibility become, fit for employments which are legally open to the stupidest and basest of the other sex, or else that however fit they may be, those employments shall be interdicted to them, in order to be preserved for the exclusive benefit of males. . . .

It will perhaps be sufficient if I confine myself in the details of my argument, to functions of a public nature: since, if I am successful as to those, it probably will be readily granted that women should be admissible to all other occupations. . . . And here let me begin . . . [with] the suffrage, both parliamentary and municipal. . . .

. . . To have a voice in choosing those by whom one is to be governed, is a means of self-protection due to every one, though he were to remain for ever excluded from the function of governing. . . . Under whatever conditions, and within whatever limits, men are admitted to the suffrage, there is not a shadow of justification for not admitting women under the same. The majority of the women of any class are not likely to differ in political opinion from the majority of the men of the same class, unless the question be one in which the interests of women, as such, are in some way involved; and if they are so, women require the suffrage, as their guarantee of just and equal consideration. . . .

With regard to the fitness of women, not only to participate in elections, but themselves to hold offices or practise professions involving important public

[291]

responsibilities; I have already observed that this consideration is not essential to the practical question in dispute: since any woman, who succeeds in an open profession, proves by that very fact that she is qualified for it. And in the case of public offices, if the political system of the country is such as to exclude unfit men, it will equally exclude unfit women: while if it is not, there is no additional evil in the fact that the unfit persons whom it admits may be either women or men. . . .

. . . There is no country of Europe in which the ablest men have not frequently experienced, and keenly appreciated, the value of the advice and help of clever and experienced women of the world, in the attainment both of private and of public objects; and there are important matters of public administration to which few men are equally competent with such women; among others, the detailed control of expenditure. But what we are now discussing is not the need which society has of the services of women in public business, but the dull and hopeless life to which it so often condemns them, by forbidding them to exercise the practical abilities which many of them are conscious of, in any wider field than one which to some of them never was, and to others is no longer, open. If there is anything vitally important to the happiness of human beings, it is that they should relish their habitual pursuit [that is, they should be happy in their work]. This requisite of an enjoyable life is very imperfectly granted, or altogether denied, to a large part of mankind; and by its absence many a life is a failure, which is provided, in appearance, with every requisite of success.

Source 8 from the French Union for Women's Suffrage (Paris, 1913). Translated and reprinted in Lisa di Caprio and Merry E. Wiesner, Lives and Voices: Sources in European Women's History *(Boston: Houghton Mifflin, 2001), pp. 385–386. Reprinted by permission of the Houghton Mifflin Company.*

8. The French Union for Women's Suffrage Report, "The Question of the Vote for Women," 1913

SOME ARGUMENTS IN FAVOR OF THE VOTE FOR WOMEN

We are going to try to prove that the vote for women is a just, possible and desirable reform.

It is just that a woman vote.

A woman is subject to the law, pays direct and indirect taxes just as a man does; in a country of universal suffrage, laws ought to be established by all the taxpayers, men and women.

A woman possesses her own property; she can inherit, make a will; she has an interest in having her say in the laws relating to property.

A woman has responsibility in the family; she ought to be consulted about the laws establishing her rights and duties with respect to her husband, her children, her parents.

Women work—and in ever greater numbers; a statistic of 1896 established that at that date 6,400,000 French women were gainfully employed, that the proportion of female workers was 42 per cent of the women over thirteen years of age, and that the number of women workers was 35 per cent of the total number of workers, both male and female.

If she is in business, she, like any businessman, has interests to protect; it would be unjust for her not to be represented in the Chambers of Commerce, and in the regulatory bodies and courts dealing with commercial matters. Many questions pertaining to business can be decided only by the Municipal Councils and regulatory bodies.

If a woman is a worker or a domestic, she ought to participate as a man does in voting on unionization laws, laws covering workers' retirement, social security, the limitation and regulation of work hours, weekly days off, labor contracts, etc.

If she is a civil servant (postal employee, schoolteacher, professor), should she not have the right to give her opinions on the questions of her salary, of her service, of vacations, of the special rules to which she is subject? If she is a doctor, lawyer, writer, artist, she must fight to make her rights recognized. And the others, who do not yet work but who will have to work in view of the increasing costs of the necessities of life, will also have to fight to assure that new careers will be open to them as well as to men.

Certainly many beneficial reforms have been made on behalf of women, in the name of justice, by a legislature composed of men. But in order for them to correspond to the real rights of women it is necessary that the latter participate in their establishment.

A woman is from this day on capable of voting.

Her education has improved considerably; the elementary school curriculum for boys and girls is the same, and in coeducational schools girls profit from the instruction at least as much as boys; higher education is available to young women, secondary education is as serious in girls' secondary schools as it is in boys' secondary schools.

Woman's importance in the family is greater and greater, her moral authority and economic power are increasing; new legislation on marriage and divorce and on paternity suits tend to make her independent and allow her to develop her personality.

Finally, her special characteristics of order, economy, patience and resourcefulness will be as useful to society as the characteristics of man and will favor the establishment of laws too often overlooked until now.

The women's vote will assure the establishment of important social laws.

All women will want:

To fight against alcoholism, from which they suffer much more than men;

To establish laws of health and welfare;

To obtain the regulation of female and child labor;

To defend young women against prostitution;

Finally, to prevent wars and to submit conflicts among nations to courts of arbitration.

We will see, by studying what has been accomplished by the women's vote in countries where women have obtained it, that it is legitimate to expect that all these urgent reforms will be realized in France too when French women vote.

Source 9 from September 26, 1913, issue of the Vote, *the newspaper of the Women's Freedom League. Reprinted in Lisa di Caprio and Merry E. Wiesner,* Lives and Voices: Sources in European Women's History *(Boston: Houghton Mifflin, 2001), p. 392.*

9. Pro-suffrage Cartoon, 1913

STUDIES IN NATURAL HISTORY.
The Antysuffragyst or Prejudicidon.

The Antysuffragyst or Prejudicidon. This curious animal has the smallest brain capacity of any living creature. Its sight is so imperfect that it cannot see further than the end of its nose; but it has a wonderful capacity for discovering the stupefying plant called "Humbugwort," on which it feeds voraciously. It is closely allied to the Lunaticodon, and it is a fierce enemy of the Justiceidon.

QUESTIONS TO CONSIDER

As you have no doubt noticed, in some cases arguments on each side of the women's rights debate were grounded in fundamentally different premises: Those who rejected women's full citizenship argued that women were in their very being inferior to men, while those who supported women's rights argued that men and women were basically equal and that differences came primarily from differing opportunities for education and work. Looking at your notes, which of the authors would you see as best typifying these two positions? On what abstract principles are they basing their argument? How are they describing their opponents and supporters? Do you think there would have been much room for discussion among these authors?

Along with those who argued that men were superior and those who argued that men and women were equal, you have also no doubt noticed that some of the authors asserted that men and women were *different*, but that this difference was not necessarily a hierarchical one. You may have also noted that this emphasis on the differences between men and women, and on the complementarity of their social roles and functions, emerged in authors on both sides of the women's rights debate. How would you compare, for example, Mrs. Humphrey Ward's ideas about women's proper role in the community (Source 2) with the statements about what all women want at the end of the pamphlet by the French Union for Women's Suffrage (Source 8)? Where does Jeanne

Deroin (Source 6) seem to fit on the equal versus complementary scale? Why do you think an emphasis on complementarity led to different positions in terms of women's full citizenship?

Along with differing ideas about the relative merits of men and women and the proper limits of their social and political roles, parties on both sides of this debate had differing ideas about the proper bases of citizenship itself. Look first at Sources 1 and 3. How do Proudhon and Wright view the relationship between physical force and political rights? Between intellectual ability and political rights? Do they see these as historically variable? Now look at Deroin's argument in Source 6. How does she view the relationship between force and citizenship? What does she see as the proper basis of citizenship? Does Mill (Source 7) agree with her on this?

The tactics of women's rights groups varied from country to country; those in England ultimately turned to militant moves such as hunger strikes and other types of civil disobedience, while in most other countries women used more moderate means, such as petition drives (a political tool first developed by women's groups), lobbying, and letters of protest. Some advocates of women's rights argued that only rights exactly equal to those of men were acceptable, while others regarded incremental steps as better than nothing, that once *some* women had the vote it would be easier to gain the vote for others. Looking at Sources 6 through 8, what evidence do you see of these two opinions?

[295]

You are now ready to answer the central questions for this chapter: What arguments do supporters and opponents of women's rights give for extending or not extending full citizenship to women? How do they use language and images, particularly in portrayals of themselves and their opponents, to make their points?

EPILOGUE

Advocates of voting rights for women were ultimately successful, and suffrage was gradually extended to women around the world. Women were allowed to vote in national elections first in New Zealand in 1893 and in Finland in 1906; suffrage rights were granted in the United States and many European countries right after World War I and in Latin America, the Philippines, India, China, Japan, and the rest of Europe (except Switzerland) in the 1930s and 1940s. Although, as you have seen in this chapter, both supporters and opponents of women's suffrage expected women's voting patterns to differ sharply from those of men, in most elections they did not. After gaining suffrage, however, many women's groups turned their attention away from women's political status to other types of issues, such as educational, health, and legal reforms, or world peace.

By the 1960s, women in many parts of the world were dissatisfied with the pace at which they were achieving political and legal equality beyond the ballot box, and a second-wave women's movement began, often termed the "women's liberation movement." Women's groups pressured for an end to sex discrimination in hiring practices, pay rates, inheri-

tance rights, and the granting of credit; they opened battered-women's shelters, day-care centers, and rape crisis centers; and they pushed for university courses on women and laws against sexual harassment. The United Nations declared 1975–1985 to be the International Decade for Women, and meetings discussing the status of women around the world were held under UN auspices in Mexico City (1975), Copenhagen (1980), Nairobi (1985), and Beijing (1995). In 1979, the UN passed the Convention on the Elimination of All Forms of Discrimination Against Women (CEDAW), which as of early 2003 has been ratified by 163 countries.

Like the first movement for women's rights, the reinvigorated feminist movement sparked conservative reactions in many countries, with arguments often couched in terms of "tradition." Women's rights, it was argued, stood against "traditional family values" and had caused an increase in the divorce rate, the number of children born out of wedlock, family violence, and juvenile delinquency. Such arguments were effective in stopping some legal changes; the United States and about twenty other countries did not ratify CEDAW, and in the United States, the Equal Rights Amendment was not ratified by enough states to become law, though Canada passed a similar measure in 1960 and Australia in 1984. Although most countries in the world now officially give women and men equal voting rights—only Kuwait limits voting to men—other aspects of citizenship, such as becoming a citizen after emigration, have remained easier for men than for women. Thus certain aspects of women's rights in the twenty-first century would no doubt be pleasing to Proudhon and Wright, while others would please Deroin and Mill. Neither side would be surprised that impassioned rhetoric on this issue can still be found regularly in every type of media.

CHAPTER ELEVEN

WORLD WAR I:

TOTAL WAR

In the first days of August 1914, every major capital city in Europe was the scene of enthusiastic patriotic demonstrations in favor of the declarations of war that began World War I. All confidently predicted victory for their own nation, and all expected a short war. Emperor William II (Kaiser Wilhelm II) told German troops departing for the front, "You will be home before the leaves have fallen from the trees." The war indeed ended in autumn, but it was the autumn of 1918, not 1914. Previous military history did not prepare Europeans in any way for the war they were to undertake in 1914.

Europe's last general war had ended in 1815 with Napoleon's defeat at Waterloo. Subsequent nineteenth-century conflicts never involved all the great powers, and they were invariably short wars. The Prussians, for example, had defeated Austria in six weeks during the Austro-Prussian War of 1866. In the last nineteenth-century conflict involving

major powers, the Franco-Prussian War of 1870–1871, France and Prussia had signed an armistice after a little over twenty-seven weeks of combat.

These nineteenth-century wars after Waterloo were also highly limited conflicts, involving relatively small professional armies whose weapons and tactics differed little from those of the Napoleonic era. Civilian populations seldom felt much impact from such conflicts, although Paris endured a siege of eighteen weeks in the Franco-Prussian War.

The war on which Europeans so enthusiastically embarked in 1914 proved far different from the 1870–1871 conflict. The prewar alliance system meant that, for the first time in a century, all the great powers were at war, making the scope of the hostilities greater than in any recent fighting. Moreover, the conflict quickly became a world war as the belligerents fought one another outside Europe and as non-European powers such as Japan and the United States joined the ranks of warring nations.

Even more significant than the number of nations engaged in the conflict, however, was the nature of the war they fought. The Industrial Revolution of the nineteenth century had brought technical changes to warfare that were to transform the 1914 conflict into the Western world's first modern, total war. This would be a war of tremendous cost to both soldiers and civilians, a struggle requiring effort and sacrifice by every citizen of the warring countries.

Modern railroads and motorized transport permitted belligerent nations to bring the full weight of their new industrial strengths to the battlefields of World War I. Both sides for the first time made extensive use of the machine gun as well as new, longer-range heavy artillery. Whole new weapons systems included flame throwers, poison gas, the tank, the airplane, the lighter-than-air dirigible, and the submarine.

Generals trained in an earlier era of warfare failed at first to understand the increased destructive capacity of these new weapons and practiced military tactics of 1870 in fighting the war's first battles. As before, they attacked the enemy with massed infantrymen armed with bayonets fixed, flags flying, drums sounding, and led by officers in dress uniforms complete with white gloves. This was the kind of war Europeans had enthusiastically anticipated in 1914, but because of modern firepower, casualties in such attacks were extremely heavy—indeed, completely unprecedented.

Especially in western Europe, such losses resulted in increased reliance on what has been called the "in-fantryman's best friend," the shovel. To avoid the firepower of the new modern weaponry, opposing armies dug into the earth, and by Christmas 1914 they opposed each other in 466 miles of trenches stretching through France from the English Channel to the border of Switzerland. These trenches represented stalemate. They were separated by "No Man's Land," the open space an attacker had to cross to reach the enemy. Swept with machine gun and artillery fire and blocked by barbed wire and other obstacles, "No Man's Land" was an area that an attacking force could cross only with great losses. In such circumstances, neither side could achieve the traditional decisive breakthrough into the enemy's lines. Field Marshal Horatio Kitchener, an experienced commander of the old school of warfare and British secretary for war until 1916, expressed the frustration of many about such combat: "I don't know what is to be done—this isn't war."

In their efforts to achieve victory, generals and statesmen sought to break the stalemate in a number of ways that extended the impact of World War I. The warring nations mobilized unprecedented numbers of men; over 70 million were called to military service. Never before had so large a part of Europe's population been put in uniform: England mobilized 53 percent of its male population of military age in 1914–1918, and France and Germany called on the service of some 80 percent of their males of draft age.

Each warring government took unprecedented steps to meet its forces' needs for food, material, and ammunition. Governments rationed consumer goods to provide for their armies. England and Germany asserted extraordinary government control over raw materials, privately owned production facilities, and civilian labor in the name of war production.

Civilians felt the war in other ways, too. The stalemate meant a long war, and governments soon recognized that they could not maintain their war efforts during a long conflict if civilian morale broke. They therefore attempted to exert total control over news and public opinion, often at the expense of their citizens' rights. They censored the press, used propaganda to maintain civilian morale, and placed critics under surveillance or arrest.

The warring nations also recognized the equal importance of the home front to their enemies in achieving victory. As a result, civilians experienced the war in unprecedented ways. Blockades by surface fleets and submarine attacks on shipping aimed at slowing war production and destroying civilian morale by cutting off vital shipments of raw materials and food to enemy countries. New weapons systems also placed civilians in actual physical danger. Warring nations dropped bombs on their enemies' cities from dirigibles and primitive bomber aircraft, and long-range artillery rained shells on population centers miles from battlefronts.

This was the world's first total war; until the outbreak of another such war in 1939, participants remembered it as the "Great War." Your task in this chapter is to assess the all-encompassing nature of modern warfare through several different kinds of sources. Why was World War I different from previous wars? What impact did it have on the soldiers at the front? How did it affect civilians at home?

SOURCES AND METHOD

In this chapter we have assembled a variety of evidence, and we have arranged it to illustrate three aspects of World War I. We open with sources illustrating Europe's rush to war in 1914 amid an almost universal burst of enthusiasm and nationalist sentiment. A second group of sources presents the front-line experiences of the millions of men mobilized by their goverments for military service. Finally, a third group of sources demonstrates the war's impact on European civilians on the home front.

A large portion of this chapter's evidence consists of literary sources, the work of young intellectuals who often welcomed the war as a conflict that would sweep away a decadent cultural life and replace it with one more vital.

Many talented and well-educated men sought to hasten this cultural transformation by volunteering for military service. Front-line combat, however, soon showed these young men that they were caught up in a war unlike any previous struggle. Conscious of the uniqueness of their battlefield experience and aware that their front-line service would leave them forever changed, many made an effort to record their experiences. Letters, diaries, autobiographical works, paintings, and sketches by individual soldiers all supplement the dry official records kept by war ministries of the participating countries and give the historian an excellent sense of battlefield realities and their impact. Your main sources in this chapter comprise creative works, in the form of poetry and fiction, in which a number of talented soldiers sought to convey the experience of modern war and its effect on them.

Literature can be a valuable source for the student of history in understanding the past. We must, however, stay fully aware of its limits as well as its value. The utility of literature as a historical source is somewhat limited by its very nature: As the product of an individual, it reflects personal and social perspectives that must be identified. Most of the authors represented here, for example, came from the middle or upper classes because such individuals, not the sons of the working classes, had the education to write works of enduring significance. With such a social background, many served as officers, and the conditions they endured were in some ways better than those of the enlisted men: The war was often significantly worse for a private than for a captain.

Individuals have opinions, too, and opinions often invade war literature. The soldier often portrayed himself as a victim of forces beyond his control: a powerful government, modern technology, or the military authorities. As historians, we must note these opinions because they convey to us the individual's reaction to the war, but we must look beyond them as well to discern the objective wartime conditions the author was recording.

Not all chroniclers of the war were equally well placed to understand the war. We must ask if each work was based on actual front-line experience. If not, we should discount it as historical evidence. We must also ask if an author's work was written in the midst of war, in which case it may reflect the passions of the moment. If the work was written after the war, the author's selective memory for certain facts may have influenced his or her work. The evidence in this chapter presents works by front-line authors written at the outbreak of the war, at the time of their combat experiences, and after the war. Indeed, the great majority of literary works on the war appeared, like the literature on Vietnam, about a decade after the cessation of hostilities. Perhaps a gestation period is necessary for the minds of many to analyze the combat experience. If that is the case, we must recognize the frailty of the human memory and measure the message of postwar literature against those writings composed in the heat of battle.

Once the various viewpoints and perspectives are identified, however, a student of history can obtain an excellent sense of World War I through works of poetry and fiction. These works present the war in human terms far more vividly than do government reports and statistics. To assist your reading, some information on each of the writers presented here is in order. We turn first to the rush to war.

Rupert Brooke (1887–1915), the author of Source 1, was a graduate of Cambridge University and one of England's most promising young poets when he enlisted in September 1914 as a sublieutenant in the Royal Naval Division, a land force attached to the British navy. After brief service in Belgium in 1914, his unit was dispatched to the Middle East in 1915 as part of the British and French attack on the Turks at Gallipoli—a strategy designed to open the straits to the Black Sea so that Western supplies could reach Russia. (The attack itself, in which many Australian and New Zealand troops perished, was generally deemed a disaster.) Not quite twenty-eight years of age, Brooke died of blood poisoning en route to Gallipoli and was buried on the island of Skyros, Greece, home of Achilles of the ancient Homeric myths. The selection by Brooke presented here, the poem "Peace," reflects the romanticism characteristic of much prewar English poetry but also expresses Brooke's response to the war. What were his sensations as he watched the war engulf Europe? How does he characterize the spirit of pre–World War I Europe? What will awaken that spirit? Why do you think his poem suggests that Brooke would welcome death?

A remarkable Frenchman, Charles Péguy (1873–1914), wrote Source 2, "Blessed Are." Péguy was a talented poet and essayist, much of whose work expresses his nationalism as well as his concern for the poor and the cause of social justice. His writings also reflect a remarkable spiritual journey. Raised a Catholic, his dislike for the authoritarian character of the Church grew by the time he reached adulthood, and he declared himself an atheist about 1893. In 1908, however, he rediscovered a deep religious faith, though he kept his distance from the institutional Church and probably never participated in its sacramental life. Péguy's later writings bear witness to this religiosity as well as to his continued concern for his fellow man and his French nationalism.

Péguy was forty-one when war broke out in 1914, and he therefore qualified for the army reserve, not front-line duty. Always a man of action, however, he volunteered for active service. Commissioned a lieutenant of infantry, he died leading his men in an attack on September 5, 1914. Remember the details of his life as you read "Blessed Are." What elements of Péguy's thought does the poem combine? What was his view of war? Although Péguy's national and religious background was different from that of the English Protestant Brooke, what ideas did he share with Brooke? Why do you think other intellectuals also drew on the romanticism and nationalism of the late nineteenth and early twentieth centuries to welcome war?

Source 3, the "Hymn of Hate," is the work of the German poet Ernst Lissauer (1882–1937), who served as a private in the German army. Composed as the war broke out, the poem was soon set to music and became very popular in Germany. To appreciate its significance fully, you may wish to review in your textbook the sections on nineteenth-century nationalism and on the international rivalries that contributed to World War I. Which nation do the Germans see as their archenemy? Why, after consulting your textbook, do you think this country was so hated in Germany? What do these three sources reveal about Europeans' attitudes as they went to war in 1914?

With Source 4, we turn to the grim realities of the front-line experience. Sources 4 and 5 are actual combat photographs that offer exceptional evidence of wartime conditions. By 1914, technical advances in photography had made the camera portable enough so that it could be carried into combat zones to record the realities of war. The camera could thus show the combatants of World War I in action, and not in the posed scenes generally photographed behind the firing lines in late-nineteenth-century wars.

Source 4 is a photograph of a German infantry unit advancing in their autumn, 1912, maneuvers. The German army, like many European armies, held elaborate annual maneuvers, also sometimes called war games, prior to the outbreak of World War I in 1914. In maneuvers, large portions of the nation's army practiced the tactics that they planned to employ in the next war, and military analysts carefully observed such war games for what they revealed of an army's techniques of warfare. Those analysts observed that in 1914 all

large armies retained traditional tactics based on the advance of massed infantry units that sought ultimate engagement with the enemy in bayonet fighting. Thus, French tacticians wrote of the *attaque á outrance* ("attack at the point of a knife"), Russian regulations required infantrymen to keep bayonets fixed to their rifles in permanent readiness for such attack, and the authors of the German army's infantry manual asserted their commitment to the traditional infantry offensive "cost what it may."

Examine Source 4 for what it reveals about the tactics that the German army, like most other European forces, brought to the early days of World War I. Notice that the soldiers advance in tight formation and in straight ranks commanded by mounted officers and that they employ infantry tactics that had changed little in over two centuries. Nevertheless, the weapons of war had changed dramatically by 1914. In a real battle, these soldiers' objective would have been defended by modern artillery and machine guns capable of firing 400 or 500 rounds per minute. What effect do you think such modern firepower would have had on this attack force? Why might you conclude that such tactics revealed the lack of preparation of all armies for the realities of modern warfare in 1914? Why would you not be surprised to learn that the French army, which also used such tactics, suffered staggering losses in the war's first four months (August to December, 1914) totaling an estimated 754,000 casualties (dead, wounded, missing in action, and captured)? What tactics might seem more appropriate than those employed in the war's first months?

Source 5 is a photo of British infantry going "over the top," that is, exiting a trench and moving out into "No Man's Land," the open area between their own trenches and those of their opponents swept by artillery and machine gun fire. The specific object of this attack in April 1918 was Kemmel Hill, a high point in the Flanders region of Belgium. How have infantry tactics changed since 1914? What was the purpose of the position from which the soldiers are shown attacking? How have infantry tactics remained the same? What evidence do you find of modern military technology in this photograph? Note especially the helmets and gas masks that the soldiers wear and the barbed wire strung in front of their trench.

With Source 6, we return to the analysis of literary evidence. Novelists also drew on their wartime experiences. Henri Barbusse (1873–1935), the author of *Under Fire,* worked as a French government employee and a journalist before World War I. Politically a socialist, he was swept up by the general surge of patriotism in 1914 and volunteered for military service. He served in the French army from 1914 through the early days of the great Battle of Verdun in 1916, when he was wounded and left the service. In *Under Fire,* which was written in the trenches, he attempted to portray realistically the physical and psychological impact of modern war. The novel was recognized early as an important work and received France's most prestigious literary award, the Goncourt Prize, in 1916.

The excerpt presented as Source 6 describes an attack on the Germans by veteran French infantrymen led by their trusted Corporal Bertrand. How does Barbusse describe modern warfare?

Excerpts from a second novel, *All Quiet on the Western Front* (Source 7), offer us the view of the losing side in the war. Its author, Erich Maria Remarque (1898–1970), grew up the son of a German bookbinder. Drafted at the age of eighteen, he served in the German army from 1916 to the war's end. Remarque had already begun to write before his military service, and his *All Quiet on the Western Front* represented such a realistic picture of the war that many perceived it as an attack on German patriotism. As a consequence, the novel was among the first batch of books burned by the Nazis in 1933. How does Remarque describe the experience of modern warfare? What effect did it have on the many youthful front-line soldiers like the main character, Paul Baumer? What impact did that war have on German civilians?

Two poems conclude our literary evidence on World War I. Source 8, "Dulce et Decorum Est" ("It is sweet and fitting"), is the work of Wilfred Owen (1893–1918). Owen studied briefly at the University of London before the war, intending a career in the clergy. He enlisted in the British army in 1915, aged twenty-two, and as an infantry lieutenant served in France in the great Battle of the Somme. Owen was wounded three times in 1917 and recuperated in England, where he met Siegfried Sassoon, author of the next selection, who encouraged Owen in his writing. After recovering from his wounds, Owen again served on the western front. He received the Military Cross for bravery in October 1918 and died leading his men in an attack on November 4, 1918, one week before the war's end.

Owen's battlefield experiences shaped his poetry. "Dulce et Decorum Est" is titled with a phrase from the Roman poet Horace, whose work would have been familiar to all upper-class English schoolboys of Owen's day. How would you summarize Owen's view of the war, especially his opinion of those on the home front who blindly supported it?

Siegfried Sassoon (1886–1967), author of "The General" (Source 9), was seven years older than his friend Owen, and his poetic response to the war is the reaction of one with greater experience of life and its problems. A Cambridge graduate like Rupert Brooke, he had written poetry since his boyhood. The war transformed Sassoon from an upper-class young man who enjoyed the hunt to a postwar social activist and socialist. Although he served with great bravery as a front-line officer, he experienced an increasingly bitter sense of the war's futility. Wounded in 1917, he had a long convalescence in England and went through an emotional crisis as he attempted to balance his growing pacifism with his enduring sense of duty and the comradeship he felt with those still on the front line. Sassoon's response was to throw away his Military Cross awarded for bravery and to draft a letter of protest of the war to his com-

manding officer. Stating that a war undertaken as one of defense had become a war of conquest, he declared, "I can no longer be a party to prolong those sufferings for ends which I believe to be evil and unjust." Such a letter from an officer in wartime would normally have resulted in court-martial. Intervention of friends on his behalf led instead to Sassoon's treatment for shell shock, a common psychological problem among front-line troops. It was during his hospitalization for this treatment that Sassoon met Owen. Returning to service in 1918, Sassoon was wounded again but lived to survive the war. His poem, "The General," is very brief, but it reflects Sassoon's attitude toward the war. How does Sassoon view the general?

Participants in the war left other personal records of the conflict in the form of letters and autobiographical works. The letter in Source 10 records such a remarkable event in the midst of total war that people then, as now, tended to doubt that it ever occurred. Nevertheless, the story of this anonymous German soldier can be verified in the writings of his battlefield opponents. How had initial enthusiasm for the war and hatred of the enemy fared at the front? Why?

With Source 11, we turn to the war's impact on civilians. World War I was the first conflict to demand great participation in the war effort from women. Yet, oddly, few left extensive written records of the war's effect on them. Source 11, drawn from the Englishwoman Vera Brittain's (1893–1970) *The Testament of Youth,* is one of the few works we have by a woman. A student at Oxford when England declared war, Brittain left her studies shortly after for service as a nurse, and her book in part records the war from that vantage point. It also gives us a sense of the war's impact on those at the home front. What kind of warfare does Brittain describe the Germans as practicing? What was their objective in such warfare? What effect did the war have on Brittain?

Sources 12 through 15 are evidence of a nonpersonal nature, reports and statistics amassed by modern governments of the kind we have examined in earlier chapters. Nevertheless, such material will allow you to amplify your understanding of the impact of total warfare. Source 12, taken from the official record compiled by the U.S. army's forces occupying the Rhineland area of Germany at the war's end, describes the rations for Germany's civilian population during the last days of the war in 1918. These rations reflect the effects of a British naval blockade of the ports of Germany, established to cut the country off from imported food and strategic raw materials. Because prewar Germany was not self-sufficient in food production, the effect of such a blockade was great.

In analyzing this ration information, we must, as students of history, recognize that the supplies shown here may not completely reflect the German dietary situation. Rationing presumes that producers placed all foodstuffs at their government's disposal. In practice they did not, because rationing was based on government-regulated prices that were invariably lower than free market prices in a period of shortage. The result was a lively black market trade in foodstuffs for those who could pay higher prices.

Still, the evidence here does indicate the basic ration for many Germans. Analyze this record. What dietary basics do you find lacking or in short supply? What did German civilians eat a great deal of during the war? What cumulative effect do you think such a diet, imposed by total war, had on German civilians?

The strain of warfare was not only a matter of food and other material restrictions, however. As we noted earlier, warring governments tried to gauge and influence public opinion because they knew that total warfare would become untenable if civilian spirit broke. In Source 13 you will read a report to French police officials from the area of Grenoble in southeastern France in 1917. What does that report show about public opinion? In calling millions of men for military service, total war created tremendous labor shortages and yet another strain on civilians in all countries. Who filled the jobs vacated by men in England, according to Source 14?

The ultimate cost of the war can be measured in human lives lost. Official casualty figures, however, present considerable problems of analysis. We must first understand that all such figures are approximate. Deficiencies in wartime record keeping are part of the problem, but governments manipulated figures, too. During the war, security considerations led to consistent understatements of losses by each warring nation to prevent the enemy from knowing its manpower resources. At the war's end, some victorious governments allegedly inflated figures as a basis for postwar claims on their defeated enemies.

The figures for military deaths in Source 15 are taken from a recent study attempting to determine the best estimates of war losses from several sources, not just governmental records. Though we still must accept those figures as only approximations, they do allow a good sense of the relative losses of each country. Which suffered the greatest numerical losses? In which armies did a man mobilized for military service have the greatest chance of being killed? What do the high casualty rates of certain Eastern European countries tell you about those nations' capacities to wage modern warfare? Among the great powers, which nation lost the greatest portion of its population?

As you now read the evidence for this chapter, keep all these questions in mind. They should aid you in answering the central questions posed: Why was World War I different from previous wars? What impact did it have on soldiers at the front? How did it affect civilians at home?

THE EVIDENCE

THE RUSH TO WAR

Source 1 from Geoffrey Keynes, editor, The Poetical Works of Rupert Brooke *(London: Faber and Faber, 1960), p. 19.*

1. Rupert Brooke, "1914 Sonnet: I. Peace," 1914

Now, God be thanked Who has matched us with His hour,
　　And caught our youth, and wakened us from sleeping,
With hand made sure, clear eye, and sharpened power,
　　To turn, as swimmers into cleanness leaping,
Glad from a world grown old and cold and weary,
　　Leave the sick hearts that honour could not move,
And half-men, and their dirty songs and dreary,
　　And all the little emptiness of love!

Oh! we, who have known shame, we have found release there,
　　Where there's no ill, no grief, but sleep has mending,
　　　Naught broken save this body, lost but breath;

Nothing to shake the laughing heart's long peace there
  But only agony, and that has ending;
    And the worst friend and enemy is but Death.

Source 2 from Charles Péguy, Basic Verities: Prose and Poetry, *translated by Ann and Julian Green (New York: Pantheon, 1943), pp. 275–277.*

2. Charles Péguy, "Blessed Are," 1914

Blessed are those who died for carnal earth
Provided it was in a just war.
Blessed are those who died for a plot of ground.
Blessed are those who died a solemn death.

Blessed are those who died in great battles,
Stretched out on the ground in the face of God.
Blessed are those who died on a final high place,
Amid all the pomp of grandiose funerals.

Blessed are those who died for carnal cities.
For they are the body of the city of God.
Blessed are those who died for their hearth and their fire,
And the lowly honors of their father's house. . . .

Blessed are those who died, for they have returned
Into primeval clay and primeval earth.
Blessed are those who died in a just war.
Blessed is the wheat that is ripe and the wheat that is gathered in sheaves.

Source 3 from Ernst Lissauer, Jugend *(1914). Translated by Barbara Henderson,* New York Times, *October 15, 1914.*

3. Ernst Lissauer, "Hymn of Hate," 1914

French and Russian they matter not,
A blow for a blow and a shot for a shot;
We love them not, we hate them not,
We hold the Weichsel and Vosges-gate,[1]

1. The Germans possessed defensible boundaries against the Russians and the French. In the east, they held the Vistula (Weichsel) River in Poland as a barrier to Russain attack. In the west, they blocked the French attack with their possession of the Vosges Mountains.

We have but one—and only hate,
We love as one, we hate as one,
We have one foe and one alone.

He is known to you all, he is known to you all,
He crouches behind the dark grey flood,
Full of envy, of rage, of craft, of gall,
Cut off by waves that are thicker than blood.
Come, let us stand at the Judgment place,
An oath to swear to, face to face,
An oath of bronze no wind can shake,

An oath for our sons and their sons to take.
Come, hear the word, repeat the word,
Throughout the Fatherland make it heard.
We will never forgo our hate,
We have all but a single hate,
We love as one, we hate as one,
We have one foe, and one alone—

                    EN G L A N D!

In the Captain's mess, in the banquet hall,
Sat feasting the officers, one and all,
Like a sabre-blow, like the swing of a sail,
One seized his glass held high to hail;
Sharp-snapped like the stroke of a rudder's play,
Spoke three words only: "To the Day!"[2]
Whose glass this fate?
They had all but a single hate.
Who was thus known?
They had one foe, and one alone—

                    EN G L A N D!

Take you the folk of the Earth in pay,
With bars of gold your ramparts lay,
Bedeck the ocean with bow on bow,
Ye reckon well, but not well enough now.
French and Russian they matter not,
A blow for a blow, a shot for a shot,
We fight the battle with bronze and steel,
And the time that is coming Peace will seal.

---

2. **To the Day!:** In German naval officers' messes before World War I, it was customary to offer a
toast to "the Day," that is, the day England would be defeated.

You will hate with a lasting hate,
We will never forgo our hate,
Hate by water and hate by land,
Hate of the head and hate of the hand,
Hate of the hammer and hate of the crown,
Hate of seventy millions, choking down.
We love as one, we hate as one,
We have one foe, and one alone—

ENGLAND!

THE FRONT LINES

Source 4 from Julius Hoppenstedt, Das Volk in Waffen, *Volume 1: Das Heer. (Dachau, 1913). Reprinted in Eric Dorn Brose,* The Kaiser's Army: The Politics of Military Technology in Germany During the Machine Age, 1870–1918. *Oxford: Oxford University Press, 2001, p. 157. Photograph: Hoppenstedt, Das Heer.*

4. German Infantrymen Attack in Close Order in the Autumn, 1912, Maneuvers.

Source 5 from John Ellis, Eye-Deep in Hell: Trench Warfare in World War I *(Baltimore: The Johns Hopkins University Press, 1976), p. 90. Photo source cited: John MacClancy.*

5. British Infantry Going "Over the Top" in Attack on Kemmel Hill, April 1918

Source 6 from Henri Barbusse, Under Fire: The Story of a Squad, *translated by Fitzwater Wray (New York: E. P. Dutton, 1917), pp. 250–259.*

6. From Henri Barbusse,
Under Fire: The Story of a
Squad, **1916**

We are ready. The men marshal themselves, still silently, their blankets cross-wise, the helmet-strap on the chin, leaning on their rifles. I look at their pale, contracted, and reflective faces. They are not soldiers, they are men. They are not adventurers, or warriors, or made for human slaughter, neither butchers nor cattle. They are laborers and artisans whom one recognizes in their uniforms. They are civilians uprooted, and they are ready. They await the signal for death or murder; but you may see, looking at their faces between the vertical gleams of their bayonets, that they are simply men.

Each one knows that he is going to take his head, his chest, his belly, his whole body, and all naked, up to the rifles pointed forward, to the shells, to the bombs piled and ready, and above all to the methodical and almost infallible machine-guns—to all that is waiting for him yonder and is now so frightfully silent—before he reaches the other soldiers that he must kill. They are not careless of their lives, like brigands, nor blinded by passion like savages. In spite of the doctrines with which they have been cultivated they are not inflamed. They are above instinctive excesses. They are not drunk, either physically or morally. It is in full consciousness, as in full health and full strength, that they are massed there to hurl themselves once more into that sort of madman's part imposed on all men by the madness of the human race. One sees the thought and the fear and the farewell that there is in their silence, their stillness, in the mask of tranquillity which unnaturally grips their faces. They are not the kind of hero one thinks of, but their sacrifice has greater worth than they who have not seen them will ever be able to understand.

They are waiting; a waiting that extends and seems eternal. Now and then one or another starts a little when a bullet, fired from the other side, skims the forward embankment that shields us and plunges into the flabby flesh of the rear wall. . . .

A man arrives running, and speaks to Bertrand, and then Bertrand turns to us—

"Up you go," he says, "it's our turn."

All move at once. We put our feet on the steps made by the sappers, raise ourselves, elbow to elbow, beyond the shelter of the trench, and climb on to the parapet.

Bertrand is out on the sloping ground. He covers us with a quick glance, and when we are all there he says, *"Allons,* forward!"[3]

Our voices have a curious resonance. The start has been made very quickly, unexpectedly almost, as in a dream. There is no whistling sound in the air. Among the vast uproar of the guns we discern very clearly this surprising silence of bullets around us—

We descend over the rough and slippery ground with involuntary gestures, helping ourselves sometimes with the rifle. . . . On all sides the slope is covered by men who, like us, are bent on the descent. On the right the outline is defined of a company that is reaching the ravine by Trench 97—an old German work in ruins. We cross our wire by openings. Still no one fires on us. Some awkward ones who have made false steps are getting up again. We form up on the farther side of the entanglements and then set ourselves to topple down the slope rather faster—there is an instinctive acceleration in the movement. Several bullets arrive at last among us. Bertrand shouts to us to reserve our bombs and wait till the last moment.

But the sound of his voice is carried away. Abruptly, across all the width of the opposite slope, lurid flames burst forth that strike the air with terrible detonations. In line from left to right fires emerge from the sky and explosions from the ground. It is a frightful curtain which divides us from the world, which divides us from the past and from the future. We stop, fixed to the ground, stupefied by the sudden host that thunders from every side; then a simultaneous effort uplifts our mass again and throws it swiftly forward. We stumble and impede each other in the great waves of smoke. With harsh crashes and whirlwinds of pulverized earth, towards the profundity into which we hurl ourselves pell-mell, we see craters opened here and there, side by side, and merging in each other. Then one knows no longer where the discharges fall. Volleys are let loose so monstrously resounding that one feels himself annihilated by the mere sound of the downpoured thunder of these great constellations of destruction that form in the sky. One sees and one feels the fragments passing close to one's head with their hiss of red-hot iron plunged in water. The blast of one explosion so burns my hands, that I let my rifle fall. I pick it up again, reeling, and set off in the tawny-gleaming tempest with lowered head, lashed by spirits of dust and soot in a crushing downpour like volcanic lava. The stridor of the bursting shells hurts your ears, beats you on the neck, goes through your temples, and you cannot endure it without a cry. The gusts of death drive us on, lift us up, rock us to and fro. We leap, and do not know whither we go. Our eyes are blinking and weeping and obscured. The view before us is blocked by a flashing avalanche that fills space.

3. *Allons:* "Let's go!"

It is the barrage fire. We have to go through that whirlwind of fire and those fearful showers that vertically fall. We are passing through. We are through it, by chance. Here and there I have seen forms that spun round and were lifted up and laid down, illumined by a brief reflection from over yonder. I have glimpsed strange faces that uttered some sort of cry—you could see them without hearing them in the roar of annihilation. A brasier full of red and black masses huge and furious fell about me, excavating the ground, tearing it from under my feet, throwing me aside like a bouncing toy. I remember that I strode over a smoldering corpse, quite black, with a tissue of rosy blood shriveling on him; and I remember, too, that the skirts of the great-coat flying next to me had caught fire, and left a trail of smoke behind. On our right, all along Trench 97, our glances were drawn and dazzled by a rank of frightful flames, closely crowded against each other like men.

Forward!

Now, we are nearly running. I see some who fall solidly flat, face forward, and others who founder meekly, as though they would sit down on the ground. We step aside abruptly to avoid the prostrate dead, quiet and rigid, or else offensive, and also—more perilous snares!—the wounded that hook on to you, struggling.

The International Trench! We are there. The wire entanglements have been torn up into long roots and creepers, thrown afar and coiled up, swept away and piled in great drifts by the guns. Between these big bushes of rain-damped steel the ground is open and free.

The trench is not defended. The Germans have abandoned it, or else a first wave has already passed over it. Its interior bristles with rifles placed against the bank. In the bottom are scattered corpses. From the jumbled litter of the long trench, hands emerge that protrude from gray sleeves with red facings, and booted legs. In places the embankment is destroyed and its woodwork splintered—all the flank of the trench collapsed and fallen into an indescribable mixture. In other places, round pits are yawning. . . .

We have spread out in the trench. The lieutenant, who has jumped to the other side, is stooping and summoning us with signs and shouts—"Don't stay there; forward, forward!"

We climb the wall of the trench with the help of the sacks, of weapons, and of the backs that are piled up there. In the bottom of the ravine the soil is shot-churned, crowded with jetsam, swarming with prostrate bodies. Some are motionless as blocks of wood; others move slowly or convulsively. The barrage fire continues to increase its infernal discharge behind us on the ground that we have crossed. But where we are at the foot of the rise it is a dead point for the artillery.

A short and uncertain calm follows. We are less deafened and look at each other. There is fever in the eyes, and the cheek-bones are blood-red. Our breathing snores and our hearts drum in our bodies.

In haste and confusion we recognize each other, as if we had met again face to face in a nightmare on the uttermost shores of death. Some hurried words are cast upon this glade in hell—"It's you!"—"Where's Cocon?"—"Don't know."—"Have you seen the captain?"—"No."—"Going strong?"—"Yes."

The bottom of the ravine is crossed and the other slope rises opposite. We climb in Indian file by a stairway rough-hewn in the ground: "Look out!" The shout means that a soldier half-way up the steps has been struck in the loins by a shell-fragment; he falls with his arms forward, bareheaded, like the diving swimmer. We can see the shapeless silhouette of the mass as it plunges into the gulf. I can almost see the detail of his blown hair over the black profile of his face.

We debouch upon the height. A great colorless emptiness is outspread before us. At first one can see nothing but a chalky and stony plain, yellow and gray to the limit of sight. No human wave is preceding ours; in front of us there is no living soul, but the ground is peopled with dead—recent corpses that still mimic agony or sleep, and old remains already bleached and scattered to the wind, half assimilated by the earth.

As soon as our pushing and jolted file emerges, two men close to me are hit, two shadows are hurled to the ground and roll under our feet, one with a sharp cry, and the other silently, as a felled ox. Another disappears with the caper of a lunatic, as if he had been snatched away. Instinctively we close up as we hustle forward—always forward—and the wound in our line closes of its own accord. The adjutant stops, raises his sword, lets it fall, and drops to his knees. His kneeling body slopes backward in jerks, his helmet drops on his heels, and he remains there, bareheaded, face to the sky. Hurriedly the rush of the rank has split open to respect his immobility.

But we cannot see the lieutenant. No more leaders, then—— Hesitation checks the wave of humanity that begins to beat on the plateau. Above the trampling one hears the hoarse effort of our lungs. "Forward!" cries some soldier, and then all resume the onward race to perdition with increasing speed.

"Where's Bertrand?" comes the laborious complaint of one of the foremost runners. "There! Here!" He had stooped in passing over a wounded man, but he leaves him quickly, and the man extends his arms toward him and seems to sob.

It is just at the moment when he rejoins us that we hear in front of us, coming from a sort of ground swelling, the crackle of a machine-gun. It is a moment of agony—more serious even than when we were passing through the flaming earthquake of the barrage. That familiar voice speaks to us across the plain, sharp and horrible. But we no longer stop. "Go on, go on!"

Our panting becomes hoarse groaning, yet still we hurl ourselves toward the horizon.

"The Boches![4] I see them!" a man says suddenly.

"Yes—their heads, there—above the trench—it's there, the trench that line. It's close. Ah, the hogs!"

We can indeed make out little round gray caps which rise and then drop on the ground level, fifty yards away, beyond a belt of dark earth, furrowed and humped. Encouraged they spring forward, they who now form the group where I am. So near the goal, so far unscathed, shall we not reach it? Yes, we will reach it! We make great strides and no longer hear anything. Each man plunges straight ahead, fascinated by the terrible trench, bent rigidly forward, almost incapable of turning his head to right or to left. I have a notion that many of us missed their footing and fell to the ground. I jump sideways to miss the suddenly erect bayonet of a toppling rifle. Quite close to me, Farfadet jostles me with his face bleeding, throws himself on Volpatte who is beside me and clings to him. Volpatte doubles up without slackening his rush and drags him along some paces, then shakes him off without looking at him and without knowing who he is, and shouts at him in a breaking voice almost choked with exertion: "Let me go, let me go, *nom de Dieu!*[5] They'll pick you up directly—don't worry."

The other man sinks to the ground, and his face, plastered with a scarlet mask and void of all expression, turns in every direction; while Volpatte, already in the distance, automatically repeats between his teeth, "Don't worry," with a steady forward gaze on the line.

A shower of bullets spurts around me, increasing the number of those who suddenly halt, who collapse slowly, defiant and gesticulating, of those who dive forward solidly with all the body's burden, of the shouts, deep, furious, and desperate, and even of that hollow and terrible gasp when a man's life goes bodily forth in a breath. And we who are not yet stricken, we look ahead, we walk and we run, among the frolics of the death that strikes at random into our flesh.

The wire entanglements—and there is one stretch of them intact. We go along to where it has been gutted into a wide and deep opening. This is a colossal funnel-hole, formed of smaller funnels placed together, a fantastic volcanic crater, scooped there by the guns.

The sight of this convulsion is stupefying; truly it seems that it must have come from the center of the earth. Such a rending of virgin strata puts new edge on our attacking fury, and none of us can keep from shouting with a solemn shake of the head—even just now when words are but painfully torn from our throats—"Ah, Christ! Look what hell we've given 'em there! Ah, look!"

Driven as if by the wind, we mount or descend at the will of the hollows and the earthy mounds in the gigantic fissure dug and blackened and burned

---

4. **Boches:** a derogatory term applied by the French to German soldiers, originating from the French *caboche*, or blockhead.

5. *nom de Dieu:* "Name of God!"

by furious flames. The soil clings to the feet and we tear them out angrily. The accouterments and stuffs that cover the soft soil, the linen that is scattered about from sundered knapsacks, prevent us from sticking fast in it, and we are careful to plant our feet in this débris when we jump into the holes or climb the hillocks.

Behind us voices urge us—"Forward, boys, forward, *nom de Dieu!*"

"All the regiment is behind us!" they cry. We do not turn round to see, but the assurance electrifies our rush once more.

No more caps are visible behind the embankment of the trench we are nearing. Some German dead are crumbling in front of it, in pinnacled heaps or extended lines. We are there. The parapet takes definite and sinister shape and detail; the loopholes—we are prodigiously, incredibly close!

Something falls in front of us. It is a bomb. With a kick Corporal Bertrand returns it so well that it rises and bursts just over the trench.

With that fortunate deed the squad reaches the trench.

Pépin has hurled himself flat on the ground and is involved with a corpse. He reaches the edge and plunges in—the first to enter. Fouillade, with great gestures and shouts, jumps into the pit almost at the same moment that Pépin rolls down it. Indistinctly I see—in the time of the lightning's flash—a whole row of black demons stooping and squatting for the descent, on the ridge of the embankment, on the edge of the dark ambush.

A terrible volley bursts point-blank in our faces, flinging in front of us a sudden row of flames the whole length of the earthen verge. After the stunning shock we shake ourselves and burst into devilish laughter—the discharge has passed too high. And at once, with shouts and roars of salvation, we slide and roll and fall alive into the belly of the trench!

Source 7 from Erich Maria Remarque, All Quiet on the Western Front *(New York: Fawcett Crest, 1969), pp. 167–171, 174–175. "Im Westen Nichts Neues" copyright 1928 by Ullstein A.G.; copyright renewed 1956 by Erich Maria Remarque. "All Quiet on the Western Front" copyright 1929, 1930 by Little, Brown and Company; copyright renewed 1957, 1958 by Erich Maria Remarque.*

7. From Erich Maria Remarque, *All Quiet on the Western Front*, 1928

We have been able to bury Müller, but he is not likely to remain long undisturbed. Our lines are falling back. There are too many fresh English and American regiments over there. There's too much corned beef and white wheaten bread. Too many new guns. Too many aeroplanes.

But we are emaciated and starved. Our food is so bad and mixed up with so much substitute stuff that it makes us ill. The factory owners in Germany have grown wealthy;—dysentery dissolves our bowels. The latrine poles are always densely crowded; the people at home ought to be shown these grey, yellow, miserable, wasted faces here, these bent figures from whose bodies the colic wrings out the blood, and who with lips trembling and distorted with pain, grin at one another and say: "It is not much sense pulling up one's trousers again—"

Our artillery is fired out, it has too few shells and the barrels are so worn that they shoot uncertainly, and scatter so widely as even to fall on ourselves. We have too few horses. Our fresh troops are anæmic boys in need of rest, who cannot carry a pack, but merely know how to die. By thousands. They understand nothing about warfare, they simply go on and let themselves be shot down. A single flyer routed two companies of them for a joke, just as they came fresh from the train—before they had ever heard of such a thing as cover.

"Germany ought to be empty soon," says Kat.

We have given up hope that some day an end may come. We never think so far. A man can stop a bullet and be killed; he can get wounded, and then the hospital is his next stop. There, if they do not amputate him, he sooner or later falls into the hands of one of those staff surgeons who, with the War Service Cross in his buttonhole, says to him: "What, one leg a bit short? If you have any pluck you don't need to run at the front. The man is A1.[6] Dismiss!"

Kat tells a story that has travelled the whole length of the front from the Vosges to Flanders;—of the staff surgeon who reads the names on the list, and when a man comes before him, without looking up says: "A1. We need soldiers up there." A fellow with a wooden leg comes up before him, the staff surgeon again says A1—"And then," Kat raises his voice, "the fellow says to him: 'I already have a wooden leg, but when I go back again and they shoot off my head, then I will get a wooden head made and become a staff surgeon.' " This answer tickles us all immensely.

There may be good doctors, and there are, lots of them; all the same, every soldier some time during his hundreds of inspections falls into the clutches of one of these countless hero-grabbers who pride themselves on changing as many C3's and B3's as possible into A1's.

There are many such stories, they are mostly far more bitter. All the same, they have nothing to do with mutiny or lead-swinging. They are merely honest and call a thing by its name; for there is a very great deal of fraud, injustice, and baseness in the army.—Is it nothing that regiment after regiment returns again and again to the ever more hopeless struggle, that attack follows attack along the weakening, retreating, crumbling line?

From a mockery the tanks have become a terrible weapon. Armoured they come rolling on in long lines, and more than anything else embody for us war's horror.

We do not see the guns that bombard us; the attacking lines of the enemy infantry are men like ourselves; but these tanks are machines, their caterpillars

---

6. **A1:** the highest category of physical fitness, that is, qualified for front-line duty.

run on as endless as the war, they are annihilation, they roll without feeling into the craters, and climb up again without stopping, a fleet of roaring, smoke-belching armour-clads, invulnerable steel beasts squashing the dead and the wounded—we shrivel up in our thin skin before them, against their colossal weight our arms are sticks of straw, and our hand-grenades matches.

Shells, gas clouds, and flotillas of tanks—shattering, starvation, death.

Dysentery, influenza, typhus—murder, burning, death.

Trenches, hospitals, the common grave—there are no other possibilities.

In one attack our company commander, Bertinck, falls. He was one of those superb front-line officers who are foremost in every hot place. He was with us for two years without being wounded, so that something had to happen in the end.

We occupy a crater and get surrounded. The stink of petroleum or oil blows across with the fumes of powder. Two fellows with a flame-thrower are seen, one carries the tin on his back, the other has the hose in his hands from which the fire spouts. If they get so near that they can reach us we are done for, we cannot retreat at the moment.

We open fire on them. But they work nearer and things begin to look bad. Bertinck is lying in the hole with us. When he sees that we cannot escape because under the sharp fire we must make the most of this cover, he takes a rifle, crawls out of the hole, and lying down propped on his elbows, he takes aim. He fires—the same moment a bullet smacks into him, they have got him. Still he lies and aims again;—once he shifts and again takes his aim; at last the rifle cracks. Bertinck lets the gun drop and says: "Good," and slips back into the hole. The hindermost of the two flame-throwers is hit, he falls, the hose slips away from the other fellow, the fires squirts about on all sides and the man burns.

Bertinck has a chest wound. After a while a fragment smashes away his chin, and the same fragment has sufficient force to tear open Leer's hip. Leer groans as he supports himself on his arm, he bleeds quickly, no one can help him. Like an emptying tube, after a couple of minutes he collapses.

What use is it to him now that he was such a good mathematician at school?

The months pass by. The summer of 1918 is the most bloody and the most terrible. The days stand like angels in gold and blue, incomprehensible, above the ring of annihilation. Every man here knows that we are losing the war. Not much is said about it, we are falling back, we will not be able to attack again after this big offensive, we have no more men and no more ammunition. . . .

There are so many airmen here, and they are so sure of themselves that they give chase to single individuals, just as though they were hares. For every one German plane there come at least five English and American. For one hungry, wretched German soldier come five of the enemy, fresh and fit. For one German army loaf there are fifty tins of canned beef over there. We are not beaten, for as soldiers we are better and more experienced; we are simply crushed and driven back by overwhelmingly superior forces.

Behind us lie rainy weeks—grey sky, grey fluid earth, grey dying. If we go out, the rain at once soaks through our overcoat and clothing;—and we remain wet all the time we are in the line. We never get dry. Those who still wear high boots tie sand bags round the top so that the mud does not pour in so fast. The rifles are caked, the uniforms caked, everything is fluid and dissolved, the earth one dripping, soaked, oily mass in which lie the yellow pools with red spiral streams of blood and into which the dead, wounded, and survivors slowly sink down.

The storm lashes us, out of the confusion of grey and yellow the hail of splinters whips forth the childlike cries of the wounded, and in the night shattered life groans wearily to the silence.

Our hands are earth, our bodies clay and our eyes pools of rain. We do not know whether we still live. . . .

It is autumn. There are not many of the old hands left. I am the last of the seven fellows from our class.

Everyone talks of peace and armistice. All wait. If it again proves an illusion, then they will break up; hope is high, it cannot be taken away again without an upheaval. If there is not peace, then there will be revolution.

I have fourteen days' rest, because I have swallowed a bit of gas; in a little garden I sit the whole day long in the sun. The armistice is coming soon, I believe it now too. Then we will go home.

Here my thoughts stop and will not go any farther. All that meets me, all that floods over me are but feelings—greed of life, love of home, yearning of the blood, intoxication of deliverance. But no aims.

Had we returned home in 1916, out of the suffering and the strength of our experiences we might have unleashed a storm. Now if we go back we will be weary, broken, burnt out, rootless, and without hope. We will not be able to find our way any more.

And men will not understand us—for the generation that grew up before us, though it has passed these years with us here, already had a home and a calling; now it will return to its old occupations, and the war will be forgotten—and the generation that has grown up after us will be strange to us and push us aside. We will be superfluous even to ourselves, we will grow older, a few will adapt themselves, some others will merely submit, and most will be bewildered;—the years will pass by and in the end we shall fall into ruin.

But perhaps all this that I think is mere melancholy and dismay, which will fly away as the dust, when I stand once again beneath the poplars and listen to the rustling of their leaves. It cannot be that it has gone, the yearning that made our blood unquiet, the unknown, the perplexing, the oncoming things, the thousand faces of the future, the melodies from dreams and from books, the whispers and divinations of women, it cannot be that this has vanished in bombardment, in despair, in brothels.

Here the trees show gay and golden, the berries of the rowan stand red among the leaves, country roads run white out to the sky-line, and the canteens hum like beehives with rumours of peace.

I stand up.

I am very quiet. Let the months and years come, they bring me nothing more, they can bring me nothing more. I am so alone, and so without hope that I can confront them without fear. The life that has borne me through these years is still in my hands and my eyes. Whether I have subdued it, I know not. But so long as it is there it will seek its own way out, heedless of the will that is within me. . . .

He fell in October 1918, on a day that was so quiet and still on the whole front, that the army report confined itself to the single sentence: All quiet on the Western Front.

He had fallen forward and lay on the earth as though sleeping. Turning him over one saw that he could not have suffered long; his face had an expression of calm, as though almost glad the end had come.

Source 8 from C. Day Lewis, editor, The Collected Poems of Wilfred Owen *(New York: New Directions, 1964), p. 55.*

8. Wilfred Owen,
"Dulce et Decorum Est,"
ca 1917

Bent double, like old beggars under sacks,
Knock-kneed, coughing like hags, we cursed through sludge,
Till on the haunting flares we turned our backs
And towards our distant rest began to trudge.
Men marched asleep. Many had lost their boots
But limped on, blood-shod. All went lame; all blind;
Drunk with fatigue; deaf even to the hoots
Of tired, outstripped Five-Nines[7] that dropped behind.

Gas! Gas! Quick, boys!—An ecstasy of fumbling,
Fitting the clumsy helmets just in time;
But someone still was yelling out and stumbling
And flound'ring like a man in fire or lime . . .
Dim, through the misty panes and thick green light,
As under a green sea, I saw him drowning.

7. **Five-Nines:** one of the types of artillery used by the Germans was the 5.9-inch howitzer, which projected a very large shell in a high arc. As the barrels of such guns became worn, their accuracy was impaired.

[321]

In all my dreams, before my helpless sight,
He lunges at me, guttering, choking, drowning.

If in some smothering dreams you too could pace
Behind the wagon that we flung him in,
And watch the white eyes writhing in his face,
His hanging face, like a devil's sick of sin;
If you could hear, at every jolt, the blood
Come gargling from the froth-corrupted lungs,
Obscene as cancer, bitter as the cud
Of vile, incurable sores on innocent tongues,—
My friend, you would not tell with such high zest
To children ardent for some desperate glory,
The old Lie: Dulce et decorum est
Pro patria mori.[8]

Source 9 from Siegfried Sassoon, Collected Poems, 1908–1956 *(London: Faber and Faber, 1961), p. 75.*

9. Siegfried Sassoon, "The General," ca 1917

'Good-morning; good-morning!' the General said
When we met him last week on our way to the line.
Now the soldiers he smiled at are most of 'em dead,
And we're cursing his staff for incompetent swine.
'He's a cheery old card,' grunted Harry to Jack
As they slogged up to Arras[9] with rifle and pack.

But he did for them both by his plan of attack.

---

8. From Horace, *Odes,* III, 2, 3: "It is sweet and fitting to die for one's country."

9. **Arras:** city of northeastern France that was the site of a major British attack in April 1917. With heavy artillery bombardment and the element of surprise, the British were able to break through German lines. Unfortunately, excessive caution on the part of British commanders in exploiting their costly initial successes permitted the Germans time to regroup and deprived the British of a sweeping victory.

Source 10 from Rudolf Hoffman, editor, Der deutscher Soldat: Briefe aus dem Weltkrieg (Munich: 1937), pp. 297–298. Translated and quoted in Hanna Hafkesbrink, Unknown Germany: An Inner Chronicle of the First World War Based on Letters and Diaries (New Haven, Conn.: Yale University Press, 1948), p. 141.

10. New Year's Eve, 1914: Letter from a Former German Student Serving in France

On New Year's Eve we called across to tell each other the time and agreed to fire a salvo at 12. It was a cold night. We sang songs, and they clapped (we were only 60–70 yards apart); we played the mouth-organ and they sang and we clapped. Then I asked if they haven't got any musical instruments, and they produced some bagpipes (they are the Scots guards, with the short petticoats and bare legs) and they played some of their beautiful elegies on them, and sang, too. Then at 12 we all fired salvos into the air! . . . It was a real good "Sylvester,"[10] just like in peace-time!

THE HOME FRONT

Source 11 from Vera Brittain, The Testament of Youth: An Autobiographical Study of the Years 1900–1925 (London: Gollancz, 1981), pp. 365–366.

11. Vera Brittain: A London Air Raid, June 13, 1917

Although three out of the four persons were gone who had made all the world that I knew,[11] the War seemed no nearer a conclusion than it had been in 1914. It was everywhere now; even before Victor was buried, the daylight air-raid of June 13th "brought it home," as the newspapers remarked, with such force that I perceived danger to be infinitely preferable when I went after it, instead of waiting for it to come after me.

I was just reaching home after a morning's shopping in Kensington High Street when the uproar began, and, looking immediately at the sky, I saw the sinister group of giant mosquitoes sweeping in close formation over London. My mother, whose temperamental fatalism had always enabled her to sleep

10. **Sylvester:** Roman Catholics observe December 31 as the feast of Saint Sylvester.

11. Vera Brittain lost her fiancé and two other male friends in World War I. The fourth person, her brother Edward, was still alive in June 1917, but perished while serving with the British army in Italy later in 1917.

peacefully through the usual night-time raids, was anxious to watch the show from the roof of the flats, but when I reached the doorway my father had just succeeded in hurrying her down to the basement; he did not share her belief that destiny remained unaffected by caution, and himself derived moral support in air-raids from putting on his collar and patrolling the passages.

The three of us listened glumly to the shrapnel raining down like a thunder-shower upon the park—those quiet trees which on the night of my return from Malta[12] had made death and horror seem so unbelievably remote. As soon as the banging and crashing had given way to the breathless, apprehensive silence which always followed a big raid, I made a complicated journey to the City[13] to see if my uncle had been added to the family's growing collection of casualties.

When at last, after much negociation [sic] of the crowds in Cornhill and Bishopsgate, I succeeded in getting to the National Provincial Bank, I found him safe and quite composed, but as pale as a corpse; indeed, the whole staff of men and women resembled a morose consignment of dumb spectres newly transported across the Styx.[14] The streets round the bank were terrifyingly quiet, and in some places so thickly covered with broken glass that I seemed to be wading ankle-deep in huge unmelted hailstones. I saw no dead nor wounded, though numerous police-supervised barricades concealed a variety of gruesome probabilities. Others were only too clearly suggested by a crimson-splashed horse lying indifferently on its side, and by several derelict tradesman's carts bloodily denuded of their drivers.

These things, I concluded, seemed less inappropriate when they happened in France, though no doubt the French thought otherwise.

Source 12 from the American Military Government of Occupied Germany, 1918–1920, Report of the Officer in Charge of Civil Affairs, Third Army and American Forces in Germany (Washington, D.C.: U.S. Government Printing Office, 1943), pp. 155–156.

12. German Wartime Civilian Rations, 1918

Conditions on arrival of Third Army.—When the Third Army entered its area of occupation, it found the principal foodstuffs rationed, as had been the case for several years. In brief, the situation may be outlined thus, [:] prior to the war, the average food consumption for the German population, expressed in calories, was about 3500 calories per person per day. According to German

12. Brittain had served as a military nurse on the British island of Malta in the Mediterranean.
13. **the City:** the financial district of London.
14. **Styx:** in Greek mythology, the river that the souls of the dead must cross as they leave the world of the living.

figures, this had shrunk to 3000 calories in 1914, 2000 in 1915, 1500 in 1916, and to 1200 in the winter of 1917–1918.

All the principal foodstuffs had been rationed during the war, and, on paper at least, every resource of the Empire in the way of food was entirely under control and carefully distributed.

The ration at the beginning of the occupation was essentially as follows:

Bread	260 grams per head per day[15]
Potatoes	500 grams per head per day

The main reliance for sustenance was placed on the above two foods and, except in the large cities, where the supply was subject to much fluctuation, the amounts indicated, or more, were fairly consistently provided during the whole of the year 1919.

In addition, the following substances constituted a part of the ration in the amounts indicated:

Meat	200 grams per head per week. Frequently reduced in amount, and often not issued at all.
Fat	150–200 grams per head per week. Later became very scarce.
Butter	20 grams per head per week. Practically never issued in the ration.
Sugar	600–750 grams per head per month.
Marmalade	200 grams per head per week. Often unavailable.
Milk	Not issued at all to the population in general, on account of its scarcity. Issued only to children under 6 years of age and, on physicians' certificates, to the sick, nursing mothers, pregnant women and the aged. One half to one litre per day.

Fresh vegetables, in general, were not rationed and were fairly plentiful. Additional substances, such as rice, oats, grits, margarine, sausage, "Ersatz" (substitute) coffee, eggs, and additional flour, were added to the ration from time to time when available.

15. To convert grams to ounces, multiply grams by 0.035. Thus the German bread ration was a little over 9 ounces per day per person, and the potato ration was 17.5 ounces per person per day.

Source 13 from Jean-Jacques Becker, The Great War and the French People, *translated by Arnold Pomerans (New York: St. Martin's, 1986), pp. 232–234. Reprinted by permission of Berg Publishers.*

13. Report on French Public Opinion in the Department of the Isère

Grenoble, 17 June 1917

The Prefect[16] of the Department of Isère to the Minister of the Interior[17]
Office of the Sûreté Générale[18]

I have the honour to reply herewith to the questions contained in your confidential telegram circulated on *10 June inst.*:[19]

The inquiry I have myself conducted, or with the help of colleagues, to test the opinion of certain leading personages has shown that the morale of the people of Isère is far from satisfactory and that their exemplary spirit has suffered a general decline during the past two months. Today there is weariness bordering on dejection, a result less of the curtailment of the public diet and supply difficulties than of the disappointment caused by the failure of our armies in April,[20] the feeling that military blunders have been made, that heavy losses have been sustained without any appreciable gains, that all further offensives will be both bloody and in vain. The inactivity of Russia, whose contribution now seems highly doubtful, has accentuated the decline in morale.[21] The remarks of sol-

16. **prefect:** since the Revolution of 1789, France has been divided into departments. The chief administrative officer in each department, since the time of Napoleon, has been the prefect. The prefect historically has been an appointee of the central government and thus responsible to it and not to local interests.

17. **Minister of the Interior:** most police services in France are under the control of the central government's Ministry of the Interior.

18. **Sûreté Général:** the central police command charged with criminal investigations.

19. **inst.:** An archaic use of "instant" to mean "current." Here it is used to express "June 10th of the current year."

20. In April 1917, the French army had received a new commander, General Nivelle, who launched a massive and costly offensive to break through German lines and end the war. The offensive failed and, coming after great French losses at Verdun in 1916, provoked a mutiny in the army in which soldiers refused orders to attack until August 1917. The mutinies placed the entire French war effort at risk. Order was restored only by a new commander, General Pétain, and a new and authoritarian prime minister, Georges Clemenceau.

21. Russia had experienced a revolution in February 1917 that toppled Tsar Nicholas II from power and replaced him with a republic under a Provisional Government. Although the leaders of this government were committed to Russia's war against Germany, disorganization of Russian armies by the revolution prevented effective Russian action. Because the Russian collapse accompanied Germany's unrestricted submarine warfare against all shipping around England and the disastrous defeat of the Italian armies at Caporetto in October, 1917 was the great year of crisis for France and its allies.

diers coming back from the front are the major cause of this decline: these remarks, made in the trains, in the railway stations, in the cafés on the way home,
and then in the villages, convey a deplorable picture of the mentality of a great
number of servicemen. Each one tells of and amplifies this or that unpleasant
incident, this or that error committed by his commander, this or that useless
battle, this or that act of insubordination presented as so many acts of courage
and determination. These remarks, listened to with a ready ear by those who
are already nervous or depressed enough as it is, are then peddled about
and exaggerated with the result that discontent and anxiety are increased further. Each day, incidents in public places, particularly in the large railway stations and on the trains, reflect the most deplorable attitude in the minds of servicemen.

In the countryside, the restive mood is less obvious than it is in the towns;
the peasants work, but they do not hide the fact that 'it's been going on too
long'; they are tired of their continuous over-exertion in the fields, of the lack
of hands and of the very heavy burden of the requisitions. They are growing
more and more suspicious and indifferent to the idea of collective effort and
mutual solidarity, and to patriotic appeals, and can think only of their immediate interests and their own safety.

Growers increasingly complain about price rises, even though they probably
suffer less than others from the cost of living and even though their produce is
sold at ever higher prices.

Nevertheless, it is among the rural populations that one finds the greatest
composure and resignation.

In the towns, and particularly in the industrial centres, the more impres-
sionable and hence more excitable population—the workers, the ordinary
people—are upset about the duration of the struggle, impatient with the increasing cost of living, irritated by the considerable profits being made out of
the war by the big industrialists in their neighbourhood, and increasingly
taken in by the propagandists of the united Socialist Party and their internationalist ideas. Under the influence of the Russian Revolution they already
dream of workers' and soldiers' committees and of social revolution. These
sentiments are aired frequently at workers' meetings, called ostensibly to discuss economic or union matters, and in their paper, *Le Droit du Peuple*,[22] which
is waging a very skillful anti-war and internationalist campaign.

This attitude, together with the constant rise in the cost of living, has
fuelled a widespread demand for wage increases which the employers have
quietly met to a large degree. Unfortunately, the calm following these increases has been momentary only. The cost of living keeps rising further and it
is painful to watch each wage increase being followed directly by a corresponding increase in the price of food and the cost of board and lodging. Already those workers engaged on national defence contracts are finding that

22. ***Le Droit du Peuple:*** the *Right of the People.*

[327]

the new wage scales agreed less than two months ago for Grenoble and district have become inadequate; they are presently asking for a cost-of-living allowance of 2 francs a day and have made it quite clear that if their demand is not met there will be trouble in the streets; some of them have even gone so far as to declare that they know where to find the necessary arms, alluding to the shell and explosives factories in the suburbs of Grenoble. I know perfectly well that these remarks were presumably made in order to intimidate the citizens, but it is nevertheless symptomatic that they should have been made in the first place. When they lack the courage to speak out themselves, the factory propagandists use the women working beside them who, running smaller risks, are less restrained in their threats. The demands of the reservists in the munitions factories have been forwarded to the ministry of supply and a number of agitators have been sent away—not to the front, which would have been dangerous, but to other factories in various parts of the area. Calm has therefore been restored, but there are fears that the present lull may be temporary.

If working-class militancy were to make itself felt in the munitions factories in Grenoble and in the industrial centres of the department, it would be very difficult and extremely risky to try to control it by force: the local police force would prove inadequate, even if it were reinforced by gendarmes. It is clearly necessary to strengthen the police contingent, but this can only be done through the deferment of professional policemen serving in the territorial army or the reserve. The auxiliary policemen drawn from the ranks of the retired are admittedly men of goodwill, but they are physically and mentally worn out, and their contribution and energy are inadequate. The relocation, or rather the transfer, of some gendarmerie brigades would be very useful, but the consequent changes in domicile would involve cumbersome formalities. . . . It would not be unhelpful if an intelligent, serving special commissioner were put in charge, with particular emphasis on the surveillance of aliens who continue to move about freely in the department and can undermine the morale of our people even as these aliens go about the business of gathering information useful to the enemy.

In conclusion, I believe that the present situation, both in respect of morale and also of social stability, while not giving cause for alarm, is far from satisfactory and that it ought to be considered serious enough to call for precautionary measures, and if necessary for energetic intervention.

What is really needed to lift flagging courage and to restore confidence in the future is a military success by our armies, a major Russian offensive, or just a German retreat.

Source 14 from Report of the War Cabinet Committee on Women in British Industry *(London: His Majesty's Stationery Office, 1919).*

14. Employment of Women in Wartime British Industry

Trades	Est. Number Females Employed in July 1914	Est. Number Females Employed in July 1918	Difference Between Numbers of Females Employed in July 1914 and July 1918	Percentage of Females to Total Number Workpeople Employed		Est. Number Females Directly Replacing Males in Jan. 1918
				July 1914	July 1918	
Metal	170,000	594,000	+424,000	9	25	195,000
Chemical	40,000	104,000	+ 64,000	20	39	35,000
Textile	863,000	827,000	− 36,000	58	67	64,000
Clothing	612,000	568,000	− 44,000	68	76	43,000
Food, drink, and tobacco	196,000	235,000	+ 39,000	35	49	60,000
Paper and printing	147,500	141,500	− 6,000	36	48	21,000
Wood	44,000	79,000	+ 35,000	15	32	23,000
China and earthenware	32,000 ⎫					
Leather	23,100 ⎬	197,100	+ 93,000	4	10	62,000
Other	49,000 ⎭					
Government establishments	2,000	225,000	+223,000	3	47	197,000
Total	2,178,600	2,970,600	+792,000	26	37	704,000

Source 15 from J. M. Winter, The Great War and the British People (Cambridge, Mass.: Harvard University Press, 1986), p. 75. Reprinted by permission.

15. Estimated Military Casualties, by Nation

Country	Total Killed or Died	Total Mobilized (in thousands)	Prewar Male Pop. 15–49	Total Prewar Pop.	Total Killed		
					Per 1,000 Mobilized	Per 1,000 Males 15–49	Per 1,000 People
Britain, Ireland	723	6,147	11,540	45,221	118	63	16
Canada	61	629	2,320	8,100	97	26	8
Australia	60	413	1,370	4,900	145	44	12
New Zealand	16	129	320	1,100	124	50	15
South Africa	7	136	1,700	6,300	51	4	1
India	54	953	82,600	321,800	57	1	0
France	1,327	7,891	9,981	39,600	168	133	34
French colonies	71	449	13,200	52,700	158	5	1
Belgium	38	365	1,924	7,600	104	20	5
Italy	578	5,615	7,767	35,900	103	75	16
Portugal	7	100	1,315	6,100	70	5	1
Greece	26	353	1,235	4,900	73	21	5
Serbia	278	750	1,225	4,900	371	227	57
Rumania	250	1,000	1,900	7,600	250	132	33
Russia	1,811	15,798	40,080	167,000	115	45	11
United States	114	4,273	25,541	98,800	27	4	1
Allied Total	5,421	45,001	204,018	812,521	120	27	7
Germany	2,037	13,200	16,316	67,800	154	125	30
Austria-Hungary	1,100	9,000	12,176	58,600	122	90	19
Turkey	804	2,998	5,425	21,700	268	148	37
Bulgaria	88	400	1,100	4,700	220	80	19
Central Powers' Total	4,029	25,598	35,017	152,800	157	115	26
Total Overall	9,450	70,599	239,035	965,321	134	40	10

QUESTIONS TO CONSIDER

Now that you have read the selections, try to consider them collectively, drawing out the effects of war on the people of western Europe. First, consider the initial reaction to war. We saw in The Problem that war was universally greeted with patriotic enthusiasm. What forms did that enthusiasm assume in the poems of Brooke, Péguy, and Lissauer? What previous experience had these authors with modern warfare?

Next, assess the experience of front-line service as it is expressed in the literary and other sources. Why do you think the initial ardor for warfare wore off quickly? On whom or what did the writers lay the blame for the horrors of war? How radical was their discontent? Consider again the casualty figures in Source 15, the scenes of combat in Sources 4 and 5, and the descriptions of trench warfare in Sources 6 and 7. Remember that Barbusse wrote during the war and Remarque a decade later. Do their descriptions of modern warfare differ substantially? What do you think was uppermost in the minds of men subjected to such conditions?

The war inflicted unprecedented battle losses on every belligerent country, but societal groups within the warring countries did not suffer equally. In any combat situation, the highest casualty rate affects non-commissioned and junior officers—the sergeants, lieutenants, and captains who lead attacks at the front of their units. What social groups does Remarque's *All Quiet on the Western Front* suggest made up the officer corps of each warring nation? What postwar effect do you think the loss of such men might have?

The front-line experience had costs for those who survived, too. Why might you conclude from the German soldier's account of the holiday in 1914 that one of the war's first casualties was patriotic devotion to its cause? As the war wore on, other reactions to combat became widespread among soldiers. Barbusse said that the war created two separate Frances, front-line and civilian. Does the character of Baumer in Remarque's novel reflect a similar division in Germany? Do you think a sense of alienation was a common reaction among veterans? How would it affect adjustment to postwar civilian life? Finally, assess the poems of Wilfred Owen and Siegfried Sassoon. How might you describe the sentiments expressed in those poems? What view of military authority does Sassoon's poem express? How old were Owen and Sassoon when they began military service? Are sentiments such as theirs usual in persons so young? What was the source for these views?

World War I affected civilian populations in ways no previous conflict had. Drawing on the German ration data, how do you think you would have found German wartime conditions? Why do you think Germans suffered nutritional deficiencies? Did such shortages also affect the German military, according to Source 7?

Every belligerent country recognized that the home front was essential to victory. The areas the Germans attacked in the London bombing described by Vera Brittain certainly lacked obvious military value. The Germans also launched long-range attacks on Paris, and one shell fell on a crowded church on Good Friday, 1918, killing or injuring 200 people. What was the goal of such attacks on targets of no military value? Recall the report to the French police on public opinion in the Grenoble area. What ideas were current among civilians? Why were French authorities so concerned about public opinion?

The war had a deep impact on women, too. Source 14 clearly shows a great spurt in the employment of Englishwomen in many industries. In which industries especially did they find employment? How were these jobs probably related to the war effort? Women left certain jobs, too. Which did they abandon? Many of the industries they left traditionally offered low-paying employment for unskilled or semiskilled workers. How did wartime conditions allow women to improve their economic positions in England and, indeed, in all the warring nations? Do you think women's wartime contributions (remember that the nursing efforts of Vera Brittain and other women are not reflected in Source 14) would argue for improved postwar status for women?

The effects of World War I would be felt long after the armistice that ended hostilities in 1918. Refer to the table in Source 15. Notice the total numbers of men mobilized, recalling that in countries like France and Germany 80 percent of the military-age male population was in uniform. What effect do you think the absence of so many young men from their homes had on the birth rate during the years 1914–1918? What enduring impact did the deaths of many of these men have on their countries' birth rates? What implications could all these factors have had for future defense considerations? Among the great powers, which country suffered the greatest proportional war losses? What do you predict the public attitudes in this country might be when war threatened again within twenty years of World War I's end? Do you think the costs of war would evoke the same response in all countries?

Your examination of these issues should now allow you to answer the main questions of this chapter: Why was World War I different from previous wars? What impact did it have on the soldiers at the front? How did it affect civilians at home?

EPILOGUE

World War I permanently changed Europe and the world. As this chapter demonstrated, the conflict introduced a new kind of warfare, a total warfare that inflicted suffering on the civilian citizens of belligerent countries as well as on their men in military service. But World War I permanently changed much else, too.

The political old order of Europe expired in the trenches along with a generation of young men. The stress of modern warfare meant that no government survived politically when its war effort ended in defeat. At the war's end revolutions overthrew the old monarchies in Russia, Germany, Austria-Hungary, Bulgaria, and Turkey. The governmental change was most dramatic in Russia, where that country's wartime problems led to revolution and eventually to the world's first communist dictatorship, but everywhere defeat meant political collapse. That political collapse also contributed to numerous changes in national boundaries. The breakdown of governmental authority in many defeated countries permitted national minorities in these states to seek independence. Austria-Hungary and Turkey disappeared from the map as large, multinational empires as their subject peoples declared independence at war's end. And the Russian empire lost a large part of its western territory as Finns, Poles, Latvians, Lithuanians, Estonians, and Romanians used the moment of tsarist collapse to escape Russian rule.

World War I also facilitated the transformation of Western society. Women's labor in war industries, their work in nursing, and their participation in uniformed auxiliary services of the armed forces sustained the prewar demands of women for a political voice. In most Western countries, women gained the right to vote after World War I, a major step in attaining a status equal to that of males.

The war changed Europe economically, too. The financial needs of total warfare forced every government to borrow. The most obvious change was that the United States emerged from the war as the greatest creditor nation, but other economic changes occurred as well. As warring nations purchased raw materials and manufactured goods in the Americas and Asia during the conflict, the West's wealth began to shift out of Europe. In addition, western European nations, particularly France, faced tremendous war-related property damage whose repair would consume funds for years to come.

Another cost of the war in both economic and human terms was found among its victims. The injured and crippled had to be treated, rehabilitated, and paid pensions. The situation of England illustrates the extent of the problem. When the government finalized its pension rolls in 1929, 2,424,000 men were receiving some sort of disability pension, about 40 percent of all the soldiers who had served in the British army in the war.

The war's unhappiest result, however, was that it did not become what U.S. President Woodrow Wilson called "a war to end all wars." Rather, seeds for the next conflict were sown by the events and consequences of World War I. Total war created the desire for total victory, and the peace treaties reflected animosities produced by four years of bloody conflict. The Treaty of Versailles presented Germany with a settlement that would produce a desire for revision of the peace terms and even revenge. At the same time, the great losses of life in World War I engendered in many people in victorious nations a "never again" attitude that would lead them to seek to avoid another war at all costs. This attitude would in part result in efforts to appease a resurgent and vengeful Germany under Adolf Hitler (see Chapter 12) in the 1930s.

The alienation of former soldiers from civilian life led many to search out civilian opportunities for renewing the comradeship of the front, such as veterans' groups and paramilitary organizations. Especially in the defeated countries or in those victorious countries disappointed with their gains, this impulse had dangerous consequences. In Italy and Germany, veterans enlisted in great numbers in the ranks of uniformed right-wing organizations that became the power base for the brutal armed supporters of the dictators Mussolini and Hitler (see Chapter 12). Pledged to winning back the losses in their nations' defeats in World War I, such leaders as Hitler and Mussolini seized political power by exploiting postwar problems and resentments. Their policies were to breed a second global conflict.

CHAPTER TWELVE

SELLING A

TOTALITARIAN SYSTEM

Hitler's dictatorship differed in one fundamental point from all its predecessors in history. His was the first dictatorship in the present period of modern technical development, a dictatorship which made complete use of all technical means for the domination of its own country.

Through technical devices like the radio and the loudspeaker, eighty million people were deprived of independent thought. It was thereby possible to subject them to the will of one man. . . .

Earlier dictators needed highly qualified assistants, even at the lowest level, men who could think and act independently. The totalitarian system in the period of modern technical development can dispense with them; the means of communication alone make it possible to mechanize the lower leadership. As a result of this there arises the new type of the uncritical recipient of orders. . . . Another result was the far-reaching supervision of the citizens of the State and the maintenance of a high degree of secrecy for criminal acts.

The nightmare of many a man that one day nations could be dominated by technical means was all but realized in Hitler's totalitarian system.[1]

This was how Albert Speer, once one of Hitler's most trusted subordinates, sought to answer the question that every student of the Nazi phenomenon must ultimately ask: "How could it have happened?"[2] Because your textbook examines the roots and de-

1. Final statement by Albert Speer to the International Military Tribunal for major war criminals at Nuremberg, 1946. Quoted in Alan Bullock, *Hitler: A Study in Tyranny,* rev. ed. (New York: Harper & Row, 1964), p. 380. An architect by training, Speer (1905–1981) first attracted Hitler's attention because of his expertise in that field and talent for orchestrating party rallies. He testified at Nuremberg, "If Hitler had had any friends, I would certainly have been one of his close friends." (*Inside the Third Reich: Memoirs by Albert Speer,* translated by Richard and Clara Winston [New York: Macmillan, 1970], p. 609.) Hitler promoted Speer to minister of armaments during World War II, and in that capacity, Speer's efforts maintained German war production despite Allied bombing. As it became clear, however, that the war was lost and that Hitler was determined to fight on regardless of the cost to Germany, Speer made an attempt to assassinate the dictator.

2. See, for example, Richard F. Hamilton, *Who Voted for Hitler?* (Princeton, N.J.: Princeton University Press, 1982), p. 3.

velopment of Hitler's doctrines, we will not focus in this chapter on the horrific ideology of the Nazi movement. Rather, we will examine the question that Speer addressed, for in the political history of the West, the Nazi party was the first totalitarian movement to make full use of modern media to gain and maintain power.

In their use of modern media and campaign techniques to achieve power, Hitler and his followers built on a number of developments in Western politics, technology, and intellectual life. As we observed in Chapter 7, the nature of politics in the West had begun to change in the late nineteenth century. The right to vote in the more advanced European countries expanded to include all men and, after World War I, women as well. The increased electorate demanded new political techniques. No longer could gentleman politicians gain power by winning the support of a small, male, socially privileged electorate. A mass audience had to be addressed. Although many politicians at first refused to degrade themselves by appealing for support to such an audience, we can see emerging in late-nineteenth-century campaigns the modern political objective—and the requirement—of swaying large numbers of voters.

In 1879 and 1880, the British statesman William E. Gladstone (1809–1898) won election to Parliament from Midlothian County, Scotland, following a campaign that became the model for modern ones, especially after Gladstone built his victory into his second term as prime minister. In Midlothian Gladstone delivered

numerous public speeches. He presented many of these from the platform of his campaign train at a variety of locations, the first "whistle-stop campaign." Gladstone's campaign style found imitators in other democracies, although they did not always achieve his success. In the U.S. presidential campaign of 1896, the Democratic candidate, William Jennings Bryan (1860–1925), traveled about 18,000 miles and gave more than 600 speeches in an unsuccessful campaign against the Republican candidate, William McKinley (1843–1901). McKinley, who epitomized the old-style campaigner, simply received visitors from the press and public at the front porch of his Ohio home. Other candidates in many democracies would follow the example of Gladstone and Bryan.

Technological advances aided political leaders in their appeals for mass support. By the 1890s, developments like the Linotype machine, which mechanized typesetting, greatly reduced the price of newspapers and other printed materials for an increasingly literate public. Mass-circulation daily newspapers had tremendous potential for shaping public opinion. Political leaders also used other technological developments in delivering their messages. By 1920 the motion picture, photograph, radio, and microphone and public-address system all represented new media through which to influence the public.

At the same time that new media became available to political leaders, a greater understanding of how to influence public opinion was emerging

[336]

in the early-twentieth-century West. During World War I, many belligerent countries employed increasingly sophisticated propaganda techniques to sustain the morale of their own citizens or to erode the will to fight among enemy populations. The lessons learned on influencing public opinion were not forgotten, as we will see.[3]

Industrial mass production required mass markets, and in the United States modern advertising techniques developed to stimulate the consumption necessary to sustain production. Advertising had political applications as well. One advertising strategy is to generate interest in a new product by creating suspense about it. When the Nazis launched a new Berlin newspaper, *Der Angriff* (*The Attack*), in 1927, a poster campaign was launched to heighten interest in it. The first posters issued simply stated, "The Attack?" The next group of posters proclaimed, "The Attack takes place on July 4!" The last set of posters was informational, alerting readers that the paper would appear on Mondays, that its motto was "For the Suppressed against the Exploiters," and that "Every German man and every German woman will read 'The Attack' and subscribe to it!"[4]

Even science, particularly psychology, contributed to the understanding of human thought essential to those who sought to shape opinion. The French social psychologist Gustave Le Bon (1841–1931), for example, affected Hitler's political technique. Le Bon's ideas, although doubted today, were highly influential in the early twentieth century. A student of mass psychology, Le Bon claimed that the mind of the crowd was most susceptible to sentiment and emotion, not reason.[5]

The rapid pace of technological development and the equally swift emergence of techniques for molding public opinion meant that, by the 1920s, there existed an incompletely understood, underused, but nonetheless formidable arsenal for the politically ambitious to employ in attaining power. Forces prepared to exploit these technological and methodological developments emerged in the politically unstable environment of much of the post–World War I West.

Rooted in defeat, frustration in World War I, or the economic debacle of the Great Depression beginning in 1929, totalitarian movements emerged in many European countries. None of these movements proved more dangerous to traditional Western values than a German party that began insignificantly in 1919 as one of a multitude of right-wing, nationalist parties founded in response to the German defeat in the Great War. The party came to be known as the National Socialist German Workers' Party (Nazi), and Adolf Hitler quickly emerged not only as its leader but as a master

3. Hitler in *Mein Kampf* (translated by Ralph Manheim [Boston: Houghton Mifflin, 1943], pp. 176–186) wrote of the lessons he had drawn from Allied propaganda during World War I.

4. Described in Ernest K. Bramsted, *Goebbels and National Socialist Propaganda, 1925–1945* (East Lansing, Mich.: Michigan State University Press, 1965), p. 30.

5. Le Bon's great work was *The Crowd: A Study of the Popular Mind,* originally published in 1897 and available in German.

of the new style of politics, including political propaganda.

The successful propagandist must correctly identify the fears and hopes of the people he or she wishes to influence. In Germany after World War I, Nazi propaganda had a great number of fears and hopes to exploit. Most Germans rejected the Treaty of Versailles that ended the war. Humiliated by the treaty's assignment of war guilt to Germany, they were also angered by the huge reparations their country was forced to pay the victorious allies. German nationalists especially rejected the unilateral disarmament the treaty sought to impose on Germany. All Germans hoped for some revision of the Treaty of Versailles.

Some Germans blamed the nation's defeat on internal enemies, not on battlefield disasters. These persons, mostly conservative, identified two chief groups on which to place responsibility for the internal dissent at the war's end that had brought the overthrow of Emperor William II (Kaiser Wilhelm II) and armistice. The first groups condemned for the defeat were the parties of the left, the socialists and communists, who had participated in the revolution of 1918 that created the Weimar Republic. To many, the communists seemed the greatest threat because that party had attempted to seize power and create a Marxist state by force in the Spartacist Revolt of 1919. The communist threat, moreover, persisted after 1919. The party's voting bloc grew as the economic problems of the Great Depression intensified,

and many feared that the communists might gain power through election.

The other group on whom some Germans sought to fix the blame of their defeat was the country's small Jewish minority. Such Germans drew on nineteenth-century nationalist prejudices to allege some Jewish involvement in Germany's defeat. Certain political leaders of the early German republic, the men whose government signed the Versailles Treaty, were Jews. One prominent Jewish official, Walter Rathenau (1867–1922), died at the hands of a nationalist fanatic.

The Great Depression also increased Germans' fears after 1929. The depression hit Germany particularly hard, threatening economic ruin to many. Many parties and movements identified those fears and hopes of postwar Germans and sought to address them by rejecting the Treaty of Versailles, by portraying themselves as anticommunist or anti-Semitic, and by proposing solutions to the depression. But, as we will see, it was the skill of Hitler and the Nazis in the new politics and propaganda that allowed them to exploit most effectively Germans' fears and hopes to gain power.

It was Hitler who transformed a party that essentially had been little more than a collection of malcontents in the back room of a Munich beer hall into a movement with a considerable following in the 1920s. It was Hitler who gave the party a visual identity by adopting its symbol, the swastika, and by creating its banners. It was also Hitler who exploited the alienation of many war veterans by drawing them into the S.A. (*Sturm Abteilung*), the Storm Troopers or uniformed, paramilitary branch of the party, which was prepared to use violence and intimidation against communists and socialists. And it was Hitler who launched an abortive attempt in 1923 to seize power forcibly for his party.

Hitler's failed revolution resulted in his brief imprisonment, during which he wrote *Mein Kampf* (*My Struggle*), the political statement of his movement. On his release Hitler resolved to seek power within the political system—that is, to win power through the electoral system of the German republic. To his quest for power Hitler brought the Nazi party apparatus and symbols, his excellent oratorical ability, and, most dangerously, a keen understanding of the uses of political propaganda and modern media to mold public opinion. Aiding him in presenting his party to German voters was Joseph Goebbels (1897–1945), a man whose speaking abilities, understanding of propaganda and modern media, and political unscrupulousness rivaled Hitler's own.

In his quest for power after 1923, Hitler led the Nazis through a number of electoral campaigns. The first results of Nazi appeals to German voters disappointed many of Hitler's followers. Indeed, in elections to the Reichstag, Germany's parliament, the party's vote actually declined during the 1920s. In the elections of May 1924, it captured 6.5 percent of the vote; that total declined to 3.0 percent in December 1924 and 2.6 percent in May 1928. The party's elec-

toral breakthrough of 1930, however, reversed this trend as the Nazis increased their share of the Reichstag vote to 18.3 percent. Certainly, in achieving their victory, the Nazis' extreme nationalist message capitalized on the Young Plan of 1929, which had failed to reduce the war reparation payments to the Allies so deeply resented by many Germans. The growing severity of the Great Depression after 1929 also encouraged many Germans to look to the strong leadership that Hitler claimed to offer. As party membership and dues grew, and as Hitler secured some limited financial aid from a few wealthy opponents of the Young Plan such as Alfred Hugenberg,[6] for the first time the Nazis had sufficient funds to exploit the modern media thoroughly.

The Nazi share of the vote increased rapidly after 1930. The party especially demonstrated its media skills in 1932, when Hitler ran for president of Germany against the incumbent, the octogenarian war hero Field Marshal Paul von Hindenburg. Although Hindenburg won the election with 53 percent of the vote to Hitler's 36.8 percent, the campaign built momentum for the Nazis and

6. **Alfred Hugenberg** (1865–1951): leader of the Nationalist party and a bigoted conservative ultranationalist with tremendous wealth based in industry and great influence founded on his control of a number of newspapers and Germany's largest film and newsreel firm. His newsreels, shown regularly in German theaters, and his newspapers gave the Nazis considerable coverage. Like other conservatives, Hugenberg made the mistake of classifying Hitler with other politicians. Hitler quickly excluded Hugenberg from the government once the Nazis had gained power.

helped them to perfect their campaign style. In the Reichstag elections held in July 1932, the Nazis won 37.4 percent of the vote to become the largest single party in parliament, a distinction they retained despite a diminished Nazi 33.1 percent of the vote in Reichstag elections in November 1932. On the basis of these victories, which gave the Nazis control of the largest single bloc of seats in the Reichstag, conservative associates of President von Hindenburg finally convinced him to name Hitler chancellor or prime minister on January 30, 1933. The Nazis had gained control of the government, and German democracy was their first victim: by the end of the year the country was a one-party, totalitarian state.

To achieve power, the Nazis had persuaded substantial numbers of German voters to support their candidates. Certainly in the aftermath of Germany's defeat in 1918, the party's extreme nationalism attracted support, as did its anti-Semitism, which blamed the country's economic and political woes on its tiny Jewish minority. This Nazi political rhetoric of hatred ultimately became government policy when Hitler gained power. Anti-Semitism took on brutal form in the Holocaust. Extreme nationalism manifested itself in the Nazi goal of settling Germans in eastern Europe by pushing out the area's Slavic natives. But other German parties in the 1920s and early 1930s also expressed anti-Semitic and nationalistic ideas. Your objective in this chapter is to determine how Nazi use of modern media and techniques, such as propaganda for molding public opinion, allowed Hitler's party to draw the German voter's attention. As you assess the evidence that follows, you should ask yourself what kind of image the Nazis projected. Why did it appeal to German voters? How did the Nazis use media to aid their rise to power? As a result of your analysis, you should be able to answer in some form that most disturbing question, "How could it have happened?"

SOURCES AND METHOD

This chapter presents a variety of evidence: theoretical writings on Nazi political strategy, visual propaganda used by Nazis to publicize their cause, and observations on the public reception of Hitler's media campaign. Through individual and comparative study of these sources, you should be able to determine the nature of the attraction of the Nazis for German voters.

The evidence opens with two selections by Hitler on the means for gaining power. Sources 1 and 2 are taken from Hitler's *Mein Kampf*, which he wrote during his imprisonment in 1923–1924. In this work, often ignored in his early days, Hitler stated much of his future program, including his rabidly anti-Jewish and anti-Marxist policies and his plans to expand Germany eastward. In the evidence presented in this chapter, you will read Hitler's ideas on the use of propaganda and other tactics for coming to power. How were the ideas for seizing power that he expressed in 1924 to be realized within a decade? How would you assess his understanding of human psychology?

When you finish the Hitler materials, you will find an assortment of evidence selected to further your analysis of how the Nazis sought to win support for their party. You will be examining, in effect, a thoroughly modern public relations effort, complete with slogans. In Source 3, assess the nature of the Nazi propaganda effort as defined by its director, Joseph Goebbels. Why do you think Goebbels so closely controlled the party's propaganda?

Consider next the S.A., remembering, of course, that orders like that in Source 4 are not always rigidly obeyed by subordinates in any organization. Examine the pictorial evidence on the S.A. in Sources 5 and 6. The banners express Nazi slogans; the Regensburg S.A. banner proclaims, "Everything for the Fatherland." Nazi meetings always opened with solemn processions of such banners. What impression did the marching men seek to convey to their audience on the streets of Spandau?

Next read Source 7, the report of the brawl in the Pharus Hall in 1927. You should understand that this brawl was no accident; Goebbels deliberately scheduled the meeting to take place in a hall used by the Nazis' enemies, the communist and socialist political and labor groups. The hall, moreover, was in the heart of a left-wing, working-class district of Berlin. What could Goebbels have hoped to gain from the fight that was bound to

ensue from his provocative action in selecting such a meeting site?

The next evidence consists of posters produced by the Nazis. The poster, a traditional political medium, was used extensively by the Nazis. They relied especially on posters in their early days, before they secured the funds necessary to exploit more novel media. The poster in Source 8 was part of the propaganda campaign Nazi leaders organized for the spring 1924 German legislative elections. At the time of the elections, Hitler remained in prison as a result of his failed attempt to seize power in 1923, and his party nominally was outlawed. Thus party leaders entered the campaign as part of a right-wing, nationalist coalition, the "Völkischen Block" identified on the poster. The German word *Volk* is difficult to translate. Superficially, it may be translated as "people" or "nation," but for early-twentieth-century Germans the word had a much more complex meaning conveying the innate superiority of German culture, language, and people over non-German cultures and peoples. Thus its use to identify a right-wing, nationalistic political alliance was not accidental, and was entirely consistent with Nazi ideology. Indeed, the Nazi origins of this poster are evident in the party's insignia, the swastika, in the lower corners of the poster. Analyze the poster to ascertain what sentiments the Nazis appealed to in post–World War I Germany and to which classes they looked for support. What group did the "String-puller" represent (notice his watch chain)? What message did his identity convey to Germans?

[341]

The second poster, Source 9, conveys much about Germany in the 1920s. Why might the Nazis address females? Of what problems did this poster, issued in the midst of the depression, remind Germans? What did it promise them? The third poster, Source 10, was the work of a skilled propaganda artist, "Mjolnir" ("Hammer"), who drew cartoons extensively for the Berlin newspaper *Der Angriff*, edited by Goebbels. Analyze the artist's message by examining the faces of the Storm Troopers. What sentiment do you find there? What sort of message does this poster convey about the party and its solutions for Germany?

Another Nazi political device was the public mass meeting, designed to convey the impression of vast support for the party. It was a technique Hitler learned early while observing Social Democratic demonstrations as a youth in Vienna. He wrote in *Mein Kampf*:

> With what changed feeling I now gazed at the endless columns of a mass demonstration of Viennese workers that took place one day as they marched past four abreast! For nearly two hours I stood there watching with bated breath the gigantic human dragon slowly winding by.

As their resources increased, the Nazis perfected the mass meeting. Source 11 shows one such rally in Berlin's Sports Palace, a favored site because it seated a large audience of 12,000 persons. Events like this were always carefully staged: The aisles are lined with the party faithful, ready for the entry of the speakers, accompanied by a uniformed S.A. guard unit and party banners. Why would such an elaborate spectacle have been important to the party cause?

The Nazis also employed music as propaganda to win support. The person whose name the song bears in Source 12, Horst Wessel, was a young Nazi who wrote the words to the song as a poem. The words eventually were set to a traditional stirring tune, but Horst Wessel himself drifted away from the party in pursuit of a female prostitute. He took up residence with her and was fatally shot by her procurer, who coincidentally was a communist, in February 1930. In Goebbels's hands, Horst Wessel's misspent life was transformed into that of a hero martyred in the Nazis' cause by their communist enemies. His song became Germany's second national anthem after *Deutschland über Alles* (*Germany Above All*) in the Nazi era. In reading the song's words, identify the problems it identifies. What benefits does the song claim the party offered Germans?

Also part of Nazi political propaganda was the creation of what Goebbels himself called the "Führer (Leader) Myth." This myth, which Goebbels regarded as one of his great propaganda accomplishments, attempted to convince Germans that a strong, courageous, and brilliant Hitler personified a Germany restored from its defeat. In its more extreme manifestations, the myth almost deified Hitler, appealing to many Germans accustomed to strong rulers during the monarchy and therefore unhappy with what they believed to be the weak government of the republic. Source 13 is drawn from an elementary school textbook published shortly after the Nazis gained power, but it describes Hitler's campaign for power. What qualities did the party's propaganda apparatus wish the young to believe that Hitler possessed?

The Nazis did not come to power solely through conveying a positive image for their party and leader, however. They also used propaganda to exploit fears, employed violence to intimidate voters, and used new technologies to sway the thinking of their fellow Germans. Source 14 is a pamphlet, issued, you must remember, in the midst of the economic collapse of the early 1930s. Recall the events of Germany's past as you read it, and analyze its appeal.

The violence of the Hitler movement can best be viewed on the local level. The graph in Source 15 presents the rhythm of political life in the German town of Northeim. The number of political meetings, to which the Nazis contributed more than their share, increased sharply at election times. What else increased?

Source 16 presents the political beliefs of Dr. Joseph Goebbels, a fervent Nazi and a master of political propaganda. Convinced of his own historical importance, Goebbels kept a diary from his earliest days in politics to give future generations a

record of his thought and activities. He was still making entries in 1945 as the war ended. When Russian armies closed in on Berlin, Goebbels committed suicide. His diary, like any diary, must be used with caution, because most writers tend to put their own behavior and motivations in the best light. Nonetheless, it does offer an important perspective on Goebbels's propaganda work. Assess his command of his job as you read the selection. What new technologies did he employ in winning popular support for the Nazis?

The evidence in this chapter concludes with two observations on the impact of Nazi efforts to win support among Germans. The first is a report by a German Protestant leader noting membership losses from the Protestant youth movement to the Nazis. The second is by the American correspondent William L. Shirer (1904–1993), who covered events in Germany from 1934 to 1941. A perceptive observer of the Hitler movement, Shirer was able to assess the kind of appeal it had been building in Germany during the years before he arrived. What appeal to Germans do these two very different persons note in the Nazi movement?

Now turn to the evidence. You should read it with the foregoing considerations in mind, seeking to answer the central questions of this chapter: What image did the Nazis convey to German voters? Why did they appeal to German voters? How did the Nazis use media to aid their rise to power?

[343]

THE EVIDENCE

FUNDAMENTAL POLITICAL
STRATEGIES OF THE
NAZI PARTY

Sources 1 and 2 from Adolf Hitler, Mein Kampf, *translated by Ralph Manheim (Boston: Houghton Mifflin, 1943), pp. 178–184, 343, 582; pp. 42–44. Copyright 1943 and renewed 1971 by Houghton Mifflin Company. Reprinted by permission of Houghton Mifflin Company. All rights reserved.*

1. Hitler on the Nature and Purpose of Propaganda

The goal of a political reform movement will never be reached by enlightenment work or by influencing ruling circles, but only by the achievement of political power. Every world-moving idea has not only the right, but also the duty, of securing, those means which make possible the execution of its ideas. Success is the one earthly judge concerning the right or wrong of such an effort, and under success we must not understand, as in the year 1918, the achievement of power in itself, but an exercise of that power that will benefit the nation. Thus, a coup d'état must not be regarded as successful if, as senseless state's attorneys in Germany think today, the revolutionaries have succeeded in possessing themselves of the state power, but only if, by the realization of the purposes and aims underlying such a revolutionary action, more benefit accrues to the nation than under the past régime. Something which cannot very well be claimed for the German revolution, as the gangster job of autumn, 1918, calls itself.[7]. . .

The victory of an idea will be possible the sooner, the more comprehensively propaganda has prepared people as a whole and the more exclusive, rigid, and firm the organization which carries out the fight in practice. . . .

To whom should propaganda be addressed? To the scientifically trained intelligentsia or to the less educated masses?

It must be addressed always and exclusively to the masses.

What the intelligentsia—or those who today unfortunately often go by that name—what they need is not propaganda but scientific instruction. The content of propaganda is not science any more than the object represented in a poster is art. The art of the poster lies in the designer's ability to attract the

7. **the gangster job of autumn 1918**: the revolution of October and November 1918 that overthrew Emperor William II and established the Weimar Republic. Hitler, like many of the German right, believed that revolution to have been the work of socialists, communists, and Jews, who, by toppling the old government, had "stabbed in the back" the German army at the front in World War I and made defeat in that conflict inevitable.

attention of the crowd by form and color. A poster advertising an art exhibit must direct the attention of the public to the art being exhibited; the better it succeeds in this, the greater is the art of the poster itself. The poster should give the masses an idea of the significance of the exhibition, it should not be a substitute for the art on display. Anyone who wants to concern himself with the art itself must do more than study the poster; and it will not be enough for him just to saunter through the exhibition. We may expect him to examine and immerse himself in the individual works, and thus little by little form a fair opinion.

A similar situation prevails with what we today call propaganda.

The function of propaganda does not lie in the scientific training of the individual, but in calling the masses' attention to certain facts, processes, necessities, etc., whose significance is thus for the first time placed within their field of vision.

The whole art consists in doing this so skillfully that everyone will be convinced that the fact is real, the process necessary, the necessity correct, etc. But since propaganda is not and cannot be the necessity in itself, since its function, like the poster, consists in attracting the attention of the crowd, and not in educating those who are already educated or who are striving after education and knowledge, its effect for the most part must be aimed at the emotions and only to a very limited degree at the so-called intellect.

All propaganda must be popular and its intellectual level must be adjusted to the most limited intelligence among those it is addressed to. Consequently, the greater the mass it is intended to reach, the lower its purely intellectual level will have to be. But if, as in propaganda for sticking out a war, the aim is to influence a whole people, we must avoid excessive intellectual demands on our public, and too much caution cannot be exerted in this direction.

The more modest its intellectual ballast, the more exclusively it takes into consideration the emotions of the masses, the more effective it will be. And this is the best proof of the soundness or unsoundness of a propaganda campaign, and not success in pleasing a few scholars or young aesthetes.

The art of propaganda lies in understanding the emotional ideas of the great masses and finding, through a psychologically correct form, the way to the attention and thence to the heart of the broad masses. The fact that our bright boys do not understand this merely shows how mentally lazy and conceited they are.

Once we understand how necessary it is for propaganda to be adjusted to the broad mass, the following rule results:

It is a mistake to make propaganda many-sided, like scientific instruction, for instance.

The receptivity of the great masses is very limited, their intelligence is small, but their power of forgetting is enormous. In consequence of these facts, all effective propaganda must be limited to a very few points and must harp on these in slogans until the last member of the public understands what you want him to understand by your slogan. As soon as you sacrifice this slogan and try to be many-sided, the effect will piddle away, for the crowd can neither digest nor retain the material offered. In this way the result is weakened and in the end entirely cancelled out.

[345]

Thus we see that propaganda must follow a simple line and correspondingly the basic tactics must be psychologically sound. . . .

But the most brilliant propagandist techniques will yield no success unless one fundamental principle is borne in mind constantly and with unflagging attention. It must confine itself to a few points and repeat them over and over. Here, as so often in this world, persistence is the first and most important requirement for success.

2. Hitler on Terror in Politics

Like the woman, whose psychic state is determined less by grounds of abstract reason than by an indefinable emotional longing for a force which will complement her nature, and who, consequently, would rather bow to a strong man than dominate a weakling, likewise the masses love a commander more than a petitioner and feel inwardly more satisfied by a doctrine, tolerating no other beside itself, than by the granting of liberalistic freedom with which, as a rule, they can do little, and are prone to feel that they have been abandoned. They are equally unaware of their shameless spiritual terrorization and the hideous abuse of their human freedom, for they absolutely fail to suspect the inner insanity of the whole doctrine. All they see is the ruthless force and brutality of its calculated manifestations, to which they always submit in the end. . . .

I achieved an equal understanding of the importance of physical terror toward the individual and the masses.

Here, too, the psychological effect can be calculated with precision.

Terror at the place of employment, in the factory, in the meeting hall, and on the occasion of mass demonstrations will always be successful unless opposed by equal terror.

NAZI TECHNIQUES FOR PUBLICIZING THEIR CAUSE

Sources 3 and 4 from Jeremy Noakes and Geoffrey Pridham, editors, Documents on Nazism, 1919–1945 *(New York: Viking, 1975), pp. 103–104; pp. 163–164. Copyright © 1975 by Jeremy Noakes and Geoffrey Pridham. Reprinted by permission of Sterling Lord Literistic, Inc.*

3. Joseph Goebbels, Directives for the Presidential Campaign of 1932

(1) Reich Propaganda Department to all *Gaue*[8] and all *Gau* Propaganda Departments.

8. **Gaue:** the administrative divisions of Germany set up by the Nazi party.

. . . A striking slogan:

> Those who want everything to stay as it is vote for Hindenburg. Those who want everything changed vote for Hitler. . . .

(2) Reich Propaganda Department to all *Gaue* and all *Gau* Propaganda Departments.

. . . Hitler Poster. The Hitler poster depicts a fascinating Hitler head on a completely black background. Subtitle: white on black—"Hitler." In accordance with the Führer's wish this poster is to be put up only during the final days [of the campaign]. Since experience shows that during the final days there is a variety of coloured posters, this poster with its completely black background will contrast with all the others and will produce a tremendous effect on the masses. . . .

(3) Reich Propaganda Department
Instructions for the National Socialist Press for the election of the Reich President

1. From Easter Tuesday 29 March until Sunday 10 April inclusive, all National Socialist papers, both daily and weekly, must appear in an enlarged edition with a tripled circulation. Two-thirds of this tripled circulation must be made available, without charge, to the *Gau* leadership responsible for its area of distribution for propaganda purposes. . . .

2. From Easter Tuesday 29 March until Sunday 3 April inclusive, a special topic must be dealt with every day on the first page of all our papers in a big spread. Tuesday 29 March: Hitler as a man. Wednesday 30 March: Hitler as a fighter (gigantic achievement through his willpower, etc.). Friday 1 April: Hitler as a statesman—plenty of photos. . . .

3. On Sunday 3 April, at noon (end of an Easter truce), the great propaganda journey of the Führer through Germany will start, through which about a million people are to be reached directly through our Führer's speeches. . . . The press organization is planned so that four press centres will be set up in Germany, which in turn will pass on immediately any telephone calls to the other papers of their area, whose names have been given them.

4. S.A. Order 111 of Adolf Hitler, 1926

1. The SA will appear in public only in closed formation. This is at the same time one of the most powerful forms of propaganda. The sight of a large number of men inwardly and outwardly uniform and disciplined, whose total

commitment to fighting is clearly visible or can be sensed, makes the deepest impression on every German and speaks a more convincing and inspiring language to his heart than speech, logic, or the written word is ever capable of doing.

Calm composure and natural behaviour underline the impression of strength—the strength of marching columns and the strength of the cause for which they are marching.

The inner strength of the cause makes the German conclude instinctively that it is right: "for only what is right, honest and good can release real strength." Where whole crowds purposefully risk life and limb and their livelihood for a cause (not in the upsurge of sudden mass suggestion), the cause must be great and true!

Here lies the task of the SA from the point of view of propaganda and re-cruiting. The SA leaders must gear the details and forms of their appearances to a common line.

2. This instinctive "proof of truth" is not underlined but disturbed and dissipated by the addition of logical arguments and propaganda. The fol-lowing should be avoided: cheers and heckling, posters about day-to-day controversies, abuse, accompanying speeches, leaflets, festivals, public amusements.

3. It is inappropriate for the SA to work in one way one day and differently the next, according to circumstances. The SA must always and on principle re-frain from all actual political propaganda and agitation. This should remain the task of the political leadership alone. However, each SA man is also a member of the Party and as such of course must cooperate as much as he can in the propaganda of the political leadership. But not the SA as such. Not the SA men on duty and in uniform.

The SA man is the holy freedom fighter. The member of the Party is the clever propagandist and skilled agitator. Political propaganda tries to en-lighten the opponent, to argue with him, to understand his point of view, to enter into his thoughts, to agree with him to a certain extent. But when the SA arrives on the scene, this stops. It makes no concessions. It goes all out. It only recognizes the motto (metaphorically): Kill or be killed!

4. It is forbidden for an SA to appeal to the public (or its opponents) orally or in writing, either through proclamations, announcements, leaflets, press "corrections," letters, advertisements, invitations to festivals or meetings, or in any other way.

Public consecrations of the colours and sports competitions must take place within the framework of an event organized by a local branch, which alone is-sues the invitations or announcements for it.

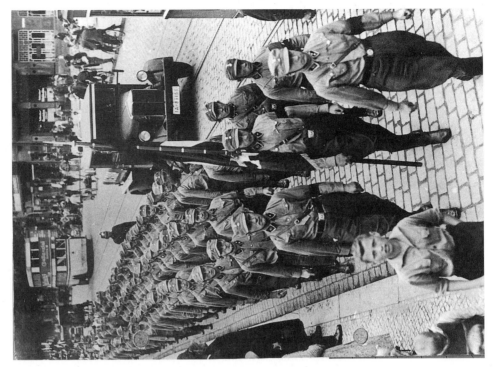

6. S.A. Propaganda Rally in Spandau, 1932

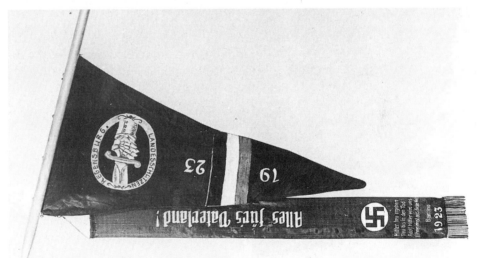

Sources 5 and 6 from Bundesarchiv, Koblenz.

5. Banners of the Regensburg
S.A.: "Everything for the
Fatherland, 1923"

[349]

7. Report of a Nazi Meeting Held in a Heavily Communist Quarter of Berlin, February 1927

On the 11th of this month the Party held a public mass meeting in the "Pharus [Beer] Halls" in Wedding, the real working-class quarter, with the subject: "The Collapse of the Bourgeois Class State." Comrade Dr Goebbels was the speaker. It was quite clear to us what that meant. It had to be visibly shown that National Socialism is determined to reach the workers. We succeeded once before in getting a foothold in Wedding. There were huge crowds at the meeting. More than 1,000 people filled the hall whose political composition was four-fifths SA to one-fifth KPD.[9] But the latter had gathered their main forces in the street. When the meeting was opened by Comrade Daluege, the SA leader, there were, as was expected, provocative shouts of "On a point of order!" After the KPD members had been told that *we,* not they, decided points of order, and that they would have the right to ask questions after the talk by Comrade Dr Goebbels, the first scuffling broke out. Peace seemed to be restored until there was renewed heckling. When the chairman announced that the hecklers would be sent out if the interruptions continued, the KPD worked themselves into a frenzy. Meanwhile, the SA had gradually surrounded the centre of the disturbance, and the Communists, sensing the danger, suddenly became aggressive. What followed all happened within three or four minutes. Within seconds both sides had picked up chairs, beer mugs, even tables, and a savage fight began. The Communists were gradually pushed under the gallery which we had taken care to occupy and soon chairs and glasses came hurtling down from there also. The fight was quickly decided: the KPD left with 85 wounded, more or less: that is to say, they could not get down the stairs as fast as they had calmly and "innocently" climbed them. On our side we counted 3 badly wounded and about 10–12 slightly. When the police appeared the fight was already over. Marxist terrorism had been bloodily suppressed.

9. **Kommunistische Partei Deutschlands:** the German Communist party.

Source 8 from Anshcläge: Ebenhausen: Langewiesche/Bradt Verlag.

8. Poster: "The String-Puller. White Collar and Manual Laborers: Vote for the Völkischen Block," 1924

10. Poster: "National Socialism: The Organized Will of the People," 1932

9. Poster: "Women! Millions of Men Are Without Work. Millions of Children Are Without a Future. Save the German Family! Vote for Adolf Hitler!," 1932

Source 11 from Bundesarchiv, Koblenz.

11. A National Socialist Rally in the Berlin Sports Palace, September 1930

Source 12 from Liederbuch der Nationalsozialistischen Deutschen Arbeiterpartei *(Munich: Zentralverlag der NSDAP, 1938). Selection translated by Julius R. Ruff.*

12. "The Horst Wessel Song," ca 1930

Raise high the banner! Close the serried ranks!
S.A. marches on with calm, firm stride.
Comrades killed by the Red Front and the Reaction[10]
March in spirit in our ranks.

Clear the streets for the brown battalions![11]
Clear the streets for the Storm Troopers!
The swastika gives hope to millions.
The day of freedom and bread is breaking.

10. **Red Front:** the *Rot Frontkämpfer Bund* or Red Fighters League, the communist opposition to the Storm Troopers. The more traditional right, the Nationalist party, which sought a restoration of a monarchy and is here called the **Reaction,** had an armed force, too, uniformed in green.
11. The S.A. uniform was brown.

[353]

The roll call is heard for the last time!
We all stand ready for the struggle!
Soon Hitler's banner will fly over every street
And Germany's bondage will soon end.

Source 13 from George L. Mosse, editor, Nazi Culture: Intellectual, Cultural, and Social Life in the Third Reich *(New York: Grosset and Dunlap, 1966), pp. 291–293. Selection translated by the editor. Used by permission of George L. Mosse.*

13. Otto Dietrich, Description of Hitler's Campaign by Airplane, 1932

On April 8, 1932, a severe storm, beyond all imagining, raged over Germany. Hail rattled down from dark clouds. Flash floods devastated fields and gardens. Muddy foam washed over streets and railroad tracks, and the hurricane uprooted even the oldest and biggest trees.

We are driving to the Mannheim Airport. Today no one would dare expose an airplane to the fury of the elements. The German Lufthansa has suspended all air traffic.

In the teeming rain stands the solid mass of the most undaunted of our followers. They want to be present, they want to see for themselves when the Führer entrusts himself to an airplane in this raging storm.

Without a moment's hesitation the Führer orders that we take off at once. We have an itinerary to keep, for in western Germany hundreds of thousands are waiting.

It is only with the greatest difficulty that the ground crew and the SA troopers, with long poles in their strong fists, manage to hold on to the wings of the plane, so that the gale does not hurl it into the air and wreck it. The giant motors begin to turn over. Impatient with its fetters, the plane begins to buck and shake, eager for the takeoff on the open runway.

One more short rearing up and our wild steed sweeps across the greensward. A few perilous jumps, one last short touch with earth, and presto we are riding through the air straight into the witches' broth.

This is no longer flying, this is a whirling dance which today we remember only as a faraway dream. Now we jump across the aerial downdrafts, now we whip our way through tattered clouds, again a whirlpool threatens to drag us down, and then it seems that a giant catapult hurls us into steep heights.

And yet, what a feeling of security is in us in the face of this fury of the elements! The Führer's absolute serenity transmits itself to all of us. In every hour of danger he is ruled by his granite-like faith in his world-historical mission, the unshakable certainty that Providence will keep him from danger for the accomplishment of his great task.

Even here he remained the pre-eminent man, who masters danger because in his innermost being he has risen far above it. In this ruthless contest between man and machine the Führer attentively follows the heroic battle of our Master Pilot Bauer as he steers straight through the gale, or quickly jumps across a whole storm field, and then again narrowly avoids a threatening cloud wall, while the radio operator on board zealously catches the signals sent by the airfields.

Source 14 from Jeremy Noakes and Geoffrey Pridham, editors, Documents on Nazism, 1919–1945 *(New York: Viking, 1975), p. 106. Copyright © 1974 by Jeremy Noakes. Reprinted by permission of Sterling Lord Literistic, Inc.*

14. Nazi Pamphlet, ca 1932

Attention! Gravediggers at work!

Middle-class citizens![12] Retailers! Craftsmen! Tradesmen!

A new blow aimed at your ruin is being prepared and carried out in Hanover!

The present system enables the gigantic concern

WOOLWORTH (America)

supported by finance capital, to build a new vampire business in the centre of the city in the Georgstrasse to expose you to complete ruin. This is the wish and aim of the black-red[13] system as expressed in the following remarks of Marxist leaders.

The Marxist Engels declared in May 1890: "If capital destroys the small artisans and retailers it does a good thing. . . ."

That is the black-red system of today!

Put an end to this system and its abettors! Defend yourself, middle-class citizen! Join the mighty organization that alone is in a position to conquer your arch-enemies. Fight with us in the Section for Craftsmen and Retail Traders within the great freedom movement of Adolf Hitler!

Put an end to the system!

Mittelstand, vote for List 8![14]

12. **Middle-class citizens:** this is a rather imprecise translation of the original German *Mittelstand.* That word, which is difficult to translate, here describes a very specific segment of society to whom the Nazis made special appeal: small shopkeepers and craftsmen whose livelihoods increasingly were threatened by competition from large department stores and big industrial concerns.

13. Prussia was governed by a coalition of the Catholic Center party and the Social Democrats. Because of its association with the Church, the Center was labeled "Black"; the leftist socialists were labeled "Red."

14. **Mittelstand:** middle-class shopkeepers and craftsmen.

Source 15 adapted from William Sheridan Allen, The Nazi Seizure of Power: The Experience of a Single German Town, 1922–1945, *revised ed. (New York: Franklin Watts, 1984), p. 321. Copyright © 1965, 1984 by William Sheridan Allen. Used with permission of the publisher, Franklin Watts, Inc.*

15. Political Violence in Northeim, Germany, 1930–1932

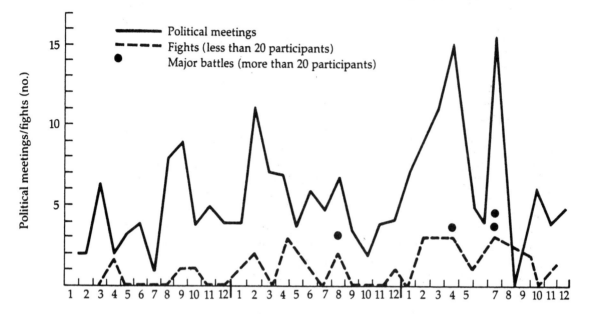

Source 16 from Joseph Goebbels, My Part in Germany's Fight, *translated by Kurt Fielder (New York: Howard Fertig, 1979), pp. 44, 47–48, 55, 66, 145–146, 214.*

16. Joseph Goebbels, *My Part in Germany's Fight,* 1934

February 29th, 1932.

Our propaganda is working at high pressure.

The clerical work is finished. Now the technical side of the fight begins. What enormous preparations are necessary to organize such a vast distribution!

Reported to the Leader (Hitler) at noon. I gave him details as to the measures we are taking. The election campaign is chiefly to be fought by means of placards and addresses. We have not much capital, but as the Party is working gratuitously a little money goes a long way.

Fifty thousand gramophone records have been made, which are so small they can be slipped into an ordinary envelope. The supporters of the Government will be astonished when they place these miniature records on the gramophone!

In Berlin everything is going well.

A film (of me) is being made and I speak a few words in it for about ten minutes. It is to be shown in all public gardens and squares of the larger cities. . . .

March 8th, 1932.

Dictate two articles and heaps of handbills. The placard war has reached its climax. Up till now we lead in the race.

Interview with the *Popolo d'Italia.*[15] I describe our methods and means of propaganda. The representative of this influential Italian paper is positively dumbfounded. "The vastest and most up-to-date propaganda of Europe." . . .

March 18th, 1932.

A critical innovation: the Leader will conduct this next campaign by plane. By this means he will be able to speak three or four times a day at various places as opportunity serves, and address about one and a half millions of people in spite of the time being so short.

April 14th, 1932.

The Leader is planning a new plane campaign for the Prussian elections. He intends to start on Sunday. His perseverance is admirable, and it is amazing how he stands the continual strain.

At work again organizing his great 'plane trips. Now we have quite a lot of experience in these matters.

An important problem is how to make use of the Leader's propaganda flights for the Press. Everything has to be minutely prepared and organized beforehand.

October 4th, 1932.

Monday: Berlin. Prepared for the Leader's meeting at Munich. Dashed off designs for seven huge placards. Things knocked off quickly and enthusiastically are always good.

It is difficult to adapt men used to editorial work to the necessities of electioneering. They are too accurate and slow. . . .

---

15. *Popolo d'Italia:* a newspaper founded by the Italian Fascist leader Mussolini in 1914 and edited by him until he gained political control of Italy in 1922, this journal was the official organ of the Fascist dictatorship in Italy by 1932. Indeed, until the newspaper ceased publication in 1943, Mussolini still set its general editorial direction and even contributed articles himself.

January 18th, 1933.

In the evening we go to see the film "Rebel," by Luis Trencker. A first-class production of an artistic film. Thus I could imagine the film of the future, revolutionary in character, with grand mass-scenes, composed with enormous vital energy. In one scene, in which a gigantic crucifix is carried out of a small church by the revolutionaries, the audience is deeply moved. Here you really see what can be done with the film as an artistic medium, when it is really understood. We are all much impressed.

February 10th, 1933.

The Sportpalast[16] is already packed by six o'clock in the evening. All the squares in the city swarm with people waiting to hear the Leader's speech. In the whole Reich twenty to thirty millions more are listening in to it.

Drag myself to the Sportpalast, still weak with the illness from which I have not yet fully recovered. On the platform first I address the Press, and then for twenty minutes at the microphone speak to the audience in the Sportpalast. It goes better than I had thought. It is a strange experience suddenly to be faced with an inanimate microphone when one is used to addressing a living crowd, to be uplifted by the atmosphere of it, and to read the effect of one's speech in the expression on the faces of one's hearers.

The Leader is greeted by frantic cheering. He delivers a fine address containing an outspoken declaration of war against Marxism. Towards the end he strikes a wonderful, incredibly solemn note, and closes with the word "Amen"! It is uttered so naturally that all are deeply moved and affected by it. It is filled with so much strength and belief, is so novel and courageous, that it is not to be compared to anything that has gone beforehand.

This address will be received with enthusiasm throughout Germany. The nation will be ours almost without a struggle.

The masses at the Sportpalast are beside themselves with delight. Now the German Revolution has truly begun.

'Phone calls from different parts of the country report on the fine effect the speech has made even over the Radio. As an instrument for propaganda on a large scale the efficacy of the Radio has not yet been sufficiently appreciated. In any case our adversaries did not recognize its value. All the better, we shall have to explore its possibilities.

16. **Sportpalast:** the Sports Palace, a large, indoor sports arena in Berlin.

THE IMPACT OF NAZI METHODS

Source 17 from Jeremy Noakes and Geoffrey Pridham, editors, Documents on Nazism, 1919–1945 *(New York: Viking, 1975), p. 108. Copyright © 1975 by Jeremy Noakes and Geoffrey Pridham. Reprinted by permission of Sterling Lord Literistic, Inc.*

17. Report on the Problem of Stemming the Spread of Nazi Ideas in the Protestant Youth Movement, 1931

The cause which at the moment is most closely associated with the name of National Socialism and with which, at a moderate estimate, certainly 70 per cent of our young people, often lacking knowledge of the facts, are in ardent sympathy, must be regarded, as far as our ranks are concerned, more as an ethical than a political matter. Our young people show little political interest. Secondary school students are not really much concerned with the study of Hitler's thoughts; it is simply something irrational, something infectious that makes the blood pulse through one's veins and conveys an impression that something great is under way, the roaring of a stream which one does not wish to escape: "If you can't feel it you will never grasp it. . . ."

All this must be taken into account when we see the ardour and fire of this movement reflected in our ranks. A pedantic and nagging approach seems to me useless, and so do all attempts, however well-intentioned, by the leader to refute the policy of National Socialism in detail. The majority of the young fight against this with a strange instinct. We must, in keeping with our responsibility, though it is difficult in individual cases, try first to influence the ethos, and in this we must maintain an attitude above parties. We must educate in such a way that this enthusiasm is duly tempered by deeper understanding and by disenchantment, that words like "national honour and dignity" do not become slogans but arouse individual responsibility so that no brash demagogues grow up among us.

Source 18 from William L. Shirer, Berlin Diary, The Journal of a Foreign Correspondent, *1934–1941 (New York: Knopf, 1941), pp. 18, 19, 21, 22, 23. Reprinted by permission of Don Congden Associates, Inc. Copyright © 1941, renewed 1969 by William L. Shirer.*

18. William L. Shirer,
Reactions to the Nazi Party
Rally at Nuremberg, 1934

NUREMBERG, *September 5*

I'm beginning to comprehend, I think, some of the reasons for Hitler's astounding success. Borrowing a chapter from the Roman church,[17] he is restoring pageantry and colour and mysticism to the drab lives of twentieth-century Germans. This morning's opening meeting in the Luitpold Hall on the outskirts of Nuremberg was more than a gorgeous show; it also had something of the mysticism and religious fervour of an Easter or Christmas Mass in a great Gothic cathedral. The hall was a sea of brightly coloured flags. Even Hitler's arrival was made dramatic. The band stopped playing. There was a hush over the thirty thousand people packed in the hall. Then the band struck up the *Badenweiler March,* a very catchy tune, and used only, I'm told, when Hitler makes his big entries. Hitler appeared in the back of the auditorium, and followed by his aides, Göring, Goebbels, Hess, Himmler, and the others, he strode slowly down the long centre aisle while thirty thousand hands were raised in salute. It is a ritual, the old-timers say, which is always followed. Then an immense symphony orchestra played Beethoven's *Egmont* Overture. Great Klieg lights played on the stage, where Hitler sat surrounded by a hundred party officials and officers of the army and navy. Behind them the "blood flag," the one carried down the streets of Munich in the ill-fated putsch. Behind this, four or five hundred S.A. standards. When the music was over, Rudolf Hess, Hitler's closest confidant, rose and slowly read the names of the Nazi "martyrs"—brown-shirts who had been killed in the struggle for power—a roll-call of the dead, and the thirty thousand seemed very moved.

In such an atmosphere no wonder, then, that every word dropped by Hitler seemed like an inspired Word from on high. Man's—or at least the German's—critical faculty is swept away at such moments, and every lie pronounced is accepted as high truth itself.

NUREMBERG, *September 7*

Another great pageant tonight. Two hundred thousand party officials packed in the Zeppelin Wiese with their twenty-one thousand flags unfurled in the searchlights like a forest of weird trees. "We are strong and will get

17. **Roman church:** the Roman Catholic church.

stronger," Hitler shouted at them through the microphone, his words echoing across the hushed field from the loud-speakers. And there, in the floodlit night, jammed together like sardines, in one mass formation, the little men of Germany who have made Nazism possible achieved the highest state of being the Germanic man knows: the shedding of their individual souls and minds—with the personal responsibilities and doubts and problems—until under the mystic lights and at the sound of the magic words of the Austrian they were merged completely in the Germanic herd. Later they recovered enough—fifteen thousand of them—to stage a torchlight parade through Nuremberg's ancient streets, Hitler taking the salute in front of the station across from our hotel.

NUREMBERG, *September* 10

(Later)—After seven days of almost ceaseless goose-stepping, speech-making, and pageantry, the party rally came to an end tonight. And though dead tired and rapidly developing a bad case of crowd-phobia, I'm glad I came. You have to go through one of these to understand Hitler's hold on the people, to feel the dynamic in the movement he's unleashed and the sheer, disciplined strength the Germans possess. And now—as Hitler told the correspondents yesterday in explaining his technique—the half-million men who've been here during the week will go back to their towns and villages and preach the new gospel with new fanaticism. . . .

QUESTIONS TO CONSIDER

This chapter posed three basic questions: What image did the Nazis convey to German voters? Why did they appeal to German voters? How did the Nazis use media to aid their rise to power?

First examine the image the party conveyed to Germans in the 1920s and early 1930s. Start by considering the highly visible uniformed wing of the party, the S.A. Why did the S.A. Order 111 (Source 4) place such emphasis on how the S.A. appeared in public? What was the Storm Trooper supposed to epitomize? How was that visual effect designed to build a certain image for the party? How might

columns of marching men and political banners contribute to this image? Reflect, too, on the mass meetings so carefully mounted by the party. What impression might they have conveyed to the average man or woman on the street? How did the Leader myth contribute to a certain image for the party? Remember that Hitler was relatively young, forty-three years of age, when he gained power. How do you think many Germans viewed a young party leader whose use of airplanes made him seem omnipresent?

With your concept of the party's image now clearly in mind, assess the Nazi appeal to voters. You may wish to review the numerous problems facing Germany in the 1920s and early 1930s that we examined in the introduction. What did the Nazis propose as solutions to the Versailles Treaty, the threat of communist takeover, and the ills of the depression? Did the Nazis convey an image that would lead Germans to believe the party could solve the country's problems? Consider the S.A. and the Leader myth. How did they reinforce a promise to restore German power?

What groups did the Nazis specifically appeal to in our evidence, and what were their specific problems? What were the alleged conditions of the workers in Source 8, the poster of "The String-Puller"? Who was threatened by the proposed Woolworth's store in Hanover (Source 14)? How did the Nazis win support in these groups?

Beyond its proposed answers to Germany's problems and its specific appeal to certain groups, the Nazi party also had a more general appeal. Reflect for a moment on the anomie that Durkheim identified as part of modern urban life (see Chapter 9). In what ways do you think participation in mass meetings might combat this feeling? What sorts of positive feelings might it seem to provide? The twentieth century, as we saw in Chapter 9, witnessed for many a weakening of both the ritual and authority of traditional religion. How do the photographs of the banners and rally (Sources 5 and 6) and Shirer's account (Source 18) indicate a conscious attempt by the Nazis to exploit this development? Why would you not be surprised to find German religious youth movements losing members to the Nazis? Why are you shocked but not surprised at the conclusion of Hitler's speech of February 10, 1933 (Source 16)?

Finally, consider the Nazis' techniques, their use of media and propaganda in achieving their goal of power. In this regard, consider the theoretical bases for Nazi propaganda. What was Hitler's view of the masses? According to Hitler, why would the masses submit to terror? Recall the account of the brawl in the Pharus Hall in Source 7. What effect might this event have had on Hitler's opponents? Reexamine the graph of violence in Northeim. Why did Nazi violence break out when it did? How did it affect the party's image?

Examine the party's use of media technology for propaganda. What was the response of the Italian journalist to Nazi propaganda, according to Goebbels (Source 16)? What new electronic media did the Nazis employ? What do you think the Nazis' level of success would have been without such modern technology as the microphone? What features of Nazi campaign technology have become part of modern campaigning?

As you consider these questions, you should have a better understanding of the Nazi seizure of power in Germany. The Nazis used technology and methods of political manipulation that were new to the modern world. To understand fully the magnitude of their political revolution in winning the German masses, conclude your examination by referring to Chapter 2 of this volume. Which social groups was Louis XIV of France trying to influence? What was his message? How have Western political strategies changed in the almost three centuries separating Louis XIV and Hitler?

EPILOGUE

Nazi media mastery and propaganda worked well enough by January 1933 for the party to secure the chancellorship for Hitler. In free elections, however, the Nazis never secured more than 44 percent of the vote.[18] Once Hitler became chancellor, the task for the party and Goebbels was to use modern media and propaganda either to win the support of the majority of Germans or at least to convince them that opposition to the new political order was futile. As had been the case with the Nazi drive for power, implicit in this effort was the threat that force would be used against the recalcitrant. But Hitler did seem to keep his promises. The Communist party was outlawed in 1933; building projects and eventually rearmament stimulated the economy and created jobs; and Germany restored its military power and defied the Treaty of Versailles. Ominously, Hitler's promises also pointed to the terrible tragedy of the Holocaust for European Jews, and to World War II. But Goebbels's propaganda machine never let Germans forget the regime's successes.

The Hitler government centralized control of all information and media in a new Ministry of Public Enlightenment and Propaganda, headed by Goebbels, which closely regulated Germany's press, film, and radio after 1933. Especially significant was Goebbels's understanding of the role of radio as a propaganda device and his use of it once in power. He said, "With the radio we have destroyed the spirit of rebellion,"[19] because the radio could bring the Nazi message into every German home. The regime saw to it that cheap radios were made available to Germans, and the number of receivers increased from 5 million in 1932 to 9.5 million in 1938. A system of government wardens notified citizens to tune in important programs, and the Propaganda Ministry increased their impact still further by setting up loudspeakers in the streets and squares of Germany during key broadcasts.

Goebbels's ministry also sought to sway opinion via the medium of film. After some early crude and unpopular efforts, Goebbels's understanding of film as a propaganda device grew greatly. He wrote in 1942 of the subtle possibilities inherent in the medium:

> Even entertainment can be politically of special value, because the moment a person becomes conscious of propaganda, propaganda becomes ineffective. However, as soon as propaganda as a tendency, as a characteristic, as an attitude remains in the background and becomes apparent through human beings, then propaganda becomes effective in every respect.[20]

18. In the last free Reichstag elections held in March 1933, the Nazis won only 43.9 percent of the vote, despite S.A. intimidation of voters and the great political advantage accruing to the party from Hitler's position as chancellor. The Nazis finally secured a Reichstag majority only when Hitler expelled the Communist members from the Chamber.

19. Quoted in Roger Manvell and Heinrich Fraenkel, *Doctor Goebbels: His Life and Death* (London: Heinemann, 1960), pp. 127–128.

20. Joseph Goebbels, *Tagebuch*, unpublished sections, in Institut für Zeitgeschichte, Munich, entry for March 1, 1942. Quoted in David Welch, *Propaganda and the German Cinema, 1933–1945* (Oxford: Clarendon Press, 1983), p. 45.

Armed with such methods, the Nazi regime was able to retain power, mobilize its citizens for war, and sustain their morale throughout much of World War II. There was opposition to the dictatorship, including a number of plots against Hitler himself, but the regime managed to contain such active resistance within a minority of the population. Modern media and propaganda techniques and a message that attracted many, combined with the omnipresent threat of state police power, proved to be effective devices that aided the regime in maintaining its ascendancy. Such employment of modern media and propaganda techniques, supported by the police power of the state, would characterize many later twentieth-century totalitarian regimes.

CHAPTER THIRTEEN

BERLIN: THE CRUX OF THE COLD

WAR, 1945–1990

On April 25, 1945, at Torgau, Germany, American soldiers invading the country from the west met and shook hands with Russian soldiers of the Soviet Union advancing from the east. Their encounter that day, followed within days by the Soviet capture of the German capital of Berlin, seized the attention of much of the world. It marked victory over the Hitler regime after a worldwide conflict that had taken the lives of as many as 60 million persons, and it reflected the hopes of people everywhere for a postwar era of peace and understanding.[1] Few at that time would have imagined that the World War II allies—the United States, Britain, and France in the west and the Soviet Union in the east—would so fundamentally disagree on their treatment of Germany that the country would remain divided for over four decades, in part along the Elbe River where the armies met in 1945. Even fewer would have imagined that out of those disagreements, and others initially focused on Central and Eastern European matters, would develop a new conflict, a "Cold War" that would occasionally verge on a "hot" war, that is, a third, worldwide conflict in the twentieth century. Indeed, conflict between the Western powers and the Soviet Union dominated

---

1. The number of World War II deaths will always be approximate because of loss of records and the massive numbers of civilians who perished with little or no documentation, including some 6 million victims of the Holocaust and large numbers of persons killed by military bombing of civilian populations. However, recent research in Russia and Eastern Europe made possible by the end of the Cold War has forced historians to raise their estimates of military and civilian mortality in World War II. They now estimate deaths in the Soviet Union alone at about 25 million persons, a level of loss that certainly shaped the Soviet Union's response to defeated Germany.

much of the second half of the twentieth century, and it is by examining one of the chief sources of that conflict, the postwar treatment of Germany and especially its capital, Berlin, that we may study the Cold War in microcosm. Berlin, in fact, produced two major international crises in relations between the Western allies and the Soviet Union.

Two generations of historians have now examined and debated the origins of the Cold War. The view, once widely held in the West, that it was the result of aggressive Soviet attempts at worldwide domination has been tempered in recent years, especially as historians have been able to examine records that became available after the breakup of the Soviet Union in 1991. The growing scholarly consensus is that each side bore some responsibility for the Cold War. Indeed, the common need to defeat Hitler's Germany in World War II concealed fundamental differences between the Western powers and the Soviet Union. Certainly these differences were ideological: The United States, Britain, and France possessed democratic political institutions and capitalist, free enterprise economic systems while the Soviet Union was a Communist party dictatorship under Joseph Stalin (1879–1953) with a state-dominated economic life. Such ideological differences led the Western powers to intervene militarily against Communist forces in Russia in the civil war of 1918–1920 and to shun the Soviet regime diplomatically until the 1930s. But Cold War differences also were strategic in origin. Stalin and his diplomats sought a post–

World War II reorganization of Europe that would shield their country from any repetition of the costly German invasions that it had sustained in the two world wars of the twentieth century. Achievement of this goal all but mandated Soviet domination of the countries of Eastern Europe to create a buffer zone between the Soviet Union and Germany. At the same time, many British and American statesmen envisioned a postwar Europe in which nations like Italy, Greece, and others would fall within a sphere of influence dominated by the Western powers. Germany, in the center of Europe, thus was of vital strategic importance to both the Soviets and the Western powers, and neither side was prepared to see the other dominate this country.

Such considerations contributed to a growing mistrust between the wartime allies even before the defeat of Germany. Stalin, for example, suspected that the Anglo-American negotiations that led to Italy's changing sides in 1943 were a first step toward integrating Germany's former ally into a Western sphere of influence. He also believed that the United States and Britain deliberately delayed their invasion of France until 1944 in order to impose more of the war's burden on the Soviets. American and British statesmen, for their part, grew increasingly uneasy late in the war at unilateral Soviet occupations of Poland and other Eastern European countries that clearly aimed at postwar communist domination of these lands. Thus, statesmen sought at a number of international conferences during and just after the war in Europe to resolve differences between the Western allies and the Soviets on the war's conduct and the postwar order. A Moscow conference of foreign ministers in October 1943, for example, created a European Advisory Commission (EAC) composed of American, British, and Russian officials to work out the details of Germany's postwar treatment. This group's plan, one whose authors believed would govern defeated Germany only until the Allies worked out a permanent postwar settlement, divided the country into zones of occupation. A line partially following the Elbe River separated a Soviet eastern zone of occupation from British and American zones of occupation in the west. Such a division left the country's capital, Berlin, 110 miles within the Soviet zone of occupation, but, as a symbol of joint victory, the EAC plan divided that city into American, British, and Soviet sectors of occupation.

Successive wartime conferences only slightly modified this basic division of Germany while failing to resolve other fundamental issues about the defeated power. Thus, at Yalta in February 1945, American president Franklin D. Roosevelt (1882–1945), British prime minister Winston Churchill (1874–1965), and Stalin agreed to create a French zone of occupation within the American and British zones in Germany and their sectors of Berlin. They did this at the behest of the British, who, heeding Roosevelt's view that all American troops would leave Europe within two years of the war's end, wished to involve another Western power in the occupation. The

statesmen also agreed on the broad general principle that their occupation policy in Germany would emphasize de-Nazification of the political system, democratization of government, and demilitarization of society. But they failed to agree on the specific policies that would achieve these principles.

At Potsdam in July and August 1945, American president Harry S Truman (1884–1972) and British prime minister Clement Attlee (1883–1967) did agree with Stalin to set up an Allied Control Council for the administration of occupied Germany that was composed of the powers' military commanders in each zone.[2] But the allied heads of government set down only a general agenda for the council, the ideological disagreements of the Western allies and the Soviets were great, and the French government, which initially favored a permanently divided and weakened Germany, often blocked common policy efforts just after the war. Thus, the four occupation zones evolved from the first without any common policies. This posed great problems, because the Soviets occupied the eastern agricultural lands of Germany while the Western powers occupied the industrial heartland, which produced only 40 percent of its food needs.

2. President Roosevelt died in April 1945, and Vice President Truman assumed his office. Winston Churchill represented Britain at the opening of the conference, but his Conservative party lost control of the House of Commons in the elections of 1945, and the Labour party leader, Clement Attlee, replaced him as prime minister.

The possibility of common solutions to problems in Germany diminished as relations between the Soviets and the Western powers became increasingly tense. Soviet insecurities mounted with America's abrupt termination of wartime Lend Lease aid in May 1945 after victory in Europe and the successful employment of atomic bombs by the United States to end the war against Japan in August 1945. At the same time, Soviet actions increasingly alarmed Western policymakers. Stalin violated his promises of free elections in Poland, and Soviet officials clearly sought to facilitate communist domination of other governments in Eastern European countries occupied by their Red Army (Czechoslovakia, Hungary, Bulgaria, and Romania). In addition, when a communist insurgency erupted in Greece at the war's end and the Soviet Union began to apply pressure on Turkey to revise the treaty limiting the movement of Soviet warships through the Turkish Straits, American and British statesmen began to fear that Stalin sought a massive expansion of the territory dominated by his country.

The United States government responded to this perceived threat in two important policy initiatives in 1947 that further embittered East–West relations. Militarily, President Truman extended assistance to Greece and Turkey while offering such aid to all other countries resisting communist takeover. This Truman Doctrine created an American policy of "containment" of communist expansion that would be the keystone of postwar United States foreign policy. It

meant, too, that American forces remained in Europe not for two years after the end of World War II, as Roosevelt had expected, but for two generations. Economically, American secretary of state George C. Marshall announced a plan of economic assistance to war-torn Europe—the Marshall Plan—to rebuild the Continent and restore its prosperity in order to encourage noncommunist governmental institutions. The United States offered this aid to all European countries, but the Soviets perceived it as a scheme to draw countries into the orbit of the United States. Thus, the Soviets rejected Marshall Plan aid, blocked attempts by Czechoslovakia and Poland to participate in the plan, and forced the removal of noncommunist officials from several Eastern European governments. The Western powers particularly resented a coup in Czechoslovakia, a country with democratic traditions, which replaced a coalition government with a communist one in February 1948.

Developments in Germany reflected such growing tension as the occupation zones increasingly diverged politically. In the eastern zone, the Soviets stripped the area of much of its industrial stock as reparations for their losses in the war and created a one-party state dominated by the Socialist Unity party (SED) led by the Communist Walter Ulbricht. They sought to use this party to win control of Berlin's municipal government, too, in the elections of 1946, but Berliners, recalling the brutality of the Red Army in their city at the end of the war, rejected the party's candidates. One-party government became the lot of Soviet-occupied East Berlin; the Western powers' sectors maintained a free, multiparty political system. Beyond Berlin, in their zones of occupation in western Germany, American, British, and French officials also permitted free elections. Officials chosen in those elections met with SED officials in Munich in June 1947 to discuss the creation of a government for a unified Germany. Disagreement on the nature of a new German government, however, was immediate, and SED representatives walked out of the meeting at its very outset.

If the failure of the Munich conference ruled out immediate unification of the Soviet and western occupation zones, American and British officials evolved an alternative plan. Their plan was the result of serious problems in the western zones of Germany, where they faced the ongoing need to supply large quantities of food for the civilian population because, as we have seen, western Germany was not self-sufficient in food production. The Americans and the British opted to rebuild the western German economy so that their former enemies could exchange manufactured goods in the world market for their own food needs. This decision had important consequences.

The Americans and British began by economically merging their zones on January 1, 1947, to coordinate economic policy on a larger scale. The French zone also eventually joined this entity, and the Western powers' next step in German economic recovery was much-needed currency reform. At war's end the occupying

powers had replaced Hitler-era currency with occupation Reichsmarks, which quickly lost their value as the Soviets printed them in vast quantities to meet their costs of occupation. As merchants increasingly refused to accept this devalued currency, German economic life stagnated and a barter system became widespread in which the most universally accepted currency was American cigarettes. Despite this disastrous situation, the Soviets resisted American-sponsored currency reform because to them it represented a plan to integrate western Germany economically into the sphere of the United States. When the Americans proceeded with currency reform without Soviet approval, they violated the Potsdam agreement, which mandated joint action on this issue, and the Soviets terminated meetings of the Allied Control Council after March 1948 as the Western powers prepared to introduce the new currency, the Deutschmark. Then in June 1948, a meeting of representatives of Western democratic nations including the United States, Britain, France, Belgium, the Netherlands, and Luxembourg authorized a meeting of the German states under Western occupation to begin to prepare a constitution for their unification as one nation.

From the Soviet point of view, this progress toward currency reform and the unification of the Western occupation zones put control of western Germany increasingly beyond Soviet grasp, and it seems to have prompted Stalin to take several steps. Many historians view the resulting crisis as the beginning of the Cold War. On April 1,

1948, Soviet officials began to interfere with the Western allies' rail and highway transport into Berlin to make the position of the allied garrisons there more difficult. In addition, they ordered the eastern zone to adopt a new currency, the Ostmark. But when Soviet officials attempted to force the Berlin municipal assembly on June 23, 1948, to adopt their zone's currency instead of the Deutschmark, a clear move to bring the entire city under greater Soviet economic control, they provoked a crisis. The city's assembly rejected the Ostmark, and Soviet officials halted all traffic into Berlin by highway, water, and railroad in what came to be called the Berlin Blockade. Stalin intended either to block the new currency and the unification of the western zones or to starve the city into submission and to force the withdrawal of the Western allies from Berlin. Germany was too important a prize to let the Western powers integrate it more closely into their economic and political system. Indeed, Stalin said as much during the blockade, telling Western diplomats to give up the currency reform and western German unification and "You shall no longer have any difficulties. That may be done even tomorrow. . . ."[3]

Clearly the Western allies could not give in to Soviet demands; Germany had great strategic importance for them, too. But the Western response to the blockade had to be a cautious one. Postwar budget cuts

had left the United States armed forces in no condition to fight a war in 1948. Thus, the suggestion of the American military governor in Germany, General Lucius D. Clay, that an armed convoy protected by Western soldiers force its way, if necessary, into Berlin had to be rejected. Such an act might well have provoked a war. Instead, on June 26, 1948, the United States Air Force (USAF) and the British Royal Air Force (RAF) began to fly supplies over the Soviet zone of occupation into Berlin along the three air corridors to the city from the west that had been established in wartime agreements. This mission, the Berlin Airlift, required that the USAF and RAF transport all of the food and fuel required by a city of 2.5 million civilians as well as by their own garrisons there. At a minimum, these needs amounted to 3,000 tons of coal and 2,500 tons of food daily. In all, the USAF and the RAF sent 276,926 flights into Berlin before the Soviets ended the blockade on May 12, 1949. At its peak, the airlift landed one transport airplane in Berlin every 63 seconds, twenty-four hours per day, to permit the western sectors of the city to remain free of Soviet control. In the course of the blockade relations between the Western allies and the Soviets only worsened. In April 1949, the United States sponsored the creation of the North Atlantic Treaty Organization (NATO), an alliance whose chief aim was the defense of Western Europe against the Soviets. The following month, the western zones of Germany adopted a constitution and became the Federal Republic of Germany (often called "West Germany"),

3. Quoted in John Lewis Gaddis, *We Now Know: Rethinking Cold War History* (Oxford: Clarendon Press, 1997), p. 112.

a step the Soviet zone echoed when it declared itself the German Democratic Republic (often called "East Germany"). In the years following, the two Germanys went their separate ways. The Federal Republic rapidly rebuilt its economy in what has been called an "economic miracle," and its citizens came to enjoy one of the world's highest standards of living. Moreover, the Western powers increasingly integrated it into their military and economic systems. The Federal Republic also rebuilt its armed forces and assumed a part in NATO, just as it played a role in founding the organization that became the European Union (see Chapter 15). In the German Democratic Republic, the dictatorial one-party rule of the SED imposed a communist economic system on the country, collectivizing agriculture, nationalizing industry, and launching a drive to transform heavily agricultural East Germany into an industrial power, that consumed much of the nation's resources and made life there austere in the extreme. The East German government sought to enforce its citizens' acquiescence in this situation with an extensive secret police network designed to root out dissent. As a result, large numbers of people fled the Democratic Republic for West Germany, and by the end of the 1950s as many as 4 million persons—20 percent of the area's 1945 population—had left. Such population loss was disastrous for East Germany, especially because the refugees were disproportionately young and well educated, the very people necessary to accomplish communist goals in the east. Certainly,

too, the continuing flight of the most talented citizens of the Democratic Republic was an enduring embarrassment to its regime and to the Soviet Union.

The East German regime sought to stop such emigration by making flight a crime and by better policing its 860-mile-long border with West Germany. But tighter border controls drove increasing numbers of East Germans to Berlin, where the four-power occupation of the city still permitted free movement between the sectors of the Western allies and the Soviet Union. Indeed, departure from the Democratic Republic there could be as simple as boarding a subway in the Soviet zone and detraining in the western sector of Berlin.

While East Germans fled their homes in great numbers in the 1950s, the Cold War continued and became more dangerous when the Soviets acquired atomic weapons. With nuclear warfare between the NATO powers and the Soviets a possibility, Europe settled into a tense equilibrium for a time, despite uprisings in Eastern Europe (East Berlin, 1953; Poland and Hungary, 1956) and many late 1940s and 1950s Cold War confrontations outside of Europe. Thus, a communist insurgency toppled an American-supported regime in China in 1949, and in 1950 through 1953 American-led United Nations forces fought North Korean and communist Chinese forces for control of the Korean peninsula. In addition, a communist-led uprising in Indochina (Cambodia, Laos, and Vietnam) against French rule led to the defeat of the colonial power and increasing American involvement there as part of the containment policy.

Only in 1958 did a major Cold War crisis again confront Europe, but the issue was still Germany. By that time, however, the new leader of the Communist party of the Soviet Union and the country's premier, Nikita S. Khrushchev (1894–1971), was directing policy. For Khrushchev, the continuing flight of refugees from East Germany impeded that state's economic development and demanded resolution. At the same time, he seems to have calculated that the growing nuclear and missile power of the Soviet Union would mean that the United States and its allies would not risk war over Berlin. The result was a second Berlin crisis.

Khrushchev demanded that the wartime Allies sign peace treaties with the two Germanys and that all occupying forces evacuate Berlin, leaving the capital a free city. The United States and the Western allies could not accept this proposal, of course, because it left East Germany in communist hands while raising the possibility of all of Berlin slipping into the Soviet sphere. Nevertheless, negotiations between the two sides opened under Khrushchev's threat to sign a treaty unilaterally with the Democratic Republic. East–West tensions remained high as John F. Kennedy (1917–1963) assumed the American presidency in 1961, and they grew as East Germans, frightened by the prospect of a settlement that would close the Berlin escape route, hastened to flee westward. Between January 1, 1961, and August 13, 1961, 159,700 persons left behind all that they owned and fled the German Democratic Republic. This was a greater number of refugees than in all of 1959.

When Kennedy and Khrushchev met in Vienna in June 1961, neither side offered any concessions on Berlin, and the Soviet leader adopted a bellicose attitude that even he conceded in his memoirs might have been perceived by the American president as threatening war. Following the meeting both leaders announced large military build-ups. But the Kennedy administration, while preparing to defend the Western sectors of Berlin, clearly signaled that it was not prepared to fight a war if the Soviets and the East Germans confined their actions to stopping the flow of refugees. Thus, before dawn on August 13, 1961, the German Democratic Republic began construction of a wall separating the eastern sector of Berlin from those occupied by the Western powers to stop its citizens' flights to the West. East German police closely guarded the wall and used deadly force against persons attempting to escape. The wall's construction shocked Americans and Western Europeans. But despite a tense face-off between American and Soviet tanks at Checkpoint Charlie (the only point where American and allied officials could cross to East Berlin after the wall's construction) on October 27, 1961, the great powers avoided war over Berlin a second time.

Berlin brought the Western allies and the Soviet Union perilously close to war twice in less than a decade and a half as part of the enduring conflict known as the Cold War. Your problem in this chapter is to examine the causes of the Cold War and especially the roots of the conflict over Berlin. What were the origins of the Cold War? How did the Berlin crises develop out of wartime agreements? What strategic considerations made Berlin so essential to both the Western allies and the Soviets?

SOURCES AND METHOD

Modern government produces a vast written record that is of great value to the student of history in understanding a country's foreign policy, and much material is readily available. Treaties, for example, are widely disseminated in the press and in government publications because many democratic governments, like that of the United States, require that legislative bodies ratify the commitments that they contain. Less well known is the record of what went into the making of foreign policy, since policymakers often draw on top-secret analyses of strategic matters drawn up by military, diplomatic, and security officials. National law in most countries governs the release of such documents for study, and in most cases scholars and the public can see such records only after a considerable lapse of time, in some cases fifty years or more, or when the contents of the records no longer compromise national security. Because the Cold War is now over, records of the latter sort are becoming available to historians, and the present chapter combines such records with those more traditionally made available to researchers for examination of the Berlin crises.

Source 1 is a record of the Potsdam Conference (technically called the "Berlin Conference"; Potsdam is a suburb of Berlin) concluded on August 2, 1945. Nations maintain extensive written records of such international meetings because they often result in treaties that have the effect of international law. The United States, for example, published a written record of the conference more than 2,700 pages in length.[4] Source 1 is the Potsdam protocol that Clement Attlee, Harry Truman, and Joseph Stalin signed on behalf of their respective nations on August 2, 1945. A protocol is an official diplomatic document summarizing the agreements reached at an international meeting, and that at Potsdam dealt with the very broad range of issues that arose with the end of World War II in Europe. But the statesmen were especially concerned with Germany, and the excerpts from the Potsdam protocol in Source 1 offer you a synopsis of the arrangements made to govern Germany as well as the legal background for much of the Cold War confrontation over Berlin. Why do you conclude that the signatories to the Potsdam agreement viewed their arrangements for Germany as temporary

---

4. *Foreign Relations of the United States. Diplomatic Papers: The Conference of Berlin (The Potsdam Conference), 1945*, 2 vols. (Washington, D.C.: United States Government Printing Office, 1960).

in nature? The signatory powers concluded treaties with Italy, Romania, Bulgaria, Hungary, and Finland, Germany's wartime allies, in the course of 1947. Why do you think the statesmen at Potsdam might have expected that a treaty with Germany shortly would have followed these agreements? What sort of postwar policies did the Allies seek to impose on Germany? Given the very different governmental systems of the signatory powers, why do you think that they might have interpreted differently such words as *democracy*? What was the clear message of the Potsdam agreement in regard to such postwar developments in Germany as separate currency systems and, indeed, separate governments for East and West Germany?

Source 2 is a map of Europe after World War II showing the division of Germany and Berlin into occupation zones, the territorial changes resulting from World War II, and the demarcation point between Soviet and Western spheres in Europe, a line Churchill called "the Iron Curtain." Policymakers frequently consult maps drawn up by their security services to better understand the strategic implication of their decisions. What strategic difficulties does the map reveal in a joint American, British, French, and Soviet occupation of Berlin? How did the war permit the Soviet Union to add territory to protect itself better from future attacks from Germany? How did Communist party domination of the Eastern European countries make these nations part of the buffer zone that the Soviets wished to create on their

western border? According to the map, what was the strategic importance of Germany to both sides in the Cold War?

Source 3 is an example of the kind of government record that is seldom published. It is a top-secret report from the Soviet Union's ambassador to the United States, Nikolai Novikov, to the foreign minister, Viacheslav Molotov, sent in 1946. Ambassadors for centuries have provided their governments with such secret information on the countries in which they represent their nations; indeed, intelligence gathering was one of the original functions of such diplomatic representatives. The intent of Novikov's communication was to provide the foreign minister with the latest intelligence on American foreign policy goals. Molotov apparently paid close attention to the report; he annotated it (the underlining in the text is his), and he kept it handy in his personal files. Soviet authorities believed that it played a key role in shaping their government's strategic thinking about the United States in the 1950s, and they thus released it to Western scholars in 1990 at a conference in the last days of the Soviet Union. What sort of wartime calculations did Novikov impute to Americans? What sort of policy outlook did he identify in America after the death of President Roosevelt? What specifically did Novikov see the United States doing in Germany? What did he see as America's postwar goal in the world? How did Germany fit into this plan? Why would this increase the strategic importance of Germany to the Soviets? How did the Soviet definition of *democracy* differ from that which the Americans would have assigned to it? To which country did this report assign all of the blame for the emerging Cold War? How might its message have affected the Cold War's early days, especially since Novikov predicted a war?

If ambassadors long have provided their governments with strategic information, modern states also have created specialized intelligence agencies to gather data on foreign nations, if necessary through spying. Such agencies also analyze the data they collect and make policy recommendations to their governments. The United States developed such an agency during World War II, the Office of Strategic Services (OSS), and after the war President Truman decided to centralize the government's intelligence activities in the Central Intelligence Group (CIG) that he created in January 1946. In 1947, the National Security Act replaced the CIG with the Central Intelligence Agency (CIA), which still provides intelligence data to American policymakers. The analyses of security data collected by the CIG/CIA almost always are classified "Secret" or "Top Secret" and are meant for the use of the president and his closest advisers in making national policy. During the early Cold War years, the intelligence agencies sent daily, weekly, and monthly summaries and analyses of events to the president and his advisers. The intelligence analyses received by these statesmen played a considerable role in shaping American policy in the Cold War and in the Berlin Blockade, and Source 4 offers three brief excerpts from such reports that were de-

classified by the government after the end of the Cold War in the late 1990s.

Source 4A is a general statement of the Soviet threat to the United States by American intelligence analysts written in 1948. How did American experts characterize the general relationship between the United States and the Soviet Union? What did they see as the long-term goals of the Soviet Union? Did these experts perceive a worldwide threat to the United States? How did the Americans' vision of the Soviet Union compare with Novikov's vision of the United States in Source 3? Under what circumstances might the Cold War CIA analysts envisioned erupt into a "hot" war? Did such circumstances exist in 1948? Source 4B is from a weekly summary of events written in the first days of the Berlin Blockade. What did CIA analysts see as the Soviet Union's primary goal in cutting off Berlin? Why did they see gaining control of the city itself as almost a secondary goal? How do you think such an analysis stiffened American determination to maintain the Western allies' position in Berlin? How is this analysis consistent with that of the agency in 1946? How did CIA analysts describe the attitude of Berliners in the western sectors of the city toward Soviet domination? How might this have affected American policy? Source 4C is from a weekly summary of events written as the Berlin Blockade came to an end in 1949. What consistent Soviet goal for Germany did CIA analysts identify? How did analysts envision the Soviets achieving this goal? Why would Germany remain a preoccupation of

American Cold War policy even as the roads and railroads to Berlin were reopened? How did the CIA attempt to guide American statesmen with predictions of the Soviet attitude in upcoming negotiations?

Sources 5 and 6 provide us with a much closer vantage point for observing matters in Germany than that of CIA analysts in Washington. These sources are from the papers of General Lucius D. Clay (1897–1978), who served first as American military governor in Germany from the war's end to 1947 and then as commander of all United States forces in Europe until 1949. It was General Clay who coordinated American policy in Germany and who had to deal directly with the Berlin crisis in 1948–1949. Source 5 is Clay's response to the impact of the American War Department's decision to reduce food shipments to the American zone in Germany in 1946. Recalling from Chapter 4 that a daily human food intake equal to 2,400 calories is necessary to sustain moderate labor, what do you conclude about the food situation in the American zone of Germany? What sort of German responses to these food shortages did Clay foresee? How might such American difficulties in provisioning their occupation zone have encouraged the economic reforms that contributed to the Berlin Blockade crisis of 1948 and 1949?

Source 6 is a radio communication from General Clay to Assistant Secretary of War William H. Draper, Jr., during the Berlin Blockade. Clay's position made him extremely influential in Washington policymaking circles, and

this communication is revealing about the thinking of American policymakers early in the crisis. Given the options posed in the communication, did the United States seem firmly determined, at first, to resist the blockade? What did Clay see at stake in the Berlin Blockade? Why did he believe retreat from Berlin was not possible? What does this tell you about his view of the Soviet threat? How did Clay propose to show American force in the Berlin Blockade?

Source 7 presents excerpts from the text of the treaty establishing the North Atlantic Treaty Organization (NATO) in 1949. The treaty came as a direct response to events of 1948, including the Berlin Blockade and a coup in Czechoslovakia that brought that country under complete communist control. What sort of an alliance is NATO? Its original members were the United States, Belgium, Britain, Canada, Denmark, France, Iceland, Italy, Luxembourg, the Netherlands, Norway, and Portugal. Assessing this list of nations, against whom was their alliance clearly directed? What impact do you think such an alliance had on East–West relations in Europe? What impact do you think the creation in 1955 of an opposing alliance system, the Warsaw Pact (the Soviet Union, Albania, Bulgaria, Czechoslovakia, the German Democratic Republic, and Romania), had on those relations?

With Source 8 we turn our attention to the second Berlin crisis, that of 1961. Source 8 is an *aide-mémoire*, a diplomatic document that summarizes a proposal. Nikita Khrushchev handed it to John F. Kennedy at the Vienna meeting as his first step in reopening with a new American administration his proposal of 1958 for a treaty with Germany. The great powers conducted post–World War II international relations in an age of electronic media that focused public attention as never before on the national policy of countries like the United States and the Soviet Union. Reading Source 8, why might you conclude that part of its purpose was propaganda in the Cold War? How did it portray both East and West Germany and the motives of the Soviet Union? Why do you think that the United States failed to accept Khrushchev's invitation to draft a treaty with Germany? What role would a post-treaty West Germany have had in NATO? What sort of Berlin did the Soviets envision? From the American standpoint, would this new status for the city have provided an opportunity for communist control of the former Western sectors of the city? What sort of consistency do you find in American policy regarding Berlin in the postwar era?

Source 9 is a radio and television report to the Soviet people by Khrushchev on his Vienna meeting with Kennedy. Certainly propaganda is part of the purpose of this speech, but it also is a fundamental statement of Soviet policy and as such is an important part of the documentary evidence on the Berlin situation. In the course of his speech, Khrushchev restated his proposal for a treaty with Germany. But he added much that alarmed statesmen in the West. Of what does he accuse the United States and other Western powers? What do

you make of Khrushchev's references to military force, especially when he asserts "times are different now," apparently referring to the Soviets' possession of nuclear weapons? Remember that he made this statement as the Soviet Union began a build-up of its military forces. What effect do you think Khrushchev's statement that East Germany would control access to a post-treaty Berlin had on Western statesmen?

Source 10 is President Kennedy's response to Khrushchev on July 25, 1961. Again, it is a statement in the form of a radio and television address. The president sought to build support at home for his policies by addressing the Berlin issue in this fashion, but he also sent several messages to the Soviets. What was the most obvious message? What effect could the president's announcement of an American military build-up, a partial mobilization of the nation's reserve forces, and the preparation of civilian bomb shelters have had on the Soviets? But there was a less obvious message in the speech, too. To whose defense did the president commit American arms? You will note that Kennedy emphasized American commitment to West Berlin, not to all of Berlin. If you had been a Soviet diplomat skilled in analyzing language, you would immediately have noted the distinction. What conclusions would you have drawn? At the same time, prominent figures in Washington, like the chairman of the Senate Foreign Relations Committee, J. William Fulbright, suggested in interviews that while the United States

[377]

would fight to remain in West Berlin, it would not resist measures to terminate the immediate problem for the Soviets, the flood of refugees. How would Soviet observation of signals such as this have shaped their actions? Why might you conclude that the president was forcing Khrushchev to back down from his threats while giving him a way out of the crisis short of war?

As you now read the evidence for this chapter, keep this background information and the questions it raised in mind. It will aid you in answering the central questions of this chapter. What were the origins of the Cold War? How did the Berlin crises develop out of wartime agreements? What strategic considerations made Berlin so essential to both the Western allies and the Soviets?

THE EVIDENCE

Source 1 from Germany, 1947–1949: The Story in Documents *(Washington, D. C.: U. S. Government Printing Office for the Department of State Division of Publications, 1950), pp. 47–57.*

1. Protocol of the Proceedings of the Berlin Conference

There is attached hereto the agreed protocol of the Berlin Conference.

JOSEPH V. STALIN
HARRY TRUMAN
C. R. ATTLEE

PROTOCOL OF THE PROCEEDINGS OF THE BERLIN CONFERENCE

The Berlin Conference of the Three Heads of Government of the U.S.S.R., U.S.A., and U.K., which took place from July 17 to August 2, 1945, came to the following conclusions:

I. Establishment of a Council of Foreign Ministers

A. The Conference reached the following agreement for the establishment of a Council of Foreign Ministers to do the necessary preparatory work for the peace settlements:

"(1) There shall be established a Council composed of the Foreign Ministers of the United Kingdom, the Union of Soviet Socialist Republics, China, France, and the United States. . . .

"(3) (i) As its immediate important task, the Council shall be authorized to draw up, with a view to their submission to the United Nations, treaties of peace with Italy, Rumania, Bulgaria, Hungary and Finland, and to propose settlements of territorial questions outstanding on the termination of the war in Europe. The Council shall be utilized for the preparation of a peace settlement for Germany to be accepted by the Government of Germany when a government adequate for the purpose is established.

II. The Principles To Govern the Treatment of Germany in the Initial Control Period

A. Political Principles

1. In accordance with the Agreement on Control Machinery in Germany, supreme authority in Germany is exercised, on instructions from their respective Governments, by the Commanders-in-Chief of the armed forces of the United States of America, the United Kingdom, the Union of Soviet Socialist Republics, and the French Republic, each in his own zone of occupation, and also jointly, in matters affecting Germany as a whole, in their capacity as members of the Control Council.

2. So far as is practicable, there shall be uniformity of treatment of the German population throughout Germany.

3. The purposes of the occupation of Germany by which the Control Council shall be guided are:

(i) The complete disarmament and demilitarization of Germany and the elimination or control of all German industry that could be used for military production. . . .

(ii) To convince the German people that they have suffered a total military defeat and that they cannot escape responsibility for what they have brought upon themselves, since their own ruthless warfare and the fanatical Nazi resistance have destroyed German economy and made chaos and suffering inevitable.

(iii) To destroy the National Socialist Party and its affiliated and supervised organizations, to dissolve all Nazi institutions, to ensure that they are not revived in any form, and to prevent all Nazi and militarist activity or propaganda.

(iv) To prepare for the eventual reconstruction of German political life on a democratic basis and for eventual peaceful cooperation in international life by Germany. . . .

9. The administration in Germany should be directed towards the decentralization of the political structure and the development of local responsibility. To this end:

(i) local self-government shall be restored throughout Germany on democratic principles and in particular through elective councils as rapidly as is consistent with military security and the purposes of military occupation;

(ii) all democratic political parties with rights of assembly and of public discussion shall be allowed and encouraged throughout Germany;

(iii) representative and elective principles shall be introduced into regional, provincial and state (Land) administration as rapidly as may be justified by the successful application of these principles in local self-government;

(iv) for the time being, no central German Government shall be established. Notwithstanding this, however, certain essential central German administrative departments, headed by State Secretaries, shall be established, particularly in the fields of finance, transport, communications, foreign trade and industry. Such departments will act under the direction of the Control Council.

10. Subject to the necessity for maintaining military security, freedom of speech, press and religion shall be permitted, and religious institutions shall be respected. Subject likewise to the maintenance of military security, the formation of free trade unions shall be permitted.

B. Economic Principles

11. In order to eliminate Germany's war potential, the production of arms, ammunition and implements of war as well as all types of aircraft and sea-going ships shall be prohibited and prevented. Production of metals, chemicals, machinery and other items that are directly necessary to a war economy shall be rigidly controlled and restricted to Germany's approved post-war peacetime needs. . . . Productive capacity not needed for permitted production shall be removed in accordance with the reparations plan recommended by the Allied Commission on Reparations and approved by the Governments concerned or if not removed shall be destroyed. . . .

14. During the period of occupation Germany shall be treated as a single economic unit. To this end common policies shall be established in regard to:

(a) mining and industrial production and its allocation;

(b) agriculture, forestry and fishing;

(c) wages, prices and rationing;

(d) import and export programs for Germany as a whole;

(e) currency and banking, central taxation and customs;

(f) reparation and removal of industrial war potential;

(g) transportation and communications.

In applying these policies account shall be taken, where appropriate, of varying local conditions.

Source 3 from Houghton Mifflin.

2. Map of Europe after World War II

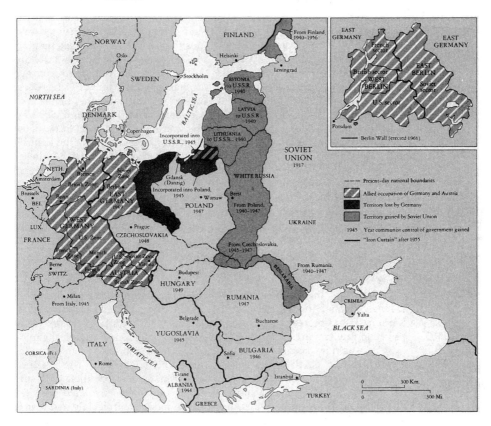

Source 3 from Kenneth M. Jensen, ed., Origins of the Cold War, Revised Edition: The Novikov, Kennan, and Roberts "Long Telegrams" of 1946 *(Washington, D.C.: United States Institute of Peace, 1991), pp. 3–31. Copyright © 1993 by the Endowment of the United States Institute of Peace. Used with permission by the United States Institute of Peace, Washington, D.C.*

3. The Novikov Telegram, Washington, September 27, 1946

U.S. Foreign Policy in the Postwar Period

[All italics replicate the underlining of Foreign Minister Viacheslav Molotov.]

The foreign policy of the United States, which reflects the imperialist tendencies of American monopolistic capital, is characterized in the postwar period by a striving *for world supremacy*.[5] This is the real meaning of the many statements by President Truman and other representatives of American ruling circles: that the United States has the right to lead the world. All the forces of American diplomacy—the army, the air force, the navy, industry, and science—are enlisted in the service of this foreign policy. For this purpose broad plans for expansion have been developed and are being implemented through diplomacy and the establishment of a system of naval and air bases stretching far beyond the boundaries of the United States, through the arms race, and through the creation of ever newer types of weapons.

The foreign policy of the United States is conducted now *in a situation that differs greatly* from the one that existed in the prewar period. This situation does not fully conform to the calculations of those reactionary circles which hoped that during the Second World War they would succeed in avoiding, at least for a long time, the main battles in Europe and Asia. They calculated that the United States of America, if it was unsuccessful in completely avoiding direct participation in the war, would enter it only at the last minute, when it could easily affect the outcome of the war, completely ensuring its interests.

In this regard, it was thought that the main competitors of the United States would be crushed or greatly weakened in the war, and the United States by virtue of this circumstance would assume *the role of the most powerful factor* in resolving the fundamental questions of the postwar world. These calculations were also based on the assumption, which was very widespread in the United States in the initial stages of the war, that the Soviet Union, which had been subjected to the attack of German Fascism in June 1941, would also be exhausted or even completely destroyed as a result of the war. . . .

Europe has come out of the war with a completely dislocated economy, and the economic devastation that occurred in the course of the war cannot be overcome in a short time. All of the countries of Europe and Asia are experi-

5. Molotov's marginal notation to this sentence was: "A difference from [the] prewar [period]?"

encing a colossal need for consumer goods, industrial and transportation equipment, etc. Such a situation provides American monopolistic capital with *prospects for enormous shipments of goods and the importation of capital* into these countries—a circumstance that would permit it to infiltrate their national economies.

Such a development would mean a serious strengthening of the economic position of the United States in the whole world and would be a stage on the road to world domination by the United States. . . .

At the same time *the USSR's international position is currently stronger than it was in the prewar period.*[6] Thanks to the historical victories of Soviet weapons, the Soviet armed forces are located on the territory of Germany and other formerly hostile countries, thus guaranteeing that these countries will not be used again for an attack on the USSR. In formerly hostile countries, such as *Bulgaria, Finland, Hungary, and Romania*, democratic reconstruction has established regimes that have undertaken to strengthen and maintain friendly relations with the Soviet Union. In the Slavic countries that were liberated by the Red Army or with its assistance—*Poland, Czechoslovakia, and Yugoslavia*—democratic regimes have also been established that maintain relations with the Soviet Union on the basis of agreements on friendship and mutual assistance.

The enormous relative weight of the USSR in international affairs in general and in the European countries in particular, the independence of its foreign policy, and the economic and political assistance that it provides to neighboring countries, both allies and former enemies, has led to the growth of the political influence of the Soviet Union in these countries and to the further strengthening of democratic tendencies in them.

Such a situation in Eastern and Southeastern Europe cannot help but be regarded by the American imperialists as an obstacle in the path of the expansionist policy of the United States. . . .

Obvious indications of the U.S. effort to establish world dominance are also to be found in the increase in military potential in peacetime and in the establishment of a large number of naval and air bases both in the United States and beyond its borders.

In the summer of 1946, for the first time in the history of the country, Congress passed a law *on the establishment of a peacetime army, not on a volunteer basis but on the basis of universal military service.* The size of the army, which is supposed to amount to about one million persons as of July 1, 1947, was also increased significantly. The size of the navy at the conclusion of the war decreased quite insignificantly in comparison with war-time. At the present time, the American navy occupies first place in the world, leaving England's navy far behind, to say nothing of those of other countries. . . .

Along with maintaining a large army, navy, and air force, the budget provides that these enormous amounts also will be spent on establishing a very extensive system of naval and air bases in the Atlantic and Pacific oceans. . . .

---

6. **USSR:** the Union of Soviet Socialist Republics, the formal name of the Soviet Union.

The establishment of American bases on islands that are often 10,000 to 12,000 kilometers from the territory of the United States and are on the other side of the Atlantic and Pacific oceans clearly indicates *the offensive nature of the strategic concepts* of the commands of the U.S. army and navy. . . .

All of these facts show clearly that a decisive role in the realization of plans for world dominance by the United States is played by its armed forces. . . .

The "hard-line" policy with regard to the USSR announced by Byrnes[7] after the rapprochement of the reactionary Democrats with the Republicans is at present the main obstacle on the road to cooperation of the Great Powers.[8] It consists mainly of the fact that in the postwar period the United States no longer follows a policy of strengthening cooperation among the Big Three (or Four) but rather has striven to undermine the unity of these countries.[9] The *objective* has been to *impose* the will of other countries on the Soviet Union. . . .

The present policy of the American government with regard to the USSR is also directed at limiting or dislodging the influence of the Soviet Union from neighboring countries. In implementing this policy in former enemy or Allied countries adjacent to the USSR, the United States attempts, at various international conferences or directly in these countries themselves, to support reactionary forces with *the purpose of creating obstacles to the process of democratization of these countries. In so doing, it also attempts to secure positions for the penetration of American capital into their economies.* Such a policy is intended to weaken and overthrow the democratic governments in power there, which are friendly toward the USSR, and replace them in the future with new governments that would obediently carry out a policy dictated from the United States. In this policy, the United States receives full support from English diplomacy.

One of the most important elements in the general policy of the United States, which is directed toward limiting the international role of the USSR in the postwar world, is the *policy with regard to Germany.* In Germany, the United States is taking measures to strengthen reactionary forces for the purpose of opposing democratic reconstruction. Furthermore, it displays special insistence on accompanying this policy with completely inadequate measures for the demilitarization of Germany.

The American occupation policy does not have the objective of eliminating the remnants of *German Fascism* and rebuilding German political life *on a democratic basis,* so that Germany might cease to exist as an aggressive force. The United States is not taking measures *to eliminate the monopolistic associations* of German industrialists on which German Fascism depended in preparing ag-

---

7. **Byrnes:** United States Secretary of State James F. Byrnes. Byrnes took office in 1945, and Novikov imputed to him and President Truman an anti-Soviet foreign policy.

8. Molotov also marked the underlined phrase with a check for added emphasis.

9. **Big Three, Big Four:** the "Big Three" refers to Britain, the Soviet Union, and the United States, the great powers whose leaders shaped the postwar world at Yalta and Potsdam. With the addition of France, this group was the "Big Four."

gression and waging war. Neither is any *agrarian* reform being conducted to eliminate large landholders, who were also a reliable support for the Hitlerites. Instead, the United States is considering the possibility *of terminating the Allied occupation* of German territory before the main tasks of the occupation—the de-militarization and democratization of Germany—have been implemented. This would create the prerequisites for the revival of an imperialist Germany, which the United States plans to use in a future war on its side.

The numerous and extremely hostile statements by American government, political, and military figures with regard to the Soviet Union and its foreign policy are very characteristic of the current relationship between the ruling cir-cles of the United States and the USSR. . . .

The basic goal of this anti-Soviet campaign of American "public opinion" is to exert political pressure on the Soviet Union and compel it to make conces-sions. Another, no less important goal of the campaign is the attempt *to create an atmosphere of war psychosis* among the masses, who are weary of war, thus making it easier for the U.S. government to carry out measures for the mainte-nance of high military potential. . . .

Of course, all of these measures for maintaining a high military potential are not goals in themselves. They are only intended *to prepare the conditions for win-ning world supremacy* in a new war, the date for which, to be sure, cannot be de-termined now by anyone, but which is contemplated by the most bellicose cir-cles of American imperialism.

Careful note should be taken of the fact that the preparation by the United States for a future war is being conducted with the prospect of *war against the Soviet Union*, which in the eyes of American imperialists is the main obstacle in the path of the United States to world domination. . . .

[signed]
N. Novikov

Source 4 from Woodrow J. Kuhns, ed., Assessing the Soviet Threat: The Early Cold War Years *(Washington, D.C.: Center for the Study of Intelligence of the Central Intelligence Agency, 1997), pp. 61, 220–221, 243, 311–312.*

4A. Report 60-48, Central Intelligence Agency, Office of Reports and Estimates

[As in Source 3, italics replicate underlining in the original document.]

THREATS TO THE SECURITY OF THE UNITED STATES SUMMARY

1. For the foreseeable future the USSR will be the only power capable of threatening the security of the United States. The Soviet regime, moreover, is essentially and implacably inimical toward the United States.

2. The power of the USSR to endanger the security of the United States is a consequence not only of Soviet strength, but also of the weakness and instability prevalent in Europe and Asia and of weaknesses in the military posture of the United States. The principal restraint on hostile Soviet action is the greater potential strength of the United States. . . .

4. In general, the probable basic intentions of the Kremlin for the next decade are:

a. To avoid war with the United States, but to exploit to the utmost, within that limitation, the coercive power inherent in the preponderance of Soviet military strength in Eurasia, relying on the disinclination of the United States to resort to war.

b. To build up as rapidly as possible the war potential of the Soviet orbit, in an effort to equal and surpass, eventually, the war potential of the United States.

c. To wage political, economic, and psychological warfare against the United States and its allies, with a view to undermining their potential strength and increasing the relative strength of the USSR: in particular, to prevent or retard the recovery and coalition of Western Europe and the stabilization of the situation in the Near East and Far East.

d. To exploit every opportunity presented by the weakness and instability of neighboring states to expand the area of Soviet domination by political and subversive means.

5. Although the Kremlin is unlikely to resort deliberately to war to gain its ends within the next decade, it would do so if ever it came to consider such a course expedient, particularly if convinced that time was on the side of the United States. In this respect the situation will remain critical pending the successful accomplishment of US efforts to redress the balance of power. Moreover, there is constant danger of war through accident or miscalculation.

6. In any case, the fundamental hostility of the Soviet Government toward the United States and its formidable military power require, in common prudence, that the United States be prepared for the eventuality of war with the USSR.

4B. Central Intelligence Agency
Weekly Summary, July 2, 1948

Western Europe

GERMANY

The Soviet Union has further threatened the position of the western powers in Berlin by increasing existing restrictions on communications between the city and the western zones. The recent Soviet action in cutting off all rail communications and road and barge traffic represents the near-maximum curtailment of ground facilities within Soviet capabilities. On 23 June when the new embargoes were put into effect, the western sectors had food stocks adequate for a six-week minimum German ration and fuel stocks to supply light, power, and water for three weeks. The Soviet action, ostensibly taken in retaliation against the western decision to introduce the new west German currency in Berlin, has two possible objectives: either to force the western powers to negotiate on Soviet terms regarding Germany, or failing that, to force a western power withdrawal from Berlin.

The USSR does not seem ready to force a definite showdown but for the present appears more inclined to compel the western powers to negotiate locally regarding Berlin in the hope that such negotiations could be broadened to include Soviet demands on major issues such as the Ruhr. . . .

4C. Central Intelligence Agency
Weekly Summary, May 6, 1949

Eastern Europe

SOVIET UNION

German Objectives

Soviet agreement to lift the Berlin blockade and enter into four-power discussions on Germany does not represent any change in the Soviet objective to establish a Germany which will eventually fall under Soviet domination. It is still too early, however, to predict the sincerity of the Soviet desire to achieve an understanding with the West on Germany or the extent of the concessions the USSR would make in order to reach an agreement. . . . Progress of the CFM alone, therefore, will demonstrate whether the USSR: (1) has agreed to enter into four-power discussions to sound out the western position and retrieve itself from the unfavorable situation created by the Berlin blockade; or (2) now considers it a sounder strategy to seek a "neutral" Germany in order to delay the final consolidation of the West German state and give the USSR some voice in all Germany.[10]

CFM Proposals

Initial Soviet proposals at the forthcoming CFM will be designed to appeal strongly to an increasingly articulate German nationalism. After attempting to secure a commitment on postponing the West German state, the USSR will probably propose a general settlement for all Germany based on a return to four-power cooperation and the Yalta and Potsdam agreements. The Soviet terms will include. . .: (1) establishment of a centralized government for all Germany; (2) conclusion of a peace treaty and withdrawal of occupation

10. **CFM:** Council of Foreign Ministers, that is, a high-level meeting of the diplomats who headed their countries' respective foreign policy offices.

troops within one year; and (3) control over Ruhr production and distribution by the US, the USSR, the UK, and France. Depending primarily upon the intensity of the Soviet desire to obtain the withdrawal of US troops from Europe, the USSR may later in the negotiations seek a "compromise" agreement. Such a compromise might involve the acceptance of a federal government composed of the East and West German zonal organizations. The USSR would insist, however, that such a federation be established in a manner which, in addition to not threatening Soviet political and economic control in East Germany, would provide for sufficient Soviet influence in West Germany to offer reasonable prospects for subsequently establishing a centralized Germany not wholly western-oriented and susceptible to eventual Soviet domination.

Sources 5 and 6 from Jean Edward Smith, ed., The Papers of General Lucius D. Clay: Germany, 1945–1949, *2 vols. (Bloomington: Indiana University Press, 1974), 1:180–181; 2:743–746. Reprinted with the permission of Indiana University Press.*

5. Food Situation in U.S. Zone

18 March 1946

From CLAY for MCNARNEY[11]

Recommend the dispatch of the following Eyes Only cable from you to General Eisenhower:[12]

"Clay advises me that War Department requires an immediate reduction in the present German ration from 1550 calories to 1313 calories with no shipments of food prior to 1 July except to replace French loan.[13] No assurance is provided for supplies after 1 July which would permit any increase in the reduced ration. The present ration is inadequate to sustain a working population. Health authorities have indicated time and time again that it is insufficient to maintain health over any long period of time. The reduced ration is insufficient to maintain a living standard even for a short period. Sickness and malnutrition are certain to result. Even more important, the population will be incapable of the work necessary in reviving even a minimum economy with a consequent increased financial burden to the United States. While the difficulties in maintaining a higher ration in the U.S. zone than in the adjacent French and British zones are recognized, I believe the reduced ration to be less than

11. **McNarney:** General Joseph T. McNarney, who succeeded General Dwight D. Eisenhower as commander of American forces in Europe in November 1945. Eisenhower had returned to the United States to serve as army chief of staff. Clay was seeking more impact for the message by asking McNarney to send it out under his signature.

12. **Eyes Only:** a security notation indicating that the message was secret and was to be read only by the person to whom it was addressed.

13. **French loan:** refers to food supplies dispatched to the American zone from the French zone to meet the food needs of German citizens there.

the ration allowed in the Russian zone. . . .

"Our reduction in occupational forces has been based on a stabilized U.S. zone in which reasonable food supplies were available for the German people. I do not believe that the reduced ration is sufficient to prevent disease and unrest. Therefore I shall have to reconsider the size of the occupational forces required to maintain order and security.

6. The Berlin Blockade

19 July 1948

TOP SECRET—EYES ONLY

From CLAY for DRAPER

Have received copy of cablegram from Douglas[14] to [Under Secretary of State] Lovett of 17 July which suggests that we are now faced with three alternatives: (A) to abandon Berlin at the risk of losing Europe; (B) to abandon Berlin but under strong commitments to western European nations which would serve to salvage some prestige; and (C) to attempt through the employment of all devices at our command to remain in Berlin.

We might avoid or defer being faced with these alternatives if we now agree to a quadripartite discussion of the entire German problem at governmental level and concurrently suspend our program in western Germany pending such discussion.

Certainly, last November when the Council of Foreign Ministers broke up and again this spring in meetings with the French and British in the London Conference, we recognized fully the probabilities of Soviet counter-measures, and certainly we must have made the decision then that we had to go ahead if democracy was to take the initiative in Europe. This we did, and also added an even greater deterrent to the Soviet expansion policy which was the adoption of the European Recovery Program.[15] The very violence of Soviet reaction now is proof of the success of our several programs to restore and build up democracy in Europe. Having committed ourselves to a course of action to this end and having backed it with large sums of money, can we afford now to throw it away as we encounter our first major evidence of Soviet resistance?

Of course it would be difficult if not impossible for the three western nations to refuse to discuss the German problem with Russia. However, we should refuse to discuss the problem if it means abandonment or suspension of our program in western Germany. No solution of the German problem can be found which does not give USSR a voice in the Ruhr. A failure on our part to establish a German government now could only be interpreted as weakness and apprehension on our part. Even if it were now possible with Soviet partici-

14. **Douglas:** Lewis Douglas was American ambassador to Britain at this time.

15. European Recovery Program (ERP): the Marshall Plan.

pation to establish a unified Germany, could we afford to include it in the ERP, and if we could afford it would not Soviet participation in such a government prevent it from attaining any success[?] Increased production from a western Germany oriented toward western European recovery must be conceded by all as essential to a successful program for European recovery. If we give up that opportunity, can we hope to carry the ERP to a successful conclusion? No final solution of the German problem is possible until ERP has invigorated western Europe so that it may develop a military strength which makes Soviet domination of Europe impossible. I doubt if such a military strength would be developed with Germany under quadripartite control. We have gone too far with western Europe to have any hope of establishing a quadripartite control of Germany which would not retard the development of western Europe and a unified Germany can come now with safety only when the balance of power in Europe is restored.

Soviet measures now being taken must be based on one of two premises: (A) the first premise is that the Soviet Government, recognizing the rising tide of anti-communistic forces under European recovery, are [*sic*] determined to exert pressures to retard such recovery to the point of, but short of, war. In other words, they are still bluffing but will continue to do so until it is absolutely evident that their bluff is being called. In such case they will recede. To support this premise there is their evident lack of real readiness for war and their lack of preparation for immediate and major war in Europe.

(B) The second premise is that the Soviet Government has now made up its mind that European recovery can be stopped only by war. Having advised their population for three years now that America is getting ready to attack the USSR, it would be their intent to force us to the first overt act so that they could charge us with being the aggressor. If this premise is correct, war will come now because the USSR has determined it to be inevitable and that time is against the USSR. If war has been determined, it will not be fought to gain possession of Berlin, and the pressures now being exerted in Berlin if we withdraw will be applied elsewhere next, probably in Vienna, and will continue until we are provoked into an act of war. The Soviet Government may well believe that with passing time our position will become relatively stronger than at present, and hence if the USSR does want war it is to their advantage for it to come sooner rather than later. There are no reports of military movements to support this premise except the very large expenditure programs of the Soviet Government during the past three years to maintain its military establishment.

While I fully appreciate the importance of diplomatic procedures to include the further exchange of notes, the placing of the issue before the United Nations, the imposing of sanctions elsewhere, and any other measures which seem feasible, we must recognize that all of these measures take time under which our own situation may well deteriorate. Moreover, unless we and the western nations take far more vigorous measures for preparedness than we are taking now, we can only hope that the passage of time will make us really prepared for war. Certainly the Soviet Government during this same period of time, with its absolute control of the Soviet economy, can be increasing its own efforts to prepare for war at an accelerated rate. Thus, a delay, if war is inevitable, does not necessarily find the West better prepared. . . .

. . .It is only by a showing of force which is in the nature of an armed reconnaissance that we can determine the real intent of the Soviet Government.

Our right to move an armed force for garrison purposes into and out of Berlin, as far as I know, has not been questioned. The movement of such a force could be stopped only by attack.[16] This attack would not occur unless the Soviet Government is determined upon a war course. If it has so determined, a retreat now will merely be followed by pressure elsewhere within a matter of weeks or months. If war is inevitable, the time that we can gain by retreat now is so relatively short that it has little value.

The choice before us is a hard choice. However, if we do decide to retreat now, this retreat will not save us from again and again having to choose between retreat and war. With each retreat we will find ourselves confronted with the same problem but with fewer and fewer allies on our side.

I am sending this radio to you personally rather than officially to the Department as I realize that my views and comments go beyond my responsibilities as theater commander. Thus I leave to you entirely the decision as to how you use these views, if at all. I shall keep no copy here. However, I cannot but feel that the world today is facing the most critical issue that has arisen since Hitler placed his policy of aggression in motion. In fact, the Soviet Government has more force immediately at its disposal than did Hitler to accomplish his purpose. Only America can exert the world leadership, and only America can provide the strength to stop this policy of aggression here and now. The next time may be too late. I believe determined action will stop it short of war. It cannot be stopped without the serious risk of war.

16. Clay alludes here to the plan he put forward early in the crisis for "calling the bluff" of the Soviets. Because they alleged that they had closed land routes to Berlin because of "technical problems," that is, destroyed bridges and other obstacles, Clay proposed sending a force of American, British, and French troops, equipped with artillery as well as bridging equipment, from the west across the Soviet zone to Berlin. Of course, such an armed incursion into the Soviet zone risked war.

Source 7 from Lawrence Friedman, ed., Europe Transformed: Documents on the End of the
Cold War *(New York: St. Martin's Press, 1990), pp. 14–15.*

7. The North Atlantic Treaty,
April 4, 1949

The Parties to this Treaty *reaffirm* their faith in the purposes and principles of the Charter of the United Nations and their desire to live in peace with all peoples and all governments.

They *are determined* to safeguard the freedom, common heritage and civilization of their peoples, founded on the principles of democracy, individual liberty and the rule of law.

They *seek to promote* stability and well-being in the North Atlantic area.

They are *resolved* to unite their efforts for collective defence and for the preservation of peace and security.

They therefore agree to this North Atlantic Treaty:

Article 1

The Parties undertake, as set forth in the Charter of the United Nations, to settle any international dispute in which they may be involved by peaceful means in such a manner that international peace and security and justice are not endangered, and to refrain in their international relations from the threat or use of force in any manner inconsistent with the purposes of the United Nations.

Article 2

The Parties will contribute toward the further development of peaceful and friendly international relations by strengthening their free institutions, by bringing about a better understanding of the principles upon which these institutions are founded, and by promoting coalitions of stability and well-being. They will seek to eliminate conflict in their international economic policies and will encourage economic collaboration between any or all of them.

Article 3

In order more effectively to achieve the objectives of this Treaty, the Parties, separately and jointly, by means of continuous and effective self-help and mutual aid, will maintain and develop their individual and collective capacity to resist armed attack.

Article 4

The Parties will consult together whenever, in the opinion of any of them, the territorial integrity, political indepedence or security of any of the Parties is threatened.

Article 5

The Parties agree that an armed attack against one or more of them in Europe or North America shall be considered an attack against them all and consequently they agree that, if such an armed attack occurs, each of them, in exercise of the right of individual or collective self-defence recognized by Article 51 of the Charter of the United Nations, will assist the Party or Parties so attacked by taking forthwith, individually and in concert with the other Parties, such action as it deems necessary, including the use of armed force, to restore and maintain the security of the North Atlantic area. . . .

Source 8 from Department of State Bulletin 45 *(1961): 231–233.*

8. Soviet Aide-Mémoire
of June 4, 1961

Official translation

1. The years-long delay in arriving at a peace settlement with Germany has largely predetermined the dangerous course of events in Europe in the postwar period. The major decisions of the Allies on the eradication of militarism in Germany, which once were considered by the Governments of the United States and the U.S.S.R. as the guarantee of stable peace, have been implemented only partially and now are actually not being observed in the greater part of German territory. Of the Governments of the two German States that were formed after the war, it is only the Government of the German Democratic Republic that recognizes and adheres to those agreements. The Government of the Federal Republic of Germany openly proclaims its negative attitude to those agreements, cultivates sabre-rattling militarism and advocates the review of the German frontiers and the results of the Second World War. It tries to establish a powerful military base for its aggressive plans, to kindle a dangerous hotbed of conflicts on German soil, and to set the former Allies in the anti-Hitler coalition against each other.

The Western Powers have allowed the Federal Republic of Germany to start accumulating armaments and setting up an army, which are clearly in excess of defense needs. . . .

2. The Soviet Government is earnestly striving towards removing the sources of tension between the United States and the U.S.S.R. and to proceed to constructive, friendly cooperation. The conclusion of a German peace treaty would allow the two countries to come much closer to the attainment of this goal. The U.S.S.R. and the United States fought together against Hitlerite Germany. Their common duty is to conclude a German peace treaty and thereby create a reliable guarantee that German soil will never again give birth to forces that could plunge the world into a new and even more devastating war. If the desire of the Soviet Union to consolidate peace and to prevent the unleashing of a new world war in Europe does not run counter to the intentions of the United States Government, then it will not be difficult to reach agreement. . . .

4. The Soviet Government is not pursuing the goal of harming the interests of the United States or other Western Powers in Europe. It does not propose to change anything either in Germany or in West Berlin in favor of any one State or group of States. The U.S.S.R. deems it necessary in the interests of consolidating peace formally to recognize the situation which has developed in Europe after the war, to legalize and to consolidate the inviolability of the existing German borders, to normalize the situation in West Berlin on the basis of reasonable consideration for the interests of all the parties concerned.

In the interests of achieving agreement on a peace treaty the Soviet Union does not insist on the immediate withdrawal of the Federal Republic of Germany from NATO. Both German States could for a certain period, even after the conclusion of a peace treaty, remain in the military alliances to which they now belong. . . .

5. The conclusion of a German peace treaty would also solve the problem of normalizing the situation in West Berlin. Deprived of a stable international status, West Berlin at present is a place where the Bonn revanchist[17] circles continually maintain extreme tension and organize all kinds of provocations very dangerous to the cause of peace. We are duty-bound to prevent a development where intensification of West German militarism could lead to irreparable consequences due to the unsettled situation in West Berlin.

At present, the Soviet Government does not see a better way to solve the West Berlin problem than by transforming it into a demilitarized free city. The implementation of the proposal to turn West Berlin into a free city, with the interests of all parties duly taken into consideration, would normalize the situation in West Berlin. The occupation regime now being maintained has already outlived itself and has lost all connection with the purposes for which it was established, as well as with the Allied agreements concerning Germany that established the basis for its existence. The occupation rights will naturally be ter-

---

17. **Bonn revanchist:** Bonn was the West German capital; revanchists seek revenge, a desire that Soviet cold war officials consistently imputed to the government of Chancellor Konrad Adenauer.

minated upon the conclusion of a German peace treaty, whether it is signed with both German States or only with the German Democratic Republic, within whose territory West Berlin is located.

The position of the Soviet Government is that the free city of West Berlin should have unobstructed contacts with the outside world and that its internal regulations should be determined by the freely expressed will of its population. The United States as well as other countries would naturally have every possibility to maintain and develop their relations with the free city. In short, West Berlin, as the Soviet Government sees it, should be strictly neutral. Of course, the use of Berlin as a base for provocative activities, hostile to the U.S.S.R., the G.D.R. or any other State, cannot be permitted in the future, nor can Berlin be allowed to remain a dangerous hotbed of tension and international conflicts. . . .

Source 9 *from* The Soviet Stand on Germany: Nine Key Documents Including Diplomatic Papers and Major Speeches by N.S. Khrushchev *(New York: Crosscurrents Press, a division of International Book Company, Moscow, 1961), pp. 22, 30, 34–36, 38.*

9. Radio and Television Address to the Soviet Union by Nikita S. Khrushchev, July 15, 1961

DEAR COMRADES, FRIENDS:

As you know, I recently returned from Vienna where for two days I met and had comprehensive talks with John F. Kennedy, the President of the United States of America.

Many materials were published in our press, just as in the entire world press, on this score. Many of you have already read the memoranda which were handed to President Kennedy. The first memorandum dealt with the question of ending nuclear weapons tests; and the other, with the conclusion of a peace treaty with Germany and a solution of the West Berlin problem on this basis.[18] Obviously many of you also read President Kennedy's radio and television speech, which was published in full in our newspapers. Thus Soviet public opinion is well informed about the views which the United States President set forth and his appraisal of our meeting. . . .

Permit me now to turn to the German question, which occupied an important place in our talks with President Kennedy.

The Soviet Government has repeatedly stated its position on this question. And the Western powers cannot complain that they do not know our proposals sufficiently well. We have done and are doing everything to convince the Governments of Britain, the United States of America, France, and the other

18. This is the *aide-mémoire* in Source 8.

nations which took part with us in the war against Hitler Germany that the absence of a peace treaty with Germany has created a deeply abnormal and dangerous situation in Europe.

It has always been recognized that peace treaties should be concluded after wars between states have ended. This has already become a custom and, if you wish, a standard of international law. Instances of this can also be found in international practice after the end of World War II. Peace treaties with Italy and the other states that fought on the side of Hitler Germany were signed more than fourteen years ago. The United States of America, Britain and the other countries concluded a peace treaty with Japan in 1951. But the governments of these selfsame countries will not countenance the conclusion of a peace treaty with Germany.

Every person, if not deprived of common sense, understands that the signing of a peace treaty is the road toward improving relations between states. The refusal to sign a peace treaty and the perpetuation of the occupational regime in West Berlin are directed at continuing the cold war, and who can say where lies the borderline between a cold war and a war in the full sense of the word? Surely it is clear that a cold war is a period of preparation, of accumulating forces for war.

I speak of all this so that everyone may understand the gravity of the danger incurred by any further delay in the conclusion of a German peace treaty.

When we suggest signing a peace treaty with Germany and turning West Berlin into a free city, we are accused of wanting, allegedly, to deprive the Western powers of access to this city. But that is a wrong and an unworthy argument. The granting to West Berlin of the status of a free city would mean that all countries of the world wishing to maintain economic and cultural ties with this city would have the right and opportunity freely to maintain these ties. Of course, agreement would have to be reached with the country across whose territory pass the communications that link West Berlin with the outside world. That is normal. Otherwise the sovereignty of the state in which West Berlin is situated would be jeopardized. . . .

When the Soviet Government suggests concluding a peace treaty and normalizing on this basis the situation in West Berlin, it wants only peace, it wants to remove from relations between states everything that causes friction and could cause a dangerous conflict. It is not the socialist countries but the Western powers that are throwing out a challenge to the world, when despite common sense they declare that they will not recognize the conclusion of a peace treaty and will seek to preserve the occupation regime in West Berlin, which they—if you please—conquered. That is not a policy of peace; that is trampling on the most elementary norms in relation between states. It is a desire to preserve a state of extreme tension in international relations and, moreover, it is a threat of war.

The Soviet Union and our friends do not want war, and we will not start it. But we will defend our sovereignty, will fulfill our sacred duty to defend our freedom and independence. If any country violates peace and crosses the borders—land, air or water—of another, it will assume full responsibility for the consequences of the aggression and will receive a proper rebuff.

The world press has published many comments on our meetings and talks with President Kennedy. Among these comments there are many sensible statements made in the United States, in Britain, in France and in West Germany, not to mention the German Democratic Republic and the other socialist countries. But there are hate-ridden persons, deprived of common sense, who oppose negotiations with the Soviet Union and call for a crusade against communism. . . .

The governments of some countries have announced in advance that they will not take part in a peace conference. The Soviet Union will, of course, regret it if some countries evade the signing of a German peace treaty; we have always wanted and still want all countries of the anti-Hitler coalition to take part in the peaceful settlement of the German question.

But even should certain countries refuse to take part in the negotiations on the conclusion of a peace treaty, that will not stop us; together with other countries which do desire it, we shall sign a peace treaty with the two German states. Should Federal Germany not agree to sign a peace treaty, we shall sign it with the German Democratic Republic alone, which has long declared her desire to conclude a peace treaty and has agreed to the formation on her territory of a free city of West Berlin.

There are some in the West who threaten us, saying that if we sign a peace treaty it will not be recognized, and that even arms will be brought into play to prevent its implementation.

Evidently they forget that times are different now. If even in the past the "position of strength" policy was useless against the Soviet Union, then now it is more than ever doomed to failure. The Soviet Union is against the use of force in relations between states. We stand for a peaceful settlement of controversial questions between states. However, we are capable of giving a proper rebuff to any use of force, and we have what is needed to defend our interests. . . .

Source 10 from Public Papers of the Presidents of the United States: John F. Kennedy, Containing the Public Messages, Speeches and Statements of the President, January 20 to December 31, 1961 *(Washington, D.C.: U.S. Government Printing Office, 1962), pp. 533–536.*

10. Radio and Television Report to the American People on the Berlin Crisis, July 25, 1961

Good evening:

Seven weeks ago tonight I returned from Europe to report on my meeting with Premier Khrushchev and the others. His grim warnings about the future of the world, his aide memoire on Berlin, his subsequent speeches and threats which he and his agents have launched, and the increase in the Soviet military budget that he has announced, have all prompted a series of decisions by the Administration and a series of consultations with the members of the NATO organization. In Berlin, as you recall, he intends to bring to an end, through a stroke of the pen, *first* our legal rights to be in West Berlin—and *secondly* our ability to make good on our commitment to the two million free people of that city. That we cannot permit. . . .

We are there as a result of our victory over Nazi Germany—and our basic rights to be there, deriving from that victory, include both our presence in West Berlin and the enjoyment of access across East Germany. . . .

Thus, our presence in West Berlin, and our access thereto, cannot be ended by any act of the Soviet government. The NATO shield was long ago extended to cover West Berlin—and we have given our word that an attack upon that city will be regarded as an attack upon us all. . . .

We do not want to fight—but we have fought before. . . .

We cannot and will not permit the Communists to drive us out of Berlin, either gradually or by force. For the fulfillment of our pledge to that city is essential to the morale and security of Western Germany, to the unity of Western Europe, and to the faith of the entire Free World. . . .

The new preparations that we shall make to defend the peace are part of the long-term build-up in our strength which has been underway since January. They are based on our needs to meet a world-wide threat, on a basis which stretches far beyond the present Berlin crisis. Our primary purpose is neither propaganda nor provocation—but preparation.

A first need is to hasten progress toward the military goals which the North Atlantic allies have set for themselves. In Europe today nothing less will suffice. We will put even greater resources into fulfilling those goals, and we look to our allies to do the same.

The supplementary defense build-ups that I asked from the Congress in March and May have already started moving us toward these and our other defense goals. They included an increase in the size of the Marine Corps, improved readiness of our reserves, expansion of our air and sea lift, and stepped-up procurement of needed weapons, ammunition, and other items. . . .

But even more importantly, we need the capability of placing in any critical area at the appropriate time a force which, combined with those of our allies, is large enough to make clear our determination and our ability to defend our rights at all costs—and to meet all levels of aggressor pressure with whatever levels of force are required. We intend to have a wider choice than humiliation or all-out nuclear action.

While it is unwise at this time either to call up or send abroad excessive numbers of these troops before they are needed, let me make it clear that I intend to take, as time goes on, whatever steps are necessary to make certain that such forces can be deployed at the appropriate time without lessening our ability to meet our commitments elsewhere. . . .

Accordingly, I am now taking the following steps:

(1) I am tomorrow requesting the Congress for the current fiscal year an additional $3,247,000,000 of appropriations for the Armed Forces.

(2) To fill out our present Army Divisions, and to make more men available for prompt deployment, I am requesting an increase in the Army's total authorized strength from 875,000 to approximately 1 million men.

(3) I am requesting an increase of 29,000 and 63,000 men respectively in the active duty strength of the Navy and the Air Force.

(4) To fulfill these manpower needs, I am ordering that our draft calls be doubled and tripled in the coming months; I am asking the Congress for authority to order to active duty certain ready reserve units and individual reservists, and to extend tours of duty; . . .

We have another sober responsibility. To recognize the possibilities of nuclear war in the missile age, without our citizens knowing what they should do and where they should go if bombs begin to fall, would be a failure of responsibility. In May, I pledged a new start on Civil Defense. . . . Tomorrow, I am requesting of the Congress new funds for the following immediate objectives: to identify and mark space in existing structures—public and private—that could be used for fall-out shelters in case of attack; to stock those shelters with food, water, first-aid kits and other minimum essentials for survival; to increase their capacity; to improve our air-raid warning and fall-out detection systems, including a new household warning system which is now under development; and to take other measures that will be effective at an early date to save millions of lives if needed. . . .

A fundamental cause of the Cold War may be found in each of the great powers' understanding, or misunderstanding, of the other. Begin your analysis of the Cold War's origins by considering the Soviet view of the United States. What view was Novikov expressing when he wrote of the "imperialist tendencies of American capital"? What American actions during World War II did Novikov allege were part of the American policy? How did he see postwar American business as a tool of this policy? Where did the military establishment fit into American plans for Novikov? What was his vision of his own country's motives as it pursued "democratic reconstruction" in Eastern Europe? Why did he conclude that the ultimate American goal was war against the Soviet Union? Fifteen years after Novikov wrote, Nikita Khrushchev made his radio and television address. What views of the United States and its allies did this Soviet leader express? Do you think that his assertion that there were some in the West who wished to perpetuate Cold War tensions as well as "hate-ridden persons, deprived of common sense" was simply propaganda, or might he have believed what he said? After all, American students of Soviet policy in the 1940s and 1950s consistently reported that Soviet leaders were not well informed about foreign countries.

Next, consider the American vision of the Soviets. What objectives did CIA analysts ascribe to the Soviet Union? Why did they envision the So-

viet Union as the worldwide enemy of the United States and its European allies? What chances for war between the Soviet Union and the United States existed according to the CIA? What did General Clay believe were the goals of the Soviet Union? Why did he compare its threat to that of Hitler? Why was he prepared to risk war against the Soviets?

Finally, consider the specific issue of Germany and its capital. What does the map suggest about the strategic viability of the American-British-French position in Berlin after World War II? How do you think the Western allies maintained their position in Berlin for almost two generations, given the numerical superiority of Soviet forces in the region? Was it perhaps because they convinced Soviet authorities that they were prepared to fight a general war over the German capital? What sort of machinery had the Potsdam agreement set up for administering occupied Germany? In retrospect, what sort of differences between the Western allies and the Soviets might have been foreseen in establishing this machinery? What did Soviet observers like Novikov believe that the Americans were doing in Germany? For their part, how did American policymakers understand Soviet actions in Germany? How, for example, did General Clay characterize the Soviet threat in the first Berlin crisis, even as he noted that he had no evidence of Soviet troop movements to give tangible form to that threat?

Once you have analyzed the perspectives of both sides in the Cold War, you should be ready to address this chapter's central questions. What were the origins of the Cold War? How did the Berlin crises develop out of wartime agreements? What strategic consideration made Berlin so essential to both the Western allies and the Soviet Union?

EPILOGUE

The construction of the Berlin Wall in 1961 dramatically decreased the number of East Germans fleeing to the West by surrounding the western sectors of the German capital with a wall twenty-nine miles in length that was guarded by heavily armed policemen. Nonetheless, East Germans continued to attempt to escape; some tunneled under the wall, others attempted to smash through the barriers with trucks, and a few tried to climb over it. Many failed in such attempts, as did Peter Fechter, an eighteen-year-old who tried to scale the wall in August 1962. Shot in the back and stomach by East German border guards as he climbed the wall, Fechter fell back into the eastern sector, where East German guards left him unattended for an hour, despite his calls for help, as he bled to death. Fechter's tragic fate sparked anti-Soviet riots in West Berlin, and it, and other incidents like it, dramatized the human price of a wall that divided a city as well as families.

Beyond Germany the Cold War continued for another generation. Discovery of Soviet missiles in Cuba, ninety miles off the American coast, provoked the last great direct confrontation between the United States and the Soviet Union in 1962. Although the Kennedy administration forced the removal of the missiles, a costly arms race between the Americans and the Soviets ensued. The United States also fought a long war in Vietnam against communist forces there. But by the early 1970s, an era of *détente*—improvement in East–West relations—developed. Improved relations between West Germany and the Soviets were essential in this process, and in 1970 Chancellor Willy Brandt did something no earlier West German leader had done by officially recognizing Germany's World War II territorial losses in the east (see Source 2) to the Soviet Union and Poland. His government was able to build on this first step in improving relations with Eastern block countries by negotiating rights for West Germans to visit relatives in East Germany. The Western allies also concluded an important agreement with the Soviets in the Quadripartite Agreement of 1972, which fully recognized the Western powers' rights of access to Berlin. The German capital then faded from the world's attention until events of the 1980s propelled it back into the news.

In 1985 the Soviet Union got new leadership in Mikhail Gorbachev. Recognizing that the restrictive economic and intellectual life of the Soviet Union made competition with the West increasingly difficult, Gorbachev announce a policy of *perestroika* (restructuring of government to achieve more democracy) and *glas-*

nost (greater freedom of expression). He also sought better relations with the United States and other Western powers. Most importantly, however, Gorbachev was unwilling, or unable, to maintain Soviet domination of the nations of Eastern Europe, and beginning in the late 1980s these states increasingly asserted their rights to be free political systems. In East Germany, the SED dictatorship faced growing dissatisfaction among its citizens, and in 1989 opposition groups began to protest for the first time in years. East Germans also expressed their dissatisfaction once again by leaving their country when the opportunity arose. Thus, when neighboring Hungary opened its western border to the free movement of people, 25,000 East Germans with travel permits for vacations in that country simply left for the West by way of Hungary in just three days in September 1989.

Indeed, throughout 1989 the SED regime had growing difficulties maintaining its accustomed control in East Germany. The number of protests demanding fundamental political and economic changes grew in size and number throughout the year and forced changes in a party leadership that ultimately proved incapable of controlling events. Finally, on November 9, 1989, the authorities ceased to enforce their control of the Berlin Wall, and free movement between the eastern and western sectors of Berlin resumed. In the first four days of such freedom, 4.3 million East Germans crossed into West Berlin. Most returned home, but many stayed in the western zone. As the East German regime grew increasingly weak, it joined with West Germany to take the first steps toward German reunification. The wall at last came down, and on July 1, 1990, East Germany adopted the currency and free economic system of West Germany. The final obstacle to German reunification fell when the Soviets dropped their long-standing objection to a reunified Germany belonging to NATO. Thus, in the so-called Two (East and West Germany) Plus Four (Britain, France, the Soviet Union, and the United States) Treaty of 1990, the World War II Allies finally signed a treaty ending occupation and paving the way for German unification. A unified German state, holding membership in NATO, became a reality at midnight on October 3, 1990, and the Cold War issue of Berlin ceased to threaten the world's peace.

CHAPTER FOURTEEN

THE PERILS OF PROSPERITY:

THE UNREST OF

YOUTH IN THE 1960s

THE PROBLEM

Commuters just emerging from subway exits in the university district of Paris on the evening of Friday, May 3, 1968, must have been bewildered. They stepped out into a neighborhood transformed since morning into a war zone in which police and students battled over the future of France's governmental and economic systems. These commuters witnessed a conflict in which French students, like students in many other countries in 1968, called into question a material prosperity purchased, in their view, with a loss of individual liberty in the face of the power of the modern state and giant industrial concerns.

The postwar Western world indeed was experiencing unprecedented prosperity by the late 1960s. The United States enjoyed the world's highest living standard. In Western Europe, the European Economic Community (or EEC), also called the

Common Market, served as a key instrument for economic recovery and growth for war-ravaged France, West Germany, Italy, Belgium, the Netherlands, and Luxembourg. Non-EEC countries, including Great Britain and the Scandinavian nations, also shared in this economic success. Even in communist Eastern Europe, war damage was repaired and the socialist economies of the region produced standards of living for their peoples substantially improved over those of the early postwar years.

Behind the façade of material success, however, were a number of problems that led to widespread unrest, especially among the young, in the 1960s. Part of the basis for this discontent may be found in the very economic success of the postwar period. Several Western countries, including France and Great Britain, encouraged growth by government intervention in the economy or national ownership of industries. The economic life of communist Eastern Europe, of course, was entirely

Chapter 14

The Perils of

Prosperity:

The Unrest of

Youth in

the 1960s

under government control. The result was a growing state economic bureaucracy in which the individual had little voice. The nature of the economic growth was unsettling, too. The West was entering a new phase of industrialization. New and sophisticated industries, such as computers and electronics, flourished; the service sector of the economy grew while older heavy industries declined in importance. The result was deep concern among many workers, who found little demand for their traditional skills and who felt powerless to avoid unemployment or underemployment. Worker dissatisfaction with the existing system only increased with economic recessions like that of 1968 in France, which added to unemployment and reduced the buying power of those who retained their jobs. Economic growth, for many, was not an unqualified success.

Many European students were dissatisfied with the system of higher education. A partial reason may be found in the West's great population growth after World War II. The postwar baby boom of 1946–1964, which affected both Europe and America, coincided with a prosperity that permitted Western democracies to provide their youth with greater educational opportunity than had been offered any earlier generation. In two decades student populations vastly increased. From 1950 to 1970, university enrollments increased from 123,000 to 651,000 in France; from 190,000 to 561,000 in Italy; from 117,000 to 410,000 in West Germany; and from 67,200 to 250,000 in Great Britain.[1] But often the quality of the educational experience declined as the system strained to cope with unprecedented enrollments. University faculty and facilities failed to grow as fast as their student bodies, resulting in crowded lecture halls and student-faculty ratios that went as high as 105 to 1 in Italy and rendered professors inaccessible to students.

Other problems also affected the student population. University curricula often provided a traditional education that did little to prepare a student to succeed in the new service-oriented economy. When European governments decreed half-hearted curriculum reforms to respond to economic change, they often, as in France, extended a student's course of study. The university also seemed divorced from the real problems of society, such as poverty and crime, a fact reflected in the rarity of sociology courses dealing with those problems.

These curricular problems and the impersonal nature of the modern university led to student demands for sweeping change in the educational establishment. The students wished a voice in the decisions that affected them. They increasingly demanded a say in what was taught, who taught, and how the universities were administered. As we will see, such demands also reflected the feelings of many nonstudents who bitterly felt their inability to affect the modern institutions that controlled their lives.

1. B. R. Mitchell, ed., *European Historical Statistics,* abridged ed. (New York: Columbia University Press, 1978), pp. 396–400.

Students of the 1960s were disappointed and angered by educational shortcomings, but they were even more frustrated by their inability to effect political change. The student generation of the 1960s was physically more mature than any previous generation, thanks to improved nutrition. Their sense of adulthood was heightened by the spread of techniques of birth control that freed women from the fear of pregnancy outside of marriage and fostered a youthful revolt against traditional sexual mores. That revolt could have political ramifications; a slogan frequently heard among French students in 1968 was: "Every time I make love I want to make the revolution; every time I make the revolution I want to make love." But these self-consciously mature young people could change little around them. Everywhere, those under twenty-one were eligible for military service but had no right to vote. Nor had students even a voice in their universities' governance. Typically, European governments controlled universities through centralized bureaucracies. In France, for example, such minor events as student dances had to be approved by the Ministry of Education.

Yet for all the dissatisfaction among students and workers, traditional twentieth-century political ideologies offered scant appeal. The cold war had polarized Europe for twenty years, and neither of the opposing doctrines—Russian communism or the democratic capitalism of the United States—offered real answers to student demands. Indeed, in a political sense both doctrines increas-ingly lost credibility for students. For some, the democratic ideals of the United States no longer seemed attractive because of that nation's increasingly unpopular war in Vietnam. Many saw that Southeast Asian conflict, which engaged about 500,000 American servicemen by 1968, as a war to uphold a favored minority in South Vietnam through military involvement. Those who looked toward a communist vision of a better world similarly were disappointed. The Soviet Union, with its regimented society, inefficient economy, and forceful crushing of dissent in its East German, Polish, and Hungarian satellites in the 1950s, was hardly the best advertisement for Marxian socialism.

Ideological disillusionment led a minority of students to radical doctrines rejecting orthodox Marxism as well as liberal democracy. The ideas of Leon Trotsky, a Marxist who rejected the need for a bureaucracy in a socialist state, attracted some. The example of Mao Zedong, the Chinese revolutionary, stirred other students to reject all authority and to attempt to rally working people to the cause of revolutionary change. Still others were attracted by nineteenth-century anarchist thought that rejected any hierarchy of control over the individual. Some also found inspiration in the revolutionary activism of Cuba's Fidel Castro and Che Guevara. Common to all was the belief that the institutions of society favored the rich, manipulated the poor, and substituted materialism bred of postwar economic growth for individual liberty and any high-minded questioning of the

Chapter 14

The Perils of

Prosperity:

The Unrest of

Youth in

the 1960s

established order. Everywhere student demands could be summed up as calls for participation by individuals in all the decisions that shaped their lives, a concept that French students labeled *autogestion.*

Whatever their ideology, student radicals sought confrontation with established governmental and educational authority in the hope of garnering a mass following for change among the nonrevolutionary majority of students, workers, and others. The radicals increasingly found student followers in many countries. Unrest due to the Vietnam War was widespread on campuses in the United States from the mid-1960s. In Europe, riots began in Italy in 1965 at the universities of Milan and Trento as students demanded a voice in academic policy. Italian unrest continued into the late 1960s, when student radicals combined ideas for a complete overthrow of traditional society with their demands for educational change. Incidents rooted in the desire for political change were common to German and British universities, too. In most of these countries, however, youthful radicals generated little support beyond their campuses. France was the only Western European country in which youthful unrest spread beyond students and thus threatened the existence of the government.

In 1968 France had been led for ten years by President Charles de Gaulle, the seventy-eight-year-old hero of World War II whose imperial style of government only increased the extreme state centralization traditional in that country. Significantly, too, France was suffering an economic recession that heightened the discontent of many workers. Problems began at the new Nanterre campus of the University of Paris. Placed amid slums housing immigrant workers, this modern university center seemed to radicals a dramatic illustration of the failings of modern consumer society. Led by the anarchist Daniel Cohn-Bendit in a protest of university regulations, Nanterre students forced the closing of their campus in the spring of 1968.

Nanterre radicals next focused their attention on the main campus of the University of Paris, at the Sorbonne, after university authorities had begun disciplinary action against Cohn-Bendit and others on May 3, 1968. As police removed protesting student radicals from the Sorbonne, antipolice violence erupted among crowds of students around the university. The very appearance of the police on university grounds provoked student anger. University confines were normally beyond the jurisdiction of the police, who had last entered the Sorbonne in 1791. The crowd threw rocks and, more dangerously, the heavy cobblestones of Paris streets. Police beat students brutally, and the broadcast of such scenes on the evening television news generated widespread support for the radicals, who now demanded a change in France's government.

For the next two weeks, the university district of Paris was the scene of street fighting between police and students that drew on the traditions of a Paris that had often defied government in the past.[2] Ominously for the government, the student unrest spread to other parts of society. On May 13, 1968, unions scheduled a twenty-four-hour general strike to protest police brutality, despite the opposition of the large French Communist party, which feared the unorthodoxy of the spreading revolt. On May 14 workers began to occupy factories and to refuse to work, the young among them demanding, like the students, a voice in decisions affecting them. For other workers, improved wages were a demand. Within a week, perhaps as many as 10 million workers nationwide had seized their factories and were on strike. Even professionals in broadcasting, sports, and other fields joined the strike. The country was paralyzed, and the government seemed on the brink of collapse as opposition leaders began to discuss alternative regimes.

As the government faltered, both sides in the confrontation clearly saw the significance of the growing revolt. Cohn-Bendit characterized it as "a whole generation rising against a certain sort of society— bourgeois society." A leader of the establishment, France's Prime Minister Georges Pompidou, defined the revolt as one against modern society itself. Even the authoritarian de Gaulle heard the message, conceding on May 19, "Reform yes, anarchy no."[3]

Prime Mister Pompidou began to defuse the crisis by offering wage increases to the striking unions. Faced with destroying the consumer society or enjoying more of its benefits, many striking workers quickly chose the latter option. Then, on May 29, de Gaulle flew to West Germany, assured himself of the support of French army units stationed there in case of the need of force, and returned to Paris to end the crisis. Addressing the nation on radio the next day, the president refused to resign as the protesters demanded and instead dissolved the National Assembly, calling for new elections to that body. The maneuver saved the government's cause. The protesters could not call repressive a government that was willing to risk its control of the legislature in elections called ahead of schedule. Although student radicals tried to continue the revolt, most workers accepted proffered pay increases and new elections and returned to work. De Gaulle's supporters won a majority of the seats in the National Assembly on June 23, 1968, and the president retained the power to govern.

As students and workers battled police in France, equally dramatic events were moving to a climax across Europe in Czechoslovakia.

---

2. Students fought much as Parisians had in the eighteenth and nineteenth centuries, tearing up paving stones and piling them with overturned vehicles and fallen trees to create street barricades from behind which they fought police. When the student revolt ended, the government paved cobblestone streets with asphalt.

3. In the present context, *anarchy* is probably the best English word to convey briefly what de Gaulle meant. De Gaulle probably sought a certain effect by using an army colloquialism, *chien lit,* which even the French press had difficulty expressing adequately. It means making "a mess in one's own bed"—in other words, "fouling one's own nest."

Chapter 14

The Perils of

Prosperity:

The Unrest of

Youth in

the 1960s

Although unrest in democratic France and one-party Czechoslovakia displayed differences, the revolts in both countries had common roots in a rejection of highly centralized and unresponsive authority.

Czechoslovakia, an industrialized country with Western democratic traditions, experienced a coup in 1948 that established a communist government. The leaders of that regime, party First Secretaries Klement Gottwald (1948–1953) and Antonín Novotný (1953–1968), were steadfast followers of authoritarian Stalinist communism, even though the Soviet Union itself began a process of "de-Stalinization" after 1956. But by 1967 Novotný's style of communism was becoming increasingly unacceptable to Czechoslovakians in two chief regards. The most basic problem concerned the nation's two largest ethnic groups: the Czechs and the Slovaks. For a long time the Slovaks had been unhappy with Czech domination of both the Communist party and the state apparatus. The Novotný regime perpetuated this Czech domination as the Slovaks clamored for a stronger voice in national affairs.

Even more fundamental than the regime's ethnic difficulties, however, was its rigid and authoritarian Stalinist communism. Economically, this meant a managed economy, oriented toward heavy industrial goods rather than consumer items, that was hampered by centralized control, no profit motive, and low productivity. The nation had experienced serious economic problems since 1962. Politically, Novotný's government gave the country rigid control by a small party inner circle sustained by a secret police, press censorship, and extreme curbs on intellectual freedom.

A series of events led to change in Czechoslovakia through the efforts of the younger generation of party officials, intellectuals, and students. As in France, loss of support for the regime began among those who were being groomed in the educational system as future leaders, not with the materially deprived. Pressure for change in the country's highest leadership mounted as Novotný's authoritarian style of government resisted reform and economic problems persisted.

In 1963 the Slovak branch of the Communist party named a new first secretary, the reform-minded Alexander Dubček. In a country where literature long had been politicized, writers began to desert the regime; at the Congress of Czechoslovak Writers in June 1967, they demanded an end to censorship and freedom for their craft. Other intellectuals also grew restive with the regime. But, as in France, it was young people who brought matters to a crisis point. Cries of "We want freedom, we want democracy" and "A good communist is a dead communist" punctuated traditional student May Day observances in 1966 and resulted in arrests by policemen whom the students called "Gestapo," after the Nazi security police. The government responded forcefully, expelling from the universities and drafting into the army leaders of student organizations who had called for more freedom. Nonetheless, opposition to the Novotný regime not only continued but increased, especially after the events of October 31, 1967. On that night, as on numerous previous occasions, an electrical failure left the large complex of student dormitories in Prague, the capital, without light. Students took up candles and began a procession chanting "We want light," a phrase that could indicate far more than their need for electric power. The brutal acts of the police in confronting the students outraged public opinion, thus strengthening reform elements in the party's Central Committee sufficiently for them to gain a majority in that body. On January 5, 1968, the reformers replaced Novotný with the Slovak Alexander Dubček as first secretary of the national Communist party. On March 22, 1968, war hero Ludvik Svoboda replaced Novotný as president of the nation. A bloodless revolution had occurred in Prague.

The spring of 1968 was an exhilarating one for the people of Czechoslovakia. Dubček announced his intention to create "socialism with a human face," a socialism that would allow "a fuller assertion of the personality than any bourgeois democracy," a socialism that would be "profoundly democratic." Rigid press censorship ended, as did other controls on the individual. But Dubček soon found himself in a difficult position. Permitted freedom of expression for the first time in twenty years, Czechoslovaks demanded far more, including even a free political system with a role for noncommunist parties. Such developments, however, threatened neighboring communist dictatorships in East Germany and Poland and risked depriving the So-

viet Union of strategically located Czechoslovakia in its Warsaw Pact alliance system.

On August 21, after having watched developments in Prague for months with growing alarm, the Soviet Union acted. Troops from the Soviet Union, East Germany, Hungary, Poland, and Bulgaria entered Czechoslovakia. In the largest movement of troops in Europe since 1945, they forcibly ended the "Prague Spring" experiment.

The Soviets were met with widespread passive nationalist resistance. The majority of the population seemed to wish continuation of reform, but earlier unrest in Eastern Europe, as in the failed Hungarian revolt of 1956, had demonstrated the futility of civilians' active opposition to Soviet arms. Students again took part in resistance, however, and two, Jan Palach and Jan Zajíc, burned themselves alive in early 1969 in protest. Force prevailed, however, and Soviet pressure ensured the gradual replacement of Dubček and his reform leadership with men more subservient to Moscow's wishes. Soviet party First Secretary Leonid Brezhnev announced that events in Czechoslovakia represented an expression of what came to be called the "Brezhnev Doctrine"—that is, the Soviet Union's policy to act against any threat to the stability of an East European communist regime.

Those supporting change in both France and Czechoslovakia were acutely aware of the need to sway public opinion in their favor. This task was made difficult by government controls of the media: In

Chapter 14

The Perils of

Prosperity:

The Unrest of

Youth in

the 1960s

France, the radio and television systems were state-controlled; in Czechoslovakia, the regime controlled not only electronic media but the press as well. Your problem in this chapter is to analyze events in France and Czechoslovakia in 1968 by examining the materials issued by those who sought to rally support for change. Deprived of media controlled by the political establishment, proponents of change issued leaflets, posters, and cartoons designed to win support. What aspects of the modern state and economy provoked the events of 1968? What vision of the future did the leaders of the French and Czechoslovakian movements embrace? How did they propose to achieve it?

SOURCES AND METHOD

Modern political causes seek to mobilize support in various ways. Because posters, pamphlets, and other publications as well as simple slogans scrawled on walls all aim to energize support for a movement by publicizing its ideas, analyzing such materials provides a broad understanding of the goals and methods of any cause. In this chapter we have assembled two groups of evidence, one relating to the French disorders and the other to the Czechoslovakian reform movement of 1968.

Let us consider the French evidence first. Source 1 is a pamphlet distributed to striking workers by the March 22 Movement, a student group whose name commemorated the student upheaval at the Nanterre campus. It appeared on May 21, 1968. What were the students' goals for the future society and economy of France? What were the aims of workers in their strike? How did student leaders try to unify student and worker causes in this pamphlet? Source 2, a leaflet that appeared on May 22, 1968, was issued by a number of student and worker groups. Consider the views expressed here about President de Gaulle, the government, and the economy. Would the authors have been satisfied only with the departure of de Gaulle from the political scene? What do you deduce from their refusal of "summit negotiations" with government and management? To whom does the leaflet appeal? What vision of the future does it advocate?

You must analyze the language of Source 3 to understand the message it seeks to convey. This is a list of slogans that the student Sorbonne Occupation Committee suggested to its followers on May 16, 1968. Note the locations proposed for such slogans. The one advocating the end of bureaucrats was painted across a large mural in the Sorbonne administration building. How did this and some of the other suggested locations reflect student attitudes toward authority? Now turn to the words themselves. Slogans are important in politics; as we noted in Chapter 12, the simpler they are, the more easily they can be spread to influence large numbers of people. Each side of the 1968 confrontations sought to dismiss the validity of the other's ideas by extreme and often inaccurate name calling. In France as well as in the United States and other countries, students referred to policemen as "pigs" or "fascists." French students' chants of "CRS—SS!" likened the riot police, the CRS (*Compagnies Républicaines de Securité*), to the Nazi SS (*Schutz Staffeln* or security echelon, whose insignia resembled a sharp double *S*). The students' opponents responded in kind, often calling them "commies." What views of their opponents do the students convey in these slogans? What sort of society do they advocate? What methods do they advocate for their cause?

With the French Sources 4 through 12, you must analyze pictorial attempts to mobilize opinion. The artists conveyed these messages graphically in pictures, with a minimum of words. Here you must ascertain the nature of the message and the goals of the students and workers.

The visual evidence is of several types. In 1968 posters appeared all over the university district of Paris in defiance of long-standing laws against posters on public buildings. Often they were fairly sophisticated in execution because many advanced art students put their skills in the service of the May revolt. The political cartoon also flourished in a number of new radical publications in Paris. The cartoons presented here originated in *L'enragé* (*The Madman*), a publication that consisted entirely of cartoons critical of established authority in France.

Cartoons and posters often magnify the physical characteristics of public figures, sometimes to ridicule but also to make perfectly clear the subject of the message. Thus you will find the prominent nose of President de Gaulle quite exaggerated, as well as certain poses. De Gaulle often embellished his speeches by raising both arms, the same gesture he used when leading the singing of the national anthem, *La Marseillaise*, a frequent occurrence after a public address. This pose is duplicated in the cartoons and posters along with his uniform of a French general, complete with the cylindrical cap known as a *kepi*, making him instantly recognizable. Artists further identified de Gaulle by including in their pictures the Cross of Lorraine, the symbol of his World War II resistance movement, with its two transverse bars.

In analyzing the material, remember that political posters and cartoons, though based on real events, are not intended to report those occurrences accurately. They are meant instead to affect public opinion. By carefully examining the posters and cartoons, you can discover the artists' views of events and how they wished to sway public opinion. What action does each picture represent? What message is the artist trying to convey? What reaction does he or she wish to evoke in viewers? What do the pictures tell you about the participants, methods, and aspirations of the French movement?

Now let us examine the Czechoslovakian sources. The Czechoslovakian writings should be examined

[411]

Chapter 14

The Perils of

Prosperity:

The Unrest of

Youth in

the 1960s

with the same methods you applied to the French. Source 13 is a tract that circulated illegally in Czechoslovakian literary circles as early as April 1967 and was republished in a Prague student publication in March 1968. Notice first the use of language. What effect do the authors seek in condemning their opponents as "knaves"? What view does the statement as a whole express toward established ideologies, both Soviet Marxist and U.S. capitalist? What methods for change are advocated? Did young Czechoslovakians follow the course of action recommended in the tenth commandment? Why should the intellectuals, students, and professors be the leaders in change?

Source 14 is an extract from a statement that appeared in an influential publication, *Literární Listy* (*Literary Papers*), the journal of the Czechoslovakian Writers' Union. *Literární Listy* was the chief forum in 1968 in which intellectuals expressed their views on reform. It had a large circulation (300,000 copies in June 1968), and it published the manifesto for change, "Two Thousand Words." Source 14 appeared on March 5, 1968, as one of a number of replies to the question of the nation's political future posed by the editors: "Wherefrom, with Whom, and Whither?" The answer reprinted here was made by Ivan Sviták, a philosophy professor and reform leader. Notice his choice of language. Who, in his view, was the

enemy of change? How does he characterize these people? What sort of social and political system did Czechoslovakian intellectuals seek?

Sources 15 through 20 are cartoons drawn from *Literární Listy* and its successor, *Listy*. Use the same methods of analysis here as you employed with the French posters and cartoons. You again will note exaggeration of certain physical features to clarify the cartoon's message. Alexander Dubček had a large nose, as de Gaulle did, and it was exaggerated by Czechoslovak cartoonists, just as French artists exaggerated de Gaulle's nose.

The Czechoslovakian cartoonists represented here also used symbols to illuminate their messages. The Phrygian cap worn by the woman in Source 15, for example, represents revolution and liberty. Dubček is depicted in Source 16 as Jánašík, a legendary Slovak "Robin Hood." Source 19 shows the Soviet president Leonid Brezhnev as Saint Florian. Old statues of this saint stand in many Czechoslovakian villages because he was thought to offer protection from fire.

Using the analytical methods described here, you should be able to answer the central questions of this chapter: What aspects of the modern state and economy provoked the events of 1968? What vision of the future did leaders of the French and Czechoslovakian movements embrace? How did they propose to achieve it?

THE EVIDENCE

FRANCE

Sources 1 through 3 from Vladimir Fišera, editor, Writing on the Wall, May 1968: A Documentary Anthology (London: Allison & Busby, 1978), pp. 133–134; p. 137; pp. 125–126. Reprinted by permission of W. H. Allen Publishers.

1. The March 22 Movement, "Your Struggle Is Our Struggle," May 21, 1968

We are occupying the faculties, you are occupying the factories. Aren't we fighting for the same thing? Higher education only contains 10 percent workers' children. Are we fighting so that there will be more of them, for a democratic university reform? That would be a good thing, but it's not the most important. These workers' children would just become like other students. We are not aiming for a worker's son to be a manager. We want to wipe out segregation between workers and management.

There are students who are unable to find jobs on leaving university. Are we fighting so that they'll find jobs, for a decent graduate employment policy? It would be a good thing, but it is not vital. Psychology or sociology graduates will become the selectors, the planners and psychotechnicians who will try to organise your working conditions; mathematics graduates will become engineers, perfecting maximum-productivity machines to make your life even more unbearable. Why are we, students who are products of a middle-class life, criticising capitalist society? The son of a worker who becomes a student leaves his own class. For the son of a middle-class family, it could be his opportunity to see his class in its true light, to question the role he is destined for in society and the organisation of our society. We refuse to become scholars who are out of touch with real life. We refuse to be used for the benefit of the ruling class. We want to destroy the separation that exists between those who organise and think and those who execute their decisions. We want to form a classless society; your cause is the same as ours.

You are asking for a minimum wage of 1,000 francs in the Paris area, retirement at sixty, a 40-hour week for 48 hours' pay.

These are long-standing and just demands: nevertheless, they seem to be out of context with our aims. Yet you have gone on to occupy factories, take your managers as hostages, strike without warning. These forms of struggle have been made possible by perseverance and lengthy action in various enterprises, and because of the recent student battles.

Chapter 14

The Perils of

Prosperity:

The Unrest of

Youth in

the 1960s

These struggles are even more radical than our official aims, because they go further than simply seeking improvements for the worker within the capitalist system, [;] they imply the destruction of the system. They are political in the true sense of the word: you are fighting not to change the Prime Minister, but so that your boss no longer retains his power in business or society. The form that your struggle has taken offers us students the model for true socialist activity: the appropriation of the means of production and of the decision-making power by the workers.

Our struggles converge. We must destroy everything that seeks to alienate us (everyday habits, the press, etc.). We must combine our occupations in the faculties and factories.

Long live the unification of our struggles!

2. "Producers, Let Us Save Ourselves," May 22, 1968

To ten million strikers, to all workers:

No to parliamentary solutions, with de Gaulle going and the bosses staying.

No to summit negotiations which give only a new lease of life to a moribund capitalism.

No more referenda. No more spectacles.

Don't let anybody speak for us. Maintain the occupation of all workplaces.

To continue the struggle, let us put all the sectors of the economy which are hit by the strike at the service of the fighting workers.

Let us prepare today our power of tomorrow (direct food-supplies, the organisation of public services: transport, information, housing, etc.).

In the streets, in the local committees, wherever we are, workers, peasants, wage-earners, students, teachers, school students, let us organise and coordinate our struggles.

FOR THE ABOLITION OF THE EMPLOYERS, FOR WORKERS' POWER.

3. Sorbonne Occupation Committee, Slogans to Be Circulated by Any Means, May 16, 1968

(leaflets—announcements over microphones—comics—songs—painting on walls—texts daubed over the paintings in the Sorbonne—announcements in the cinema during the film, or stopping it in the middle—texts written on the posters in the underground—whenever you empty your glass in the bistro—before making love—after making love—in the lift)

Occupy the factories.

Power to the workers' councils.

Abolish class society.

Down with a society based on commodity production and the spectacle.

Abolish alienation.

An end to the university.

Mankind will not be happy until the last bureaucrat has been strung up by the guts of the last capitalist.

Death to the pigs.

Free the four people arrested for looting on 6 May.

Chapter 14

The Perils of

Prosperity:

The Unrest of

Youth in

the 1960s

THE ENEMY

Sources 4 through 8 from Bibliothèque Nationale, Les Affiches de Mai 68 ou l'imagination graphique *(Paris: Bibliothèque Nationale, 1982), p. 64; p. 15; p. 9; p. 63; p. 47.*

4. Poster, May 1968

6. Poster: "Light Salaries, Heavy Tanks," May 1968

SALAIRES LEGERS

CHARS LOURDS

5. Poster: "Let Us Smash the Old Gears!,"
May 1968

BRISONS

LES VIEUX ENGRENAGES

7. Poster: "Beauty Is in the Street!," May 1968

8. Poster: "Less than 21 Years of Age: Here Is Your Ballot!," May 1968

MOINS DE 21ANS voici votre bulletin de VOTE

LA BEAUTÉ EST DANS LA RUE

Source 9 from Jean-Jacques Pauvert, editor, L'enragé: collection complète des 12 numéros introuvables, mai–novembre 1968 *(Paris: Jean-Jacques Pauvert, 1978).*

9. Cartoon, June 10, 1968

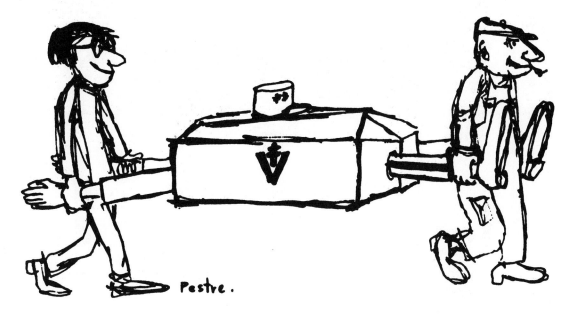

Chapter 14
The Perils of
Prosperity:
The Unrest of
Youth in
the 1960s

THE STUDENTS' VISION

Sources 10 and 11 from Bibliothèque Nationale, Les Affiches de Mai 68 ou l'imagination graphique, *p. 10; p. 24.*

10. Cartoon: "Each One of Us Is the State," May 1968

L'ETAT C'EST CHACUN DE NOUS

11. Cartoon: "Popular Power," May 1968

Chapter 14

The Perils of

Prosperity:

The Unrest of

Youth in

the 1960s

THE STUDENTS IN DEFEAT

Source 12 from Pauvert, L'enragé: collection complète des 12 numéros introuvables, mai–novembre 1968.

12. Cartoon, June 17, 1968

CZECHOSLOVAKIA

Sources 13 and 14 from Ivan Sviták, The Czechoslovak Experiment, 1968-1969 *(New York: Columbia University Press, 1971), pp. 17-18; p. 16. Reprinted by permission of the author.*

13. "Ten Commandments for a Young Czechoslovak Intellectual," March 1968

There are no more knaves than before; it is only that their field of activity is larger. . . . And so all of us are living in close collaboration with a few knaves.

LUDVÍK VACULÍK, in Orientation, 1967[4]

1. Do not collaborate with knaves. If you do, you inevitably become one of them. Engage yourself against the knaves.

2. Do not accept the responsibility forced upon you by the knaves for their own deeds. Do not believe such arguments as "we are all responsible," or the social problems touch "all of us," or "everyone has his share of guilt." Openly and clearly dissociate yourself from the deeds of the knaves and from arguments that you are responsible for them.

3. Do not believe any ideology that consists of systems of slogans and words which only speculate about your feelings. Judge people, political parties, and social systems concretely, according to the measure of freedom they give, and according to how tolerable the living conditions are. Judge them according to results, not words.

4. Do not solve only the narrow generational problems of youth; understand that the decisive problems are common to all human beings. You cannot solve them by postulating the demands of young men, but by vigorously defending the problems of all people. Do not complain about the privileges of one generation, but fight for human rights.

5. Do not consider the given social relations as constant. They are changing in your favor. Look forward. If you do not want to be wrong today, you must think from the point of view of the year 2000.

6. Do not think only as a Czech or a Slovak, but consider yourself a *European*. The world will sooner adapt to Europe (where Eastern Europe belongs) than to fourteen million Czechs and Slovaks. You live neither in America nor in the Soviet Union; you live in Europe.

---

4. **Ludvík Vaculík:** a novelist and one of the leaders of the Czechoslovakian reform movement; he also drafted the manifesto "Two Thousand Words."

Chapter 14

The Perils of

Prosperity:

The Unrest of

Youth in

the 1960s

7. Do not succumb to utopias or illusions; be dissatisfied and critical. Have the sceptical confidence of a negotiator, but have confidence in the purpose of your negotiations. The activity has its own value.

8. Do not be afraid of your task in history and be courageous in intervening in history. The social changes and transformations of man take place, no doubt, without regard to you, but to understand these changes and to influence them with the limited possibilities of an individual is far better than to accept the fatal inevitability of events.

9. Do not negotiate out of good motives alone; negotiate with sound arguments and with consideration of what you can achieve. A good deed can rise from a bad motive and vice versa. The motives are forgotten, but deeds remain.

10. Do not let yourself be *shot* in the fight between the interests of the power blocs. *Shoot* when in danger. Are you not in danger right now when you collaborate with the few knaves? Are you a knave?

14. Ivan Sviták, "Wherefrom, with Whom, and Whither?," March 5, 1968

From totalitarian dictatorship toward an open society, toward the liquidation of the power monopoly and toward the effective control of the power elite by a free press and by public opinion. From the bureaucratic management of society and culture by the "hard-line thugs" (C. Wright Mills)[5] toward the observance of fundamental human and civil rights, at least to the same extent as in the Czechoslovakia of bourgeois democracy. With the labor movement, without its *apparatchiks*;[6] with the middle classes, without their groups of willing collaborators; and with the intelligentsia in the lead. The intellectuals of this country must assert their claim to lead an open socialist society toward democracy and humanism.

5. **C. Wright Mills** (1916–1962): a Columbia University sociologist, the author of influential books including *White Collar* and *The Power Elite* and a severe critic of modern institutions.

6. *apparatchik*: a Russian word describing an individual who is part of the existing power structure.

THE PEOPLE'S VISION

Sources 15 and 16 from Literární Listy, *in Sviták,* The Czechoslovak Experiment, 1968–
1969, *p. 2; p. 51.*

15. Cartoon: "If There Are No Complications the Child Should Be Born in the Ninth Month," 1968

Chapter 14
The Perils of
Prosperity:
The Unrest of
Youth in
the 1960s

16. Cartoon, 1968

THE ENEMY

Source 17 from Literární Listy, *in Robin Alison Remington, editor,* Prague in Winter: Documents on Czechoslovak Communism in Crisis *(Cambridge, Mass.: M.I.T. Press, 1969), p. 289.*

17. Cartoon, "Workers of All Countries Unite—Or I'll Shoot!," August 28, 1968

Chapter 14
The Perils of
Prosperity:
The Unrest of
Youth in
the 1960s

Sources 18 and 19 from Literární Listy, *in Sviták,* The Czechoslovak Experiment, 1968–1969, *p. 196; p. 155.*

18. Cartoon: "Liberté, Egalité, Freundschaft!" ("Liberty, Equality, Friendship!"), 1968

IN DEFEAT

19. Cartoon: "But There Is No Fire!," 1969

Chapter 14

The Perils of

Prosperity:

The Unrest of

Youth in

the 1960s

Source 20 from Listy, *in Remington,* Prague in Winter, *p. 373.*

20. Cartoon: "It Is Only a Matter of a Few Tactical Steps Back," January 30, 1969

JDE JENOM O NĚKOLIK

TAKTICKÝCH ÚSTUPKŮ..

Vladimír Jiránek

QUESTIONS TO CONSIDER

France and Czechoslovakia are two very different countries at opposite ends of Europe. Let us compare the events of 1968 as they unfolded in these two locations. Do they illustrate a common response to problems basic to modern life in the noncommunist and communist West?

Consider first the demands of French and Czechoslovakian protest leaders. Examine again the written and visual evidence, and consider the protesters' views on working conditions in France. What problems do they identify in Sources 1, 2, and 3? How are these problems defined graphically? Why do you think that the artist in Source 4 portrayed modern capitalism as a puppeteer? What is the significance of the puppeteer's appearance? Why did the artist show de Gaulle as part of the industrial gears of France in Source 5? Turn next to the Czechoslovakian statements on working conditions. Notice particularly Source 14, with its references to management by "hard-line thugs" and "apparatchiks." What great lie about communism (whose slogan is "Workers of the World Unite!") do the Czechoslovakians discern in Source 17? What common theme do you find in French and

Czechoslovakian protesters' ideas on the conditions of labor in the modern economy?

Next consider the political vision of the 1968 activists. Take the French first. What sort of government did the formulators of Source 3 envision? How is that idea amplified in Sources 9, 10, and 11? These cartoons spell their messages in words, but their art contains a message, too. Look closely at Source 10. How does the artist see the individual faring against big government, industrial giants, and powerful unions? What solution does the artist propose in the caption? Which groups did the creator of Source 11 hope would seize political power? Does the same message appear in Source 9? Who is being buried? What does his body represent? Notice the clothing and grooming of the pallbearers. Can you identify the occupational groups that the artist hopes will seize power after the burial?

The Czechoslovakians also had a political vision. Review Sources 13 and 14. What political outlook do these statements express? What groups did Czechoslovakian reformers expect to lead change? Combine this message with Source 15. How do the reformers regard their chances for success? How were the political visions of the French and Czechoslovakian reformers similar?

Both movements also expressed images of their opponents and the methods to be employed in their struggles. What sort of action does the artist of Source 7 recommend to the French? What secondary message do you think underlies the portrayal of the fighter as a woman? Source 8 shows a close-up view of a Parisian paving stone. What message do you find in its accompanying statement? In Sources 6 and 12, we find some statements of the reformers' view of the opposition and its power. Why do you think the artist pictured a silhouette of a tank in Source 6? The final French selection, Source 12, is a cartoon that appeared on the cover of *L'enragé* after the defeat of the students and workers. What significance do you find in the portrayal of de Gaulle? What has crippled him? What supports him? What view of the government does the shape of his crutches convey?

The Czechoslovakian sources also characterize the reformers' opposition and their chances of success. In Source 15 what does the woman's obvious pregnancy represent? When does Dubček predict the birth? How long did the Czechoslovakian experiment in greater democracy actually last? What does Dubček's strange activity in Source 16 convey about the artist's view of the future? Sources 18 and 19 are cartoons that appeared as the Soviet Union and its Warsaw Pact allies invaded Czechoslovakia. The inspiration for Source 18 is the painting by Eugène Delacroix, *Liberty Leading the People,* in which a bare-breasted female Liberty (in a Phrygian cap) leads revolutionaries to freedom. In our cartoon, however, the artist portrays Liberty as Walter Ulbricht, the head of the East German Communist party. What is the artist's view of the friendship of this Liberty? The cartoon also employs a modified version of the motto of the French Revolution of 1789, "*Liberté,*

[431]

Chapter 14

The Perils of

Prosperity:

The Unrest of

Youth in

the 1960s

Egalité, Fraternité" ("Liberty, Equality, Brotherhood"), rendered as *"Liberté, Egalité, Freundschaft"* (German for "friendship"). Considering the preceding twenty-five years of European history, why might the artist have used French for "Liberty" and "Equality" while using German for the last word? Why is Brezhnev/ Florian in Source 19 pouring water on a house representing Czechoslovakia (CSSR: Czechoslovak Socialist Republic)? Why does Dubček object? What significance do you ascribe to the difference in the two figures' sizes?

The last cartoon, Source 20, reflects Czechoslovakia in defeat. Many alleged that making peace with the country's Russian conquerors would be simple: "It is only a matter of a few tactical steps back!" Where do the steps backward lead in this case? What does this tell us about the fate of the reform movement? What common sentiment do you detect in the French and Czechoslovakian evidence regarding the reformers' chances for meaningful success in the face of the modern state?

Answering these questions should prepare you to formulate your replies to the central questions of this chapter: What aspects of the modern state and economy provoked the events of 1968? What vision of the future did leaders of the French and Czechoslovakian movements embrace? How did they propose to achieve it?

EPILOGUE

As you continue your reading on the history of Western civilization through the events of the 1970s, 1980s, and 1990s, it will become clear that the student unrest in France and other parts of Western Europe as well as events in Czechoslovakia is of enduring importance.

Perhaps in partial response to this agitation, significant political changes occurred in much of the West in the 1970s and 1980s. In most Western democracies, eighteen-year-olds won the vote. In many countries, too, at least a partial reversal of political centralization began, perhaps in some measure stemming from youthful demands for more "power to the people." This impulse to diminish state authority defied ideological labels: In France and Sweden it was begun by socialist governments, whereas in the United States it has been the work of conservative administrations. No country, however, has yet approached the French students' vision of autogestion.

In France, where student movements amassed the broadest nonstudent support, other changes occurred. His power tarnished by the events of 1968, de Gaulle resigned within a year of the student strikes over a minor issue of government reform. Universities and their curricula were radically restructured in an attempt to meet some student demands, and working conditions in the factories were improved. Even in France, however, fundamental educational and industrial policy re-

[432]

mained firmly in the hands of government officials and corporate managers. Student political activism and bitter labor disputes, many originating in issues raised in 1968, persist.

Elsewhere, the student revolt garnered less support, produced fewer changes, and led some frustrated student radicals to turn their energies from protest to brutal political violence in the 1970s. In West Germany, some student radicals formed terrorist groups like the Baader-Meinhof gang, which lashed out violently at West German symbols of the conservative consumer society and American military installations. The Red Brigades terrorist groups in Italy had the same roots and objectives.

In the 1980s youthful discontent in Western Europe partially manifested itself in the Green movement. Especially strong in West Germany, this movement represents the continued alienation of many from the West's industrial economy and modern society. The Green movement attacks the effects of modern industry on our environment and particularly the failure of traditional governing parties effectively to address environmental issues. The Greens in West Germany also advocated an end to their country's participation in the North Atlantic Treaty Organization (NATO). While not always well organized, Greens entered the political life of a number of countries and by 1992 had elected members to parliaments in Germany and Switzerland as well as to the European Parliament. Indeed, in 1998, the Greens became part of the governing coalition (with the Social Democratic party) in Germany, and the party's leader became foreign minister. Such a governing role led the Greens to accept NATO membership for Germany.

Eastern Europe felt the effects of Soviet actions in Czechoslovakia in 1968 for two decades, as those seeking political, economic, and social change in that region consciously confined reform within the boundaries established by the Brezhnev Doctrine. Discontent with communist rule and Soviet domination, however, grew in the 1980s, led by the rise in Poland of an independent, noncommunist labor movement, Solidarity. By the late 1980s, events in the Soviet Union also actually fostered change in Eastern Europe. Soviet President Mikhail Gorbachev (1985–1991) proclaimed a policy of *glasnost* (openness) and *perestroika* (restructuring) and abandoned the Brezhnev Doctrine, allowing Eastern European nations to determine their own destinies. The result was a largely peaceful revolution in 1989, when one-party communist political systems collapsed in Poland, Hungary, East Germany, Romania, and Czechoslovakia. Indeed, by the end of 1991, the ultimate result of Gorbachev's new path was the dissolution of the Soviet Union and its one-party communist political system, replaced by the Commonwealth of Independent States. Events in Czechoslovakia provide an example of the rapidity of Eastern European change in 1989 and remind us of the enduring importance of the events of 1968 in promoting that change.

In Czechoslovakia the rigid, one-party communist rule reimposed by Soviet arms in 1968 proved particu-

Chapter 14

The Perils of

Prosperity:

The Unrest of

Youth in

the 1960s

larly resistant to change. The government dealt harshly with those favoring change: 500,000 dissidents lost their party memberships, hundreds of thousands of others linked with reform endured exclusion from professional employment for which they were qualified, and Dubček found himself demoted to work as a mechanic. Nevertheless, opposition continued. In January 1977, a number of dissidents established Charter 77 to pressure the government to respect human rights. Its leaders included the playwright Václav Havel and the philosopher Jan Patocka. Havel spent five years in prison for his reform efforts, and Patocka died after police questioning, but by the mid-1980s the success of Solidarity in Poland and the reforms of Gorbachev in the Soviet Union inspired new hope for change.

In 1988 widespread demonstrations against the communist regime began, despite the authorities' consistently forceful responses to this dissent. The year 1989 opened with a massive demonstration commemorating the twentieth anniversary of the death of the student Jan Palach protesting the loss of the Prague Spring reforms. Indeed, a demonstration by students was key in bringing down the communist government. On November 17, 1989, the authorities permitted a seemingly harmless student observance in Prague of the fiftieth anniversary of an act of student resistance to Czechoslovakia's occupation by Germany in World War II. The commemorative event quickly turned into a demonstration for greater democracy that drew

100,000 participants. Armed riot police brutally dispersed the unarmed crowd, seriously injuring 291 and arresting over 100 persons. But the brutality revolted the country, especially as unfounded rumors of a student death circulated, and opposition to the government dramatically rose. Students seized university buildings. Reformers, led by Havel, who had recently been released from prison, founded Civic Forum in the Czech lands and Public Against Violence in Slovakia to coordinate resistance. A general strike on November 27 brought the country to a virtual halt, and additional demonstrations for democracy were widespread in late November and in December. Faced with great opposition, Communist party leaders finally relinquished power in late December. The country's legislature selected a new presiding officer for its deliberations, Alexander Dubček, the reformer of 1968, and a new president for the country, the playwright Václav Havel. In what has been called the "Velvet Revolution" because so little bloodshed occurred, Czechoslovakia reestablished the democratic system it had lost in the coup of 1948. The newly democratic Czechoslovakia was not safe, however, from some of the problems that had undone its former communist regime. By 1992 long-standing nationalist tensions between the country's two chief language groups, the Czechs and the Slovaks, broke the country into two separate nation-states, the Czech Republic and Slovakia. Thus, many of the issues of 1968, here, as elsewhere, still affect the West.

CHAPTER FIFTEEN

BEYOND THE NATION-STATE:

THE EUROPEAN UNION

The history of modern Europe—and indeed that of the world as a whole—has been written largely in terms of the nation-state, a sovereign political unit generally governing one language group and expressing the unique interests of that group. The conflicting interests of the nation-states of Europe, of course, produced the recurring wars on that continent in the modern period. But after World War II, a unique experiment, still in progress today, began in Europe with the objective of creating a union of nations that would create peace and prosperity on the Continent by serving the common interests of all member countries, not just the narrow interests of one. Nothing like this experiment, now called the European Union, had ever been tried before.

The experiment was born amid the problems created by World War II. That war accelerated the rise of two superpowers, the United States and the Soviet Union, leaving a much-diminished role in the postwar world for traditional European powers like France. Like many other nations, France struggled in the late 1940s to rebuild from the war's destruction, but also to limit the ability of its former enemy, Germany, to make future war. France blocked American and British efforts to rebuild occupied West Germany and sought to restrict its access to the coal and steel output of the German industrial heartland in the Ruhr and Saar regions. This policy understandably generated considerable friction with France's allies and created much ill will in West Germany in the first years after the end of the war. At the same time, however, some Europeans sought to achieve peace on the Continent and to rebuild its war-torn economy not through confrontation with former enemies but through federalism, that is, an economic and political union of European nations, a "United States of Europe" that one day might equal the superpowers in economic importance. The most influential advocate of this idea after World War II was Jean Monnet (1888–1979), a French economist of international influence who also directed planning for the postwar economic reconstruction of France. Monnet needed access to West German coal and steel for French recovery at the very time that British and American diplomats were pressuring French foreign minister Robert Schuman (1886–1963) to compromise on his country's opposition to their plans for German economic reconstruction. Monnet presented Schuman with a plan to put the coal and steel resources of France and Germany under a supranational authority, that is, one that did not represent the interests of a single nation and that therefore could deprive Germany of sufficient resources for military adventure while still providing France the coal and steel that it needed. Schuman quickly proposed Monnet's plan, which came to be called "the Schuman Plan" despite Monnet's authorship, to West Germany. That country, recognizing the plan as a way to improve relations with France and its allies, readily agreed to negotiations, and Belgium, the Netherlands, Luxembourg, and Italy soon participated as well. The result of these multilateral negotiations was the European Coal and Steel Community (ECSC) of 1952 in which all six countries pooled their coal and steel resources.

Building the ECSC was no easy matter, however, because the need for supranational authority had to be balanced with traditional national interests. The institutions of the ECSC reflected a delicate compromise that we will find forming a blueprint for other institutions of European federalism. A supranational High Authority, led from 1952 to 1955 by Jean Monnet, regulated prices, production, and marketing of coal and steel in the member countries, while another supranational body, the Court of Justice, enforced the terms of the ECSC treaty and adjudicated disputes. A Council of Ministers, drawn from the cabinets of member states, advised the High Authority and represented national interests, as did a Common Assembly composed of members of the parliaments of the ECSC nations.

As the ECSC took shape, the American and British desire to rearm West Germany elicited a French plan for a European Defense Community (EDC), again inspired by Monnet. If West Germany was to be rearmed, France sought to place its former enemy's forces into a European army under supranational control. The other four ECSC members, Belgium, Italy, Luxembourg, and the Netherlands, joined France and West Germany in negotiations to create such a defense force, and the Treaty of Paris of 1952 actually created it. The same nations also began negotiating a plan for a European Political Community (EPC). But ultimately neither of these plans produced new institutions. The French parliament proved unwilling to cede national control of armed forces to a supranational authority and refused to ratify the EDC treaty. The EPC scheme perished with the EDC treaty.

Reluctance to embrace supranational institutions was not uniquely French, however. The British government, concerned to protect its national prerogatives and not to endanger either its unique relationship with the United States or its traditional trade and military arrangements with its former colonies in the British Commonwealth of Nations, rejected opportunities for full membership in the ECSC, the EDC, and the EPC. Nevertheless, European federalists, inspired by the success of the ECSC in restoring its members' economic strength, continued to work for their goal of a more united Europe, and Jean Monnet left the High Authority of the ECSC in 1955 to found the Action Committee for a United States of Europe. Thus, in 1957, Belgium, France, Italy, Luxembourg, the Netherlands, and West Germany signed important new agreements in Rome.

The Rome treaties created two new supranational organizations, the European Atomic Energy Community (EURATOM) to undertake peaceful atomic research and the European Economic Community (EEC) to weld the six countries into one economic unit without import taxes (tariffs) on trade between them. EURATOM and the EEC took their place alongside the ECSC, and the institutions of the EEC, like those of the ECSC, reflected the founders' need to balance federalist ideals with national sentiment and interest in the pursuit of European integration. As amended over the years, the basic agreement creating the EEC, often referred to simply as the "Treaty of Rome" remains one of the governing documents of what we today call the European Union.

Two EEC institutions are supranational. The Commission, headquartered in Brussels, Belgium, is the executive branch of the EEC and is composed of representatives of the member states. The Treaty of Rome charged the Commission, led by a president, with acting in the interests of the Community, not individual nations, and in that capacity it administers policy through its own civil service and proposes new policy initiatives to the Council of Ministers (see below). The EEC's judicial branch, the European Court of Justice, joined in 1975 by a Court of Auditors for financial matters, is the other supranational EEC institution; it adjudicates disputes and enforces Community regulations. Indeed, the court's early decisions established an essential legal precedent for any federal entity: just as in the United States, where federal law has primacy over state law, the regulations of the EEC supersede the laws of individual member nations.

Two institutions of the EEC give voice to national interests. The Council of Ministers, comprising ministerial representatives from each member nation, initially was the chief policymaking body of the EEC. The Treaty of Rome required its unanimous vote to decide matters of essential policy, but only a qualified majority vote (with each country assigned votes according to its population) for other decisions. The European Parliament, like the Council, reflects national interests. Under the initial terms of the Treaty of Rome, it comprised members of the parliaments of the signatory nations; since 1979 it has been directly elected. Its original role was largely as an advisory body for the Council and the Commission, but its voice in Community affairs has grown in recent years.

Thus structured, the EEC began operation on January 1, 1958, and quickly proved to be an economic success. Industrial production boomed as trade barriers fell and manufacturers gained new European markets; indeed, trade between the original six members increased 50 percent in the period from 1958 to 1960. Such growth soon elicited requests by nonmember countries to join the EEC, the most important of these from Britain, which had rejected opportunities to play a founding role in the ECSC. Negotiations for British entry into the EEC were difficult; the British were reluctant to cede national authority to the supranational institutions of the EEC, and their ties to the United States and the Commonwealth remained strong. Thus, French president Charles de Gaulle, perhaps jealous of the role Britain might play in the EEC, blocked British membership in 1963 and again in 1967 (EEC enlargement required a unanimous vote of the Council). Nevertheless, European integration continued as the Commission in 1970 secured regular sources of revenue. Largely funded from the common tariff on goods imported into the EEC and a percentage of the value-added tax collected by all members, these reunions supported Community activities like the Common Agricultural Policy, which provides price supports to farmers to ensure Europe's food supply.

France eventually dropped its objections to British membership, and the EEC experienced its first enlargement in 1973. Britain, Denmark, Ireland, and Norway secured admission to the EEC, but subsequent events proved that some of these states retained reservations about the federal ideal. Norwegians, in fact, rejected membership in a referendum largely fought over their fears of losing national control of their fisheries, agriculture, and newly discovered offshore oil resources. For their part, the British and the Danes proved to be unenthusiastic supporters of further European integration, and the British soon demanded to renegotiate the financial terms of their entry into the EEC. Such internal difficulties, combined with a deep recession and high inflation in the 1970s, meant that the EEC undertook few new moves toward greater integration for almost a decade after the Community's first enlargement.

In the 1980s and 1990s, however, the EEC resumed both its membership growth and its progress in building the federal ideal with the rise of new leaders like François Mitterand (president of France, 1981–1995), Helmut Kohl (German chancellor, 1982–1998), and Jacques Delors (president of the EEC Commission, 1985–1995). Enlargement of the Community confronted the EEC with both opportunities and challenges. Certainly, the admission of Austria, Finland, and Sweden to the Community on January 1, 1995, added members to the EEC whose affluence contributed to the common institutions and commitments. But the admission applications of Greece, Portugal, and Spain presented signal new challenges to the Community. All three were emerging democracies in the early 1980s, and EEC leaders correctly reasoned that membership, which required democratic political processes, would help to strengthen those nations' new governments. All three were also significantly poorer than the other members of the EEC, and all required significant economic development assistance and Common Agricultural Policy funds. Nevertheless, Greece joined the EEC in 1981, and Portugal and Spain entered in 1986. The original Community of six became one of fifteen with these admissions of the 1980s and 1990s.

The collapse of communist regimes in the former satellite states of the Soviet Union and the disintegration of Yugoslavia in 1989–1991 presented the Community with additional applicants for membership as the nations of Central and Eastern Europe developed democratic governments and capitalist economic systems. Thus, at a meeting in December 2002, the Community offered membership, subject to ratification by the applicant nations, to Cyprus, the Czech Republic, Estonia, Hungary, Latvia, Lithuania, Malta, Poland, Slovakia, and Slovenia. The admission of these nations at once represented the post–Cold War reunification of Europe and the Community's greatest challenge of growth as it began to expand into a union of twenty-five very diverse nations.

First and foremost, such enlargement presents a problem of identity. Can such a large community find common purpose and identity? Moreover, should it expand further? Romania and Bulgaria already are negotiating for admission in 2007, and their addition will push the Community's eastern border to that of Turkey. That country, a NATO member with only a tiny part of its territory on the European Continent and an overwhelming Muslim population, also is clamoring for membership. Negotiations for Turkish admission may begin in 2004, but some prominent Western Europeans, like former French president Valéry Giscard d'Estaing, oppose Turkish membership. Giscard, who chaired the EU Constitutional Convention in 2002–2003, asserted that Turkey is not a European state and that its admission would destroy the idea of a united Europe.

More tangibly, these potential members present economic challenges to the Community because, while all have growing economies, they are far poorer than its present members. Most of them, indeed, are poorer than Portugal was when that nation joined. Moreover, their combined population is large (75 million persons, one-fifth of the population of the Community prior to their admission) and will require vast sums of economic development and agriculture assistance from Brussels to raise them to Community levels of per capita wealth. Indeed, the Community will spend $42 billion in these new member states in just the period 2004–2006.

As the Community grew in the late twentieth and early twenty-first centuries, it also intensified its integration efforts. In the process, non-elected Community officials, instead of elected national officials, increasingly made decisions affecting the administration of Europe. Indeed, as integration increased in the 1990s, 40 percent of the new laws passed by the parliament of the Netherlands were not Dutch-initiated legislation, but acts passed to conform Dutch law to regulations from the Community's administration in Brussels. Some Europeans, in fact, began to talk about a "democratic deficit" in the Community.

The first major integrative step of the 1980s was the Single European Act (SEA) of 1986, designed to complete the work begun by the Treaty of Rome. Despite that treaty's removal of tariff barriers to trade, other practical obstacles to the free movement of goods, capital, and people persisted in the differences between Community members' national regulations governing such matters as transportation, banking, certain consumer goods, and professional qualifications to practice professions like law and medicine. Thus, the SEA required the harmonization of literally thousands of regulations of member countries under the direction of the EEC Commission to more completely unify the economic life of the EEC.

The next step in the integrative process was the most sweeping to date. The Treaty on European Union of 1992, negotiated at Maastricht in the Netherlands and generally referred to as the Treaty of Maastricht, created a new federative structure, the European Union (EU), under the institutions of the EEC. The EU subsumed the ECSC, EURATOM, and the EEC and established a European

Monetary Union (EMU) to create a common currency for the Community. And the Maastricht treaty dramatically expanded the competence of the central authorities of the EU at the expense of the traditional prerogatives of the nation-state in four chief ways that the authors of the EPC would never have dared to imagine. The result of the Maastricht treaty at times has been considerable tension between the policy expressions of the federal ideal and the traditional role of the nation-state.

First, the treaty endowed citizens of each member state with citizenship in the EU. Such citizenship carried rights that affected the national policies of EU members in a number of spheres, including education, culture, consumer protection, and social and economic development. The treaty also mandated fundamental changes in members' electoral processes because it granted EU citizens the right to vote and run for the European Parliament in any member nation.

Second, Maastricht's provision for the EMU projected the EU deeply into the economic policies of its members. The establishment of a stable common currency, which came to be called the *euro*, required that member nations adhere to strict EMU limits on public debt. These limits often required budget and program cuts by member states that their legislatures would otherwise have found politically unacceptable. A common currency also required the establishment of a European Central Bank to which EMU members ceded their national banks' powers to issue currency, regulate the money supply, and set interest rates. These dramatic cessions of national economic prerogatives prompted Britain, Denmark, and Sweden to remain outside of the currency plan, and they retained their traditional national currencies.

Third, Maastricht provided for a Common Foreign and Security Policy to which the policies of EEC member states would conform. The EEC members long had cooperated in some spheres of foreign policy, most significantly in extending aid to developing countries outside of Europe. But evolution of a comprehensive common foreign policy has proven difficult. The conduct of foreign policy is one of the fundamental powers of the nation-state, and EEC members have very different diplomatic positions. Some, like Austria, Finland, Ireland, and Sweden, are traditionally neutral; others, like Britain, belong to NATO and retain close ties to the United States. Thus the EU, despite its immense economic strength, proved incapable of common action to protect lives and property when civil war erupted in the disintegrating Yugoslavian state in the 1990s. Only slowly has the EU worked toward limited common foreign policy efforts. The Amsterdam Treaty of 1997 facilitated foreign policy action by establishing "common strategies" that required a majority vote of the council, not unanimity, for implementation. And plans were progressing in 2003 for a Rapid Response Force of 60,000 EU soldiers to forcefully project Community foreign policy into global trouble spots. But the EU has a long way to go before its foreign policy significance matches that of its economic resources.

Finally, Maastricht provided for cooperation on police and judicial matters, other traditional concerns of the nation-state. While certainly EU nations long have cooperated in police matters, and all definitely want to control crime, the treaty also sought cooperation in the very controversial area of immigration and border control. The full ramifications of this aspect of the treaty are still evolving because many members are reluctant to cede national control of their borders.

The two EU treaties signed since Maastricht largely addressed matters of Community administration. Thus, the Amsterdam Treaty of 1997 sought to deal with the "democratic deficit" by giving the elected European Parliament more power over the non-elected European Commission, and the Treaty of Nice of 2001 increased the number of areas in which the Council could act without a unanimous vote. When all was said and done, however, the EU remained a cumbersome administrative apparatus, and in 2002 a constitutional convention opened to draft a new operating document. As those debates developed, the most divisive question remained that which had vexed Jean Monnet and the founders of the ECSC half a century earlier: the role of the institutions, policies, and traditions of the nation-state in a supranational community.

Jean Monnet believed that a peaceful "United States of Europe" would be built in small, discrete steps, and we may use his thought to begin to frame the central questions of this chapter. What were the goals of Monnet and the drafters of the Treaty of

Rome? What were those small steps that, cumulatively, produced European unity and a half-century of peace on the Continent? How have they created an economically prosper-

ous EU, and what is its role in the world today? Finally, what is the role for the European nation-state in this new order?

SOURCES AND METHOD

In the previous chapters of *Discovering the Western Past,* you have encountered many of the diverse sources employed by historians in doing their work of reconstructing the past. In this final chapter of the book, you will be asked to combine many of the sorts of sources that you earlier analyzed with several new kinds of evidence to better understand the European Union and the unique experiment that it represents in the history of the West. The variety of sources represented in this chapter reflect the efforts of historians to identify and employ all of the evidence available to them.

Source 1 is a selection from Robert Schuman's declaration proposing the ECSC. As you saw in Chapter 13, public statements by foreign policy officials often have two goals: to muster the support of voters at home and to place a diplomatic initiative before the leaders of another state. How did Schuman's declaration combine these two goals? How did it seek to realize French interests while achieving the federalist goals of Monnet? What do you think Schuman's proposal offered Germany, at the time a defeated and isolated state? Even with the obvious balancing of supranational and national goals in the

Schuman Plan, how did it mark a whole new era in European international relations, especially between France and Germany?

Source 2 requires that you apply some of the skills of quantitative analysis that you learned in Chapter 4. Source 2A is a table illustrating production and consumption levels in the ECSC during its period of transition into the new Community. The rates of production increases for the period 1949 through 1952 were artificially inflated in several ways. They reflected large rates of growth from an artificially small production level caused by the destruction of plants and equipment in World War II, and they also recorded temporary production increases to supply forces in both the Korean conflict and the French war in Indochina. The end of the Korean War thus accounted for a decrease in 1953 production, but it also marked the return of a period of peace characterized by solid growth in production for the civilian sector of the economy. How much did general production in the ECSC member states increase in the first five years of the Community, 1952 though 1957? How much did production in the metals industries increase in the same period? What do you conclude from the figures for consumption for this period? How do they indicate economic recovery? Source 2B illustrates trade between the ECSC members. Compare the increase in trade with the increases in production. Why might you conclude that the founders' goal of making the ECSC members closer trading partners was being realized in the first five years of the organization's life? How might such figures prompt member states to investigate ways to draw still closer together?

Source 3 is an excerpt from the *Memoirs* of Jean Monnet. Recall from Chapter 2 the great value of the memoirs of influential persons when they are subjected to critical historical analysis. How does Monnet's narrative account of ECSC success accord with the data in Source 2? Why did Monnet regard the ECSC as something much more than an economic success? What future did Monnet envision for Europe?

Source 4 presents excerpts from a treaty, a form of evidence often employed by historians. Treaties are agreements between governments that bind their signatories to abide by their terms, and modern treaties are essentially similar in format. Thus, the Treaty of Rome in Source 4 begins with a descriptive title followed by a preamble that enumerates the heads of state of the signatory powers, states the treaty's purpose, and lists the plenipotentiaries (diplomats empowered by a government to act on its behalf) who signed the treaty. The text of the treaty follows the preamble, and such texts of modern treaties on complex issues like trade can be detailed and lengthy documents. Indeed, the full Treaty of Rome creating the EEC fills an entire volume. Examine the preamble to the Treaty of

Rome. What were the general objectives of this treaty's signatories? Does the preamble suggest that those signing it believed that they were creating a simple economic union or that they were building the foundation for more comprehensive federal institutions? What goals did the treaty's signers announce in Part One of the treaty? Turn next to the articles in Part Two of the treaty. How would Title I of that part restructure European trade? What sort of policy did the treaty's Title II create in the agricultural sector of the economy? Why might you conclude that achieving the treaty's agricultural goals would lead to expensive farm subsidy programs? Did members of the EEC give up part of the traditional power of independent nations to control their borders when they agreed to Title III? The treaty's terms also required that members coordinate their laws in certain areas. Why might you see these requirements as also limiting the traditional lawmaking authority of independent nations?

Source 5 provides statistical evidence of how well the EEC did its economic work in its first thirty years of life, in this case realizing the goal in the preamble to the Treaty of Rome of "reducing the differences existing between the various regions and the backwardness of the less favored regions." The table illustrates changes in the gross domestic product (the total value of a nation's output of goods and services less payments on foreign investments) per capita in EEC members. Gross domestic product per capita is a good indicator of the prosperity of a nation's people, and this table, like other data sets that you have analyzed, uses a base of 100 for the average gross domestic product per capita for the twelve members of the EEC in each period. What were the poorest nations in 1960? How did their gross domestic product per capita change between 1960 and 1990? Remembering that the data for each period indicate only a nation's status relative to the total gross domestic product for the whole Community and that no nation actually grew poorer, what changes occurred among the wealthiest nations in the 1960 to 1990 period? What do you think helped propel those changes?

Source 6 presents additional quantitative data on gross domestic product. This data set, however, presents total gross domestic product from the EU countries in comparative perspective. Does the gross domestic product of any single European country approach those of the United States and Japan? How does the gross domestic product of the EU compare to those of the United States and Japan? Why do you think such statistical data justified the hope of the European Community's founders that it would emerge as one of the world's economic superpowers? Why do you find Europe's economic role in the world far different from its political and military role as demonstrated in the Yugoslavian crisis of the 1990s?

Source 7 presents population data on the EU and other countries. How does the population of the current EU compare to those of the United States, Japan, and the People's Republic of China? How does that of the EU as it

will be enlarged in 2004 compare? Does the EU as yet exercise a political role in the world commensurate with this population? Note the long-range population projections for the nations in the table, which reflect the diminishing fertility rates characteristic of increasingly prosperous populations in most countries, except for the United States, where immigration in part will increase the population. What world role do you project for the EU in half a century?

With Source 8 and 9 we present material reflecting the reaction of the various peoples of the EU to the Community, its organizations, and ultimately the supranational idea for which they stand. Source 8 is a series of cartoons from the famous English journal of humor and political comment, *Punch*, published from 1841 to 1992. You have already analyzed cartoons and their ability to capture or shape public opinion. Here, again, you should apply such analysis to this series by one of *Punch's* longtime cartoonists, Mahood, that appeared on the eve of the British referendum on continued membership in the EEC in 1975. Why do you think that many persons voting in the referendum found the situations portrayed here both humorous and unsettling? Why do you find that the artist portrayed British life turned upside down by EEC membership? Considering that one-third of all voters in the referendum voted "No" on the EEC and that even in the early twenty-first century British opinion remains quite deeply divided on further integration of Britain into Europe, why do you think Mahood's sketches aptly caught the British unease with European federalism?

Sources 9A and 9B chart the results of the extensive public opinion polling regularly done by the EU. Source 9A charts support for EU membership in the member nations. Which countries' citizens most frequently saw membership as a bad thing? Note the frequency of the "bad" responses in traditionally neutral countries like Sweden, Finland, and Austria. Why do you think the negative responses were numerous in these countries? Note the frequency of "bad" responses in Britain. Recalling the cartoons in Source 8, as well as Britain's attempts to renegotiate the terms of its entry into the EEC and its rejection of the euro, why are you not surprised by that country's views on the EU? Source 9B shows how Europeans believe the EU will influence their lives in five years. How did respondents view the future? What conclusions do you draw from these data? Do significant numbers of Europeans appear to have moved beyond the nation-state in their allegiances?

Source 10 asks you to analyze the meanings of symbols, which, as we saw in Chapters 2 and 12, can carry important unwritten messages. Source 10 presents photographs of the new euro (∈) currency issued by the European Union beginning on January 1, 2002, to replace the national currencies of Austria, Belgium, Finland, France, Germany, Greece, Ireland, Italy, Luxembourg, the Netherlands, Portugal, and Spain.

The coining and printing of money long has been an act with unique sig-

nificance in the history of the West because, as a fundamental function of government, it symbolizes the sovereignty of the state. The coinage of monarchies traditionally bore the image of the sovereign, reflecting that figure's claim to absolute power within the realm. And while republics traditionally struck different symbols on their coinage, their magistrates, like monarchs, regarded the issuance of money as a fundamental symbol of their political authority. Counterfeiting currency thus has always been a serious offense in Western law, and in medieval and early modern Europe the manufacture and circulation of false money was a crime of *lese majesty*, that is, a fundamental attack on the authority of the state punishable with the death penalty. Given such a traditional linkage between the production of money and national sovereignty, why is the adoption of the euro by twelve states such a significant event?

Examine the photographs of the various denominations of euro banknotes (Source 10A). Like most non-American currency, the notes differ in size and color by denomination. Thus, if our illustrations were in color, you would note that the five-euro note is gray in color, the ten-euro red, and so forth. European authorities asked the Austrian designer of these notes to create bills illustrating "the ages and styles" of Europe while also showing the flag of the European Union, a blue banner with a circle of twelve gold stars. Why do you think the designer chose bridges and windows of various periods to illustrate these notes? Why do you think the

[445]

designer deliberately failed to portray any existing bridges or windows from the great historic sites of Europe and instead drew bridges and windows typifying those of the chief architectural styles of the Continent's long history. Why do you find no representations on the bills of any actual European site or individual European? The designer's only concession to the linguistic individuality of the European nations resulted from the functional necessity to indicate the issuing agency, the European Central Bank (thus the notes show the bank's initials in five linguistic forms: BCE, ECB, EZB, EKT, EKP), and to show the name of the currency in both the Latin and Greek alphabets. Why do you think the designer created the notes in such a way? How do these notes and the symbols on them illustrate the goals of the European Union?

One euro contains 100 cents, and Source 10B illustrates the coinage issued by the European Union in denominations from 1 cent to 2 euros. The work of a Belgian designer, the coins' denomination sides are uniform throughout Europe. But each country issues its own coins and applies a unique design to the obverse of the coin, even though all euro coins circulate freely throughout the entire euro zone. Compare the illustrated examples of coins of the French Republic and the Kingdom of the Netherlands. Each symbolically celebrates national tradition. The French 1-, 2-, and 5-cent coins bear images of Marianne, the female symbol of the republic employed on French coinage for over two centuries. The French

10-, 20-, and 50-cent coins carry the figure of another traditional symbol of the republic, a woman sowing seeds. The French 1- and 2-euro coins bear the image of a tree of life, perhaps representing the liberty trees decorated by patriots during the Revolution of 1789. The tree is surmounted by the motto of the republic, "Liberty, Equality, Fraternity," and imposed on it is the abbreviation of the nation's official name, "RF" for "République française" (French Republic). The coins of the Netherlands celebrate a quite different tradition; like coins of old they carry the image of the monarch, Queen Beatrix. What is the significance of the uniform denominational side on the euro coins? Why do you think the authorities permitted national designs on the obverse of the coins? How does this overall design scheme reflect the enduring influence of the nation-state in Europe in 2001?

The final piece of evidence, Source 11, is an excerpt from a series of interviews conducted by the French scholar Dominique Wolton (DW in the series of questions and answers that constitute this source) with Jacques Delors (JD) that were published in book form. As president of the European Commission during the expansion and redefinition of the European Union in the 1980s and 1990s, Delors was arguably the most influential figure of his generation in the European Community. How does Delors believe that the traditional nation-state must change? How does he define the role of the nation-state in a modern, federated Europe? Why might you conclude that he envisions a sharing of traditional governmental functions between the EU and the nation-state because there are certain things that the state does best?

Your goal with the evidence that follows is to examine the economic and political experiment that we call the European Union to see how it has changed the Continent and the role of the traditional nation-state over the last five decades. What were the goals of Monnet and the drafters of the Treaty of Rome? What were the small steps that, taken cumulatively, produced European unity and a half-century of peace on the Continent? How have they created an economically prosperous EU, and what is its role in the world today? Finally, what is the role for the European nation-state in this new order?

Source 1 from Leiden University Historical Institute, The Schuman Plan Collection (http://www.let.leidenuniv.nl/history/rtg/res1/schumanplan.html).

1. Declaration of French Foreign Minister Robert Schuman, May 9, 1950

World peace cannot be safeguarded without the making of creative efforts proportionate to the dangers which threaten it. The contribution which an organized and living Europe can bring to civilization is indispensable to the maintenance of peaceful relations. In taking upon herself for more than 20 years the role of champion of a united Europe, France has always had as her essential aim the service of peace. A united Europe was not achieved and we had war.[1] Europe will not be made all at once, or according to a single plan. It will be built through concrete achievements which first create a de facto solidarity. The coming together of the nations of Europe requires the elimination of the age-old opposition of France and Germany. Any action taken must in the first place concern these two countries. With this aim in view, the French Government proposes that action be taken immediately on one limited but decisive point: It proposes that Franco-German production of coal and steel as a whole be placed under a common High Authority, within the framework of an organization open to the participation of the other countries of Europe. The pooling of coal and steel production should immediately provide for the setting up of

1. An earlier French foreign minister, Aristide Briande (1862–1932), had proposed a plan for European union in May 1930.

[447]

common foundations for economic development as a first step in the federation of Europe, and will change the destinies of those regions which have long been devoted to the manufacture of munitions of war, of which they have been the most constant victims. The solidarity in production thus established will make it plain that any war between France and Germany becomes not merely unthinkable, but materially impossible. The setting up of this powerful productive unit, open to all countries willing to take part and bound ultimately to provide all the member countries with the basic elements of industrial production on the same terms, will lay a true foundation for their economic unification. This production will be offered to the world as a whole without distinction or exception, with the aim of contributing to raising living standards and to promoting peaceful achievements. In this way, there will be realized simply and speedily that fusion of interest which is indispensable to the establishment of a common economic system; it may be the leaven from which may grow a wider and deeper community between countries long opposed to one another by sanguinary divisions. By pooling basic production and by instituting a new High Authority, whose decisions will bind France, Germany and other member countries, this proposal will lead to the realization of the first concrete foundation of a European federation indispensable to the preservation of peace. To promote the realization of the objectives defined, the French Government is ready to open negotiations on the following bases: The task with which this common High Authority will be charged will be that of securing in the shortest possible time the modernization of production and the improvement of its quality; the supply of coal and steel on identical terms to the French and German markets, as well as to the markets of other member countries; the development in common of exports to other countries; the equalization and improvement of the living conditions of workers in these industries. . . .

Source 2 from William Diebold, Jr., The Schuman Plan: A Study in Economic Cooperation, 1950–1959 (New York: Frederick A. Praeger for the Council on Foreign Relations, 1959), pp. 568, 575.

2A.

COMMUNITY PRODUCTION AND CONSUMPTION DURING THE TRANSITIONAL PERIOD

	Production			Consumption		Index of Industrial Production	
	Coal	Coke	Steel	Coal	Steel[2]	General[3]	Metal-Using Industries
			(millions of tons)				*(1953 equals 100)*
1929	237.2	60.6	35.6				
1949	209.4	44.1	28.7	218.1	23.0	70	67
1952	238.9	62.4	41.9	246.5	33.2	95	97
1953	237.0	61.5	39.7	233.4	32.8	100	100
1954	241.7	59.8	43.8	241.8	36.5	111	113
1955	246.4	68.6	52.6	261.2	43.7	124	132
1956	249.1	74.8	56.8	218.9	46.4	135	146
1957	247.9	77.2	59.8	280.9	48.2	143	155
			Percentage Increase				
1929–57	4.5	27.4	68.0				
1949–52	14.1	41.5	46.0	13.0	44.3	35.7	44.8
1952–57	3.8	23.7	42.7	14.0	45.2	50.5	59.8

2B.

TRADE WITHIN THE COMMUNITY, 1952–1957

	Iron & Steel	Coal	Coke	Iron Ore	Scrap
		(millions of tons)			
1952	2.1	16.3	8.1	9.4	.4
1953	2.9	19.9	7.1	10.5	1.1
1954	4.2	23.6	7.0	10.8	1.2
1955	5.7	23.3	9.0	13.5	1.2
1956	5.1	19.7	9.1	14.1	1.3
1957	5.7	19.8	9.3	14.3	1.1
		Percentage Increase			
1952–55	171.4	42.9	11.1	43.6	200.0
1952–57	171.4	21.5	14.8	52.1	175.0

Note: Belgium and Luxembourg are treated as a unit for steel but separately for all other products. France and the Saar are combined in all figures.

2. Includes products not covered by the treaty.

3. Not including building or the food, drink, and tobacco industries.

Source 3 from Jean Monnet, Memoirs, *Introduction by George W. Ball, translated by Richard Mayne (Garden City, N.Y.: Doubleday and Co., a division of Bantam Doubleday Dell Publishing Group, Inc., 1978), pp. 392–393. Used by permission of Doubleday, a division of Random House, Inc.*

3. From Jean Monnet, *Memoirs*

We took a great deal of trouble, in fact, to keep to the deadlines we had imposed on ourselves. One by one, the barriers were removed and the prophecies of doom were confounded. Production and trade increased; and steel prices, resisting cyclical pressure, rose far less rapidly than elsewhere in the world. The Italian steel industry flourished beyond all expectations, while the Belgian coalmines overcame their previous backwardness with help from their more advanced competitors. Producers, with a general picture of the Community's needs before them, were able to invest wisely; and consumers, now at last publicly informed of the real price situation, could choose where to purchase their supplies. But the success of the ECSC went far beyond these material achievements. It meant that frontier barriers were definitively on the way out, that sovereignty could be delegated, and that common institutions worked well. This proof remained valid even when the inevitable difficulties arose. It was more valid still in later economic crises, which the Common Market overcame better than its separate member States could have done. Above all, it was now clear that the ECSC method was indeed the way to establish the greatest solidarity among peoples. I spelled out the lesson before the Common Assembly:[4]

"We can never sufficiently emphasize that the six Community countries are the fore-runners of a broader united Europe, whose bounds are set only by those who have not yet joined. Our Community is not a coal and steel producers' association: it is the beginning of Europe."

The beginning of Europe was a political conception; but, even more, it was a moral idea. Europeans had gradually lost the ability to live together and combine their creative strength. There seemed to be decline in their contribution to progress and to the civilization which they themselves had created—doubtless because in a changing world they no longer had institutions capable of leading them ahead. National institutions had proved that they were ill-adapted to this task. The new Community institutions, it seemed to me, were the only vehicle through which Europeans could once more deploy the exceptional qualities they had displayed in times past. . . .

---

4. **Common Assembly**: the assembly of the ECSC.

Source 4 from Tufts University treaty collection (http://www.tufts.edu/departments/
fletcher/multi/texts/rome/preamble.txt); *original, 1957 text from J.A.S. Grenville and
Bernard Wasserstein, eds.,* The Major International Treaties of the Twentieth Century: A
History and Guide with Texts, *2 vols. (London and New York: Routledge, 2001) 1: 530–544.*

4. Preamble from the Treaty Between Belgium, the Federal Republic of Germany, France, Italy, Luxembourg, and the Netherlands Establishing the European Economic Community (Treaty of Rome), March 25, 1957

His Majesty The King of the Belgians, the President of the Federal Republic of Germany, the President of the French Republic, the President of the Italian Republic, Her Royal Highness The Grand Duchess of Luxembourg, Her Majesty The Queen of the Netherlands,

Determined to lay the foundations of an ever closer union among the peoples of Europe,

Resolved to ensure the economic and social progress of their countries by common action to eliminate the barriers which divide Europe,

Affirming as the essential objective of their efforts the constant improvement of the living and working conditions of their peoples,

Recognising that the removal of existing obstacles calls for concerted action in order to guarantee steady expansion, balanced trade and fair competition,

Anxious to strengthen the unity of their economies and to ensure their harmonious development by reducing the differences existing between the various regions and the backwardness of the less favoured regions,

Desiring to contribute, by means of a common commercial policy, to the progressive abolition of restrictions on international trade,

Intending to confirm the solidarity which binds Europe and the overseas countries and desiring to ensure the development of their prosperity, in accordance with the principles of the Charter of the United Nations,

Resolved by thus pooling their resources to preserve and strengthen peace and liberty, and calling upon the other peoples of Europe who share their ideal to join in their efforts,

Have decided to create a European Economic Community and to this end have designated as their Plenipotentiaries: [Then follows a list of diplomatic representatives.],

Who, having exchanged their full powers, found in good and due form, Have
agreed as follows:

Part One: Principles

Article 1. By this Treaty, the High Contracting Parties establish among themselves a European Economic Community.

Article 2. The Community shall have as its task, by establishing a common
market and progressively approximating the economic policies of Member
States, to promote throughout the Community a harmonious development of
economic activities, a continuous and balanced expansion, an increase in stability, an accelerated raising of the standard of living and closer relations between the States belonging to it.

Article 3. For the purposes set out in Article 2, the activities of the Community
shall include, as provided in this Treaty and in accordance with the time table
set out therein:

(a) the elimination, as between Member States, of customs duties and of
quantitative restrictions on the import and export of goods, and of all other
measures having equivalent effect:

(b) the establishment of a common customs tariff and of a common commercial policy towards third countries;

(c) the abolition, as between Member States, of obstacles to freedom of
movement for persons, services and capital;

(d) the adoption of a common policy in the sphere of agriculture;

(e) the adoption of a common policy in the sphere of transport;

(f) the institution of a system ensuring that competition in the common market is not distorted;

(g) the application of procedures by which the economic policies of Member
States can be coordinated and disequilibria in their balance of payments reme-
died;

(h) the approximation of the laws of Member States to the extent required
for the proper functioning of the common market;

(i) the creation of a European Social Fund in order to improve employment
opportunities for workers and to contribute to the raising of their standard of
living;

(j) the establishment of a European Investment Bank to facilitate the economic expansion of the Community by opening up fresh resources;

(k) the association of the overseas countries and territories in order to increase trade and to promote jointly economic and social development.

Article 4. 1. The tasks entrusted to the Community shall be carried out by the
following institutions:

an Assembly,

a Council,

a Commission,
a Court of Justice. . . .

Article 6. 1. Member States shall, in close cooperation with the institutions of the Community, coordinate their respective economic policies to the extent necessary to attain the objectives of this Treaty. . . .

Article 7. Within the scope of application of this Treaty, and without prejudice to any special provisions contained therein, any discrimination on grounds of nationality shall be prohibited. . . .

Article 8. 1. The common market shall be progressively established during a transitional period of twelve years. . . .[5]

Part Two: Foundations of the Community

TITLE 1: FREE MOVEMENT OF GOODS

Article 9. 1. The Community shall be based upon a customs union which shall cover all trade in goods and which shall involve the prohibition between Member States of customs duties on imports and exports and of all charges having equivalent effect; and the adoption of a common customs tariff in their relations with third countries. . . .

TITLE II: AGRICULTURE

Article 38. 1. The common market shall extend to agriculture and trade in agricultural products. 'Agricultural products' means the products of the soil, of stock-farming and of fisheries and products of first-stage processing directly related to these products. . . .

Article 39. 1. The objectives of the common agricultural policy shall be:

(a) to increase agricultural productivity by promoting technical progress and by ensuring the rational development of agricultural production and the optimum utilization of the factors of production, in particular labour;

(b) thus to ensure a fair standard of living for the agricultural community, in particular by increasing the individual earnings of persons engaged in agriculture;

(c) to stabilize markets;

(d) to assure the availability of supplies;

(e) to ensure that supplies reach consumers at reasonable prices. . . .

---

5. In practice, the establishment of the EEC proved so successful that the member nations were able to end this transition period early, on July 1, 1968.

TITLE III: FREE MOVEMENT OF PERSONS, SERVICES AND CAPITAL

Chapter 1: Workers

Article 48. 1. Freedom of movement for workers shall be secured within the Community by the end of the transitional period at the latest.

2. Such freedom of movement shall entail the abolition of any discrimination based on nationality between workers of the Member States as regards employment, remuneration and other conditions of work and employment.

3. It shall entail the right, subject to limitations justified on grounds of public policy, public security or public health:

(a) to accept offers of employment actually made;

(b) to move freely within the territory of Member States for this purpose;

(c) to stay in a Member State for the purpose of employment in accordance with the provisions governing the employment of nationals of that State laid down by law, regulation or administrative action;

(d) to remain in the territory of a Member State after having been employed in that State, subject to conditions which shall be embodied in implementing regulations to be drawn up by the Commission. . . .

Source 5 from Loukas Tsoukalis, "Regional Policies and Redistribution," Chapter 8 of The New European Economy, The Politics and Economics of Integration, *2nd ed. (Oxford: Oxford University Press, 1993). Reprinted in Richard T. Griffiths, ed.,* The Economic Development of the EEC *(Cheltenham, U.K. and Lyme, N.H.: Edward Elgar Publishing, Ltd., 1997), p. 469.*

5. Divergence of GDP per Capita, 1960–1990

	1960	1970	1975	1980	1985	1990
Belgium	95.4	98.9	103.1	104.1	101.6	102.6
Denmark	118.3	115.2	110.5	107.8	115.8	108.2
Germany	117.9	113.2	109.9	113.6	114.2	112.8
Greece	38.6	51.6	57.3	58.1	56.7	52.6
Spain	60.3	74.7	81.9	74.2	72.5	77.8
France	105.8	110.4	111.8	111.6	110.6	108.6
Ireland	60.8	59.5	62.7	64.0	65.2	69.0
Italy	86.5	95.4	94.6	102.5	103.1	103.1
Luxembourg	158.5	141.4	126.7	118.5	122.4	125.6
Netherlands	118.6	115.8	115.5	110.9	107.0	103.1
Portugal	38.7	48.9	52.2	55.0	52.0	55.7
United Kingdom	128.6	108.5	105.9	101.1	104.2	105.1
EC-12	100.0	100.0	100.0	100.0	100.0	100.0

Note: Per capita GDP is given at current market prices and purchasing power parities.

Source 6 from Eurostat, the Statistical Office of the European Communities, online at http://europa.eu.int/comm/eurostat/Public/datashop/print-catalogue/EN?catalogue=Eurostat.

6. Gross Domestic Product of EU Countries and Other Selected Nations, 1990–2000[6]

Gross Domestic Product at Market Prices. Current Series in Million ECU/EUR[7]

	1990	1991	1992	1993	1994	1995	1996	1997	1998	1999	2000
EU-15[8]	:	5 779 473	6 025 169	6 042 446	6 334 523	6 588 340	6 919 958	7 287 921	7 632 029	8 016 767	8 524 371
B	156 489	164 435	175 718	184 590	197 140	211 708	212 654	216 405	224 312	235 538	248 338
DK	105 048	108 446	113 694	118 541	128 024	137 793	144 155	149 169	155 881	165 366	176 490
D	:	1 432 638	1 561 740	1 670 845	1 763 760	1 880 187	1 878 200	1 863 492	1 916 381	1 974 200	2 025 534
EL	66 168	73 081	77 024	79 771	84 353	89 888	97 972	107 010	108 466	117 080	122 986
E	402 618	444 901	464 098	426 007	425 439	446 882	480 536	495 627	525 437	565 483	608 787
F	957 587	987 210	1 040 541	1 089 370	1 139 320	1 188 1o1	1 224 606	1 241 129	1 297 574	1 350 159	1 404 775
IRL	37 248	38 648	41 447	42 570	46 148	50 890	57 628	70 608	77 240	89 029	103 470
I	867 836	939 613	951 165	849 037	863 369	839 041	971 065	1 029 991	1 068 802	1 107 779	1 165 677
L	:	..	..	..	:	13 833	14 313	15 563	16 886	18 433	20 934
NL	231 859	244 524	258 503	277 767	293 923	317 324	324 479	332 654	351 648	373 664	401 089
A	127 315	136 573	146 955	158 511	168 108	179 840	182 364	181 645	188 646	196 658	204 843
P	56 253	65 534	75 479	73 635	76 303	82 614	88 576	94 192	100 714	108 214	115 255
FIN	107 732	99 829	83 851	73 565	84 369	98 898	100 523	108 072	115 256	120 491	131 670
S	:	..	..	164 188	174 216	183 597	206 273	210 815	213 702	226 494	246 619
UK	780 695	836 147	828 109	823 509	878 109	867 743	936 614	1 171 548	1 271 085	1 368 181	1 547 903
IS	4 977	5 469	5 363	5 199	5 280	5 330	5 717	6 523	7 245	8 093	9 459
NO	90 923	95 224	97 607	99 128	103 600	112 089	124 026	136 703	131 685	144 091	175 506
CH	180 062	188 248	188 344	202 173	220 482	235 052	233 328	225 895	234 268	242 803	259 582
US	4 557 196	4 830 880	4 867 832	5 672 359	5 930 383	5 657 888	6 153 332	7 335 177	7 833 012	8 696 570	10 708 897
CA	458 906	483 846	447 776	482 942	475 675	452 667	484 597	563 995	550 049	615 699	770 482
JP	2 406 152	2 818 298	2 933 484	3 738 206	4 053 961	4 046 234	3 699 213	3 807 064	3 523 100	4 224 698	5 145 362

6. Country abbreviations: B: Belgium; DK: Denmark; D: Germany; EL: Greece; E: Spain; F: France; IRL: Ireland; I: Italy; L: Luxembourg; NL: Netherlands; A: Austria; P: Portugal; FIN: Finland; S: Sweden; UK: United Kingdom of Great Britain and Northern Ireland; IS: Iceland; NO: Norway; CH: Switzerland; US: United States; CA: Canada; JP: Japan.

7. ECU: European currency unit (the predecessor of the euro).

8. EU 15: the EEC/EU member nations prior to the planned twenty-first-century admissions of Central and Eastern European countries.

Source 7 from The World Almanac and Book of Facts, 2003 (New York: World Almanac
Books, 2003), pp. 856–857.

7. Population of the European Union, Countries Due for 2004 Admission, and Other Selected Nations (in Thousands)

Country	2002	2025	2050
EU 15:			
Belgium	10,275	9,533	7,609
Denmark	5,369	5,334	4,476
Germany	83,252	75,372	57,429
Greece	10,645	10,473	8,362
Spain	40,077	36,841	29,405
France	59,766	57,806	48,219
Italy	57,716	50,352	38,290
Ireland	3,883	3,913	3,600
Luxembourg	449	447	360
Netherlands	16,068	15,852	12,974
Austria	8,170	7,822	6,136
Portugal	10,084	9,012	7,256
Finland	5,184	5,009	4,170
Sweden	8,877	9,158	8,052
United Kingdom	59,778	59,985	54,116
Total EU 15	379,593	356,909	290,454
EU 2004 admissions:			
Bulgaria	7,621	7,292	5,905
Czech Republic	10,257	10,128	8,626
Estonia	1,416	1,237	1,047
Cyprus	767	870	878
Latvia	2,367	1,965	1,659
Lithuania	3,601	3,417	3,063
Hungary	10,075	9,374	7,684
Malta	397	391	325
Poland	38,625	40,117	36,465
Romania	22,318	21,417	18,483
Slovenia	1,933	1,864	1,484
Slovakia	5,422	5,718	5,215
Total EU 25	484,392	460,699	381,288
United States	280,562	335,360	394,241
Japan	126,975	119,865	101,334
China	1,284,304	1,407,739	1,322,435

8. Mahood's Ideal Europe Would Combine Cultural Freedom with Complete Mobility of Labour[9]

1. His Holiness the Pope at work on his mural at Sandy Row, Belfast while His Reverence Big Ian Paisley is on a Sabbatical in Rome retouching the Michelangelos and preparing for canonization.

2. The Arts Council of Britain has come to the aid of the European wine industry by sponsoring a tour by the Scunthorpe Morris dancers. With choreography by Lord Feather. It looks like being a vintage year.

3. Maria Callas singing Wagner in Gaelic during her summer season for the Scottish Tourist Board. While Herr Franz-Josef Strauss is appearing three times daily in Loch Ness, Sir Christopher Soames is busking in Brussels.

4. Highspot of the Cup Final was referee Roland Petit's superb entrachat as he sent off Malcolm Macdonald for clumsy lifts. When Bianca Jagger scored the winning goal for Luton Town the crowd sang excerpts from *Pelleas et Melisande.*

9. **Et, tu, William**: Latin for "And you William," based on Caesar's words to one of his assassins as he died in Shakespeare's play *Julius Caesar*, Act III, scene 1. "William" refers to King William III of England, whose victory over the Irish Catholic supporters of King James II at the Battle of the Boyne in 1690 is annually commemorated by a provocative and sometimes violent parade by Protestants through Catholic neighborhoods in Belfast. **Belfast**: the chief city of Northern Ireland, torn since the 1970s by violence between Protestants and Catholics. **Ian Paisley**: Northern Irish Protestant clergyman and leader of the Democratic Unionist party who is a prominent anti-Catholic leader. **canonization**: the process by which a person is classified a saint in the Roman Catholic Church. **Morris dance**: an English folk dance featuring a hobbyhorse and dancers in costume. **Maria Callas**: a Greek-born opera soprano (1923–1977). **Gaelic**: Celtic language spoken in parts of Scotland and Ireland. **Franz-Josef Strauss**: West German politician (1915–1988) who led the Christian Social Union party in Bavaria. **Loch Ness**: Scottish lake said to be inhabited by a monster. **Sir Christopher Soames**: British member of the European Commission in Brussels in 1975. **busking**: playing music in the street. **Roland Petit**: French ballet dancer and choreographer. **entrachat**: usually spelled "entrechat," this is a ballet leap in which the dancer repeatedly crosses his legs and sometimes beats them together. **Malcolm Macdonald**: the star of the Newcastle United soccer team in the 1970s. **Bianca Jagger**: the Nicaraguan-born wife of British rock star Mick Jagger in the 1970s. *Pelleas et Melisande*: an opera by the French composer Claude Debussy (1862–1918).

[457]

Source 9 from Eurobarometer 56 (April 2002), pp. 20, 48. Available online at: http://europa. eu.int/comm/Public_opinion/archies/eb/eb56_en.pdf.

9A.

Support for European Union Membership

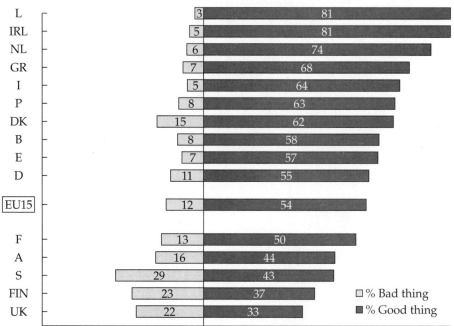

Percentage "don't know" and "neither good nor bad" not shown

9B.

The Perceived Role of the EU in People's Daily Life in 5 Years

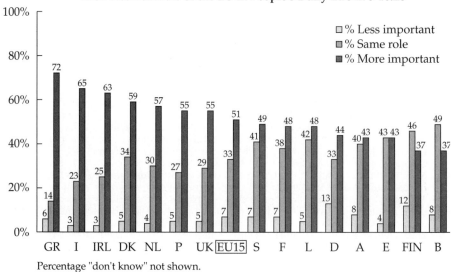

Percentage "don't know" not shown.

Source 10 from "The Euro Banknotes and Coin" (Frankfurt: The European Central Bank, 2002)

10A. Euro Banknotes

10B. Euro Coins

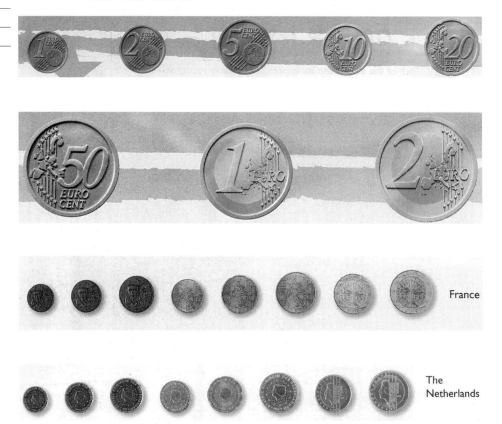

France

The
Netherlands

Source 11 from Jacques Delors, L'Unité d'un homme: Entretiens avec Dominique Wolton (Paris: Editions Odile Jacob, 1994), pp. 285–286. Translated by Julius R. Ruff.

11. From Interviews with Jacques Delors

JD: First, a profession of faith. I never believed, like militant Europeans, in the disappearance of nations. I am not among those who believe that historical evolution leads to the passing of nations.

DW: You are not like Denis de Rougement. . . .[10]

JD: No. . . . Because the nation represents a fundamental element of personal identity and common heritage. Certainly, the nation's traditional identity now must take different forms than those condemnable ones that exalted one nation at the expense of others. The nation can no longer define itself in terms of centuries-old adversaries, nor in terms of a monarch or religion. . . . Thus, the modern nation has difficulty defining itself because it can no longer do so in terms of antagonisms or exaltation of its superiority over others.

DW: Paradoxically, could Europe contribute to the rebirth of the national idea?

JD: Yes, if the construction of united Europe seemed to some to be a threat to the nation. . . . But the nation cannot be defined simply by saying "no" to the European community, since this institution is built on a voluntary association of sovereign nations expressed in treaties. If these sovereign nations agreed to share the exercise of a part of their sovereignty, it was because they believed that this served the national interest. The nation defines both rights and policy. That is the reason why certain prerogatives of the nation, especially in the realm of the most common public services, like education, health, and social policy, must remain in the hands of the state and will justify its existence. At the same time the nation can express social harmony between citizens, and solidarity between rich and poor, young and old. The European community will not take these fundamental tasks from the nations. The community can assist them . . . but it is up to the nation to define its concept of society and social welfare.

10. **Denis de Rougement**: a Swiss-born, French-language philosopher (1906–1985) and European federalist who anticipated the demise of the nation-state.

QUESTIONS TO CONSIDER

This final chapter of *Discovering the Western Past* may prompt you to reflect on all that you have read in this volume because its subject, an ongoing experiment in economic and political federation that has brought Europe peace and prosperity, apparently breaks a cycle of recurring conflict that many see characterizing the modern West. How did this break with the past, in the middle of a century marked by the costliest wars in human history, come about?

Begin first with ideas. What fundamental ideas infused the Schuman proposal? How did its solution to years of Franco-German conflict blend both supranational ideals and practical politics? How did the first, limited steps toward European unity reflect Jean Monnet's belief that much could be built on small, practical steps that solved very real problems? Why did Jean Monnet believe that the governments of nation-states in the twentieth century were ill suited to achieving European peace and unity? Why, however, do you believe that it would have been impossible, in 1952, as today, to create one government for all of Europe? The institutions Monnet influenced most, those of the ECSC and the EEC, retained a role for the nation-state in a modern Europe with supranational administration of certain spheres of activity. Why did the nation-state remain important in the thought of Jacques Delors? What future can you envision for the traditional nation-state?

Move next to the practical aspects of European unity. It would not have been achieved, as Delors suggested, had there not been real benefits in European federation for the nations of the continent. What practical political benefits did the Schuman Plan offer France and Germany in 1952? What economic benefits did the resulting ECSC give its participants to encourage them to persevere with other supranational economic arrangements? How has the realization of a completely open European economy expanded the purview of the institutions of the EU into ever more aspects of Europeans' lives and even challenged the traditional authority of the nation-state in some spheres?

Finally, reflect on where the EU experiment will lead Europe. What problems will accrue as the Community expands to twenty-five nations? Can the EU retain its important economic role in the world despite projections that Europeans will constitute a far smaller share of the globe's population in half a century? Can Europeans, ultimately, agree to move beyond economic matters and use the EU to forge a common foreign policy?

As you complete this chapter, reflect once more on the history of the West since 1500. Has it been entirely one of conflict? Ultimately, could the experiment that we call the European Union have achieved realization without a common intellectual and cultural heritage on which all educated Europeans drew by the late twentieth century? Despite their obvious linguistic and cultural differences, Europeans, especially with the end of the cold war, ideally frame their policies within shared values, including democratic principles of government, respect for the rights of the individual, and concern for the welfare of all citizens.

EPILOGUE

The European Union at the start of the twenty-first century is a far different organization than that of the European Coal and Steel Community of 1952. The Union is an economic and political federation soon to be composed of twenty-five European nations. Its quest for prosperity and peace through European economic unity based on the free movement of goods and people has broadened its activities dramatically over almost half a century. Indeed, in the first decade of the twenty-first century, the extent of its activities almost duplicates those of a nation-state. Equipped with its own executive and judicial branches, and served by a supranational civil service that numbers almost 20,000 employees, the Union makes economic policy, issues money, judges relevant cases in its own courts, endeavors to pursue a common foreign policy, and is preparing to field an armed force. The range of such activities has caused some to question the long-term viability of the traditional European nation-state.

The evidence that you considered in this chapter demonstrated the developmental path followed by Europe from the European Coal and Steel Community to the European Union. Our evidence also should suggest to you that the Union will confront new challenges over the coming years. In the process of weighing such evidence on historical questions, we hope that you have developed habits of critical thinking that will serve you in whatever you choose for your life's work. Historians cannot predict the future, but of one thing we can be sure: In this information age, you will be bombarded with mountains of evidence requiring analysis.

[463]